London 2012
Olympic Games and Paralympic Games

Olympic Park Map —Inside front cover

Introduction—2

Olympic Park Venues
Aquatics Centre —2,104
Basketball Arena —2,104
BMX Track —2,104
Copper Box —2,104
Eton Manor —2,104
Olympic Stadium —2,104
Riverbank Arena —3,104
Velodrome —3,104
Water Polo Arena —3,104

London Venues
Earls Court —3,106
ExCeL —3,107
Greenwich Park —3,107
Hampton Court Palace —3,105
Horse Guards Parade —3,106
Hyde Park —4,106
Lord's Cricket Ground —4,106
North Greenwich Arena —4,107
The Mall —4,106
The Royal Artillery Barracks —4,107
Wembley Arena —4,109
Wembley Stadium —4,109
Wimbledon —4,109

Out of London
Brands Hatch —4,104
City of Coventry Stadium —4,104
Eton Dorney —4,105
Hadleigh Farm —4,105
Hampden Park Stadium, Glasgow —5,105
Lee Valley White Water Centre —5,108
Millennium Stadium, Cardiff —5,108
Old Trafford Stadium, Manchester —5,108
St. James' Park Stadium, Newcastle upon Tyne —5,108
Weymouth and Portland —5,109

Live sites —5
Transport —5
Journey Planner —5

Torch Relays —6-10
Games Venue Maps —104-109

This summer London and the UK will come alive with the world's largest sporting events when London 2012 begins. The London 2012 Olympic and Paralympic Games will encompass 30 days of competition with 14,723 athletes and millions of people gathered here to enjoy the sporting and cultural action.

Olympic Heritage
The first ancient Olympic Games can be traced back to 776 BC. They were dedicated to the Olympian gods and staged on the plains of Olympia in Greece. The modern Olympic Games were founded by French-born athlete, poet and educator Pierre de Coubertin (1863–1937).

Olympic Games
In 2012 London will host a Games like never before, drawing on the UK's proud Olympic heritage. In 1908, London stood in as Host City for Rome after an eruption of Mount Vesuvius. It was the first time that the athletes paraded under national flags at the start of the Games. London again stepped in at the last minute to host the first Games after World War II. It was the first time that they were shown on home television.

Paralympic Games
The London 2012 Paralympic Games are being planned together with the Olympic Games. In 1948, Dr Ludwig Guttmann organised a sports competition that involved World War II soldiers with spinal cord injuries based at Stoke Mandeville Hospital. The competition took place between sports clubs and other hospitals on the same day as the Opening Ceremony of the London 1948 Olympic Games. Four years later, athletes from Holland joined in, creating the forerunner of the Paralympic Games. The first official Paralympic Games, rather than one aimed to help war veterans, was that held in Rome in 1960.

Olympic Torch Relay
An important element of the Olympic Games of Ancient Greece, the Flame is lit from the sun's rays at the Temple of Hera in Olympia.
For details of both the Olympic Torch and Paralympic Torch Relay routes see pages 6-10.

Cultural Olympiad
The London 2012 Cultural Olympiad is the largest cultural celebration in the history of the modern Olympic and Paralympic Movements. The London 2012 Festival, will bring leading artists from all over the world to create the UK's biggest ever festival; a chance for everyone to celebrate London 2012 through dance, music, theatre, the visual arts, film and digital innovation and leave a lasting legacy for the arts in the UK.

Legacy
After the Games the Olympic Park will be transformed into one of the largest urban parks created in Europe for more the 150 years. The world class sports facilities will be adapted for use by sports clubs and the local community as well as by elite athletes.

Aquatics Centre

The Aquatics Centre will be the venue for Swimming, Paralympic Swimming, Diving, Synchronised Swimming and the swimming element of the Modern Pentathlon. The venue features a spectacular wave-like roof that is 160m long and up to 80m wide.

Diving
Diving requires acrobatic excellence and supreme coordination skills, as athletes dive from heights of up to 10m.

Swimming
There are four strokes used in Olympic competition: Freestyle, Backstroke, Breaststroke and Butterfly. The 10km Marathon Swimming will be held in the Serpentine within Hyde Park.

Synchronised Swimming
Synchronised Swimmers use pin-point precision and immense stamina to deliver beautiful routines in the pool.

Paralympic Swimming
Swimmers are classified according to their functional ability to perform each stroke, and compete against athletes in their own classification.

Basketball Arena

The fourth-largest venue on the Olympic Park and one of the largest ever temporary venues built for any Games.

Basketball
Preliminaries and women's quarter-finals are held here at the Basketball Arena. All other rounds take place in the North Greenwich Arena.

Handball
Venue for the Handball men's quarter-finals, all semi-finals and all medal matches. All other rounds take place in the Copper Box.

Wheelchair Basketball
Preliminary games will be split between the Basketball Arena and North Greenwich Arena. All quarter-finals, semi-finals and medal games will take place at North Greenwich Arena.

Wheelchair Rugby
Played indoors on a regulation-size basketball court by teams of four, contact between wheelchairs is permitted, but physical contact is outlawed.

BMX Track

The purpose built BMX Track will be reconfigured after the Games to form part of a new VeloPark with a mountain bike track and road-cycle circuit.

BMX Racing
Inspired by motocross, BMX Racing is the most recent discipline to have been added to the Olympic programme.

Copper Box

This Olympic Park venue will be adapted after the Games to become a multi-use sports centre for community use, athlete training and small- to medium-sized events.

Handball
Preliminary rounds of both the men's and women's competitions, as well as the women's quarter-finals, will take place here. The competition will then move to the Basketball Arena, also in the Olympic Park.

Modern Pentathlon
Fencing, the first element of Modern Pentathlon takes place here. Swimming takes place in the Aquatics Centre, riding and the combined running/shooting events in Greenwich Park.

Goalball
Goalball is played by visually impaired athletes using a ball with bells inside, athletes wear blackout masks on the playing court, which allows persons with varying degrees of vision to participate together.

Eton Manor

It is intended that Eton Manor will be transformed after the Games into sporting facilities for local and regional communities.

Wheelchair Tennis
Invented in 1976, Wheelchair Tennis is one of the fastest-growing wheelchair sports in the world.

Olympic Stadium

The Olympic Stadium will host the Athletics and Paralympic Athletics events at the London 2012 Games, as well as the Opening and Closing Ceremonies.

Athletics
One of the most popular sports is also the biggest, Athletics, with 2,000 athletes competing in 47 events. There are four main strands to the Athletics competion: track events, such as the 100m; field events, which include the High Jump and the Shot Put; combined events such as the Decathlon, a mix of track and field elements; and road events, among them the Marathon.

Paralympic Athletics

Athletics will also be the largest sport at the Paralympic Games with 1,100 athletes competing. Some athletes compete in wheelchairs or throwing frames, others with prostheses, and others with the guidance of a sighted companion.

Riverbank Arena

The Riverbank Arena is located in the Olympic Park.

Hockey

Until the 1970s, hockey was always played on grass. However, top-level matches now take place on water-based synthetic-turf pitches.

Paralympic 5-a-side Football

Played by visually impaired athletes using a ball with a noise-making device inside, the pitch is surrounded with a rebound wall. The sport is played with no throw-ins and no offside rule.

Paralympic 7-a-side Football

Follows modified FIFA rules; the playing field is smaller, as are the goals. Teams are made up of ambulant cerebral palsy athletes, featuring players with varying levels of disability.

Velodrome

Purpose built within the Olympic Park it features a distinctive sweeping roof design reflecting the geometry of the cycling track. After the Games a new mountain bike course and road-cycle circuit will be added to create a VeloPark for the local community, sports clubs and elite athletes.

Cycling - Track

Cycling has a long history in the UK. As early as 1870, large crowds were drawn to races held on indoor wooden tracks. There are ten Olympic Track Cycling events (five for men, five for women): The Sprint, The Keirin, the Team Sprint, Team Pursuit and the Omnium.

Paralympic Cycling - Track

The competition features athletes with a visual impairment, cerebral palsy, amputations or other physical disabilities competing on bicycles, tricycles, tandems and hand cycles.

Water Polo Arena

A temporary Olympic Park venue adjacent to the Aquatics Centre.

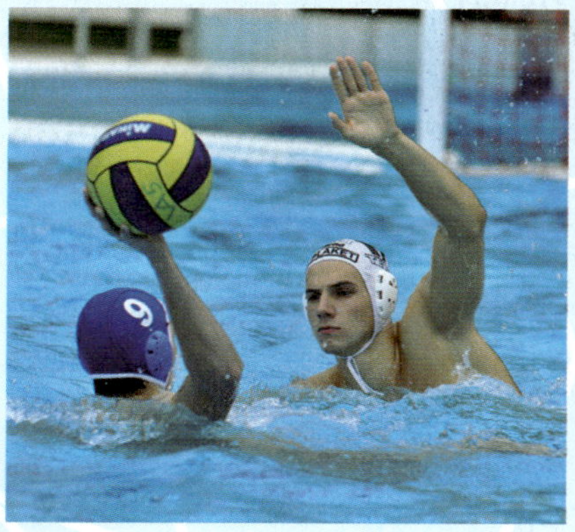

Water Polo

Water Polo developed during the 19th century as an aquatic version of rugby, played informally in rivers and lakes. The version of the game that survives today is closer to Handball.

Earls Court

A west London major venue for exhibitions, conferences and events.

Volleyball

The dynamic, competitive sport of Volleyball made its Olympic debut in 1964.

ExCeL

A London Docklands exhibition and conference centre, its arenas will host a range of Olympic and Paralympic sports.

Boxing

Men's Boxing events will be joined on the Olympic programme by a women's competition for the first time. Boxing featured at the original Olympic Games in the 7th century BC.

Fencing

Although sword fighting dates back thousands of years, Fencing really came of age as a sport in the 19th century.

Judo

Developed from jujitsu and established as a sport in the late 19th century, contests will be a five-minute whirlwind of combat, with athletes attempting a combination of throws and holds in a bid to defeat their opponents.

Table Tennis

Table Tennis, based on the same basic principles as Tennis, is a spectacle that blends power, speed, skill and subtlety.

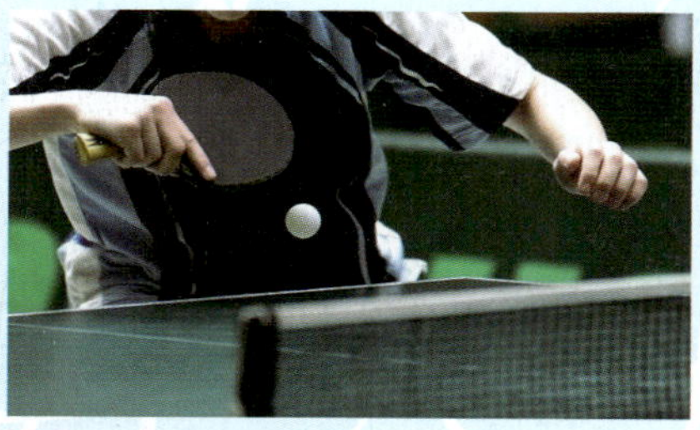

Taekwondo

'Taekwondo' translates into English as 'the way of foot and fist' – an accurate description of this martial art - landing powerful kicks and punches on your opponent.

Weightlifting

The aim of Weightlifting is simple, to lift more weight than anyone else resulting in pure sporting theatre. The strongest competitors may lift more than three times their body weight.

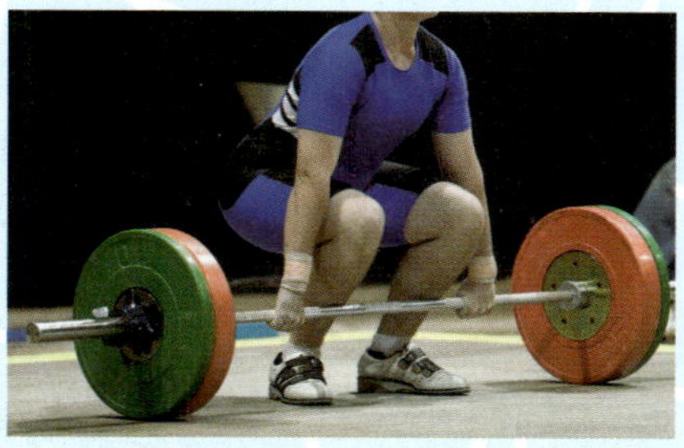

Wrestling

Recognised as one of the world's oldest sports, Wrestling was first held at the ancient Olympic Games in 708 BC.

Boccia

Boccia is a target sport that tests muscle control and accuracy, demanding extreme skill and concentration. Players must be in a seated position within a throwing box at one end of the playing court.

Paralympic Judo

Contested by visually impaired athletes, the mats have different textures to indicate the competition area and zones.

Paralympic Table Tennis

A permanent part of the Paralympic programme since the first Games in 1960, it is also one of the largest with 29 medal events and 300 athletes.

Powerlifting

Powerlifting is a bench-press competition – competitors are classified by bodyweight alone.

Volleyball (Sitting)

Sitting Volleyball emerged in the Netherlands in the 1950s, a combination of Volleyball and a German game called Sitzbal.

Wheelchair Fencing

Athletes compete in wheelchairs fastened to the floor, resulting in a fierce, fast-moving battle of tactics and technique.

Greenwich Park

Greenwich Park will host the Olympic and Paralympic Equestrian competitions, plus the combined running and shooting element of the Modern Pentathlon. Situated on the south bank of the River Thames in south east London.

Equestrian - Dressage

Dressage events will be a test of both athletic prowess and supreme elegance.

Equestrian - Eventing

Featuring dressage, cross-country and a dramatic jumping finale, the Eventing competition shows an all-encompassing test of Equestrian skill.

Equestrian - Jumping

Known as 'show jumping' in the UK, the Jumping competition will require horse and rider to navigate a short course with precision, speed and perfect technique.

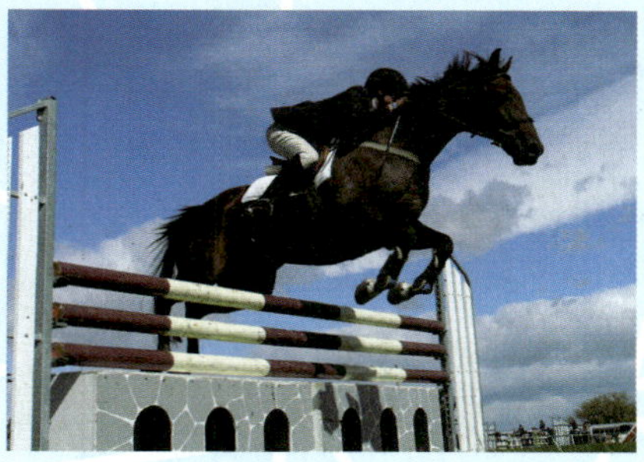

Modern Pentathlon

Riding and combined running/shooting will be staged here in Greenwich Park. Fencing will be in the Copper Box, Swimming in the Aquatics Centre - both venues in the Olympic Park.

Paralympic Equestrian

Athletes with a disability have long taken part in Equestrian activities, originally as a means of rehabilitation and recreation. Classified across five grades to ensure that the tests can be judged on the skill of the rider, regardless of their disability.

Hampton Court Palace

Hampton Court Palace is one of London's historic Royal Palaces. It is located in the London Borough of Richmond upon Thames in south-west London.

Cycling - Road

The Olympic Road Cycling programme includes two events. Time Trials begin and finish at Hampton Court Palace, Road Racing will begin and end on The Mall.

Horse Guards Parade

Horse Guards Parade is situated between Whitehall and St James's Park. A temporary beach will be created with 3,000 tonnes of imported sand.

Beach Volleyball

Beach Volleyball is similar to the indoor game, although it is played by teams of two, instead of teams of six.

Hyde Park

Within London's West End this extensive park abuts Mayfair and Knightsbridge.

Swimming - Marathon

The Swimming 10km Marathon event takes place in the Serpentine lake. All other swimming events are held in the Olympic Park Aquatics Centre.

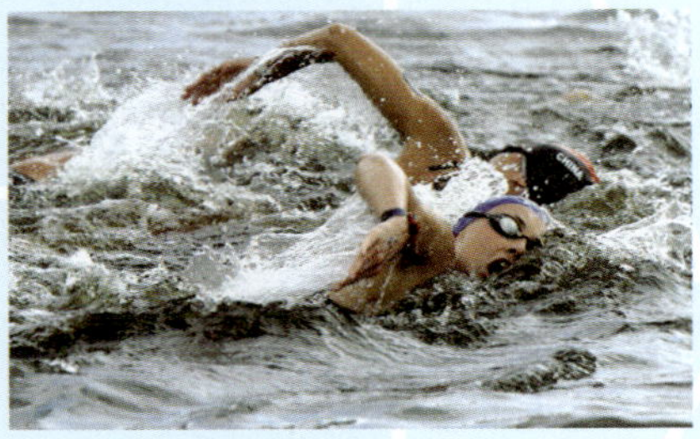

Triathlon

Triathlon races combine swimming, cycling and running, in that order. Events are conducted over a variety of distances. There are no heats; both the men's and women's events consist of a single race.

Lord's Cricket Ground

Lord's is the home of cricket. It is located in St John's Wood, north-west London, near Regent's Park.

Archery

Archery dates back around 10,000 years; developed as a competitive activity in medieval England, it is now practised in more than 140 countries around the world.

North Greenwich Arena

Built for the Millennium celebrations, and transformed into a sports and entertainment venue, the arena is sited on the south side of the River Thames.

Basketball

Men's quarter-finals and women's semi-finals onwards are held here, preliminaries and women's quarter-finals are held at the Basketball Arena, Olympic Park.

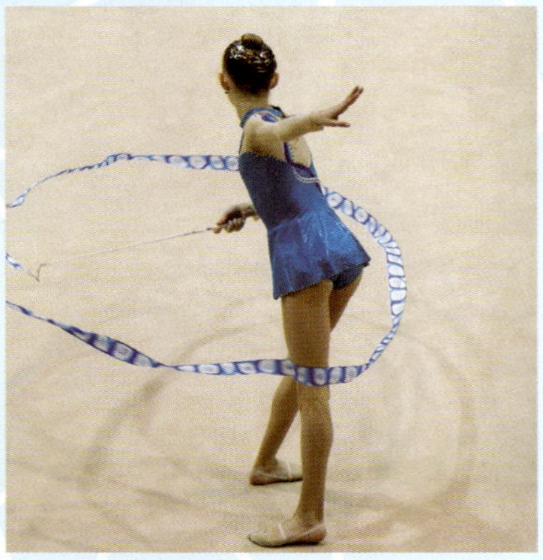

Gymnastics - Artistic

The grace, strength and skill of Olympic gymnasts have been astonishing audiences since the Games in Ancient Greece.

Gymnastics - Trampoline

Trampoline is the newest of the three Gymnastics disciplines making its Olympic debut at Sydney in 2000.

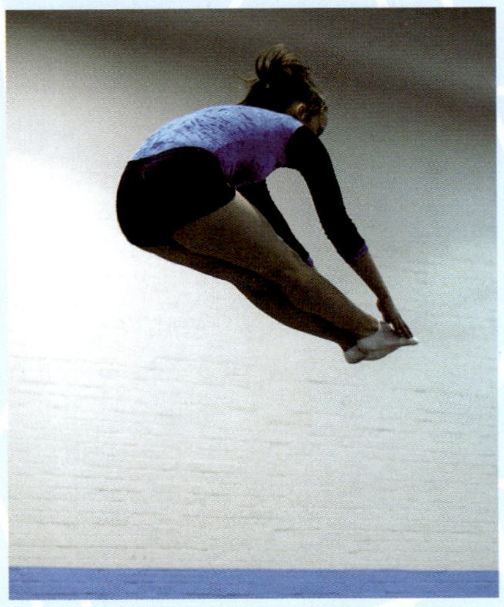

Wheelchair Basketball

Preliminary games will be split between the Olympic Park Basketball Arena and North Greenwich Arena. All quarter-finals, semi-finals and medal games will take place here.

The Mall

This famous ceremonial route connects Buckingham Palace and Trafalgar Square.

Athletics - Marathon and Race Walk

The start and finish points for the Olympic Games Marathon and Race Walk. At London 1908, the Marathon distance was extended from around 25 miles to 26.2 miles (42.195 kilometres) so that it finished in front of the Royal Box. This distance became standard for the Marathon and is still used today.

Cycling - Road Racing

The start and finish point for Cycling Road Racing events. There are two Road Cycling events for both men and women. Time Trials take place at Hampton Court Palace.

Paralympic Athletics - Marathon

Men's and women's Marathons will be held on the streets of central London, starting and finishing on The Mall.

The Royal Artillery Barracks

Located south of the River Thames in Woolwich the Barracks are a historic military site dating from 1776.

Shooting

Olympic Shooting events fall broadly into three types: Pistol, Rifle and Shotgun events. Having been practised competitively for centuries, the sport of Shooting is now popular all over the world.

Paralympic Archery

Paralympic Archery consists of both standing and wheelchair events for individuals and teams.

Paralympic Shooting

Athletes with different disabilities compete together in two classes – for athletes who can support the weight of their firearm themselves, and for athletes who use a shooting stand to support their arm.

Wembley Arena

A flagship live music and sport venue, in north-west London.

Badminton

One of the most dynamic Olympic sports, Badminton made its full Olympic debut at Barcelona 1992.

Gymnastics - Rhythmic

Rhythmic Gymnastics is a combination of gymnastics and dance. Scores are awarded for difficulty, artistry and execution.

Wembley Stadium

England's national stadium is situated in north-west London.

Football

The competition will encompass five other co-Host City stadia with the finals for both the men's and women's competition being played at Wembley.

Wimbledon

The home of the All England Lawn Tennis and Croquet Club. Wimbledon staged the tennis competition for London's first Olympic Games in 1908.

Tennis

The Tennis competition will feature five medal events including Mixed Doubles, making its first appearance since 1924. Situated in south west London about 12 miles from the Olympic Park.

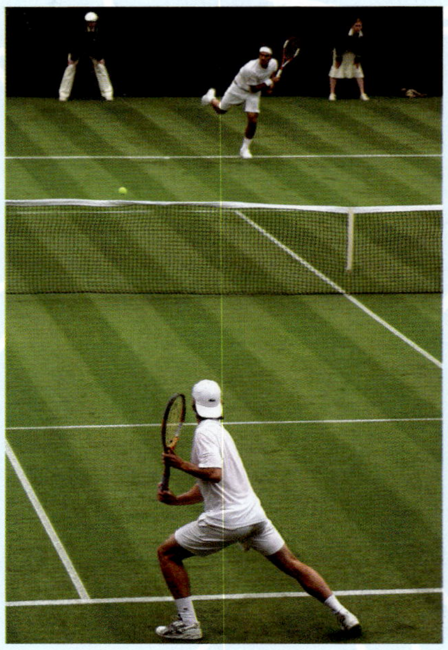

Brands Hatch

Brands Hatch motor racing circuit in Kent is approximately 20 miles south-east of the Olympic Park.

Paralympic Cycling - Road

Athletes with a visual impairment, cerebral palsy, amputations or other physical disabilities compete on bicycles, tricycles, tandems and hand cycles.

City of Coventry Stadium

City of Coventry Stadium is situated close to the city centre.

Football

The competition will encompass five other co-Host City stadia with the final at Wembley.

Eton Dorney

Eton Dorney is located near Windsor Castle, about 25 miles west of London.

Canoe Sprint

Races will be held over three distances with the fastest races taking just 30 seconds to complete. Canoe Slalom takes place at Lee Valley White Water Centre.

Rowing

The 14 Olympic Rowing events range from the Single Sculls, featuring solo rowers, to the Eights, contested by teams of eight rowers plus a cox.

Paralympic Rowing

Appearing at the Paralympic Games for only the second time. Adaptive rowing boats are equipped with special seats, which vary according to the disability of the athlete.

Hadleigh Farm

Hadleigh Farm, with its ideal mountain biking terrain, is to the east of London in Essex.

Cycling - Mountain Bike

Rocky paths, tricky climbs and technical descents will provide plenty of challenges for riders in the competition.

Hampden Park Stadium

Glasgow's Hampden Park stadium is situated a few miles south of the city centre.

Football

Hampden Park will host eight matches, over five days, three men's games and five women's including the women's quarter final on the 3rd August.

Lee Valley White Water Centre

Lee Valley White Water Centre is located in the River Lee Country Park 30km north of the Olympic Park. After the Games this new centre will become a venue for canoeing, kayaking and white water rafting.

Canoe Slalom

Modelled on slalom skiing, the sport was first staged on flat water, but was later switched to white water rapids. The competitions consist of timed runs down a white water course with up to 25 gates. Canoe Sprint takes place at Eton Dorney Rowing Centre.

Millennium Stadium

Cardiff Millennium Stadium is situated close to the city centre on the banks of the River Taff.

Football

The Millennium Stadium will host 11 matches, over eight days, and will host the men's Bronze medal play-off on 10th August.

Old Trafford Stadium

Manchester's Old Trafford stadium is a few miles south of the city centre.

Football

Old Trafford will host nine matches over seven days, including one of the men's and women's semi finals.

St. James' Park Stadium

Newcastle upon Tyne's St. James' Park stadium is situated close to the city centre.

Football

St. James' Park, Newcastle will host six match days with nine matches, including both a men's and women's quarter final.

Weymouth and Portland

This beautiful bay setting has some of the best natural sailing waters in the UK.

Sailing

The competition will host 10 Sailing events featuring a variety of craft from dinghies and keelboats, to windsurfing boards.

Paralympic Sailing

Paralympic sailing will consist of three mixed events.

Live Sites

Live Sites are big screen and event spaces in urban centres nationwide providing a unique combination of free sports screenings, cultural entertainment and ticketed concerts. Each site will be ticketed to control numbers, with some event tickets needing to be purchased; however, access to the Live Sites during most of the Games will be free to the public.

Live Sites will include:
Belfast - City Hall
Birmingham - Victoria Square
Bradford - Centenary Square
Bristol - Millennium Square, Waterfront
Cardiff - The Hayes
Coventry - Millennium Place, Hales Street
Derby - Market Place
Dover - Market Square
Edinburgh - Festival Square
Leeds - Millennium Square
Leicester - Humberstone Gate
Manchester - Exchange Square
Middlesbrough - Centre Square
Norwich - Chapelfield Shopping Centre
Plymouth - Armada Way
Portsmouth - Guildhall Square
Swansea - Castle Square
Swindon - Wharf Green
Waltham Forest - Town Square, Walthamstow
Woolwich - General Gordon Place

TRANSPORT

For up-to-date travel details and bookings

www.london2012.com/travel

London 2012 is aiming for a 'public transport' Games, there will be no parking at or near any venue. You can travel to each venue using different types of public transport, or by walking or cycling.

2012 Games park-and-ride

- Secure park-and-ride sites with limited space will be provided at convenient locations.
- Park-and-ride services must be booked in advance: www.firstgroupgamestravel.com
- Venues with park-and-ride facilities during the Olympic Games include: the Olympic Park, ExCeL, Greenwich Park (30 July only), Eton Dorney, Hadleigh Farm, the Lee Valley White Water Centre and Weymouth and Portland.
- Venues with park-and-ride facilities during the Paralympic Games include: the Olympic Park, ExCeL, and Eton Dorney.

Blue Badge Parking

Blue Badge Parking spaces are available for spectators who hold a valid Blue Badge or recognised national disability permit.
- Blue Badge Parking spaces must be booked in advance: www.firstgroupgamestravel.com

Rail

The National Rail network connects London and all the co-Host Cities for the London 2012 venues. Extra Rail services will be provided to Games venues, and trains will run later from London to key destinations up to approximately two hours away, such as Birmingham, Manchester, Leeds and Cardiff.

Shuttle Buses

Shuttle buses will be provided from some recommended stations to London 2012 and co-Host City venues, particularly where these stations are more than a short walk away from the venue entrance. These shuttles will be low-floor accessible buses and the service will be available for all spectators.

2012 Games coach services

- During the Olympic Games coach services will be provided to the Olympic Park, ExCeL, Greenwich Park (30 July only) and Weymouth and Portland from a range of locations outside the M25. Coaches will pick up from bus stops and bus stations throughout Great Britain.
- During the Paralympic Games, 2012 Games coach services will be provided to the Olympic Park and ExCeL
- All passengers on the coach services will have a dedicated seat or wheelchair space.
- All seats and wheelchair spaces on 2012 Games coach services must be booked in advance: www.firstgroupgamestravel.com/direct-coaching

Venues in London

London's transport system will be very busy, so you should allow plenty of time to travel to, from and between venues. Check the information on travelling to your event to find out where your venue is, the best way to get there and how long your journey will take between the recommended stations serving venues.
London is well-served by public transport with travel options including the London Underground, London Overground, Docklands Light Railway, National Rail, buses and river services.

Outer London venues

Some sporting events are being held in venues on the outskirts of London, including Eton Dorney, the Lee Valley White Water Centre and Hadleigh Farm. All of these venues are linked to London by National Rail services.

Co-Host Cities and Towns

The co-Host Cities are Cardiff, Coventry, Glasgow, Manchester, Newcastle upon Tyne (all for Football) and Weymouth and Portland (Sailing). They all have National Rail stations with direct links to London, although some of these venues are significant distances from the capital.

Travel tickets

London 2012 ticket holders can benefit from a range of special travel tickets for the Games. Spectators with a ticket for a Games event in London will receive a one-day Games Travelcard for the day of that event valid within zones 1 to 9. This includes London Underground (Tube), London Overground, Docklands Light Railway (DLR), buses, trams and National Rail services, including the Javelin® service between St Pancras International and Stratford International stations, but excluding the Heathrow, Stansted or Gatwick Express trains, or taxis and private hire vehicles.

2012 Games spectator journey planner

www.london2012.com/getting-to-the-games

Plan your journey using the 2012 Games spectator journey planner. It will provide you with:
- Estimated journey times to and from Games venues from anywhere in Great Britain.
- Estimated walking and cycling time to and from recommended stations to Games venues.
- Timetable information to allow Games ticket holders to plan their travel.
- Links to travel booking sites to enable Games ticket holders to purchase travel tickets in advance of travel.
- Recommended routes to make your journey as easy as possible.

Useful websites

London 2012 Information:
www.london2012.com

Rail:
National Rail Enquiries
www.nationalrailgamestravel.co.uk

Coach, park-and-ride & Blue Badge:
www.firstgroupgamestravel.co.uk

Eurostar:
www.eurostar.com

National Express Coach Enquiries:
www.nationalexpress.co.uk

Green Line Coaches:
www.greenline.co.uk

Public transport outside London:
www.traveline.org.uk

London Travel Information
www.tfl.gov.uk

London Tourist Information
www.visitlondon.com
Hotels, places to visit, events, travel and other important information.

Accessibility Information
www.london2012.com/accessibility
www.inclusivelondon.com

Picture credits:
© www.Bigstock.com: **2** (3.5.6.7.8.) **3** (1.2.3.4.5.6.7.9.) **4** (2.3.5.6.8.) **5** (3.)
© www.iStockphoto.com: **2** (4.) **3** (10.) **5** (1.)
© www.Shutterstock.com: **3** (8.) **4** (4.7.9.) **5** (2.)
© A-Z Maps: **4** (10.)
© ODA: **2** (1.2.) **4** (1.) Inside back cover (1.2.)

Every possible care has been taken to ensure that, to the best of our knowledge, the information contained in this atlas is accurate at the date of publication 01.2012

Torch Relays

LONDON
Greenwich
Newham
Tower Hamlets
Hackney
Waltham Forest 64
Redbridge
Barking & Dagenham
Havering
Bexley 65
Lewisham
Bromley
Croydon
Sutton
Merton
Wandsworth 66
Kingston
Richmond
Hounslow
Hillingdon
Ealing 67
Harrow
Brent
Barnet
Enfield
Haringey 68
Camden
Islington
City
Southwark
Lambeth
Kensington & Chelsea
Hammersmith & Fulham
Westminster 69
Olympic Park 70
E N G L A N D
Scarborough
Filey
Bridlington
Pickering
Thirsk
Aiskew
Bedale
Ripon
Knaresborough
Harrogate
Ilkley
Wetherby
Boston Spa
Tadcaster
Harewood
32 YORK
Beverley
37 HULL
Brough
Headlingley
Potternewton
Barkston Ash
Harehills
Richmond Hill
Selby
Bradford
LEEDS 37
Beeston
Hunslet
Monk Fryston
Camblesforth
Halifax
Brighouse
Morley
Castleford
Dewsbury
Batley
Pontefract
Goole
Huddersfield
Wakefield
Ackworth Moor Top
Immingham
Grimsby
39 CLEETHORPES
Kexbrough
Darton
Barnsley
Lundwood
Cundy Cross
Dunsville
Hatfield
Armthorpe
Doncaster
Warmsworth
Scunthorpe
Brigg
Wrawby
Thrybergh
Dalton
Conisbrough
Chapeltown
Ecclesfield
Rotherham
Parson Cross 38
SHEFFIELD
Louth
Legbourne
Withern
Mablethorpe
Trusthorpe
Maltby le Marsh
Sutton-on-Sea
Mumby
Hogsthorpe
Ingoldmells
Winthorpe
Skegness
Wainfleet All Saints
Wrangle
Boston
Buxton
Chesterfield
Calow
Boughton
Tuxford
East Markham
Saxilby
40 LINCOLN
Kirton
Bolsover
Edwinstowe
Darlton
Bracebridge Heath
Bakewell
Darley Dale
Matlock
Glapwell
Mansfield
Kelham
Newark-on-Trent
Balderton
Ashbourne
NOTTINGHAM
41
West Bridgford
Radcliffe-on-Trent
Grantham
Sleaford
42 DERBY
Burton upon Trent
Hoton
Wymeswold
Melton Mowbray
Loughborough
Asfordby
Quorn
Bourne
Thurlby
Moulton
Holbeach
Whaplode
Spalding
Market Deeping
Long Sutton
South Wootton
King's Lynn
East Rudham
West Rudham
Fakenham
Holt
Cromer
Aylsham
NORWICH 47
Acle
Filby
Great Yarmouth
Lowestoft
Lichfield
Streethay
Hopwas
Tamworth
Langham
Oakham
Stamford
45 LEICESTER
PETERBOROUGH
46
Uppingham
Bloxwich
Birchills
Walsall
West Bromwich
Oldbury
Oadby
Kibworth Harcourt
Foxton
Dingley
Corby
Lubenham
Market Harborough
Geddington
Kettering
Isham
43 BIRMINGHAM
COVENTRY
44
Solihull
Earlswood
Kenilworth
Warwick
Royal Leamington Spa
Rugby
Dunchurch
Wellingborough
Huntingdon
St. Ives
Newmarket
Bury St. Edmunds
50
CAMBRIDGE
Reydon
Wrentham
Southwold
Kelsale
Saxmundham
Wickham Market
Aldeburgh
Melton
Ufford
Woodbridge
Alcester
Stratford-upon-Avon
Northampton
Alderminster
Newbold on Stour
Wickhamford
Chipping Campden
Bedford
Cotton End
Milton Keynes
Letchworth Garden City
Saffron Walden
Haverhill
IPSWICH 48
Felixstowe
Buckingham
Bletchley
Newport
Stansted Mountfitchet
CHELTENHAM
Kirtlington
Winslow
Bicester
Whitchurch
Dunstable
LUTON
51
Stevenage
Welwyn Garden City
Bishop's Stortford
Colchester
Woodstock
Kidlington
Waddesdon
Aylesbury
St. Albans
Harlow
Hatfield Peverel
CHELMSFORD
Heybridge
Maldon
OXFORD 52
STOKE MANDEVILLE
24hr Relay to London
Hemel Hempstead
Hatfield
Hertford
Ware
49
Waltham Cross
Waltham Abbey
Brentwood
Cirencester
Abingdon
Crowmarsh Gifford
Bisham (Bisham Abbey)
Wallingford
Nettlebed
Henley-on-Thames
Maidenhead
Slough
Herongate
Basildon
Rayleigh
Hadleigh
Southend-on-Sea
LONDON
See London Inset
Grays
Westgate-on-Sea
Birchington
Margate
Cliftonville
St. Peters
Broadstairs
Ramsgate
Swindon
Chiseldon
Windsor
Gravesend
Higham
Rochester
Chatham
Gillingham
St. Lawrence
Cliffsend
Great Stonar
Upstreet
Sturry
Sandwich
Calne
Marlborough
Theale
Ascot
53
READING
Bracknell
Egham
Faversham
Harrietsham
Canterbury
Sholden
Deal
Newbury
Thatcham
Riverhead
Seal
Borough Green
62
MAIDSTONE
Challock
Thanington
Tidworth
Ludgershall
Basingstoke
GUILDFORD 63
Dorking
Redhill
Godstone
Sevenoaks
Reigate
Bletchingley
Shere
Westcott
Godalming
Copthorne
Felbridge
Crawley
East Grinstead
Royal Tunbridge Wells
Crowborough
Hamstreet
Ashford
61 DOVER
Folkestone
Hythe
Sandgate
Andover
Amesbury
Wilton
54 SALIBURY
Barford St. Martin
Kings Worthy
Winchester
Rogate
Easebourne
Petworth
Petersfield
Midhurst
Tillington
Duncton
Rye
SOUTHAMPTON
57
Lyndhurst
Fareham
Bridgemary
Chichester
Westergate
Arundel
Lancing
West Blatchington
Lewes
St. Leonards-on-Sea
60 HASTINGS
Pevensey
Bexhill-on-Sea
Pevensey Bay
Eastbourne
Whitchurch
Brockenhurst
Lymington
Gosport
58
North Bersted
South Bersted
Woodgate
Bognor Regis
Worthing
59
BRIGHTON & HOVE
Wallisdown
Branksome
Hamworthy
Christchurch
55
Boscombe
Totland
Yarmouth
East Cowes
Newport
PORTSMOUTH
BOURNEMOUTH
Carisbrooke
Ashley Cross
Swanage
ISLE OF WIGHT
Southampton to St. Peter Port (Guernsey)
St. Helier (Jersey) to Fareham
Southampton to St. Peter Port
St. Peter Port
GUERNSEY
St. Helier to Fareham
JERSEY
St. Helier
Jersey and Guernsey lie 85 miles south of Weymouth

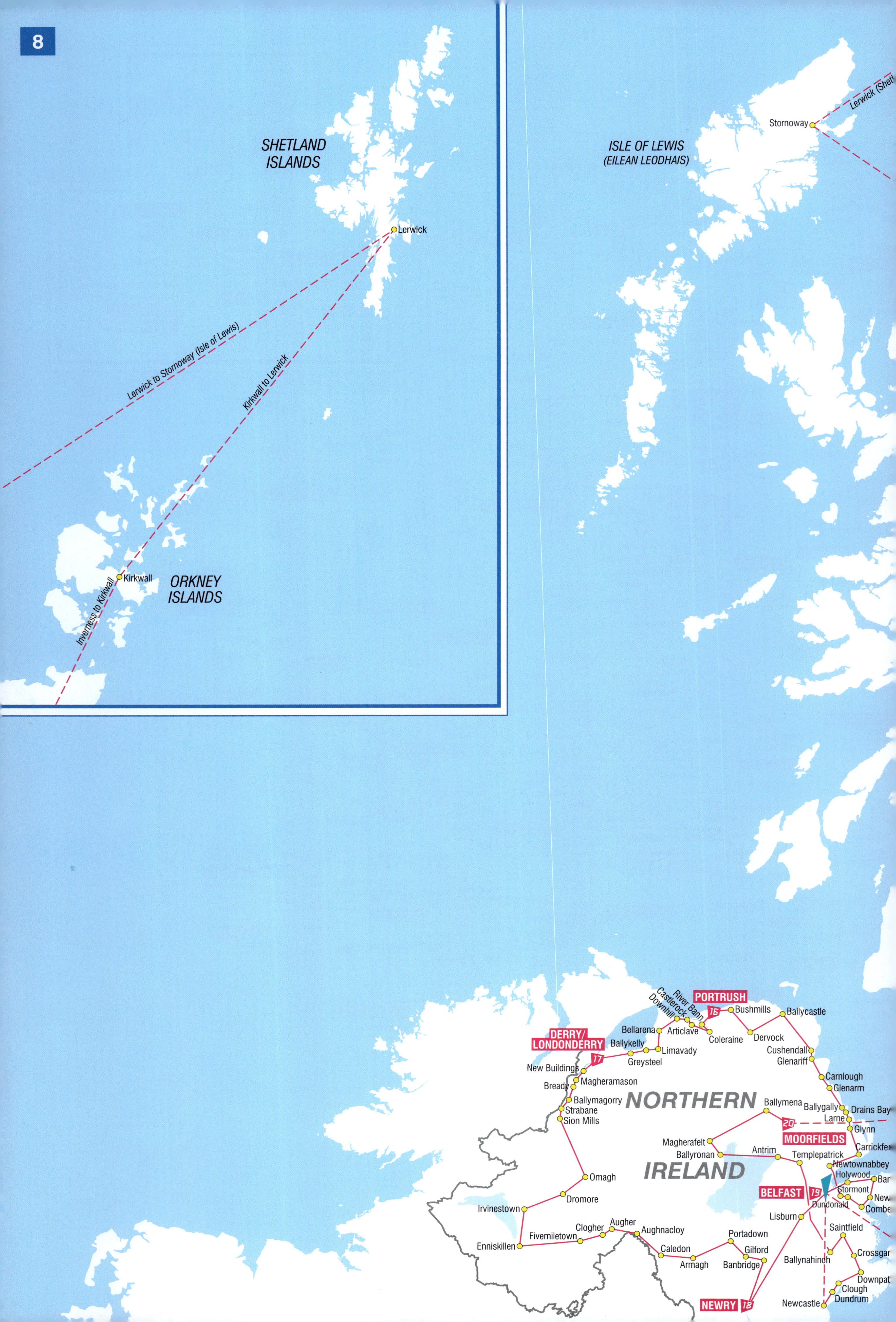

SHETLAND ISLANDS
Lerwick
Lerwick to Stornoway (Isle of Lewis)
Kirkwall to Lerwick
Kirkwall
ORKNEY ISLANDS
Inverness to Kirkwall
ISLE OF LEWIS
(EILEAN LEODHAIS)
Stornoway
PORTRUSH
16
Bushmills
Ballycastle
River Bann
Castlerock
Downhill
Bellarena
Articlave
Coleraine
Dervock
DERRY/
LONDONDERRY
Ballykelly
Limavady
Greysteel
17
Cushendall
Glenariff
New Buildings
Magheramason
Bready
Carnlough
Glenarm
Ballymagorry
Strabane
Sion Mills
NORTHERN
IRELAND
Ballymena
Ballygally
Drains Bay
Larne
20
Glynn
MOORFIELDS
Magherafelt
Ballyronan
Antrim
Templepatrick
Newtownabbey
Holywood
Stormont
BELFAST
19
Dundonald
Omagh
Dromore
Irvinestown
Lisburn
Saintfield
Clogher
Augher
Aughnacloy
Fivemiletown
Enniskillen
Caledon
Armagh
Portadown
Gilford
Banbridge
Ballynahinch
Crossgar
Clough
Dundrum
Newcastle
NEWRY
18

Inverness to Kirkwall (Orkney Islands)
Stornoway to Inverness
SCOTLAND
INVERNESS 22
Drumnadrochit
Lewiston
Invermoriston
Fort Augustus
Spean Bridge
Fort William
North Ballachullish
Glencoe
Tyndrum
Crianlarich
Tarbet
Luss
Dumbarton
Grantown-on-Spey
Carrbridge
Aviemore
Tomintoul
Crathie
Ballater
Dinnet
Kincardine O'Neil
Aboyne
Banchory
Drumoak
Peterculter
Cults
Bieldside
24 ABERDEEN
Stonehaven
Marykirk
Hillside
Montrose
Brechin
Forfar
Meigle
Woodside
Coupar Angus
Burrelton
Scone Palace
Balbeggie
Scone
25 DUNDEE
Perth
Leuchars
Newburgh
Dairsie
Guardbridge
Cupar
Abernethy
St. Andrews
Milnathort
Kinross
Dunblane
Bridge of Allan
Alloa
Crook of Devon
Stirling
Cairneyhill
Dunfermline
Crossford
Larbert
Camelon
Skinflats
Falkirk
Hopetoun House
Cumbernauld
EDINBURGH
Broxburn
26
Musselburgh
Duddingston
Dalkeith
Loanhead
Lasswade
Milton Bridge
Bilston
Penicuik
Eddleston
Peebles
Walkerburn
Innerleithen
Galashiels
Selkirk
Earlston
Gordon
Greenlaw
Duns
Chirnside
Foulden
Berwick-upon-Tweed
Port Glasgow
Clydebank
Bearsden
Kilmacolm
GLASGOW 21
Rutherglen
Giffnock
Lochwinnoch
Beith
Barrmill
Dunlop
Stewarton
Kilmaurs
Kilmarnock
Ayr
Alloway
Maidens
Turnberry
Maybole
Kirkoswald
Girvan
Ballantrae
Cairnryan
Stranraer
Cairnryan/Stranraer to Belfast
Bamburgh
ALNWICK 27
Hipsburn
Warkworth
Amble
Ashington
Newbiggin-by-the-Sea
Morpeth
Choppington
Bedlington
Blyth
Hartford
Whitley Bay
North Shields
Cullercoats
Wallsend
Tynemouth
NEWCASTLE UPON TYNE 28
South Shields
Howdon
Whitburn
Hexham
Prudhoe
Riding Mill
Blaydon
Gateshead
Stocksfield
Low Fell & Chowdene
Sunderland
Moorside
Consett
Castleside
Langley Park
Sherburn
Haswell Plough
Esh
29
Peterlee
Horden
Tow Law
DURHAM
Sherburn Hill
Blackhall Colliery
Hartlepool
Bishop Auckland
Sedgefield
Billingham
Redcar
Marske-by-the-sea
Saltburn-by-the-sea
Brotton
Carlin How
Loftus
Hinderwell
Lythe
Sandsend
Whitby
Shildon
Middridge
Newton Aycliffe
Stockton-on-Tees
30
High Beaumont Hill
Harrogate Hill
Darlington
MIDDLESBROUGH
Dumfries
Annan
Eastriggs
Gretna
33 CARLISLE
Wigton
Aspatria
Maryport
Flimby
Workington
Cockermouth
Keswick
Whitehaven
Penrith
Appleby-in-Westmorland
Brough
Barnard Castle
Richmond
Leyburn
Aysgarth
Bedale
Aiskew
Northallerton
Thirsk
Pickering
Grasmere
Ambleside
BOWNESS-ON-WINDERMERE 34
Kendal
Laxey
ISLE OF MAN
Castletown to Belfast

Torch Relays

Olympic Torch Relay

Lit in Greece, the Olympic Flame arrives in the UK on 18 May 2012. The Olympic Flame will travel to within 10 miles of 95 per cent of people in the UK, Isle of Man, Guernsey and Jersey during the 70-day Olympic Torch Relay. 8,000 people from around the UK will carry the Olympic Flame, the last Torchbearer lights the cauldron at the Olympic Games Opening Ceremony.

Paralympic Torch Relay

On consecutive days over the August Bank Holiday 2012, each nation of the UK will host a unique Torch lighting event that will use the power of human energy to ignite a flame. Each of the four Flames will be taken to Stoke Mandeville where they will be joined together in a special ceremony to create the Paralympic Flame. Teams of Torchbearers will then carry the Flame during a 24 hour Relay to the Opening Ceremony of the Paralympic Games.

Day 1 19 May
Land's End
Sennen
Newlyn
Penzance
Marazion
Rosudgeon
Ashton
Breage
Helston
Falmouth
Truro
Newquay
St Stephen
St Austell
Stenalees
Bugle
Lanivet
Bodmin
Liskeard
Saltash
Plymouth

Day 2 20 May
Plymouth
Brixton
Yealmpton
Modbury
Kingsbridge
West Charleton
Chillington
Torcross
Stoke Fleming
Dartmouth
Totnes
Paignton
Torquay
Teignmouth
Exeter

Day 3 21 May
Exeter
Okehampton
Folly Gate
Hatherleigh
Merton
Great Torrington
Bideford
Sticklepath
Barnstaple
Wrafton
Braunton
Knowle
Ilfracombe
Combe Martin
Lynton
Lynmouth
Porlock
Minehead
Dunster
Carhampton
Washford
Williton
Taunton

Day 4 22 May
Taunton
Ilminster
Yeovil
Ilchester
Somerton
Street
Glastonbury
Coxley
Wells
Croscombe
Shepton Mallet
Frome
Southwick
Trowbridge
Bradford on Avon
Bath
Bitton
Longwell Green
Hanham
Bristol

Day 5 23 May
Bristol
Flax Bourton
Backwell Farleigh
Backwell West Town
Nailsea
Failand
Leigh Woods
Bristol
Chippenham
Calne
Malborough
Chiseldon
Wroughton
Royal Wootton Bassett
Swindon
Cirencester
Stroud
Painswick
Brockworth
Shurdington
Cheltenham

Day 6 24 May
Gloucester
Maisemore
Hartpury
Corse and Staunton
Ledbury
Bartestree
Lugwardine
Hereford
Leominster
Ludlow
Clee Hill
Cleobury Mortimer
Far Forest
Callow Hill
Bewdley
Kidderminster
Droitwich Spa
Fernhill Heath
Worcester

Day 7 25 May
Worcester
Powick
Malvern
Malvern Wells
Ross-on-Wye
Monmouth
Raglan
Abergavenny
Brynmawr
Blaenavon
Abersychan
Pontypool
Newport
Cardiff

Day 8 26 May
Cardiff
Dinas Powys
Barry
Caerphilly
Pontypridd
Merthyr Tydfil
Treherbert
Ynyswen
Treorchy
Nant-y-moel
Ogmore Vale
Bryncethin
Bridgend
Laleston
Pyle
Margam
Taibach
Port Talbot
Briton Ferry
Neath
Swansea

Day 9 27 May
Swansea
Llanelli
Burry Port
Kidwelly
Carmarthen
Haverfordwest
Fishguard
Newport
Cardigan/Aberteifi
Sarnau
Brynhoffnant
Llanarth
Aberaeron
Llanon
Llanrhystud
Aberystwyth

Day 10 28 May
Aberystwyth
Bow Street
Tal-y-bont
Tre Taliesin
Machynlleth
Dolgellau
Llan Ffestiniog
Blaenau Ffestiniog
Porthmadog
Criccieth
Pwllheli
Bontnewydd
Caernarfon
Y Felinheli
Bangor

Day 11 29 May
Beaumaris
Menai Bridge
Conwy
Deganwy
Llandudno
Penrhyn Bay
Rhos on Sea
Colwyn Bay
Old Colwyn
Abergele
Towyn
Kinmel Bay
Rhyl
Rhuddlan
Connah's Quay
Shotton
Queensferry
Harwarden
Saltney
Chester

Day 12 30 May
Chester
Wrexham
Rhostyllen
Acrefair
Trevor
Oswestry
Pant
Llanymynech
Welshpool
Shrewsbury
Cressage
Much Wenlock
Benthall
Broseley
Ironbridge
Telford
Newport
Gnosall
Haughton
Stafford
Shelton
Stoke-on-Trent

Day 13 31 May
Stoke-on-Trent
Cobridge
Burslem
Middleport
Crewe
Congleton
Macclesfield
Knutsford
Tatton Park
Runcorn
Widnes
Warrington
Lowton
Abram
Wigan
Scholes
Ince
Hindley
Westhoughton
Bolton

Day 14 1 June
Bolton
Horwich
Chorley
Euxton
Croston
Burscough
Ormskirk
Southport
Ainsdale
Formby
Crosby
St Helen's
Huyton
Knotty Ash
Old Swan
Liverpool
Birkenhead
Liverpool

Day 15 2 June
Liverpool
Douglas, Isle of Man
Laxey, Isle of Man
Onchan, Isle of Man
Ballasalla, Isle of Man
Castletown, Isle of Man

Day 16 3 June
Belfast
Holywood
Bangor
Newtownards
Comber
Dundonald
Stormont
Newtownabbey
Carrickfergus
Glynn
Larne
Drains Bay
Ballygally
Glenarm
Carnlough
Glenariff
Cushendall
Ballycastle
Dervock
Bushmills
Portrush

Day 17 4 June
River Bann
Coleraine
Articlave
Castlerock
Downhill
Bellarena
Limavady
Ballykelly
Greysteel
Derry / Londonderry

Day 18 5 June
Derry / Londonderry
New Buildings
Magheramason
Bready
Ballymagorry
Strabane
Sion Mills
Omagh
Dromore
Irvinestown
Enniskillen
Fivemiletown
Clogher
Augher
Aughnacloy
Caledon
Armagh
Portadown
Gilford
Banbridge
Newry

Day 19 6 June
Dublin
Newry
Lisburn
Belfast

Day 20 7 June
Newcastle
Dundrum
Clough
Downpatrick
Crossgar
Saintfield
Ballynahinch
Templepatrick
Antrim
Ballyronan
Magherafelt
Ballymena
Moorfields

Day 21 8 June
Stranraer
Cairnryan
Ballantrae
Girvan
Turnberry
Maidens
Kirkoswald
Maybole
Alloway
Ayr
Kilmarnock
Kilmaurs
Stewarton
Dunlop
Barrmill
Beith
Lochwinnoch
Kilmacolm
Port Glasgow
Rutherglen
Glasgow
Giffnock
Glasgow

Day 22 9 June
Glasgow
Bearsden
Clydebank
Dumbarton
Luss
Tarbet
Crianlarich
Tyndrum
Glencoe
North Ballachullish
Fort William
Spean Bridge
Fort Augustus
Invermoriston
Lewiston
Drumnadrochit
Inverness

Day 23 10 June
Kirkwall, Orkney Islands
Lerwick, Shetland Islands

Day 24 11 June
Stornoway, Isle of Lewis
Inverness
Aviemore
Carrbridge
Grantown-on-Spey
Tomintoul
Crathie
Ballater
Dinnet
Aboyne
Kincardine O'Neil
Banchory
Drumoak
Peterculter
Bieldside
Cults
Aberdeen

Day 25 12 June
Aberdeen
Stonehaven
Marykirk
Hillside
Montrose
Brechin
Forfar
Meigle
Coupar Angus
Woodside
Burrelton
Balbeggie
Scone
Scone Palace
Perth
Abernethy
Newburgh
Cupar
Dairsie
Guardbridge
Leuchars
Dundee

Day 26 13 June
St. Andrews
Milnathort
Kinross
Crook of Devon
Alloa
Bridge of Allan
Dunblane
Stirling
Cumbernauld
Larbert
Camelon
Falkirk
Skinflats
Cairneyhill
Crossford
Dunfermline
Hopetoun House
Broxburn
Edinburgh

Day 27 14 June
Edinburgh
Duddingston
Musselburgh
Dalkeith
Lasswade
Loanhead
Bilston
Milton Bridge
Penicuik
Eddleston
Peebles
Innerleithen
Walkerburn
Selkirk
Galashiels
Earlston
Gordon
Greenlaw
Duns
Chirnside
Foulden
Berwick-upon-Tweed
Bamburgh
Alnwick

Day 28 15 June
Alnwick
Hipsburn
Warkworth
Amble
Ashington
Newbiggin-by-the-Sea
Ashington
Choppington
Morpeth
Hartford
Bedlington
Blyth
Whitley Bay
Cullercoats
Tynemouth
North Shields
Howdon
Wallsend
Newcastle Upon Tyne

Day 29 16 June
Gateshead
South Shields
Whitburn
Sunderland
Low Fell & Chowdene
Blaydon
Prudhoe
Stocksfield
Hexham
Riding Mill
Consett
Moorside
Castleside
Tow Law
Esh
Langley Park
Durham

Day 30 17 June
Durham
Sherburn
Sherburn Hill
Haswell Plough
Peterlee
Horden
Blackhall Colliery
Hartlepool
Billingham
Sedgefield
Bishop Auckland
Shildon
Middridge
Newton Aycliffe
High Beaumont Hill
Harrogate Hill
Darlington
Stockton-on-Tees
Middlesbrough

Day 31 18 June
Middlesbrough
Redcar
Marske-by-the-Sea
Saltburn-by-the-Sea
Brotton
Carlin How
Loftus
Hinderwell
Lythe
Sandsend
Whitby
Pickering
Scarborough
Filey
Bridlington
Beverley
Hull

Day 32 19 June
Hull
Brough
Goole
Camblesforth
Selby
Monk Fryston
Barkston Ash
Tadcaster
Boston Spa
Wetherby
Harewood
Knaresborough
Harrogate
Ripon
York

Day 33 20 June
York
Thirsk
Northallerton
Aiskew
Bedale
Aysgarth
Leyburn
Richmond
Barnard Castle
Brough
Appleby-in-Westmorland
Penrith
Carlisle

Day 34 21 June
Dumfries
Annan
Eastriggs
Gretna
Carlisle
Wigton
Aspatria
Maryport
Flimby
Workington
Whitehaven
Cockermouth
Keswick
Grasmere
Ambleside
Bowness-on -Windermere

Day 35 22 June
Kendal
Milnthorpe
Carnforth
Bolton-le-Sands
Hest Bank
Morecambe
Lancaster
Garstang
St Michael's on Wyre
Fleetwood
Cleveleys
Blackpool

Day 36 23 June
Lytham St Anne's
Warton
Preston
Blackburn
Accrington
Burnley
Crawshawbooth
Reedsholme
Rawtenstall
Rochdale
Heywood
Bury
Whitefield
Prestwich
Higher Broughton
Cheetham Hill
Manchester

Day 37 24 June
Salford
Trafford
Moss Side
Rusholme
Longsight
Levenshulme
Stockport
Ashton-under-Lyne
Oldham
Marsh
Huddersfield
Brighouse
Halifax
Bradford
Keighley
Skipton
Ilkley
Headingley
Potternewton
Harehills
Richmond Hill
Leeds

Day 38 25 June
Leeds
Hunslet
Beeston
Morley
Batley
Dewsbury
Wakefield
Castleford
Pontefract
Ackworth Moor Top
Lundwood
Cundy Cross
Barnsley
Darton
Kexbrough
Chapeltown
Ecclesfield
Parson Cross
Sheffield

Day 39 26 June
Sheffield
Rotherham
Dalton
Thrybergh
Conisbrough
Warmsworth
Doncaster
Armthorpe
Dunsville
Hatfield
Scunthorpe
Brigg
Wrawby
Immingham
Grimsby
Cleethorpes

Day 40 27 June
Grimsby
Louth
Legbourne
Withern
Maltby le Marsh
Mablethorpe
Trusthorpe
Sutton-on-Sea
Mumby
Hogsthorpe
Ingoldmells
Winthorpe
Skegness
Wainfleet All Saints
Wrangle
Boston
Sleaford
Bracebridge Heath
Lincoln

Day 41 28 June
Lincoln
Saxilby
Darlton
East Markham
Tuxford
Kirton
Boughton
Edwinstowe
Mansfield
Kelham
Newark-on-Trent
Balderton
Grantham
Radcliffe-on-Trent
West Bridgford
Nottingham

Day 42 29 June
Nottingham
Glapwell
Bolsover
Calow
Chesterfield
Matlock
Darley Dale
Bakewell
Buxton
Ashbourne
Derby

Day 43 30 June
Derby
Burton upon Trent
Streethay
Lichfield
Hopwas
Tamworth
Great Wyrley
Newtown
Bloxwich
Leamore
Birchills
Walsall
Willenhall
Wolverhampton
Dudley
Oldbury
West Bromwich
Smethwick
Birmingham

Day 44 1 July
Birmingham
Solihull
Earlswood
Astwood Bank
Redditch
Alcester
Evesham
Wickhamford
Broadway
Chipping Campden
Newbold on Stour
Alderminster
Stratford-upon-Avon
Warwick
Royal Leamington Spa
Kenilworth
Coventry

Day 45 2 July
Coventry
Rugby
Dunchurch
Northampton
Wellingborough
Isham
Kettering
Geddington
Corby
Dingley
Market Harborough
Lubenham
Foxton
Kibworth Harcourt
Oadby
Leicester

Day 46 3 July
Leicester
Quorn
Loughborough
Hoton
Wymeswold
Asfordby
Melton Mowbray
Langham
Oakham
Uppingham
Stamford
Peterborough

Day 47 4 July
Peterborough
Market Deeping
Thurlby
Bourne
Spalding
Moulton
Whaplode
Holbeach
Long Sutton
King's Lynn
South Wootton
West Rudham
East Rudham
Fakenham
Holt
Cromer
Aylsham
Norwich

Day 48 5 July
Norwich
Acle
Filby
Great Yarmouth
Lowestoft
Wrentham
Reydon
Southwold
Kelsale
Saxmundham
Aldeburgh
Wickham Market
Ufford
Melton
Woodbridge
Felixstowe
Ipswich

Day 49 6 July
Ipswich
Colchester
Hatfield Peverel
Heybridge
Maldon
Rayleigh
Southend-on-Sea
Hadleigh
Basildon
Grays
Herongate
Brentwood
Chelmsford

Day 50 7 July
Chelmsford
Harlow
Waltham Abbey
Waltham Cross
Hertford
Ware
Bishop's Stortford
Stansted Mountfitchet
Newport
Saffron Walden
Haverhill
Bury St Edmunds
Newmarket
Cambridge

Day 51 8 July
Cambridge
St Ives
Huntingdon
Bedford
Cotton End
Letchworth Garden City
Stevenage
Welwyn Garden City
Hatfield
St Albans
Hemel Hempstead
Luton

Day 52 9 July
Luton
Dunstable
Milton Keynes
Bletchley
Buckingham
Winslow
Whitchurch
Aylesbury
Stoke Mandeville
Aylesbury
Waddesdon
Bicester
Kirtlington
Woodstock
Kidlington
Oxford

Day 53 10 July
Oxford
Abingdon
Wallingford
Crowmarsh Gifford
Nettlebed
Henley-on-Thames
Bisham (Bisham Abbey)
Maidenhead
Slough
Windsor
Egham
Ascot
Bracknell
Reading

Day 54 11 July
Reading
Theale
Thatcham
Newbury
Basingstoke
Kings Worthy
Winchester
Andover
Ludgershall
Tidworth
Amesbury
The Winterbournes
Salisbury

Day 55 12 July
Salisbury
Wilton
Barford St Martin
Fovant
Ludwell
Shaftesbury
Fontmell Magna
Iwerne Minster
Stourpaine
Blandford Forum
Winterborne Whitechurch
Milborne St Andrew
Puddletown
Dorchester
Winterbourne Abbas
Bridport
Chideock
Lyme Regis
Burton Bradstock
Abbotsbury
Portesham
Chickerell
Wyke Regis
Osprey Quay, Portland
Weymouth

Day 56 13 July
Portland Bill
Southwell
Weston
Easton
Portland
Fortuneswell
Weymouth
Preston
Osmington
Winfrith Newburgh
Wool
Corfe Castle
Swanage
Stoborough
Wareham
Sandford
Lytchett Minster
Upton
Hamworthy
Poole
Ashley Cross
Branksome
Wallisdown
Bournemouth

Day 57 14 July
Bournemouth
Boscombe
Christchurch
Lyndhurst
Brockenhurst
Lymington
Totland
Yarmouth
Carisbrooke
Newport
East Cowes
Southampton

Day 58 15 July
Southampton
St Peter Port, Guernsey
St Helier, Jersey
Fareham
Bridgemary
Gosport
Portsmouth

Day 59 16 July
Portsmouth
Petersfield
Rogate
Midhurst
Easebourne
Tillington
Petworth
Duncton
Chichester
North Bersted
South Bersted
Bognor Regis
Woodgate
Westergate
Arundel
Worthing
Lancing
West Blatchington
Brighton & Hove

Day 60 17 July
Brighton & Hove
Crawley
Copthorne
Felbridge
East Grinstead
Royal Tunbridge Wells
Crowborough
Lewes
Eastbourne
Pevensey Bay
Pevensey
Bexhill-on-Sea
St Leonards-on-Sea
Hastings

Day 61 18 July
Hastings
Rye
Hamstreet
Ashford
Hythe
Sandgate
Folkestone
Dover

Day 62 19 July
Deal
Sholden
Sandwich
Great Stonar
Cliffsend
St Lawrence
Ramsgate
Broadstairs
St Peters
Cliftonville
Margate
Westgate-on-Sea
Birchington
Upstreet
Sturry
Canterbury
Thanington
Faversham
Chalk
Harrietsham
Maidstone

Day 63 20 July
Maidstone
Chatham
Gillingham
Rochester
Higham
Gravesend
Borough Green
Seal
Sevenoaks
Riverhead
Godstone
Bletchingley
Redhill
Reigate
Dorking
Westcott
Shere
Godalming
Guildford

Day 64 21 July
Greenwich
Newham
Tower Hamlets
Hackney
Waltham Forest

Day 65 22 July
Redbridge
Barking & Dagenham
Havering
Bexley

Day 66 23 July
Lewisham
Bromley
Croydon
Sutton
Merton
Wandsworth

Day 67 24 July
Kingston
Richmond
Hounslow
Hillingdon
Ealing

Day 68 25 July
Harrow
Brent
Barnet
Enfield
Haringey

Day 69 26 July
Camden
Islington
City
Southwark
Lambeth
Kensington & Chelsea
Hammersmith & Fulha
Westminster

Day 70 27 July
London, Olympic Park

Paralympic Torch

August
Flame lighting venues
24 London
25 Belfast
26 Edinburgh
27 Cardiff

Creating the Paralympi Flame
28 Stoke Mandeville

Paralympic Torch Rela
29 Opening Ceremony

Great Britain Road A-Z Atlas

London 2012 Games

Olympic Park map ....Inside front cover

Venues, sports and Travel information.........2-5

Torch Relays...................6-10

London Main Road Map

Greater London main road network including the M25 and its approach roads.................................96-103

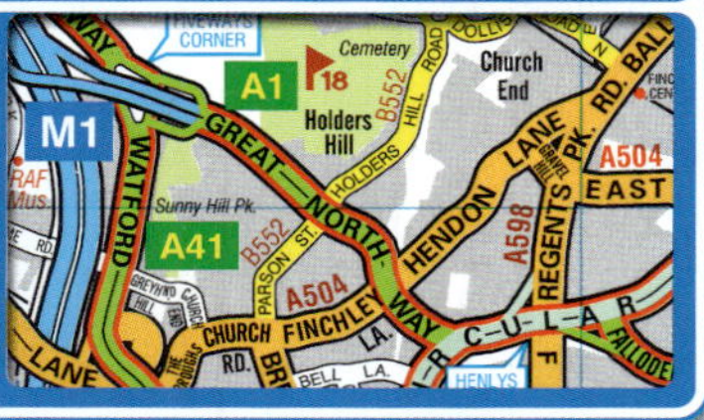

Journey Route Planning maps

Southern Britain........12-13

Northern Britain........14-15

Mileage Chart...................16

Games Venue maps

Access maps to all London 2012 venues.............................104-109

Motorway Junctions

Details of motorway junctions with limited interchange...........................17

Junction	M67	
1	Eastbound Westbound	Access from A57 eastbound only Exit to A57 westbound only
1a	Eastbound Westbound	No access, exit to A6017 only No exit, access from A6017 only
2	Eastbound Westbound	No exit, access from A57 only No access, exit to A57 only

Over 32,000 Index References

Including cities, towns, villages, hamlets and locations......................110-132

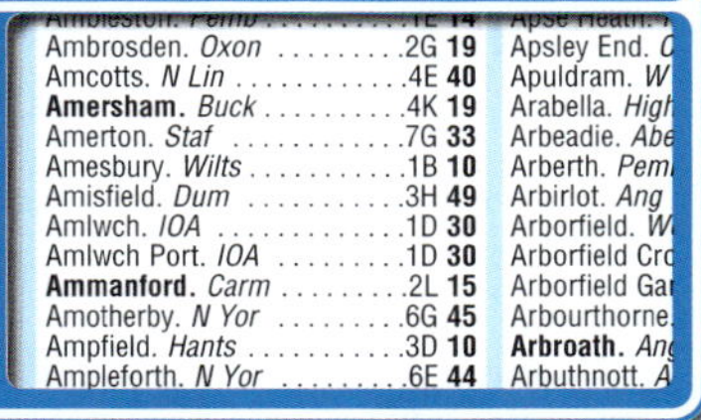

Great Britain Road map section

Key to map pages ....back cover

Reference..............................18

Road Maps..................19-95

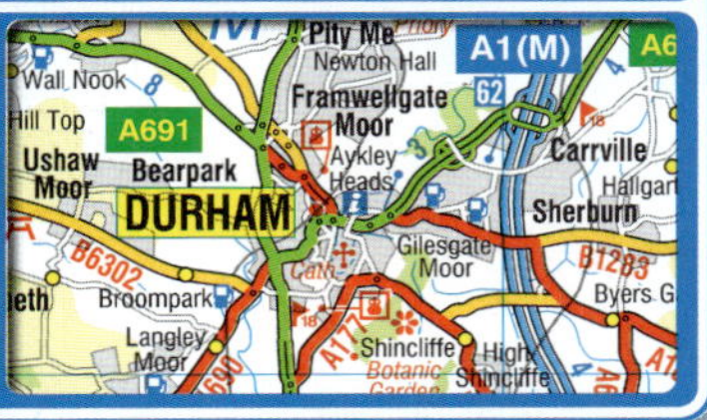

Direct
Customer Service

If you experience difficulty obtaining any of our 300 titles, please contact us direct for help and advice.

www.az.co.uk

Tel: 01732 783422 Fax: 01732 780677

Geographers' A-Z Map Company Ltd. Fairfield Road, Borough Green, Sevenoaks, Kent TN15 8PP

Retail Sales: 01732 783422 Trade Sales: 01732 781000 www.az.co.uk

Edition 26* 2012. Copyright © Geographers' A-Z Map Company Limited. An AtoZ Publication

Every possible care has been taken to ensure that, to the best of our knowledge, the information contained in this atlas is accurate at the date of publication. However, we cannot warrant that our work is entirely error free and whilst we would be grateful to learn of any inaccuracies, we do not accept any responsibility for loss or damage resulting from reliance on information contained within this publication.

The representation on the maps of a road, track or footpath is no evidence of the existence of a right of way.

PocketGPSWorld.com's CamerAlert is a self-contained speed and red light camera warning system for SatNavs and Android or Apple iOS smartphones/tablets. Visit www.cameralert.co.uk to download.

Mapping sourced from Ordnance Survey

ISLE OF MAN
IRISH SEA
CARDIGAN BAY
BRISTOL CHANNEL
ENGLISH
REPUBLIC OF IRELAND
WALES
CYMRU
Old Trafford
See Pages 5 & 108
Millennium Stadium
See Pages 5 & 108
Weymouth and Portland
See Pages 5 & 109
Peel
Douglas
Castletown
Newry
Warrenpoint
Newcastle
Dundalk
Carrickmacross
Drogheda
Kells
Navan
DUBLIN
Dun Laoghaire
Bray
Kildare
Naas
Wicklow
Carlow
Arklow
Gorey
Enniscorthy
New Ross
Wexford
Rosslare Harbour
Barrow-in-Furness
Ulverston
Morecambe
Heysham
Lancaster
Kirkby Lonsdale
Fleetwood
Blackpool
Lytham St.Anne's
Preston
Blackburn
Southport
Chorley
Darwen
Bolton
Bury
Wigan
Formby
LIVERPOOL
St. Helens
Wallasey
Birkenhead
Warrington
Sale
Runcorn
Ellesmere Port
Northwich
Chester
Crewe
Amlwch
Holyhead
(Caergybi)
Llangefni
Beaumaris
Llandudno
Rhyl
Conwy
Colwyn Bay
(Bae Colwyn)
Bangor
Llanrwst
Denbigh
(Dinbych)
Flint
(Y Fflint)
Mold
(Yr Wyddgrug)
Caernarfon
Betws-y-Coed
Ruthin
(Rhuthun)
Wrexham
(Wrecsam)
Nantwich
STOKE-ON-TRENT
Llan Ffestiniog
Llangollen
Whitchurch
Porthmadog
Pwllheli
Bala
(Y Bala)
Oswestry
(Croesoswallt)
Ellesmere
Wem
Market Drayton
Barmouth
(Abermaw)
Dolgellau
Llanfyllin
Shrewsbury
Newport
Oakengates
Telford
Welshpool
(Y Trallwng)
Wolverhampton
Tywyn
Machynlleth
Montgomery
(Trefaldwyn)
Church Stretton
Bridgnorth
Llanidloes
Newtown
(Y Drenewydd)
Bishop's Castle
Aberystwyth
Llangurig
Ludlow
Kidderminster
Rhayader
(Rhaeadr Gwy)
Knighton
(Tref-Y-Clawdd)
Presteigne
(Llanandras)
Aberaeron
New Quay
(Ceinewydd)
Llandrindod Wells
Leominster
Worcester
Lampeter
(Llanbedr Pont Steffan)
Builth Wells
(Llanfair-ym-Muallt)
Kington
Fishguard
(Abergwaun)
Cardigan
(Aberteifi)
Great Malvern
Hereford
Llandovery
(Llanymddyfri)
St. David's
(Tyddewi)
Brecon
(Aberhonddu)
Carmarthen
(Caerfyrddin)
Ross-on-Wye
Tewkesbury
Llandeilo
Abergavenny
(Y Fenni)
Monmouth
(Trefynwy)
Gloucester
Haverfordwest
(Hwlffordd)
Ammanford
(Rhydaman)
Merthyr Tydfil
(Merthyr Tudful)
Milford Haven
(Aberdaugleddau)
St. Clears
Ebbw Vale
Tredegar
Abertillery
Aberdare
(Aberdâr)
Pembroke
(Penfro)
Tenby
(Dinbych-y-Pysgod)
Llanelli
Neath
(Castell-nedd)
Pontypool
(Pontypwl)
Chepstow
(Cas-gwent)
Cwmbran
Nailsworth
SWANSEA
(Abertawe)
Pontypridd
Caerphilly
(Caerffili)
Port Talbot
Newport
(Casnewydd)
Malmesbury
Porthcawl
Bridgend
(Pen-y-Bont-Ar Ogwr)
CARDIFF
(Caerdydd)
Penarth
BRISTOL
Cork
Barry
(Barri)
Weston-Super-Mare
Bath
Trowbridge
Radstock
Frome
Wells
Lynton
LUNDY
Ilfracombe
Minehead
Watchet
Williton
Burnham-on-Sea
Glastonbury
Shepton Mallet
Barnstaple
Bridgwater
Taunton
Wincanton
Bideford
Great Torrington
South Molton
Wellington
Sherborne
Yeovil
Tiverton
Bude
Holsworthy
Honiton
Chard
Crewkerne
Blandford Forum
Okehampton
Exeter
Sidmouth
Bridport
Launceston
Exmouth
Lyme Regis
Dorchester
Padstow
Wadebridge
Tavistock
Ashburton
Dawlish
Teignmouth
Weymouth
Fortuneswell
Bodmin
Liskeard
Saltash
Buckfastleigh
Newton Abbot
Torquay
Newquay
Lostwithiel
Devonport
Totnes
Paignton
Brixham
Looe
PLYMOUTH
Redruth
St. Austell
Truro
Dartmouth
St. Ives
Camborne
Kingsbridge
Salcombe
St. Just
Penzance
Falmouth
Helston
LAND'S END
ISLES OF SCILLY
Guernsey
Jersey
St. Malo
Roscoff
Santander

REFERENCE
MOTORWAY WITH NUMBER
M4
Service Area
MOTORWAY
(Under Construction/Proposed)
MOTORWAY JUNCTIONS
PRIMARY ROUTE
A5
A ROAD
A272
NATIONAL BOUNDARY
LONDON 2012 VENUES
Old Trafford
Brands Hatch
SCALE
0 10 20 30 40 Miles
0 10 20 30 40 50 60 Kilometres
NORTH SEA
City of Coventry Stadium
See Pages 4 & 104
Lee Valley White Water Centre
See Pages 5 & 108
London Venues
See Pages 3,4 & 105-109
Olympic Park Venues
See Pages 2,3 & 104
Hadleigh Farm
See Pages 4 & 105
Brands Hatch
See Pages 4 & 104
Eton Dorney
See Pages 4 & 105
Rotterdam
Zeebrugge
Esbjerg
Hook of Holland
Ostend
Dieppe
Bilbao
Caen
Cherbourg
Guernsey
Jersey
Le Havre
St. Malo
Santander
Cherbourg
Guernsey
Jersey
St. Malo
Humber
THE WASH
ENGLAND
FRANCE
CHANNEL
Channel Tunnel
ISLE OF WIGHT
Scarborough
Filey
Thirsk
Leyburn
Ripon
Malton
Bridlington
Knaresborough
Harrogate
Wetherby
Ilkley
YORK
Driffield
Hornsea
LEEDS
BRADFORD
Selby
Beverley
KINGSTON UPON HULL
Withernsea
Hedon
Castleford
Halifax
Huddersfield
Wakefield
Pontefract
Goole
Immingham
Grimsby
Cleethorpes
Scunthorpe
Barnsley
Doncaster
Rotherham
Gainsborough
Market Rasen
Louth
Mablethorpe
SHEFFIELD
Worksop
Chesterfield
Buxton
Lincoln
Horncastle
Skegness
Bakewell
Matlock
Mansfield
Leek
Alfreton
Hucknall
Newark-on-Trent
Ashbourne
Ilkeston
NOTTINGHAM
Sleaford
Boston
Hunstanton
Cromer
Wells-next-the-Sea
DERBY
Beeston
Grantham
Uttoxeter
Burton upon Trent
Loughborough
Melton Mowbray
Bourne
Spalding
King's Lynn
Fakenham
North Walsham
Coalville
Lichfield
Tamworth
LEICESTER
Oakham
Stamford
Wisbech
Swaffham
NORWICH
Great Yarmouth
Walsall
Hinckley
Peterborough
Downham Market
Wymondham
Nuneaton
Market Harborough
Oundle
March
Lowestoft
BIRMINGHAM
Solihull
COVENTRY
Rugby
Corby
Kettering
Ramsey
Ely
Thetford
Diss
Bungay
Southwold
Halesworth
Warwick
Royal Leamington Spa
Daventry
Wellingborough
Northampton
Huntingdon
St. Ives
Bury St. Edmunds
Redditch
Stratford-upon-Avon
Bedford
St. Neots
Cambridge
Newmarket
Stowmarket
Aldeburgh
Evesham
Newport Pagnell
Haverhill
Hadleigh
Ipswich
Banbury
Milton Keynes
Royston
Saffron Walden
Sudbury
Felixstowe
Chipping Norton
Buckingham
Letchworth Garden City
Stevenage
Bishop's Stortford
Halstead
Harwich
Cheltenham
Stow-on-the-Wold
Bicester
Dunstable
Luton
Welwyn Garden City
Braintree
Colchester
Woodstock
Aylesbury
Hemel Hempstead
St. Albans
Hertford
Harlow
Clacton-on-Sea
OXFORD
Thame
Chelmsford
Cirencester
Witney
Chesham
Abingdon
High Wycombe
Amersham
Epping
Watford
Enfield
Romford
Swindon
Wallingford
Wantage
Henley-on-Thames
Maidenhead
Slough
Basildon
Southend-on-Sea
READING
Windsor
Staines
LONDON
Dartford
Tilbury
Gravesend
Sheerness
Herne Bay
Margate
Broadstairs
Ramsgate
Marlborough
Newbury
Wokingham
Bracknell
Wimbledon
Rochester
Devizes
Camberley
Woking
Croydon
Sandwich
Canterbury
Leatherhead
Reigate
Sevenoaks
Maidstone
Deal
Andover
Basingstoke
Aldershot
Guildford
Dorking
East Grinstead
Tonbridge
Dover
Alton
Farnham
Godalming
Crawley
Royal Tunbridge Wells
Tenterden
Ashford
Folkestone
Hythe
Winchester
Horsham
Salisbury
Romsey
Eastleigh
Midhurst
Petersfield
Haywards Heath
Uckfield
Rye
New Romney
SOUTHAMPTON
Ringwood
Gosport
Havant
Chichester
Worthing
Lewes
Hastings
Bexhill
Christchurch
Lymington
PORTSMOUTH
Bognor Regis
BRIGHTON
Newhaven
Eastbourne
Bournemouth
Yarmouth
Cowes
Ryde
Newport
Sandown
Swanage
Dunkerque
Calais
Boulogne
St. Omer
Le Touquet-Paris-Plage
Montreuil
St. Pol
Abbeville
Dieppe
Amiens

UNST
YELL
FETLAR
SHETLAND ISLANDS
WHALSAY
Bergen
FOULA
Lerwick
Scalloway
BRESSAY
Sumburgh
FAIR ISLE
WESTRAY
EDAY
SANDAY
ROUSAY
STRONSAY
SHAPINSAY
Stromness
Kirkwall
ORKNEY ISLANDS
HOY
SOUTH RONALDSAY
John o'Groats
Scrabster
Thurso
OUTER HEBRIDES
Stornoway (Steòrnabhagh)
ISLE OF LEWIS (EILEAN LEODHAIS)
Tarbert (Tairbeart)
Leverburgh (An t-Ob)
HARRIS (NA HEARADH)
Lochmaddy (Loch nam Madadh)
NORTH UIST (UIBHIST A TUATH)
BENBECULA (BEINN NA FAOGHLA)
Uig
Dunvegan
Portree
RAASAY
SOUTH UIST (UIBHIST A DEAS)
ISLE OF SKYE
Lochboisdale (Loch Baghasdail)
BARRA (BARRAIGH)
Castlebay (Bagh a' Chaisteil)
CANNA
RÙM
Mallaig
EIGG
MUCK
INNER HEBRIDES
COLL
Kilchoan
Acharacle
Tobermory
TIREE
ISLE OF MULL
IONA
COLONSAY
JURA
ISLAY
Port Ellen
GIGHA
Portrush
Portstewart
Ballycastle
Coleraine
Letterkenny
Londonderry
NORTHERN IRELAND
Larne
Ballymena
Ardara
Strabane
Antrim
Donegal
Lough Neagh
Ballyshannon
Omagh
Crumlin
BELFAST
Dungannon
Enniskillen
Armagh
Sligo
Ballina
Monaghan
Downpatrick
Newry
Newcastle
Warrenpoint

NORTH SEA
NORTH SEA
SCOTLAND
Hampden Park
See Pages 5 & 105
St. James' Park
See Pages 5 & 108
Amsterdam
Moray Firth
Firth of Forth
Solway Firth
Loch Ness
Loch Lomond
ISLE OF BUTE
ISLE OF ARRAN
ISLE OF MAN
John o'Groats
Scrabster
Thurso
Wick
Tongue
Scourie
Lochinver
Helmsdale
Lairg
Brora
Golspie
Ullapool
Bonar Bridge
Dornoch
Tain
Poolewe
Gairloch
Alness
Invergordon
Cromarty
Kinlochewe
Torridon
Achnasheen
Dingwall
Fortrose
Nairn
Lossiemouth
Elgin
Forres
Banff
Portsoy
Fraserburgh
Keith
Aberchirder
Turriff
Peterhead
Huntly
Rothes
Dufftown
Inverness
Strathcarron
Grantown-on-Spey
Oldmeldrum
Ellon
Inverurie
ABERDEEN
Invermoriston
Fort Augustus
Aviemore
Kingussie
Invergarry
Newtonmore
Braemar
Ballater
Banchory
Peterculter
Stonehaven
Spean Bridge
Fort William
Inverbervie
Glencoe
Pitlochry
Brechin
Kirriemuir
Montrose
Aberfeldy
Blairgowrie
Forfar
Dunkeld
Arbroath
Dundee
Carnoustie
Oban
Perth
Crianlarich
Crieff
St. Andrews
Auchterarder
Cupar
Inveraray
Callander
Dunblane
Kinross
Glenrothes
Pittenweem
Doune
Methil
Stirling
Alloa
Dunfermline
Kirkcaldy
Cowdenbeath
Helensburgh
North Berwick
Kilsyth
Dunbar
Dumbarton
Falkirk
EDINBURGH
Haddington
GLASGOW
Greenock
Clydebank
Bathgate
Musselburgh
Dunoon
Wemyss Bay
Airdrie
Dalkeith
Rothesay
Kennacraig
Paisley
Livingston
Penicuik
Eyemouth
Largs
Hamilton
Motherwell
Duns
East Kilbride
Berwick-upon-Tweed
Ardrossan
Lanark
Lauder
Galashiels
Coldstream
Irvine
Kilmarnock
Peebles
Troon
Biggar
Kelso
Wooler
Brodick
Prestwick
Selkirk
Ayr
Cumnock
Alnwick
Hawick
Jedburgh
Maybole
Sanquhar
Moffat
Amble
Girvan
Ashington
Morpeth
Langholm
New Galloway
Lockerbie
Bedlington
Blyth
Whitley Bay
Dumfries
NEWCASTLE UPON TYNE
Tynemouth
South Shields
Cairnryan
Castle Douglas
Annan
Newton Stewart
Gatehouse of Fleet
Hexham
Gateshead
Washington
Sunderland
Dalbeattie
Carlisle
Brampton
Stanley
Stranraer
Wigtown
Kirkcudbright
Consett
Seaham
Durham
Tow Law
Whithorn
Alston
Peterlee
Maryport
Cockermouth
Penrith
Hartlepool
Workington
Bishop Auckland
Keswick
Appleby-in-Westmorland
Newton Aycliffe
Stockton-on-Tees
Redcar
Whitehaven
Brough
MIDDLESBROUGH
Egremont
Barnard Castle
Darlington
Whitby
Ambleside
Windermere
Richmond
Catterick
Ramsey
Ravenglass
Coniston
Northallerton
Peel
Kendal
Leyburn
Thirsk
Kirkby

Mileage Chart and Journey Times

This chart shows the distance in miles and journey time between two cities or towns in Great Britain. Each route has been calculated using a combination of motorways, primary routes and other major roads. This is normally the quickest, though not always the shortest route.

Average journey times are calculated whilst driving at the maximum speed limit. These times are approximate and do not include traffic congestion or convenience breaks.

To find the distance and journey time between two cities or towns, follow a horizontal line and vertical column until they meet each other.

For example, the 285 mile journey from London to Penzance is approximately 4 hours and 59 minutes.

Great Britain

Journey times

	Aberystwyth	Ayr	Birmingham	Bradford	Brighton	Bristol	Cambridge	Cardiff	Carlisle	Coventry	Derby	Doncaster	Dover	Edinburgh	Exeter	Fort William	Glasgow	Gloucester	Harwich	Holyhead	Inverness	Ipswich	Kendal	Kingston upon Hull	Leeds	Leicester	Lincoln	Liverpool	Manchester	Middlesbrough	Newcastle upon Tyne	Norwich	Nottingham	Oxford	Penzance	Perth	Plymouth	Portsmouth	Reading	Salisbury	Sheffield	Shrewsbury	Southampton	Southend-on-Sea	Stoke-on-Trent	Swansea	Thurso	Worcester	York	London
Aberdeen	8:21	3:31	7:13	6:28	9:56	8:26	8:15	8:55	4:08	7:27	7:09	6:25	10:16	2:39	9:38	3:38	2:50	7:55	9:32	7:41	2:30	9:08	4:55	6:51	6:16	7:40	7:07	6:13	6:01	5:16	4:39	9:18	7:14	8:18	11:22	1:48	10:16	9:33	8:57	9:21	6:42	7:07	9:25	9:22	6:28	9:31	4:52	7:35	6:07	9:03
Aberystwyth		6:34	2:34	3:27	5:21	2:44	4:00	2:29	4:24	2:52	2:56	3:45	5:41	6:20	3:51	8:13	5:53	2:34	5:17	2:29	8:39	4:53	3:40	4:20	3:29	3:18	4:11	2:39	2:54	4:34	5:07	5:03	3:17	3:43	5:35	6:41	4:29	4:27	3:50	4:01	3:41	1:47	4:18	4:56	2:48	1:48	11:00	2:19	4:00	4:28
Ayr			5:28	4:28	8:11	6:42	6:31	7:10	2:24	5:43	5:25	4:41	8:32	1:48	7:54	3:03	0:48	6:11	7:48	5:56	3:51	7:24	3:10	5:06	4:32	5:55	5:22	4:29	4:16	3:56	3:28	7:34	5:29	6:34	9:37	1:53	8:31	7:49	7:13	7:37	4:57	5:23	7:40	7:37	4:43	7:46	6:12	5:50	4:22	7:16
Birmingham				2:15	3:04	1:41	1:43	2:09	3:16	0:36	1:01	1:40	3:25	5:12	2:53	7:05	4:45	1:10	3:01	2:59	7:31	2:37	2:32	2:21	2:05	1:01	1:55	1:49	1:46	2:55	3:28	2:46	1:08	1:27	4:36	5:33	3:30	2:42	2:06	2:39	1:36	0:59	2:33	2:39	1:02	2:44	9:52	0:49	2:21	2:11
Bradford					4:30	3:34	2:43	4:03	2:17	2:19	1:34	0:53	4:37	4:17	4:46	6:06	3:46	3:03	4:01	2:49	6:31	3:37	1:32	1:18	0:28	2:02	1:35	1:22	0:57	1:32	2:06	3:46	1:37	3:05	6:29	4:33	5:24	4:20	3:44	4:18	1:00	2:15	4:12	3:50	1:36	4:38	8:52	2:42	0:59	3:32
Brighton						2:49	2:09	3:26	6:00	2:42	3:15	3:53	1:53	7:53	3:41	9:49	7:29	2:47	2:19	5:39	10:14	2:20	5:15	4:35	4:19	2:57	3:43	4:32	4:29	5:08	5:42	3:05	3:21	1:58	5:24	8:16	4:18	1:14	1:39	1:54	3:49	3:45	1:35	1:41	3:45	4:01	12:35	3:07	4:35	1:27
Bristol							3:02	0:56	4:31	1:44	2:21	2:59	3:18	6:27	1:37	8:20	6:00	0:47	3:27	4:13	8:45	3:28	3:46	3:41	3:25	2:17	3:11	3:03	3:01	4:15	4:48	3:58	2:28	1:30	3:20	6:48	2:14	2:03	1:26	1:37	2:56	2:14	1:54	2:58	2:17	1:30	11:07	1:07	3:41	2:07
Cambridge								3:28	4:20	1:30	1:52	2:03	2:06	6:04	4:11	8:09	5:49	2:29	1:28	4:20	8:35	1:04	3:56	2:37	2:34	1:25	1:47	3:12	3:10	3:19	3:52	1:13	1:41	1:55	5:54	6:37	4:49	2:34	1:51	2:47	2:15	2:26	2:35	1:19	2:26	4:03	10:56	2:08	2:45	1:17
Cardiff									4:58	2:15	2:48	3:27	3:54	6:54	2:02	8:47	6:27	1:16	4:03	4:23	9:13	4:03	4:14	4:09	3:53	2:46	3:39	3:31	3:28	4:42	5:16	4:31	2:55	2:05	3:46	7:15	2:40	2:38	2:01	2:12	3:23	2:24	2:29	3:33	2:44	0:53	11:34	1:35	4:09	2:43
Carlisle										3:30	3:12	2:28	6:19	2:08	5:41	4:01	1:41	3:58	5:35	3:44	4:27	5:11	0:58	2:54	2:19	3:43	3:10	2:16	2:04	1:44	1:15	5:21	3:17	4:21	7:25	2:29	6:19	5:36	5:00	5:24	2:45	3:10	5:28	5:25	2:31	5:34	6:48	3:38	2:10	5:07
Coventry											1:03	1:41	3:05	5:29	2:55	7:22	5:02	1:12	2:49	3:13	7:48	2:21	2:49	2:23	2:06	0:45	1:39	2:06	2:03	2:56	3:30	2:31	1:09	1:04	4:38	5:50	3:32	2:19	1:43	2:17	1:37	1:18	2:11	2:20	1:19	2:49	10:09	0:56	2:22	1:53
Derby												0:57	3:33	4:58	3:31	7:02	4:42	1:48	3:09	2:52	7:27	2:45	2:28	1:39	1:23	0:49	1:24	1:45	1:42	2:13	2:46	2:55	0:33	1:51	5:14	5:29	4:08	3:06	2:30	3:04	0:54	1:21	2:58	2:48	0:53	3:22	9:49	1:27	1:39	2:19
Doncaster													3:58	4:13	4:12	6:19	3:59	2:30	3:21	3:17	6:44	2:57	2:16	0:56	0:43	1:27	0:55	1:48	1:25	1:28	2:02	3:07	1:02	2:30	5:56	4:46	4:50	3:45	3:09	3:43	0:30	2:13	3:36	3:11	1:44	4:04	9:05	2:09	0:54	2:57
Dover														7:56	4:14	10:08	7:48	3:16	2:16	5:59	10:34	2:17	5:35	4:29	4:26	3:14	3:40	4:52	4:49	5:11	5:45	3:02	3:34	2:27	5:57	8:36	4:51	2:23	2:08	2:50	4:06	4:05	2:38	1:37	4:05	4:29	12:55	3:36	4:38	1:34
Edinburgh															7:38	3:01	1:05	5:55	7:20	5:41	3:02	6:56	2:55	4:38	4:04	5:26	4:54	4:13	4:00	3:00	2:23	7:06	5:01	6:18	9:21	1:02	8:16	7:33	6:57	7:21	4:29	5:07	7:25	7:09	4:28	7:30	5:24	5:34	3:54	6:57
Exeter																9:31	7:11	1:58	4:36	5:24	9:56	4:37	4:57	4:52	4:36	3:28	4:22	4:14	4:12	5:26	5:59	5:07	3:39	2:46	1:54	7:59	0:53	2:38	2:43	1:55	4:07	3:25	2:27	4:02	3:28	2:37	12:18	2:18	4:52	3:16
Fort William																	2:26	7:49	9:26	7:35	1:32	9:02	4:49	6:44	6:10	7:34	7:00	6:07	5:54	5:34	5:06	9:12	7:07	8:12	11:15	2:09	10:10	9:27	8:51	9:15	6:35	7:01	9:19	9:16	6:22	9:24	4:04	7:28	6:01	8:56
Glasgow																		5:28	7:05	5:13	3:08	6:41	2:28	4:23	3:49	5:12	4:39	3:46	3:33	3:13	2:45	6:51	4:46	5:51	8:54	1:10	7:48	7:06	6:30	6:54	4:14	4:40	6:57	6:55	4:01	7:03	5:29	5:07	3:40	6:36
Gloucester																			3:25	3:42	8:14	3:22	3:15	3:10	2:54	1:46	2:39	2:32	2:29	3:43	4:17	3:31	1:56	1:11	3:39	6:16	2:33	2:00	1:24	1:42	2:24	1:42	1:52	2:56	1:45	1:49	10:35	0:36	3:10	2:05
Harwich																				5:38	9:53	0:42	5:13	3:55	3:52	2:43	3:05	4:30	4:28	4:37	5:10	1:32	2:59	2:26	6:20	7:55	5:14	2:49	2:17	3:12	3:33	3:44	3:01	1:09	3:44	4:38	12:14	3:26	4:03	1:42
Holyhead																					7:58	5:16	2:59	3:39	2:49	3:23	3:52	1:53	2:13	3:53	4:26	5:25	3:15	4:06	7:06	6:00	6:00	5:21	4:45	5:05	3:06	2:10	5:12	5:18	2:11	4:33	10:19	3:19	3:19	4:47
Inverness																						9:27	5:14	7:10	6:35	7:59	7:26	6:32	6:20	5:41	5:04	9:37	7:33	8:37	11:41	2:10	10:35	9:52	9:16	9:40	7:01	7:26	9:44	9:41	6:47	9:50	2:31	7:54	6:26	9:21
Ipswich																							4:50	3:31	3:28	2:20	2:41	4:06	4:04	4:13	4:46	1:08	2:35	2:27	6:21	7:31	5:15	2:50	2:18	3:13	3:09	3:20	3:02	1:10	3:20	4:39	11:50	3:02	3:39	1:43
Kendal																								2:44	1:53	3:02	3:00	1:36	1:23	1:38	1:59	5:00	2:54	3:41	6:44	3:13	5:38	4:56	4:20	4:44	2:22	2:30	4:47	4:53	1:50	4:53	7:32	2:57	2:04	4:22
Kingston upon Hull																									1:08	2:08	0:58	2:13	1:49	1:54	2:27	3:18	1:43	3:10	6:36	5:12	5:30	4:25	3:49	4:23	1:11	2:53	4:17	3:43	2:25	4:44	9:31	2:49	1:02	3:39
Leeds																										1:53	1:25	1:23	0:58	1:20	1:53	3:37	1:27	2:55	6:21	4:38	5:15	4:10	3:34	4:08	0:50	2:16	4:02	3:40	1:37	4:29	8:57	2:34	0:46	3:23
Leicester																											1:16	2:17	2:14	2:42	3:15	2:27	0:46	1:32	5:11	6:01	4:05	2:47	2:11	2:45	1:23	1:43	2:39	2:29	1:24	3:20	10:20	1:25	2:08	2:01
Lincoln																												2:31	2:02	2:11	2:44	2:20	0:59	2:28	6:07	5:29	5:01	3:43	3:07	3:41	1:07	2:33	3:34	2:54	2:10	4:16	9:48	2:21	1:35	2:51
Liverpool																													0:48	2:28	3:01	4:16	2:10	2:56	6:00	4:33	4:54	4:11	3:35	3:59	1:52	1:25	4:03	4:09	1:06	3:48	8:53	2:13	1:54	3:39
Manchester																														2:03	2:36	4:12	1:51	2:52	5:55	4:22	4:49	4:07	3:30	3:55	1:14	1:41	3:58	4:04	1:01	4:04	8:41	2:08	1:29	3:37
Middlesbrough																															0:55	4:20	2:15	3:43	7:09	3:40	6:03	4:58	4:22	4:56	1:43	3:20	4:50	4:24	2:40	5:17	8:02	3:22	1:05	4:12
Newcastle upon Tyne																																4:54	2:49	4:17	7:43	3:03	6:37	5:32	4:56	5:30	2:17	3:54	5:24	4:58	3:14	5:51	7:25	3:56	1:43	4:46
Norwich																																	2:44	2:58	6:51	7:40	5:45	3:31	2:48	3:43	3:18	3:29	3:32	2:00	3:28	5:06	11:59	3:10	3:48	2:13
Nottingham																																		1:57	5:23	5:34	4:17	3:12	2:36	3:10	0:57	1:44	3:04	2:49	1:18	3:31	9:53	1:36	1:42	2:25
Oxford																																			4:30	6:40	3:24	1:28	0:45	1:25	2:25	2:08	1:19	1:56	2:09	2:40	10:59	1:31	3:10	1:15
Penzance																																				9:43	1:41	4:22	4:27	3:39	5:51	5:09	4:11	5:46	5:12	4:20	14:02	4:02	6:36	4:59
Perth																																					8:37	7:54	7:18	7:42	5:03	5:28	7:46	7:43	4:49	7:52	4:30	5:55	4:28	7:24
Plymouth																																						3:16	3:20	2:32	4:44	4:02	3:04	4:39	4:05	3:14	12:55	2:55	5:29	3:54
Portsmouth																																							1:18	0:52	3:39	3:23	0:32	2:11	3:23	3:13	12:13	2:20	4:25	1:39
Reading																																								1:22	3:01	2:45	1:09	1:46	2:45	2:37	11:35	1:44	3:47	0:56
Salisbury																																									3:37	3:09	0:40	2:37	3:12	2:47	12:02	2:02	4:22	1:52
Sheffield																																										2:08	3:32	3:22	1:40	3:59	9:22	2:04	1:11	2:53
Shrewsbury																																											3:16	3:22	1:04	2:45	9:46	1:23	2:46	2:53
Southampton																																												2:26	3:15	3:05	12:05	2:12	4:16	1:40
Southend-on-Sea																																													3:21	4:09	12:02	3:03	3:51	1:07
Stoke-on-Trent																																														3:18	9:08	1:23	2:09	2:53
Swansea																																															12:11	2:10	4:44	3:18
Thurso																																																10:15	8:47	11:43
Worcester																																																	2:49	2:24
York																																																		3:39

Distance in miles

	Aberdeen	Aberystwyth	Ayr	Birmingham	Bradford	Brighton	Bristol	Cambridge	Cardiff	Carlisle	Coventry	Derby	Doncaster	Dover	Edinburgh	Exeter	Fort William	Glasgow	Gloucester	Harwich	Holyhead	Inverness	Ipswich	Kendal	Kingston upon Hull	Leeds	Leicester	Lincoln	Liverpool	Manchester	Middlesbrough	Newcastle upon Tyne	Norwich	Nottingham	Oxford	Penzance	Perth	Plymouth	Portsmouth	Reading	Salisbury	Sheffield	Shrewsbury	Southampton	Southend-on-Sea	Stoke-on-Trent	Swansea	Thurso	Worcester	York
Aberystwyth	471
Ayr	181	324
Birmingham	423	114	272
Bradford	377	159	196	124
Brighton	596	258	441	169	263
Bristol	505	122	375	88	215	129
Cambridge	487	198	366	102	156	117	167
Cardiff	525	106	377	106	233	168	42	201
Carlisle	229	232	89	183	107	345	286	256	288
Coventry	442	134	297	18	124	157	102	84	129	200
Derby	418	137	269	41	88	188	134	99	159	180	43
Doncaster	371	192	239	95	40	232	184	117	210	150	94	57
Dover	620	315	477	195	284	81	194	118	233	393	180	208	244
Edinburgh	126	340	75	284	198	466	377	326	379	91	303	266	212	444
Exeter	581	199	425	161	282	170	75	323	107	336	166	213	257	244	439
Fort William	159	430	136	391	305	568	478	456	486	198	415	387	345	591	131	549
Glasgow	146	322	36	291	203	468	378	355	384	96	313	282	245	491	46	449	100
Gloucester	473	109	317	53	171	152	35	132	53	228	59	93	149	189	331	107	435	324
Harwich	568	258	411	170	224	130	203	64	234	323	152	167	185	129	397	262	524	419	171
Holyhead	452	96	315	151	158	330	204	252	209	226	167	156	169	358	316	279	423	323	189	331
Inverness	105	492	198	449	353	620	536	490	558	260	458	421	369	601	157	607	63	162	496	554	481
Ipswich	538	268	420	156	210	125	206	54	240	311	138	155	171	127	381	264	510	409	177	21	307	538
Kendal	280	182	139	151	62	324	235	215	232	50	170	136	99	344	141	307	248	146	200	279	180	310	268
Kingston upon Hull	398	235	255	139	68	243	228	134	239	165	123	94	37	254	230	290	367	255	195	204	218	387	189	127
Leeds	359	171	198	119	9	256	209	144	226	111	117	74	32	275	190	279	309	208	167	217	162	345	197	72	60
Leicester	445	155	294	43	99	163	118	70	140	214	24	30	73	183	282	189	412	312	83	146	182	431	125	166	98	97
Lincoln	411	208	249	87	80	207	170	88	192	178	76	53	41	206	247	241	376	274	135	152	204	402	124	140	46	72	52
Liverpool	354	120	199	99	67	267	180	179	169	110	113	90	89	294	201	240	308	213	142	265	95	370	236	75	126	73	110	118
Manchester	349	128	204	87	37	252	167	159	188	117	99	58	51	273	208	239	315	215	132	230	120	363	211	72	96	42	95	87	34
Middlesbrough	289	233	181	174	69	316	265	196	287	92	175	130	84	316	147	337	279	192	230	266	226	306	253	77	88	64	154	127	134	106
Newcastle upon Tyne	252	266	146	209	98	345	300	232	312	58	209	165	115	350	104	369	237	153	263	297	257	263	287	88	130	96	188	153	167	136	40
Norwich	536	270	348	163	185	174	234	62	256	280	142	146	142	169	351	284	478	378	193	72	289	505	44	249	145	178	112	103	222	177	221	252
Nottingham	416	155	267	54	78	191	140	84	165	188	52	15	48	210	256	218	386	286	108	165	177	410	140	141	92	72	27	37	107	68	128	159	118
Oxford	497	151	335	68	167	106	73	92	106	267	57	101	138	142	358	151	465	365	47	134	208	515	128	223	175	162	76	123	168	157	218	253	159	104
Penzance	688	301	552	269	394	279	184	343	218	463	278	316	369	355	551	109	663	561	217	374	388	715	375	419	412	391	310	359	353	344	449	481	393	323	261
Perth	86	366	85	336	245	509	412	370	422	134	346	309	254	485	43	487	103	59	362	439	360	113	424	184	273	233	326	290	244	254	191	148	394	299	404	598
Plymouth	619	232	461	203	325	206	111	274	159	372	209	254	300	286	485	43	592	490	150	305	322	648	305	348	326	323	231	284	299	281	379	412	327	255	193	75	529
Portsmouth	579	231	440	147	274	50	95	132	138	357	132	184	231	137	448	127	555	455	114	161	303	603	158	308	268	245	166	209	254	237	315	360	200	191	83	235	486	170
Reading	538	180	399	103	213	79	77	90	112	309	90	138	184	115	402	141	506	406	75	129	264	554	126	263	209	207	113	168	193	197	264	295	152	129	25	251	445	184	60
Salisbury	538	178	383	121	245	82	53	140	101	312	113	159	207	158	400	91	510	408	73	177	262	569	177	265	251	230	132	187	213	208	287	318	200	162	65	201	443	132	43	57
Sheffield	390	173	235	79	40	225	163	121	193	154	75	35	21	268	230	245	352	250	139	185	164	387	176	102	66	33	68	46	74	40	102	133	144	37	137	361	273	293	228	160	203
Shrewsbury	419	73	260	47	100	216	116	140	107	171	64	67	114	249	262	175	369	267	77	215	104	424	195	125	163	102	79	123	59	67	166	203	196	86	105	286	309	218	195	147	150	85
Southampton	564	213	401	128	235	64	75	129	122	330	114	167	201	150	433	106	528	426	98	157	287	590	162	276	249	230	136	189	235	215	288	320	190	162	66	217	476	149	20	47	23	206	175
Southend-on-Sea	549	258	431	152	220	85	177	64	211	342	129	168	185	89	395	226	548	438	152	57	303	549	57	283	200	213	139	156	255	225	262	299	99	160	105	337	439	269	117	98	132	197	173	126
Stoke-on-Trent	381	108	243	47	75	217	127	137	140	150	64	36	74	236	241	202	348	248	95	201	122	410	179	121	117	78	55	87	56	36	142	173	171	55	118	311	287	241	201	147	168	50	35	183	199
Swansea	529	76	368	124	220	209	80	236	41	279	150	184	244	264	370	154	477	375	91	279	172	578	279	249	262	229	174	226	168	187	293	323	286	178	144	266	446	196	175	147	136	202	124	159	245	159
Thurso	212	584	304	557	461	728	644	589	640	352	552	529	475	706	262	715	169	268	604	657	589	108	654	402	492	453	544	510	463	471	410	367	613	519	621	823	220	758	709	662	664	506	523	682	659	502	631
Worcester	448	96	309	29	135	162	62	119	73	220	46	68	124	197	306	136	418	311	28	168	151	480	174	169	166	146	72	118	108	101	203	229	180	85	57	244	350	177	146	95	101	103	49	124	150	65	97	572
York	345	193	201	129	34	269	227	151	237	116	129	84	33	269	187	289	314	214	181	232	185	344	200	81	38	24	108	76	96	65	48	83	176	84	174	400	230	331	257	217	244	54	132	244	214	114	268	450	164
London	537	228	440	118	203	53	118	61	151	309	97	129	171	76	403	179	511	404	116	86	277	562	82	263	214	195	103	155	211	209	251	283	117	128	59	285	451	216	84	41	92	166	161	82	43	161	187	669	136	211

Scale to Map Pages

1:250,000 = 3.946 miles to 1 inch (2.54 cm) / 2.5 km to 1 cm

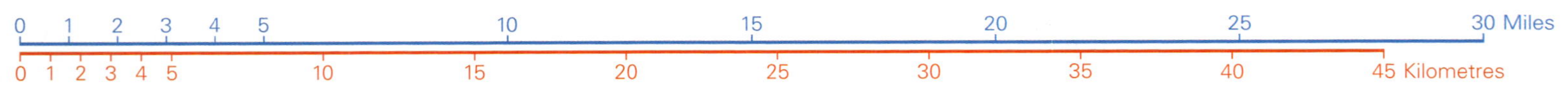

Limited Interchange Motorway Junctions are shown on the mapping pages by red junction indicators 2

M1

Junction		
2	Northbound	No exit, access from A1 only
	Southbound	No access, exit to A1 only
4	Northbound	No exit, access from A41 only
	Southbound	No access, exit to A41 only
6a	Northbound	No exit, access from M25 only
	Southbound	No access, exit to M25 only
17	Northbound	No access, exit to M45 only
	Southbound	No exit, access from M45 only
19	Northbound	Exit to M6 only, access from A14 only
	Southbound	Access from M6 only, exit to A14 only
21a	Northbound	No access, exit to A46 only
	Southbound	No exit, access from A46 only
24a	Northbound	Access from A50 only
	Southbound	Exit to A50 only
35a	Northbound	No access, exit to A616 only
	Southbound	No exit, access from A616 only
43	Northbound	Exit to M621 only
	Southbound	Access from M621 only
48	Eastbound	Exit to A1(M) northbound only
	Westbound	Access from A1(M) southbound only

M2

Junction		
1	Eastbound	Access from A2 eastbound only
	Westbound	Exit to A2 westbound only

M3

Junction		
8	Eastbound	No exit, access from A303 only
	Westbound	No access, exit to A303 only
10	Northbound	No access from A31
	Southbound	No exit to A31
13	Southbound	No access from A335 to M3 leading to M27 Eastbound

M4

Junction		
1	Eastbound	Exit to A4 eastbound only
	Westbound	Access from A4 westbound only
21	Eastbound	No exit to M48
	Westbound	No access from M48
23	Eastbound	No access from M48
	Westbound	No exit to M48
25	Eastbound	No exit
	Westbound	No access
25a	Eastbound	No exit
	Westbound	No access
29	Eastbound	No exit, access from A48(M) only
	Westbound	No access, exit to A48(M) only
38	Westbound	No access, exit to A48 only
39	Eastbound	No access or exit
	Westbound	No exit, access from A48 only
42	Eastbound	No access from A48
	Westbound	No exit to A48

M5

Junction		
10	Northbound	No exit, access from A4019 only
	Southbound	No access, exit to A4019 only
11a	Southbound	No exit to A417 westbound
18a	Northbound	No access from M49
	Southbound	No exit to M49

M6

Junction		
3a	Eastbound	No exit to M6 Toll
	Westbound	No access from M6 Toll
4	Northbound	No exit to M42 northbound No access from M42 southbound
	Southbound	No exit to M42 No access from M42 southbound
4a	Northbound	No exit, access from M42 southbound only
	Southbound	No access, exit to M42 only
5	Northbound	No access, exit to A452 only
	Southbound	No exit, access from A452 only
10a	Northbound	No access, exit to M54 only
	Southbound	No exit, access from M54 only
11a	Northbound	No exit to M6 Toll
	Southbound	No access from M6 Toll
20	Northbound	No exit to M56 eastbound
	Southbound	No access from M56 westbound
24	Northbound	No exit, access from A58 only
	Southbound	No access, exit to A58 only
25	Northbound	No access, exit to A49 only
	Southbound	No exit, access from A49 only
30	Northbound	No exit, access from M61 northbound only
	Southbound	No access, exit to M61 southbound only
31a	Northbound	No access, exit to B6242 only
	Southbound	No exit, access from B6242 only
45	Northbound	No access onto A74(M)
	Southbound	No exit from A74(M)

M6 Toll

Junction		
T1	Northbound	No exit
	Southbound	No access
T2	Northbound	No access or exit
	Southbound	No access
T5	Northbound	No exit
	Southbound	No access
T7	Northbound	No access from A5
	Southbound	No exit
T8	Northbound	No exit to A460 northbound
	Southbound	No exit

M8

Junction		
8	Eastbound	No exit to M73 northbound
	Westbound	No access from M73 southbound
9	Eastbound	No access, exit only
	Westbound	No exit, access only
13	Eastbound	No access from M80 southbound
	Westbound	No exit to M80 northbound
14	Eastbound	No access, exit only
	Westbound	No exit, access only
16	Eastbound	No exit, access only
	Westbound	No access, exit only
17	Eastbound	No exit, access from A82 only
	Westbound	No access, exit to A82 only
18	Westbound	No exit, access only
19	Eastbound	No exit to A814 eastbound
	Westbound	No access from A814 westbound
20	Eastbound	No exit, access only
	Westbound	No access, exit only
21	Eastbound	No access, exit only
	Westbound	No exit, access only
22	Eastbound	No exit, access from M77 only
	Westbound	No access, exit to M77 only
23	Eastbound	No exit, access from B768 only
	Westbound	No access, exit to B768 only
25	Eastbound & Westbound	Access from A739 southbound only Exit to A739 northbound only
25a	Eastbound	Access only
	Westbound	Exit only
28	Eastbound	No exit, access from airport only
	Westbound	No access, exit to airport only

M9

Junction		
1a	Northbound	No access, exit to M9 spur only
	Southbound	No exit, access from M9 spur only
2	Northbound	No exit, access from B8046 only
	Southbound	No access, exit to B8046 only
3	Northbound	No access, exit to A803 only
	Southbound	No exit, access from A803 only
6	Northbound	No exit, access only
	Southbound	No access, exit to A905 only
8	Northbound	No access, exit to M876 only
	Southbound	No exit, access from M876 only
Junction with A90	Northbound	Exit onto A90 westbound only
	Southbound	Access from A90 eastbound only

M11

Junction		
4	Northbound	No exit, access from A406 eastbound only
	Southbound	No access, exit to A406 westbound only
5	Northbound	No access, exit to A1168 only
	Southbound	No exit, access from A1168 only
8a	Northbound	No access, exit only
	Southbound	No exit, access only
9	Northbound	No access, exit only
	Southbound	No exit, access only
13	Northbound	No access, exit only
	Southbound	No exit, access only
14	Northbound	No access from A428 eastbound No exit to A428 westbound
	Southbound	No exit, access from A428 eastbound only

M20

Junction		
2	Eastbound	No access, exit to A20 only (access via M26 Junction 2a)
	Westbound	No exit, access only (exit via M26 Jun.2a)
3	Eastbound	No exit, access from M26 eastbound only
	Westbound	No access, exit to M26 westbound only
11a	Eastbound	No access from Channel Tunnel
	Westbound	No exit to Channel Tunnel

M23

Junction		
7	Northbound	No exit to A23 southbound
	Southbound	No access from A23 northbound

M25

Junction		
5	Clockwise	No exit to M26 eastbound
	Anti-clockwise	No access from M26 westbound
Spur to A21	Northbound	No exit to M26 eastbound
	Southbound	No access from M26 westbound
19	Clockwise	No access, exit only
	Anti-clockwise	No exit, access only
21	Clockwise & Anti-clockwise	No exit to M1 southbound No access from M1 northbound
31	Northbound	No access, exit only (access via Jun.30)
	Southbound	No exit, access only (exit via Jun.30)

M26

Junction		
Junction with M25 (M25 Jun.5)	Eastbound	No access from M25 clockwise or spur from A21 northbound
	Westbound	No exit to M25 anti-clockwise or spur to A21 southbound
Junction with M20 (M20 Jun.3)	Eastbound	No exit to M20 westbound
	Westbound	No access from M20 eastbound

M27

Junction		
4	Eastbound & Westbound	No exit to A33 southbound (Southampton) No access from A33 northbound
10	Eastbound	No exit, access from A32 only
	Westbound	No access, exit to A32 only

M40

Junction		
3	N.W bound	No access, exit to A40 only
	S.E bound	No exit, access from A40 only
7	N.W bound	No access, exit only
	S.E bound	No exit, access only
13	N.W bound	No access, exit only
	S.E bound	No exit, access only
14	N.W bound	No exit, access only
	S.E bound	No access, exit only
16	N.W bound	No exit, access only
	S.E bound	No access, exit only

M42

Junction		
1	Eastbound	No exit
	Westbound	No access
7	Northbound	No access, exit to M6 only
	Southbound	No exit, access from M6 northbound only
8	Northbound	No exit, access from M6 southbound only
	Southbound	Exit to M6 northbound only Access from M6 southbound only

M45

Junction		
Junction with M1 (M1 Jun.17)	Eastbound	No exit to M1 northbound
	Westbound	No access from M1 southbound
Junction with A45 east of Dunchurch	Eastbound	No access, exit to A45 only
	Westbound	No exit, access from A45 northbound only

M48

Junction		
Junction with M4 (M4 Jun.21)	Eastbound	No exit to M4 westbound
	Westbound	No access from M4 eastbound
Junction with M4 (M4 Jun.23)	Eastbound	No access from M4 westbound
	Westbound	No exit to M4 eastbound

M53

Junction		
11	Northbound & Southbound	No access from M56 eastbound, no exit to M56 westbound

M56

Junction		
1	Eastbound	No exit to M60 N.W bound No exit to A34 southbound
	S.E bound	No access from A34 northbound
	Westbound	No access from M60
2	Eastbound	No exit, access from A560 only
	Westbound	No access, exit to A560 only
3	Eastbound	No access, exit only
	Westbound	No exit, access only
4	Eastbound	No exit, access only
	Westbound	No access, exit only
7	Westbound	No access, exit only
8	Eastbound	No access or exit
	Westbound	No exit, access from A556 only
9	Eastbound	No access from M6 northbound
	Westbound	No exit to M60 southbound
10a	Northbound	No exit, access only
	Southbound	No access, exit only
15	Eastbound	No exit to M53
	Westbound	No access from M53

M57

Junction		
3	Northbound	No exit, access only
	Southbound	No access, exit only
5	Northbound	No exit, access from A580 westbound only
	Southbound	No access, exit to A580 eastbound only

M58

Junction		
1	Eastbound	No exit, access from A506 only
	Westbound	No access, exit to A506 only

M60

Junction		
2	N.E bound	No access, exit to A560 only
	S.W bound	No exit, access from A560 only
3	Eastbound	No access from A34 southbound
	Westbound	No exit to A34 northbound
4	Eastbound	No exit to M56 S.W bound No exit to A34 northbound
	Westbound	No access from A34 southbound No access from M56 eastbound
5	N.W bound	No access from or exit to A5103 southbound
	S.E bound	No access from or exit to A5103 northbound
14	Eastbound	No exit to A580 No access from A580 westbound
	Westbound	No exit to A580 eastbound No access from A580
16	Eastbound	No exit, access from A666 only
	Westbound	No access, exit to A666 only
20	Eastbound	No access from A664
	Westbound	No exit to A664
22	Westbound	No access from A62
25	S.W bound	No access from A560 / A6017
26	N.E bound	No access or exit
27	N.E bound	No access, exit only
	S.W bound	No exit, access only

M61

Junction		
2&3	N.W bound	No access from A580 eastbound
	S.E bound	No exit to A580 westbound
Junction with M6 (M6 Jun.30)	N.W bound	No exit to M6 southbound
	S.E bound	No access from M6 northbound

M62

Junction		
23	Eastbound	No access, exit to A640 only
	Westbound	No exit, access from A640 only

M65

Junction		
9	N.E bound	No access, exit to A679 only
	S.W bound	No exit, access from A679 only
11	N.E bound	No exit, access only
	S.W bound	No access, exit only

M66

Junction		
1	Northbound	No access, exit to A56 only
	Southbound	No exit, access from A56 only

M67

Junction		
1	Eastbound	Access from A57 eastbound only
	Westbound	Exit to A57 westbound only
1a	Eastbound	No access, exit to A6017 only
	Westbound	No exit, access from A6017 only
2	Eastbound	No exit, access from A57 only
	Westbound	No access, exit to A57 only

M69

Junction		
2	N.E bound	No exit, access from B4669 only
	S.W bound	No access, exit to B4669 only

M73

Junction		
1	Southbound	No exit to A721 eastbound
2	Northbound	No access from M8 eastbound No exit to A89 eastbound
	Southbound	No exit to M8 westbound No access from A89 westbound
3	Northbound	No exit to A80 S.W bound
	Southbound	No access from A80 N.E bound

M74

Junction		
1	Eastbound	No access from M8 Westbound
	Westbound	No exit to M8 Westbound
3	Eastbound	No exit
	Westbound	No access
3a	Eastbound	No access
	Westbound	No exit
7	Northbound	No exit, access from A72 only
	Southbound	No access, exit to A72 only
9	Northbound	No access or exit
	Southbound	No access, exit to B7078 only
10	Southbound	No exit, access from B7078 only
11	Northbound	No exit, access from B7078 only
	Southbound	No access, exit to B7078 only
12	Northbound	No access, exit to A70 only
	Southbound	No exit, access from A70 only

M77

Junction		
Junction with M8 (M8 Jun.22)	Northbound	No exit to M8 westbound
	Southbound	No access from M8 eastbound
4	Northbound	No exit
	Southbound	No access
6	Northbound	No exit to A77
	Southbound	No access from A77
7	Northbound	No access from A77 No exit to A77

M80

Junction		
1	Northbound	No access from M8 westbound
	Southbound	No exit to M8 eastbound
4a	Northbound	No access
	Southbound	No exit
6a	Northbound	No exit
	Southbound	No access
8	Northbound	No access from M876
	Southbound	No exit to M876

M90

Junction		
2a	Northbound	No access, exit to A92 only
	Southbound	No exit, access from A92 only
7	Northbound	No exit, access from A91 only
	Southbound	No access, exit to A91 only
8	Northbound	No access, exit to A91 only
	Southbound	No exit, access from A91 only
10	Northbound	No access from A912 Exit to A912 northbound only
	Southbound	No exit to A912 Access from A912 southbound only

M180

Junction		
1	Eastbound	No access, exit only
	Westbound	No exit, access from A18 only

M606

Junction		
2	Northbound	No access, exit only

M621

Junction		
2a	Eastbound	No exit, access only
	Westbound	No access, exit only
4	Southbound	No exit
5	Northbound	No access, exit to A61 only
	Southbound	No exit, access from A61 only
6	Northbound	No exit, access only
	Southbound	No access, exit only
7	Eastbound	No access, exit only
	Westbound	No exit, access only
8	Northbound	No access, exit only
	Southbound	No exit, access only

M876

Junction		
Junction with M80 (M80 Jun.5)	N.E bound	No access from M80 southbound
	S.W bound	No exit to M80 northbound
Junction with M9 (M9 Jun.8)	N.E bound	No exit to M9 northbound
	S.W bound	No access from M9 southbound

A1(M)

Junction		
Hertfordshire Section		
2	Northbound	No access, exit only
	Southbound	No exit, access from A1001 only
3	Southbound	No access, exit only
5	Northbound	No exit, access only
	Southbound	No access or exit
Cambridgeshire Section		
13a	Northbound	No exit to B1043
	Southbound	No access from B1043
14	Northbound	No exit, access only
	Southbound	No access, exit only
Leeds Section		
40	Southbound	Exit to A1 southbound only
43	Northbound	Access from M1 eastbound only
	Southbound	Exit to M1 westbound only
Durham Section		
57	Northbound	No access, exit to A66(M) only
	Southbound	No exit, access from A66(M)
65	Northbound	Exit to A1 N.W bound and to A194(M) only
	Southbound	Access from A1 S.E bound and from A194(M) only

A3(M)

Junction		
4	Northbound	No access, exit only
	Southbound	No exit, access only

Aston Expressway A38(M)

Junction		
Junction with Victoria Road, Aston	Northbound	No exit, access only
	Southbound	No access, exit only

A48(M)

Junction		
Junction with M4 (M4 Jun.29)	N.E bound	Exit to M4 eastbound only
	S.W bound	Access from M4 westbound only
29a	N.E bound	Access from A48 eastbound only
	S.W bound	Exit to A48 westbound only

Mancunian Way A57(M)

Junction		
Junction with A34 Brook Street, Manchester	Eastbound	No access, exit to A34 Brook Street, southbound only
	Westbound	No exit, access only

Leeds Inner Ring Road A58(M)

Junction		
Junction with Park Lane / Westgate	Southbound	No access, exit only

Leeds Inner Ring Road A64(M) (continuation of A58(M))

Junction		
Junction with A58 Clay Pit Lane	Eastbound	No access
	Westbound	No exit

A66(M)

Junction		
Junction with A1(M) (A1(M) Jun.57)	N.E bound	Access from A1(M) northbound only
	S.W bound	Exit to A1(M) southbound only

A74(M)

Junction		
18	Northbound	No access
	Southbound	No exit

Newcastle Central Motorway A167(M)

Junction		
Junction with Camden Street	Northbound	No exit, access only
	Southbound	No access or exit

A194(M)

Junction		
Junction with A1(M) (A1(M) Jun.65) and A1 Gateshead Western By-Pass	Northbound	Access from A1(M) only
	Southbound	Exit to A1(M) only

Reference

Motorway (M1)
Autoroute
Autobahn

Motorway Under Construction
Autoroute en construction
Autobahn im Bau

Motorway Proposed
Autoroute prévue
Geplante Autobahn

Motorway Junctions with Numbers
Unlimited Interchange 4
Limited Interchange 5

Autoroute échangeur numéroté
Echangeur complet
Echangeur partiel

Autobahnanschlußstelle mit Nummer
Unbeschränkter Fahrtrichtungswechsel
Beschränkter Fahrtrichtungswechsel

Motorway Service Area (with fuel station)
with access from one carriageway only

Aire de services d'autoroute (avec station service)
accessible d'un seul côté

Rastplatz oder Raststätte (mit tankstelle)
Einbahn

Major Road Service Areas (with fuel station) with 24 hour facilities
Primary Route — Class A Road

Aire de services sur route prioritaire (avec station service) Ouverte 24h sur 24
Route à grande circulation — Route de type A

Raststätte (mit tankstelle) Durchgehend geöffnet
Hauptverkehrsstraße — A- Straße

Truckstop (selection of)
Sélection d'aire pour poids lourds
Auswahl von Fernfahrerrastplatz

Primary Route (A41)
Route à grande circulation
Hauptverkehrsstraße

Primary Route Junction with Number (5)
Echangeur numéroté
Hauptverkehrsstraßenkreuzung mit Nummer

Primary Route Destination (DOVER)
Route prioritaire, direction
Hauptverkehrsstraße Richtung

Dual Carriageways (A & B roads)
Route à double chaussées séparées (route A & B)
Zweispurige Schnellstraße (A- und B- Straßen)

Class A Road (A129)
Route de type A
A-Straße

Class B Road (B177)
Route de type B
B-Straße

Narrow Major Road (passing places)
Route prioritaire étroite (possibilité de dépassement)
Schmale Hauptverkehrsstaße (mit Überholmöglichkeit)

Major Roads Under Construction
Route prioritaire en construction
Hauptverkehrsstaße im Bau

Major Roads Proposed
Route prioritaire prévue
Geplante Hauptverkehrsstaße

Safety Cameras with Speed Limits
Single Camera (30)
Multiple Cameras located along road (50)
Single & Multiple Variable Speed Cameras (V)

Radars de contrôle de vitesse
Radar simple
Radars multiples situés le long de la route
Radars simples et multiples de contrôle de vitesse variable

Sicherheitskameras mit Tempolimit
Einzelne Kamera
Mehrere Kameras entlang der Straße
Einzelne und mehrere Kameras für variables Tempolimit

Fuel Station
Station service
Tankstelle

Gradient 1:5 (20%) **& steeper**
(ascent in direction of arrow)
Pente égale ou supérieure à 20% (dans le sens de la montée)
20% Steigung und steiler (in Pfeilrichtung)

Toll (TOLL)
Barrière de péage
Gebührenpflichtig

Mileage between markers (8)
Distence en miles entre les flèches
Strecke zwischen Markierungen in Meilen

Railway and Station
Voie ferrée et gare
Eisenbahnlinie und Bahnhof

Level Crossing and Tunnel
Passage à niveau et tunnel
Bahnübergang und Tunnel

River or Canal
Rivière ou canal
Fluß oder Kanal

County or Unitary Authority Boundary
Limite de comté ou de division administrative
Grafschafts- oder Verwaltungsbezirksgrenze

National Boundary
Frontière nationale
Landesgrenze

Built-up Area
Agglomération
Geschloßene Ortschaft

Village or Hamlet
Village ou hameau
Dorf oder Weiler

Wooded Area
Zone boisée
Waldgebiet

Spot Height in Feet (• 813)
Altitude (en pieds)
Höhe in Fuß

Relief above 400' (122m)
Relief par estompage au-dessus de 400' (122m)
Reliefschattierung über 400' (122m)

National Grid Reference (kilometres) (100)
Coordonnées géographiques nationales (Kilomètres)
Nationale geographische Koordinaten (Kilometer)

Page Continuation (48)
Suite à la page indiquée
Seitenfortsetzung

Area covered by Main Route map (MAIN ROUTE 97)
Répartition des cartes des principaux axes routiers
Von Karten mit Hauptverkehrsstrecken

Tourist Information

Airport
Aéroport
Flughafen

Airfield
Terrain d'aviation
Flugplatz

Heliport
Héliport
Hubschrauberlandeplatz

Battle Site and Date (1066)
Champ de bataille et date
Schlachtfeld und Datum

Castle (open to public)
Château (ouvert au public)
Schloß / Burg (für die Öffentlichkeit zugänglich)

Castle with Garden (open to public)
Château avec parc (ouvert au public)
Schloß mit Garten (für die Öffentlichkeit zugänglich)

Cathedral, Abbey, Church, Friary, Priory
Cathédrale, abbaye, église, monastère, prieuré
Kathedrale, Abtei, Kirche, Mönchskloster, Kloster

Country Park
Parc régional
Landschaftspark

Ferry (vehicular, sea)
(vehicular, river)
(foot only)

Bac (véhicules, mer)
(véhicules, rivière)
(piétons)

Fähre (auto, meer)
(auto, fluß)
(nur für Personen)

Garden (open to public)
Jardin (ouvert au public)
Garten (für die Öffentlichkeit zugänglich)

Golf Course (9 hole) (18 hole)
Terrain de golf (9 trous) (18 trous)
Golfplatz (9 Löcher) (18 Löcher)

Historic Building (open to public)
Monument historique (ouvert au public)
Historisches Gebäude (für die Öffentlichkeit zugänglich)

Historic Building with Garden (open to public)
Monument historique avec jardin (ouvert au public)
Historisches Gebäude mit Garten (für die Öffentlichkeit zugänglich)

Horse Racecourse
Hippodrome
Pferderennbahn

Lighthouse
Phare
Leuchtturm

Motor Racing Circuit
Circuit Automobile
Automobilrennbahn

Museum, Art Gallery
Musée
Museum, Galerie

National Park
Parc national
Nationalpark

National Trust Property
(open) NT
(restricted opening) NT
(National Trust for Scotland) NTS NTS

National Trust Property
(ouvert)
(heures d'ouverture)
(National Trust for Scotland)

National Trust- Eigentum
(geöffnet)
(beschränkte Öffnungszeit)
(National Trust for Scotland)

Nature Reserve or Bird Sanctuary
Réserve naturelle botanique ou ornithologique
Natur- oder Vogelschutzgebiet

Nature Trail or Forest Walk
Chemin forestier, piste verte
Naturpfad oder Waldweg

Place of Interest (Monument •)
Site, curiosité
Sehenswürdigkeit

Picnic Site
Lieu pour pique-nique
Picknickplatz

Railway, Steam or Narrow Gauge
Chemin de fer, à vapeur ou à voie étroite
Eisenbahn, Dampf- oder Schmalspurbahn

Theme Park
Centre de loisirs
Vergnügungspark

Tourist Information Centre
Syndicat d'initiative
Information

Viewpoint (360 degrees) (180 degrees)
Vue panoramique (360 degrés) (180 degrés)
Aussichtspunkt (360 Grade) (180 Grade)

Visitor Information Centre
Centre d'information touristique
Besucherzentrum

Wildlife Park
Réserve de faune
Wildpark

Windmill
Moulin à vent
Windmühle

Zoo or Safari Park
Parc ou réserve zoologique
Zoo oder Safari-Park

***Please note:** symbols have been enlarged for clarity*

ISLES OF SCILLY
The Isles of Scilly lie 28 miles WSW of Land's End
Round Island
St. Helen's
White Island
BRYHER
Tean
ST. MARTIN'S
TRESCO
EASTERN ISLES
Samson
Maypole
Hugh Town
ST. MARY'S
Crim Rocks
Annet
Gugh
Western Rocks
ST. AGNES
Bishop Rock
Hugh Town to Penzance 2hrs. 40mins. (Seasonal)
ATLANTIC OCEAN
TREVOSE HEAD
Padstow
Newquay
St. Columb Major
Perranporth
St. Agnes
TRURO
REDRUTH
CAMBORNE
St. Ives
Hayle
PENZANCE
FALMOUTH
Penryn
Helston
St. Just
Sennen
LAND'S END
MOUNT'S BAY
St. Clement's Isle
Penzance to Hugh Town 2hrs. 40mins. (Seasonal)
Mullion
Lizard
LIZARD POINT
Coverack
St. Keverne
The Manacles
Black Head
St. Mawes
Veryan
Gull Rock
Nare Head
Probus
Ladock
Indian Queens
A30
A39
A390
A394
A3075
A3058
A3078
A3083
A3071

ENGLISH
CORNWALL
BODMIN MOOR
Launceston
Bodmin
Liskeard
Wadebridge
Padstow
St. Columb Major
St. AUSTELL
Lostwithiel
Fowey
Looe
East Looe
West Looe
Saltash
Torpoint
Callington
Camelford
Tintagel
Boscastle
Mevagissey
St. Austell Bay
Mevagissey Bay
Veryan Bay
Whitsand Bay
Talland Bay
Port Isaac Bay
Padstow Bay
Tintagel Head
Rumps Point
Pentire Point
Gulland Rock
Gull Rock
Dodman Point
Chapel Point
Black Head
Gribbin Head
Pencarrow Head
Rame Head
Penlee Point
Nare Head
Greeb Point
Drake's Island
The Sound
St. George's or Looe Island
Eddystone Rocks
Plymouth to: Roscoff 6hrs. (Seasonal) Santander 20hrs. (Seasonal)
A30
A38
A39
A390
A391
A388
A392
A3058
A374
A395
B3254
B3266
B3314
A B C D E F
1 2 3 4 5 6 7 8
22
19

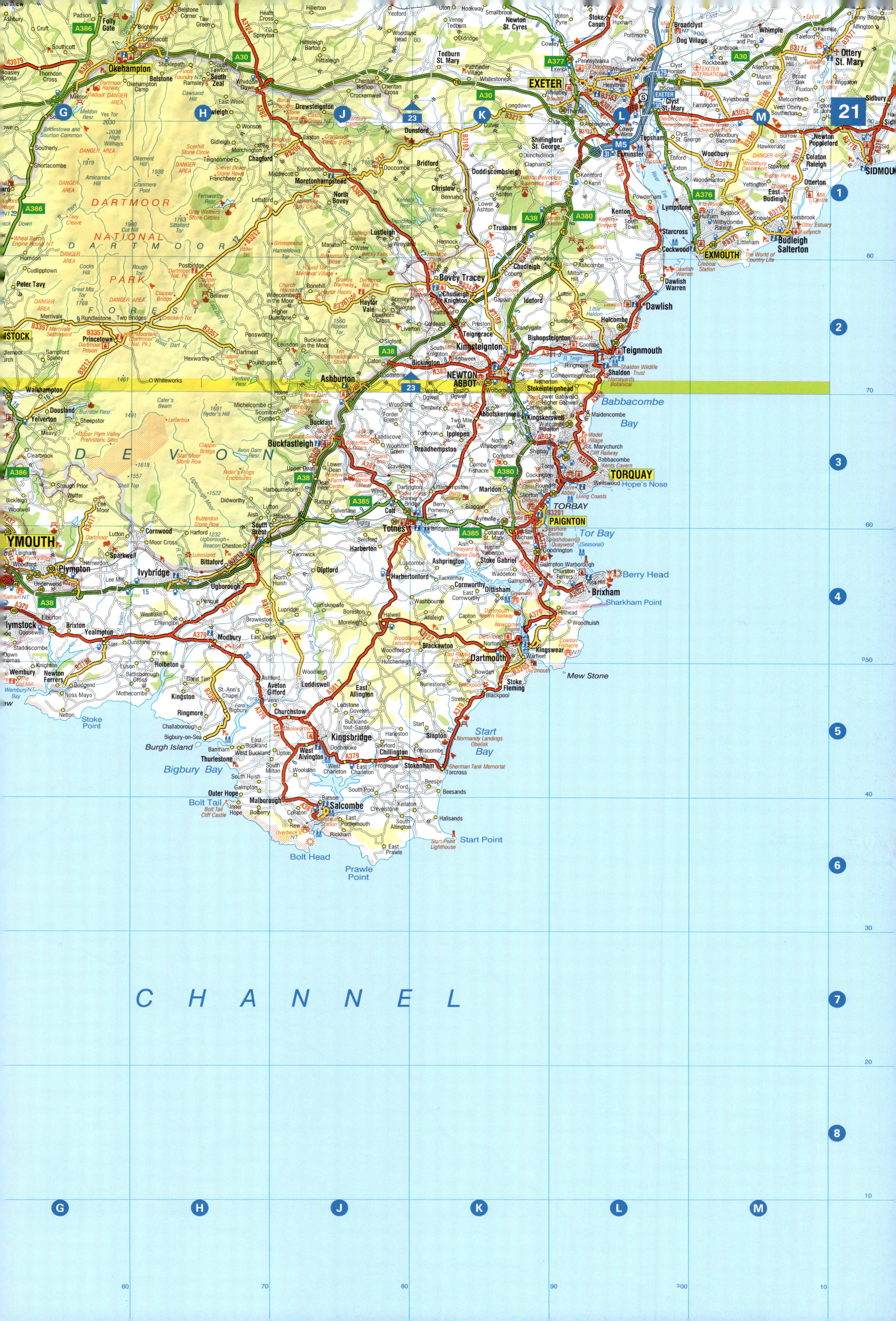
21
Okehampton
EXETER
Ottery St. Mary
Sidbury
DARTMOOR
NATIONAL
PARK
FOREST
D E V O N
Moretonhampstead
Chagford
Bovey Tracey
Dawlish
Teignmouth
Kingsteignton
NEWTON ABBOT
Ashburton
Buckfastleigh
Babbacombe Bay
TORQUAY
Hope's Nose
TORBAY
PAIGNTON
Tor Bay
Berry Head
Brixham
Sharkham Point
Totnes
Dartmouth
Kingswear
Mew Stone
Stoke Fleming
Start Bay
Start Point
Kingsbridge
Salcombe
Bolt Head
Prawle Point
Bolt Tail
Bigbury Bay
Burgh Island
Ivybridge
Plympton
YMOUTH
Yelverton
Princetown
Exmouth
Budleigh Salterton
Lympstone
Starcross
Topsham
Stoke Point
C H A N N E L
A30
A38
A380
A385
A379
A386
A377
A376
M5
23
1
2
3
4
5
6
7
8
G
H
J
K
L
M

LUNDY
North West Point
South West Point
Rat Island
Bird Observatory
Lundy to: Bideford 2hrs. (Seasonal) Ilfracombe 1hr. 45mins. (Seasonal)
Ilfracombe to Lundy 1hr. 45mins. (Seasonal)
Bideford to Lundy 2hrs. (Seasonal)
BARNSTAPLE OR BIDEFORD BAY
Bull Point
Rockham Bay
Morte Point
Mortehoe
Woolacombe
Morte Bay
Baggy Point
Croyde Bay
Croyde
Georgeham
Saunton
Braunton
DANGER AREA
Appledore
Northam
Westward Ho!
Abbotsham
BIDEFORD
East-the-Water
HARTLAND POINT
Windbury Point
Hartland Quay
Hartland
Clovelly
Stoke
Welcombe
Knaps Longpeak
Morwenstow
Higher Sharpnose Point
Lower Sharpnose Point
Kilkhampton
Bude Bay
Flexbury
Bude
Stratton
Marhamchurch
Holsworthy
Bradworthy
Sutcombe
Widemouth Bay
Dizzard Point
Crackington Haven
Cambeak
Week St. Mary
Whitstone
Fire Beacon Point
Boscastle
Tintagel Head
Tintagel
Gull Rock
Camelford
CORNWALL
BODMIN MOOR
Launceston
North Petherwin
South Petherwin
Altarnun
Lifton
Milton Abbot
Rumps Point
The Mouls
Port Isaac Bay
Port Isaac
Portquin Bay
Pentire Point
Padstow Bay
Newland
Gulland Rock
Trevone
Padstow
Wadebridge
St. Minver
Rock
St. Issey
St. Mabyn
St. Breward
Blisland
Bodmin
Lanivet
Cardinham
St. Neot
Liskeard
Dobwalls
Callington
Calstock
Gunnislake
St. Mawgan
St. Columb Major
A39
A30
A38
A388
A390
A3072
A386
A395
A391
B3263
B3266
B3314
B3254
B3248
22
30
31
19
A
B
C
D
E
F
1
2
3
4
5
6
7
8

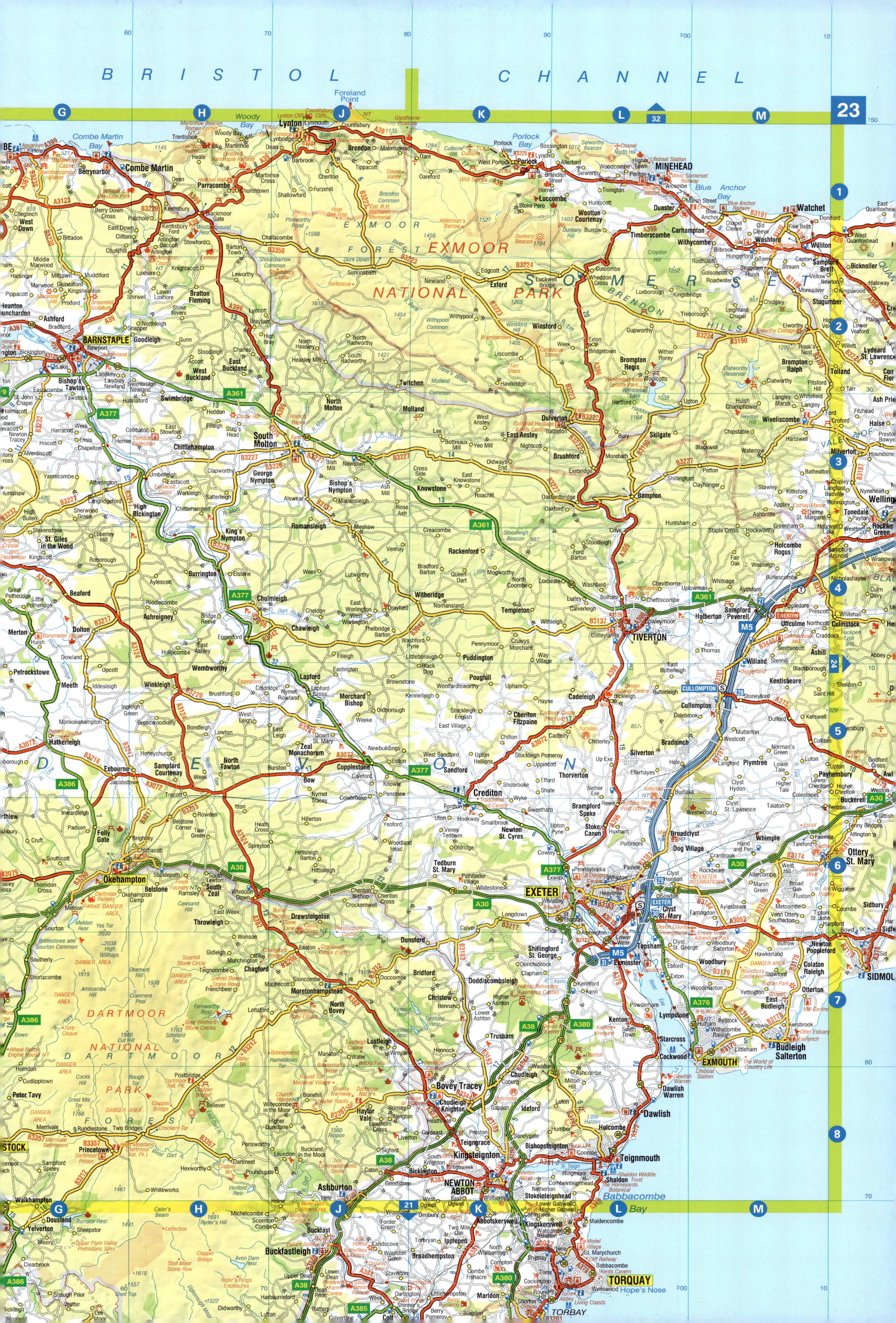

BRISTOL CHANNEL
23
EXMOOR NATIONAL PARK
EXMOOR FOREST
SOMERSET
BRENDON HILLS
DEVON
DARTMOOR
DARTMOOR NATIONAL PARK
DARTMOOR FOREST
Foreland Point
Porlock Bay
Combe Martin Bay
Blue Anchor Bay
Babbacombe Bay
Woody Bay
Combe Martin
Lynton
Lynmouth
Porlock
MINEHEAD
Dunster
Watchet
Williton
BARNSTAPLE
Bishop's Tawton
South Molton
Dulverton
Bampton
Wiveliscombe
Milverton
Wellington
TIVERTON
Cullompton
Crediton
EXETER
Exmouth
Budleigh Salterton
Sidmouth
Ottery St. Mary
Okehampton
Chagford
Moretonhampstead
Bovey Tracey
Dawlish
Teignmouth
Kingsteignton
NEWTON ABBOT
Ashburton
Buckfastleigh
Princetown
Kingskerswell
TORQUAY
TORBAY
Hope's Nose
Yelverton
Dousland
A39
A361
A377
A30
A38
A380
A386
A396
A3072
M5

London 2012 Venue
BRIDGWATER BAY
BURNHAM-ON-SEA
BRIDGWATER
TAUNTON
Glastonbury
Wells
Cheddar
Street
Shepton Mallet
Midsomer Norton
YEOVIL
Sherborne
Crewkerne
Chard
Ilminster
Honiton
Ottery St. Mary
SIDMOUTH
Budleigh Salterton
Seaton
Axminster
Lyme Regis
Bridport
DORCHESTER
Weymouth and Portland
SEE PAGES 5 & 109
S O M E R S E T
D E V O N
LYME BAY
ENGLISH

25
SALISBURY PLAIN
WILTSHIRE
CRANBORNE CHASE
NEW FOREST NATIONAL PARK
DORSET
CHANNEL
ISLE OF WIGHT
ISLE OF PORTLAND
ISLE OF PURBECK
POOLE BAY
HENGISTBURY HEAD
DURLSTON HEAD
ST. ALDHELM'S OR ST. ALBAN'S HEAD
TROWBRIDGE
Westbury
FROME
WARMINSTER
Ludgershall
Tidworth
Amesbury
SALISBURY
Shaftesbury
Gillingham
Blandford Forum
Wimborne Minster
Ringwood
Ferndown
POOLE
BOURNEMOUTH
CHRISTCHURCH
Highcliffe
Barton on Sea
Milford on Sea
New Milton
Lymington
Wareham
Swanage
Corfe Castle
Wilton
Mere
Hindon
Tisbury
Fordingbridge
Downton
Romsey
Totland
Colwell Bay
Alum Bay
THE NEEDLES
Brownsea Island
Sandbanks
Poole Harbour
Christchurch Bay
Studland Bay
Swanage Bay
Durlston Bay
Kimmeridge
Worth Matravers
Stalbridge
Sturminster Newton
Milton Abbas
Puddletown
Bere Regis
Verwood
Cranborne
Sixpenny Handley
A30
A303
A36
A350
A338
A354
A31
A35
A348
A351
A352
A3049
M27
Poole to:
Cherbourg 4hrs. 30mins. (Seasonal)
Cherbourg 2hrs. 30mins. (Fast Ferry, Seasonal)
Guernsey 2hrs. 30mins. (Fast Ferry, Seasonal)
Jersey 3hrs. 30mins. (Fast Ferry, Seasonal)
St. Malo 4hrs. 30mins. (Fast Ferry, Seasonal)
Weymouth to:
Guernsey 2hrs. (Fast Ferry)
Jersey 3hrs. 30mins. (Fast Ferry)
St. Malo 5hrs. 30mins. (Fast Ferry)
G
H
J
K
L
M
80
90
400
10
20
30
70

WILTSHIRE
SALISBURY PLAIN
HAMPSHIRE
ENGLISH
THE SOLENT
NEW FOREST NATIONAL PARK
ISLE OF WIGHT
ISLE OF PURBECK
Ludgershall
Tidworth
Andover
Amesbury
Durrington
Salisbury
Wilton
Winchester
Romsey
Eastleigh
Southampton
Totton
Hythe
Ringwood
Fordingbridge
Wimborne Minster
Poole
Bournemouth
Christchurch
New Milton
Lymington
Brockenhurst
Lyndhurst
Swanage
Cowes
East Cowes
Newport
Yarmouth
Freshwater
Hamble-le-Rice
Netley
Lee-on-the-Solent
Stubbington
Stockbridge
Whitchurch
Overton
Upavon
Ferndown
Verwood
Hengistbury Head
The Needles
Durlston Head
St. Catherine's Point
Poole Bay
Christchurch Bay
Studland Bay
Swanage Bay
Barton on Sea
Milford on Sea
Keyhaven
Calshot
Fawley
Beaulieu
Dibden Purlieu
Chandler's Ford
Bishop's Waltham
Hedge End
Cranborne
Sixpenny Handley
Tisbury
M27
M3
M271
A303
A338
A36
A31
A354
A350
A30
A34
A343
A27
A35
A33
Poole to:
Cherbourg 4hrs. 30mins. (Seasonal)
Cherbourg 2hrs. 30mins. (Fast Ferry, Seasonal)
Guernsey 2hrs. 30mins. (Fast Ferry, Seasonal)
Jersey 3hrs. 30mins. (Fast Ferry, Seasonal)
St. Malo 4hrs. 30mins. (Fast Ferry, Seasonal)
A
B
C
D
E
F
1
2
3
4
5
6
7
8

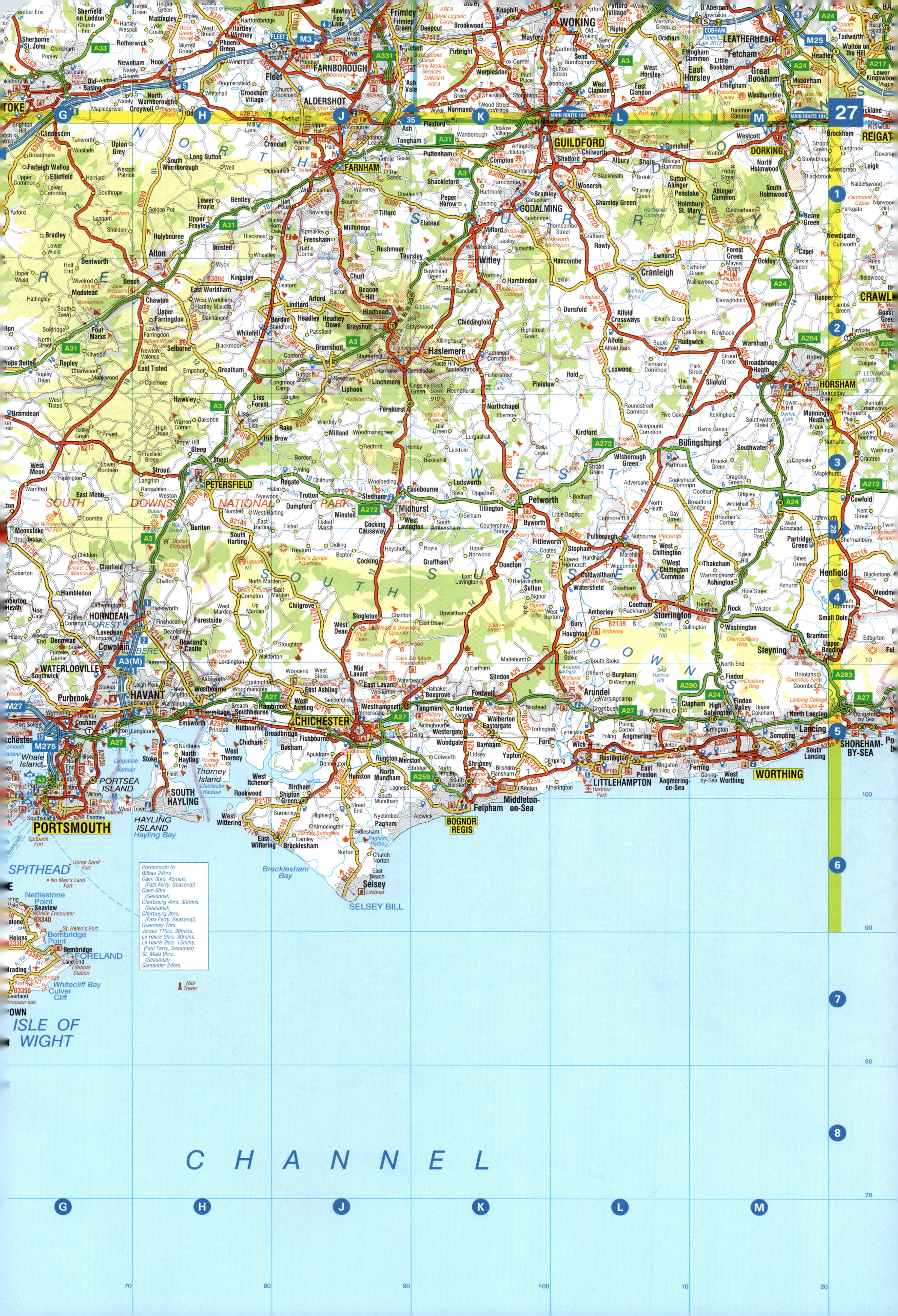

27
WOKING
GUILDFORD
GODALMING
FARNHAM
ALDERSHOT
FARNBOROUGH
Fleet
LEATHERHEAD
DORKING
REIGATE
HORSHAM
Haslemere
Cranleigh
Petworth
Midhurst
PETERSFIELD
Alton
CHICHESTER
HAVANT
WATERLOOVILLE
PORTSMOUTH
SOUTH HAYLING
HAYLING ISLAND
Hayling Bay
BOGNOR REGIS
Selsey
SELSEY BILL
LITTLEHAMPTON
Arundel
WORTHING
SHOREHAM-BY-SEA
Lancing
Steyning
Storrington
Pulborough
Billingshurst
Henfield
SOUTH DOWNS NATIONAL PARK
SOUTH DOWNS
WEST SUSSEX
SPITHEAD
ISLE OF WIGHT
Bracklesham Bay
PORTSEA ISLAND
Portsmouth to:
Bilbao 24hrs.
Caen 3hrs. 45mins.
(Fast Ferry, Seasonal)
Caen 6hrs.
(Seasonal)
Cherbourg 4hrs. 30mins.
(Seasonal)
Cherbourg 3hrs.
(Fast Ferry, Seasonal)
Guernsey 7hrs.
Jersey 11hrs. 30mins.
Le Havre 5hrs. 30mins.
Le Havre 3hrs. 15mins.
(Fast Ferry, Seasonal)
St. Malo 9hrs.
(Seasonal)
Santander 24hrs.
C H A N N E L
G
H
J
K
L
M
1
2
3
4
5
6
7
8

London 2012 Venue
28
RICHMOND
WIMBLEDON
KINGSTON UPON THAMES
NEW MALDEN
MORDEN
MERTON
MITCHAM
STREATHAM
LEWISHAM
WOOLWICH
CATFORD
ELTHAM
BECKENHAM
BROMLEY
CHISLEHURST
SIDCUP
Bexley
Bexleyheath
ERITH
DARTFORD
Dartford-Thurrock River Crossing
GRAYS
TILBURY
GRAVESEND
Northfleet
Swanley
ORPINGTON
CROYDON
SUTTON
CARSHALTON
WALLINGTON
EWELL
EPSOM
PURLEY
BANSTEAD
COULSDON
WARLINGHAM
CATERHAM
Biggin Hill
Oxted
REDHILL
REIGATE
DORKING
Westerham
SEVENOAKS
Kemsing
West Kingsdown
Brands Hatch
SEE PAGES 4 & 104
STROOD
ROCHESTER
CHATHAM
Snodland
MAIDSTONE
Walderslade
TONBRIDGE
Hildenborough
Edenbridge
Lingfield
HORLEY
CRAWLEY
EAST GRINSTEAD
Forest Row
Southborough
ROYAL TUNBRIDGE WELLS
Pembury
Paddock Wood
Crowborough
Wadhurst
Ticehurst
Cranbrook
Hawkhurst
HORSHAM
HAYWARDS HEATH
Cuckfield
BURGESS HILL
Hurstpierpoint
Hassocks
Uckfield
Heathfield
Crowhurst
Battle
ASHDOWN FOREST
SOUTH DOWNS NATIONAL PARK
LEWES
Ringmer
HAILSHAM
Polegate
Willingdon
EASTBOURNE
BEACHY HEAD
Pevensey
Pevensey Bay
Langney Point
BEXHILL
Norman's Bay
SEAFORD
NEWHAVEN
Newhaven to: Dieppe 4hrs
Peacehaven
Rottingdean
Saltdean
Woodingdean
BRIGHTON
HOVE
Portslade-by-Sea
SHOREHAM-BY-SEA
SOUTHWICK
Henfield
Steyning
WORTHING
Sompting
South Lancing
ENGLISH
A
B
C
D
E
F
1
2
3
4
5
6
7
8
M25
M23
M26
M20
M2
A21
A22
A23
A24
A26
A27
A264
A272
MAIN ROUTE 101
MAIN ROUTE 102
MAIN ROUTE 103
36
27
100
90
20
30
40
50
60
70

29
SHEERNESS
Isle of Grain
Minster
Queenborough
Leysdown-on-Sea
ISLE OF SHEPPEY
Warden Point
SITTINGBOURNE
FAVERSHAM
WHITSTABLE
HERNE BAY
Herne Bay
Whitstable Bay
MARGATE
Westgate on Sea
Birchington
ISLE OF THANET
BROADSTAIRS
RAMSGATE
NORTH FORELAND
Foreness Point
South Channel
Pegwell Bay
Sandwich Bay
Sandwich
The Small Downs
The Downs
DEAL
Walmer
Kingsdown
St. Margaret's at Cliffe
St. Margaret's Bay
SOUTH FORELAND
DOVER
Dover to: Calais 1hr. 10mins. Dunkirk 2hrs.
Ramsgate to Ostend 4hrs.
CHANNEL TUNNEL Folkestone to Calais 35mins.
STRAIT OF DOVER
CANTERBURY
Sturry
Herne
Fordwich
Aylesham
Wingham
Ash
Harbledown
Chartham
Bridge
Barham
Lenham
Harrietsham
Charing
Wye
ASHFORD
Hothfield
Great Chart
Kingsnorth
Mersham
Sellindge
CHANNEL TUNNEL
Hawkinge
Capel-le-Ferne
FOLKESTONE
Sandgate
HYTHE
Saltwood
Lympne
East Wear Bay
Dymchurch
St. Mary's Bay
New Romney
Greatstone-on-Sea
Lydd
Lydd-on-Sea
Dungeness
DUNGENESS
ROMNEY MARSH
WALLAND MARSH
Brookland
Hamstreet
Tenterden
Woodchurch
Appledore
Wittersham
Isle of Oxney
Rye
Rye Harbour
Camber
Rye Bay
Winchelsea
Winchelsea Beach
West Road
Fairlight
Fairlight Cove
HASTINGS
Biddenden
High Halden
St. Michaels
Rolvenden
Headcorn
Smarden
Bethersden
Pluckley
Egerton
Hollingbourne
MAIDSTONE
MEDWAY
Faversham
CHANNEL
CHANNEL TUNNEL
ASHFORD
EUROSTAR (Passengers only)
EUROTUNNEL (Vehicles only)
Brabourne Lees
Sellindge
Hamstreet
Newchurch
Appledore Heath
Lympne
HYTHE
FOLKESTONE
Elham
Densole
Alkham
Whitfield
DOVER
Hawkinge
Capel-le-Ferne
FOLKESTONE CHANNEL TUNNEL TERMINAL
Junction 11a
Junction 12
Junction 13
FOLKESTONE
SCALE
3 Miles
6 Kms
CALAIS
Grand-Fort Philippe
Gravelines
Sangatte
Coquelles
Escalles
Wissant
Guines
Ardres
Audruicq
CALAIS CHANNEL TUNNEL TERMINAL
Junction 41
Junction 42
SNCF Fréthun International Station

PEMBROKESHIRE COAST NATIONAL PARK
(PARC CENEDLAETHOL ARFORDIR PENFRO)
MYNYDD PRESELI
PEMBROKESHIRE
ST. BRIDES BAY
BROAD SOUND
Milford Haven
ST. DAVID'S HEAD
Ramsey Island
Ynys Bery
Green Scar
Rickets Head
Stack Rocks
Tower Point
Skomer Island
Wooltack Point
Midland Isle
Grassholm Island
Gateholm Island
Skokholm Island
Dale Point
Thorn Island
St. Ann's Head
Sheep Island
Pembroke to Rosslare 3hrs. 45mins.
Freshwater West
Linney Head
Crow Rock
Toes
St. Govan's Head
Stackpole Head
Trewent Point
Old Castle Head
St. Margaret's Island
Caldey Island
Chapel Point
Giltar Point
Caldey Sound
Monkstone Point
Goodwick (Wdig)
Fishguard (Abergwaun)
Newport (Trefdraeth)
Penbwchdy
Penclegyr
Carreg-gwylan-fach
Penllechwen
St. David's (Tyddewi)
Solva
Whitchurch
Newgale
Roch
Camrose
Broad Haven
Little Haven
Walton West
Marloes
Dale
St. Ishmael's
Herbrandston
HAVERFORDWEST (Hwlffordd)
MILFORD HAVEN (Aberdaugleddau)
Neyland
Pembroke Dock (Doc Penfro)
Pembroke (Penfro)
Angle
Castlemartin
Bosherston
Manorbier
Lamphey
Narberth (Arberth)
Kilgetty
Saundersfoot
Tenby (Dinbych-y-Pysgod)
Amroth
Templeton
Whitland
Maenclochog
Letterston
Wolf's Castle
Prendergast
A40
A487
A477
A478
A4076
LUNDY
North West Point
South West Point
Rat Island
Lundy to: Bideford 2hrs. (Seasonal) Ilfracombe 1hr. 45mins (Seasonal)
A
B
C
D
E
F
1
2
3
4
5
6
7
8
38
22

CARMARTHENSHIRE
FOREST OF BRECHFA
BLACK MOUNTAIN
Llandovery
(Llanymddyfri)
Llandeilo
CARMARTHEN
(Caerfyrddin)
St. Clears
Laugharne
Kidwelly
(Cydweli)
Pembrey
Burry Port
LLANELLI
GORSEINON
Pontarddulais
Ammanford
(Rhydaman)
Pontardawe
Ystalyfera
Ystradgynlais
Clydach
Morriston
SWANSEA
(Abertawe)
NEATH
(Castell-nedd)
Skewen
Briton Ferry
Baglan
PORT TALBOT
Margam
Pyle
PORTHCAWL
Sker Point
Tusker Rock
AFAN FOREST PARK
MAESTEG
Mumbles
(Mwmbwls)
Mumbles Head
Swansea Bay
(Bae Abertawe)
Swansea to Cork 10hrs.
GOWER
Burry Holms
Llanmadoc
Rhossili
Rhossili Bay
WORMS HEAD
(Penrhyn-gwyr)
Port-Eynon
Port-Eynon Point
Oxwich Bay
Pwlldu Head
Whiteford Point
Pendine
(Pentywyn)
Ginst Point
CARMARTHEN BAY
(BAE CAERFYRDDIN)
BRISTOL CHANNEL
SWANSEA WEST
PONT ABRAHAM
Foreland Point
ILFRACOMBE
Ilfracombe to Lundy 1hr. 45mins. (Seasonal)
Combe Martin
Combe Martin Bay
Lynton
Lynmouth
Woody Bay
Bull Point
Morte Point
Rockham Bay
Woolacombe
Morte Bay
Berrynarbor
Parracombe
Brendon
EXMOOR
A40
A48
A483
A465
A4138
M4

London 2012 Venue
32
BRECON BEACONS NATIONAL PARK
(PARC CENEDLAETHOL BANNAU BRYCHEINIOG)
BRECON BEACONS
Brecon (Aberhonddu)
MERTHYR TYDFIL (Merthyr Tudful)
TREDEGAR
EBBW VALE (Glyn Ebwy)
BLAENAU GWENT
ABERTILLERY
ABERGAVENNY (Y Fenni)
HEREFORD
TORFAEN
PONTYPOOL (Pontypŵl)
CWMBRAN
NEWPORT (Casnewydd)
NEWPORT
ABERDARE (Aberdâr)
MOUNTAIN ASH (Aberpennar)
PONTYPRIDD
CAERPHILLY (Caerffili)
NEATH (Castell-nedd)
NEATH PORT TALBOT
MAESTEG
BRIDGEND (Pen-y-Bont Ar Ogwr)
PORTHCAWL
THE VALE OF GLAMORGAN
Cowbridge
CARDIFF (Caerdydd)
Millennium Stadium
SEE PAGES 5 & 108
Penarth
BARRY (Barri)
Barry Island
Sully Island
Flat Holm
Steep Holm
WESTON-SUPER-MARE
BRISTOL CHANNEL
BRIDGWATER BAY
MOUTH OF
BURNHAM-ON-SEA
MINEHEAD
Watchet
EXMOOR
Nash Point
Tusker Rock
Sker Point
Breaksea Point
Lavernock Point
Sand Point
M4
M5
A40
A470
A465
A48
A4232

CHELTENHAM
GLOUCESTER
Tewkesbury
Ross-on-Wye
Ledbury
Newent
Winchcombe
Bishop's Cleeve
Cinderford
Lydney
MONMOUTH
(Trefynwy)
CHEPSTOW
(Cas-gwent)
STROUD
CIRENCESTER
Dursley
Nailsworth
Tetbury
Wotton-under-Edge
Malmesbury
Thornbury
Yate
Chipping Sodbury
MANGOTSFIELD
BRISTOL
Avonmouth
Portishead
Nailsea
Kingswood
KEYNSHAM
BATH
CHIPPENHAM
Corsham
Calne
MELKSHAM
DEVIZES
TROWBRIDGE
Bradford-on-Avon
Westbury
FROME
WARMINSTER
Radstock
Midsomer Norton
Shepton Mallet
Wells
Cheddar
Yatton
Congresbury
Caldicot
FOREST OF DEAN
SOUTH GLOUCESTERSHIRE
NORTH SOMERSET
BATH & N.E. SOMERSET
RIVER SEVERN
SALISBURY PLAIN
M4
M5
M48
M49
M32
M50
A40
A48
A46
A38
A37
A36
A4
A429
A417
A419
A350

CHELTENHAM
Winchcombe
Prestbury
Charlton Kings
Andoversford
Withington
Northleach
Bourton-on-the-Water
Stow-on-the-Wold
Moreton-in-Marsh
Chipping Norton
Charlbury
Woodstock
Kidlington
Bicester
Burford
WITNEY
Eynsham
OXFORD
Carterton
Bampton
Faringdon
Lechlade on Thames
Fairford
CIRENCESTER
Cricklade
Highworth
Wantage
ABINGDON
Didcot
Shrivenham
SWINDON
Royal Wootton Bassett
Wroughton
Calne
Marlborough
Hungerford
NEWBURY
Thatcham
DEVIZES
Pewsey
Ludgershall
ANDOVER
Tidworth
Amesbury
Durrington
Market Lavington
Upavon
Aldbourne
Lambourn
GLOUCESTERSHIRE
COTSWOLD
OXFORDSHIRE
VALE OF WHITE HORSE
WEST BERKSHIRE
WILTSHIRE
SALISBURY PLAIN
HAMPSHIRE
M4
M40
M5
A40
A44
A34
A338
A346
A419
A420
A417
A429
A436
A361
A4
A303
A342
A343
A415
A4260

41
42
33
26

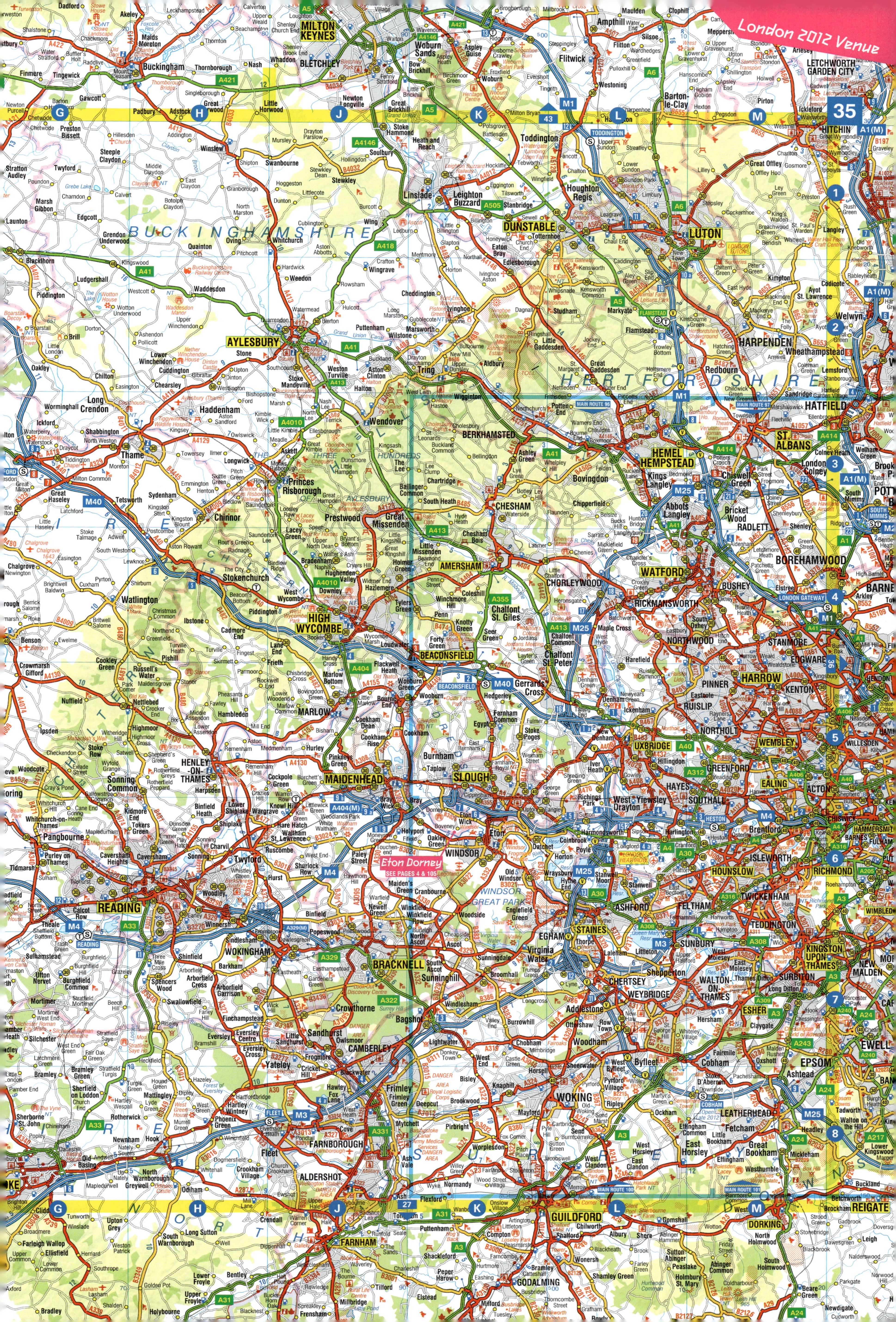
London 2012 Venue
35
BUCKINGHAMSHIRE
HERTFORDSHIRE
MILTON KEYNES
BLETCHLEY
Buckingham
Woburn Sands
Ampthill
Flitwick
LETCHWORTH GARDEN CITY
HITCHIN
Leighton Buzzard
DUNSTABLE
LUTON
Houghton Regis
Toddington
AYLESBURY
Tring
HARPENDEN
HATFIELD
ST. ALBANS
BERKHAMSTED
HEMEL HEMPSTEAD
Wendover
Princes Risborough
Thame
Haddenham
CHESHAM
AMERSHAM
Great Missenden
Chinnor
Stokenchurch
HIGH WYCOMBE
BEACONSFIELD
WATFORD
RICKMANSWORTH
CHORLEYWOOD
BOREHAMWOOD
RADLETT
NORTHWOOD
HARROW
STANMORE
EDGWARE
PINNER
RUISLIP
UXBRIDGE
WEMBLEY
MARLOW
HENLEY-ON-THAMES
MAIDENHEAD
SLOUGH
WINDSOR
Eton Dorney
SEE PAGES 4 & 105
READING
Twyford
WOKINGHAM
BRACKNELL
Sunninghill
Crowthorne
Sandhurst
CAMBERLEY
Yateley
FARNBOROUGH
ALDERSHOT
Fleet
FARNHAM
GUILDFORD
GODALMING
WOKING
Bagshot
EGHAM
STAINES
ASHFORD
FELTHAM
HOUNSLOW
ISLEWORTH
RICHMOND
TWICKENHAM
TEDDINGTON
KINGSTON UPON THAMES
NEW MALDEN
SURBITON
WALTON-ON-THAMES
WEYBRIDGE
CHERTSEY
Addlestone
Sunbury
Shepperton
ESHER
EPSOM
EWELL
LEATHERHEAD
Ashtead
DORKING
REIGATE
Cobham
Byfleet
HAYES
SOUTHALL
GREENFORD
EALING
ACTON
West Drayton
Yiewsley
Brentford
WINDSOR GREAT PARK
Pangbourne
Caversham
Woodley
Burghfield
Mortimer
Tadley
Hook
Odiham
Crondall
WILLESDEN
BARNET
POTTERS BAR
Welwyn
Wheathampstead
Redbourn
Kings Langley
Abbots Langley
Bushey
Elstree

Lee Valley
White Water Centre
SEE PAGES 5 & 100
Olympic Park Venues
SEE PAGES 2, 3 & 104
LONDON
SEE PAGES 3,4 & 105-109
Brands Hatch
SEE PAGES 4 & 104
HERTFORDSHIRE
ESSEX
KENT
SURREY
LETCHWORTH GARDEN CITY
HITCHIN
STEVENAGE
BISHOP'S STORTFORD
SAFFRON WALDEN
HERTFORD
WELWYN GARDEN CITY
HARLOW
HATFIELD
ST ALBANS
CHELMSFORD
POTTERS BAR
EPPING
CHESHUNT
WALTHAM ABBEY
BOREHAMWOOD
ENFIELD
LOUGHTON
CHIGWELL
BRENTWOOD
BILLERICAY
BASILDON
BARNET
ROMFORD
HORNCHURCH
UPMINSTER
ILFORD
BARKING
DAGENHAM
STRATFORD
WOOLWICH
DARTFORD
GRAVESEND
TILBURY
GRAYS
ROCHESTER
CHATHAM
MAIDSTONE
SEVENOAKS
TONBRIDGE
BROMLEY
CROYDON
SUTTON
KINGSTON UPON THAMES
RICHMOND
EPSOM
REIGATE
REDHILL
HORLEY
DORKING
WEMBLEY
EALING
WATFORD
River Thames
A
B
C
D
E
F
1
2
3
4
5
6
7
8

London 2012 Venue
37
Harwich to: Esbjerg 18hrs. Hook of Holland 6hrs. 15mins.
FELIXSTOWE
Harwich
COLCHESTER
Wivenhoe
Brightlingsea
CLACTON-ON-SEA
Walton-on-the-Naze
Frinton-on-Sea
Holland-on-Sea
The Naze
Hamford Water
Horsey Island
Coggeshall
Kelvedon
Tiptree
MERSEA ISLAND
West Mersea
Virley Channel
Colne Point
Sales Point
MALDON
Osea Island
Northey Island
RIVER BLACKWATER
Bradwell-on-Sea
Tillingham
Southminster
Burnham-on-Crouch
Holliwell Point
Foulness Point
Foulness Sands
FOULNESS ISLAND
Maplin Sands
Wallasea Island
Potton Island
Hockley
Ashingdon
RAYLEIGH
Rochford
Great Wakering
SOUTHEND-ON-SEA
SHOEBURY NESS
Shoeburyness
Hadleigh Farm
SEE PAGES 4 & 105
N O R T H
S E A
SHEERNESS
Isle of Grain
Queenborough
Minster
Warden Point
Leysdown-on-Sea
ISLE OF SHEPPEY
Isle of Harty
Shell Ness
WHITSTABLE
Whitstable Bay
HERNE BAY
Herne Bay
SITTINGBOURNE
FAVERSHAM
CANTERBURY
MARGATE
Westgate on Sea
Birchington
ISLE OF THANET
BROADSTAIRS
RAMSGATE
Ramsgate to Ostend 4hrs.
North Foreland
Foreness Point
South Channel
Pegwell Bay
Sandwich
Sandwich Bay
DEAL
The Downs
St. Margaret's at Cliffe
St. Margaret's Bay
SOUTH FORELAND
DOVER
Aylesham
Wingham
Lenham
Harrietsham
Charing
Challock
Wye
ASHFORD
Hollingbourne
Headcorn
Pluckley

CARDIGAN BAY
(BAE CEREDIGI
Cardigan Island
Cemaes Head
Pwllygranant
Ynys-Lochtyn
Cwmtudu
STRUMBLE HEAD
DINAS HEAD
Carregwastad Point
Pen Brush
Penbwchdy
Penclegyr
Carreg-gwylan-fach
Fishguard Bay (Bae Abergwaun)
Newport Bay (Bae Trefdraeth)
Trwyn-y-bwa
Fishguard to:
Rosslare 3hrs. 30mins.
Rosslare 1hr. 50mins.
(Fast Ferry, Seasonal)
PEMBROKESHIRE COAST NATIONAL PARK
PEMBROKESHIRE
(PARC CENEDLAETHOL ARFORDIR PENFRO)
MYNYDD PRESELI
Fishguard (Abergwaun)
Goodwick (Wdig)
Cardigan (Aberteifi)
Newport (Trefdraeth)
St. Dogmaels (Llandudoch)
Newcastle Emlyn (Castell Newydd Emlyn)
Aberporth
Llangranog
Penbryn
Y Ferwig
Cilgerran
Llechryd
Llandygwydd
Moylgrove (Trewyddel)
Nevern (Nanhyfer)
Eglwyswrw
Dinas Cross
Boncath
Crymych
Llanfyrnach
Mathry
Trefin
Castlemorris
Letterston
Little Newcastle
Puncheston (Cas-Mael)
Henry's Moat (Castell Hendre)
Maenclochog
Wolf's Castle
Whitchurch
Llanrian
Ambleston
New Moat
Llangolman
Efailwen
Glandy Cross
Llanboidy
Llandyfriog
Troedyraur
Rosebush
Spittal
Treffgarne
Walton East
Llys-y-fran
Llanycefn
A487
A40
A478
A484
A486
B4582
B4332
B4313
B4329
B4331
B4330
B4548
B4546
B4333
B4334
B4571
CARMART

Barmouth
(Abermaw)
Barmouth Bay
(Bae Bermo)
Fairbourne
Dolgellau
CADAIR IDRIS
Cross Foxes
Dinas Mawddwy
Mallwyd
Llwyngwril
Abergynolwyn
Corris
G W Y N E D D
Tonfanau
Tywyn
Bryncrug
Aberdovey
(Aberdyfi)
Pennal
Machynlleth
Penegoes
Cemmaes Road
Cemmaes
Llanbrynmair
Carno
Talerddig
Derwenlas
Glaspwll
Furnace
Eglwys Fach
Ynyslas
Borth
Tal-y-bont
Upper Borth
Llandre
Bow Street
Rhyd-meirionydd
Talybont
ABERYSTWYTH
The Bar
Penparcau
Llanbadarn Fawr
Capel Bangor
Ponterwyd
PLYNLIMON
(PUMLUMON FAWR)
Llanidloes
Llangurig
Trefeglwys
Staylittle
Devil's Bridge
(Pontarfynach)
Llanfarian
Llanilar
Pont-rhyd-y-groes
Cwmystwyth
Llanrhystud
Carreg Ti-pw
Llangwyryfon
Lledrod
Tregaron
Pontrhydfendigaid
Ystrad Meurig
Rhayader
(Rhaeadr Gwy)
St. Harmon
Llansantffraed Cwmdeuddwr
Elan Valley
C A M B R I A N   M O U N T A I N S
P O W Y S
Aberaeron
Llan-non
Pennant
Cross Inn
Bethania
Llangeitho
Llanddewi Brefi
Llanfair Clydogau
Lampeter
(Llanbedr Pont Steffan)
Cilcennin
Trefilan
Talsarn
Llannerch Aeron
Llanarth
Mydroilyn
Cwrtnewydd
Llanwnnen
Llanybydder
Rhydowen
Capel Dewi
Llanfihangel-ar-Arth
Pencader
Cwmann
Pumsaint
Caio
Llansawel
Talley
Llanwrda
Llandovery
(Llanymddyfri)
Cilycwm
Rhandirmwyn
Cynghordy
Llanwrtyd Wells
(Llanwrtud)
Beulah
Garth
Builth Wells
(Llanfair-ym-Muallt)
Builth Road
Newbridge on Wye
Llanwrthwl
Nantmel
Abergwesyn
Tirabad
MYNYDD EPPYNT
Trecastle
Sennybridge
Llandeilo
Llangadog
Myddfai
Brechfa
FOREST OF BRECHFA
Llanfynydd
Ffairfach
Nantgaredig
C A R M A R T H E N S H I R E
BRECON BEACONS
A470
A487
A44
A483
A485
A482
A40
A493
A489
A458
A4120
46
47
31
32
40
G
H
J
K
L
M
1
2
3
4
5
6
7
8

40
A
B
C
D
E
F
1
2
3
4
5
6
7
8
47
39
32
SHREWSBURY
Welshpool
(Y Trallwng)
Guilsfield
Llanfair Caereinion
Castle Caereinion
Berriew
Montgomery
(Trefaldwyn)
Newtown
(Y Drenewydd)
Kerry
Llanidloes
Rhayader
Llandrindod Wells
(Llandrindod)
Builth Wells
(Llanfair-ym-Muallt)
Brecon
(Aberhonddu)
Talgarth
Hay-on-Wye
(Y Gelli Gandryll)
Clyro
Kington
Presteigne
(Llanandras)
Knighton
(Tref-y-Clawdd)
Bishop's Castle
Clun
Church Stretton
Craven Arms
Ludlow
Leominster
HEREFORD
Pontesbury
Minsterley
Westbury
Chirbury
Leintwardine
Wigmore
Weobley
Pembridge
Eardisland
Madley
Peterchurch
Dorstone
Ewyas Harold
Pontrilas
Kentchurch
Abbey Dore
Bromyard
Shobdon
New Radnor
RADNOR FOREST
P O W Y S
S H R O P S
H E R E F O R D S
B L A C K M O U N T A I N S
WALES
ENGLAND
A5
A458
A483
A470
A489
A488
A44
A438
A479
A40
A49
A4113
A4110
A465
A480
A4103

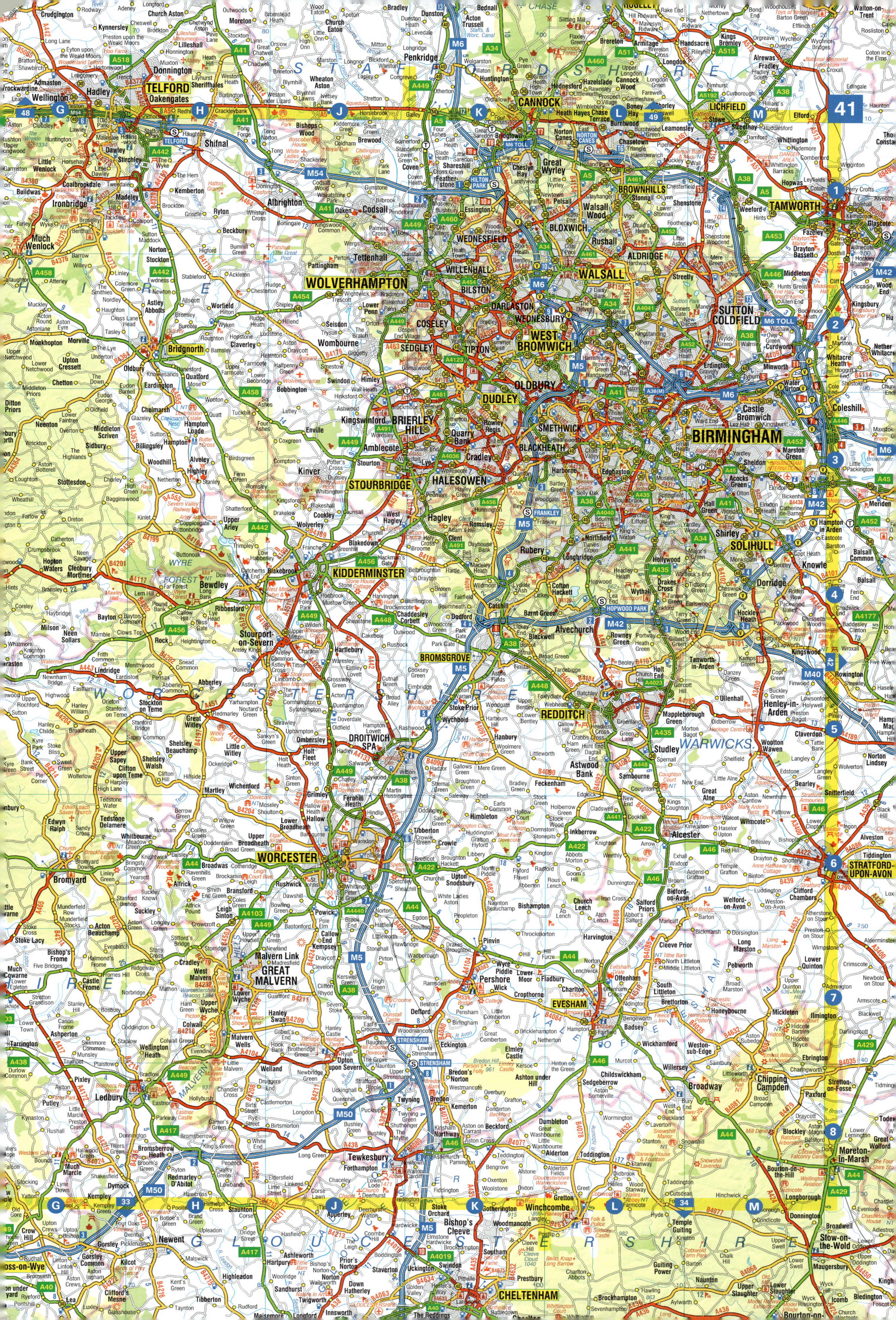
TELFORD
Oakengates
Wellington
Hadley
Donnington
Shifnal
Ironbridge
Much Wenlock
Bridgnorth
WOLVERHAMPTON
Tettenhall
Codsall
Albrighton
Penkridge
CANNOCK
Cheslyn Hay
Great Wyrley
WEDNESFIELD
WILLENHALL
BLOXWICH
WALSALL
BROWNHILLS
LICHFIELD
TAMWORTH
ALDRIDGE
BILSTON
DARLASTON
WEDNESBURY
COSELEY
SEDGLEY
TIPTON
WEST BROMWICH
OLDBURY
DUDLEY
SUTTON COLDFIELD
BIRMINGHAM
SMETHWICK
BLACKHEATH
BRIERLEY HILL
Kingswinford
Amblecote
STOURBRIDGE
HALESOWEN
Cradley
Hagley
Kinver
SOLIHULL
Shirley
Knowle
Dorridge
Castle Bromwich
Coleshill
Rubery
KIDDERMINSTER
Bewdley
Stourport-on-Severn
BROMSGROVE
Alvechurch
REDDITCH
Henley-in-Arden
Studley
WARWICKS
DROITWICH SPA
WORCESTER
Alcester
STRATFORD-UPON-AVON
Malvern Link
GREAT MALVERN
Pershore
EVESHAM
Upton upon Severn
Ledbury
Tewkesbury
Winchcombe
Bishop's Cleeve
CHELTENHAM
Broadway
Chipping Campden
Moreton-in-Marsh
Stow-on-the-Wold
Newent
Shipston-on-Stour
STAFFORDSHIRE
WORCESTERSHIRE
GLOUCESTERSHIRE
WYRE FOREST
M5
M6
M6 TOLL
M42
M40
M50
M54
A449
A38
A5
A46
A44
A435
A456
A442
A4123

London 2012 Venue
City of Coventry Stadium
SEE PAGES 4 & 104
LEICESTER
COVENTRY
NUNEATON
HINCKLEY
RUGBY
DAVENTRY
NORTHAMPTON
WARWICK
ROYAL LEAMINGTON SPA
STRATFORD-UPON-AVON
KENILWORTH
BEDWORTH
ATHERSTONE
TAMWORTH
BANBURY
BRACKLEY
BICESTER
MARKET HARBOROUGH
WIGSTON
COALVILLE
Ashby-de-la-Zouch
Barrow upon Soar
Loughborough
Buckingham
Towcester
Southam
Shipston-on-Stour
Chipping Norton
Moreton-in-Marsh
Chipping Campden
LEICESTERSHIRE
WARWICKSHIRE
NORTHAMPTONSHIRE
OXFORDSHIRE
BUCKINGHAMSHIRE
M1
M6
M40
M42
M45
M69
A5
A45
A46
A423
A43
A14

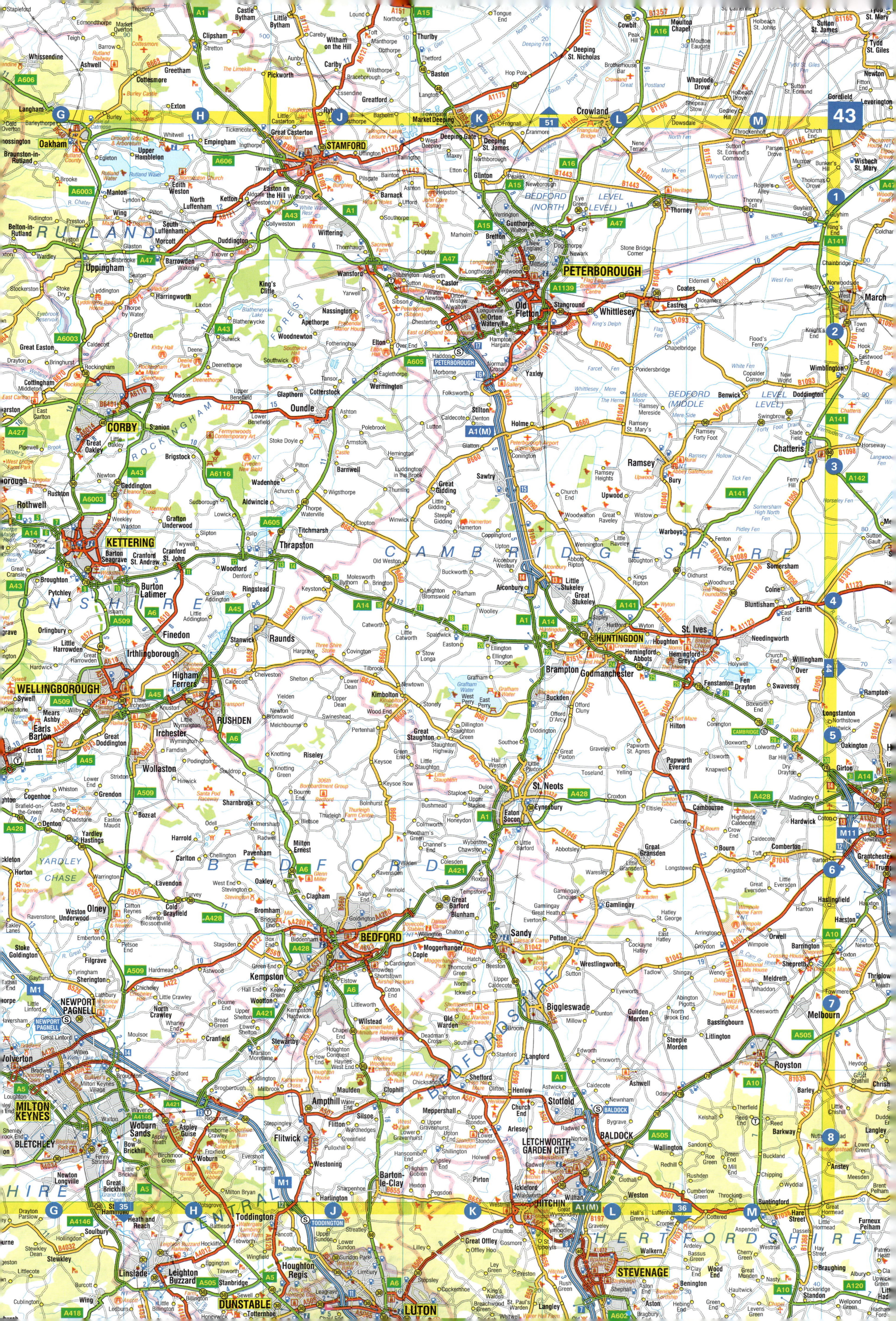
RUTLAND
Oakham
Uppingham
Stamford
Market Deeping
Deeping St. James
Crowland
Peterborough
Old Fletton
Whittlesey
March
Chatteris
Ramsey
Warboys
Somersham
St. Ives
Huntingdon
Godmanchester
St. Neots
Eynesbury
Eaton Socon
Sandy
Biggleswade
Royston
Baldock
Letchworth Garden City
Hitchin
Stevenage
Luton
Dunstable
Houghton Regis
Toddington
Leighton Buzzard
Linslade
Ampthill
Flitwick
Bedford
Kempston
Olney
Newport Pagnell
Milton Keynes
Bletchley
Wolverton
Rushden
Higham Ferrers
Irthlingborough
Wellingborough
Earls Barton
Wollaston
Irchester
Raunds
Thrapston
Oundle
Kettering
Burton Latimer
Finedon
Rothwell
Corby
Desborough
CAMBRIDGESHIRE
BEDFORDSHIRE
NORTHAMPTONSHIRE
HERTFORDSHIRE
ROCKINGHAM FOREST
YARDLEY CHASE
BEDFORD LEVEL (NORTH LEVEL)
BEDFORD LEVEL (MIDDLE LEVEL)
A1
A1(M)
A6
A14
A43
A45
A47
A421
A428
A505
A507
A509
A605
A6116
M1
M11

44
WISBECH
Downham Market
Swaffham
March
Chatteris
Littleport
Ely
Feltwell
Brandon
Thetford
THETFORD FOREST PARK
Mundford
Watton
Methwold
Mildenhall
Soham
Newmarket
BURY ST. EDMUNDS
CAMBRIDGESHIRE
CAMBRIDGE
Cottenham
Histon
Great Shelford
Sawston
Linton
Haverhill
Clare
Sudbury
Long Melford
Lavenham
Royston
Melbourn
Saffron Walden
Great Dunmow
Halstead
BRAINTREE
Coggeshall
BISHOP'S STORTFORD
Stansted Mountfitchet
Thaxted
Finchingfield
Castle Hedingham
Great Yeldham
Stoke by Clare
Kedington
Ixworth
Elveden
Lakenheath
Icklingham
Upwell
Outwell
Wimblington
Doddington
Haddenham
Sutton
Wilburton
Stretham
Burwell
Fordham
Kentford
Moulton
Dullingham
Balsham
Fulbourn
Girton
Impington
Milton
Waterbeach
Longstanton
Willingham
Swavesey
Harston
Barrington
Orwell
Barley
Barkway
Elmdon
Newport
Debden
Ashdon
Steeple Bumpstead
Wethersfield
Sible Hedingham
Earls Colne
Wakes Colne
Ickworth
Ingham
Culford
Barnham
Euston
Honington
Bardwell
NORFOLK
SUFFOLK
ESSEX
A10
A11
A14
A47
A134
A142
A505
A1065
A1066
A1101
A1122
A1123
A120
A131
M11

45
NORWICH
GREAT YARMOUTH
LOWESTOFT
Caister-on-Sea
Gorleston-on-Sea
Hopton on Sea
Kessingland
Southwold
Beccles
Bungay
Halesworth
Wymondham
Attleborough
Diss
Eye
Stowmarket
Framlingham
Saxmundham
Leiston
Aldeburgh
Wickham Market
WOODBRIDGE
IPSWICH
FELIXSTOWE
Harwich
Manningtree
Hadleigh
COLCHESTER
Walton-on-the-Naze
Wivenhoe
Acle
Wroxham
THE BROADS
Orford Ness
Hollesley Bay
Aldeburgh Bay
Hemsby Hole
The Naze
Hamford Water
Harwich to: Esbjerg 18hrs. Hook of Holland 6hrs. 15mins.

Middle Mouse (Ynys Badrig)
The Skerries (Ynysoedd y Moelrhoniaid)
West Mouse (Maen y Bugael)
East Mouse (Ynys Amlwch)
Point Lynas (Trwyn Eilian)
Carmel Head (Trwyn y Gader)
Holyhead to:
Dublin 3hrs. 15mins.
Dublin 1hr. 20mins. (Fast Ferry)
Dun Laoghaire 1hr. 50mins. (Fast Ferry)
HOLYHEAD BAY (BAE CAERGYBI)
Cemaes
Amlwch
Penysarn
Llanfairynghornwy
Llanfechell
Ynys Dulas
Dulas Bay
IRI
Moelfre
Llanerchymedd
Salt Island
HOLYHEAD (Caergybi)
ANGLESEY (YNYS MÔN)
Red Wharf Bay
Puffin Island (Ynys Seiriol)
Beaumaris
Valley
Bodedern
Llangefni
Pentraeth
Llanfairfechan
Trearddur
Menai Bridge (Porthaethwy)
Rhosneigr
Llanfaelog
Cymyran Bay
Llanfair Pwllgwyngyll
BANGOR
Aberffraw
Bethesda
CAMBRIAN
Newborough (Niwbwrch)
Malltraeth Bay
Llanddwyn Island (Ynys Llanddwyn)
CAERNARFON
Abermenai Point
CAERNARFON BAY
(BAE CAERNARFON)
Llanberis
GLYDER FAWR
SNOWDONIA NATIO
SNOWDON (YR WYDDFA)
(PARC CENEDLAE
Penygroes
Talysarn
Clynnog-fawr
Beddgelert
Trefor
Trwyn y Gorlech
Carreg Ddu
Morfa Nefyn
Nefyn
Pistyll
LLŶN PENINSULA
Tudweiliog
Llanystumdwy
Criccieth
Porthmadog
Penrhyndeudraeth
Maentwrog
Pwllheli
Pen-ychain
Carreg yr Imbill
TREMADOG BAY (BAE TREMADOG)
Harlech
Penrhyn Mawr
Botwnnog
Llanbedrog
Trwyn Llanbedrog
Braich Anelog
Aberdaron
Abersoch
Braich y Pwll
BARDSEY SOUND (SWNT ENLLI)
Pen y Cil
Ynys Gwylan-fawr
St. Tudwal's Islands
Trwyn yr Wylfa
Trwyn Cilan
Bardsey Island (Ynys Enlli)
Llanbedr
Dyffryn Ardudwy
CARDIGAN BAY
(BAE CEREDIGION)
Barmouth (Abermaw)
Barmouth Bay (Bae Bermo)
Fairbourne
Llwyngwril
Tywyn
Aberdyfi
A B C D E F
1 2 3 4 5 6 7 8
38

47
LIVERPOOL BAY
IRISH SEA
Liverpool to Dublin 8hrs.
Liverpool to Douglas 2hrs. 30mins. (Fast Ferry, Seasonal)
Birkenhead to: Belfast 8hrs. Douglas 4hrs. 15mins. (Seasonal)
Great Ormes Head (Pen-y-Gogarth)
Little Ormes Head
LLANDUDNO
CONWY BAY
Penrhyn Bay
Rhos-on-Sea
COLWYN BAY (Bae Colwyn)
Colwyn Bay
Abergele Roads
Conwy
Deganwy
Llandudno Junction
Abergele
RHYL
Prestatyn
Point of Ayr
Hilbre Islands
HOYLAKE
West Kirby
WALLASEY
BIRKENHEAD
BEBINGTON
CROSBY
BOOTLE
HESWALL
NESTON
Little Neston
Parkgate
RIVER DEE (AFON DYFRDWY)
ENGLAND
WALES
Holywell (Treffynnon)
FLINTSHIRE
Flint (Y Fflint)
CONNAH'S QUAY
BUCKLEY (Bwcle)
Mold
St. Asaph (Llanelwy)
Denbigh
Ruthin (Rhuthun)
CONWY
Penmaenmawr
Llanrwst
Betws-y-Coed
GWYDYR FOREST PARK
MOUNTAINS
SNOWDONIA NATIONAL PARK
PARC CENEDLAETHOL ERYRI
CLOCAENOG FOREST
DENBIGHSHIRE
WREXHAM
Gresford
Llangollen
Ruabon
Chirk
OSWESTRY (Croesoswallt)
Bala (Y Bala)
Llyn Tegid
Cerrigydrudion
Corwen
Pentrefoelas
Llyn Brenig
Llyn Celyn
Dolgellau
Dinas Mawddwy
Mallwyd
Llanfyllin
Llyn Efyrnwy (Lake Vyrnwy)
Llanwddyn
POWYS
CAMBRIAN MOUNTAINS
COED Y BRENIN FOREST PARK
Aberangell
Welshpool (Y Trallwng)
Llanfair Caereinion
Castle Caereinion
Machynlleth
Llanbrynmair
Trawsfynydd
Blaenau Ffestiniog
Dolwyddelan
Guilsfield (Cegidfa)
Four Crosses
Llansantffraid
Llanymynech
BERWYN

48
CROSBY
BOOTLE
WALLASEY
BIRKENHEAD
BEBINGTON
LIVERPOOL
ST. HELENS
HAYDOCK
PRESCOT
HUYTON
GOLBORNE
NEWTON-LE-WILLOWS
WARRINGTON
WIDNES
RUNCORN
ELLESMERE PORT
FRODSHAM
NESTON
MANCHESTER
SALFORD
STRETFORD
URMSTON
SALE
ALTRINCHAM
CHEADLE
WILMSLOW
KNUTSFORD
NORTHWICH
CONNAH'S QUAY
CHESTER
BUCKLEY
WINSFORD
MIDDLEWICH
CONGLETON
SANDBACH
CREWE
NANTWICH
KIDSGROVE
ALSAGER
WREXHAM
Wrecsam
NEWCASTLE-UNDER-LYME
Whitchurch
MARKET DRAYTON
OSWESTRY
SHREWSBURY
TELFORD
Wellington
CHESHIRE WEST & CHESTER
CHESHIRE EAST
WREXHAM
FLINTSHIRE
SHROPSHIRE
ENGLAND
WALES
RIVER MERSEY
A
B
C
D
E
F
1
2
3
4
5
6
7
8
M6
M53
M56
M62
M54
M57
M60
A41
A49
A51
A53
A54
A55
A5
A483
A534
A530
A556
A500
A34
A442
A458
A518

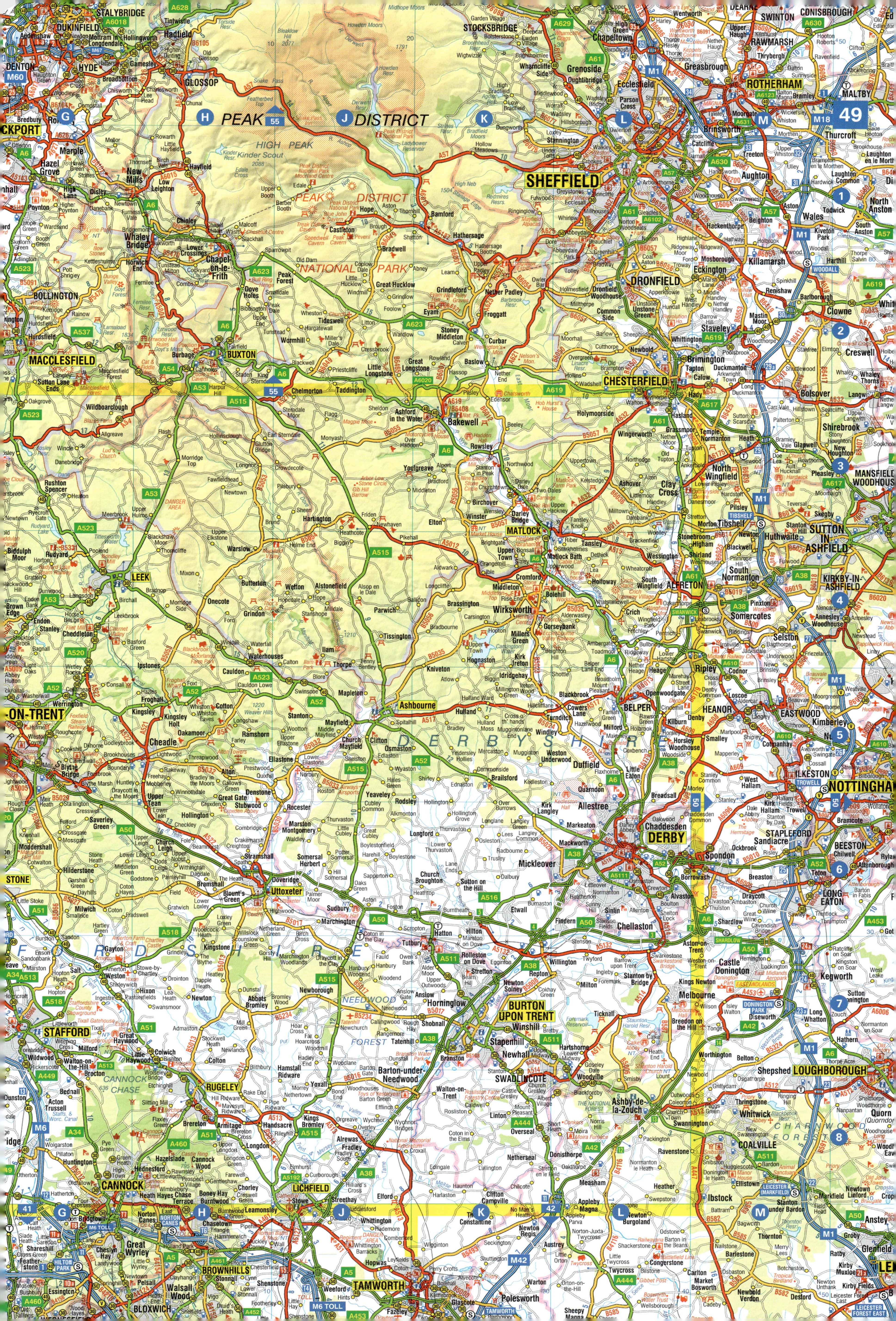

49
PEAK DISTRICT
HIGH PEAK
PEAK DISTRICT NATIONAL PARK
DERBYSHIRE
STALYBRIDGE
DUKINFIELD
HYDE
DENTON
GLOSSOP
Hadfield
STOCKSBRIDGE
Grenoside
Chapeltown
Ecclesfield
SWINTON
CONISBROUGH
RAWMARSH
ROTHERHAM
MALTBY
SHEFFIELD
Marple
New Mills
Hayfield
Whaley Bridge
Chapel-en-le-Frith
BOLLINGTON
MACCLESFIELD
BUXTON
Castleton
Hathersage
Bamford
Hope
Tideswell
DRONFIELD
Eckington
Killamarsh
Staveley
CHESTERFIELD
Bolsover
Clowne
Bakewell
Ashford in the Water
Rowsley
Chelmorton
Taddington
Youlgreave
Hartington
Matlock
Darley Dale
Wirksworth
Cromford
Clay Cross
North Wingfield
Tibshelf
Shirebrook
MANSFIELD WOODHOUSE
SUTTON IN ASHFIELD
KIRKBY-IN-ASHFIELD
Alfreton
South Normanton
Somercotes
LEEK
Cheadle
Ashbourne
Belper
Ripley
HEANOR
EASTWOOD
Kimberley
ILKESTON
NOTTINGHAM
DERBY
Duffield
Allestree
Spondon
Borrowash
Sandiacre
Stapleford
Beeston
LONG EATON
Uttoxeter
Tutbury
Melbourne
Castle Donington
Kegworth
BURTON UPON TRENT
Swadlincote
Ashby-de-la-Zouch
Coalville
LOUGHBOROUGH
Shepshed
STAFFORD
Rugeley
CANNOCK
LICHFIELD
TAMWORTH
BROWNHILLS
Walsall Wood
BLOXWICH
Barton-under-Needwood
Ibstock
Measham
STONE
-ON-TRENT

50
ROTHERHAM
RAWMARSH
SWINTON
CONISBROUGH
MALTBY
New Rossington
Bawtry
Harworth
Misterton
GAINSBOROUGH
Blyton
Kirton in Lindsey
Dinnington
North Anston
Carlton in Lindrick
WORKSOP
RETFORD
Clowne
Creswell
Whitwell
Staveley
Eckington
Killamarsh
DRONFIELD
CHESTERFIELD
Bolsover
Shirebrook
Warsop
Clipstone
Edwinstowe
Ollerton
Tuxford
Markham Moor
THE DUKERIES
NOTTINGHAMSHIRE
MANSFIELD WOODHOUSE
MANSFIELD
SUTTON IN ASHFIELD
KIRKBY IN ASHFIELD
ALFRETON
Ripley
HEANOR
EASTWOOD
HUCKNALL
Rainworth
Blidworth
Ravenshead
Calverton
Southwell
Bilsthorpe
Farnsfield
NEWARK-ON-TRENT
Collingham
Saxilby
Skellingthorpe
Waddington
North Hykeham
ARNOLD
CARLTON
NOTTINGHAM
ILKESTON
DERBY
Spondon
BEESTON
STAPLEFORD
Sandiacre
WEST BRIDGFORD
Radcliffe on Trent
Bingham
Cotgrave
Keyworth
Ruddington
Clifton
LONG EATON
Castle Donington
Kegworth
Melbourne
East Leake
LOUGHBOROUGH
Shepshed
COALVILLE
Ibstock
Mountsorrel
Quorn
Sileby
Syston
Birstall
Anstey
Thurmaston
LEICESTER
MELTON MOWBRAY
Asfordby
Oakham
RUTLAND
GRANTHAM
Bottesford
Barrowby
Colsterworth
Great Gonerby
Asfordby Hill
LEICESTERSHIRE
CHARNWOOD FOREST
M1
A1
A1(M)
A46
A52
A60
A6
A614
A617
A606
A607
A631
A57
A38
A50
A453
A47
A15
A17

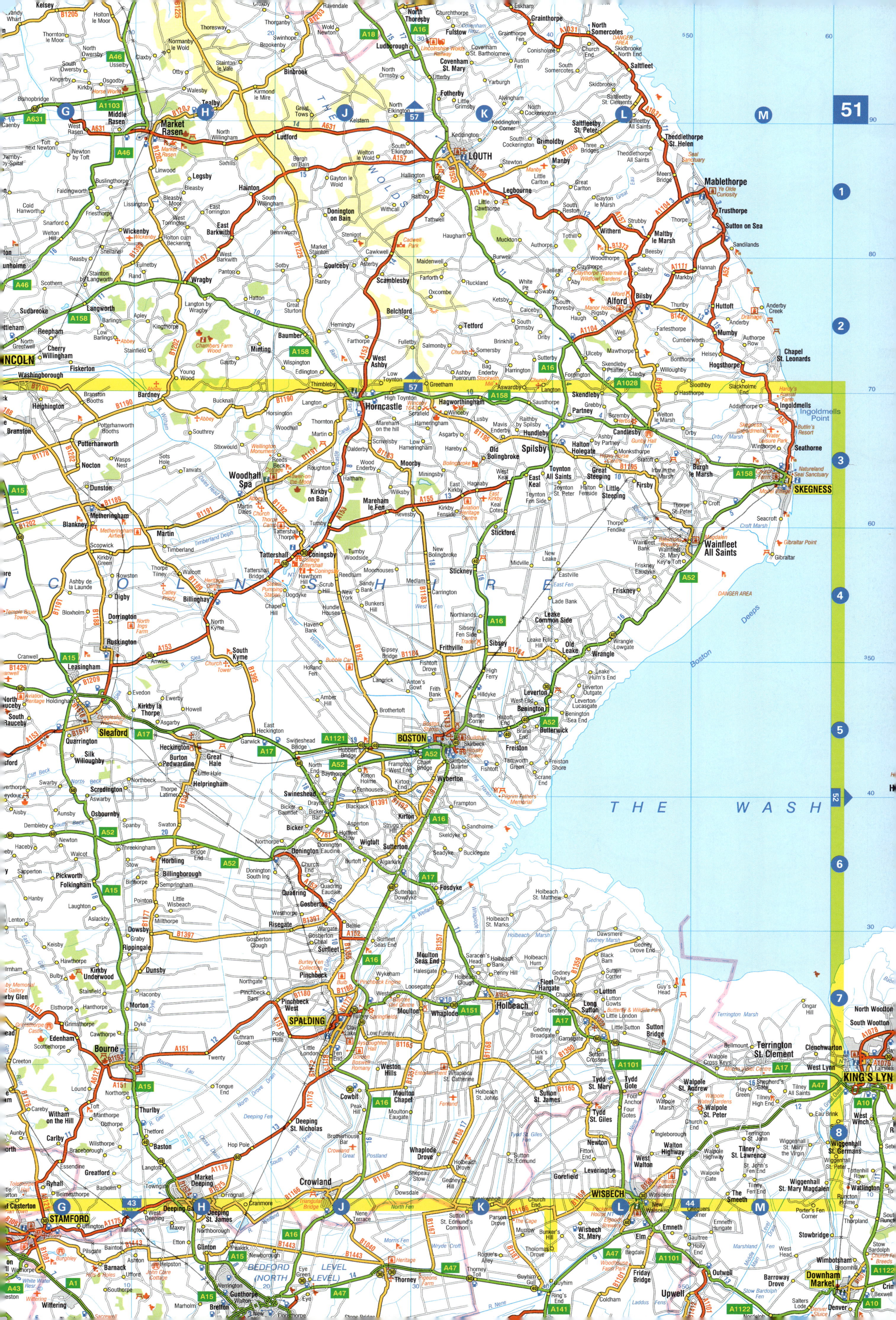

51
LOUTH
Market Rasen
Mablethorpe
Sutton on Sea
Alford
Horncastle
Spilsby
Skegness
Woodhall Spa
Coningsby
Wainfleet All Saints
Sleaford
BOSTON
THE WASH
SPALDING
Holbeach
Bourne
STAMFORD
Market Deeping
Crowland
WISBECH
KING'S LYNN
Downham Market
Terrington St. Clement
Long Sutton
THE WOLDS
57
52
43
44

THE WASH
N O R T
Scolt Head Island
Brancaster Bay
Holkham Bay
Ingoldmells Point
Gibraltar Point
Boston Deeps
Alford
Skegness
Ingoldmells
Chapel St. Leonards
Hogsthorpe
Mumby
Huttoft
Spilsby
Burgh le Marsh
Wainfleet All Saints
Friskney
Wrangle
Old Leake
Leverton
Benington
Freiston
Holbeach
Long Sutton
Sutton Bridge
Terrington St. Clement
King's Lynn
Hunstanton
Old Hunstanton
Heacham
Snettisham
Dersingham
Sandringham
Castle Rising
North Wootton
South Wootton
Clenchwarton
West Lynn
Wisbech
March
Chatteris
Upwell
Outwell
Downham Market
Denver
Southery
Littleport
Feltwell
Hockwold cum Wilton
Brandon
Thetford
Thetford Forest Park
Mundford
Swaffham
Marham
Shouldham
Narborough
Castle Acre
Fakenham
Wells-next-the-Sea
Burnham Market
Brancaster
Docking
Great Massingham
Little Massingham
Harpley
East Rudham
Gayton
Grimston
Middleton
Watton
Shipdham
Necton
Litcham
Mileham
Hempton
Walsingham
Holkham
Stiffkey
Wighton
Sculthorpe
Syderstone
Thornham
Ringstead
Sedgeford
Fring
Great Bircham
Emneth
Walpole St. Andrew
Walpole St. Peter
Tydd St. Giles
Gorefield
Leverington
Wimbotsham
Stow Bardolph
Hilgay
Methwold
Northwold
Stoke Ferry
Fincham
Wereham
Beachamwell
Gooderstone
Oxborough
Manea
Doddington
Wimblington
Prickwillow
Lakenheath
Little Downham
A16
A52
A158
A1028
A17
A47
A10
A1101
A141
A142
A148
A149
A134
A1065
A1122
A11
A1066
44
51
C
D
E
F
A
B
1
2
3
4
5
6
7
8

NORTH SEA
CROMER
Sheringham
Holt
Aylsham
North Walsham
Mundesley
Happisburgh
Wroxham
NORWICH
GREAT YARMOUTH
LOWESTOFT
Gorleston-on-Sea
Caister-on-Sea
Beccles
Bungay
Wymondham
Attleborough
Reepham
Kessingland
THE BROADS
Hemsby Hole
A47
A140
A146
A143
A148
A149
A11
A12
A1042
A1117
A1145
45

FLEETWOOD
CLEVELEYS
BLACKPOOL
LYTHAM ST. ANNE'S
PRESTON
FULWOOD
BLACKBURN
DARWEN
Clitheroe
LEYLAND
CHORLEY
SOUTHPORT
FORMBY
ORMSKIRK
SKELMERSDALE
WIGAN
BOLTON
RAMSBOTTOM
FARNWORTH
LEIGH
ATHERTON
WORSLEY
SWINTON
ECCLES
URMSTON
SALE
CROSBY
BOOTLE
WALLASEY
BIRKENHEAD
BEBINGTON
HOYLAKE
West Kirby
HESWALL
LIVERPOOL
KIRBY
ST. HELENS
PRESCOT
HUYTON
WARRINGTON
WIDNES
RUNCORN
ELLESMERE PORT
FRODSHAM
NORTHWICH
KNUTSFORD
WINSFORD
CHESTER
CONNAH'S QUAY
BUCKLEY
Mold
Flint
Holywell
LIVERPOOL BAY
RIVER MERSEY
FOREST OF BOWLAND
LANCASHIRE
CHESHIRE WEST & CHESTER
ENGLAND
WALES
Liverpool to: Dublin 8hrs.
Liverpool to: Douglas 2hrs. 30mins. (Fast Ferry, Seasonal)
Birkenhead to: Belfast 8hrs. Douglas 4hrs. 15mins. (Seasonal)
M6
M55
M65
M61
M58
M57
M62
M53
M56
A B C D E F
1 2 3 4 5 6 7 8
58
48
47

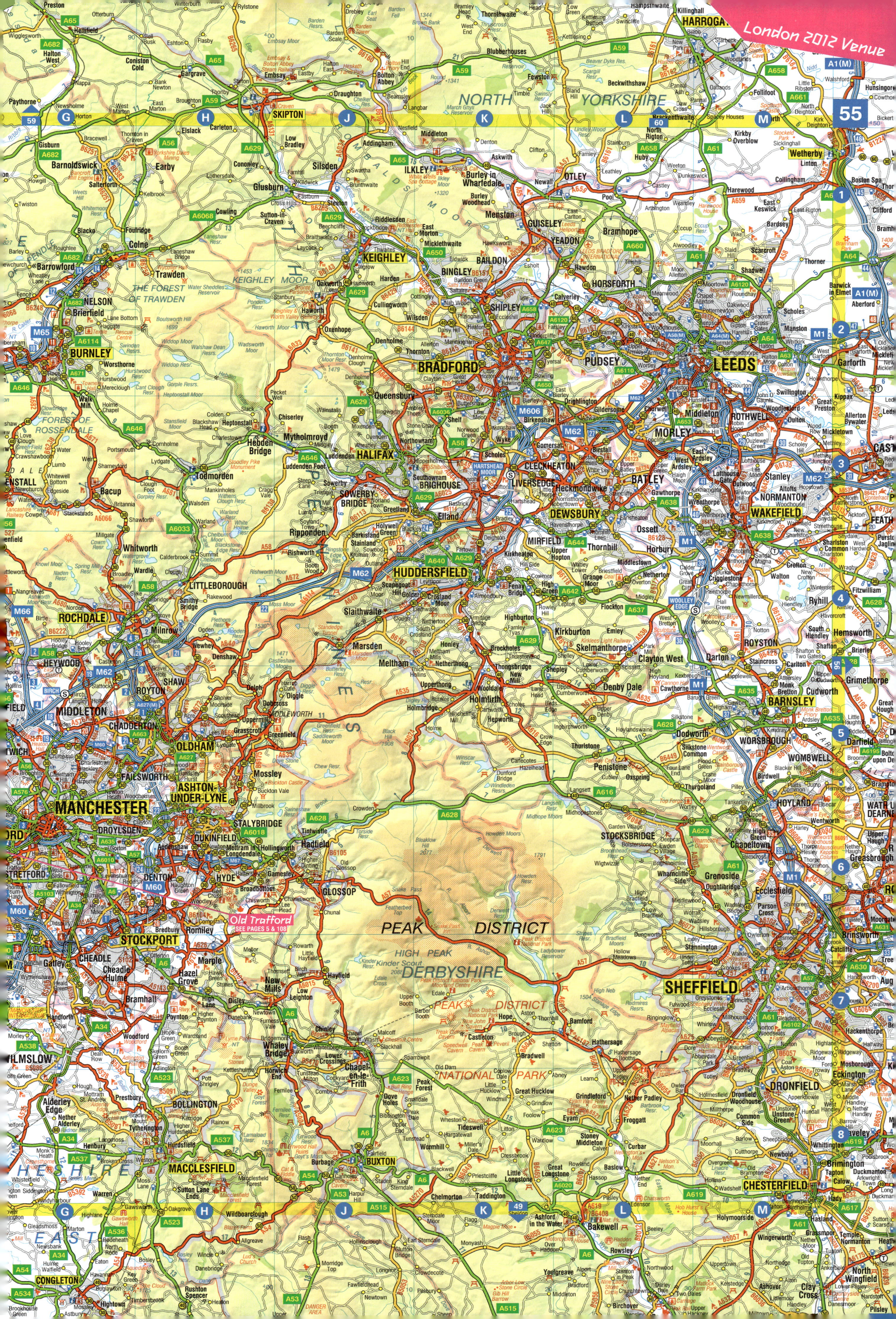
London 2012 Venue
55
NORTH YORKSHIRE
HARROGATE
SKIPTON
ILKLEY
OTLEY
KEIGHLEY
BURNLEY
BRADFORD
LEEDS
PUDSEY
HALIFAX
HUDDERSFIELD
DEWSBURY
WAKEFIELD
BARNSLEY
ROCHDALE
OLDHAM
MANCHESTER
STOCKPORT
SHEFFIELD
CHESTERFIELD
MACCLESFIELD
BUXTON
CONGLETON
PEAK DISTRICT
DERBYSHIRE
PEAK DISTRICT NATIONAL PARK
Old Trafford
SEE PAGES 5 & 108

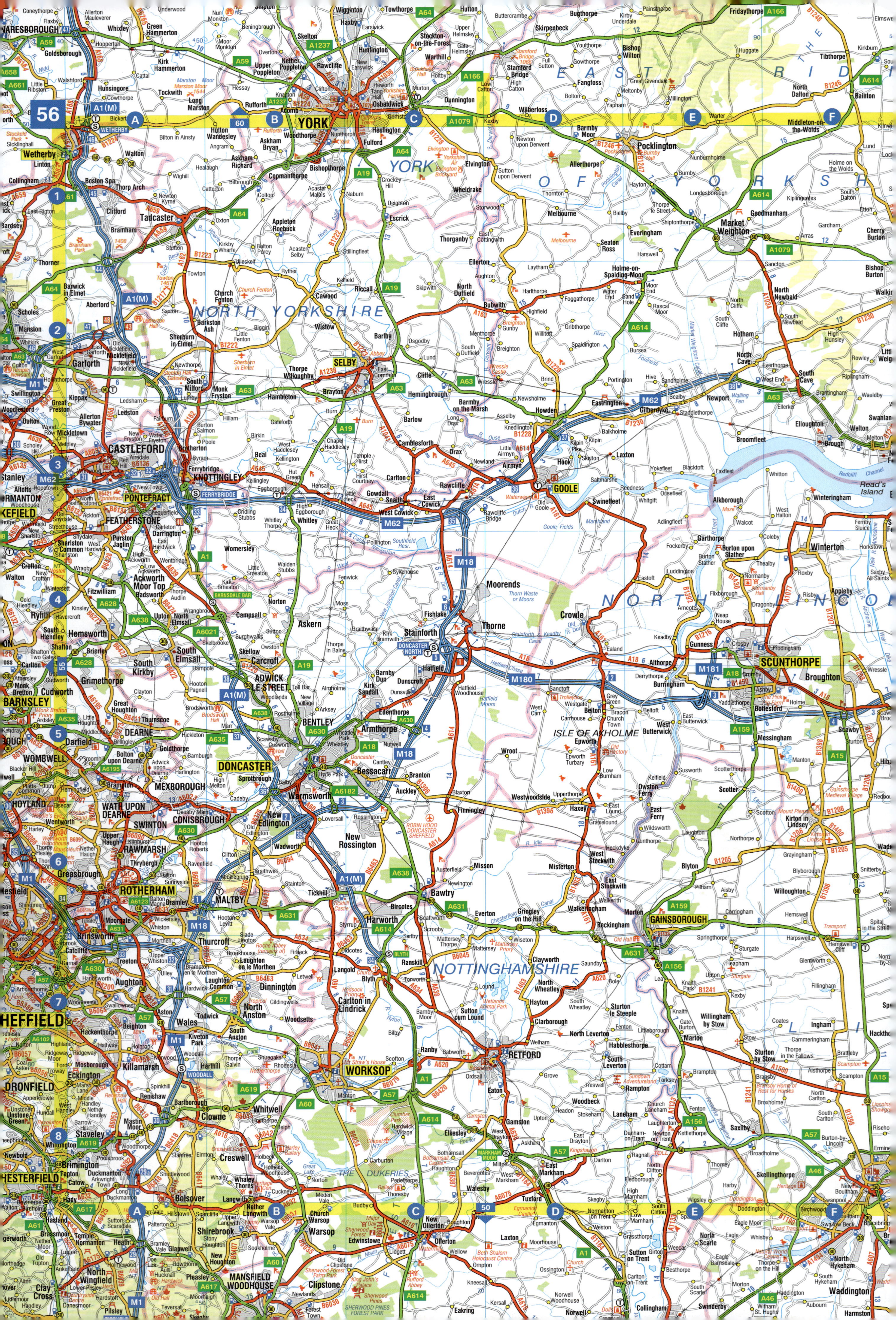
56
YORK
NORTH YORKSHIRE
EAST RIDING OF YORKSHIRE
NORTH LINCOLNSHIRE
NOTTINGHAMSHIRE
ISLE OF AXHOLME
THE DUKERIES
SHERWOOD PINES FOREST PARK
Wetherby
Tadcaster
SELBY
Pocklington
Market Weighton
Garforth
CASTLEFORD
PONTEFRACT
KNOTTINGLEY
FEATHERSTONE
GOOLE
Howden
Thorne
Stainforth
Hatfield
SCUNTHORPE
BARNSLEY
DONCASTER
Armthorpe
Bessacarr
MEXBOROUGH
CONISBROUGH
WATH UPON DEARNE
ROTHERHAM
MALTBY
New Rossington
Bawtry
Harworth
GAINSBOROUGH
WORKSOP
RETFORD
SHEFFIELD
DRONFIELD
CHESTERFIELD
Bolsover
Shirebrook
MANSFIELD WOODHOUSE
Clipstone
Ollerton
New Ollerton
Tuxford
Saxilby
North Hykeham
Waddington
Clowne
Staveley
Eckington
Killamarsh
Dinnington
North Anston
Wales
Carlton in Lindick
Blyth
Misterton
Haxey
Epworth
Crowle
Brough
Broughton
Messingham
Kirton in Lindsey
Scotter
Hemsworth
South Elmsall
South Kirkby
Askern
Adwick le Street
Bentley
Sprotbrough
Warmsworth
New Edlington
Tickhill
Wombwell
Hoyland
Swinton
Rawmarsh
Thurcroft
Aughton
Swallownest
A1(M)
M1
M18
M62
M180
M181
A1
A19
A64
A63
A614
A1079
A15
A57
A631
A638
A18
A156
A617
A619
A60
A46
A630
A616
A6102
A61
A628
A6021
A162
A166
A1237
A59
A658
A661
A620
A159
A6182
A6195
A6123
A6135
A163
A645
A6023
A635

DRIFFIELD
Wansford
Foston on the Wolds
Lissett
Ulrome
Skipsea
Beeford
North Frodingham
Hutton Cranswick
Dunnington
Hornsea
Atwick
Sigglesthorne
Leconfield
Leven
Catwick
BEVERLEY
Molescroft
Walkington
Skirlaugh
Withernwick
Mappleton
Aldbrough
Wawne
Dunswell
COTTINGHAM
Sproatley
Hilston
Tunstall
Roos
Willerby
Kirk Ella
Anlaby
Sutton-on-Hull
Marfleet
Hedon
Preston
Burstwick
Withernsea
KINGSTON UPON HULL
HESSLE
Keyingham
Ottringham
Patrington
Hollym
Holmpton
Easington
Barton upon Humber
New Holland
Barrow upon Humber
RIVER HUMBER
Paull Holme Sands
Sunk Island Sands
Trinity Sands
SPURN HEAD
Spurn Heritage Coast
N O R T H
S E A
Immingham
Immingham Dock
Grimsby Roads
GRIMSBY
CLEETHORPES
Mouth of the Humber
Hull to: Rotterdam (Europoort) 10hrs. Zeebrugge 12hrs. 30mins.
Humberston
Ulceby
Brocklesby
Keelby
Healing
Laceby
Scartho
NORTH EAST LINCOLNSHIRE
Waltham
New Waltham
Holton le Clay
Tetney
North Cotes
Marshchapel
Grainthorpe
Brigg
Barnetby le Wold
Caistor
Nettleton
Grasby
North Kelsey
Binbrook
Ludborough
Covenham St. Mary
Fotherby
Saltfleet
Theddlethorpe St. Helen
LOUTH
Legbourne
Manby
Mablethorpe
Sutton on Sea
Market Rasen
Ludford
Tealby
Middle Rasen
Withern
Alford
Huttoft
Mumby
Hogsthorpe
Chapel St. Leonards
Ingoldmells
Ingoldmells Point
Wragby
Horncastle
Spilsby
Woodhall Spa
Skegness
Burgh le Marsh
Partney
Tetford
Belchford
Donington on Bain
Goulceby
THE WOLDS
LINCOLNSHIRE
G
H
J
K
L
M
1
2
3
4
5
6
7
8
M180
A15
A180
A46
A16
A18
A631
A157
A158
A165
A1079
A1035
A1033
A1031
A1104
A1028
A52
A153
A1173
A160
A1103
A164
A63

Maryport
Workington
Seaton
Cockermouth
Keswick
Whitehaven
Cleator Moor
Egremont
St. Bees
St. Bees Head
Saltom Bay
Moss Bay
Distington
Lamplugh
Loweswater
Buttermere
Braithwaite
Thornthwaite
Threlkeld
Penruddock
Greystoke
Mungrisdale
Glenridding
Patterdale
Ambleside
Grasmere
Troutbeck
Windermere
Bowness-on-Windermere
Hawkshead
Coniston
Torver
Satterthwaite
Newby Bridge
Grange-over-Sands
Cartmel
Flookburgh
Ulverston
Dalton-in-Furness
Barrow-in-Furness
Walney Island
North Walney
Vickerstown
Foulney Island
Piel Island
Sheep Island
Roa Island
Askam in Furness
Kirkby-in-Furness
Broughton in Furness
Millom
Haverigg
Silecroft
Bootle
Selker Bay
Ravenglass
Drigg
Seascale
Gosforth
Calder Bridge
Holmrook
Eskdale Green
Boot
Santon Bridge
Ulpha
Holme Island
Chapel Island
Humphrey Head Point
Morecambe Bay
Lancaster Sound
Morecambe
Heysham
Lancaster
Middleton
Overton
Sunderland Point
Cockerham
Fleetwood
Rossall Point
Preesall
Cleveleys
Thornton
Pilling
Winmarleigh
Nateby
Bolton-le-Sands
Carnforth
Silverdale
Arnside
Milnthorpe
Levens
Staveley
Crook
Lindale
Heysham to Douglas 3hrs. 30mins.
Skiddaw
Skiddaw Forest
Helvellyn
Scafell Pike
Scafell
Copeland Forest
Furness Fells
Grizedale Forest
The Old Man of Coniston
Cumbrian Mountains
Lake District National Park
Furness
A595
A596
A66
A591
A590
A5092
A683
A585
M6
A
B
C
D
E
F
1
2
3
4
5
6
7
8

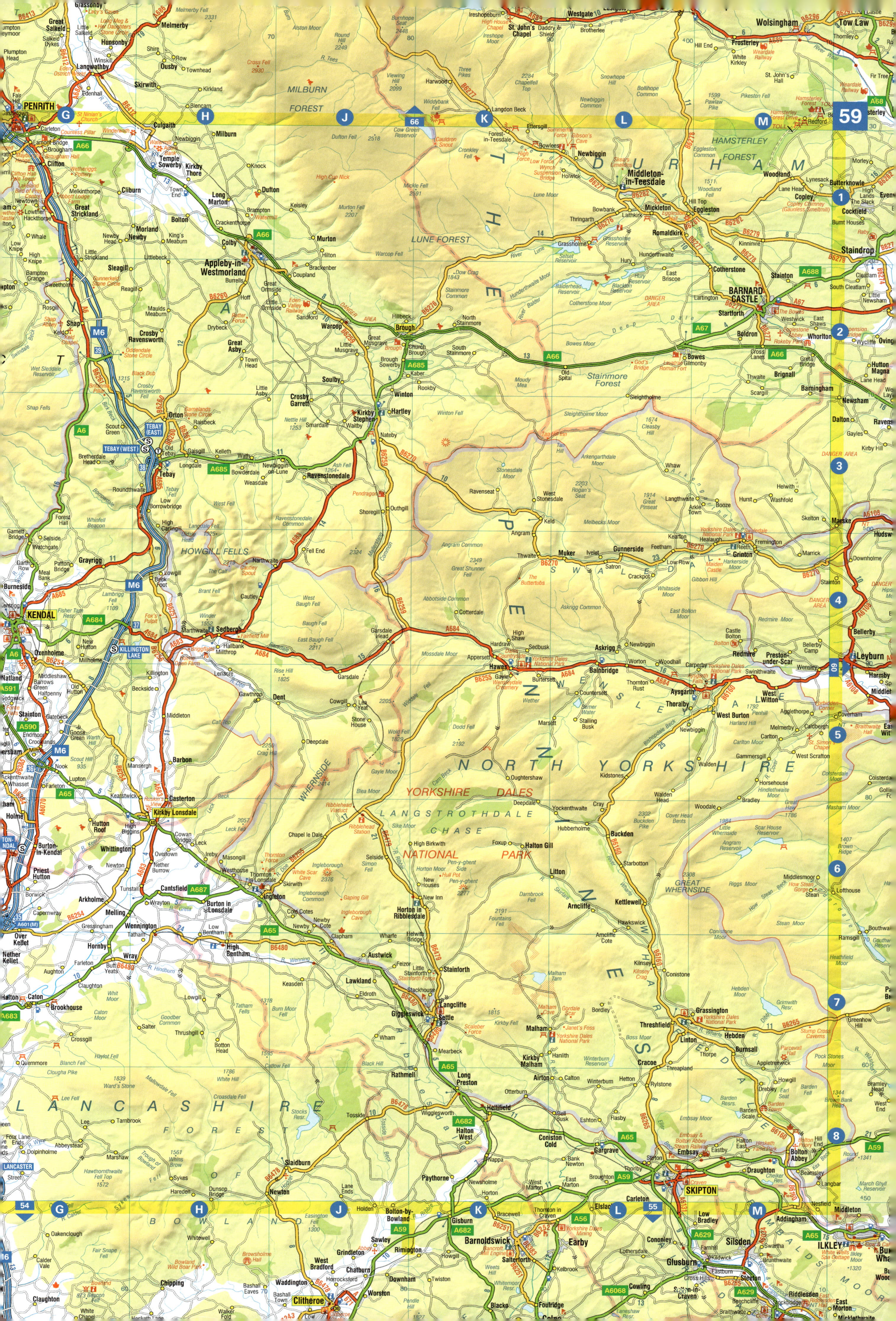
PENRITH
Appleby-in-Westmorland
Kirkby Stephen
Brough
Tebay
Sedbergh
KENDAL
Kirkby Lonsdale
Ingleton
Settle
Long Preston
Hellifield
Gisburn
Barnoldswick
Earby
SKIPTON
Grassington
Kettlewell
Buckden
Aysgarth
Leyburn
Hawes
Bainbridge
Askrigg
Reeth
Gunnerside
Muker
Keld
Middleton-in-Teesdale
BARNARD CASTLE
Staindrop
Wolsingham
Tow Law
Cotherstone
Bowes
Barningham
Newsham
Richmond
Silsden
ILKLEY
Clitheroe
Burton in Lonsdale
High Bentham
Horton in Ribblesdale
Sedbergh
Ravenstonedale
Orton
Shap
Great Asby
Warcop
Langwathby
Culgaith
Kirkby Thore
Long Marton
Dufton
MILBURN FOREST
LUNE FOREST
Stainmore Forest
HOWGILL FELLS
HAMSTERLEY FOREST
DURHAM
NORTH YORKSHIRE
YORKSHIRE DALES NATIONAL PARK
LANGSTROTHDALE CHASE
GREAT WHERNSIDE
WHERNSIDE
LANCASHIRE
FOREST OF BOWLAND
THE PENNINES
SWALEDALE
WENSLEYDALE
M6
A66
A685
A683
A684
A65
A59
A682
A629
A688
A6108
A687
B6479
B6255
B6270
B6160
B6265
B6480
B6478
B6276
B6277
B6278
B6279
B6282

60
67
59
55
A
B
C
D
E
F
1
2
3
4
5
6
7
8
Tow Law
Crook
Willington
Spennymoor
Bishop Auckland
Ferryhill
Sedgefield
Trimdon
Wingate
Hart
HARTLEPOOL
Hartlepool Bay
Seaton Carew
Tees Bay
TEESSIDE
REDCAR
Marske-by-the-Sea
Saltburn-by-the-Sea
Skelton
Guisborough
Billingham
STOCKTON-ON-TEES
MIDDLESBROUGH
Thornaby-on-Tees
Eston
Great Ayton
Stokesley
Yarm
Newton Aycliffe
Shildon
Staindrop
Barnard Castle
DARLINGTON
Gainford
Piercebridge
Winston
Hurworth-on-Tees
Croft-on-Tees
Scotch Corner
Richmond
Catterick Garrison
Catterick
Leyburn
Middleham
Bedale
Northallerton
Thirsk
Masham
Ripon
Pateley Bridge
Knaresborough
HARROGATE
Wetherby
Tadcaster
YORK
Easingwold
Helmsley
Kirkbymoorside
Ilkley
Otley
Guiseley
Yeadon
Burley in Wharfedale
Menston
Boroughbridge
DURHAM
NORTH YORK MOORS
CLEVELAND HILLS
HAMBLETON HILLS
NORTH YORKSHIRE
REDCAR & CLEVELAND
A1(M)
A19
A66
A66(M)
A167
A168
A170
A171
A172
A174
A59
A61
A64
A658
A659
A660
A661
A684
A688
A689
A1079
A1237

NORTH SEA
Skinningrove
Loftus
Boulby
Staithes
Captain Cook & Staithes Heritage
Easington
Liverton Mines
Liverton
Port Mulgrave
Hinderwell
Runswick Bay
Runswick
Roxby
Borrowby
Newton Mulgrave
Ellerby
Kettleness
Goldsborough
Lythe
Sandsend
East Row
WHITBY
Captain Cook Memorial
Saltwick Bay
Scaling Dam
Scaling Dam Reservoir
Mickleby
West Barnby
East Barnby
Ugthorpe
Raithwaite
Dunsley
Newholm
Ruswarp
Briggswath
Aislaby
Sleights
Stonegate
Lealholm
Houlsyke
Danby
Glaisdale
Egton
Egton Bridge
Grosmont
Lease Rigg
Esk Valley
Green End
Beck Hole
Goathland
Hutton Mulgrave
Golden Grove
Stainsacre
Sneaton
Ugglebarnby
Sneatonthorpe
Long Lease
High Hawsker
Low Hawsker
Ness Point or North Cheek
Raw
Fylingthorpe
Robin Hood's Bay
Old Coastguard Station
Boggle Hole
Coastal Centre
Old Peak or South Cheek
Ravenscar
Peak Alum Works
The Hermitage
A171
A169
A174
B1266
B1416
B1447
B1366
YORK MOORS
NORTH YORK MOORS
PARK
Fylingdales Moor
Lilla Cross
Burn Howe Rigg
Rosedale Moor
Loose Howe
Pike Hill Moor
Wheeldale Moor
Wheeldale Roman Road
North Yorkshire Moors Railway
Low Bell End
Rosedale Abbey
Goathland Moor
Saltergate
Malo Cross
Blakey Topping
Langdale Forest
Staintondale
Staintondale Shire Horse Farm
Crowdon
Harwood Dale Forest
Harwood Dale
Cloughton Newlands
Cloughton
Burniston
Hole of Horcum
Skelton Tower
Stape
Hartoft End
Spaunton Moor
Lastingham
Spaunton
Hutton-le-Hole
Levisham
Lockton
Newton-on-Rawcliffe
Cropton
Cropton Brewery
Cawthorne
Appleton-le-Moors
Bickley
Langdale End
Broxa
Silpho
Suffield
Hackness
Scalby
Scalby Mills
Sea Life
North Bay Railway
Throxenby
Newby
Everley
Barrowcliff
SCARBOROUGH
Falsgrave
Low Dalby
Dalby Forest
Dalby Forest Drive
Wykeham Forest
North Moor
A170
A165
A64
Sinnington
Wrelton
Aislaby
Middleton
Newbridge
Pickering
Kirkbymoorside
Marton
Normanby
Ellerburn
Thornton-le-Dale
Wilton
Allerston
Ebberston
Snainton
Brompton
Sawdon
East Ayton
West Ayton
Hutton Buscel
Ruston
Wykeham
Seamer
Irton
Crossgates
Eastfield
Osgodby
Cayton Bay
Cayton
Lebberston
The Wyke
Gristhorpe
Newbiggin
Lifeboat Station
Filey
B1415
B1258
B1261
B1039
A1039
Salton
Flamingo Land
Little Barugh
Great Barugh
Kirby Misperton
Brawby
High Marishes
Low Marishes
Yedingham
THE CARRS
Willerby
Flixton
Staxton
Folkton
Muston
Primrose Valley
Royal Oak
Hunmanby Sands
Hunmanby
Butterwick
Little Habton
Great Habton
Ryton
Wykeham
Scampston
Scampston Hall
East Knapton
West Knapton
East Heslerton
West Heslerton
Sherburn
Ganton
Potter Brompton
Fordon
Reighton
Speeton
Buckton
Bempton
FLAMBOROUGH HEAD
Danes Dyke
Flamborough
Marton
Sewerby
Sewerby Hall
Bondville Miniature Village
Lifeboat Station
BRIDLINGTON
Harbour
Hilderthorpe
West Hill
Bridlington Bay
Amotherby
Eden Camp
Broughton
Appleton-le-Street
Swinton
Malton
Old Malton
Norton-on-Derwent
Rillington
Wintringham
Thorpe Bassett
Scagglethorpe
Place Newton
Settrington
Coneysthorpe
Castle Howard
Whitewall Corner
Menethorpe
Welburn
Crambeck
Huttons Ambo
Langton
Kennythorpe
Westow
Burythorpe
Leavening
Acklam
Howsham
Leppington
Scrayingham
Foxholes
Wold Newton
Burton Fleming
Butterwick
Helperthorpe
Weaverthorpe
Thwing
Octon
Grindale
Boynton
Rudston
Rudston Monolith
Gypsey Race
Carnaby
John Bull World of Rock
Bessingby
Park Rose Birds of Prey
Haisthorpe
Thornholme
Wilsthorpe
Fraisthorpe
North Grimston
High Mowthorpe
West Lutton
East Lutton
Duggleby
Kirby Grindalythe
Birdsall
Wharram le Street
Wharram Percy Deserted Medieval Village
Sledmere
Sledmere House
Cowlam
Cottam
Langtoft
Kilham
West End
Norman Manor House
Ruston Parva
Harpham
Burton Agnes
Lowthorpe
Nafferton
Little Kelk
Great Kelk
Gransmoor
Barmston
Lissett
Ulrome
East End
West End
Skipsea
Skipsea Brough
Dringhoe
Upton
Gembling
Foston on the Wolds
Beeford
Dunnington
Atwick
Bewholme
Burdale
Towthorpe
Thixendale
Fimber
Sir Tatton Sykes's Monument
WOLDS
Wetwang
Great Kencale
Garton-on-the-Wolds
Elmswell
Little Driffield
DRIFFIELD
Wansford
Skerne
Brigham
Church End
North Frodingham
Bugthorpe
Painsthorpe
Kirby Underdale
Fridaythorpe
Skirpenbeck
Youlthorpe
Gowthorpe
Bishop Wilton
Full Sutton
Stamford Bridge
High Catton
Fangfoss
Great Givendale
Huggate
Tibthorpe
Kirkburn
Southburn
Hutton
Hutton Cranswick
Rotsea
Bolton
Meltonby
Yapham
Millington
North Dalton
Bainton
Warter
Wilberfoss
Middleton-on-the-Wolds
Kilnwick
Watton
Watton Priory
Hempholme
Barmby Moor
Pocklington
Burnby Hall
Allerthorpe
Nunburnholme
Burnby
Londesborough
Hayton
Thorpe le Street
Shiptonthorpe
Market Weighton
Goodmanham
Arras
Holme on the Wolds
South Dalton
Kiplingcotes
Etton
Lund
Beswick
Lockington
Scorborough
Cherry Burton
Arram
Leconfield
Aike
Burshill
Brandesburton
Little Leven
Leven
Leven Canal
Routh
Tickton
Catwick
Little Catwick
Long Riston
Sigglesthorne
Seaton
Hornsea Mere
Goxhill
Hornsea
Hornsea Burton
Rolston
Mappleton
Great Hatfield
Little Hatfield
Rise
Great Cowden
Sutton upon Derwent
Thornton
Melbourne
Bielby
Everingham
Seaton
EAST RIDING OF YORKSHIRE
A1079
A614
A166
A1035
A164
B1253
B1248
B1251
B1252
B1249
B1246
B1247
B1257
B1229
B1255
B1259
B1242
B1244
B1243
B1228
56
57
G
H
J
K
L
M
1
2
3
4
5
6
7
8

Clanyard Bay
Kilstay Bay
Laggantalluch Head
Kirkmaiden
Drummore
Cailiness Point
Maryport
Crammag Head
Maryport Bay
Port Kemp
MULL OF GALLOWAY
Little Scares
Scares
Big Scare
Point of Cairndoon
Glasserton
Fell of Carleton
Port Castle Bay
St. Ninian's Cave
Isle of Whithorn
Chapel
Cairn Head
BURROW HEAD
B7004
B7041
PAGE NOT CONTINUED
I R I S H
S E A
POINT OF AYRE
The Ayres
Rue Point
The Lhen
Dhowin
Cranstal
Bride
Jurby East
Andreas
Shellag Point
Jurby West
Jurby Head
Regaby
Ballasalla
Sandygate
Ramsey Bay
The Cronk
St. Judes
Dhoor
Ramsey
Sulby
Churchtown
Ballaugh
Orrisdale
Orrisdale Head
Ravensdale
Glen Auldyn
Port e Vullen
Maughold Head
Lewaigue
Maughold
Ballajora
Port Mooar
North Barrule
Kirk Michael
Bishopscourt Glen
Glen Wyllin
SNAEFELL
Slieau Dhoo
Clagh Ouyr
Corrany
Cornaa
Glen Mona
Port Cornaa
Ballacamane Beg
Ballaleigh
Barregarrow
Sulby Resr.
Snaefell Mountain Railway
Dhoon
Gob y Deigan
Knocksharry
Cronk-y-Voddy
Dhoon Glen
Bulgham Bay
St. Patrick's Isle
Peel
Ballagyr
Lambfell Moar
Rhenass Waterfall
Glen Helen
Colden
Injebreck Resr.
Laxey
Laxey Wheel
Laxey Head
Old Laxey
Contrary Head
Ballig
St. John's
Patrick
Slieau Ruy
Greeba Castle
Baldwin
Ballacannell
Laxey Bay
Baldrine
ISLE OF MAN
Clay Head
Glen Maye
Lower Foxdale
Hillberry
Onchan
Dalby Point
Niarbyl
Dalby
Foxdale
Crosby
Glen Vine
Strang
Union Mills
Willaston
Groudie Glen Railway
Port Groudle
Onchan Head
Niarbyl Bay
South Barrule
Braaid
Cooil
Spring Valley
DOUGLAS
Douglas Bay
Douglas Head
Close Clark
Kewaigue
Stroin Vuigh
Ballamodha
St. Mark's
Newtown
Horses Home
Quine's Hill
Little Ness
Ronague
Kerristal
Fleshwick Bay
Lingague
Grenaby
Port Soderick
Isle of Man Steam railway
Santon Head
Bradda
Bradda Head
Ballabeg
Colby
Ballasalla
Port Erin
Four Roads
Ship Burial
The Howe
Port St. Mary
Castletown
Derby Fort
Derbyhaven
St. Michael's Island
Chambered Cairn
The Sound
Cregneash
Kitterland
National Folk Museum
Nautical Museum
Old House of Keys
SPANISH HEAD
Calf of Man
Dreswick Point
Douglas to:
Belfast 2hrs.45mins. (Fast Ferry, Seasonal)
Birkenhead 4hrs. 15mins. (Seasonal)
Heysham 3hrs. 30mins.
Dublin 2hrs. 45mins. (Fast Ferry, Seasonal)
Liverpool 2hrs. 30mins. (Fast Ferry, Seasonal)
A B C D E F
1 2 3 4 5 6 7 8

63
Mayhole
Maybole
Dunure
Culzean Bay
Maidenhead Bay
Maidens
Turnberry Bay
Turnberry
Kirkoswald
Matthew's Port
Dipple
Crosshill
Kilgrammie
Wallacetown
Dailly
Old Dailly
Girvan
McKechnie Institute
Glendoune
Woodland Bay
Penkill
Dalquhairn
Barr
Pinmore
CARRICK
CHANGUE FOREST
Lendalfoot
Straid
Merkland
Bennane Head
Ballantrae Bay
Colmonell
Pinwherry
Poundland
Knockdolian
SOUTH AYRSHIRE
Heronsford
Ballantrae
Barrhill
Downan Point
Currarie Port
Low Ballochdowan
Chirmorie
Cairnryan to: Larne 1hr. (Fast Ferry, Seasonal) Larne 2hrs.
Stranraer to: Belfast 2hrs 10mins. (Fast Ferry, Seasonal) Belfast 3hrs.
Milleur Point
Corsewall Point
Barnhills
Portencalzie
Finnarts Bay
Glenwhilly
Polbae
Dounan Bay
Kirkcolm
Cairnryan
Airies
The Wig
Portobello
Loch Ryan
DUMFRIES & GALLOWAY
Balmurrie
Slouchnawen Bay
Leswalt
New Luce
Innermessan
Glenstockadale
Stranraer
Castle Kennedy
Broadsea Bay
Dunragit
Glenluce
I R I S H S E A
Black Head
Lochans
Mark
Portpatrick
Stoneykirk
Kilfillan
Stairhaven
Auchenmalg
Port of Spittal Bay
Kildonan
Kirklauchline
Sandhead
L U C E B A Y
Auchenmalg Bay
Garheugh Port
Cairngarroch Bay
Cairngarroch
Money Head
Float Bay
Low Ardwell
Ardwell
Chapel Rossan Bay
Milton Point
Ardwell Point
Balgowan Point
Port William
Mull of Logan
Port Logan Bay
Port Logan
Terally Point
Barsalloch Point
Cairnywellan Head
Clanyard Bay
Kilstay Bay
Laggantalluch Head
Kirkmaiden
Drummore
Cailiness Point
Maryport
Crammag Head
Maryport Bay
Scares
Port Kemin
MULL OF GALLOWAY
Achinhoan Head
Johnston's Point
Polliwilline Bay
Macharioch
Cove Point
Sheep Island
Sanda Island
Ailsa Craig
Copeland Island
NORTHERN IRELAND
Donaghadee
PAGE NOT CONTINUED
68
69
70
62
64

Maybole
Kirkmichael
Crosshill
Straiton
Dalmellington
Patna
Waterside
New Cumnock
Sanquhar
Kirkconnel
Wanlockhead
Leadhills
EAST AYRSHIRE
SOUTH AYRSHIRE
CARRICK
CARRICK FOREST
CHANGUE FOREST
Loch Doon
Carsphairn
DUNDEUGH FOREST
THE GLENKENS
GALLOWAY FOREST PARK
MERRICK
GLENTROOL FOREST
Glentrool Village
RHINNS OF KELLS
St. John's Town of Dalry
Balmaclellan
New Galloway
Moniaive
Penpont
Thornhill
Tynron
Corsock
CAIRN EDWARD FOREST
KIRROUGHTREE FOREST
DUMFRIES
GALLOWAY
PENNINGHAME FOREST
Newton Stewart
Minnigaff
CAIRNSMORE OF FLEET
Creetown
Kirkcowan
Wigtown
Bladnoch
THE MACHARS
Kirkinner
Sorbie
Garlieston
Whithorn
Isle of Whithorn
Port William
Glasserton
Monreith Bay
Burrow Head
Wigtown Bay
Islands of Fleet
Gatehouse of Fleet
LAURIESTON FOREST
GLENGAP FOREST
Laurieston
Castle Douglas
Dalbeattie
DALBEATTIE FOREST
Kirkcudbright
Tongland
Twynholm
Borgue
Dundrennan
Auchencairn
Kippford or Scaur
Rockcliffe
Hestan Island
Little Ross
Abbey Head
Port Mary
Rascarrel Bay
Crossmichael
Haugh of Urr
Kirkpatrick Durham
Crocketford or Ninemile Bar
Springholm
Carsluith
Ravenshall Point
Eggerness Point
Port Allen
Portyerrock Bay
Cairn Head
Point of Cairndoon
Barsalloch Point
Milton Point
Port Castle Bay
A77
A75
A76
A712
A713
A714
A702
A762
A711
A746
A747
A755
A762
B7079
B729

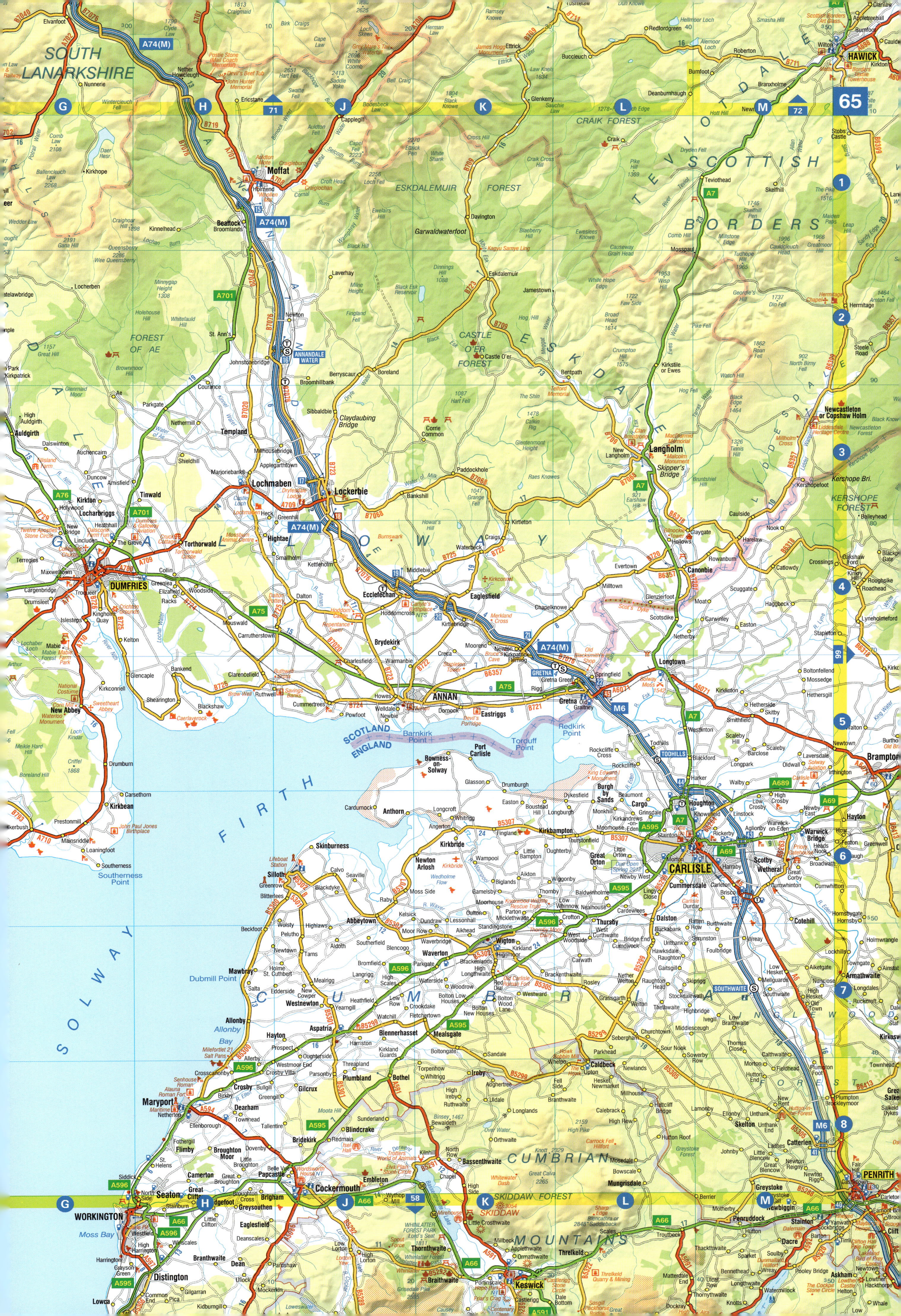

SOUTH LANARKSHIRE
A74(M)
Moffat
Beattock
ESKDALEMUIR
FOREST
Eskdalemuir
Garwaldwaterfoot
CRAIK FOREST
Craik
SCOTTISH
BORDERS
TEVIOTDALE
HAWICK
Hawick
Teviothead
Mosspaul
Hermitage
Newcastleton or Copshaw Holm
Kershopefoot
KERSHOPE FOREST
LIDDESDALE
ESKDALE
Langholm
Skipper's Bridge
Canonbie
Bentpath
CASTLE O'ER FOREST
FOREST OF AE
Lochmaben
Lockerbie
Templand
Johnstonebridge
Boreland
Kirkpatrick Fleming
Ecclefechan
Eaglesfield
Middlebie
ANNAN
Eastriggs
Gretna
Gretna Green
Springfield
Longtown
DUMFRIES
Dumfries
Torthorwald
Collin
Carrutherstown
Clarencefield
Ruthwell
Cummertrees
Powfoot
New Abbey
Glencaple
Kirkbean
Carsethorn
Southerness
Southerness Point
SOLWAY FIRTH
SCOTLAND
ENGLAND
Bowness-on-Solway
Port Carlisle
Burgh by Sands
Kirkbampton
Kirkbride
Anthorn
Cardurnock
Skinburness
Silloth
Abbeytown
Newton Arlosh
Wigton
Dalston
Thursby
CARLISLE
Carlisle
Houghton
Wetheral
Scotby
Brampton
Hayton
Warwick Bridge
Cumwhinton
Armathwaite
Southwaite
Plumpton
Calthwaite
Catterlen
Skelton
Greystoke
PENRITH
Penrith
Penruddock
Dacre
Stainton
Allonby
Allonby Bay
Dubmill Point
Mawbray
Maryport
Aspatria
Bothel
Ireby
Caldbeck
Hesket Newmarket
Sebergham
Mealsgate
Plumbland
Gilcrux
Dearham
Flimby
Seaton
WORKINGTON
Workington
Moss Bay
Harrington
Distington
Lowca
Cockermouth
Bridekirk
Papcastle
Embleton
Bassenthwaite
Braithwaite
Keswick
Threlkeld
SKIDDAW
SKIDDAW FOREST
CUMBRIAN
MOUNTAINS
CUMBRIA
Thornthwaite
WHINLATTER FOREST PARK
A7
A75
A701
A709
A710
A595
A596
A66
A689
A69
M6
B7076
B6357
B5299
B5305
71
72
58

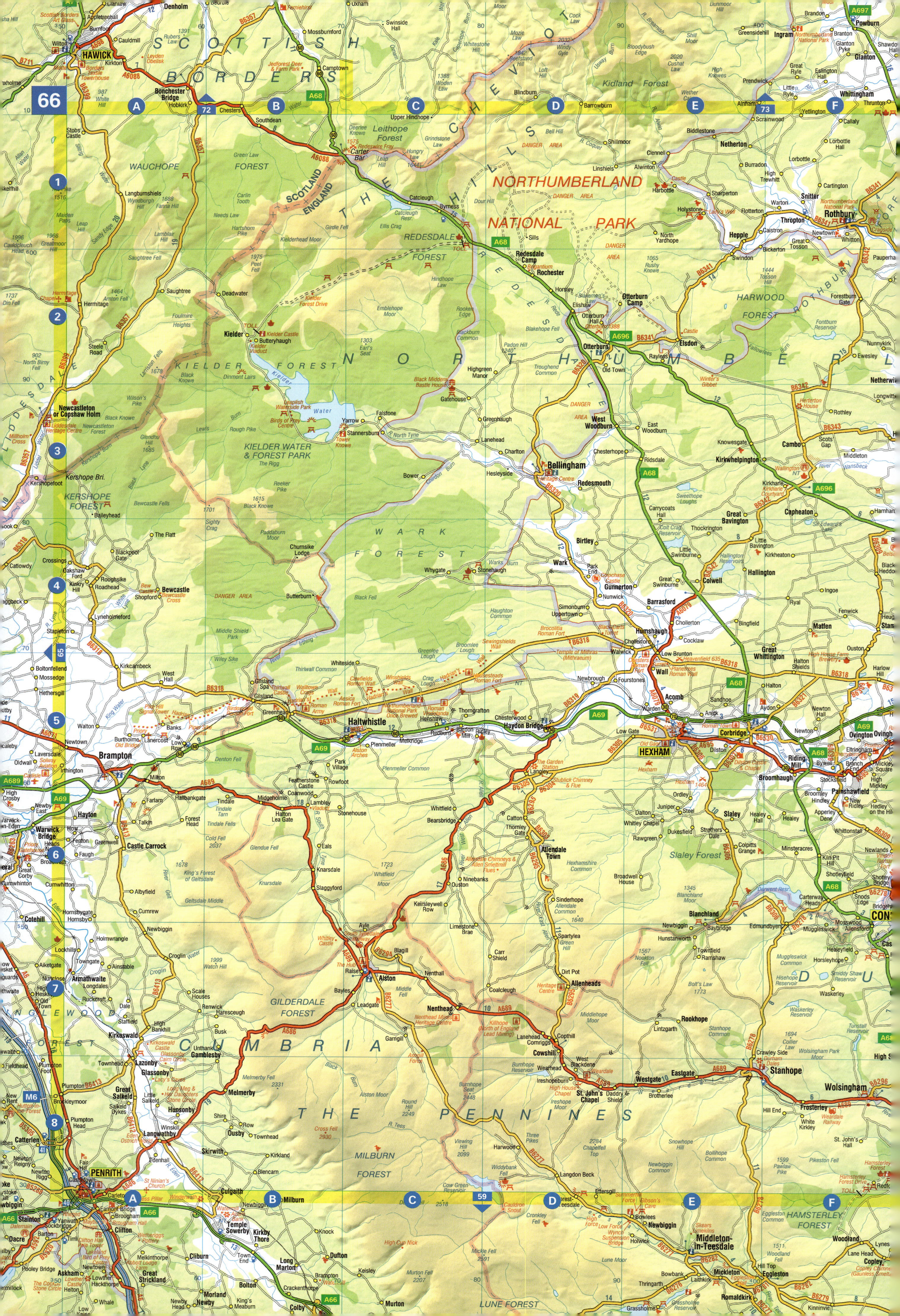
SCOTTISH BORDERS
HAWICK
WAUCHOPE FOREST
SCOTLAND
ENGLAND
THE CHEVIOT HILLS
NORTHUMBERLAND NATIONAL PARK
Kidland Forest
REDESDALE FOREST
KIELDER FOREST
KIELDER WATER & FOREST PARK
NORTHUMBERLAND
HARWOOD FOREST
Rothbury
Otterburn
Bellingham
Kielder
Newcastleton or Copshaw Holm
KERSHOPE FOREST
WARK FOREST
Haltwhistle
Haydon Bridge
HEXHAM
Corbridge
Brampton
Alston
Allendale Town
Slaley Forest
Stanhope
Wolsingham
GILDERDALE FOREST
CUMBRIA
THE PENNINES
MILBURN FOREST
PENRITH
Middleton-in-Teesdale
HAMSTERLEY FOREST
LUNE FOREST
A68
A69
A696
A686
A689
A66
72
73
65
59

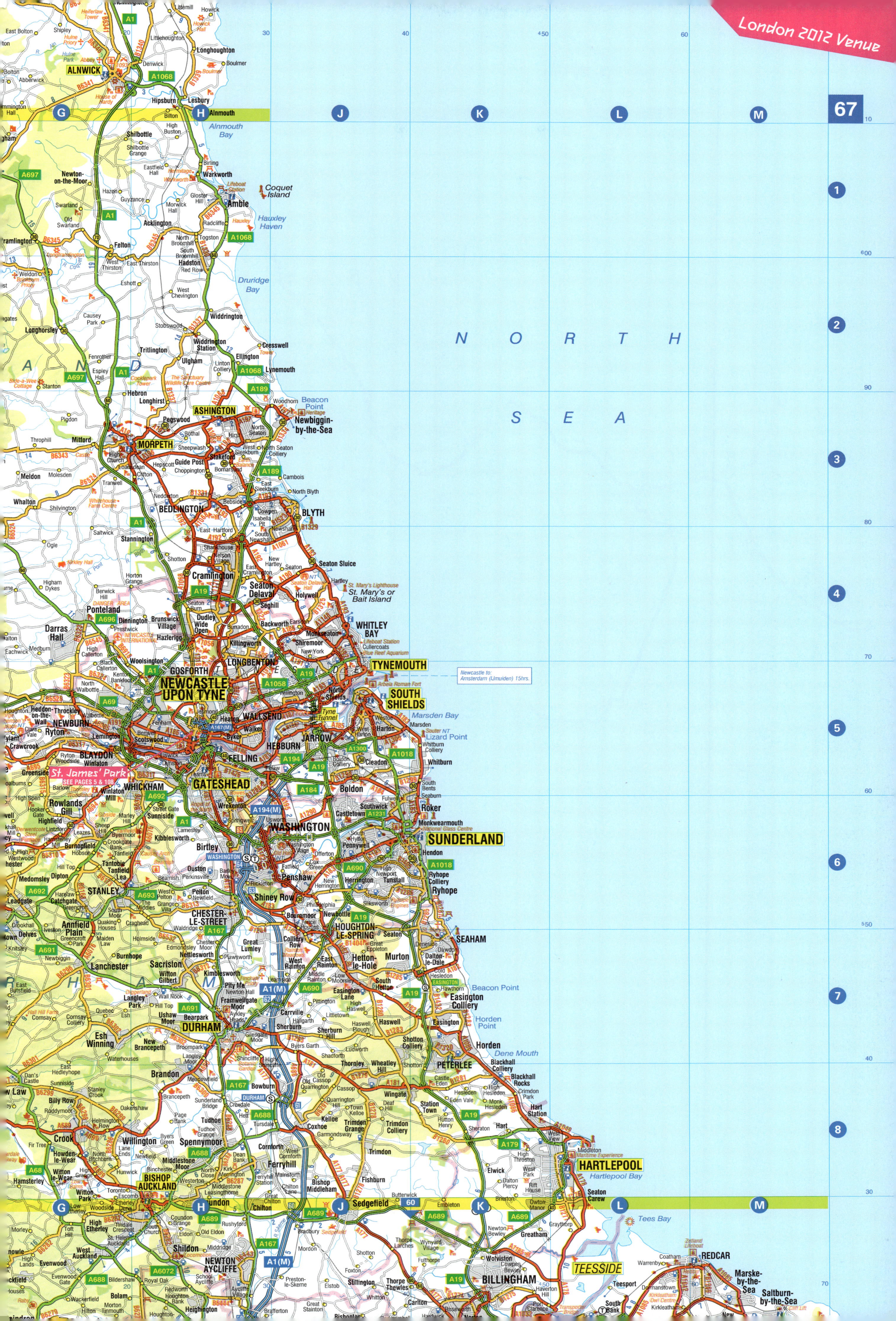
London 2012 Venue
NORTH SEA
ALNWICK
Alnmouth
Alnmouth Bay
Warkworth
Coquet Island
Amble
Hauxley Haven
Druridge Bay
Widdrington
Cresswell
Lynemouth
Beacon Point
Newbiggin-by-the-Sea
ASHINGTON
MORPETH
BEDLINGTON
BLYTH
Seaton Sluice
St. Mary's or Bait Island
Cramlington
Seaton Delaval
Ponteland
WHITLEY BAY
TYNEMOUTH
Newcastle to: Amsterdam (Ijmuiden) 15hrs.
NEWCASTLE UPON TYNE
GOSFORTH
LONGBENTON
SOUTH SHIELDS
Marsden Bay
Lizard Point
WALLSEND
HEBBURN
JARROW
Tyne Tunnel
NEWBURN
BLAYDON
Ryton
St. James' Park
SEE PAGES 5 & 108
WHICKHAM
GATESHEAD
FELLING
Boldon
Roker
SUNDERLAND
WASHINGTON
Birtley
Rowlands Gill
STANLEY
CHESTER-LE-STREET
Penshaw
Shiney Row
HOUGHTON-LE-SPRING
Ryhope
SEAHAM
Annfield Plain
Lanchester
Sacriston
Great Lumley
Hetton-le-Hole
Murton
Beacon Point
Easington Colliery
Horden Point
Horden
Dene Mouth
DURHAM
PETERLEE
Esh Winning
Brandon
Crook
Willington
Spennymoor
Ferryhill
Trimdon
HARTLEPOOL
Hartlepool Bay
BISHOP AUCKLAND
Sedgefield
Tees Bay
Shildon
NEWTON AYCLIFFE
BILLINGHAM
TEESSIDE
REDCAR
Marske-by-the-Sea
Saltburn-by-the-Sea
A1
A1(M)
A19
A68
A167
A189
A690
A691
A692
A693
A696
A697
A1018
A1058
A1068
A194(M)
A179
A181
A688
A689

COLONSAY
Scalasaig
Kiloran
Port a' Bhàta
Rubha Dubh
Eilean Leathann
Eilean a' Chladaich
Dubh Eilean
ORONSAY
Eilean nan Ron
Eilean Ghaoideamal
Ceann Riobha
Corpach Bay
Glendebadel Bay
Shian Bay
JURA
JURA FOREST
PAPS OF JURA
Lussagiven
Ardlussa
Inverlussa
Lussa Point
Gob Dubh
Tarbert
Craighouse
Small Isles
Feolin Ferry
Port Askaig
Lagg
Knockrome
Ardfernal
Leargybreck
Keils
Cabrach
Ardfin
Brosdale Island
Port na Birlinne
Na Cùiltean
Rubha na Tràille
Am Fraoch Eilean
Glas Eilean
Rubh'an t-Sailein
Rubh' a' chrois-aoinidh
RUBHA A'MHAIL
Post Rocks
Rubha Bholsa
Nave Island
Eilean Beag
Ardnave Point
Rubha Lamanais
Saligo Bay
Coul Point
Machir Bay
Kilchiaran Bay
ISLAY
Portnahaven
Port Wemyss
Orsay
RHINNS POINT
Port Gleann na Gaoidh
Port Charlotte
Bruichladdich
Bowmore
Bridgend
Ballygrant
Keills
Bunnahabhain
Caol Ila
Carraig Dhubh
Loch Indaal
Laggan Point
Laggan Bay
Port Ellen
Laphroaig
Lagavulin
Ardbeg
Texa
THE OA
MULL OF OA
Rubha na Meise Bàine
Rubha nan Leacan
Port Alsaig
Slugaide Glas
Dùn Mòr Ghil
Eilean Imersay
Rubha na Cainmhich
Eilean Bhride
Eilean Craobhach
Eilean a' Chuirn
Ardmore Point
Claggain Bay
Carraig Mhòr
McArthur's Head
ARGYLL & BUTE
SOUND OF JURA
Sound of Islay
Kennacraig to Port Askaig 2hrs
Kennacraig to Port Ellen 2hrs 20mins
Colonsay to Port Askaig 1hr 10mins (Seasonal)
ISLE OF GIGHA
Ardminish
Gigalum Island
Cara Island
Mull of Cara
Craro Island
West Tarbert Bay
East Tarbert Bay
Druimyeon Bay
Eilean Garbh
An Dubh-sgeir
Gamhna Gigha
Sound of Gigha
A' Chleit
Ronachan Point
Ardpatrick Point
West Loch Tarbert
Clachan
Tayinloan
Killean
Muasdale
Glenacardoch Point
Port a' Bhorrain
Glenbarr
Bellochantuy Bay
Bellochantuy
Port Corbert
Machrihanish Bay
Machrihanish
Campbeltown
Drumlemble
Stewarton
Island Davaar
Eararale Point
Rubha Dùin Bhàin
Rubha' a' Mharaiche
MULL OF KINTYRE
Rubha Chlachan
Port Mean
Southend
Brunerican Bay
Cove Point
Black Point
Sheep Island
Sanda Island
Polliwilline Bay
Achinhoan Head
KINTYRE
KNAPDALE
Tayvallich
Eilean Dubh
Carsaig Bay
Eilean nan Coinean
Eilean Loain
Island of Danna
Keillmore
Kilmory
Bàgh na Dojde
Eilean Mor
Point of Knap
Miller's Bay
Kilberry Head
Kilberry
Port Mòr
Ardpatrick
Rubh' a' Bhacain
Port nan Laogh
Ruadh Sgeir
Rubha nam Bàrr
Ardnoe Point
Rubha Garbh-ard
Garbh Rèisa
RATHLIN ISLAND
BENMORE HEAD
74
A
B
C
D
E
F
1
2
3
4
5
6
7
8
A83
A846
A847
B8016
B842
B843

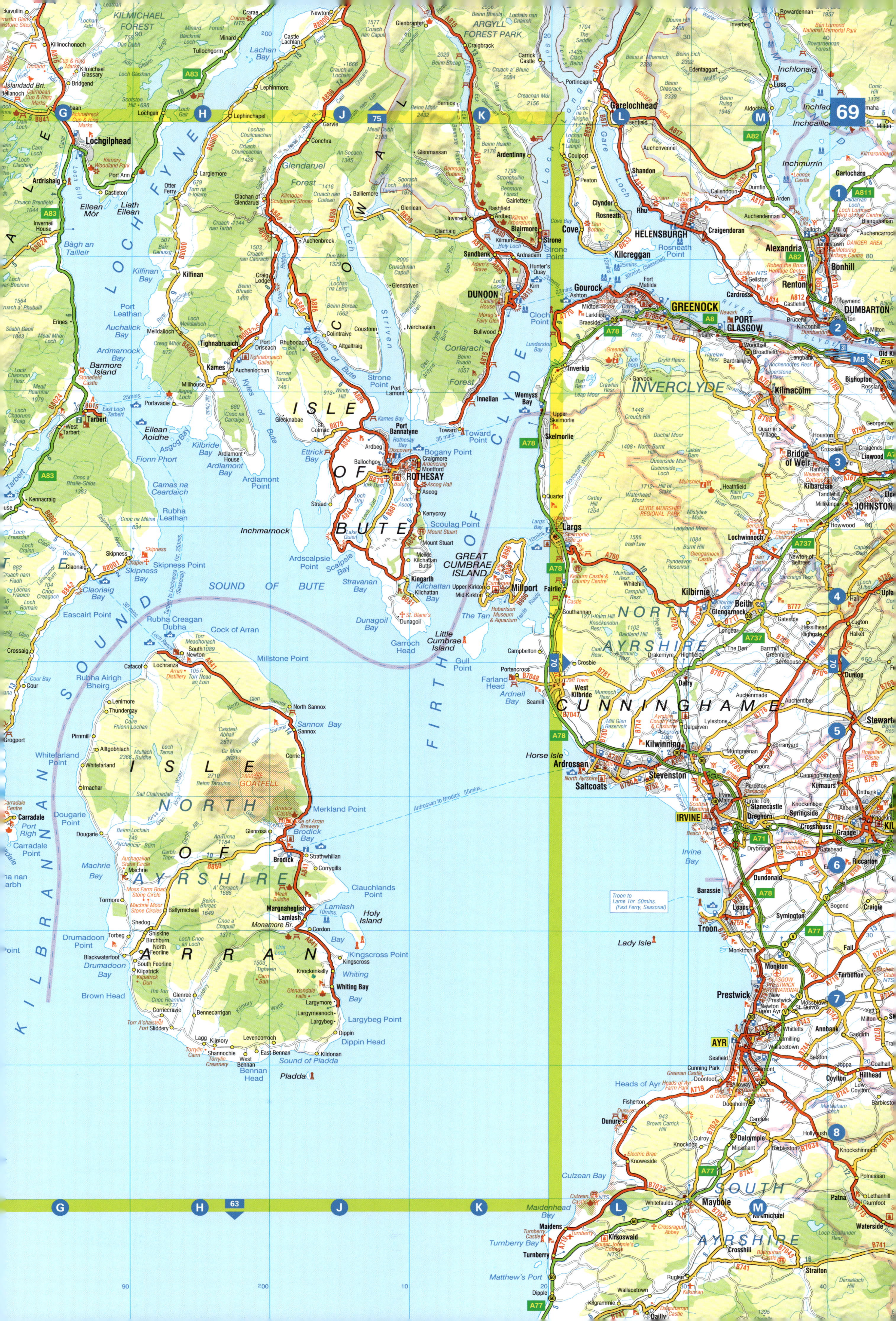
KILMICHAEL FOREST
ARGYLL FOREST PARK
Lochgilphead
Ardrishaig
LOCH FYNE
COWAL
Glendaruel Forest
Tighnabruaich
Kames
Portavadie
Tarbert
Dunoon
Sandbank
Holy Loch
Kilmun
Strone Point
Ardentinny
Garelochhead
Gare Loch
Loch Long
Cove
Kilcreggan
Rosneath
Rhu
Shandon
HELENSBURGH
Alexandria
Bonhill
Renton
DUMBARTON
Gourock
GREENOCK
PORT GLASGOW
Inverkip
Wemyss Bay
Skelmorlie
INVERCLYDE
Kilmacolm
Bridge of Weir
Kilbarchan
JOHNSTONE
Lochwinnoch
ISLE OF BUTE
Kyles of Bute
Port Bannatyne
ROTHESAY
Kingarth
Inchmarnock
SOUND OF BUTE
GREAT CUMBRAE ISLAND
Millport
Little Cumbrae Island
Largs
Fairlie
FIRTH OF CLYDE
Skipness
Claonaig
KILBRANNAN SOUND
Lochranza
ISLE OF ARRAN
NORTH AYRSHIRE
Goatfell
Brodick
Brodick Bay
Lamlash
Holy Island
Whiting Bay
Kildonan
Pladda
Blackwaterfoot
Machrie
Pirnmill
West Kilbride
Ardrossan
Saltcoats
Stevenston
Kilwinning
CUNNINGHAME
Dalry
Kilbirnie
Beith
Dunlop
Stewarton
Kilmaurs
IRVINE
Dreghorn
Troon
Lady Isle
Prestwick
Monkton
AYR
Heads of Ayr
Dunure
Maybole
Culzean Bay
Maidens
Turnberry
Kirkoswald
Crosshill
SOUTH AYRSHIRE
Dalrymple
Patna
Coylton
Annbank
Tarbolton
Symington
Kilmarnock
Ardrossan to Brodick 55mins.
Troon to Larne 1hr. 50mins. (Fast Ferry, Seasonal)
G
H
J
K
L
M
63
75
70

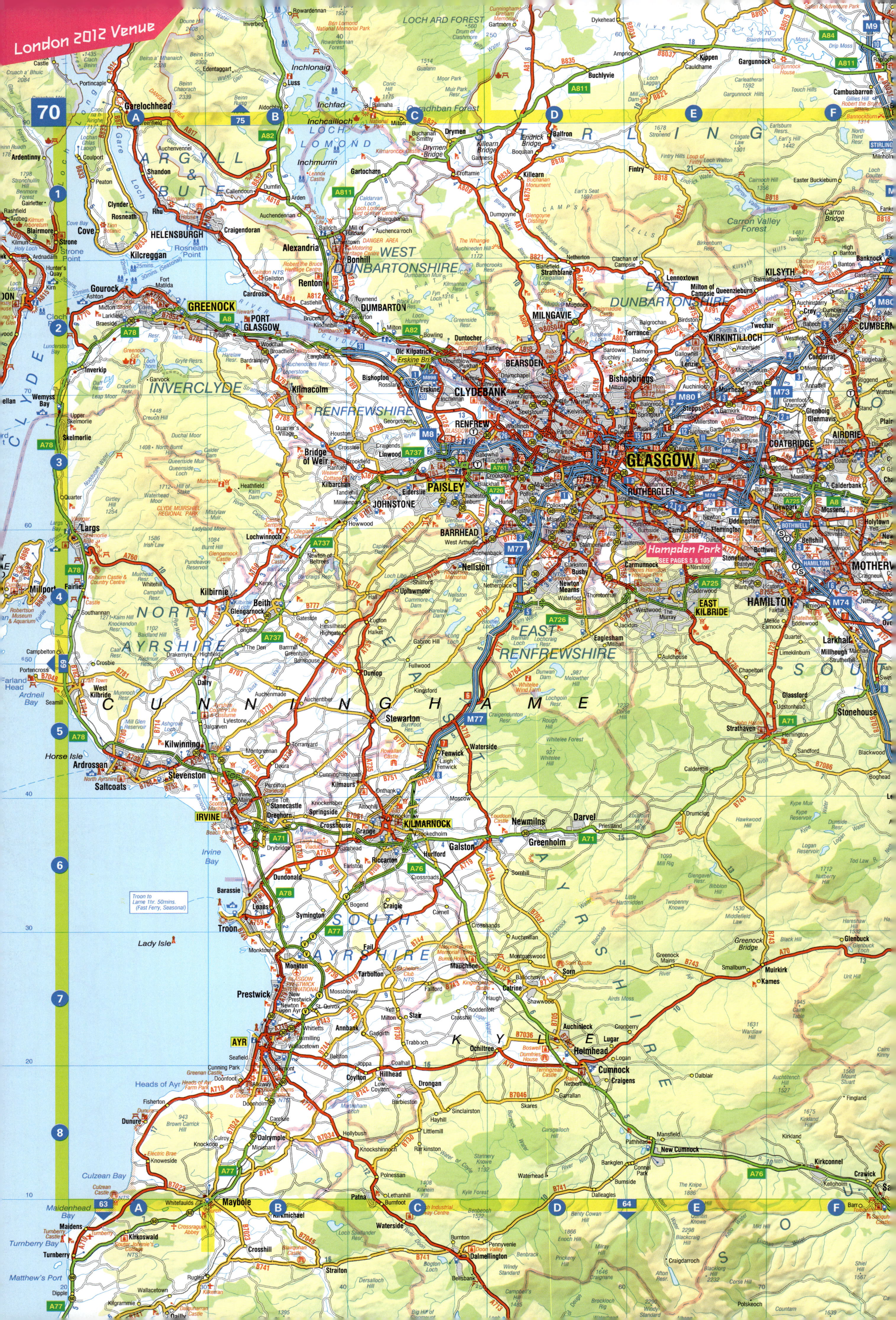
London 2012 Venue
Hampden Park
SEE PAGES 5 & 105
GLASGOW
PAISLEY
CLYDEBANK
RENFREW
RUTHERGLEN
HAMILTON
EAST KILBRIDE
MOTHERWELL
COATBRIDGE
AIRDRIE
KILSYTH
KIRKINTILLOCH
BEARSDEN
MILNGAVIE
BISHOPBRIGGS
DUMBARTON
HELENSBURGH
GREENOCK
PORT GLASGOW
KILMARNOCK
IRVINE
AYR
Ardrossan
Saltcoats
Largs
Troon
Prestwick
Maybole
Cumnock
Stewarton
Kilwinning
Johnstone
Barrhead
Newton Mearns
Strathaven
Galston
Newmilns
Darvel
ARGYLL & BUTE
WEST DUNBARTONSHIRE
EAST DUNBARTONSHIRE
INVERCLYDE
RENFREWSHIRE
EAST RENFREWSHIRE
NORTH AYRSHIRE
SOUTH AYRSHIRE
CUNNINGHAME
KYLE
STIRLING
LOCH LOMOND
FIRTH OF CLYDE
Heads of Ayr
Culzean Bay
Maidenhead Bay
Turnberry Bay
Lady Isle
Horse Isle
Millport
Troon to Larne 1hr. 50mins. (Fast Ferry, Seasonal)
A B C D E F
1 2 3 4 5 6 7 8
75
63
64
69

EDINBURGH
FIRTH OF FORTH
DUNFERMLINE
KIRKCALDY
GRANGEMOUTH
FALKIRK
ALLOA
Clackmannan
Cowdenbeath
Lochgelly
Buckhaven
Dysart
Burntisland
Aberdour
Kinghorn
Inverkeithing
Rosyth
Inchkeith
Inchmickery
Cramond Island
BO'NESS
Linlithgow
Bathgate
Armadale
LIVINGSTON
Broxburn
Kirkliston
South Queensferry
North Queensferry
Dalmeny
Currie
Balerno
Leith
Portobello
MUSSELBURGH
Prestonpans
Cockenzie and Port Seton
Tranent
DALKEITH
Bonnyrigg
Loanhead
Lasswade
Newtongrange
Gorebridge
Penicuik
MIDLOTHIAN
WEST LOTHIAN
Whitburn
Blackburn
Shotts
Fauldhouse
Carluke
LANARK
LANARKSHIRE
Carstairs
Carnwath
Biggar
Peebles
Innerleithen
Walkerburn
Eddleston
West Linton
Carlops
Broughton
Douglas
Abington
Crawford
Leadhills
Wanlockhead
Moffat
Tweedsmuir
Elvanfoot
Crawfordjohn
SCOTTISH BORDERS
ETTRICK FOREST
CRAIK FOREST
ESKDALEMUIR FOREST
Cardrona Forest
Glentress Forest
Denny
Larbert
Stenhousemuir
Bonnybridge
Airth
Kincardine
Culross
Oakley
Tillicoultry
Alva
Tullibody
Crossgates
Kelty
Cardenden
Auchterderran
Pentland Hills
Moorfoot Hills
Heriot
Pathhead
Stow
Yarrow
Ettrickbridge
Tushielaw
Craik
Davington
M8
M9
M90
M74
A74(M)
A1
A7
A68
A70
A71
A72
A701
A702
A703
A720
A985
A977
A92
A90
A199

FIRTH OF FORTH
EDINBURGH
Leith
Portobello
MUSSELBURGH
Prestonpans
Cockenzie and Port Seton
Tranent
Haddington
North Berwick
Dirleton
Gullane
Aberlady
Aberlady Bay
Gosford Bay
East Linton
Dunbar
Longniddry
Dalkeith
Bonnyrigg
Newtongrange
Gorebridge
Penicuik
Loanhead
Lasswade
Currie
Balerno
Kirknewton
Broxburn
Winchburgh
Newbridge
South Queensferry
North Queensferry
Dalmeny
Cramond
Inchkeith
Inchmickery
Inchcolm
Burntisland
Kinghorn
KIRKCALDY
Dysart
East Wemyss
Buckhaven
Cowdenbeath
Lochgelly
Lochore
Ballingry
Kelly
Auchterderran
Cardenden
Aberdour
Dalgety Bay
Inverkeithing
Rosyth
Crossgates
Fidra
Craigleith
Bass Rock
Eyebroughy
Gullane Bay
MIDLOTHIAN
EAST LOTHIAN
LAMMERMUIR
LAUDERDALE
MOORFOOT HILLS
PENTLAND HILLS
SOUTHERN UPLANDS
SCOTTISH BORDERS
ETTRICK FOREST
TEVIOTDALE
ESKDALEMUIR FOREST
WAUCHOPE FOREST
CRAIK FOREST
Glentress Forest
Cardrona Forest
Elibank and Traquair Forest
Yair Hill Forest
Peebles
Innerleithen
Walkerburn
Galashiels
Melrose
Selkirk
Hawick
Jedburgh
Lauder
Stow
St. Boswells
Newtown St. Boswells
Earlston
Gordon
Denholm
Ancrum
Bonchester Bridge
West Linton
Carlops
Dolphinton
Skirling
Broughton
Tweedsmuir
Moffat
Ettrickbridge
Yarrow
Tushielaw
Buccleuch
Clovenfords
Gattonside
Midlem
Lilliesleat
Longformacus
Westruther
Gifford
Garvald
Pencaitland
Humbie
Fala
Pathhead
Heriot
Eddleston
Romannobridge
Mountain Cross
Blyth Bridge
Drumelzier
Kirkurd
Stobo
Lyne
Manor
Traquair
Yarrow Feus
Mountbenger
St. Mary's Loch
Loch of the Lowes
Megget Reservoir
Talla Reservoir
Teviothead
Newmill
Stobs Castle
Chesters
Southdean
Cappercleuch
Camptown
A1
A68
A7
A72
A701
A702
A703
A697
A6091
A199
A720
A90
M9
M8
M90
A92
A985
A74(M)

71
77
65

N O R T H S E A
Barns Ness
East Barns
Skateraw
Thorntonloch
Innerwick
Reed Point
Cove
Siccar Point
Fast Castle Head
Cockburnspath
Oldhamstocks
ST. ABB'S HEAD
St. Abbs
Coldingham Bay
Coldingham
Eyemouth
Gunsgreenhill
Burnmouth
Ross
Reston
Ayton
Grantshouse
Houndwood
Abbey St. Bathans
Ellemford
Auchencrow
Whitchester
Millburn Bridge
Preston
Chirnside
Edrom
Duns
Foulden
Hutton
Paxton
Allanton
Lamberton
Marshall Meadows
BERWICK-UPON-TWEED
Tweedmouth
Spittal
East Ord
Redshin Cove
Scremerston
Polwarth
Gavinton
Nisbet Hill
Whitsome
Fishwick
Horncliffe
Loanend
Horndean
Fogo
Fogorig
Greenlaw
Swinton
Ladykirk
Norham
Shoreswood
Murton
Thornton
West Allerden
M E R S E
Simprim
Leitholm
Upsettlington
Grindon
Felkington
Duddo
Ancroft
Cheswick
Goswick
Haggerston
Berrington
Beal
Fenham
Fenwick
Lambden
Eccles
Castle Heaton
Coldstream
Lennel
Cornhill-on-Tweed
Melkington
Etal
Barmoor
Lowick
West Kyloe
East Kyloe
Buckton
Kyloe Hills
Detchant
Elwick
Ross
Middleton
Belford
Easington
Bamburgh
Budle Bay
Waren Mill
HOLY ISLAND
Holy Island
Keel Head
Castle Point
Burrows Hole
Longstone
Staple Sound
FARNE ISLANDS
Inner Sound
Seahouses
Carr End
North Sunderland
Beadnell
Beadnell Bay
Snook Point
Embleton Bay
Embleton
Craster
Dunstanburgh
Stichill
Ednam
Birgham
Carham
Wark
West Learmouth
Barelees
Crookham
Branxton
Ford
Kelso
Sprouston
Hadden
Pressen
Flodden
Kimmerston
Fenton
Nesbit
Doddington
Holburn
Hetton Steads
North Hazelrigg
South Hazelrigg
Chatton
Lyham
Warenton
Bellshill
Adderstone
Lucker
Warenford
Newham
Swinhoe
Preston
Ellingham
Tughall
Heiton
Lempitlaw
Mindrum
Downham
Thornington
Milfield
Pawston
Kilham
Howtel
Lanton
Coupland
Yeavering
Westnewton
Kirknewton
Akeld
Humbleton
Wooler
Shotton
Kirk Yetholm
Town Yetholm
Hethpool
Earle
Middleton Hall
Haugh Head
Chillingham
Hepburn
Eckford
Morebattle
Linton
Primsidemill
SCOTLAND
ENGLAND
THE CHEVIOT
N O R T H U M B E R L A N D
C H E V I O T H I L L S
Cessford
Whitton
Mowhaugh
Sourhope
Langleeford
Ilderton
Roseden
Roddam
Wooperton
Newtown
Eglingham
North Charlton
South Charlton
Rock
Rennington
Brandon
Powburn
Beanley
Ingram
Branton
Glanton
Shawdon Hall
Titlington
East Bolton
Shipley
ALNWICK
Denwick
Longhoughton
Boulmer
Howick
Littlehoughton
Lesbury
Alnmouth
Alnmouth Bay
Hipsburn
Whittingham
Thrunton
Lemmington Hall
Edlingham
Callaly
Yetlington
Prendwick
Alnham
Scrainwood
Kidland Forest
Barrowburn
Blindburn
Hindhope
Leithope Forest
Shillmoor
Linshiels
Alwinton
Clennell
Biddlestone
Netherton
Burradon
Lorbottle
Harbottle
Sharperton
Holystone
Flotterton
Snitter
Thropton
Rothbury
Warton
Hepple
Newtown
NORTHUMBERLAND NATIONAL PARK
Catcleugh
Byrness
Shilbottle
Newton-on-the-Moor
Swarland
Old Swarland
Acklington
Warkworth
Birling
Amble
Hauxley
Hauxley Haven
Coquet Island
Togston
Longframlington
A1
A1107
A6105
A6112
A697
A698
A699
A1068
A68
B6438
B6355
B6437
B6460
B6461
B6470
B6456
B6465
B6396
B6352
B6401
B6351
B6353
B6354
B6525
B6348
B6349
B6346
B6347
B6341
B6342
B6340
B6339
B6345
B1340
B1339
B1338
G H J K L M
1 2 3 4 5 6 7 8
66
67

Quinish Point
Caliach Point
Tobermory
Calve Island
Dervaig
AROS
MORVERN
Treshnish Point
Treshnish Isles
Ensay
Haunn
Burg
Calgary
Kengharair
Ardnacross
Drimnin
Kilmory
Lochuisge
Kingairloch
Camasnacroise
Rhemore
Killundine
Fiunary Forest
Claggan
Larachbeg
Achranich
Lochaline
Glensanda
Eilean nan Caorn
Port Ramsay
Eilean Loch Oscair
Rubh a' Chaoil
Cairn na Burgh Beg
Fladda
Eilean Dioghlum
Lunga
Gometra
Loch Tuath
ULVA
Ulva House
Ballygown
Fanmore
Lagganulva
Oskamull
Crannich
Aros Mains
Aros Castle
Salen
Rubha Mòr
Fishnish
Garmony
Kellan
Killiechronan
Gruline
Knock
Eorsa
Loch na Keal
ISLE OF MULL
Tomsleibhe
Craignure
Duart Point
Duart Castle
Lochdon
Oakbank
RUBHA AN RIDIRE
Bernera Island
LISMORE
Achnacroish
Eilean Dubh
Creag Island
Pladda Island
Eilean Musdile
Rubha Garbh-àird
Màisgeir
Eilean na Creiche
Little Colonsay
Samalan Island
Inch Kenneth
Staffa
Gribun
Derryguaig
BEN MORE
Erisgeir
Ardmeanach
Rubha na h Uamha
Tavool House
Tiroran
Port na Croise
Loch Scridain
Strathcoil
Loch Spelve
Croggan
Grass Point
Eilean nan Gamhna
Ganavan
OBAN
Kerrera
Dunollie
Bach Island
Dubh Sgeir
Rubha Seanach
Pulpit Hill
Kilbride
Cleigh
Eilean Annraidh
Rubha nan Cearc
IONA
Baile Mòr
Fionnphort
Kintra
Fidden
Bunessan
ROSS OF MULL
BROLASS
Pennyghael
Lochbuie
Carsaig
Carsaig Bay
Loch Buie
Ardchrishnish
Torrans
Loch Uisg
Minard Point
Kilninver
Erraid
Eilean nam Muc
Eilean a' Chalmain
Ardalanish Bay
Rubh' Ardalanish
Uisken
Rubha nam Bràithrean
Malcolm's Point
Frank Lockwood's Island
Eilean Dùin
Insh Island
SEIL
Clachan Seil
Balvicar
Easdale
Ellenabeich
Cuan
Melfort
Kilmelford
West Reef
Torran Rocks
Sgeir Dhoirbh
Dubh-fheith
SLATE ISLANDS
Garbh Eileach
Belnahua
Fladda
Cullipool
Torsa
Garvellachs
Eilean Dubh Mòr
Eileach an Naoimh
Lunga
Guirasdeal
LUING
Toberonochy
Shuna
Rubh' a' Chnaip
Arduaine
Craobh Haven
Barravullin
FIRTH OF LORN
Rubha nam Faoilean
SCARBA
Kilmory Lodge
Gulf of Corryvreckan
Eilean Mhic Chrion
Ardfern
Kintraw
Eilean Ona
Rèisa Mhic Phaidean
Rèisa an t-Sruith
Eilean Righ
Island Macaskin
Garbh Rèisa
Kilmartin
Port na Cuilce
Kiloran Bay
Port Ceann a' Gharraidh
COLONSAY
Port a' Bhàta
Scalasaig
Kiloran
Eilean a' Chladaich
Garvard
Rubha Dubh
Eilean Leathann
Glengarrisdale Bay
Rubh' a' Bhacain
Glendebadel Bay
Port nan Laogh
Ruadh Sgeir
Rubha Garbh-ard
Ardnoe Point
Crinan
Rubha nam Bàrr
Bellanoch
Cairnbaan
Corpach Bay
Lochgilphead
Dubh Eilean
ORONSAY
Eilean nan Ron
Eilean Ghaoideamal
Ceann Riobha
Shian Bay
Ardlussa
Ardlussa Bay
Lussa Point
Gob Dubh
Eilean Dubh
Carsaig Bay
Eilean nan Coinean
Tayvallich
Achnamara
Ardrishaig
Eilean Loain
Eilean Mòr
Rubh'an t-Sailein
Rubh' a' chrois-aoinidh
Tarbert
Keillmore
Post Rocks
RUBHA A'MHAIL
Rubha Bholsa
JURA
Lagg
Island of Danna
Bàgh an Tailleir
Nave Island
Eilean Beag
Ardnave Point
Gortantaoid
Bunnahabhain
Port Doir' a' Chrorain
An Dùnan
Bàgh na Dojde
Eilean Mor
Kilmory
Point of Knap
KNAPDALE
Caolisport
Jura Forest
Paps of Jura
Knockrome
Ardfernal
Leargybreck
Craighouse
Small Isles
Port Askaig
Keills
Ballygrant
Kilmeny
ISLAY
Bridgend
Sound of Islay
Glas Eilean
Ardfin
Cabrach
Port na Birlinne
Na Cùiltean
Rubha na Tràille
Am Fraoch Eilean
Brosdale Island
Miller's Bay
Kilberry Head
Port Mòr
Kilberry
Tarbert
Kennacraig
Barmore Island
Sound of Jura
Erines
Whitehouse
Carse House
Loch Fyne
Carraig Dhubh
Blackrock
Bruichladdich

75
RANNOCH MOOR
RANNOCH
PERTH & KINROSS
BREADALBANE
LORN
ARGYLL
STIRLING
LOCH LOMOND AND THE TROSSACHS NATIONAL PARK
QUEEN ELIZABETH FOREST PARK
ARGYLL FOREST PARK
COWAL
ISLE OF BUTE
FIRTH OF CLYDE
INVERCLYDE
WEST DUNBARTONSHIRE
BEN CRUACHAN
BEN MORE
BEN LOMOND
BEN VORLICH
BEINN IME
BEN VENUE
Ballachulish
Glencoe
Kingshouse
Bridge of Orchy
Tyndrum
Crianlarich
Dalmally
Taynuilt
Connel
Inveraray
Arrochar
Tarbet
Luss
Balquhidder
Aberfoyle
Drymen
Helensburgh
Alexandria
Dumbarton
Greenock
Port Glasgow
Gourock
Dunoon
Rothesay
Clydebank
Paisley
Renfrew
Bearsden
Johnstone
Inverkip
Skelmorlie
Wemyss Bay
Kilmacolm
Bridge of Weir
Strachur
Lochgoilhead
Garelochhead
Tighnabruaich
Port Bannatyne
Appin
Port Appin
Rannoch Station
Bridge of Gaur
Loch Creran
Loch Etive
Loch Awe
Loch Fyne
Loch Long
Loch Lomond
Loch Katrine
Loch Tulla
Loch Lyon
A82
A85
A83
A815
A828
A814
A811
A8
A78
A737
M8
69
70
80
76
G
H
J
K
L
M
1
2
3
4
5
6
7
8

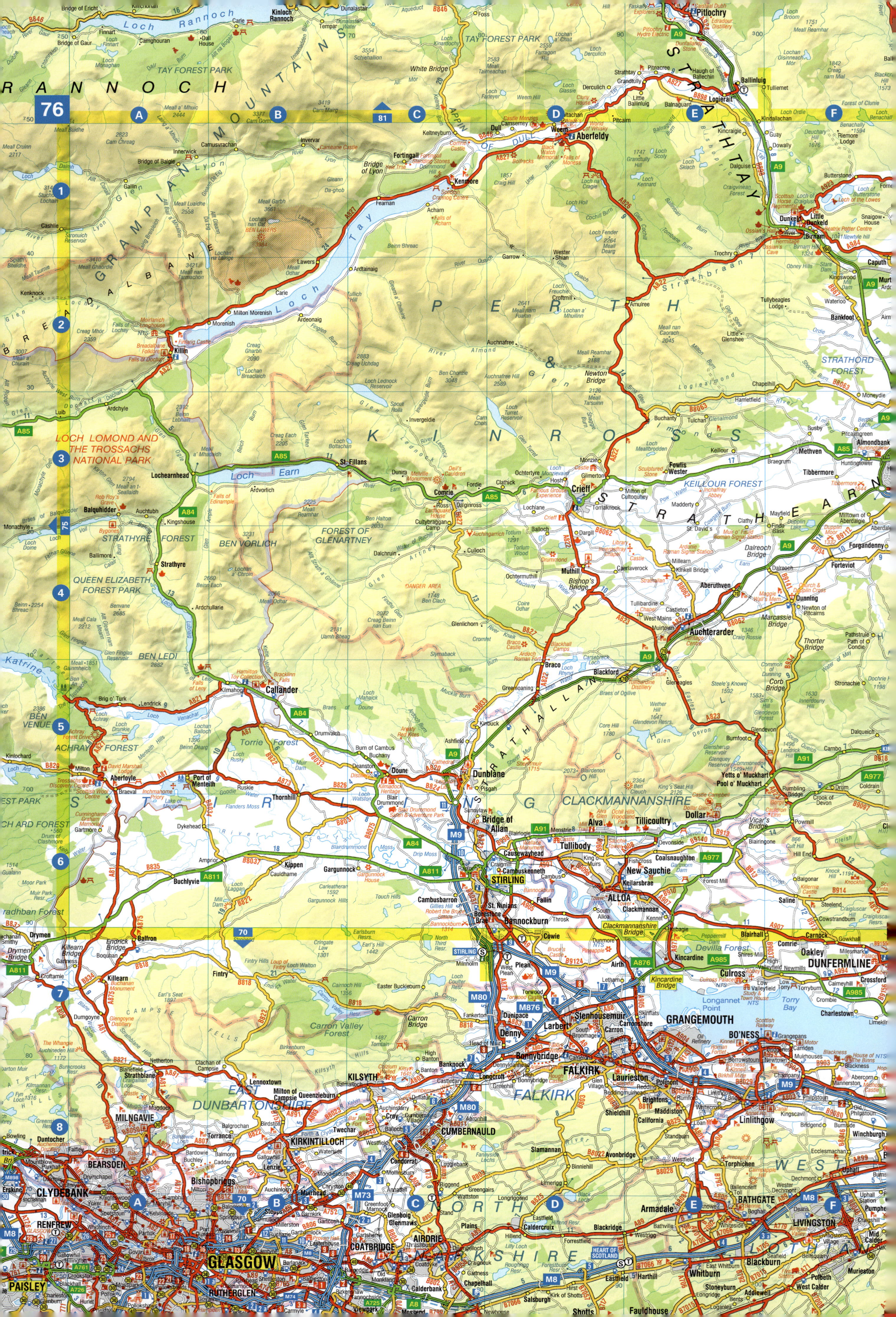
RANNOCH
Loch Rannoch
Kinloch Rannoch
TAY FOREST PARK
GRAMPIAN MOUNTAINS
BREADALBANE
Pitlochry
STRATHTAY
Logierait
Aberfeldy
Weem
Dull
Kenmore
Fortingall
Bridge of Lyon
Loch Tay
Killin
Lawers
Ben Lawers
Dunkeld
Birnam
PERTH & KINROSS
STRATHBRAAN
Amulree
Glen Almond
Newton Bridge
Crieff
Comrie
St Fillans
Loch Earn
Lochearnhead
LOCH LOMOND AND THE TROSSACHS NATIONAL PARK
Balquhidder
STRATHYRE FOREST
Strathyre
BEN VORLICH
FOREST OF GLENARTNEY
QUEEN ELIZABETH FOREST PARK
BEN LEDI
Callander
Loch Katrine
BEN VENUE
ACHRAY FOREST
Aberfoyle
Port of Menteith
Doune
Dunblane
STRATHEARN
STRATHALLAN
Muthill
Auchterarder
Braco
Blackford
Methven
Dunning
Forteviot
CLACKMANNANSHIRE
OCHIL
Dollar
Alva
Tillicoultry
Tullibody
Bridge of Allan
STIRLING
Bannockburn
ALLOA
Clackmannan
Kincardine
DUNFERMLINE
Culross
Oakley
Kippen
Buchlyvie
Balfron
Drymen
Killearn
Fintry
Carron Valley Forest
CAMPSIE FELLS
Denny
Larbert
Stenhousemuir
GRANGEMOUTH
BO'NESS
Bonnybridge
FALKIRK
Polmont
Linlithgow
KILSYTH
CUMBERNAULD
EAST DUNBARTONSHIRE
MILNGAVIE
KIRKINTILLOCH
BEARSDEN
CLYDEBANK
Bishopbriggs
GLASGOW
RENFREW
PAISLEY
RUTHERGLEN
COATBRIDGE
AIRDRIE
NORTH LANARKSHIRE
WEST LOTHIAN
Armadale
BATHGATE
LIVINGSTON
Whitburn
Blackburn
Harthill
Shotts
Fauldhouse
Slamannan
Avonbridge
M8
M9
M80
M73
A9
A84
A85
A811
A91
A977
A985
A876

STRATHMORE
ANGUS
SIDLAW HILLS
FIRTH OF TAY
FIRTH OF FORTH
FIFE
HOWE OF FIFE
CARSE OF GOWRIE
EAST LOTHIAN
MIDLOTHIAN
MONTROSE
Ferryden
Kirriemuir
FORFAR
Glamis
Alyth
Blairgowrie
Rattray
Coupar Angus
Meigle
Newtyle
Friockheim
Inverkeilor
Letham
Carmyllie
ARBROATH
Arbroath Signal Tower
Auchmithie
Arbirlot
Carnoustie
Monifieth
Broughty Ferry
DUNDEE
Tay Road Bridge
Tay Bridge
Newport-on-Tay
Tayport
Wormit
Buddon Ness
Tentsmuir Forest
PERTH
Scone
Kinfauns
Errol
Longforgan
Invergowrie
Balmerino
Leuchars
Guardbridge
St. Andrews
St. Andrews Bay
Buddo Ness
Boarhills
Kingsbarns
Fife Ness
Crail
Cupar
Newburgh
Auchtermuchty
Strathmiglo
Falkland
Freuchie
Ladybank
Springfield
Ceres
Largoward
Anstruther
Pittenweem
St. Monans
Elie
Earlsferry
Colinsburgh
Kilconquhar
Lower Largo
Leven
Methil
Buckhaven
East Wemyss
Coaltown of Wemyss
West Wemyss
Kennoway
Markinch
GLENROTHES
Leslie
Kinross
Loch Leven
Milnathort
Scotlandwell
Lochore
Ballingry
Kelty
Lochgelly
Cardenden
Auchterderran
Cowdenbeath
Dysart
KIRKCALDY
Kinghorn
Burntisland
Aberdour
Dalgety Bay
Inverkeithing
North Queensferry
Forth Bridge
South Queensferry
Cramond Island
Inchkeith
Inchcolm
Inchmickery
Isle of May
Chapel Ness
Ruddons Point
Saucher Point
Largo Bay
Gosford Bay
Aberlady Bay
Gullane Bay
Eyebroughy
Fidra
Lamb
Craigleith
Bass Rock
North Berwick
Dirleton
Gullane
Aberlady
Longniddry
Cockenzie and Port Seton
Prestonpans
Tranent
Macmerry
Pencaitland
Haddington
East Linton
Dunbar
Whitekirk
Stenton
Garvald
Gifford
EDINBURGH
Leith
Newhaven
Portobello
MUSSELBURGH
DALKEITH
Loanhead
Bonnyrigg
Newtongrange
Gorebridge
Currie
Balerno
Kirknewton
Kirkliston
Ormiston
Pathhead
Oldhamstocks
Innerwick
Spott
West Barns
Barns Ness
M90
A90
A92
A91
A1
A199
A720
A68
M8

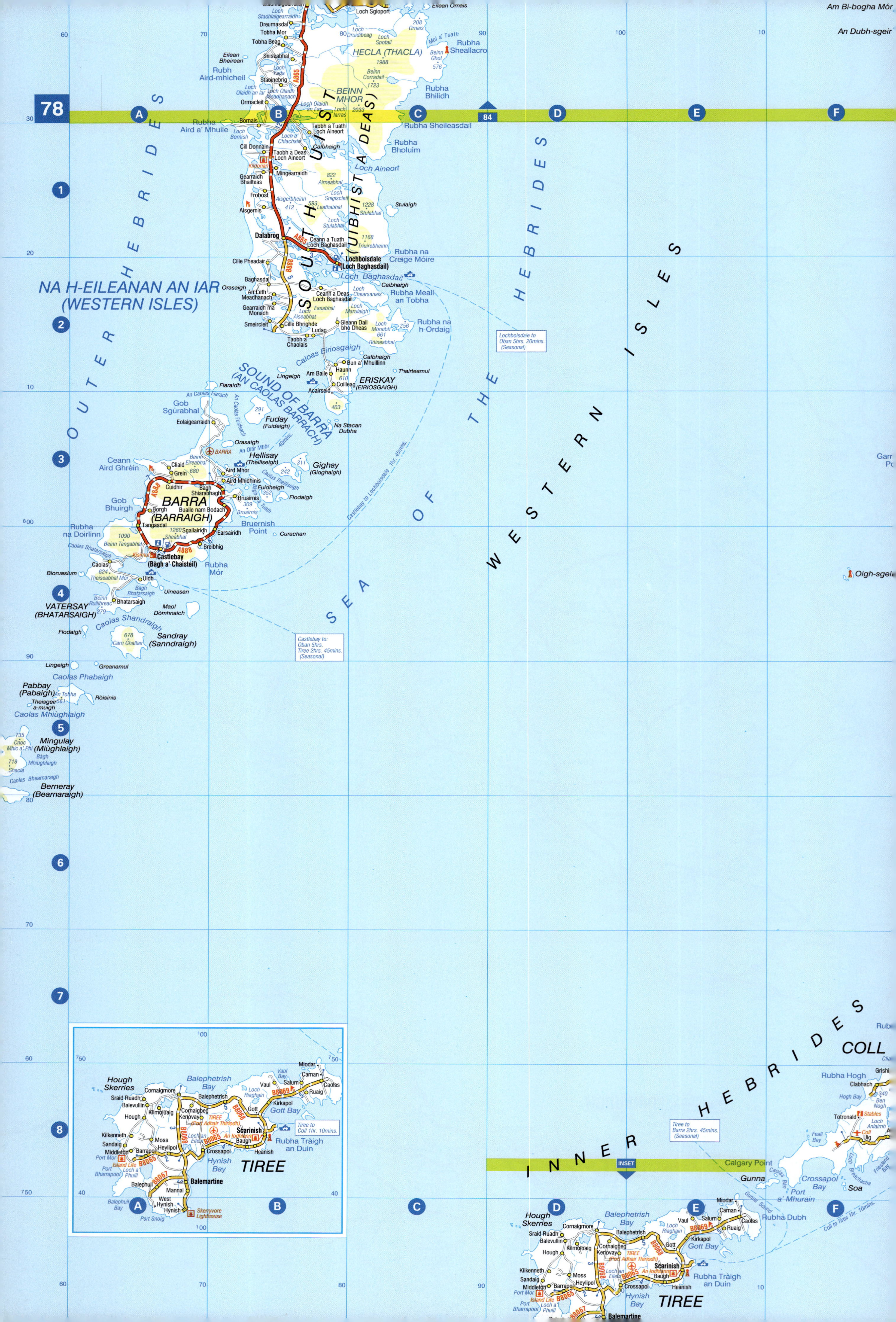

84
OUTER HEBRIDES
NA H-EILEANAN AN IAR (WESTERN ISLES)
SOUTH UIST (UIBHIST A DEAS)
HECLA (THACLA)
BEINN MHOR
Lochboisdale (Loch Baghasdail)
Dalabrog
Loch Aineort
Rubha Sheileasdail
Rubha na Creige Móire
Rubha Meall an Tobha
Rubha na h-Ordaig
Lochboisdale to Oban 5hrs. 20mins. (Seasonal)
ERISKAY (EIRIOSGAIGH)
SOUND OF BARRA (AN CAOLAS BARRACH)
Fuday (Fuideigh)
Hellisay (Theilliseigh)
Gighay (Gioghaigh)
BARRA (BARRAIGH)
Castlebay (Bàgh a' Chaisteil)
Rubha Mòr
Bruernish Point
VATERSAY (BHATARSAIGH)
Sandray (Sanndraigh)
Castlebay to: Oban 5hrs. Tiree 2hrs. 45mins. (Seasonal)
Pabbay (Pabaigh)
Mingulay (Miùghlaigh)
Berneray (Bearnaraigh)
SEA OF THE HEBRIDES
SEA OF THE WESTERN ISLES
INNER HEBRIDES
COLL
TIREE
Scarinish
Balemartine
Gott Bay
Hynish Bay
Rubha Tràigh an Duin
Tiree to Coll 1hr. 10mins.
Tiree to Barra 2hrs. 45mins. (Seasonal)
Calgary Point
Hough Skerries
Balephetrish Bay
Crossapol Bay
Rubha Hogh
Am Bi-bogha Mór
An Dubh-sgeir
Oigh-sgeir
INSET

79
ISLE OF SKYE
MINGINISH
CUILLIN HILLS
BLA BHEINN
SCALPAY
CROWLIN ISLANDS
Kyle of Lochalsh
Kyleakin
Broadford
Plockton
SOAY
Elgol
SLEAT
Armadale
Sound of Sleat
Mallaig
Morar
NORTH MORAR
SOUTH MORAR
KNOYDART
ARISAIG
Sound of Arisaig
CANNA
Sanday
RÙM
NATIONAL NATURE RESERVE
Kinloch
EIGG
Cleadale
Sound of Eigg
MUCK
SOUND OF RÙM
SEA OF THE HEBRIDES
INNER HEBRIDES
MOIDART
ARDNAMURCHAN
Point of Ardnamurchan
Kilchoan
Salen
Acharacle
Strontian
SUNART
Loch Sunart
MORVERN
Lochaline
Tobermory
ISLE OF MULL
Sound of Mull
AROS
Calgary Bay
Dervaig
Fladda
Lunga
Treshnish Isles
Glenfinnan
Lochailort
Glenelg
Eilean Shona
Samalaman Island
Cairns of Coll
Eag na Maoile
Arinagour
Eilean Ormsay
Talisker Bay
Carbost
Sligachan
Glamaig
A87
A830
A861
A884
A851
A863
85
74
80

80
86
79
74
75
A
B
C
D
E
F
1
2
3
4
5
6
7
8
Kishorn Island
Stromeferry
Plockton
Kyle of Lochalsh
Loch Alsh
Glas Eilean
Ardintoul Point
Dornie
Eilean Donan
Glenelg
Loch Duich
Shiel Bridge
Morvich
Inverinate
Ratagan
Cannich
Tomich
Glen Affric
Affric Lodge
Cluanie Inn
Loch Cluanie
Ceannacroc Bridge
Dalchreichart
Torgyle
Dundreggan
A87
A887
A82
A830
A861
A884
A828
A86
Fort Augustus
Invergarry
Laggan
Loch Garry
Loch Quoich
Kinloch Hourn
Barrisdale Bay
KNOYDART
NORTH MORAR
SOUTH MORAR
LOCH ARKAIG
Loch Arkaig
Achnacarry
Clunes
Gairlochy
Spean Bridge
Roybridge
GLEN SPEAN
Loch Lochy
GREAT GLEN
Glenfinnan
Kinlocheil
Loch Eil
Corpach
Caol
Banavie
FORT WILLIAM
BEN NEVIS
AONACH BEAG
MAMORE FOREST
Kinlochleven
Kinlochmore
North Ballachulish
South Ballachulish
Ballachulish
Glencoe
Onich
Corran
ARDGOUR
SUNART
Strontian
Inversanda
Kingairloch
Loch Linnhe
Eilean Balnagowan
Shuna Island
Portnacroish
Appin
Port Appin
Lismore
Glen Etive
Dalness
Kingshouse
Altnafeadh
Black Corries
Blackwater Reservoir
RANNOCH
BLACK MOUNT
NORTH WEST HIGHLANDS
BEINN FHADA OR BEN ATTOW
FIVE SISTERS
GLEN SHIEL
Glen Moriston
Creran

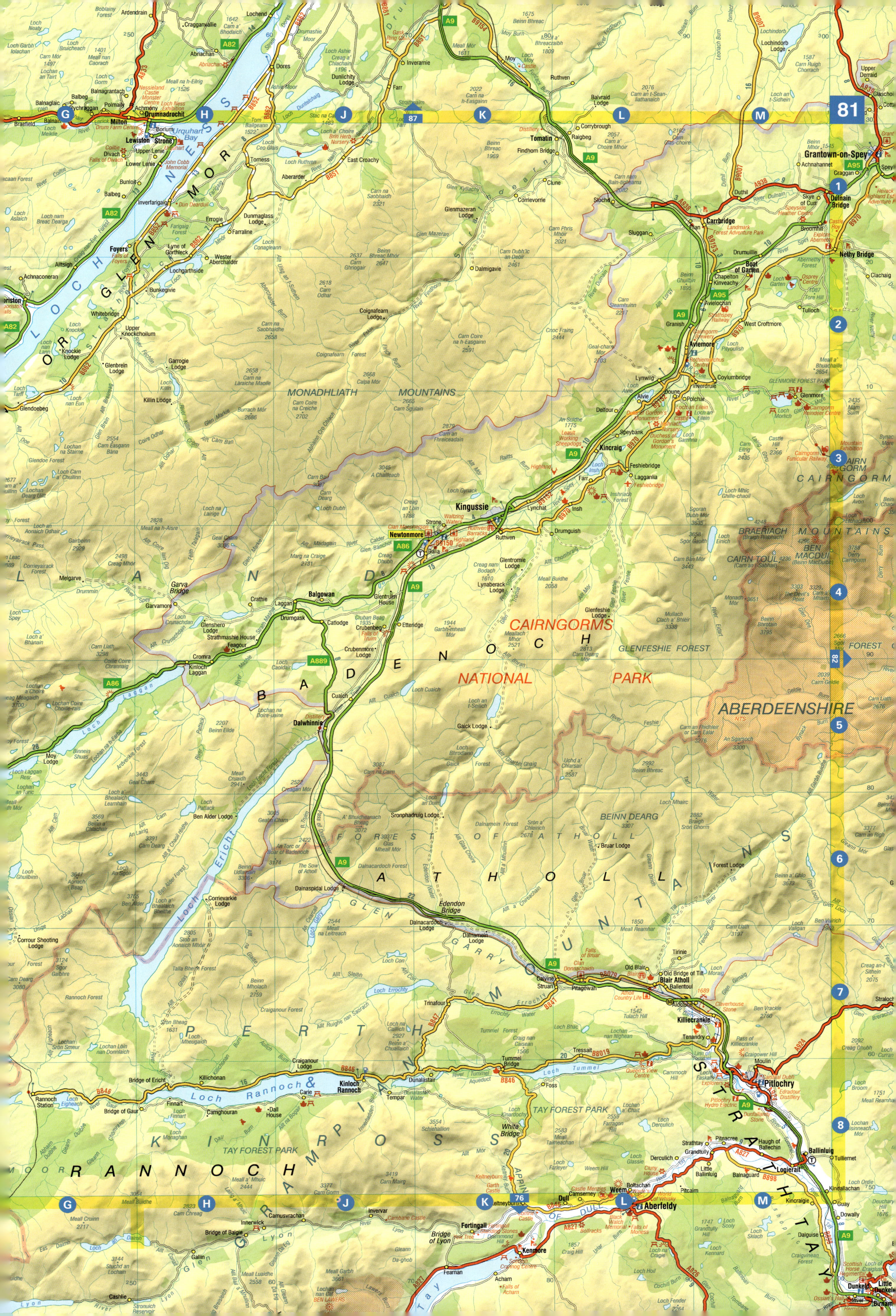
Drumnadrochit
Milton
Lewiston
Strone
Urquhart Bay
Loch Ness
Invermoriston
Foyers
Inverfarigaig
Dores
Inverarnie
Farr
Tomatin
Grantown-on-Spey
Dulnain Bridge
Carrbridge
Nethy Bridge
Boat of Garten
Aviemore
Glenmore
Kincraig
Kingussie
Newtonmore
Ruthven
Laggan
Dalwhinnie
MONADHLIATH MOUNTAINS
LOCH NESS
CAIRNGORM
CAIRN TOUL
BEN MACDUI
BRAERIACH
CAIRNGORMS NATIONAL PARK
GLENFESHIE FOREST
ABERDEENSHIRE
BADENOCH
FOREST OF ATHOLL
ATHOLL MOUNTAINS
Loch Ericht
Ben Alder Lodge
Dalnaspidal Lodge
Edendon Bridge
Dalnacardoch Lodge
Blair Atholl
Killiecrankie
Pitlochry
Ballinluig
Logierait
Dunkeld
Aberfeldy
Kenmore
Fortingall
Weem
Tummel Bridge
Kinloch Rannoch
Loch Rannoch
Loch Tummel
Rannoch Station
Bridge of Gaur
TAY FOREST PARK
RANNOCH
GRAMPIAN
PERTH
STRATH TAY
A9
A82
A86
A889
A95
A938
A827
B846
B847
B8019
87
76
82

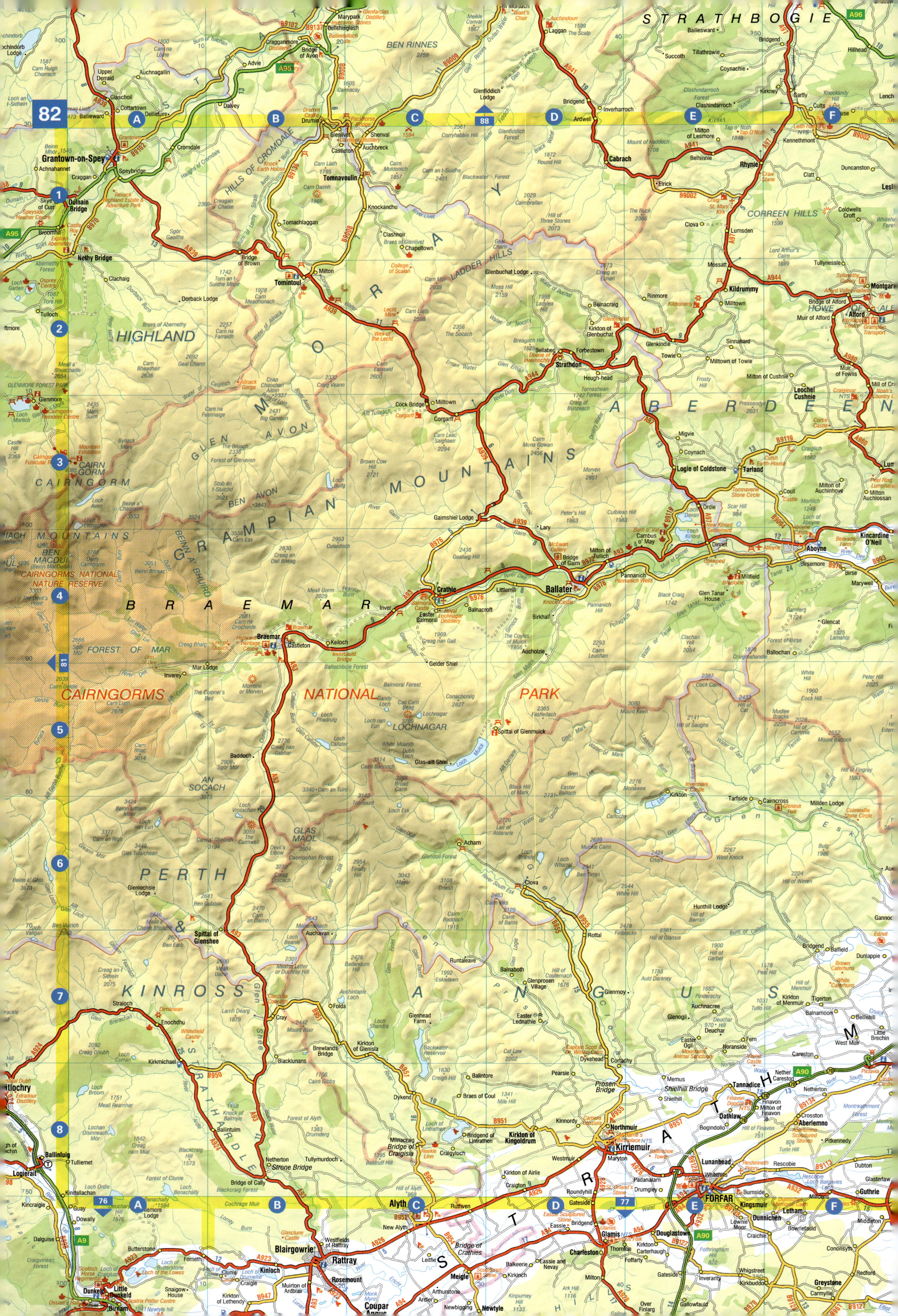

STRATHBOGIE
BEN RINNES
Grantown-on-Spey
Dulnain Bridge
Nethy Bridge
Tomintoul
Tomnavoulin
Knockandhu
Chapeltown
Cabrach
Rhynie
Lumsden
CORREEN HILLS
Kildrummy
Alford
HOWE OF ALFORD
HILLS OF CROMDALE
LADDER HILLS
HIGHLAND
MORAY
ABERDEEN
Glenmore
CAIRN GORM
CAIRNGORM
GRAMPIAN MOUNTAINS
BEN AVON
BEN MACDUI
CAIRNGORMS NATIONAL NATURE RESERVE
BRAEMAR
Braemar
Crathie
Ballater
Aboyne
Kincardine O'Neil
Tarland
Logie of Coldstone
Cock Bridge
Corgarff
Strathdon
Gairnshiel Lodge
FOREST OF MAR
CAIRNGORMS NATIONAL PARK
LOCHNAGAR
Spittal of Glenmuick
GLAS MAOL
PERTH & KINROSS
Spittal of Glenshee
AN SOCACH
Kirkton of Glenisla
Clova
Tarfside
STRATHARDLE
Kirkmichael
Ballintuim
Bridge of Cally
Blairgowrie
Rattray
Alyth
Kirriemuir
Northmuir
FORFAR
Glamis
Tannadice
Aberlemno
Letham
Kingsmuir
Douglastown
Charleston
Meigle
Coupar Angus
Dunkeld
Birnam
Ballinluig
Logierait
Kinloch
Rosemount
Pitlochry
STRATHMORE
ANGUS

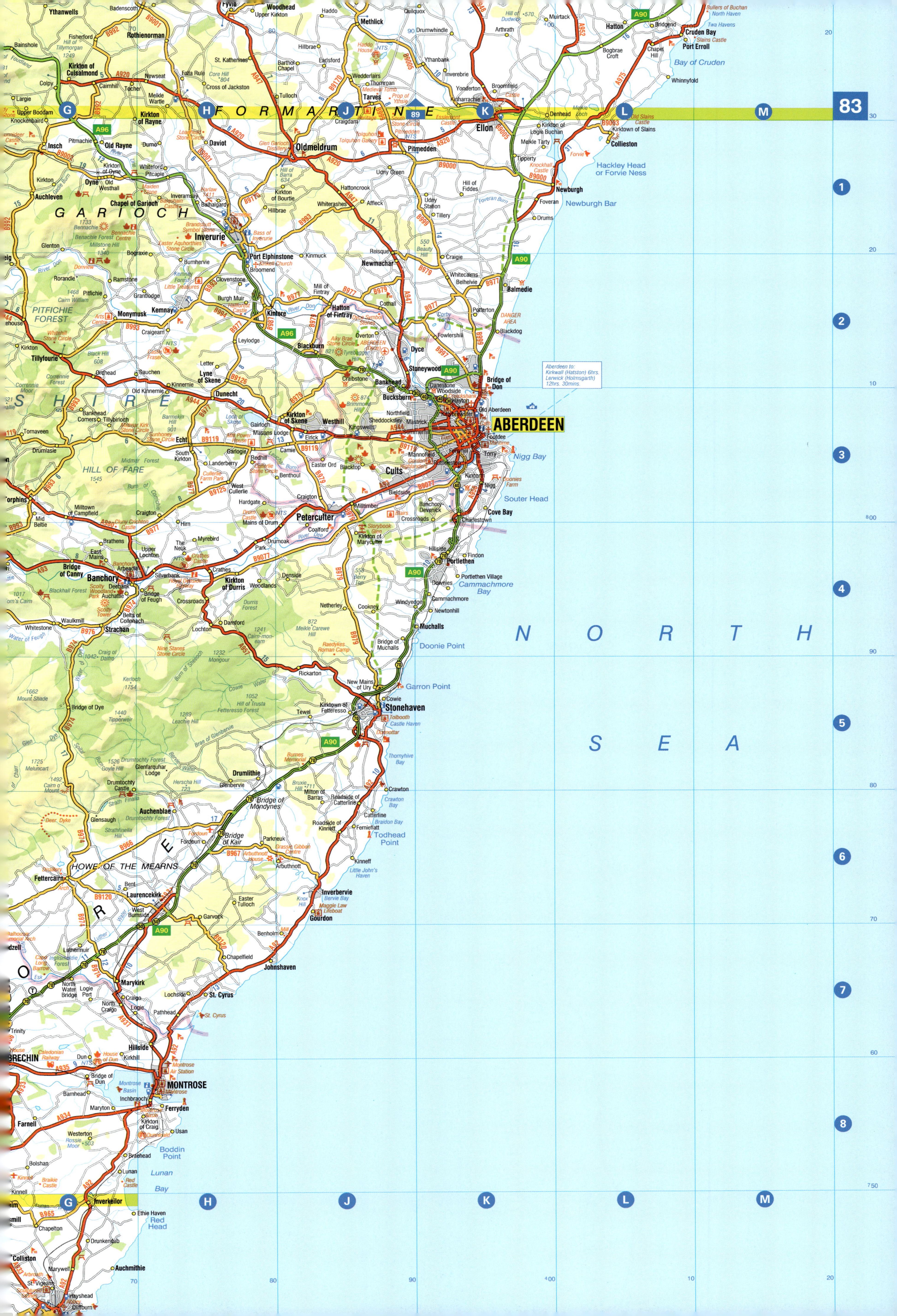

ABERDEEN
N O R T H
S E A
F O R M A R T I N E
G A R I O C H
Stonehaven
Montrose
Peterculter
Banchory
Inverurie
Oldmeldrum
Ellon
Kintore
Westhill
Cults
Portlethen
Newburgh
Collieston
Cruden Bay
Port Erroll
Bay of Cruden
Hackley Head or Forvie Ness
Newburgh Bar
Balmedie
Blackdog
Bridge of Don
Old Aberdeen
Nigg Bay
Souter Head
Cove Bay
Newtonhill
Muchalls
Doonie Point
Garron Point
Crawton
Todhead Point
Inverbervie
Gourdon
Johnshaven
St. Cyrus
Ferryden
Usan
Boddin Point
Lunan Bay
Red Head
Inverkeilor
Laurencekirk
Fettercairn
Auchenblae
Drumlithie
HOWE OF THE MEARNS
HILL OF FARE
PITFICHIE FOREST
Echt
Dyce
Blackburn
Kemnay
Monymusk
Tillyfourie
Torphins
Strachan
Marykirk
BRECHIN
Farnell
Auchmithie
Aberdeen to: Kirkwall (Hatston) 6hrs. Lerwick (Holmsgarth) 12hrs. 30mins.
A90
A96

OUTER HEBRIDES
NA H-EILEANAN AN IAR
(WESTERN ISLES)
THE LITTLE MINCH
WESTERN
SOUND OF HARRIS (CAOLAS NA HEARADH)
SOUND OF MONACH (CAOLAS MHONACH)
NORTH HARRIS
(CEANNA TUATH NA HEARADH)
SOUTH HARRIS
(CEANN A DEAS NA HEARADH)
HARRIS (NA HEARADH)
NORTH UIST
(UIBHIST A TUATH)
BENBECULA
(BEINN NA FAOGHLA)
SOUTH UIST
(UIBHIST A DEAS)
SCARP
Huisinis
Rubha Huisinis
Horsanais
Gobhaig
Rubha Leacach
Sòdhaidh Beag
Sòdhaidh Mòr
Loch a Siar
Iosaigh
TARANSAY
(TARASAIGH)
Ben Rà
Paibeil
Rubha Sgeirigin
Aird Nisabost
Horgabost
Seilebost
Losgaintir
Tarbert
(Tairbeart)
Bun Abhainn Eadarra
Aird Asaig
Miabhag
Clisham
Taigh a Bhuirgh
Na Buirgh
Scarasta
Sgarasta Mhor
TOE HEAD
(GOB AN TOBHA)
Copaigh
Rubha Màs a' Chnuic
Ceapabhal
Rubh' an Teampaill
An Taobh Tuath
Kyles Lodge
Leverburgh
(An t-Ob)
Ensay
(Easaigh)
Killegray
(Ceileagraigh)
Eilean Chalmainis
Roghadal
Bhalaigh
RENNISH POINT
(RUBHA REINIS)
Rubha Chuidhtinis
Fionnsabhagh
Liceasto
Greosabhagh
Aird Mhighe
Caolas Stocinis
Eilean Stocinis
Langaigh
Gilsaigh
Lingeigh
Sgarabhaigh
Grodhaigh
Siolaigh
Siolaigh Bheag
Caolas Shiolaigh
Rubha Bhreinis
PABBAY
(PABAIGH)
Cuidhnis
Caolas Spuir
Caolas Phabaigh
BERNERAY
(BEÀRNARAIGH)
Boreray
(Boraraigh)
Rubha Bhoisnis
Brusta
Ruisigearraidh
Baile
Borgh
Rhaiteam
Torogaigh
Sgeir a' Chàil
Aird a' Mhòrain
Rubha Bheilis
Lingeigh
Port nan Long
Baile MhicPhail
Orasaigh
Clachan Shannda
Sursaigh
Opasaigh
Taghaigh
Bhacasaigh
Thermatraigh
Tobha-Beag
Bàgh a' Chàise
Lochportain
Gròdaigh
Rubha an Dùine
Haskeir Island
(Eilean Hasgeir)
Haskeir Eagach
Rubha Ghriminis
Griminis
Scolpaig
Vallay
(Bhalaigh)
Ceathramh Meadhanach
Greinetobht
Solas
Malacleit
Trumaisgearraidh
Rubha Mhànais
Baile Mhartainn
Hosta
Taigh a Ghearraidh
Hogha Gearraidh
Aird an Rùnair
Causamul
Baile Raghaill
Paiblesgearraidh
Paibeil
Baile Mor
Ceann a Bhàigh
Rubha Port Scolpaig
Rubh' Arnal
Kirkibost Island
(Eilean Chircebost)
Deasker
Huskeiran
Ceann Iar
Siolaigh
Ceann Ear
Stòcaidh
Heisker or Monach Islands
(Theisgeir no na h-Eileanan Monach)
Cladach a Chaolais
Cladach Chircebost
Cladach Iolaraigh
Bhorogaigh
Clachan na Luib
Lochmaddy
(Loch nam Madadh)
Rubha an Fhigheadair
Rubha nam Plèac
Lochmaddy to Uig 1hr. 40mins.
An t-Aigeach
Langais
Loch Euphort
Saighdinis
Druim Saighdinis
Teanna Mhachair
Samhla
Baleshare
(Baile Sear)
Cairinis
Baile Uachdrach
Baile Iochdrach
Cladach Chairinis
EAVAL (EABHAL)
Eigneig Mhòr
Eigneig Bheag
Liernis
Flodaigh Beag
Flodaigh Mòr
Baile Glas
Grimsay
(Griomasaigh)
Bagh Mor
Scotbheinn
Ceallan
Eilean Fhlodaigh
Ronay
(Ronaigh)
Ròisinis
Maragaidh Mòr
Oitir Mhòr
Beul an Toim
Baile Mhanaich
Aird
Uachdar
Gramasdail
Baile nan Cailleach
Griminis
Torlum
Borgh
Nan Eilean
Lionacleit
Loch Uisgebhagh
Màithidh Riabhach
Creag Ghoraidh
Haclait
Rubha Cam nan Gall
Wiay
(Fuidhaigh)
Lionacuidhe
Aird a Mhachair
Cill Amhlaidh
Iochdar
Carnan
Aird Mhor
Bagh nam Faoileann
Steiseigh
Loch a Charnain
Sanndabhaig
Gasaidh
DANGER AREA
Geirinis
Our Lady of the Isles Statue
Glas-eileanan
Liursaigh Dubh
Groigearraidh
Caolas Liubharsaigh
Stadhlaigearraidh
Loch Sgioport
Eilean Ornais
Dreumasdal
Tobha Mor
Tobha Beag
HECLA (THACLA)
Rubha Sheallacro
Eilean Bheirean
Snìseabhal
Rubh Aird-mhicheil
Staoinebrig
BEINN MHOR
Rubha Bhilidh
Ormacleit
Rubha Sheileasdail
Bornais
Rubha Aird a' Mhuile
Taobh a Tuath Loch Aineort
Cill Donnain
Taobh a Deas Loch Aineort
Calbhaigh
Rubha Bholuim
Loch Aineort
Mingearraidh
Gearraidh Bhailteas
Frobost
Aisgernis
Stulaigh
Dalabrog
Ceann a Tuath
DUNVEGAN HEAD
Galtrigill
Borreraig
An Ceannaich
Lower Milovaig
Upper Milovaig
Oisgill Bay
Waterstein
Lephin
Borrodale
Glendale
Fasnaquarrie
Moonen Bay
Ramasaig
Hoe Rape
Hoe Point
Am Bi-bogha Mór
An Dubh-sgeir
A
B
C
D
E
F
1
2
3
4
5
6
7
8
78

85
PARK (PAIRC)
Eilean Shiphoirt
Eilean Liubhaird
Srianach
A' Chabag
Leumrabhagh
Gob Rubh' Uisinis
SOUND OF SHIANT (CAOLAS NAN EILEAN)
Shiant Islands (Na H-Eileanan Mora)
Garbh Eilean
Eilean Mhuire
Eilean an Taighe
Rubh' a' Bhaird
Geodha Dubh
Rubha Crago
SCALPAY (SCALPAIGH)
Eilean Glas
ISLES
Tarbert to Uig 1hr. 40mins.
Uig to Tarbert 1hr. 40mins.
Uig to Lochmaddy 1hr. 40mins.
Fladda-chùain
Sgeir nam Maol
Eilean Trodday
Rubha Hunish
Rubha na h-Aiseig
Kilmaluag Bay
An t-Iasgair
Tulm Bay
Lùb Score
Sgeir Eirin
Eilean Flodigarry
Staffin Bay
Staffin Island
Camas Mòr
Balgown
Uig
Uig Bay
Eilean Iosal
Eilean Creagach
Ascrib Islands
LOCH SNIZORT
Kilt Rock
Rubha nam Brathairean
Staffin
Portree
TROTTERNISH
THE STORR
Leac Tressirnish
Bearreraig Bay
Holm Island
Eilean Fladday
Eilean Tigh
Eilean Garbh
RONA
Port an Fhearainn
Garbh Eilean
RAASAY
SOUND OF RAASAY
INNER SOUND
Manish Point
Rubha ná Leac
Eilean Mòr Greshornish Point
Lyndale Point
WATERNISH
Sgeir nam Biast
Dunvegan
Harlosh Point
Harlosh Island
Tarner Island
Wiay
Oronsay
Loch Bracadale
Macleod's Maidens
IDRIGILL POINT
Rubha nan Clach
Talisker Bay
Bracadale
Carbost
Sligachan
GLAMAIG
SCALPAY
Longay
Pabay
Guillamon Island
Broadford
Kyleakin
Kyle of Lochalsh
Plockton
CROWLIN ISLANDS
Eilean Mòr
Eilean Beag
Sgeir Dhearg
Eilean na Bà
Kishorn Island
Applecross
Applecross Bay
Sgeir Ghlas
Sgeir na Trian
Rubha na Fearn
Rubha Chuaig
Loch Torridon
Shieldaig
Lower Diabaig
Port Henderson
Gairloch
Loch Gairloch
Eilean Horrisdale
Longa Island
Melvaig
Rubha Reidh
Eilean Furadh Mòr
Rubha nan Sasan
Loch Carron
Loch Alsh
Glas Eilean
Ardintoul Point
MINGINISH
CUILLIN HILLS
BLA BHEINN
An Dubh-sgeir
Stac an Tuill
SKYE
ISLE OF SKYE

A
B
C
D
E
F
1
2
3
4
5
6
7
8
Rubha Coigeach
Eilean Mór
Enard Bay
Eilean Mullagrach
Isle Ristol
Glas-leac Mór
Badentarbat Bay
Achiltibuie
Tanera Beg
Tanera Mór
Ullapool to Stornoway 2hrs. 40mins.
Glas-leac Beag
Summer Isles
Horse Island
Eilean Dubh
Priest Island
Bottle Island
Carn nan Sgeir
C O I G A C H
CUL MOR
CROMALT HILLS
Isle Martin
Ullapool
Loch Broom
Little Loch Broom
Greenstone Point
Rubha Beag
Gruinard Island
Gruinard Bay
Laide
Eilean Furadh Mór
Rubha nan Sasan
Isle of Ewe
Loch Ewe
Poolewe
Gairloch
Eilean Horrisdale
Eilean Subhainn
Loch Maree
AN TEALLACH
BEINN DEARG
SLIOCH
W E S T E R   R O S S
H I G H L A N D S
Kinlochewe
Achnasheen
BEINN EIGHE
LIATHACH
Torridon
Shieldaig
Shieldaig Island
Lower Diabaig
Inveralligin
STRATHCONON FOREST
W E S T
Lochcarron
Kishorn Island
Loch Carron
Stromeferry
Plockton
Kyle of Lochalsh
Loch Alsh
Glas Eilean
Ardintoul Point
N O R T H
Loch Monar
Loch Mullardoch
Cannich
Lochluichart
Garve
Aultguish Inn
Loch Glascarnoch
Loch Fannich
Knockan
Elphin
Ledmore
Inchnadamph
Lubcroy
Oykel Bridge
Loch Duich
Dornie
A835
A832
A896
A890
A87
A837
A831
91
80

Loch Shin
Lairg
Dalchork
Colaboll
Rhian
Shinness
Achnairn
Tirryside
Saval
Lairg Muir
Balloan
Tomich
Rhian Breck
Torroble
Invershin
Inveran
Culrain
Achnahanat
Altass
Rosehall
Invercassley
Doune
Dalnessie
West Langwell
East Langwell
Dalreavoch
Rhilochan
Knockarthur
Achvoan
Rogart
Little Rogart
Dalmore
Pittentrail
Morvich
Mound Rock
Little Torboll
Kirkton
Golspie
Backies
Uppat
Dunrobin
Brora
Dalchalm
West Clyne
Clynelish
East Clyne
Achrimsdale
Gordonbush
Balnacoil
Lothbeg
Lothbeg Point
Crackaig
Kilmote
Lothmore
Portgower
Gartymore
West Helmsdale
Marrel
Navidale
Helmsdale
Loch Fleet
Littleferry
Skelbo
Skelbo Street
Embo
Embo Street
Dornoch
Littletown
Cuthill
Camore
Evelix
Birichen
Fleuchary
Astle
Rearquhar
Badninish
Achvaich
Clashmore
Ospisdale
Bardnabeinne
Spinningdale
Whiteface
Lonemore
Bonar Bridge
Ardgay
Kincardine
Gledfield
Lower Gledfield
Oldtown
Ardchronie
Airdens
Migdale
Tulloch
Balblair
Wester Fearn
Easter Fearn
Dounie
Edderton
Ardmore
Tarlogie
Morangie
Glenmorangie Distillery
Tain
Hilton
Inver
Lower Arboll
Toulvaddie
Tarrel
Portmahomack
Bindal
Wilkhaven
Tarbat Ness
Tarbat Discovery Centre
Seafield
Rockfield
Lochslin
Lower Pitkerrie
Geanies
Hill of Fearn
Fearn
Hilton of Cadboll
Balintore
Shandwick
Ankerville
Arabella
Tullich
Wester Rarichie
Port an Righ
Pitcalnie
Nigg
Nigg Bay
Hill of Nigg
Balnabruaich
Nigg Ferry
Castlecraig
Balnapaling
Cromarty
Newton
Sutors of Cromarty
Blue Head
McFarquhar's Cave
Hugh Miller
Dornoch Firth
Cromarty Firth
Moray Firth
Cromarty Bay
Udale Bay
Invergordon
Saltburn
Rosskeen
Alness
Alness Bay
Dalmore
Obsdale
Achnagarron
Milton
Kildary
Pitmaduthy
Marybank
Scotsburn
Hartmount
Lamington
Kilmuir
Barbaraville
Delny
Polio
Balintraid
Broomhill
Tomich
Newmore
Rhicullen
Coillemore
Badachonacher
Nonikiln
Achandunie
Dalnavie
Ardross
Strathy
Stittenham
Contullich
Crosshills
Evanton
Drummond
Swordale
Ardullie
Foulis
Mountgerald
Kinbeachie
Culbo
Findon Mains
Culbokie
Braefindon
Resolis
Newmills
Springfield
Jemimaville
Davidston
Muirton
Easter Brae
Wester Brae
Mount High
Whitebog
Ferryton
Balblair
Alnessferry
Cullicudden
Black Isle
Killen
Rosemarkie
Fortrose
Rosemarkie Bay
Chanonry Point
Avoch
Avoch Bay
Easter Suddie
Belmaduthy
Munlochy
Munlochy Bay
Tore
Kilcoy
Drynie Park
Redcastle
Milton
Arpafeelie
Bogallan
Allanfearn
Kilmuir
Drumsmittal
Craigton
Charlestown
North Kessock
South Kessock
Craigton
Inverness
Culloden
Smithton
Balloch
Westhill
Milton of Culloden
Beauly Firth
Beauly
Kirkhill
Bunchrew
Leachkin
Clachnaharry
Muir of Ord
Ardnagrask
Conon Bridge
Maryburgh
Dingwall
Strathpeffer
Fodderty
Auchterneed
Bottacks
Knockfarrel
Jamestown
Contin
Craigdarroch
Tarvie
Tollie
Urray
Arcan
Marybank
Muir of Fairburn
Windhill
Rheindown
Dunmore
Ruisaurie
Farley
Kiltarlity
Kilmorack
Balchraggan
Belladrum
The Aird
Fanellan
Breakachy
Eskadale
Culburnie
Camault Muir
Erchless Castle
Struy
Glaich
Ardendrain
Cragganvallie
Abriachan
Dochgarroch
Dores
Essich
Scaniport
Inverarnie
Farr
Daviot
Craggiemore
Lochend
Ardersier
Fort George
Gollanfield
Lochside
Croy
Cantraywood
Cantraybruich
Clephanton
Cawdor
Easter Galcantray
Wester Galcantray
Clunas
Urchany
Nairn
Auldearn
Kingsteps
Tradespark
Moss-side
Firhall
Balmakeith
Drumm
Whiteness Head
Blackhills
Boath
Littlemill
Geddes
Redburn
Ferness
Glenferness Mains
Dava
Lochindorb Lodge
Dulnain Bridge
Carrbridge
Grantown-on-Spey
Tomatin
Findhorn Bridge
Corrybrough
Moy
Ruthven
Balvraid Lodge
Dunlichity Lodge
Loch Ness
Drumnadrochit
Lewiston
Strone
Milton
Balnain
Urquhart Castle
Inverfarigaig
Errogie
Torness
Aberarder
East Croachy
Slochd
Dulnain
Kildermorie Lodge
Wyvis Lodge
Ben Wyvis
Culzie Lodge
Loch Glass
Garbat Forest
Easter Ross
Strath Oykel
Amatnatua
Croich
The Craigs
Alladale Lodge
Glencalvie Lodge
Glencassley Castle
Dounie
Soyal
Culeave
Corriemulzie
Diebidale Forest
Freevater Forest
Aultnamain Inn
Glen Glass
Nairn
A9
A836
A839
A949
A862
A82
A96
A835
A832
A834
A8
A939
A95
A940
Culbin Forest
Dyke
Brodie
Forres
Conicavel
Logie
Dunphail
Relugas
Glenernie
Upper Derraid
Dava
Glaschoil

N O R T H
A
B
C
D
E
F
1
2
3
4
5
6
7
8
Burghead Bay
Spey Bay
Cullen Bay
Logie Head
Sandend Bay
Redhyt Point
Lossiemouth
Branderburgh
Burghead
Hopeman
Cummingstown
Findhorn
Findhorn Bay
Kinloss
Culbin Forest
FORRES
Dyke
Rafford
Dallas
Elgin
Bishopmill
New Elgin
Lhanbryde
Urquhart
Garmouth
Kingston
Mosstodloch
Fochabers
Buckie
Portgordon
Portknockie
Findochty
Cullen
Portsoy
Fordyce
Keith
Newmill
Rothes
Archiestown
Craigellachie
Charlestown of Aberlour
Dufftown
Huntly
Rothiemay
Milltown of Rothiemay
Cairnie
STRATHBOGIE
BEN RINNES
Glenlivet
Tomnavoulin
Tomintoul
Grantown-on-Spey
Nethy Bridge
Dulnain Bridge
Cromdale
HILLS OF CROMDALE
HIGHLAND
Rhynie
Kildrummy
Alford
Lumsden
Strathdon
Cabrach
Logie of Coldstone
Tarland
Glenmore
CAIRNGORMS
NATIONAL
PARK
LADDER HILLS
CORREEN HILLS
CAIRN GORM
CAIRNGORM
M O U N T A I N S
GLEN AVON
BEN AVON
A96
A95
A941
A98
A939
A97
A944
82

SEA
NORTH SEA
BUCHAN
ABERDEENSHIRE
FORMARTINE
GARIOCH
ABERDEEN
Fraserburgh
Peterhead
Kinnaird Head
Fraserburgh Bay
Cairnbulg Point
Inverallochy
St. Combs
Inzie Head
Rattray Head
Crimond
St. Fergus
Rosehearty
Sandhaven
Troup Head
Pennan Head
Pennan
Quarry Head
Gamrie Bay
Crovie
Gardenstown
Head of Garness
Knock Head
Boyndie Bay
Boyne Bay
Whitehills
Inverboyndie
Boyndie
Banff
Macduff
Turriff
Aberchirder
New Aberdour
New Pitsligo
Strichen
New Byth
Garmond
Cuminestown
Fyvie
Woodhead
Maud
New Deer
Old Deer
Mintlaw
Stuartfield
Longside
Fetterangus
New Leeds
Rathen
Memsie
Auchnagatt
Methlick
Tarves
Ellon
Hatton
Cruden Bay
Port Erroll
Bay of Cruden
Boddam
Collieston
Hackley Head or Forvie Ness
Newburgh
Newburgh Bar
Pitmedden
Oldmeldrum
Rothienorman
Kirkton of Culsalmond
Insch
Old Rayne
Kirkton of Rayne
Oyne
Chapel of Garioch
Inverurie
Port Elphinstone
Kintore
Newmachar
Hatton of Fintray
Balmedie
Blackdog
Dyce
Stoneywood
Bridge of Don
Bankhead
Bucksburn
Westhill
Kirkton of Skene
Lyne of Skene
Dunecht
Echt
Cults
Kemnay
Monymusk
Tillyfourie
PITFICHIE FOREST
HILL OF FARE
Nigg Bay
Souter Head
Aberdeen to: Kirkwall (Hatston) 6hrs. Lerwick (Holmsgarth) 12hrs. 30mins.
A90
A96
A98
A947
A920
A950
A952
A975
A981
A948
83
G
H
J
K
L
M
1
2
3
4
5
6
7
8

ATLANTIC OCEAN
OUTER HEBRIDES
NA H-EILEANAN AN IAR (WESTERN ISLES)
ISLE OF LEWIS (EILEAN LEODHAIS)
BUTT OF LEWIS (RUBHA ROBHANAIS)
Eoropaidh
Port Nis
Sgiogarstaigh
Meall Geal
NIS
Toa Galson
Roinn a' Bhuic
Rubha Bhlanisgaidh
Cellar Head
Aird Barvas
Rinn Druim Tallig
Barabhas
Leac Dubh Gob Hais
TOLSTA HEAD (CEANN or RUBHA THOLASTAIDH)
PAGE NOT CONTINUED
Rubha Caol
Carlabhagh
Gallan Head (An Gallan Uigeach)
GREAT BERNERA (BEARNARAIGH)
Breascleit
Acha Mor
Vatisker Point
Coll Sands
TIUMPAN HEAD (RUBHA AN T-SIUMPAIN)
Broad Bay (Loch aTuath)
Tràigh Mhealaboist
Newmarket
STORNOWAY (STEÒRNABHAGH)
Sanndabhaig
EYE PENINSULA (AN RUBHA)
Gob Shilldinish
Stornoway to Ullapool 2hrs. 40mins.
Aird Mòr Mangurstadh
Aird Feinis
Aird Bhreinis
Eilean Mhealasta
Morsgail Forest (Frith Mhorsgail)
Liurbost
Rubha Raerinis
Baile Ailein
SCARP
Rubha Huisinis
NORTH HARRIS
(CEANNA TUATH NA HEARADH)
Eilean Shiphoirt
PARK (PAIRC)
A' Chabag
Eilean Liubhaird
Srianach
Horsanais
Rubha Leacach
Sòdhaidh Mòr
TARANSAY (TARASAIGH)
Iosaigh
Tarbert (Tairbeart)
Gob Rubh' Uisinis
Rubh' a' Bhaird
SOUND OF SHIANT (CAOLAS NAN EILEAN)
Shiant Islands (Na h-Eileanan Mora)
Eilean Mhuire
Eilean an Taighe
Rubha Sgeirigin
Rubha Màs a' Chnuic
Sound of Taransay (Caolas Tarasaigh)
Aird Nisabost
Rubha Crago
SCALPAY (SCALPAIGH)
Eilean Glas
Loch An Tairbeairt
HARRIS (NA HEARADH)
SOUTH HARRIS

ATLANTIC
OCEAN
PAGE NOT CONTINUED
CAPE WRATH
Duslic
Stack Clò Kearvaig
Kearvaig
Bay of Keisgaig
A' Ghoil
Faraid Head
Balnakeil Bay
Balnakeil
Durness
Sangomore
Smoo Cave
Craft Village
Eilean Hoan
Leirinmore
Sangobeg
Eilean Cluimhrig
Rispond
Whiten Head or An Ceann Geal
Keoldale
Achiemore
Kyle of Durness
Loch Eriboll
Portnancon
Laid
Eilean Choraidh
Eriboll
Polla
Hope
Ben Hope
Sheigra
Balchrick
Blairmore
Droman
Oldshore Beg
Oldshoremore
Eilean an Ròin Mòr
Kinlochbervie
Badcall
Inshegra
Achriesgill
Rhuvoult
Achlyness
Rhiconich
Gualin House
Ardmore Point
Ardmore
Skerricha
Fanagmore
Tarbet
Foindle
Handa Island
Laxford Bridge
Badnabay
Scourie Bay
Scourie
Scourie More
Rubh' Aird an t-Sionnaich
Upper Badcall
Lower Badcall
Badcall Bay
Eilean a Bhreitheimh
Meall Mór
Lochstack Lodge
Lone
Achfary
FOINAVEN
Arkle
Duartmore Bridge
Calbha Beag
Calbha Mór
Eddrachillis Bay
Kylestrome
Kylesku
Unapool
Newton
Point of Stoer
Old Man of Stoer
Sgeir nan Gall
Oldany Island
Eilean Chrona
Cluas Deas
Culkein
Culkein Drumbeg
Drumbeg
Nedd
Oldany
Achnacarnin
Rhubha Stoer
Clashmore
Clashnessie
Balchladich
Glenleraig
Bay of Stoer
Stoer
Clachtoll
Clachtoll Broch
HIGHLAND
QUINAG
Lochassynt Lodge
Kinloch
Merkland Lodge
Corriekinloch
Achmelvich Bay
Achmelvich
Rhicarn
Brackloch
Rubha Rodha
Baddidarach
Lochinver
Soyea Island
Strathan
Kirkaig Point
A' Chleit
Badnaban
Inverkirkaig
Falls of Kirkaig
SUILVEN
CANISP
Inchnadamph
Ardvreck
BEN MORE ASSYNT
Inchnadamph Bone Caves
Overscaig
Fiag Bridge
Duchally
Rubha Coigeach
Eilean Mór
Enard Bay
Reiff
Altandhu
Brea of Achnahaird
Inverpolly Lodge
Inverpolly Forest
CUL MOR
Elphin
Ledmore
Altnacealgach
Benmore Lodge
Knockan
Knockan Crag
Eilean Mullagrach
Isle Ristol
Polbain
Badentarbat
Glas-leac Mór
Badentarbat Bay
Achiltibuie
Polglass
Tanera Beg
Tanera Mór
Summer Isles
Badenscallie
Glas-leac Beag
Horse Island
Achduart
Culnacraig
COIGACH
Priest Island
Eilean Dubh
Bottle Island
Carn nan Sgeir
Drumrunie
CROMALT HILLS
Strathcanaird
Linneraineach
Glencassley Castle
Invercassley
Rosehall
Lubcroy
Crask Inn
Mudale
Gobernuisgach Lodge
Alltnacaillich
Dun Dornaigil
Arscaig
Sallachy
Fiag Lodge
A838
A837
A894
A835
B801
B869
86
87
92
G
H
J
K
L
M

ATLANTIC OCEAN
HIGHLAND
STRATHY POINT
Whiten Head or An Ceann Geal
Eilean Clùimhrig
Eilean nan Ron
Neave or Coombe Island
Rabbit Islands
Farr Point
Kirtomy Point
Ardmore Point
Red Point
Brims Ness
BEN HOPE
BEN KLIBRECK
Tongue
Bettyhill
Armadale
Strathy
Portskerra
Melvich
Reay
Kinbrace
Helmsdale
Brora
Lairg
Loch Loyal
Loch Naver
Loch Shin
Kyle of Tongue
Altnaharra
Syre
Crask Inn
Forsinard
Kildonan
Rogart
Dalchork
Colaboll
Tomich
Balloan
Achany
Rosehall
Gordonbush
Lothbeg Point
Ord Point
Navidale
Marrel
Portgower
Crakaig
Lothmore
Kintradwell
Dalchalm
Uppat
Backies
Doll
West Clyne
East Clyne
Achrimsdale
Altnabreac
Dalnawillan Lodge
Glutt Lodge
Achentoul
Lochside
Garvault
Rimsdale
Badanloch Lodge
Borrobol Lodge
Altanduin
Ben Armine Lodge
Balnacoil
Dalnessie
Grummore
Mudale
Skail
Rhifail
Carnachy
Archargary
Skelpick
Borgie
Skerray
Torrisdale
Coldbackie
Rhitongue
Dalcharn
Braetongue
Ribigill
Kinloch Lodge
Loch Loyal Lodge
Hope
Achuvolcrach
Melness
Talmine
Skinnet
Midtown
Strathan
Achininver
Midfield
Lubinvullin
Achinahuagh
Modsarie
Clashaddy
Achtoty
Swordly
Crask
Kirtomy
Farr
Clerkhill
Invernaver
Achina
Leckfurin
Aultivullin
Totegan
Brawl
Aultiphurst
Lednagullin
Baligill
Bowside Lodge
Achiemore
Upper Bighouse
Craigtown
Dalhalvaig
Croick
Trantlebeg
Trantlemore
Bighouse
Fresgoe
Isauld
Lower Dounreay
Upper Dounreay
Buldoo
Achreamie
Shebster
Skiall
Forss
Crosskirk
Lythmore
Stemster
Janetstown
Newlands of Geise
Westfield
Achscrabster
Broubster
Shurrery
Brawlbin
Dorrery
Knockglass
Scrabster
Dounreay
Shinness
Achnairn
Achfrish
Tirryside
Rhian
Rhian Bridge
Arscaig
Flag Bridge
Sallachy
Saval
Lairg Muir
Gruids
Torroble
Rhian Breck
Muie
Tressady
Ardachu
Dalmore
Little Rogart
Pittentrail
Achvoan
East Langwell
West Langwell
Dalreavoch
Rhilochan
Knockarthur
Torrish
Kildonan
Craggie
Wag
Auldbea
Braemore
Gobernuisgeach
Oudsdale
West Helmsdale
East Helmsdale
Gartymore
A836
A838
A897
A9
A839
B871
B873
A836
A839
87
91

HOY
ORKNEY ISLANDS
SOUTH RONALDSAY
PENTLAND FIRTH
NORTH SEA
Flotta
Burray
St. Margaret's Hope
South Walls
Swona
Island of Stroma
Pentland Skerries
DUNNET HEAD
DUNCANSBY HEAD
John o' Groats
Stacks of Duncansby
Dunnet Bay
Dunnet
Castletown
Thurso East
Halkirk
Gills Bay
Sinclair's Bay
Wick
Wick Bay
South Head
Noss Head
Sealky Head
Helman Head
Sarclet Head
Halberry Head
Lybster
Dunbeath
Latheron
Watten
Keiss
Tang Head
Brough Head
Freswick Bay
Skirza Head
Ness Head
Thrumster
Ulbster
Loch Watten
Stromness 1hr. 30mins.
A9
A99
A836
A882
B876
B870
B874
B9041
94
G
H
J
K
L
M
1
2
3
4
5
6
7
8

ORKNEY ISLANDS
MAINLAND
HOY
ROUSAY
WESTRAY
SANDAY
EDAY
STRONSAY
SHAPINSAY
SOUTH RONALDSAY
North Ronaldsay
Papa Westray
Egilsay
Wyre
Gairsay
Burray
Flotta
Graemsay
Swona
South Walls
Island of Stroma
Pentland Skerries
PENTLAND FIRTH
WESTRAY FIRTH
STRONSAY FIRTH
NORTH RONALDSAY FIRTH
THE NORTH SOUND
Scapa Flow
Kirkwall
Stromness
Finstown
St. Margaret's Hope
Dunnet
DUNNET HEAD
DUNCANSBY HEAD
Castletown
John o' Groats
Stacks of Duncansby
SHETLAND ISLANDS
Fair Isle
Fair Isle lies about 27 miles ENE of North Ronaldsay
Stromness to: Scrabster 1hr. 30mins.
Kirkwall (Hatston) to: Aberdeen 7hrs. 15mins. Lerwick (Holmsgarth) 7hrs. 45mins.
PAGE NOT CONTINUED
SCALE: 4.734 miles to 1 inch 1:300,000
15 Miles
20 Kilometres
93

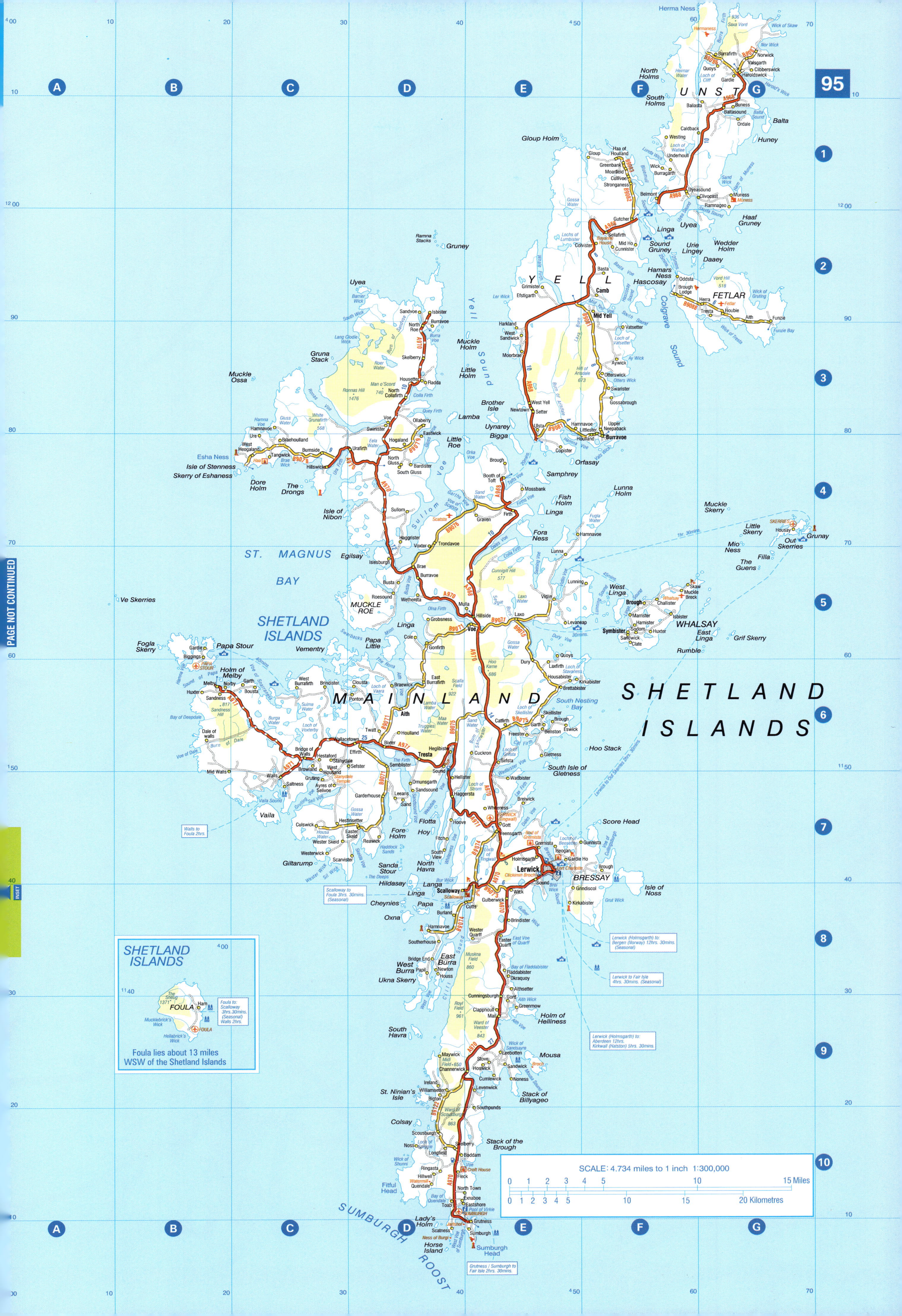
SHETLAND ISLANDS
UNST
YELL
FETLAR
MAINLAND
WHALSAY
BRESSAY
MUCKLE ROE
SHETLAND ISLANDS
ST. MAGNUS BAY
SUMBURGH ROOST
Herma Ness
Haroldswick
Baltasound
Uyeasound
Belmont
Gutcher
Mid Yell
Burravoe
Papa Stour
Vementry
Voe
Brae
Aith
Walls
Tresta
Whiteness
Lerwick
Scalloway
Sandwick
Sumburgh
Sumburgh Head
Fitful Head
Lady's Holm
Mousa
Isle of Noss
Out Skerries
Grunay
Ve Skerries
Foula
Vaila
Fair Isle
SCALE: 4.734 miles to 1 inch 1:300,000
15 Miles
20 Kilometres
Foula lies about 13 miles WSW of the Shetland Islands
PAGE NOT CONTINUED

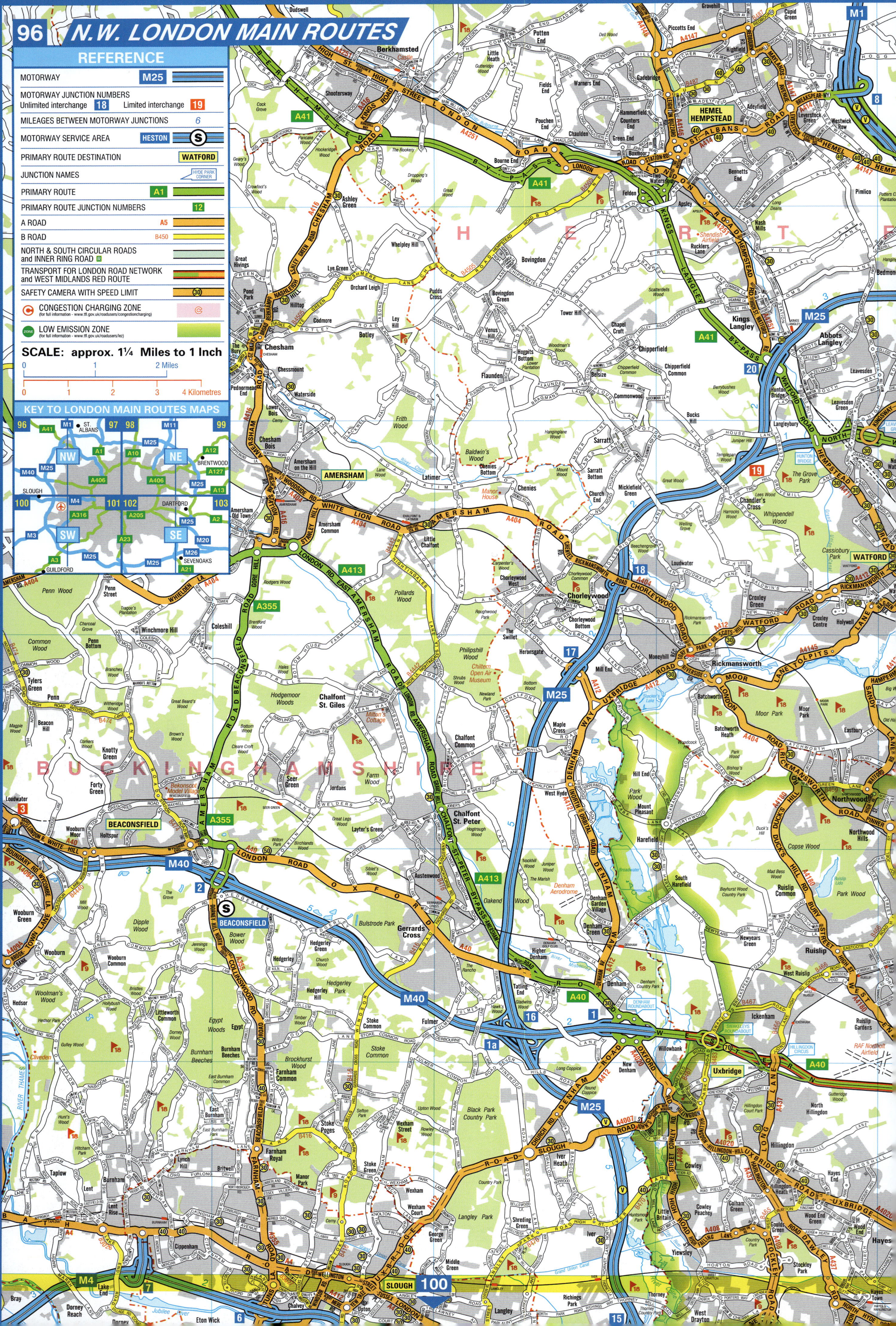
REFERENCE
MOTORWAY M25
MOTORWAY JUNCTION NUMBERS
Unlimited interchange 18 Limited interchange 19
MILEAGES BETWEEN MOTORWAY JUNCTIONS 6
MOTORWAY SERVICE AREA HESTON S
PRIMARY ROUTE DESTINATION WATFORD
JUNCTION NAMES HYDE PARK CORNER
PRIMARY ROUTE A1
PRIMARY ROUTE JUNCTION NUMBERS 12
A ROAD A5
B ROAD B450
NORTH & SOUTH CIRCULAR ROADS and INNER RING ROAD
TRANSPORT FOR LONDON ROAD NETWORK and WEST MIDLANDS RED ROUTE
SAFETY CAMERA WITH SPEED LIMIT 30
CONGESTION CHARGING ZONE
LOW EMISSION ZONE
SCALE: approx. 1¼ Miles to 1 Inch
0 1 2 Miles
0 1 2 3 4 Kilometres
KEY TO LONDON MAIN ROUTES MAPS
96 97 98 99 100 101 102 103
NW NE SW SE
ST. ALBANS
BRENTWOOD
SLOUGH
DARTFORD
GUILDFORD
SEVENOAKS
Berkhamsted
HEMEL HEMPSTEAD
Kings Langley
Abbots Langley
Chesham
Amersham
AMERSHAM
Chorleywood
Rickmansworth
WATFORD
Chalfont St. Giles
Chalfont St. Peter
Gerrards Cross
BEACONSFIELD
Denham
Uxbridge
Northwood
Ruislip
Hillingdon
Stoke Poges
Burnham
SLOUGH
Hayes
Iver
Langley
Bovingdon
Chipperfield
Sarratt
Harefield
HERTS
BUCKINGHAMSHIRE
M25
M40
M4
A41
A413
A355
A40
100

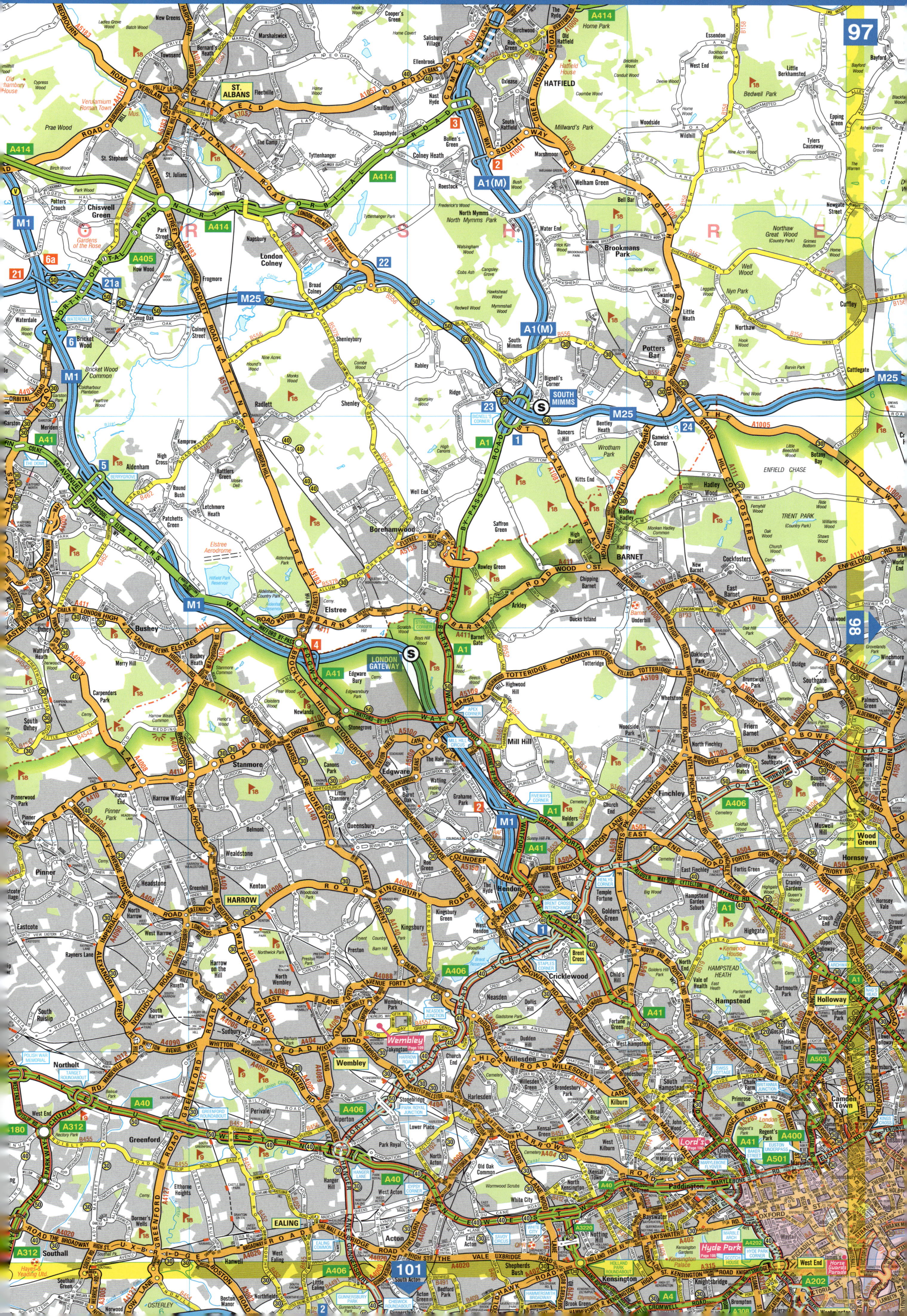

ST. ALBANS
HATFIELD
Hatfield House
Welham Green
Brookmans Park
North Mymms Park
London Colney
Colney Heath
Chiswell Green
St. Stephens
Bricket Wood
Radlett
Shenley
South Mimms
Potters Bar
Cuffley
Northaw
Borehamwood
Elstree
Aldenham
Bushey
Watford
BARNET
Hadley
Cockfosters
Enfield Chase
Trent Park
Southgate
Mill Hill
Edgware
Stanmore
Harrow Weald
Pinner
HARROW
Kenton
Kingsbury
Hendon
Finchley
Golders Green
Hampstead
Highgate
Hornsey
Wood Green
Holloway
Camden Town
Cricklewood
Willesden
Neasden
Wembley
Sudbury
Northolt
Greenford
Southall
EALING
Acton
Hanwell
Kensington
Paddington
Marylebone
Hyde Park
Kilburn
Queensbury
Eastcote
Ruislip
M1
M25
A1(M)
A1
A41
A406
A40
A414
A405
LONDON GATEWAY
Wembley
Lord's
86
101

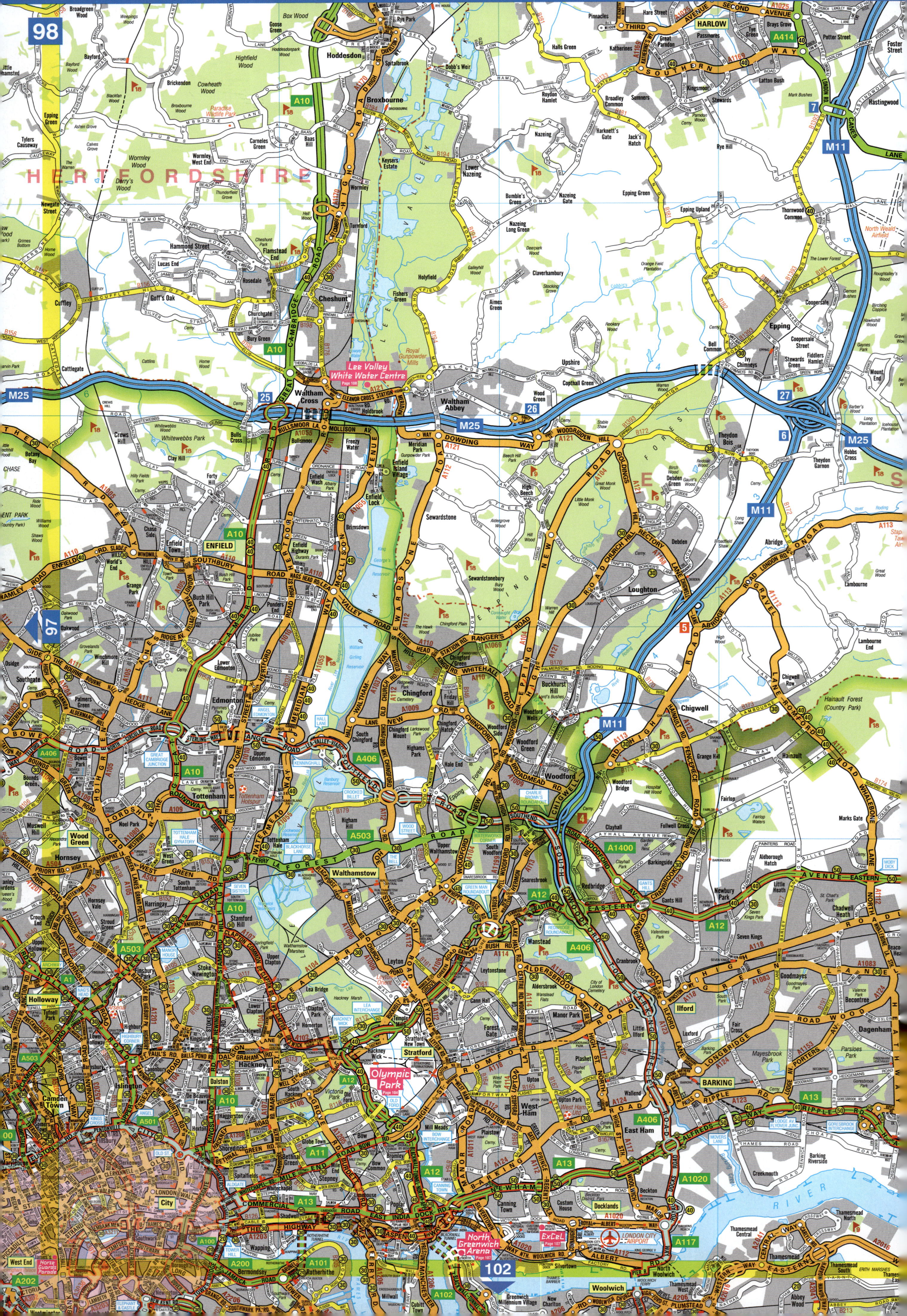
HERTFORDSHIRE
Hoddesdon
Broxbourne
Wormley
Cheshunt
Waltham Cross
Waltham Abbey
Lee Valley White Water Centre
Royal Gunpowder Mills
Nazeing
Lower Nazeing
Roydon Hamlet
Harlow
Epping
Epping Green
Epping Upland
Theydon Bois
Coopersale
Loughton
Chigwell
Abridge
Enfield
Southbury
Edmonton
Chingford
Woodford
Woodford Green
Walthamstow
Tottenham
Tottenham Hotspur
Wood Green
Hornsey
Holloway
Stoke Newington
Leyton
Leytonstone
Wanstead
Redbridge
Ilford
Barkingside
Seven Kings
Goodmayes
Dagenham
Barking
East Ham
West Ham
Stratford
Olympic Park
Hackney
Dalston
Islington
Camden Town
City
Stepney
Bow
Plaistow
Canning Town
Docklands
ExCeL
North Greenwich Arena
London City Airport
Woolwich
Beckton
Thamesmead
Rotherhithe
Bermondsey
Wapping
Silvertown
Hainault Forest (Country Park)
Hainault
M25
M11
A10
A406
A12
A13
Cuffley
Goff's Oak
Crews Hill
Chase Side
RIVER THAMES

97
102

M25
A12
A13
A127
A414
A128
A129
A1306
ROMFORD
BRENTWOOD
BILLERICAY
BASILDON
Chipping Ongar
Upminster
Hornchurch
Ingatestone
Shenfield
Writtle
Stanford-le-Hope
Rainham
Aveley
South Ockendon
North Ockendon
Orsett
Grays
THURROCK
Thorndon Country Park
Weald Country Park
Hylands Park
Dagnam Park
Belhus Woods Country Park
HORNCHURCH MARSHES
RAINHAM MARSHES
WENNINGTON MARSHES
AVELEY MARSHES
MUCKING MARSHES
ORSETT FEN
103

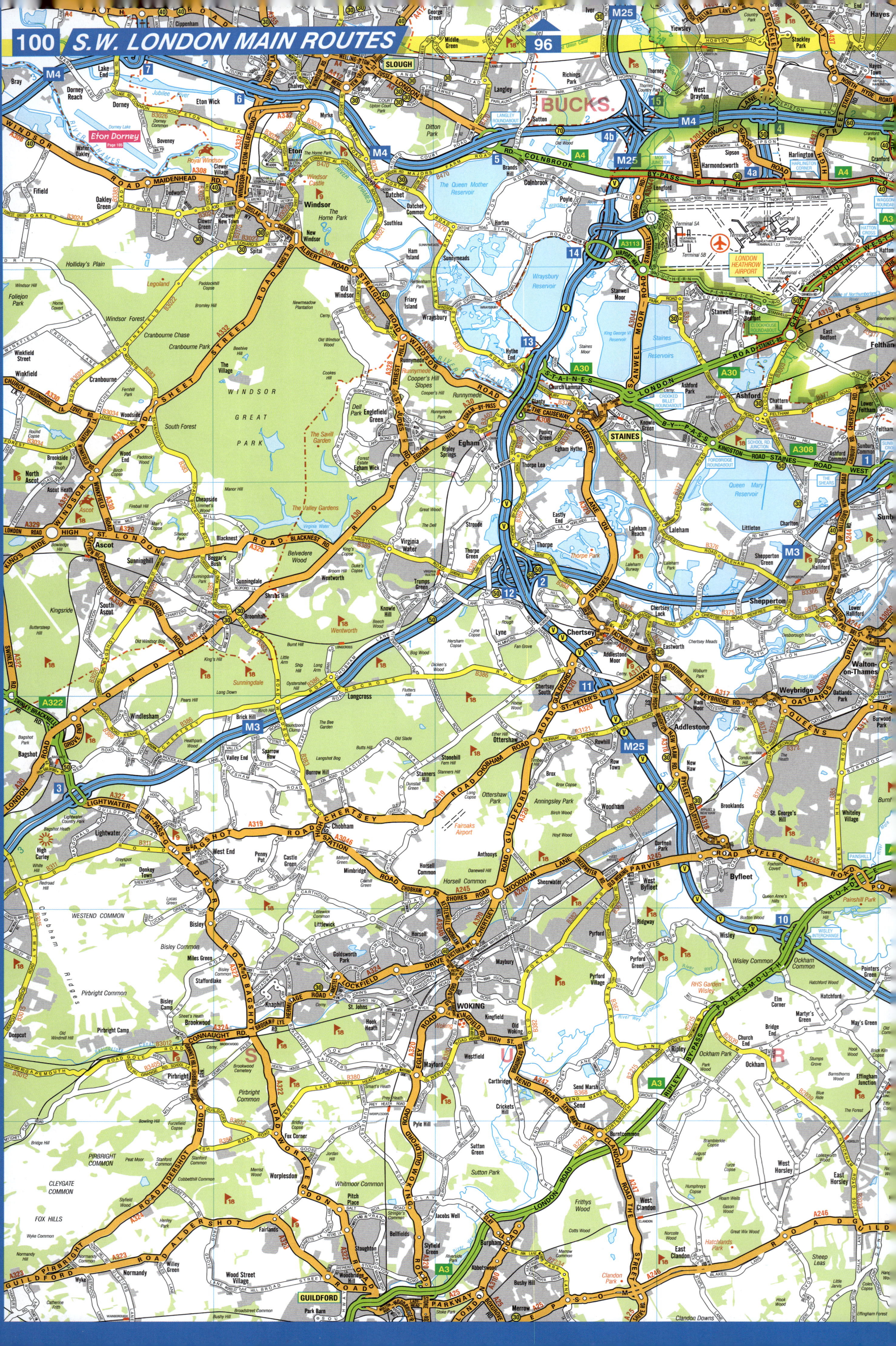

96
BUCKS.
M4
M25
M3
A4
A30
A308
A322
A329
A3
A3113
A320
A319
SLOUGH
Eton Dorney
Page 105
Windsor
Eton
Datchet
The Queen Mother Reservoir
Wraysbury Reservoir
LONDON HEATHROW AIRPORT
Colnbrook
Harmondsworth
Sipson
Harlington
Hayes
Yiewsley
West Drayton
Langley
Iver
Stanwell
Ashford
Feltham
STAINES
Egham
Englefield Green
Virginia Water
Windsor Great Park
Ascot
Sunninghill
Sunningdale
Windlesham
Bagshot
Lightwater
Chobham
Chertsey
Addlestone
Weybridge
Walton-on-Thames
Shepperton
Laleham
Thorpe
Queen Mary Reservoir
Ottershaw
Longcross
Woodham
Byfleet
West Byfleet
Pyrford
Sheerwater
WOKING
Knaphill
St. Johns
Horsell
Mayford
Send
Ripley
Ockham
Wisley
Bisley
Pirbright
Worplesdon
Jacobs Well
Burpham
Merrow
West Clandon
East Clandon
West Horsley
East Horsley
Normandy
Wood Street Village
GUILDFORD
Fairoaks Airport
Winkfield
Cranbourne
Fifield
Oakley Green
Dorney
Bray
Holliday's Plain
Legoland
West End
Brookwood
Deepcut
Sutton Green
Pyle Hill
Stoughton
Pitch Place
Send Marsh
Burntcommon
Effingham Junction

97

Ealing
Southall
Hanwell
Acton
Kensington
Hyde Park
Chiswick
Hammersmith
Earls Court
Chelsea
Brentford
Heston
Osterley
Hounslow
Isleworth
Richmond
Barnes
Fulham
Putney
Battersea
Clapham
Brixton
Wandsworth
Twickenham
Teddington
Richmond Park
Roehampton
Wimbledon
Wimbledon Common
Streatham
Tooting
Hampton
Bushy Park
Hampton Court Palace
Kingston upon Thames
New Malden
Merton
Mitcham
Morden
Surbiton
Tolworth
Worcester Park
Sutton
Carshalton
Esher
Chessington
Claygate
Cheam
Ewell
Epsom
Oxshott
Cobham
Ashtead
Banstead
Coulsdon
Purley
Leatherhead
Fetcham
Great Bookham
Tadworth
Kingswood
Walton on the Hill
Mickleham
Headley
Reigate
Redhill
Merstham
Dorking
Westhumble
North Downs
M25
M4
M23

102

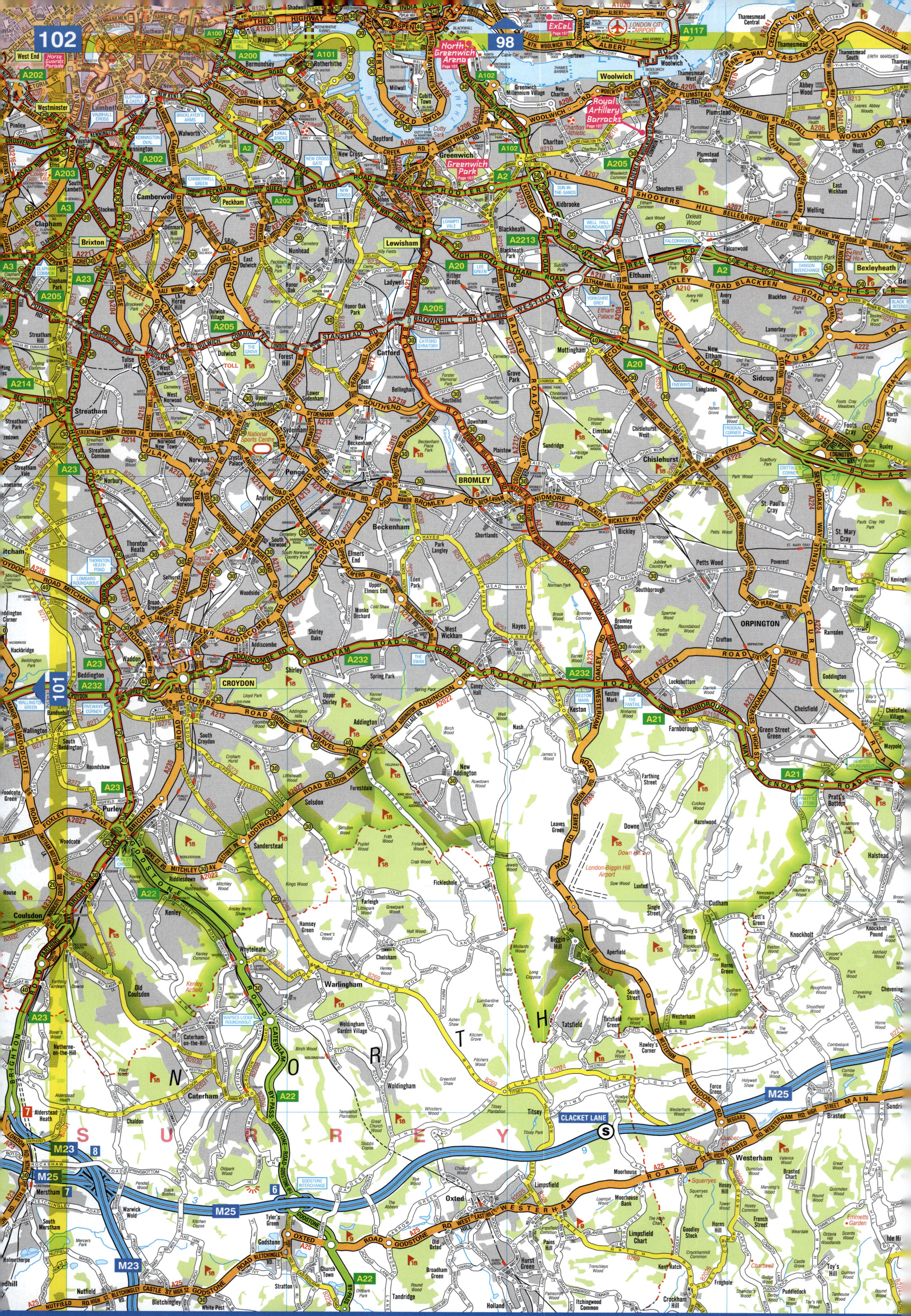

98
101
North Greenwich Arena
ExCeL
London City Airport
Royal Artillery Barracks
Greenwich Park
Woolwich
Westminster
Brixton
Clapham
Camberwell
Peckham
Lewisham
Greenwich
Deptford
Catford
Eltham
Bexleyheath
Sidcup
Streatham
Norwood
Penge
Beckenham
BROMLEY
Chislehurst
Orpington
CROYDON
West Wickham
Hayes
Keston
Farnborough
Purley
Coulsdon
Kenley
Whyteleafe
Warlingham
Caterham
Biggin Hill
Tatsfield
Westerham
Oxted
Limpsfield
Godstone
Bletchingley
Merstham
Titsey
CLACKET LANE
Green Street Green
Swanley
Knockholt
Halstead
Brasted
M25
M23
A22
A23
A20
A21
A2
A205
A232
S U R R E Y
N O R T H

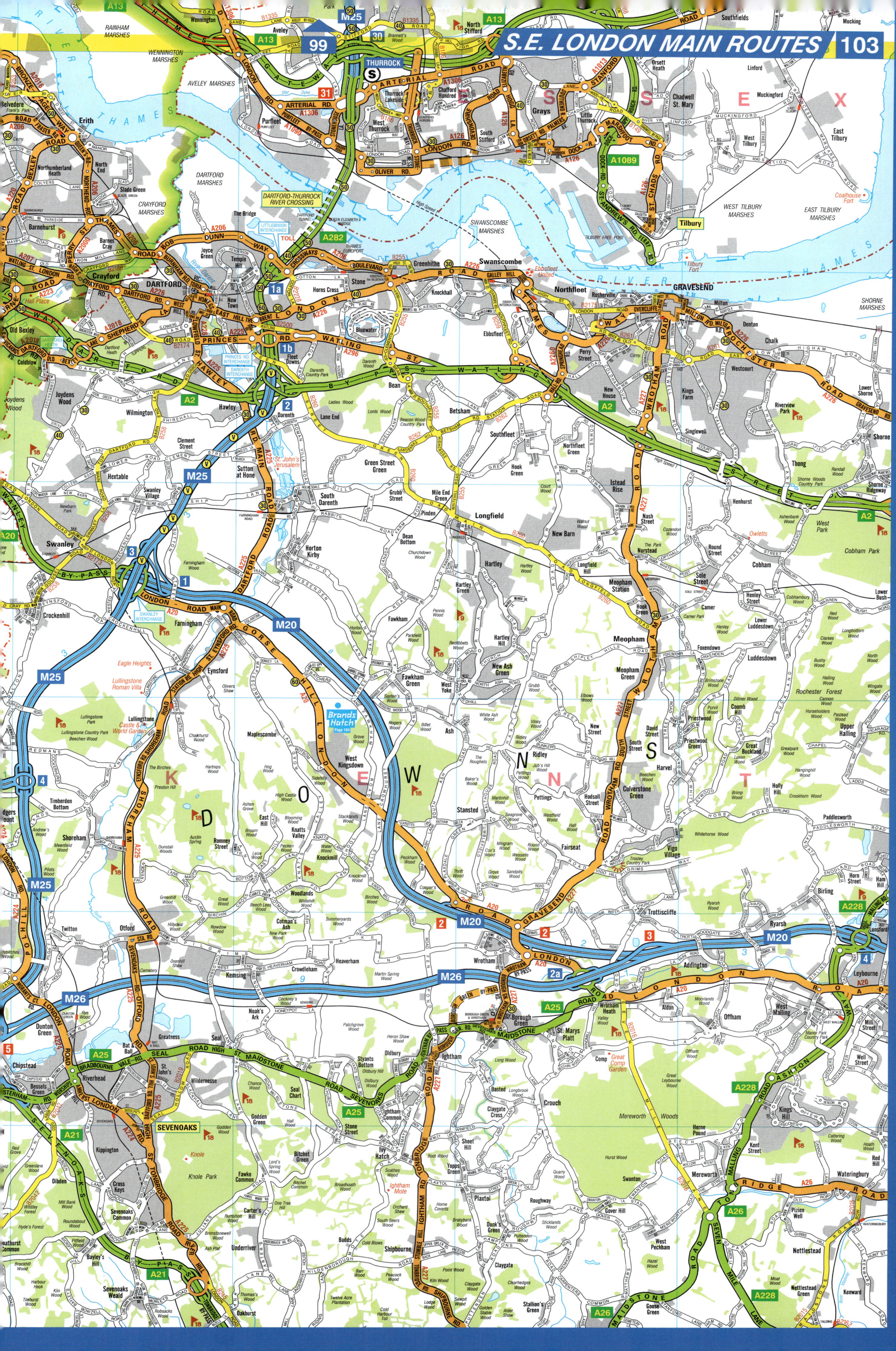
ESSEX
KENT
THAMES
RIVER THAMES
Thurrock
Grays
Tilbury
Purfleet
West Thurrock
Chafford Hundred
Little Thurrock
Chadwell St. Mary
Orsett Heath
Aveley
North Stifford
South Stifford
Erith
Crayford
DARTFORD
Stone
Greenhithe
Swanscombe
Northfleet
GRAVESEND
Bexley
Barnehurst
Wilmington
Hextable
Swanley
Crockenhill
Farningham
Eynsford
Sutton at Hone
South Darenth
Horton Kirby
Longfield
Hartley
Southfleet
Betsham
Meopham
Cobham
Shorne
Istead Rise
Culverstone Green
Vigo Village
Harvel
Birling
Ryarsh
Trottiscliffe
Addington
Wrotham
Borough Green
West Malling
Leybourne
Kings Hill
Ightham
Plaxtol
Shipbourne
Seal
Kemsing
Otford
Shoreham
SEVENOAKS
Riverhead
Chipstead
Dunton Green
Sevenoaks Weald
Knole Park
Stansted
Fairseat
West Kingsdown
Ash
New Ash Green
Fawkham Green
Mereworth
West Peckham
Wateringbury
Nettlestead
Brands Hatch
DARTFORD-THURROCK RIVER CROSSING
M25
M20
M26
A2
A13
A20
A25
A26
A227
A228
A282
A1089
99

Reference

Motorway	M4 M4 MOTORWAY
Primary Route	A12 BOW ROAD
A Road	A20 HIGH STREET
B Road	B142 DEVAS STREET
One-way Street	
Rail	Stations Tunnel
Station Name	LEYTON
Recommended Venue Stations	STRATFORD
Recommended Venue Stations for disabled spectators. Step-free and staff assistance available	
National Rail	
London Overground	
London Underground	
London DLR	DLR
Tram	
Glasgow Subway	
Newcastle Metro	M
Riverboat	
Venue Name	City of Coventry Stadium
Venue Building	
Olympic sport	
Paralympic sport	
Built-up Area	
Parks and Rivers	

Scale: 1:25344

0 — 1000 m

Olympic Park

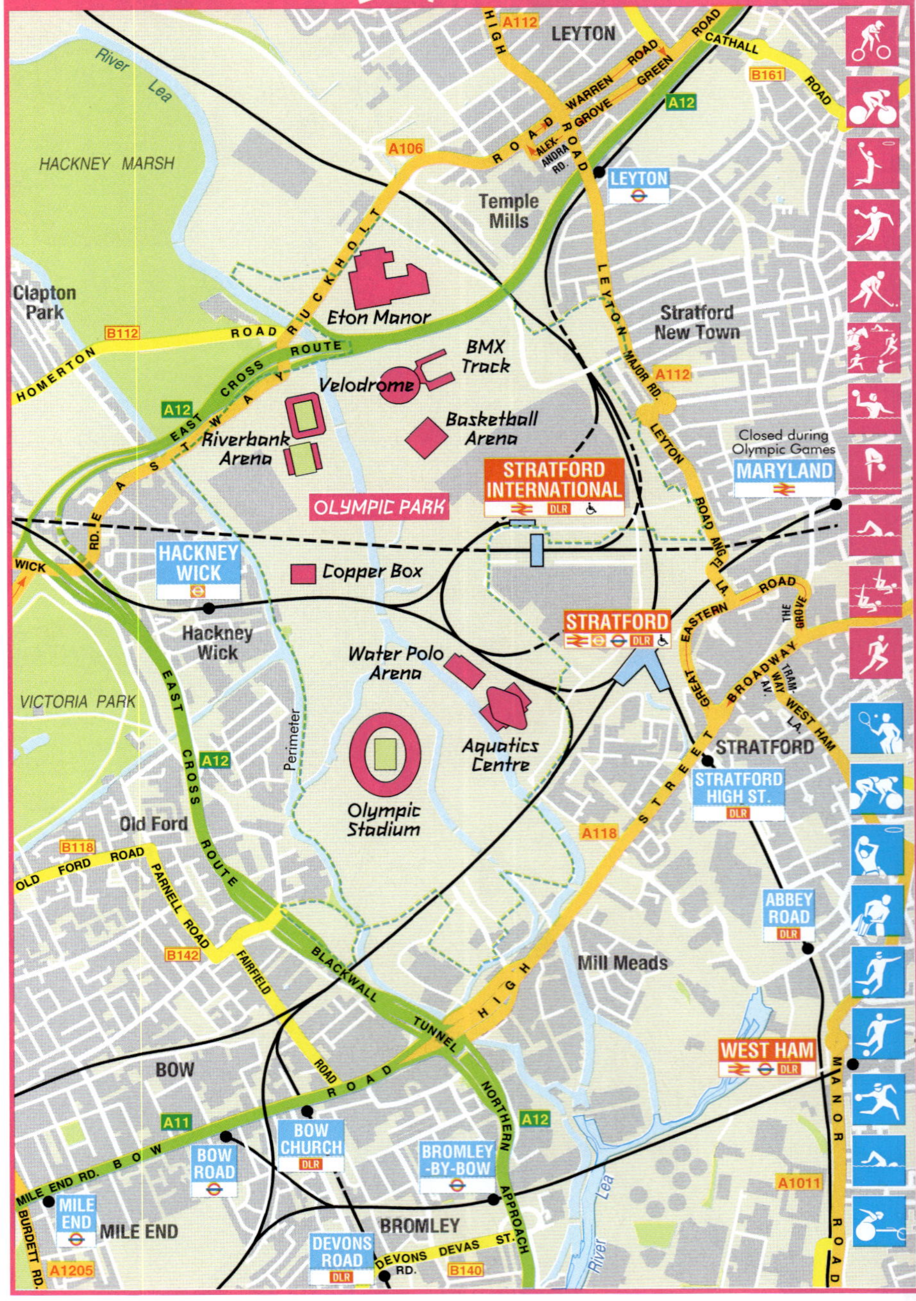

Brands Hatch

City of Coventry Stadium

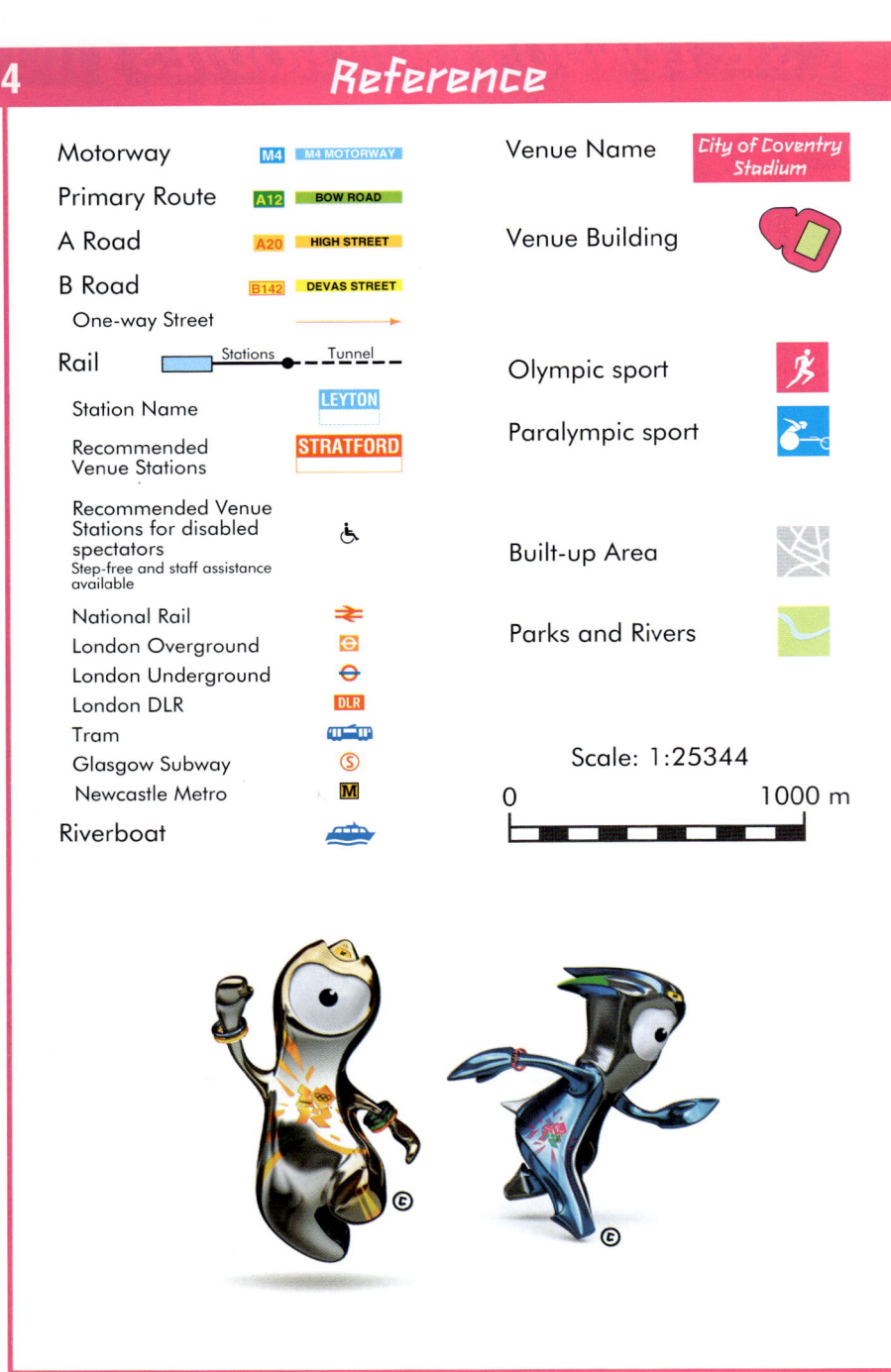

Eton Dorney

Hadleigh Farm

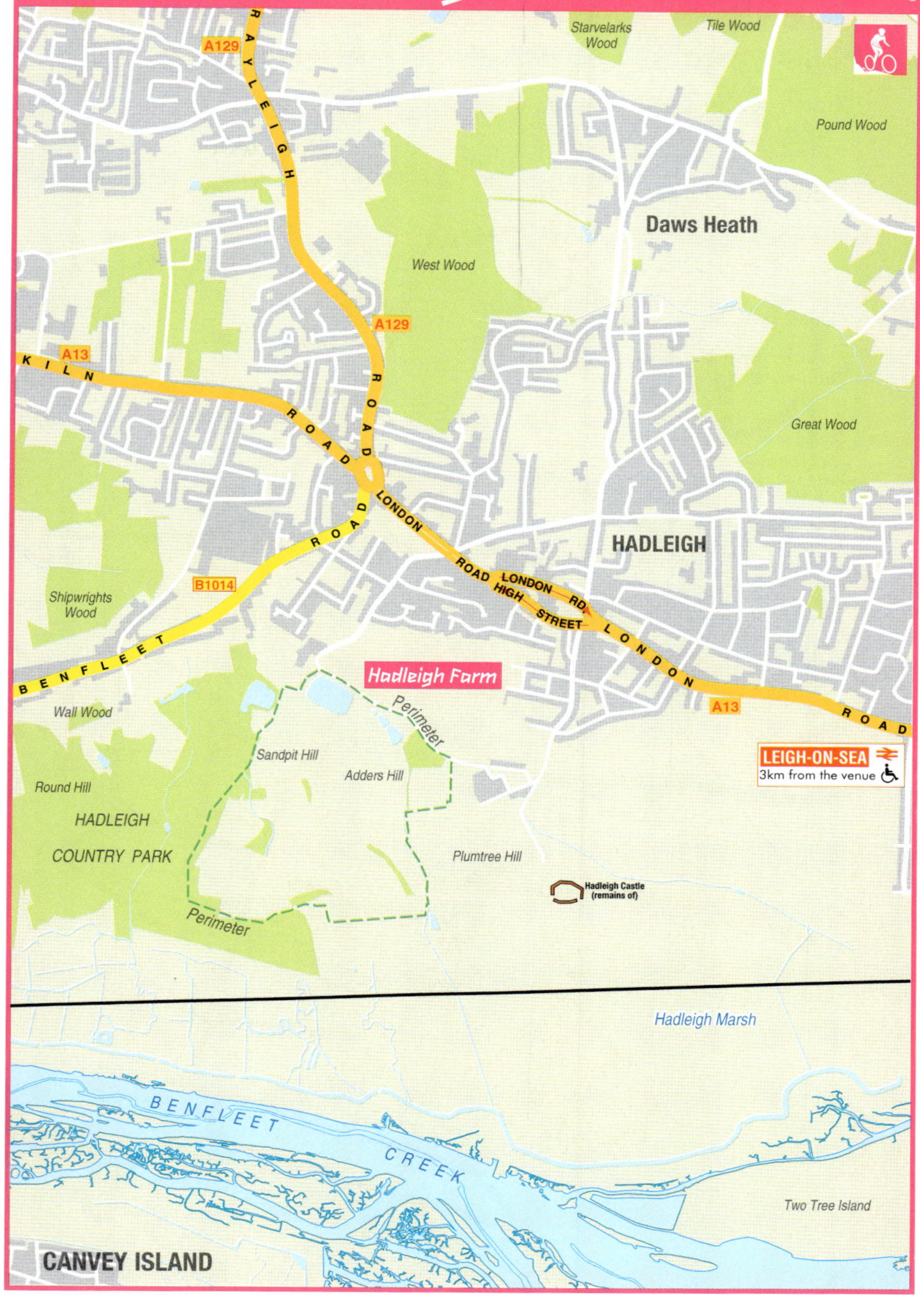

Hampden Park - Glasgow

Hampton Court Palace

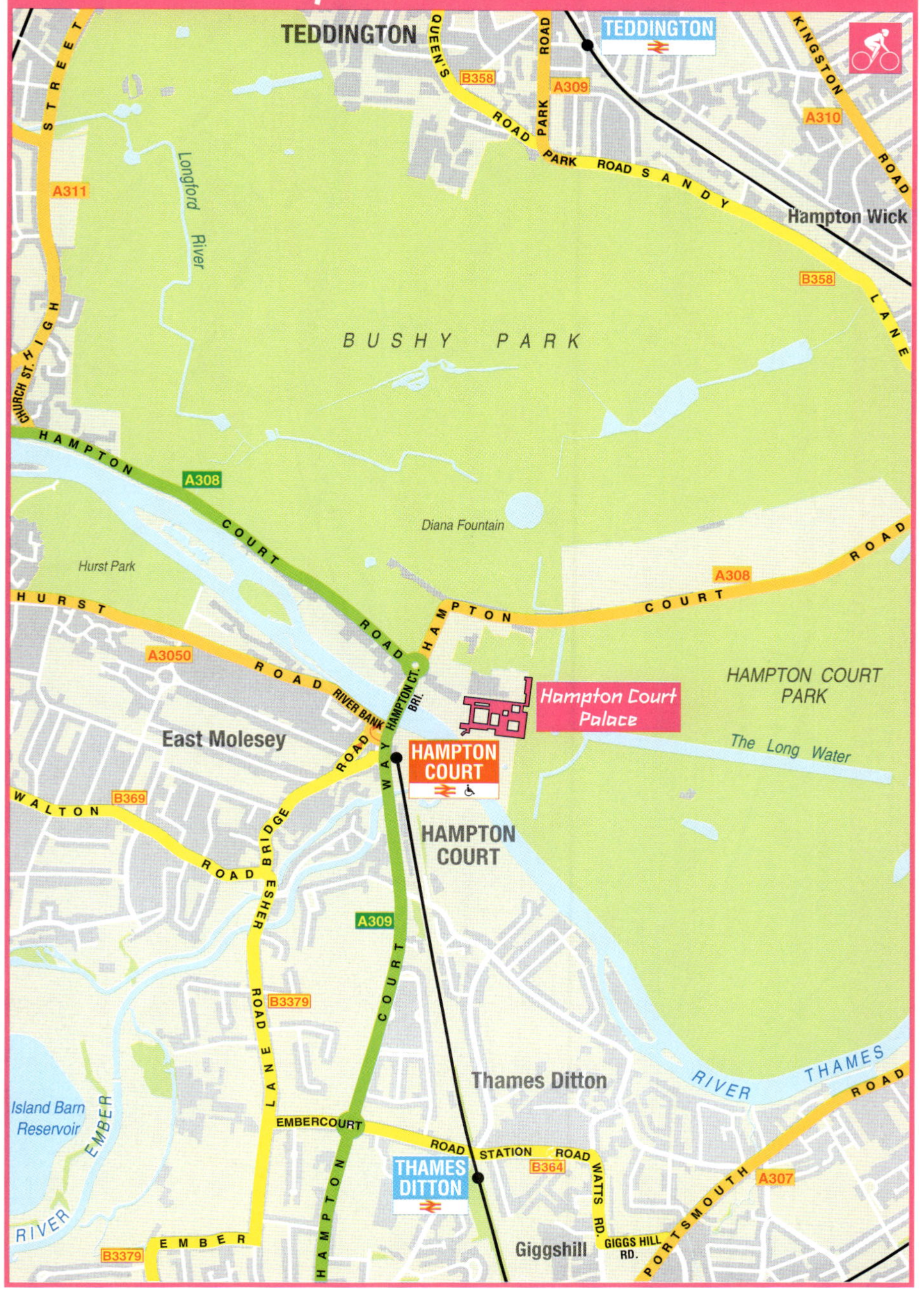

London Central Zone Earls Court • Horse Guards Parade • Hyde Park • Lord's Cricket Ground • The Mall

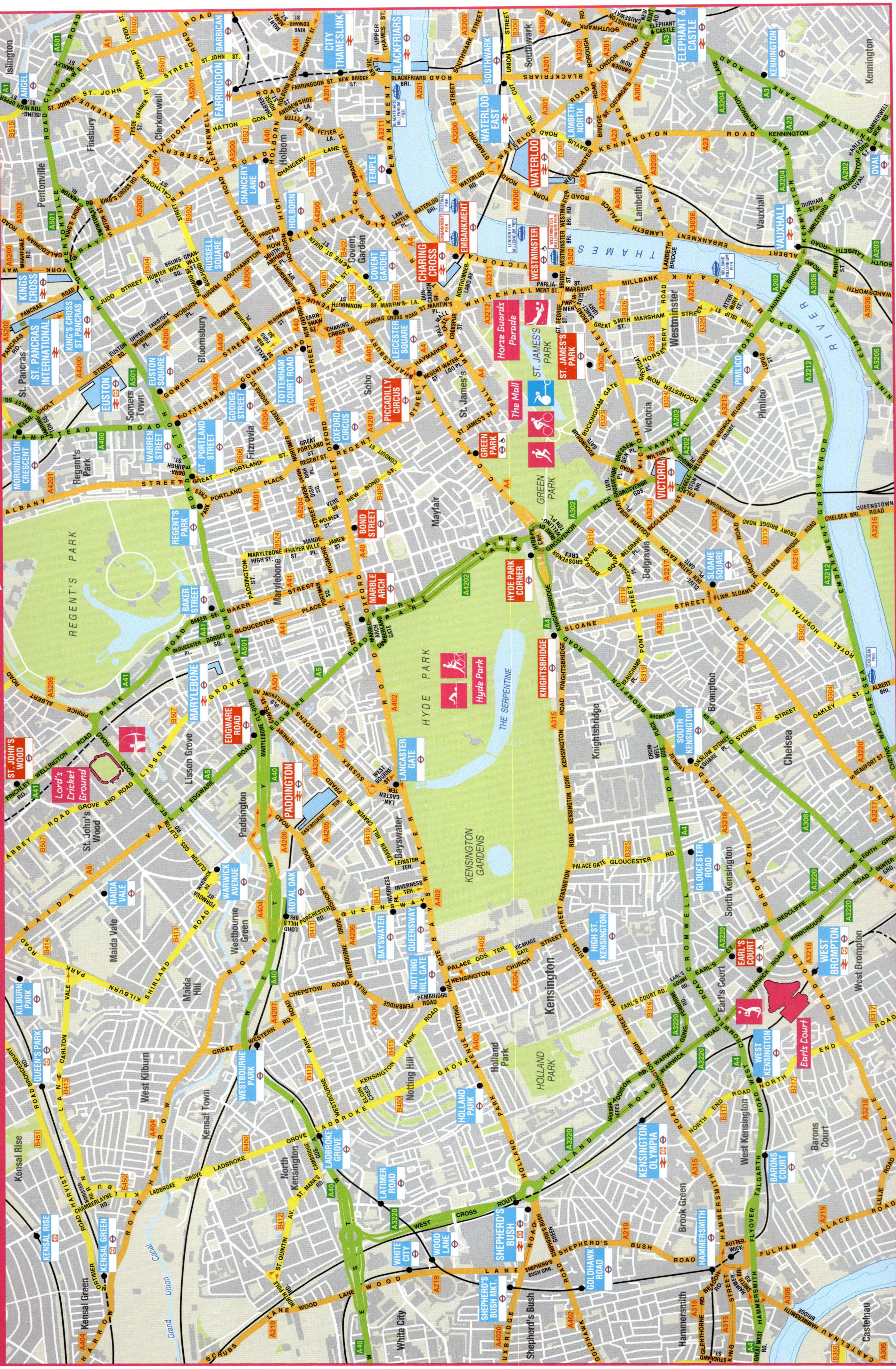

LIMEHOUSE
Ratcliff
LIMEHOUSE
LANGDON PARK
South Bromley
CANNING TOWN
CANNING TOWN
CUSTOM HOUSE
Mid Beckton
Beckton Park
BECKTON
Windsor Park
CUSTOM HOUSE for ExCeL
West Beckton
BECKTON PARK
CYPRUS
GALLIONS REACH
ROYAL VICTORIA
WESTFERRY
POPLAR
ALL SAINTS
POPLAR
BLACKWALL
EAST INDIA
LEAMOUTH
Blackwall
ExCeL
PRINCE REGENT
ROYAL ALBERT
ROYAL VICTORIA DOCK
ROYAL ALBERT DOCK
LONDON CITY AIRPORT
LONDON CITY AIRPORT
KING GEORGE V DOCK
KING GEORGE V
WEST INDIA QUAY
CANARY WHARF
HERON QUAYS
CANARY WHARF
BLACKWALL TUNNEL
Pleasure Gardens
PONTOON DOCK
WEST SILVERTOWN
SILVERTOWN
North Greenwich Arena
NORTH GREENWICH
North Greenwich
NORTH WOOLWICH
ROTHERHITHE TUNNEL
SOUTH QUAY
ISLE OF DOGS
RIVER THAMES
THAMES BARRIER
WOOLWICH FREE FERRY
Woolwich Foot Tunnel
THAMESMEAD WEST
CANADA WATER
ROTHERHITHE
Royal Arsenal West
CROSSHARBOUR
SURREY QUAYS
Cubitt Town
Millwall
MUDCHUTE
ISLAND GARDENS
New Charlton
WOOLWICH
WOOLWICH DOCKYARD
WOOLWICH ARSENAL
PLUMSTEAD
Greenwich Foot Tunnel
CHARLTON
PLUMSTEAD
CUTTY SARK for MARITIME GREENWICH
WESTCOMBE PARK
MAZE HILL
CHARLTON
Royal Artillery Barracks
DEPTFORD
GREENWICH
DEPTFORD
GREENWICH
Greenwich Park
Plumstead Common
GREENWICH PARK
WOOLWICH COMMON
NEW CROSS GATE
NEW CROSS
NEW CROSS
New Cross Gate
DEPTFORD BRIDGE
SHOOTERS HILL
St. Johns
ST. JOHNS
BLACK HEATH
Blackheath Vale
Eltham Common
ELVERSON RD
LEWISHAM
BLACKHEATH
KIDBROOKE
NUNHEAD
BROCKLEY
LEWISHAM
BLACKHEATH

Lee Valley

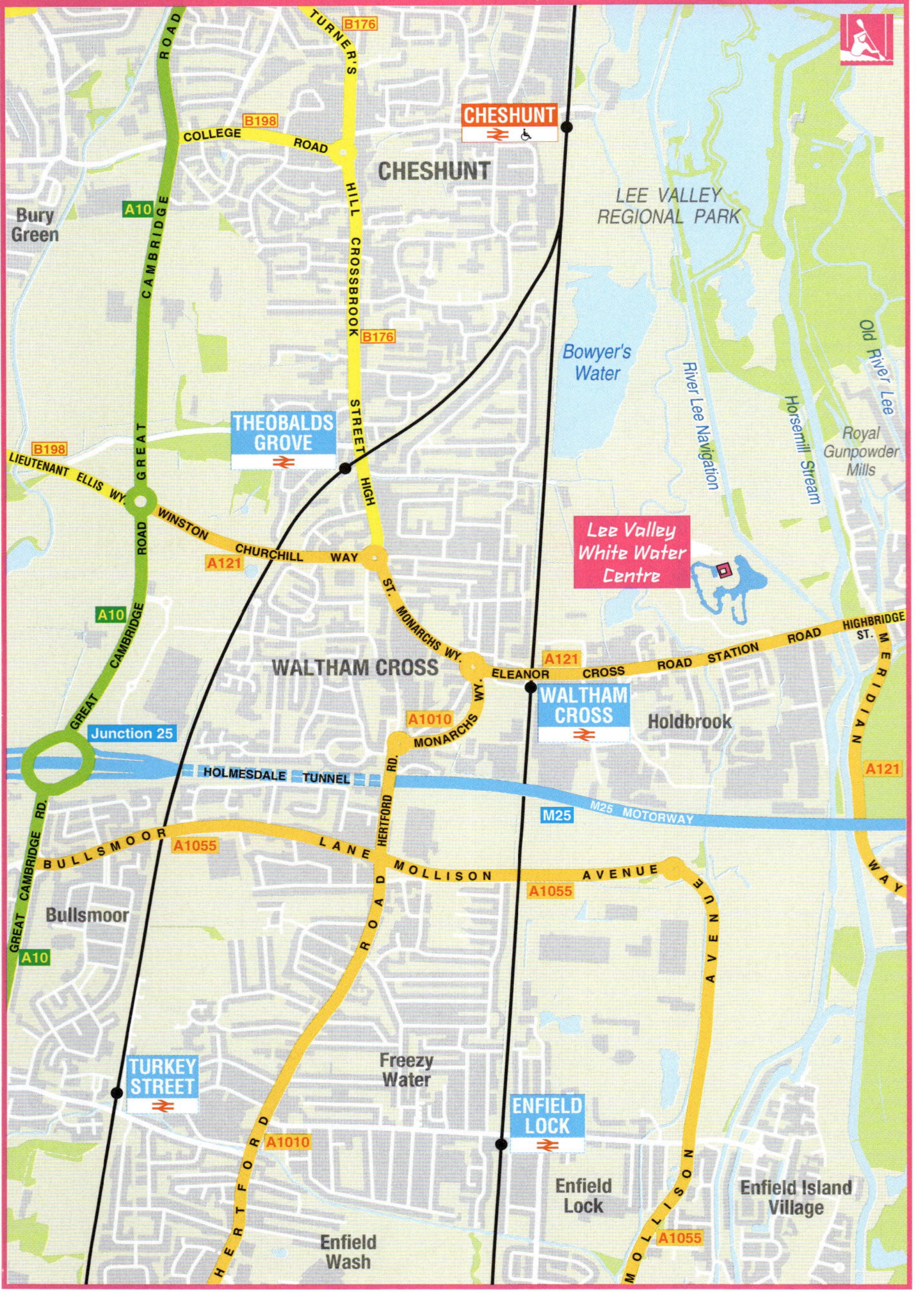

Millennium Stadium - Cardiff

Old Trafford - Manchester

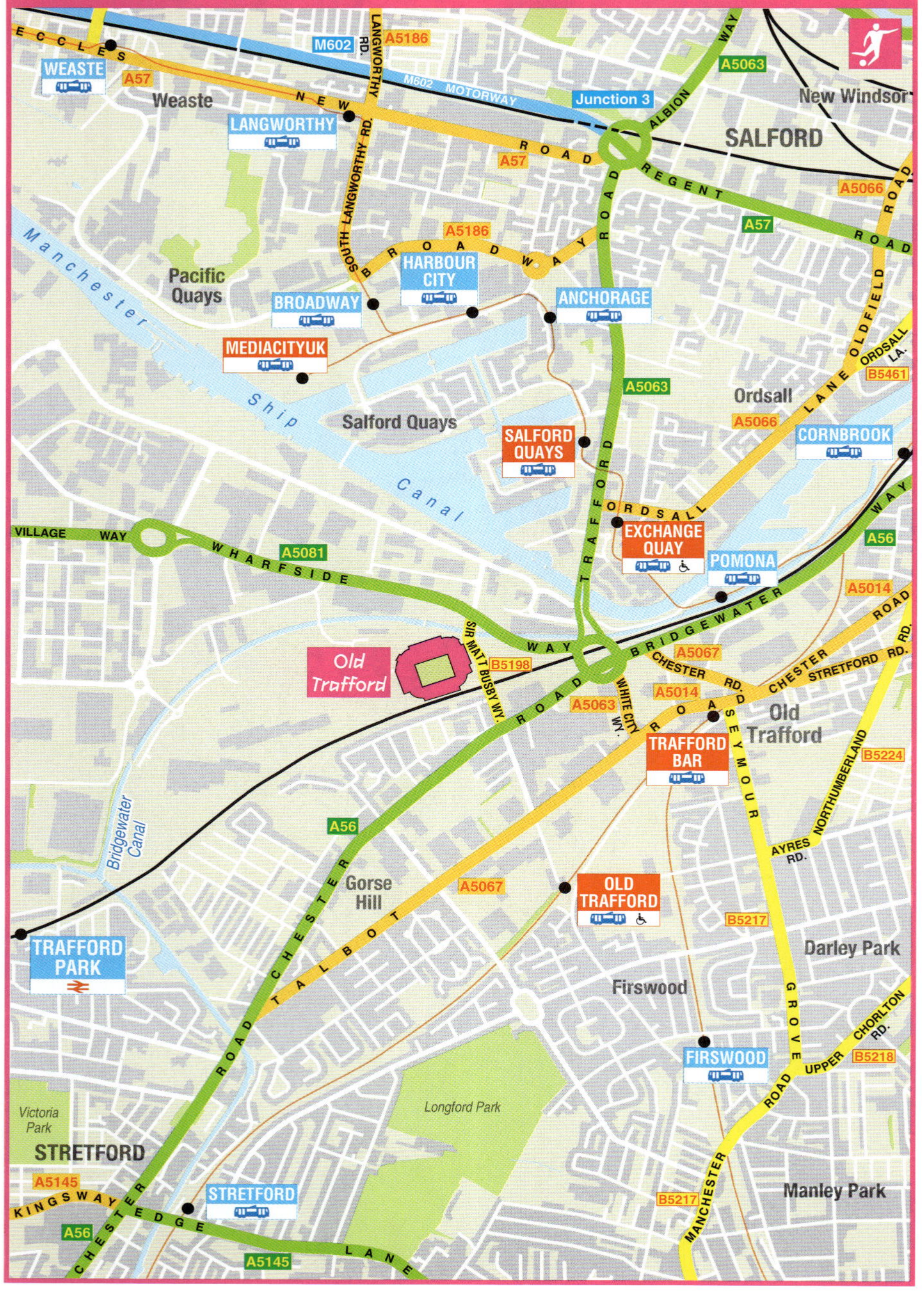

St. James' Park - Newcastle

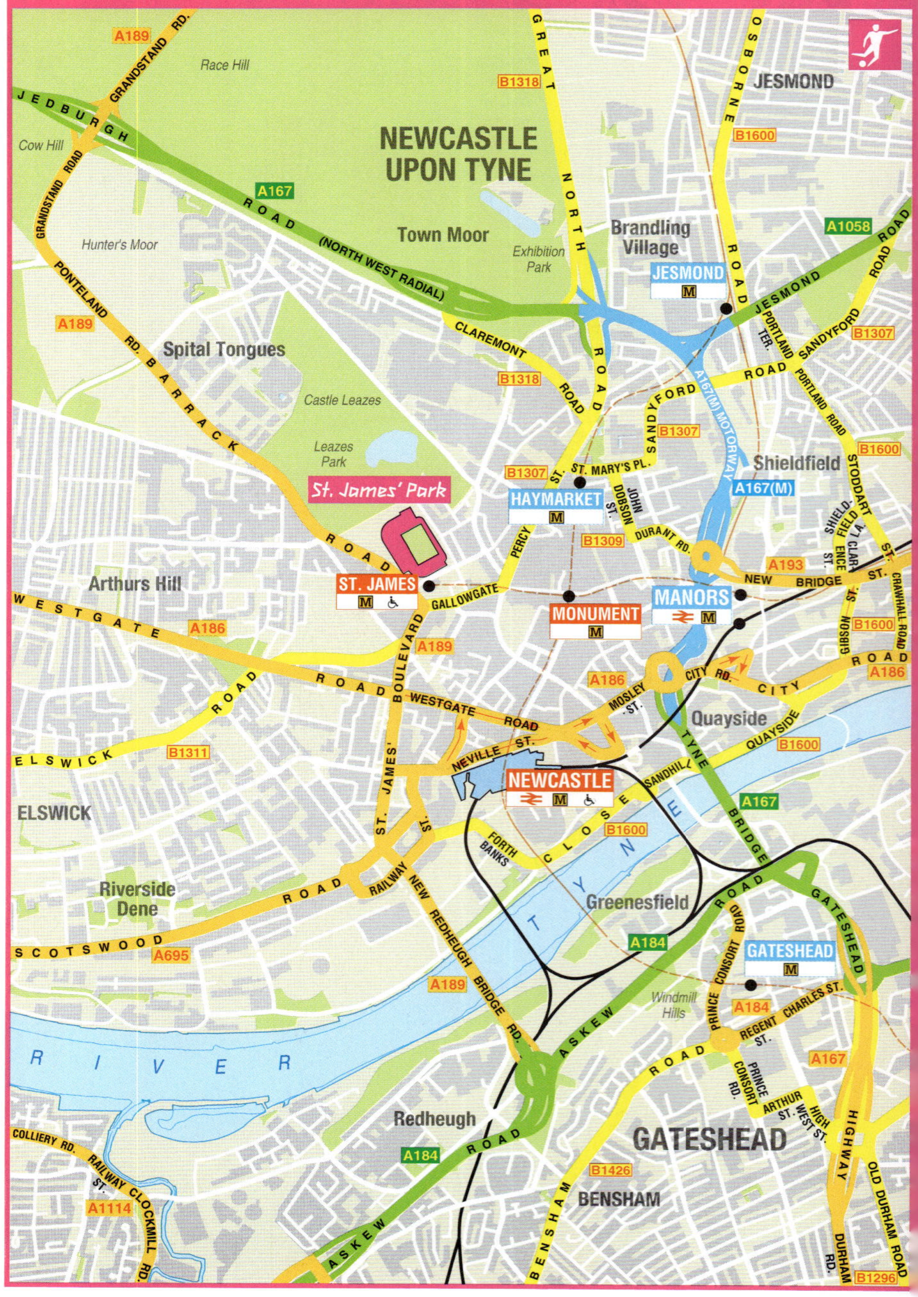

Wembley

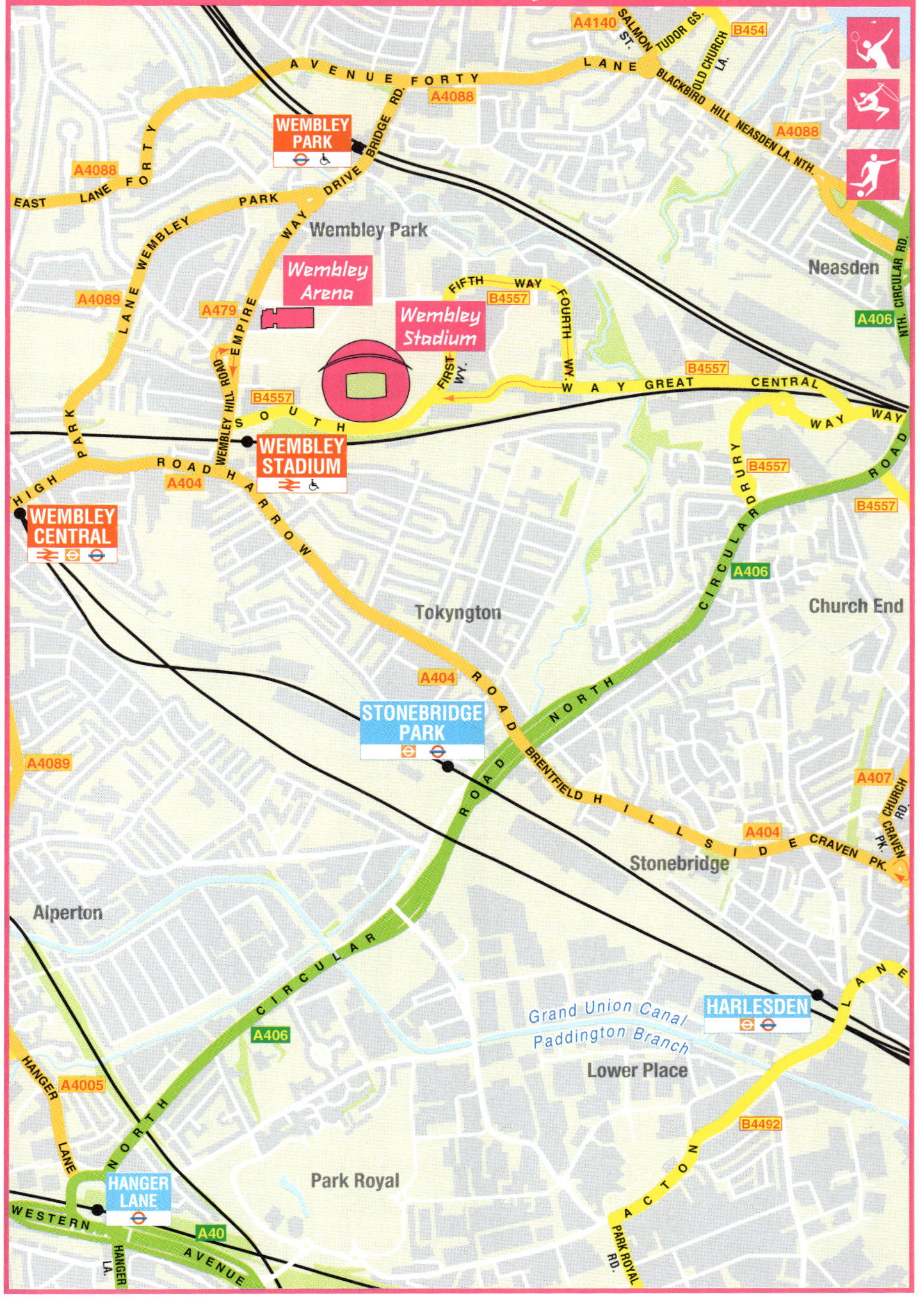

Weymouth and Portland

Wimbledon

INDEX TO CITIES, TOWNS, VILLAGES, HAMLETS, LOCATIONS, AIRPORTS & PORTS

(1) A strict alphabetical order is used e.g. An Dùnan follows Andreas but precedes Andwell

(2) The map reference given refers to the actual map square in which the town spot or built-up area is located and not to the place name.

(3) Major towns, selected airports and ports are shown in bold, i.e. **Aberdeen**. *Aber* 3K **83**

(4) Where two or more places of the same name occur in the same County or Unitary Authority, the nearest large town is also given; e.g. Achiemore. *High* . . . .3L **91** (nr. Durness) indicates that Achiemore is located in square 3L on page **91** and is situated near Durness in the Unitary Authority of Highland.

(5) Only one reference is given although due to page overlaps the place may appear on more than one page.

COUNTIES and UNITARY AUTHORITIES with the abbreviations used in this index

Aberdeen : *Aber*
Aberdeenshire : *Abers*
Angus : *Ang*
Argyll & Bute : *Arg*
Bath & N E Somerset : *Bath*
Bedford : *Bed*
Blackburn with Darwen : *Bkbn*
Blackpool : *Bkpl*
Blaenau Gwent : *Blae*
Bournemouth : *Bour*
Bracknell Forest : *Brac*
Bridgend : *B'end*
Brighton & Hove : *Brig*
Bristol : *Bris*
Buckinghamshire : *Buck*
Caerphilly : *Cphy*
Cambridgeshire : *Cambs*
Cardiff : *Card*
Carmarthenshire : *Carm*
Central Bedfordshire : *C Beds*
Ceredigion : *Cdgn*
Cheshire East : *Ches E*
Cheshire West & Chester : *Ches W*
Clackmannanshire : *Clac*
Conwy : *Cnwy*
Cornwall : *Corn*
Cumbria : *Cumb*
Darlington : *Darl*
Denbighshire : *Den*
Derby : *Derb*
Derbyshire : *Derbs*
Devon : *Devn*
Dorset : *Dors*
Dumfries & Galloway : *Dum*
Dundee : *D'dee*
Durham : *Dur*
East Ayrshire : *E Ayr*
East Dunbartonshire : *E Dun*
East Lothian : *E Lot*
East Renfrewshire : *E Ren*
East Riding of Yorkshire : *E Yor*
East Sussex : *E Sus*
Edinburgh : *Edin*
Essex : *Essx*
Falkirk : *Falk*
Fife : *Fife*
Flintshire : *Flin*
Glasgow : *Glas*
Gloucestershire : *Glos*
Greater London : *G Lon*
Greater Manchester : *G Man*
Gwynedd : *Gwyn*
Halton : *Hal*
Hampshire : *Hants*
Hartlepool : *Hart*
Herefordshire : *Here*
Hertfordshire : *Herts*
Highland : *High*
Inverclyde : *Inv*
Isle of Anglesey : *IOA*
Isle of Man : *IOM*
Isle of Wight : *IOW*
Isles of Scilly : *IOS*
Kent : *Kent*
Kingston upon Hull : *Hull*
Lancashire : *Lanc*
Leicester : *Leic*
Leicestershire : *Leics*
Lincolnshire : *Linc*
Luton : *Lutn*
Medway : *Medw*
Merseyside : *Mers*
Merthyr Tydfil : *Mer T*
Middlesbrough : *Midd*
Midlothian : *Midl*
Milton Keynes : *Mil*
Monmouthshire : *Mon*
Moray : *Mor*
Neath Port Talbot : *Neat*
Newport : *Newp*
Norfolk : *Norf*
Northamptonshire : *Nptn*
North Ayrshire : *N Ayr*
North East Lincolnshire : *NE Lin*
North Lanarkshire : *N Lan*
North Lincolnshire : *N Lin*
North Somerset : *N Som*
Northumberland : *Nmbd*
North Yorkshire : *N Yor*
Nottingham : *Nott*
Nottinghamshire : *Notts*
Orkney : *Orkn*
Oxfordshire : *Oxon*
Pembrokeshire : *Pemb*
Perth & Kinross : *Per*
Peterborough : *Pet*
Plymouth : *Plym*
Poole : *Pool*
Portsmouth : *Port*
Powys : *Powy*
Reading : *Read*
Redcar & Cleveland : *Red C*
Renfrewshire : *Ren*
Rhondda Cynon Taff : *Rhon*
Rutland : *Rut*
Scottish Borders : *Bord*
Shetland : *Shet*
Shropshire : *Shrp*
Slough : *Slo*
Somerset : *Som*
Southampton : *Sotn*
South Ayrshire : *S Ayr*
Southend-on-Sea : *S'end*
South Gloucestershire : *S Glo*
South Lanarkshire : *S Lan*
South Yorkshire : *S Yor*
Staffordshire : *Staf*
Stirling : *Stir*
Stockton-on-Tees : *Stoc T*
Stoke-on-Trent : *Stoke*
Suffolk : *Suff*
Surrey : *Surr*
Swansea : *Swan*
Swindon : *Swin*
Telford & Wrekin : *Telf*
Thurrock : *Thur*
Torbay : *Torb*
Torfaen : *Torf*
Tyne & Wear : *Tyne*
Vale of Glamorgan, The : *V Glam*
Warrington : *Warr*
Warwickshire : *Warw*
West Berkshire : *W Ber*
West Dunbartonshire : *W Dun*
Western Isles : *W Isl*
West Lothian : *W Lot*
West Midlands : *W Mid*
West Sussex : *W Sus*
West Yorkshire : *W Yor*
Wiltshire : *Wilts*
Windsor & Maidenhead : *Wind*
Wokingham : *Wok*
Worcestershire : *Worc*
Wrexham : *Wrex*
York : *York*

INDEX

A

Aston—Binley

Aston. Wok 5H 35
Aston Abbotts. Buck 1J 35
Aston Botterell. Shrp 2A 60
Aston-by-Stone. Staf 3G 41
Aston Cantlow. Warw 6M 41
Aston Clinton. Buck 2J 35
Aston Crews. Here 1E 33
Aston Cross. Glos 8H 33
Aston End. Herts 1K 36
Aston Eyre. Shrp 2G 41
Aston Fields. Worc 5K 41
Aston Flamville. Leic 2C 42
Aston Ingham. Here 1E 33
Aston juxta Mondrum. Ches E 4D 48
...

B

Babbacombe. Torb 3L 21
Babbinswood. Shrp 7A 48
Babb's Green. Herts 2B 36
Babcary. Som 3D 8
Babel. Carm 1J 39
Babell. Flin 2L 47
Babingley. Norf 7C 52
Bablock Hythe. Oxon 3B 36
Babraham. Cambs 6B 30
Babworth. Notts 1D 42
Bac. W Isl 7G 83
...

A-Z Great Britain Road Atlas 111

Binnegar. Dors 7H 25
Binniehill. Falk 2G 71
Binsoe. N Yor 6B 60
Binstead. IOW 6F 26
Binstead. W Sus 5K 27
Binsted. Hants 1H 27
Binton. Warw 6M 41
Bintree. Norf 5G 53
Binweston. Shrp 1D 40
Birch. Essx 2H 37
Birchall. Staf 4G 49
Bircham Newton. Norf 4D 52
Bircham Tofts. Norf 4D 52
Birchanger. Essx 1D 36
Birchburn. N Ayr 7H 69
Birch Cross. Staf 6J 49
Bircher. Here 5E 40
Birch Green. Essx 2H 37
Birchgrove. Card 6D 32
Birchgrove. Swan 4M 31
Birch Heath. Ches W 3C 48
Birch Hill. Ches W 8D 54
Birchill. Devn 5C 24
Birchington. Kent 7L 37
Birch Langley. G Man 5G 55
Birchley Heath. Warw 2A 42
Birchmoor. Warw 1A 42
Birchmoor Green. C Beds 8H 43
Birchover. Derbs 3K 49
Birch Vale. Derbs 7J 55
Birchview. Mor 6B 88
Birchwood. Linc 3F 50
Birchwood. Som 4B 24
Birchwood. Warr 6E 54
Bircotes. Notts 6C 56
Birdbrook. Essx 7D 44
Birdham. W Sus 5J 27
Birdholme. Derbs 3L 49
Birdingbury. Warw 5C 42
Birdlip. Glos 2M 33
Birdsall. N Yor 7H 61
Birds Edge. W Yor 5L 55
Birds Green. Essx 3D 36
Birdsgreen. Shrp 3H 41
Birdsmoorgate. Dors 5C 24
Birdston. E Dun 2E 70
Birdwell. S Yor 5M 55
Birdwood. Glos 2K 33
Birgham. Bord 6G 73
Birichen. High 2K 87
Birkby. Cumb 8H 65
Birkby. N Yor 3C 60
Birkdale. Mers 4B 54
Birkenhead. Mers 7B 54
Birkenhills. Abers 5H 89
Birkenshaw. N Lan 3E 70
Birkenshaw. W Yor 3L 55
Birkhall. Abers 4D 82
Birkhill. Ang 2J 77
Birkholme. Linc 7F 50
Birkin. N Yor 3B 56
Birley. Here 6E 40
Birling. Kent 7E 36
Birling. Nmbd 1H 67
Birling Gap. E Sus 8D 28
Birlingham. Worc 7K 41
Birmingham. W Mid 3L 41
Birmingham International Airport. W Mid 3M 41
Birnam. Per 1F 76
Birsay. Orkn 5A 94
Birse. Abers 4F 82
Birsemore. Abers 4F 82
Birstall. Leics 1D 42
Birstall. W Yor 3L 55
Birstall Smithies. W Yor 3L 55
Birstwith. N Yor 8B 60
Birthorpe. Linc 6H 51
Birtle. Lanc 4G 55
Birtley. Here 5D 40
Birtley. Nmbd 4D 66
Birtley. Tyne 6H 67
Birtsmorton. Worc 8J 41
Birts Street. Worc 8H 41
Bisbrooke. Rut 2G 43
Bisham. Wind 5J 35
Bishampton. Worc 6K 41
Bish Mill. Devn 3J 23
Bishop Auckland. Dur 1B 60
Bishopbridge. Linc 6G 57
Bishopbriggs. E Dun 2E 70
Bishop Burton. E Yor 2F 56
Bishopdown. Wilts 2B 26
Bishop Middleham. Dur 8J 67
Bishopmill. Mor 3C 88
Bishop Monkton. N Yor 7C 60
Bishop Norton. Linc 6F 56
Bishopsbourne. Kent 8K 37
Bishops Cannings. Wilts 7A 34
Bishop's Castle. Shrp 3D 40
Bishop's Caundle. Dors 4F 24
Bishop's Cleeve. Glos 1M 33
Bishop's Down. Dors 4F 24
Bishop's Frome. Here 7G 41
Bishop's Green. Essx 2E 36
Bishop's Green. Hants 7F 34
Bishop's Hull. Som 3B 24
Bishop's Itchington. Warw 6B 42
Bishops Lydeard. Som 3A 24
Bishop's Norton. Glos 1L 33
Bishop's Nympton. Devn 3J 23
Bishop's Offley. Staf 7E 48
Bishop's Stortford. Herts 1C 36
Bishops Sutton. Hants 2G 27
Bishop's Tachbrook. Warw 5B 42
Bishop's Tawton. Devn 2G 23
Bishopsteignton. Devn 8L 23
Bishopstoke. Hants 4E 26
Bishopston. Swan 5K 31
Bishopstone. Buck 2J 35
Bishopstone. E Sus 7C 28
Bishopstone. Here 7E 40
Bishopstone. Swin 5C 34
Bishopstone. Wilts 3A 26
Bishopstrow. Wilts 1H 25
Bishop Sutton. Bath 8H 33
Bishop's Waltham. Hants 4F 26
Bishopswood. Som 4B 24
Bishops Wood. Staf 1J 41
Bishopsworth. Bris 7H 33
Bishop Thornton. N Yor 7B 60
Bishopthorpe. York 1B 56
Bishopton. Darl 1C 60
Bishopton. Dum 7B 64
Bishopton. N Yor 6C 60
Bishopton. Ren 2C 70
Bishopton. Warw 6M 41
Bishop Wilton. E Yor 8G 61
Bishton. Newp 5F 32
Bishton. Staf 7H 49
Bisley. Glos 3M 33
Bisley. Surr 8K 35
Bispham. Bkpl 1B 54
Bispham Green. Lanc 4C 54
Bissoe. Corn 5E 19
Bisterne. Hants 5B 26
Bisterne Close. Hants 5C 26
Bitchfield. Linc 7F 50
Bittadon. Devn 1G 23
Bittaford. Devn 4H 21
Bittering. Norf 6F 52
Bitterley. Shrp 4F 40
Bitterne. Sotn 4E 26
Bitteswell. Leics 3D 42
Bitton. S Glo 7J 33
Bix. Oxon 5H 35
Bixter. Shet 6D 95
Blaby. Leics 2D 42
Blackawton. Devn 4K 21
Black Bank. Cambs 3B 44
Black Barn. Linc 7L 51
Blackborough. Devn 5M 23
Blackborough. Norf 6C 52
Blackborough End. Norf 6C 52
Black Bourton. Oxon 3C 34
Blackboys. E Sus 5D 28
Blackbrook. Derbs 5L 49
Blackbrook. Mers 6D 54
Blackbrook. Staf 6E 48
Blackbrook. Surr 1M 27
Blackburn. Abers 2J 83
Blackburn. Bkbn 3E 54
Blackburn. W Lot 3H 71
Black Callerton. Tyne 5G 67
Black Carr. Norf 2G 45
Black Clauchrie. S Ayr 3M 63
Black Corries. High 8E 80
Black Crofts. Arg 2G 75
Black Cross. Corn 3A 20
Blackden Heath. Ches E 8F 54
Blackditch. Oxon 3E 34
Blackdog. Abers 2K 83
Black Dog. Devn 5K 23
Blackdown. Dors 5C 24
Blackdyke. Cumb 6J 65
Blacker Hill. S Yor 5M 55
Blackfen. G Lon 6C 36
Blackfield. Hants 5E 26
Blackford. Cumb 5L 65
Blackford. Per 5D 76
Blackford. Shrp 3F 40
Blackford. Som 1D 24
(nr. Burnham-on-Sea)
Blackford. Som 3F 24
(nr. Wincanton)
Blackfordby. Leics 8L 49
Blackgang. IOW 8E 26
Blackhall. Edin 2L 71
Blackhall. Ren 3C 70
Blackhall Colliery. Dur 8K 67
Blackhall Mill. Tyne 6G 67
Blackhall Rocks. Dur 8K 67
Blackham. E Sus 4C 28
Blackheath. Essx 1J 37
Blackheath. G Lon 6B 36
Blackheath. Suff 4L 45
Blackheath. Surr 1L 27
Blackheath. W Mid 3K 41
Black Heddon. Nmbd 4F 66
Blackhill. Abers 5L 89
Blackhill. High 6H 85
Black Hill. Warw 6A 42
Blackhills. Abers 3K 89
Blackhills. High 6M 87
Blackjack. Linc 6J 51
Blackland. Wilts 7A 34
Black Lane. G Man 5F 54
Blackleach. Lanc 2C 54
Blackley. G Man 5G 55
Blackley. W Yor 4K 55
Blacklunans. Per 7B 82
Blackmill. B'end 5B 32
Blackmoor. G Man 5E 54
Blackmoor. Hants 2H 27
Blackmoor Gate. Devn 1H 23
Blackmore. Essx 3E 36
Blackmore End. Essx 8D 44
Blackmore End. Herts 2M 35
Black Mount. Arg 1K 75
Blackness. Falk 2J 71
Blacknest. Hants 1H 27
Blackney. Dors 6D 24
Blacknoll. Dors 7H 25
Black Notley. Essx 1F 36
Blacko. Lanc 1G 55
Black Pill. Swan 4L 31
Blackpool. Bkpl 2B 54
Blackpool. Devn 5K 21
Blackpool Airport. Lanc 2B 54
Blackpool Corner. Devn 6C 24
Blackpool Gate. Cumb 4A 66
Blackridge. W Lot 3H 71
Blackrock. Arg 3B 68
Blackrock. Mon 2E 32
Blackrod. G Man 4E 54
Blackshaw. Dum 5H 65
Blackshaw Head. W Yor 3H 55
Blackshaw Moor. Staf 4H 49
Blacksmith's Green. Suff 5H 45
Blacksnape. Bkbn 3F 54
Blackstone. W Sus 6A 28
Black Street. Suff 3M 45
Black Tar. Pemb 3D 30
Blackthorn. Oxon 2G 35
Blackthorpe. Suff 5F 44
Blacktoft. E Yor 3E 56
Blacktop. Aber 3J 83
Black Torrington. Devn 5F 22
Blacktown. Newp 5E 32
Blackwall Tunnel. G Lon 5B 36
Blackwater. Corn 5E 19
Blackwater. Hants 8J 35
Blackwater. IOW 7F 26
Blackwater. Som 4B 24
Blackwaterfoot. N Ayr 7G 69
Blackwell. Darl 2B 60
Blackwell. Derbs 4A 50
(nr. Alfreton)
Blackwell. Derbs 8K 55
(nr. Buxton)
Blackwell. Som 3M 23
Blackwell. Warw 7A 42
Blackwell. Worc 4K 41
Blackwood. Cphy 4D 32
Blackwood. Dum 3G 65
Blackwood. S Lan 5F 70
Blackwood Hill. Staf 4G 49
Blacon. Ches W 3A 48
Bladnoch. Dum 6B 64
Bladon. Oxon 2E 34
Blaenannerch. Cdgn 7E 38
Blaenau Dolwyddelan. Cnwy 4F 46
Blaenau Ffestiniog. Gwyn 5G 47
Blaenavon. Torf 3E 32
Blaenawey. Mon 2E 32
Blaen Celyn. Cdgn 6F 38
Blaen Clydach. Rhon 4B 32
Blaendulais. Neat 3A 32
Blaenffos. Pemb 8D 38
Blaengarw. B'end 4B 32
Blaen-geuffordd. Cdgn 3J 39
Blaengwrach. Neat 3A 32
Blaengwynfi. Neat 4A 32
Blaenllechau. Rhon 4C 32
Blaenpennal. Cdgn 5J 39
Blaenplwyf. Cdgn 4H 39
Blaenporth. Cdgn 7E 38
Blaenrhondda. Rhon 4B 32
Blaenwaun. Carm 1G 31
Blaen-y-coed. Carm 1H 31
Blaenycwm. Rhon 4B 32
Blagdon. N Som 8H 33
Blagdon. Torb 3K 21
Blagdon Hill. Som 4B 24
Blagill. Cumb 7C 66
Blaguegate. Lanc 5C 54
Blaich. High 6C 80
Blain. High 7L 79
Blaina. Blae 3E 32
Blair Atholl. Per 7L 81
Blair Drummond. Stir 6C 76
Blairgowrie. Per 1G 77
Blairhall. Fife 1J 71
Blairingone. Per 6E 76
Blairlogie. Stir 6D 76
Blairmore. Abers 6E 88
Blairmore. Arg 1K 69
Blairmore. High 4J 91
Blairquhanan. W Dun 1C 70
Blaisdon. Glos 2K 33
Blakebrook. Worc 4J 41
Blakedown. Worc 4J 41
Blake End. Essx 1F 36
Blakemere. Here 7D 40
Blakeney. Glos 3J 33
Blakeney. Norf 3G 53
Blakenhall. Ches E 5E 48
Blakenhall. W Mid 2J 41
Blakeshall. Worc 3J 41
Blakesley. Nptn 6E 42
Blanchland. Nmbd 6E 66
Blandford Camp. Dors 5J 25
Blandford Forum. Dors 5H 25
Blandford St Mary. Dors 5H 25
Bland Hill. N Yor 8B 60
Blandy. High 4B 92
Blanefield. Stir 2D 70
Blankney. Linc 3G 51
Blantyre. S Lan 4E 70
Blarmachfoldach. High 7C 80
Blarnalearoch. High 2D 86
Blashford. Hants 5B 26
Blaston. Leics 2G 43
Blatchbridge. Som 1G 25
Blathaisbhal. W Isl 4C 84
Blatherwycke. Nptn 2H 43
Blawith. Cumb 5D 58
Blaxhall. Suff 6K 45
Blaxton. S Yor 5C 56
Blaydon. Tyne 5G 67
Bleadney. Som 1D 24
Bleadon. N Som 8F 32
Blean. Kent 7K 37
Bleasby. Linc 7H 57
Bleasby. Notts 5D 50
Bleasby Moor. Linc 7H 57
Blebocraigs. Fife 4K 77
Bleddfa. Powy 5C 40
Bledington. Glos 1C 34
Bledlow. Buck 3H 35
Bledlow Ridge. Buck 4H 35
Blencarn. Cumb 8B 66
Blencogo. Cumb 7J 65
Blendworth. Hants 4H 27
Blenheim. Oxon 3F 34
Blennerhasset. Cumb 7J 65
Bletchingdon. Oxon 2F 34
Bletchingley. Surr 8B 36
Bletchley. Mil 8G 43
Bletchley. Shrp 6D 48
Bletherston. Pemb 1E 30
Bletsoe. Bed 6J 43
Blewbury. Oxon 5F 34
Blickling. Norf 5H 53
Blidworth. Notts 4B 50
Blindburn. Nmbd 8H 73
Blindcrake. Cumb 8J 65
Blindley Heath. Surr 3B 28
Blindmoor. Som 4B 24
Blisland. Corn 8B 22
Blissford. Hants 4B 26
Bliss Gate. Worc 4H 41
Blists Hill. Telf 1G 41
Blisworth. Nptn 6F 42
Blithbury. Staf 7H 49
Blitterlees. Cumb 6J 65
Blockley. Glos 8M 41
Blofield. Norf 1K 45
Blofield Heath. Norf 6K 53
Blo' Norton. Norf 4G 45
Bloomfield. Bord 7E 72
Blore. Staf 5J 49
Blount's Green. Staf 6H 49
Bloxham. Oxon 8C 42
Bloxholm. Linc 4G 51
Bloxwich. W Mid 1L 41
Bloxworth. Dors 6H 25
Blubberhouses. N Yor 8A 60
Blue Anchor. Som 1M 23
Blue Anchor. Swan 4K 31
Blue Bell Hill. Kent 7F 36
Blue Row. Essx 2J 37
Bluetown. Kent 8H 37
Blundeston. Suff 2M 45
Blunham. C Beds 6K 43
Blunsdon St Andrew. Swin 5B 34
Bluntington. Worc 4J 41
Bluntisham. Cambs 4M 43
Blunts. Corn 3E 20
Blurton. Stoke 5F 48
Blyborough. Linc 6F 56
Blyford. Suff 4L 45
Blymhill. Staf 8F 48
Blymhill Lawns. Staf 8F 48
Blyth. Nmbd 3J 67
Blyth. Notts 7C 56
Blyth. Bord 5K 71
Blyth Bank. Bord 5K 71
Blyth Bridge. Bord 5K 71
Blythburgh. Suff 4L 45
Blythe Bridge. Staf 5G 49
Blythe Marsh. Staf 5G 49
Blythe, The. Staf 7H 49
Blyton. Linc 6E 56
Boarhills. Fife 4L 77
Boarhunt. Hants 5G 27
Boarshead. E Sus 4D 28
Boar's Head. G Man 5D 54
Boars Hill. Oxon 3E 34
Boarstall. Buck 2G 35
Boasley Cross. Devn 6G 23
Boath. High 4H 87
Boat of Garten. High 2M 81
Bobbing. Kent 7G 37
Bobbington. Staf 2J 41
Bobbingworth. Essx 3D 36
Bocaddon. Corn 4C 20
Bocking. Essx 1F 36
Bocking Churchstreet. Essx 1F 36
Boddam. Abers 5M 89
Boddam. Shet 10D 95
Boddington. Glos 1L 33
Bodedern. IOA 1C 46
Bodelwyddan. Den 2K 47
Bodenham. Here 6F 40
Bodenham. Wilts 3B 26
Bodewryd. IOA 1C 46
Bodfari. Den 2K 47
Bodffordd. IOA 2D 46
Bodham. Norf 3H 53
Bodiam. E Sus 5F 28
Bodicote. Oxon 8C 42
Bodieve. Corn 8A 22
Bodinnick. Corn 4C 20
Bodle Street Green. E Sus 6E 28
Bodmin. Corn 3B 20
Bodnant. Cnwy 2H 47
Bodney. Norf 2E 44
Bodorgan. IOA 3C 46
Bodrane. Corn 3D 20
Bodsham. Kent 3K 29
Boduan. Gwyn 6C 46
Bodymoor Heath. Warw 2M 41
Bogallan. High 6J 87
Bogbrae Croft. Abers 6L 89
Bogend. S Ayr 6B 70
Boghall. Midl 3L 71
Boghall. W Lot 3H 71
Boghead. S Lan 5F 70
Bogindollo. Ang 8E 82
Bogmoor. Mor 3D 88
Bogniebrae. Abers 5F 88
Bognor Regis. W Sus 6K 27
Bograxie. Abers 2H 83
Bogside. N Lan 4G 71
Bog, The. Shrp 2D 40
Bogton. Abers 4G 89
Bogue. Dum 3D 64
Bohenie. High 5E 80
Bohortha. Corn 6F 19
Boirseam. W Isl 3E 84
Bokiddick. Corn 3B 20
Bolam. Dur 1A 60
Bolam. Nmbd 3F 66
Bolberry. Devn 6H 21
Bold Heath. Mers 7D 54
Boldon. Tyne 5J 67
Boldon Colliery. Tyne 5J 67
Boldre. Hants 6D 26
Boldron. Dur 2M 59
Bole. Notts 7D 56
Bolehall. Staf 1A 42
Bolehill. Derbs 4K 49
Bolenowe. Corn 6D 19
Boleside. Bord 6D 72
Bolham. Devn 4L 23
Bolham Water. Devn 4A 24
Bolingey. Corn 4E 19
Bollington. Ches E 8H 55
Bolney. W Sus 5A 28
Bolnhurst. Bed 6J 43
Bolshan. Ang 8G 83
Bolsover. Derbs 8A 56
Bolsterstone. S Yor 6L 55
Bolstone. Here 8F 40
Boltachan. Per 8L 81
Boltby. N Yor 5D 60
Bolton. Cumb 1H 59
Bolton. E Lot 2E 72
Bolton. E Yor 8G 61
Bolton. G Man 5F 54
Bolton. Nmbd 8L 73
Bolton Abbey. N Yor 8M 59
Bolton-by-Bowland. Lanc 1F 54
Boltonfellend. Cumb 5M 65
Boltongate. Cumb 7K 65
Bolton Green. Lanc 4D 54
Bolton-le-Sands. Lanc 7F 58
Bolton Low Houses. Cumb 7K 65
Bolton New Houses. Cumb 7K 65
Bolton-on-Swale. N Yor 4B 60
Bolton Percy. N Yor 1B 56
Bolton Town End. Lanc 7F 58
Bolton upon Dearne. S Yor 5A 56
Bolton Wood Lane. Cumb 7K 65
Bolventor. Corn 8C 22
Bomarsund. Nmbd 3H 67
Bomere Heath. Shrp 8B 48
Bonar Bridge. High 2J 87
Bonawe. Arg 2H 75
Bonby. N Lin 4G 57
Boncath. Pemb 8E 38
Bonchester Bridge. Bord 8E 72
Bonchurch. IOW 8F 26
Bond End. Staf 8J 49
Bondleigh. Devn 5H 23
Bonds. Lanc 1C 54
Bonehill. Devn 8J 23
Bonehill. Staf 1M 41
Bo'ness. Falk 1H 71
Boney Hay. Staf 8H 49
Bonham. Wilts 2G 25
Bonhill. W Dun 2B 70
Boningale. Shrp 1J 41
Bonjedward. Bord 7F 72
Bonkle. N Lan 4G 71
Bonnington. Ang 2L 77
Bonnington. Edin 3K 71
Bonnington. Kent 4J 29
Bonnybank. Fife 5J 77
Bonnybridge. Falk 1G 71
Bonnykelly. Abers 4J 89
Bonnyrigg. Midl 3M 71
Bonnyton. Ang 2J 77
Bonnytown. Fife 4L 77
Bonsall. Derbs 4K 49
Bont. Mon 2F 32
Bontddu. Gwyn 8F 46
Bont Dolgadfan. Powy 1L 39
Bontgoch. Cdgn 3J 39
Bonthorpe. Linc 8L 57
Bontnewydd. Cdgn 5J 39
Bont-newydd. Cnwy 2K 47
Bontnewydd. Gwyn 3D 46
(nr. Caernarfon)
Bont Newydd. Gwyn 5G 47
(nr. Llan Ffestiniog)
Bontuchel. Den 4K 47
Bonvilston. V Glam 6C 32
Bon-y-maen. Swan 4L 31
Booker. Buck 4J 35
Booley. Shrp 7C 48
Boorley Green. Hants 4F 26
Boosbeck. Red C 2F 60
Boot. Cumb 3C 58
Booth. W Yor 3J 55
Boothby Graffoe. Linc 4F 50
Boothby Pagnell. Linc 6F 50
Booth Green. Ches E 7H 55
Booth of Toft. Shet 4E 95
Boothstown. G Man 5F 54
Boothville. Nptn 5F 42
Booth Wood. W Yor 4J 55
Bootle. Cumb 5C 58
Bootle. Mers 6B 54
Booton. Norf 5H 53
Booze. N Yor 3M 59
Boquhan. Stir 1D 70
Boraston. Shrp 4G 41
Borden. Kent 7G 37
Borden. W Sus 3J 27
Bordlands. Bord 5K 71
Bordley. N Yor 7L 59
Bordon. Hants 2J 27
Boreham. Essx 3F 36
Boreham. Wilts 1H 25
Boreham Street. E Sus 6E 28
Borehamwood. Herts 4M 35
Boreland. Dum 2J 65
Boreston. Devn 4J 21
Borestone Brae. Stir 6D 76
Boreton. Shrp 1F 40
Borgh. W Isl 3A 78
(on Barra)
Borgh. W Isl 6B 84
(on Benbecula)
Borgh. W Isl 3D 84
(on Berneray)
Borgh. W Isl 3E 90
(on Isle of Lewis)
Borghasdal. W Isl 3E 84
Borghastan. W Isl 4B 90
Borgh na Sgiotaig. High 4H 85
Borgie. High 4B 92
Borgue. Dum 7D 64
Borgue. High 7G 93
Borley. Essx 7E 44
Borley Green. Essx 7E 44
Borley Green. Suff 5F 44
Borlum. High 1H 81
Bornais. W Isl 1B 78
Bornesketaig. High 4H 85
Boroughbridge. N Yor 7C 60
Borough Green. Kent 8E 36
Borras Head. Wrex 4A 48
Borreraig. High 6F 84
Borrobol Lodge. High 7D 92
Borrodale. High 7F 84
Borrowash. Derb 6A 50
Borrowby. N Yor 5D 60
(nr. Northallerton)
Borrowby. N Yor 2G 61
(nr. Whitby)
Borrowston. High 5J 93
Borrowstonehill. Orkn 7C 94
Borrowstoun. Falk 1H 71
Borstal. Medw 7F 36
Borth. Cdgn 3J 39
Borthwick. Midl 4M 71
Borth-y-Gest. Gwyn 6E 46
Borve. High 7J 85
Borwick. Lanc 6G 59
Bosbury. Here 7G 41
Boscastle. Corn 6B 22
Boscombe. Bour 6B 26
Boscombe. Wilts 2C 26
Boscoppa. Corn 4B 20
Bosham. W Sus 5J 27
Bosherston. Pemb 4D 30
Bosley. Ches E 3G 49
Bossall. N Yor 7G 61
Bossiney. Corn 7B 22
Bossingham. Kent 3K 29
Bossington. Som 1K 23
Bostadh. W Isl 4B 90
Bostock Green. Ches W 3D 48
Boston. Linc 5K 51
Boston Spa. W Yor 1A 56
Boswarthen. Corn 6B 19
Boswinger. Corn 5A 20
Botallack. Corn 6A 19
Botany Bay. G Lon 4A 36
Botcheston. Leics 1C 42
Botesdale. Suff 4G 45
Bothal. Nmbd 3H 67
Bothampstead. W Ber 6F 34
Bothamsall. Notts 8C 56
Bothel. Cumb 8J 65
Bothenhampton. Dors 6D 24
Bothwell. S Lan 4E 70
Botley. Buck 3K 35
Botley. Hants 4F 26
Botley. Oxon 3E 34
Botloe's Green. Glos 1K 33
Botolph Claydon. Buck 1H 35
Botolphs. W Sus 5M 27
Bottacks. High 5G 87
Bottesford. Leics 6E 50
Bottesford. N Lin 5E 56
Bottisham. Cambs 5B 44
Bottlesford. Wilts 8B 34
Bottomcraig. Fife 3J 77
Bottom o' th' Moor. G Man 4E 54
Botton. N Yor 3F 60
Botton Head. Lanc 7H 59
Bottreaux Mill. Devn 3K 23
Botus Fleming. Corn 3F 20
Botwnnog. Gwyn 6B 46
Bough Beech. Kent 3C 28
Boughrood. Powy 8B 40
Boughspring. Glos 4H 33
Boughton. Norf 1C 44
Boughton. Nptn 5F 42
Boughton. Notts 3C 50
Boughton Aluph. Kent 3J 29
Boughton Green. Kent 8F 36
Boughton Lees. Kent 3J 29
Boughton Malherbe. Kent 3G 29
Boughton Monchelsea. Kent 8F 36
Boughton under Blean. Kent 8J 37
Boulby. Red C 2G 61
Bouldnor. IOW 7D 26
Bouldon. Shrp 3F 40
Boulmer. Nmbd 8M 73
Boulston. Pemb 2D 30
Boultham. Linc 3F 50
Boulton. Derb 6L 49
Boundary. Staf 5G 49
Bounds. Here 8G 41
Bourn. Cambs 6M 43
Bournbrook. W Mid 3L 41
Bourne. Linc 7G 51
Bourne End. Bed 5J 43
Bourne End. Buck 5J 35
Bourne End. C Beds 7H 43
Bourne End. Herts 3L 35
Bournemouth. Bour 6A 26
Bournemouth Airport. Dors 6B 26
Bournes Green. Glos 3M 33
Bournes Green. S'end 5H 37
Bourne, The. Surr 1J 27
Bournheath. Worc 4K 41
Bournmoor. Dur 6J 67
Bournville. W Mid 3L 41
Bourton. Dors 2G 25
Bourton. N Som 7F 32
Bourton. Oxon 5C 34
Bourton. Shrp 2F 40
Bourton. Wilts 7A 34
Bourton on Dunsmore. Warw 4C 42
Bourton-on-the-Hill. Glos 8M 41
Bourton-on-the-Water. Glos 1B 34
Bousd. Arg 7G 79
Bousta. Shet 6C 95
Boustead Hill. Cumb 6K 65
Bouth. Cumb 5E 58
Bouthwaite. N Yor 6A 60
Boveney. Buck 6K 35
Boveridge. Dors 4A 26
Boverton. V Glam 7B 32
Bovey Tracey. Devn 8K 23
Bovingdon. Herts 3L 35
Bovingdon Green. Buck 5J 35
Bovinger. Essx 3D 36
Bovington Camp. Dors 7H 25
Bow. Devn 5J 23
Bowbank. Dur 1L 59
Bow Brickhill. Mil 8H 43
Bowbridge. Glos 3L 33
Bowburn. Dur 8J 67
Bowcombe. IOW 7E 26
Bowd. Devn 7A 24
Bowden. Devn 5K 21
Bowden. Bord 6E 72
Bowden Hill. Wilts 7M 33
Bowdens. Som 3D 24
Bowderdale. Cumb 3H 59
Bowdon. G Man 7F 54
Bower. Nmbd 3C 66
Bowerchalke. Wilts 3A 26
Bowerhill. Wilts 7M 33
Bower Hinton. Som 4D 24
Bowermadden. High 3H 93
Bowers. Staf 6F 48
Bowers Gifford. Essx 5F 36
Bowershall. Fife 6F 76
Bowertower. High 3H 93
Bowes. Dur 2L 59
Bowgreave. Lanc 1C 54
Bowhousebog. N Lan 4G 71
Bowithick. Corn 7C 22
Bowland Bridge. Cumb 5F 58
Bowlees. Dur 1L 59
Bowley. Here 6F 40
Bowlhead Green. Surr 2K 27
Bowling. W Dun 2C 70
Bowling. W Yor 2K 55
Bowling Bank. Wrex 5A 48
Bowling Green. Worc 6J 41
Bowlish. Som 1F 24
Bowmanstead. Cumb 4E 58
Bowmore. Arg 4B 68
Bowness-on-Solway. Cumb 5K 65
Bowness-on-Windermere. Cumb 4F 58
Bow of Fife. Fife 4J 77
Bowriefauld. Ang 1L 77
Bowscale. Cumb 8L 65
Bowsden. Nmbd 5J 73
Bowside Lodge. High 3D 92
Bowston. Cumb 4F 58
Bow Street. Cdgn 3J 39
Bowthorpe. Norf 1H 45
Box. Glos 3L 33
Box. Wilts 7L 33
Boxbush. Glos 1J 33
Box End. Bed 7J 43
Boxford. Suff 7F 44
Boxford. W Ber 6E 34
Boxgrove. W Sus 5K 27
Boxley. Kent 8F 36
Boxmoor. Herts 3L 35
Box's Shop. Corn 5D 22
Boxted. Essx 8F 44
Boxted. Suff 6E 44
Boxted Cross. Essx 8G 45
Boxworth. Cambs 5M 43
Boxworth End. Cambs 5M 43
Boyden End. Suff 6D 44
Boyden Gate. Kent 7L 37
Boylestone. Derbs 6J 49
Boylestonfield. Derbs 6J 49
Boyndlie. Abers 3G 89
Boynton. E Yor 7L 61
Boys Hill. Dors 4F 24
Boythorpe. Derbs 3L 49
Boyton. Corn 6E 22
Boyton. Suff 7K 45
Boyton. Wilts 2J 25
Boyton Cross. Essx 3E 36
Boyton End. Essx 8C 44
Boyton End. Suff 7D 44
Bozeat. Nptn 6H 43
Braaid. IOM 6D 62
Braal Castle. High 3G 93
Brabling Green. Suff 5J 45
Brabourne. Kent 3K 29
Brabourne Lees. Kent 3J 29
Brabster. High 3J 93
Bracadale. High 8H 85
Bracara. High 4M 79
Braceborough. Linc 8G 51
Bracebridge. Linc 3F 50
Bracebridge Heath. Linc 3F 50
Braceby. Linc 6G 51
Bracewell. Lanc 1G 55
Brackenber. Cumb 2J 59
Brackenfield. Derbs 4L 49
Brackenlands. Cumb 7K 65
Brackenthwaite. Cumb 7K 65
Brackenthwaite. N Yor 8B 60
Brackla. B'end 6B 32
Brackla. High 6L 87
Bracklesham. W Sus 6J 27
Brackletter. High 5D 80
Brackley. Nptn 8D 42
Brackley Hatch. Nptn 7E 42
Brackloch. High 7J 91
Bracknell. Brac 7J 35
Braco. Per 5D 76
Bracobrae. Mor 4F 88
Bracon. N Lin 5D 56
Bracon Ash. Norf 2H 45
Bradbourne. Derbs 4K 49
Bradbury. Dur 1C 60
Bradda. IOM 6B 62
Bradden. Nptn 7E 42
Bradenham. Buck 4J 35
Bradenham. Norf 1F 44
Bradenstoke. Wilts 6A 34
Bradfield. Essx 8H 45
Bradfield. Norf 4J 53
Bradfield. W Ber 6G 35
Bradfield Combust. Suff 6E 44
Bradfield Green. Ches E 4D 48
Bradfield Heath. Essx 1K 37
Bradfield St Clare. Suff 6F 44
Bradfield St George. Suff 5F 44
Bradford. Derbs 3K 49
Bradford. Devn 5F 22
Bradford. Nmbd 6L 73
Bradford. W Yor 2K 55
Bradford Abbas. Dors 4E 24
Bradford Barton. Devn 4K 23
Bradford Leigh. Wilts 7L 33
Bradford-on-Avon. Wilts 7L 33
Bradford-on-Tone. Som 3A 24
Bradford Peverell. Dors 6F 24
Bradiford. Devn 2G 23
Brading. IOW 7G 27
Bradley. Ches W 8D 54
Bradley. Derbs 5K 49
Bradley. Glos 4K 33
Bradley. Hants 1G 27
Bradley. NE Lin 5J 57
Bradley. N Yor 5M 59
Bradley. Staf 8F 48
Bradley. W Mid 2K 41
Bradley. W Yor 3K 55
Bradley. Wrex 4A 48
Bradley Cross. Som 8G 33
Bradley Green. Ches W 5C 48
Bradley Green. Som 2B 24
Bradley Green. Warw 1A 42
Bradley Green. Worc 5K 41
Bradley in the Moors. Staf 5H 49
Bradley Mount. Ches E 8H 55
Bradley Stoke. S Glo 5J 33
Bradlow. Here 8H 41
Bradmore. Notts 6B 50
Bradmore. W Mid 2J 41
Bradninch. Devn 5M 23
Bradnop. Staf 4H 49
Bradpole. Dors 6D 24
Bradshaw. G Man 4F 54
Bradstone. Devn 7E 22
Bradwall Green. Ches E 3E 48
Bradway. S Yor 7M 55
Bradwell. Derbs 7K 55
Bradwell. Essx 1G 37
Bradwell. Mil 8G 43
Bradwell. Norf 1M 45
Bradwell-on-Sea. Essx 3J 37
Bradwell Waterside. Essx 3H 37
Bradworthy. Devn 4E 22
Brae. High 3A 86
Brae. Shet 5D 95
Braeantra. High 4H 87
Braefield. High 8G 87
Braefindon. High 6J 87
Braegrum. Per 3F 76
Braehead. Ang 8G 83
Braehead. Dum 6B 64
Braehead. Mor 5C 88
Braehead. Orkn 3C 94
Braehead. S Lan 6G 71
(nr. Coalburn)
Braehead. S Lan 4H 71
(nr. Forth)
Braehoulland. Shet 4C 95
Braemar. Abers 4B 82
Braemore. High 6F 92
(nr. Dunbeath)
Braemore. High 4D 86
(nr. Ullapool)
Brae of Achnahaird. High 8H 91
Brae Roy Lodge. High 4F 80
Braeside. Abers 6K 89
Braeside. Inv 2A 70
Braes of Coul. Ang 8C 82
Braeswick. Orkn 4E 94
Braetongue. High 4A 92
Braeval. Stir 5A 76
Braevallich. Arg 5G 75
Braewick. Shet 6D 95
Brafferton. Darl 1B 60
Brafferton. N Yor 6D 60
Brafield-on-the-Green. Nptn 6G 43
Bragar. W Isl 4C 90
Bragbury End. Herts 1A 36
Bragleenbeg. Arg 3G 75
Braichmelyn. Gwyn 3F 46
Braides. Lanc 8F 58
Braidwood. S Lan 5G 71
Braigo. Arg 3A 68
Brailsford. Derbs 5K 49
Braintree. Essx 1F 36
Braiseworth. Suff 4H 45
Braishfield. Hants 3D 26
Braithwaite. Cumb 1D 58
Braithwaite. S Yor 4C 56
Braithwaite. W Yor 1J 55
Braithwell. S Yor 6B 56
Brakefield Green. Norf 1G 45
Bramber. W Sus 4M 27
Brambledown. Kent 6H 37
Brambridge. Hants 3E 26
Bramcote. Notts 6B 50
Bramcote. Warw 3C 42
Bramdean. Hants 3G 27
Bramerton. Norf 1J 45
Bramfield. Herts 2A 36
Bramfield. Suff 4K 45
Bramford. Suff 7H 45
Bramhall. G Man 7G 55
Bramham. W Yor 1A 56
Bramhope. W Yor 1L 55
Bramley. Hants 8G 35
Bramley. S Yor 6A 56
Bramley. Surr 1L 27
Bramley. W Yor 2L 55
Bramley Green. Hants 8G 35
Bramley Head. N Yor 8A 60
Bramley Vale. Derbs 3A 50
Bramling. Kent 8L 37
Brampford Speke. Devn 6L 23
Brampton. Cambs 4L 43
Brampton. Cumb 1H 59
(nr. Appleby-in-Westmorland)
Brampton. Cumb 5A 66
(nr. Carlisle)
Brampton. Linc 8E 56
Brampton. Norf 5J 53
Brampton. S Yor 5A 56
Brampton. Suff 3L 45
Brampton Abbotts. Here 1J 33
Brampton Ash. Nptn 3F 42
Brampton Bryan. Here 4D 40
Brampton en le Morthen. S Yor 7A 56
Bramshall. Staf 6H 49
Bramshaw. Hants 4C 26
Bramshill. Hants 7H 35
Bramshott. Hants 2J 27
Branault. High 7K 79
Brancaster. Norf 3D 52
Brancaster Staithe. Norf 3D 52
Brancepeth. Dur 8H 67
Branch End. Nmbd 5F 66
Branchill. Mor 4A 88
Brand End. Linc 5K 51
Branderburgh. Mor 2C 88
Brandesburton. E Yor 1H 57
Brandeston. Suff 5J 45
Brand Green. Glos 1K 33
Brandhill. Shrp 4E 40
Brandis Corner. Devn 5F 22
Brandish Street. Som 1L 23
Brandiston. Norf 5H 53
Brandon. Dur 8H 67
Brandon. Linc 5F 50
Brandon. Nmbd 8K 73
Brandon. Suff 3D 44
Brandon. Warw 4C 42
Brandon Bank. Cambs 3C 44
Brandon Creek. Norf 2C 44
Brandon Parva. Norf 1G 45
Brandsby. N Yor 6E 60
Brandy Wharf. Linc 6G 57
Brane. Corn 7B 19
Bran End. Essx 1E 36
Branksome. Pool 6A 26
Bransbury. Hants 1E 26
Bransby. Linc 8F 56
Branscombe. Devn 7A 24
Bransford. Worc 6H 41
Bransgore. Hants 6B 26
Bransholme. Hull 2G 57
Bransley. Shrp 4G 41
Branston. Leics 7E 50
Branston. Linc 3G 51
Branston. Staf 7K 49
Branston Booths. Linc 3G 51
Branstone. IOW 7F 26
Bransty. Cumb 2A 58
Brant Broughton. Linc 4F 50
Brantham. Suff 8H 45
Branthwaite. Cumb 8K 65
(nr. Caldbeck)
Branthwaite. Cumb 1B 58
(nr. Workington)
Brantingham. E Yor 3F 56
Branton. Nmbd 8K 73
Branton. S Yor 5C 56
Branton Green. N Yor 7D 60
Branxholme. Bord 8D 72
Branxton. Nmbd 6H 73
Brassington. Derbs 4K 49
Brasted. Kent 8C 36
Brasted Chart. Kent 8C 36
Bratch, The. Staf 2J 41
Brathens. Abers 4G 83
Bratoft. Linc 3L 51
Brattleby. Linc 7F 56
Bratton. Som 1L 23
Bratton. Telf 8D 48
Bratton. Wilts 8M 33
Bratton Clovelly. Devn 6F 22
Bratton Fleming. Devn 2H 23
Bratton Seymour. Som 3F 24
Braughing. Herts 1B 36
Braulen Lodge. High 8E 86
Braunston. Nptn 5D 42
Braunstone Town. Leic 1D 42
Braunston-in-Rutland. Rut 1G 43
Braunton. Devn 2F 22
Brawby. N Yor 6G 61
Brawl. High 3D 92
Brawlbin. High 4F 92
Bray. Wind 6K 35
Braybrooke. Nptn 3F 42
Brayford. Devn 2H 23
Bray Shop. Corn 8E 22
Braystones. Cumb 3B 58
Brayton. N Yor 2C 56
Bray Wick. Wind 6J 35
Brazacott. Corn 6D 22
Brea. Corn 5D 19
Breach. W Sus 5H 27
Breachwood Green. Herts 1M 35
Breacleit. W Isl 5B 90
Breaden Heath. Shrp 6B 48
Breadsall. Derbs 5L 49
Breadstone. Glos 3K 33
Breage. Corn 7D 19
Breakachy. High 7G 87
Breakish. High 1L 79
Bream. Glos 3J 33
Breamore. Hants 4B 26
Bream's Meend. Glos 3J 33
Brean. Som 8E 32
Breanais. W Isl 6A 90
Brearton. N Yor 7C 60
Breascleit. W Isl 5C 90
Breaston. Derbs 6A 50
Brecais Àrd. High 1L 79
Brecais Iosal. High 1L 79
Brechfa. Carm 8H 39
Brechin. Ang 8G 83
Breckles. Norf 2F 44
Brecon. Powy 1C 32
Brecon Beacons. Powy 1B 32
Bredbury. G Man 6H 55
Brede. E Sus 6G 29
Bredenbury. Here 6G 41
Breden's Norton. Worc 8K 41
Bredfield. Suff 6J 45
Bredgar. Kent 7G 37
Bredhurst. Kent 7F 36
Bredicot. Worc 6K 41
Bredon. Worc 8K 41
Bredwardine. Here 7D 40
Breedon on the Hill. Leics 7A 50
Breibhig. W Isl 4A 78
(on Barra)
Breibhig. W Isl 5E 90
(on Isle of Lewis)
Breich. W Lot 3H 71
Breightmet. G Man 4F 54
Breighton. E Yor 2D 56
Breinton. Here 8E 40
Breinton Common. Here 8E 40
Breiwick. Shet 7E 95
Brelston Green. Here 1H 33
Bremhill. Wilts 6M 33
Brenachie. High 4K 87
Brenchley. Kent 3E 28
Brendon. Devn 1J 23
Brent Cross. G Lon 5A 36
Brent Eleigh. Suff 7F 44
Brentford. G Lon 6M 35
Brentingby. Leics 8D 50
Brent Knoll. Som 8F 32
Brent Pelham. Herts 8A 44
Brentwood. Essx 4E 36
Brenzett. Kent 5J 29
Brereton. Staf 8H 49
Brereton Cross. Staf 8H 49
Brereton Green. Ches E 3E 48
Brereton Heath. Ches E 3F 48
Bressingham. Norf 3G 45
Bretby. Derbs 7K 49
Bretford. Warw 4C 42
Bretforton. Worc 7L 41
Bretherdale Head. Cumb 3G 59
Bretherton. Lanc 3C 54
Brettabister. Shet 6E 95
Brettenham. Norf 3F 44
Brettenham. Suff 6F 44
Bretton. Flin 3A 48
Bretton. Pet 1K 43
Brewer Street. Surr 8B 36
Brewlands Bridge. Ang 7B 82
Brewood. Staf 1J 41
Briantspuddle. Dors 6H 25
Bricket Wood. Herts 3M 35
Bricklehampton. Worc 7K 41
Bride. IOM 3E 62
Bridekirk. Cumb 8J 65
Bridell. Pemb 7D 38
Bridestowe. Devn 7G 23
Brideswell. Abers 6F 88
Bridford. Devn 7K 23
Bridge. Corn 5D 19
Bridge. Kent 8K 37
Bridge. Som 5C 24
Bridge End. Bed 6J 43
Bridge End. Cumb 4D 58
(nr. Broughton in Furness)
Bridge End. Cumb 7L 65
(nr. Dalston)
Bridge End. Linc 6H 51
Bridge End. Shet 8D 95
Bridgefoot. Ang 2J 77
Bridgefoot. Cumb 1B 58
Bridge Green. Essx 8A 44
Bridgehampton. Som 3E 24
Bridge Hewick. N Yor 6C 60
Bridgehill. Dur 6F 66
Bridgemary. Hants 5F 26
Bridgemere. Ches E 5E 48
Bridgemont. Derbs 7J 55
Bridgend. Abers 6F 88
(nr. Huntly)
Bridgend. Abers 6L 89
(nr. Peterhead)
Bridgend. Ang 7F 82
(nr. Brechin)
Bridgend. Ang 1J 77
(nr. Kirriemuir)
Bridgend. Arg 6F 74
(nr. Lochgilphead)
Bridgend. Arg 3B 68
(on Islay)
Bridgend. B'end 5B 32
Bridgend. Cumb 2F 58
Bridgend. Devn 5G 21
Bridgend. Fife 4J 77
Bridgend. High 6F 86
Bridgend. Mor 6D 88
Bridgend. Per 3G 77
Bridgend. W Lot 2J 71
Bridgend of Lintrathen. Ang 8C 82
Bridgeness. Falk 1J 71
Bridge of Alford. Abers 2F 82
Bridge of Allan. Stir 6C 76
Bridge of Avon. Mor 6B 88
Bridge of Awe. Arg 3H 75
Bridge of Balgie. Per 1A 76
Bridge of Brown. High 1B 82
Bridge of Cally. Per 8B 82
Bridge of Canny. Abers 4G 83
Bridge of Dee. Dum 5E 64
Bridge of Don. Aber 2K 83
Bridge of Dun. Ang 8G 83
Bridge of Dye. Abers 5G 83
Bridge of Earn. Per 4G 77
Bridge of Ericht. Per 8H 81
Bridge of Feugh. Abers 4H 83
Bridge of Forss. High 3F 92
Bridge of Gairn. Abers 4D 82
Bridge of Gaur. Per 8H 81
Bridge of Muchalls. Abers 4J 83
Bridge of Oich. High 3F 80
Bridge of Orchy. Arg 2L 75
Bridge of Walls. Shet 6C 95
Bridge of Weir. Ren 3B 70
Bridge Reeve. Devn 4H 23
Bridgerule. Devn 5D 22
Bridge Sollers. Here 7E 40
Bridge Street. Suff 7E 44
Bridgetown. Devn 3K 21
Bridgetown. Som 2L 23
Bridge Town. Warw 6A 42
Bridge Trafford. Ches W 8C 54
Bridgeyate. S Glo 6J 33
Bridgham. Norf 3F 44
Bridgnorth. Shrp 2H 41
Bridgtown. Staf 1K 41
Bridgwater. Som 2C 24
Bridister. Shet 6C 95
Bridlington. E Yor 7L 61
Bridport. Dors 6D 24
Bridstow. Here 1H 33
Brierfield. Lanc 2G 55
Brierley. Glos 2J 33
Brierley. Here 6E 40
Brierley. S Yor 4A 56
Brierley Hill. W Mid 3K 41
Brierton. Hart 8K 67
Briestfield. W Yor 4L 55
Brigg. N Lin 5G 57
Briggate. Norf 5K 53
Briggswath. N Yor 3H 61
Brigham. Cumb 8H 65
Brigham. E Yor 8K 61
Brighouse. W Yor 3K 55
Brighstone. IOW 7E 26
Brightgate. Derbs 4K 49
Brighthampton. Oxon 3D 34
Brightholmlee. S Yor 6L 55
Brightley. Devn 6H 23
Brightling. E Sus 5E 28
Brightlingsea. Essx 2J 37
Brighton. Brig 7B 28
Brighton. Corn 4A 20
Brighton Hill. Hants 1G 27
Brightons. Falk 2H 71
Brightwalton. W Ber 6E 34
Brightwalton Green. W Ber 6E 34
Brightwell. Suff 7J 45
Brightwell Baldwin. Oxon 4G 35
Brightwell-cum-Sotwell. Oxon 4F 34
Brigmerston. Wilts 1B 26
Brignall. Dur 2M 59
Brig o'Turk. Stir 5A 76
Brigsley. NE Lin 5J 57
Brigsteer. Cumb 5F 58
Brigstock. Nptn 3H 43
Brill. Buck 2G 35
Brill. Corn 7E 19
Brilley. Here 7C 40
Brimaston. Pemb 1D 30
Brimfield. Here 5F 40
Brimington. Derbs 8A 56
Brimley. Devn 8K 23
Brimpsfield. Glos 2M 33
Brimpton. W Ber 7F 34
Brims. Orkn 9A 94
Brimscombe. Glos 3L 33
Brimstage. Mers 7B 54
Brincliffe. S Yor 7M 55
Brind. E Yor 2D 56
Brindister. Shet 8E 95
Brindle. Lanc 3E 54
Brindley. Ches E 4C 48
Brindley Ford. Stoke 4F 48
Brineton. Staf 8F 48
Bringhurst. Leics 2G 43
Brington. Cambs 4J 43
Brinian. Orkn 5C 94
Briningham. Norf 4G 53
Brinkhill. Linc 8K 57
Brinkley. Cambs 6C 44
Brinklow. Warw 4C 42
Brinkworth. Wilts 5A 34
Brinscall. Lanc 3E 54
Brinscombe. Som 8G 33
Brinsley. Notts 5A 50
Brinsty Common. Here 6G 41
Brinsworth. S Yor 7A 56
Brinton. Norf 4G 53
Brisco. Cumb 6M 65
Brisley. Norf 5F 52
Brislington. Bris 6J 33
Brissenden Green. Kent 4H 29
Bristol. Bris 6H 33
Bristol International Airport. N Som 7H 33
Briston. Norf 4G 53
Britannia. Lanc 3G 55
Britford. Wilts 3B 26
Brithdir. Cphy 3D 32
Brithdir. Cdgn 7F 38
Brithdir. Gwyn 8G 47
Briton Ferry. Neat 4M 31
Britwell Salome. Oxon 4G 35
Brixham. Torb 4L 21
Brixton. Devn 4G 21
Brixton. G Lon 6B 36
Brixton Deverill. Wilts 2H 25
Brixworth. Nptn 4F 42
Brize Norton. Oxon 3D 34
Broad Alley. Worc 5J 41
Broad Blunsdon. Swin 4B 34
Broadbottom. G Man 6H 55
Broadbridge. W Sus 5J 27
Broadbridge Heath. W Sus 2M 27
Broad Campden. Glos 8M 41
Broad Chalke. Wilts 3A 26
Broadclyst. Devn 6L 23
Broadfield. Inv 2B 70
Broadfield. Pemb 3F 30
Broadfield. W Sus 4A 28
Broadford. High 1L 79
Broadford Bridge. W Sus 3L 27
Broadgate. Cumb 5C 58
Broad Green. Cambs 6C 44
Broad Green. C Beds 7H 43
Broad Green. Worc 4K 41
(nr. Bromsgrove)
Broad Green. Worc 6H 41
(nr. Worcester)
Broadhaven. High 4J 93
Broad Haven. Pemb 2C 30
Broadheath. G Man 7F 54
Broad Heath. Staf 7F 48
Broadheath. Worc 5G 41
Broadhembury. Devn 5A 24
Broadhempston. Devn 3K 21
Broad Hill. Cambs 4B 44
Broad Hinton. Wilts 6B 34
Broadholm. Derbs 5L 49
Broadholme. Linc 8E 56
Broadlay. Carm 3H 31
Broad Laying. Hants 7E 34
Broadley. Lanc 4G 55
Broadley. Mor 3D 88
Broadley Common. Essx 3C 36
Broad Marston. Worc 7M 41
Broadmayne. Dors 7G 25
Broadmere. Hants 1G 27
Broadmoor. Pemb 3E 30
Broad Oak. Carm 1K 31
Broad Oak. Cumb 4C 58
Broad Oak. Devn 6M 23
Broadoak. Dors 6D 24
(nr. Bridport)
Broad Oak. Dors 4G 25
(nr. Sturminster Newton)
Broad Oak. E Sus 6G 29
(nr. Hastings)
Broad Oak. E Sus 5E 28
(nr. Heathfield)
Broadoak. Glos 2J 33
Broadoak. Hants 4E 26
Broad Oak. Here 1G 33
Broad Oak. Kent 7K 37
Broadrashes. Mor 4E 88
Broads. Norf 1L 45
Broadsea. Abers 3K 89
Broad's Green. Essx 2E 36
Broadshard. Som 4D 24
Broadstairs. Kent 7M 37
Broadstone. Pool 6A 26
Broadstone. Shrp 3F 40
Broad Street. E Sus 6G 29
Broad Street. Kent 3K 29
(nr. Ashford)
Broad Street. Kent 8G 37
(nr. Maidstone)
Broad Street Green. Essx 3G 37
Broad, The. Here 5E 40
Broad Town. Wilts 6A 34
Broadwas. Worc 6H 41
Broadwath. Cumb 6M 65

Deadman's Cross. C Beds 7K 43
Deadwater. Nmbd 2B 66
Deaf Hill. Dur 8J 67
Deal. Kent 8M 37
Dean. Cumb 1B 58
Dean. Devn 1H 23 (nr. Combe Martin)
Dean. Devn 1J 23 (nr. Lynton)
Dean. Dors 4J 25
Dean. Hants 4F 26 (nr. Bishop's Waltham)
Dean. Hants 2E 26 (nr. Winchester)
Dean. Oxon 1D 34
Dean. Som 1F 24
Dean Bank. Dur 8H 67
Deanburnhaugh. Bord 8M 71
Dean Cross. Devn 1G 23
Deane. Hants 8F 34
Deanich Lodge. High 3F 86
Deanland. Dors 4J 25
Deanlane End. W Sus 4H 27
Dean Park. Shrp 5F 40
Dean Prior. Devn 3J 21
Dean Row. Ches E 7G 55
Deans. W Lot 3J 71
Deanscales. Cumb 1B 58
Deanshanger. Nptn 8F 42
Deanston. Stir 5C 76
Dearham. Cumb 8H 65
Dearne. S Yor 5A 56
Dearne Valley. S Yor 5M 55
Debach. Suff 6J 45
Debden. Essx 8B 44
Debden Green. Essx 4C 36 (nr. Loughton)
Debden Green. Essx 8B 44 (nr. Saffron Walden)
Debenham. Suff 5H 45
Dechmont. W Lot 2J 71
Deddington. Oxon 8C 42
Dedham. Essx 8G 45
Dedham Heath. Essx 8G 45
Deebank. Abers 4G 83
Deene. Nptn 2H 43
Deenethorpe. Nptn 2H 43
Deepcar. S Yor 6L 55
Deepcut. Surr 8K 35
Deepdale. Cumb 5J 59
Deepdale. N Lin 4G 57
Deepdale. N Yor 6K 59
Deeping Gate. Pet 1K 43
Deeping St James. Linc 1K 43
Deeping St Nicholas. Linc 8J 51
Deerhill. Mor 4E 88
Deerhurst. Glos 1L 33
Deerhurst Walton. Glos 1L 33
Deerness. Orkn 7D 94
Defford. Worc 7K 41
Defynnog. Powy 1B 32
Deganwy. Cnwy 2G 47
Deighton. N Yor 3C 60
Deighton. W Yor 4K 55
Deighton. York 1C 56
Deiniolen. Gwyn 3E 46
Delabole. Corn 7B 22
Delamere. Ches W 3C 48
Delfour. High 3L 81
Dellieture. High 6A 88
Dell, The. Suff 2L 45
Delly End. Oxon 2D 34
Delny. High 4K 87
Delph. G Man 5H 55
Delves. Dur 7G 67
Delves, The. W Mid 2L 41
Delvin End. Essx 8D 44
Dembleby. Linc 6G 51
Demelza. Corn 3A 20
Denaby Main. S Yor 6A 56
Denbeath. Fife 6J 77
Denbigh. Den 3K 47
Denbury. Devn 3K 21
Denby. Derbs 5L 49
Denby Common. Derbs 5A 50
Denby Dale. W Yor 5L 55
Denchworth. Oxon 4D 34
Dendron. Cumb 6D 58
Deneside. Dur 7K 67
Denford. Nptn 4H 43
Dengie. Essx 3H 37
Denham. Buck 5L 35
Denham. Suff 5D 44 (nr. Bury St Edmunds)
Denham. Suff 4H 45 (nr. Eye)
Denham Green. Buck 5L 35
Denham Street. Suff 4H 45
Denhead. Abers 6K 89 (nr. Ellon)
Denhead. Abers 4K 89 (nr. Strichen)
Denhead. Fife 4K 77
Denholm. Bord 8E 72
Denholme. W Yor 2J 55
Denholme Clough. W Yor 2J 55
Denholme Gate. W Yor 2J 55
Denio. Gwyn 6C 46
Denmead. Hants 4G 27
Dennington. Suff 5J 45
Denny. Falk 1G 71
Denny End. Cambs 5A 44
Dennyloanhead. Falk 1G 71
Den of Lindores. Fife 4H 77
Denshaw. G Man 4H 55
Denside. Abers 4J 83
Densole. Kent 3L 29
Denston. Suff 6D 44
Denstone. Staf 5J 49
Denstroude. Kent 7K 37
Dent. Cumb 5J 59
Den, The. N Ayr 4B 70
Denton. Cambs 3K 43
Denton. Darl 2B 60
Denton. E Sus 7C 28
Denton. G Man 6H 55
Denton. Kent 3L 29
Denton. Linc 6E 50
Denton. Norf 3J 45
Denton. Nptn 6G 43
Denton. N Yor 1K 55
Denton. Oxon 3F 34
Denver. Norf 1C 44
Denwick. Nmbd 8M 73
Deopham. Norf 1G 45
Deopham Green. Norf 2G 45
Depden. Suff 6D 44
Depden Green. Suff 6D 44
Deptford. G Lon 6B 36
Deptford. Wilts 2A 26
Derby. Derb 6L 49
Derbyhaven. IOM 7C 62
Derculich. Per 8L 81
Dereham. Norf 6F 52
Deri. Cphy 3D 32
Derril. Devn 5E 22
Derringstone. Kent 3L 29
Derrington. Shrp 2G 41
Derrington. Staf 7F 48
Derriton. Devn 5E 22
Derryguaig. Arg 2B 74
Derry Hill. Wilts 6M 33
Derrythorpe. N Lin 5E 56
Dersingham. Norf 4C 52
Dervaig. Arg 8J 79
Derwen. Den 4K 47
Derwen Gam. Cdgn 6G 39
Derwenlas. Powy 2K 39
Desborough. Nptn 3G 43
Desford. Leics 1C 42
Detchant. Nmbd 6K 73
Dethick. Derbs 4L 49
Detling. Kent 8F 36
Deuchar. Ang 7E 82
Deuddwr. Powy 8M 47
Devauden. Mon 4G 33
Devil's Bridge. Cdgn 4K 39
Devitts Green. Warw 2A 42
Devizes. Wilts 7A 34
Devonport. Plym 4F 20
Devonside. Clac 6E 76
Devoran. Corn 6E 19
Dewartown. Midl 3M 71
Dewlish. Dors 6G 25
Dewsbury. W Yor 3L 55
Dewshall Court. Here 8E 40
Dexbeer. Devn 5D 22
Dhoon. IOM 5E 62
Dhoor. IOM 4E 62
Dhowin. IOM 3E 62
Dial Green. W Sus 3K 27
Dial Post. W Sus 4M 27
Dibberford. Dors 5D 24
Dibden. Hants 5E 26
Dibden Purlieu. Hants 5E 26
Dickleburgh. Norf 3H 45
Didbrook. Glos 8L 41
Didcot. Oxon 4F 34
Diddington. Cambs 5K 43
Diddlebury. Shrp 3F 40
Didley. Here 8E 40
Didling. W Sus 4J 27
Didmarton. Glos 5L 33
Didsbury. G Man 6G 55
Didworthy. Devn 3H 21
Digby. Linc 4G 51
Digg. High 5J 85
Diggle. G Man 5J 55
Digmoor. Lanc 5C 54
Digswell. Herts 2A 36
Dihewyd. Cdgn 6G 39
Dilham. Norf 5K 53
Dilhorne. Staf 5G 49
Dillarburn. S Lan 5G 71
Dillington. Cambs 5K 43
Dilston. Nmbd 5E 66
Dilton Marsh. Wilts 1H 25
Dilwyn. Here 6E 40
Dimmer. Som 2F 24
Dimple. G Man 4F 54
Dinas. Carm 8E 38
Dinas. Gwyn 4D 46 (nr. Caernarfon)
Dinas. Gwyn 6B 46 (nr. Tudweiliog)
Dinas Cross. Pemb 8C 38
Dinas Dinlle. Gwyn 4D 46
Dinas Mawddwy. Gwyn 8H 47
Dinas Powys. V Glam 6D 32
Dinbych. Den 3K 47
Dinbych-y-Pysgod. Pemb 3F 30
Dinckley. Lanc 2E 54
Dinder. Som 1E 24
Dinedor. Here 8F 40
Dinedor Cross. Here 8F 40
Dingestow. Mon 2G 33
Dingle. Mers 7B 54
Dingleden. Kent 4G 29
Dingleton. Bord 6E 72
Dingley. Nptn 3F 42
Dingwall. High 6H 87
Dinmael. Cnwy 5K 47
Dinnet. Abers 4E 82
Dinnington. Som 4D 24
Dinnington. S Yor 7B 56
Dinnington. Tyne 4H 67
Dinorwic. Gwyn 3E 46
Dinton. Buck 2H 35
Dinton. Wilts 2A 26
Dinworthy. Devn 4E 22
Dipley. Hants 8H 35
Dippen. Arg 6F 68
Dippenhall. Surr 1J 27
Dippertown. Devn 7F 22
Dippin. N Ayr 7J 69
Dipple. S Ayr 1M 63
Diptford. Devn 4J 21
Dipton. Dur 6G 67
Dirleton. E Lot 1E 72
Dirt Pot. Nmbd 7D 66
Discoed. Powy 5C 40
Diseworth. Leics 7A 50
Dishes. Orkn 5E 94
Dishforth. N Yor 6C 60
Disley. Ches E 7H 55
Diss. Norf 4H 45
Disserth. Powy 6A 40
Distington. Cumb 1B 58
Ditchampton. Wilts 2A 26
Ditcheat. Som 2F 24
Ditchingham. Norf 2K 45
Ditchling. E Sus 6B 28
Ditteridge. Wilts 7L 33
Dittisham. Devn 4K 21
Ditton. Hal 7C 54
Ditton. Kent 8F 36
Ditton Green. Cambs 6C 44
Ditton Priors. Shrp 3G 41
Divach. High 1G 81
Dixonfield. High 3G 93
Dixton. Glos 8K 41
Dixton. Mon 2H 33
Dizzard. Corn 6C 22
Dobcross. G Man 5H 55
Dobs Hill. Flin 3A 48
Dobson's Bridge. Shrp 6B 48
Dobwalls. Corn 3D 20
Doccombe. Devn 7J 23
Dochgarroch. High 7J 87
Docking. Norf 4D 52
Docklow. Here 6F 40
Dockray. Cumb 1E 58
Doc Penfro. Pemb 3D 30
Dodbrooke. Devn 5J 21
Doddenham. Worc 6H 41
Doddinghurst. Essx 4D 36
Doddington. Cambs 2M 43
Doddington. Kent 8H 37
Doddington. Linc 3F 50
Doddington. Nmbd 6J 73
Doddington. Shrp 4G 41
Doddiscombsleigh. Devn 7K 23
Doddshill. Norf 4D 52
Dodford. Nptn 5E 42
Dodford. Worc 4K 41
Dodington. Som 1A 24
Dodington. S Glo 6K 33
Dodleston. Ches W 3A 48
Dods Leigh. Staf 6H 49
Dodworth. S Yor 5M 55
Doe Lea. Derbs 3A 50
Dogdyke. Linc 4J 51
Dogmersfield. Hants 8H 35
Dogsthorpe. Pet 1L 43
Dog Village. Devn 6L 23
Dolanog. Powy 8K 47
Dolau. Powy 5B 40
Dolau. Rhon 5C 32
Dolbenmaen. Gwyn 5E 46
Doley. Staf 7E 48
Dol-fach. Powy 1M 39 (nr. Llanbrynmair)
Dolfach. Powy 4M 39 (nr. Llanidloes)
Dolfor. Powy 3B 40
Dolgarrog. Cnwy 3G 47
Dolgellau. Gwyn 8G 47
Dolgoch. Gwyn 1J 39
Dol-gran. Carm 8G 39
Dolhelfa. Powy 4M 39
Doll. High 1L 87
Dollar. Clac 6E 76
Dolley Green. Powy 5C 40
Dollwen. Cdgn 3J 39
Dolphin. Flin 2L 47
Dolphingstone. E Lot 2M 71
Dolphinholme. Lanc 8G 59
Dolphinton. S Lan 5K 71
Dolton. Devn 4G 23
Dolwen. Cnwy 2H 47
Dolwyddelan. Cnwy 4G 47
Dol-y-Bont. Cdgn 3J 39
Dolyhir. Powy 6C 40
Domgay. Powy 8M 47
Doncaster. S Yor 5B 56
Donhead St Andrew. Wilts 3J 25
Donhead St Mary. Wilts 3J 25
Doniford. Som 1M 23
Donington. Linc 6J 51
Donington. Shrp 1J 41
Donington Eaudike. Linc 6J 51
Donington le Heath. Leics 8A 50
Donington on Bain. Linc 7J 57
Donington South Ing. Linc 6J 51
Donisthorpe. Leics 8L 49
Donkey Street. Kent 4K 29
Donkey Town. Surr 7K 35
Donna Nook. Linc 6L 57
Donnington. Glos 1B 34
Donnington. Here 8H 41
Donnington. Shrp 1F 40
Donnington. Telf 8E 48
Donnington. W Ber 7E 34
Donnington. W Sus 5J 27
Donyatt. Som 4C 24
Doomsday Green. W Sus 2M 27
Doonfoot. S Ayr 8B 70
Doonholm. S Ayr 8B 70
Dorback Lodge. High 2A 82
Dorchester. Dors 6F 24
Dorchester on Thames. Oxon 4F 34
Dordon. Warw 1A 42
Dore. S Yor 7M 55
Dores. High 8H 87
Dorking. Surr 1M 27
Dorking Tye. Suff 8F 44
Dormansland. Surr 3C 28
Dormans Park. Surr 3B 28
Dormanstown. Red C 1E 60
Dormington. Here 7F 40
Dormston. Worc 6K 41
Dorn. Glos 8A 42
Dorney. Buck 6K 35
Dornie. High 1A 80
Dornoch. High 3K 87
Dornock. Dum 5K 65
Dorrery. High 4F 92
Dorridge. W Mid 4M 41
Dorrington. Linc 4G 51
Dorrington. Shrp 1E 40
Dorsington. Warw 7M 41
Dorstone. Here 7D 40
Dorton. Buck 2G 35
Dotham. IOA 2C 46
Dottery. Dors 6D 24
Doublebois. Corn 3C 20
Dougarie. N Ayr 6G 69
Doughton. Glos 4L 33
Douglas. IOM 6D 62
Douglas. S Lan 6G 71
Douglastown. Ang 1K 77
Douglas Water. S Lan 6G 71
Doulting. Som 1F 24
Dounby. Orkn 5A 94
Doune. High 3L 81 (nr. Kingussie)
Doune. High 1G 87 (nr. Lairg)
Doune. Stir 5C 76
Dounie. High 2H 87 (nr. Bonar Bridge)
Dounie. High 3J 87 (nr. Tain)
Dounreay. High 3E 92
Doura. N Ayr 5B 70
Dousland. Devn 3G 21
Dovaston. Shrp 7A 48
Dove Holes. Derbs 8J 55
Dovenby. Cumb 8H 65
Dover. Kent 3M 29
Dovercourt. Essx 8J 45
Doverdale. Worc 5J 41
Doveridge. Derbs 6J 49
Doversgreen. Surr 3A 28
Dowally. Per 1F 76
Dowbridge. Lanc 2C 54
Dowdeswell. Glos 2A 34
Dowlais. Mer T 3C 32
Dowland. Devn 4G 23
Dowlands. Devn 6B 24
Dowles. Worc 4H 41
Dowlesgreen. Wok 7J 35
Dowlish Wake. Som 4C 24
Downall Green. Mers 5D 54
Down Ampney. Glos 4A 34
Downderry. Corn 4E 20 (nr. Looe)
Downderry. Corn 4A 20 (nr. St Austell)
Downe. G Lon 7C 36
Downend. IOW 7F 26
Downend. S Glo 6J 33
Downend. W Ber 6E 34
Down Field. Cambs 4C 44
Downfield. D'dee 2J 77
Downgate. Corn 8E 22 (nr. Kelly Bray)
Downgate. Corn 8D 22 (nr. Upton Cross)
Downham. Essx 4F 36
Downham. Lanc 1F 54
Downham. Nmbd 6H 73
Downham Market. Norf 1C 44
Down Hatherley. Glos 1L 33
Downhead. Som 1F 24 (nr. Frome)
Downhead. Som 3E 24 (nr. Yeovil)
Downholland Cross. Lanc 5B 54
Downholme. N Yor 4A 60
Downies. Abers 4K 83
Downley. Buck 4J 35
Down St Mary. Devn 5J 23
Downside. Som 8J 33 (nr. Chilcompton)
Downside. Som 1F 24 (nr. Shepton Mallet)
Downside. Surr 8M 35
Down, The. Shrp 2G 41
Down Thomas. Devn 4G 21
Downton. Hants 6C 26
Downton. Wilts 3B 26
Downton on the Rock. Here 4E 40
Dowsby. Linc 7H 51
Dowsdale. Linc 8J 51
Dowthwaitehead. Cumb 1E 58
Doxey. Staf 7G 49
Doxford. Nmbd 7L 73
Doynton. S Glo 6K 33
Drabblegate. Norf 5J 53
Draethen. Cphy 5E 32
Draffan. S Lan 5F 70
Dragonby. N Lin 4F 56
Dragons Green. W Sus 3M 27
Drakelow. Worc 3J 41
Drakemyre. N Ayr 4A 70
Drakes Broughton. Worc 7K 41
Drakes Cross. Worc 4L 41
Drakewalls. Corn 8F 22
Draughton. Nptn 4F 42
Draughton. N Yor 8M 59
Drax. N Yor 3C 56
Draycot. Oxon 3G 35
Draycote. Warw 5C 42
Draycot Foliat. Swin 6B 34
Draycott. Derbs 6A 50
Draycott. Glos 8M 41
Draycott. Shrp 2J 41
Draycott. Som 8G 33 (nr. Cheddar)
Draycott. Som 3E 24 (nr. Yeovil)
Draycott. Worc 7J 41
Draycott in the Clay. Staf 7J 49
Draycott in the Moors. Staf 5G 49
Drayford. Devn 4J 23
Drayton. Leics 2G 43
Drayton. Linc 6J 51
Drayton. Norf 6H 53
Drayton. Nptn 5D 42
Drayton. Oxon 4E 34 (nr. Abingdon)
Drayton. Oxon 7C 42 (nr. Banbury)
Drayton. Port 5G 27
Drayton. Som 3D 24
Drayton. Warw 6M 41
Drayton. Worc 4K 41
Drayton Bassett. Staf 1M 41
Drayton Beauchamp. Buck 2K 35
Drayton Parslow. Buck 1J 35
Drayton St Leonard. Oxon 4F 34
Drebley. N Yor 8M 59
Dreenhill. Pemb 2D 30
Drefach. Carm 2K 31 (nr. Meidrim)
Drefach. Carm 8F 38 (nr. Newcastle Emlyn)
Drefach. Carm 1G 31 (nr. Tumble)
Drefach. Cdgn 7G 39
Dreghorn. N Ayr 6B 70
Drellingore. Kent 3L 29
Drem. E Lot 2E 72
Dreumasdal. W Isl 8B 84
Drewsteignton. Devn 6J 23
Driby. Linc 8K 57
Driffield. E Yor 8K 61
Driffield. Glos 4A 34
Drift. Corn 7B 19
Drigg. Cumb 4B 58
Drighlington. W Yor 3L 55
Drimnin. High 8K 79
Drimpton. Dors 5D 24
Dringhoe. E Yor 8L 61
Drinisiadar. W Isl 2F 84
Drinkstone. Suff 5F 44
Drinkstone Green. Suff 5F 44
Drointon. Staf 7H 49
Droitwich Spa. Worc 5J 41
Droman. High 4J 91
Dron. Per 4G 77
Dronfield. Derbs 8M 55
Dronfield Woodhouse. Derbs 8M 55
Drongan. E Ayr 8C 70
Dronley. Ang 2J 77
Droop. Dors 5G 25
Drope. V Glam 6D 32
Droxford. Hants 4G 27
Droylsden. G Man 6G 55
Druggers End. Worc 8H 41
Druid. Den 5K 47
Druid's Heath. W Mid 1L 41
Druidston. Pemb 2C 30
Druim. High 6M 87
Druimarbin. High 6C 80
Druim Fhearna. High 2L 79
Druimindarroch. High 5L 79
Druim Saighdinis. W Isl 5C 84
Drum. Per 5F 76
Drumbeg. High 6J 91
Drumblade. Abers 5F 88
Drumbuie. Dum 3C 64
Drumbuie. High 8M 85
Drumburgh. Cumb 6K 65
Drumburn. Dum 5G 65
Drumchapel. Glas 2D 70
Drumchardine. High 7H 87
Drumchork. High 3A 86
Drumclog. S Lan 6E 70
Drumeldrie. Fife 5K 77
Drumelzier. Bord 6K 71
Drumfearn. High 2L 79
Drumgask. High 4J 81
Drumgelloch. N Lan 3F 70
Drumgley. Ang 8E 82
Drumguish. High 4K 81
Drumin. Mor 6B 88
Drumindorsair. High 7G 87
Drumlamford House. S Ayr 4M 63
Drumlasie. Abers 3G 83
Drumlemble. Arg 8E 68
Drumlithie. Abers 5H 83
Drummoddie. Dum 7A 64
Drummond. High 5J 87
Drummore. Dum 8L 63
Drummuir. Mor 5D 88
Drumnadrochit. High 8H 87
Drumnagorrach. Mor 4F 88
Drumoak. Abers 4H 83
Drumrunie. High 1D 86
Drumry. W Dun 2D 70
Drums. Abers 1K 83
Drumsleet. Dum 4G 65
Drumsmittal. High 7J 87
Drums of Park. Abers 4F 88
Drumsturdy. Ang 2K 77
Drumtochty Castle. Abers 5G 83
Drumuie. High 7J 85
Drumuillie. High 1M 81
Drumvaich. Stir 5B 76
Drumwhindle. Abers 6K 89
Drunkendub. Ang 1M 77
Drury. Flin 3M 47
Drury Square. Norf 6F 52
Drybeck. Cumb 2H 59
Drybridge. Mor 3E 88
Drybridge. N Ayr 6B 70
Drybrook. Glos 2J 33
Drybrook. Here 2H 33
Dryburgh. Bord 6E 72
Dry Doddington. Linc 5E 50
Dry Drayton. Cambs 5M 43
Drym. Corn 6D 19
Drymen. Stir 1C 70
Drymuir. Abers 5K 89
Drynachan Lodge. High 8L 87
Drynie Park. High 6H 87
Drynoch. High 8J 85
Dry Sandford. Oxon 3E 34
Dryslwyn. Carm 1K 31
Dry Street. Essx 5E 36
Dryton. Shrp 1F 40
Dubford. Abers 3H 89
Dubiton. Abers 4G 89
Dubton. Ang 8F 82
Duchally. High 8L 91
Duck End. Essx 1E 36
Duckington. Ches W 4B 48
Ducklington. Oxon 3D 34
Duckmanton. Derbs 8A 56
Duck Street. Hants 1D 26
Dudbridge. Glos 3L 33
Duddenhoe End. Essx 8A 44
Duddingston. Edin 2L 71
Duddington. Nptn 1H 43
Duddleswell. E Sus 5C 28
Duddo. Nmbd 5J 73
Duddon. Ches W 3C 48
Duddon Bridge. Cumb 5C 58
Dudleston. Shrp 6A 48
Dudleston Heath. Shrp 6A 48
Dudley. Tyne 4H 67
Dudley. W Mid 3K 41
Dudston. Shrp 2C 40
Dudwells. Pemb 1D 30
Duffield. Derbs 5L 49
Duffryn. Neat 4A 32
Dufftown. Mor 5D 88
Duffus. Mor 3B 88
Dufton. Cumb 1H 59
Duggleby. N Yor 7H 61
Duirinish. High 8M 85
Duisdalemore. High 2L 79
Duisdeil Mòr. High 2L 79
Duisky. High 6C 80
Dukesfield. Nmbd 6E 66
Dukestown. Blae 3D 32
Dukinfield. G Man 6H 55
Dulas. IOA 1D 46
Dulcote. Som 1E 24
Dulford. Devn 5M 23
Dull. Per 1D 76
Dullatur. N Lan 2F 70
Dullingham. Cambs 6C 44
Dullingham Ley. Cambs 6C 44
Dulnain Bridge. High 1M 81
Duloe. Bed 5K 43
Duloe. Corn 4D 20
Dulverton. Som 3L 23
Dulwich. G Lon 6B 36
Dumbarton. W Dun 2C 70
Dumbleton. Glos 8L 41
Dumfin. Arg 1B 70
Dumfries. Dum 4G 65
Dumgoyne. Stir 1D 70
Dummer. Hants 1F 26
Dumpford. W Sus 3J 27
Dun. Ang 7G 83
Dunagoil. Arg 4J 69
Dunalastair. Per 8K 81
Dunan. High 1K 79
Dunball. Som 1C 24
Dunbar. E Lot 2F 72
Dunbeath. High 7G 93
Dunbeg. Arg 2F 74
Dunblane. Stir 5C 76
Dunbog. Fife 4H 77
Dunbridge. Hants 3D 26
Duncanston. Abers 1F 82
Duncanston. High 6H 87
Dun Charlabhaigh. W Isl 4B 90
Dunchideock. Devn 7K 23
Dunchurch. Warw 4C 42
Duncote. Nptn 6E 42
Duncow. Dum 3G 65
Duncrievie. Per 5G 77
Duncton. W Sus 4K 27
Dundee. D'dee 2K 77
Dundee Airport. D'dee 3J 77
Dundon. Som 2D 24
Dundonald. S Ayr 6B 70
Dundonnell. High 3C 86
Dundraw. Cumb 7K 65
Dundreggan. High 2F 80
Dundrennan. Dum 7E 64
Dundridge. Hants 4F 26
Dundry. N Som 7H 33
Dunecht. Abers 3H 83
Dunfermline. Fife 1J 71
Dunford Bridge. S Yor 5K 55
Dungate. Kent 8H 37
Dunge. Wilts 8L 33
Dungeness. Kent 6J 29
Dungworth. S Yor 7L 55
Dunham-on-the-Hill. Ches W 8C 54
Dunham-on-Trent. Notts 8E 56
Dunhampton. Worc 5J 41
Dunham Town. G Man 7F 54
Dunham Woodhouses. G Man 7F 54
Dunholme. Linc 8G 57
Dunino. Fife 4L 77
Dunipace. Falk 1G 71
Dunira. Per 3C 76
Dunkeld. Per 1F 76
Dunkerton. Bath 8K 33
Dunkeswell. Devn 5A 24
Dunkeswick. N Yor 1M 55
Dunkirk. Kent 8J 37
Dunkirk. S Glo 5K 33
Dunkirk. Staf 4F 48
Dunkirk. Wilts 7M 33
Dunk's Green. Kent 8E 36
Dunlappie. Ang 7F 82
Dunley. Hants 8E 34
Dunley. Worc 5H 41
Dunlichity Lodge. High 8J 87
Dunlop. E Ayr 5C 70
Dunmaglass Lodge. High 1H 81
Dunmore. Arg 3F 68
Dunmore. Falk 1G 71
Dunmore. High 7H 87
Dunnet. High 2H 93
Dunnichen. Ang 1L 77
Dunning. Per 4F 76
Dunnington. E Yor 8L 61
Dunnington. Warw 6L 41
Dunnington. York 8F 60
Dunningwell. Cumb 5C 58
Dunnockshaw. Lanc 3G 55
Dunoon. Arg 2K 69
Dunphail. Mor 5A 88
Dunragit. Dum 6L 63
Dunrostan. Arg 1F 68
Duns. Bord 4G 73
Dunsby. Linc 7H 51
Dunscar. G Man 4F 54
Dunscore. Dum 3F 64
Dunscroft. S Yor 5C 56
Dunsdale. Red C 2F 60
Dunsden Green. Oxon 6H 35
Dunsfold. Surr 2L 27
Dunsford. Devn 7K 23
Dunshalt. Fife 4H 77
Dunshillock. Abers 5K 89
Dunsley. N Yor 2H 61
Dunsley. Staf 3J 41
Dunsmore. Buck 3J 35
Dunsop Bridge. Lanc 8H 59
Dunstable. C Beds 1L 35
Dunstal. Staf 7H 49
Dunstall. Staf 7J 49
Dunstall Green. Suff 5D 44
Dunstall Hill. W Mid 2K 41
Dunstan. Nmbd 8M 73
Dunster. Som 1L 23
Duns Tew. Oxon 1E 34
Dunston. Linc 3G 51
Dunston. Norf 1J 45
Dunston. Staf 8G 49
Dunston. Tyne 5H 67
Dunstone. Devn 4G 21
Dunston Heath. Staf 8G 49
Dunsville. S Yor 5C 56
Dunswell. E Yor 2G 57
Dunsyre. S Lan 5J 71
Dunterton. Devn 8E 22
Duntisbourne Abbots. Glos 3M 33
Duntisbourne Leer. Glos 3M 33
Duntisbourne Rouse. Glos 3M 33
Duntish. Dors 5F 24
Duntocher. W Dun 2C 70
Dunton. Buck 1J 35
Dunton. C Beds 7L 43
Dunton. Norf 4E 52
Dunton Bassett. Leics 2D 42
Dunton Green. Kent 8D 36
Dunton Patch. Norf 4E 52
Duntulm. High 4J 85
Dunure. S Ayr 8A 70
Dunvant. Swan 4K 31
Dunvegan. High 7G 85
Dunwich. Suff 4L 45
Dunwood. Staf 4G 49
Durdar. Cumb 6M 65
Durgates. E Sus 4E 28
Durham. Dur 7H 67
Durham Tees Valley Airport. Darl 2C 60
Durisdeer. Dum 1F 64
Durisdeermill. Dum 1F 64
Durkar. W Yor 4M 55
Durleigh. Som 2B 24
Durley. Hants 4F 26
Durley. Wilts 7C 34
Durley Street. Hants 4F 26
Durlow Common. Here 8G 41
Durnamuck. High 2C 86
Durness. High 3M 91
Durno. Abers 1H 83
Durns Town. Hants 6C 26
Duror. High 8B 80
Durran. Arg 5G 75
Durran. High 3G 93
Durrant Green. Kent 4G 29
Durrants. Hants 4H 27
Durrington. W Sus 5M 27
Durrington. Wilts 1B 26
Dursley. Glos 4K 33
Dursley Cross. Glos 2J 33
Durston. Som 3B 24
Durweston. Dors 5H 25
Dury. Shet 6E 95
Duston. Nptn 5F 42
Duthil. High 1M 81
Dutlas. Powy 4C 40
Duton Hill. Essx 1E 36
Dutson. Corn 7E 22
Dutton. Ches W 8D 54
Duxford. Cambs 7A 44
Duxford. Oxon 4D 34
Dwygyfylchi. Cnwy 2G 47
Dwyran. IOA 3D 46
Dyce. Aber 2J 83
Dyffryn. B'end 4A 32
Dyffryn. Carm 1H 31
Dyffryn. Pemb 8B 38
Dyffryn. V Glam 6C 32
Dyffryn Ardudwy. Gwyn 7E 46
Dyffryn Castell. Cdgn 3K 39
Dyffryn Ceidrych. Carm 1M 31
Dyffryn Cellwen. Neat 3A 32
Dyke. Linc 7H 51
Dyke. Mor 6M 87
Dykehead. Ang 7D 82
Dykehead. N Lan 3G 71
Dykehead. Stir 6A 76
Dykend. Ang 8C 82
Dykesfield. Cumb 6L 65
Dylife. Powy 2L 39
Dymchurch. Kent 5K 29
Dymock. Glos 8H 41
Dyrham. S Glo 6K 33
Dysart. Fife 6J 77
Dyserth. Den 2K 47

E

Eachwick. Nmbd 4G 67
Eadar Dha Fhadhail. W Isl 5A 90
Eagland Hill. Lanc 1C 54
Eagle. Linc 3E 50
Eagle Barnsdale. Linc 3E 50
Eagle Moor. Linc 3E 50
Eaglescliffe. Stoc T 2D 60
Eaglesfield. Cumb 1B 58
Eaglesfield. Dum 4K 65
Eaglesham. E Ren 4D 70
Eaglethorpe. Nptn 2J 43
Eagley. G Man 4F 54
Eairy. IOM 6C 62
Eakley Lanes. Mil 6G 43
Eakring. Notts 3C 50
Ealand. N Lin 4D 56
Ealing. G Lon 5M 35
Eallabus. Arg 3B 68
Eals. Nmbd 6B 66
Eamont Bridge. Cumb 1G 59
Earby. Lanc 1H 55
Earcroft. Bkbn 3E 54
Eardington. Shrp 2H 41
Eardisland. Here 6E 40
Eardisley. Here 7D 40
Eardiston. Shrp 7A 48
Eardiston. Worc 5G 41
Earith. Cambs 4M 43
Earlais. High 5H 85
Earle. Nmbd 7J 73
Earlesfield. Linc 6F 50
Earlestown. Mers 6D 54
Earley. Wok 6H 35
Earlham. Norf 1H 45
Earlish. High 5H 85
Earls Barton. Nptn 5G 43
Earls Colne. Essx 1G 37
Earls Common. Worc 6K 41
Earl's Croome. Worc 7J 41
Earlsdon. W Mid 4B 42
Earlsferry. Fife 5K 77
Earlsford. Abers 6J 89
Earl's Green. Suff 5G 45
Earlsheaton. W Yor 3L 55
Earl Shilton. Leics 2C 42
Earl Soham. Suff 5J 45
Earl Sterndale. Derbs 3H 49
Earlston. E Ayr 6C 70
Earlston. Bord 6E 72
Earl Stonham. Suff 6H 45
Earlstoun. Dum 3D 64
Earlswood. Mon 4G 33
Earlswood. Warw 4M 41
Earlyvale. Bord 4L 71
Earnley. W Sus 6J 27
Earsairidh. W Isl 4B 78
Earsdon. Tyne 4J 67
Earsham. Norf 3K 45
Earsham Street. Suff 4J 45
Earswick. York 8F 60
Eartham. W Sus 5K 27
Earthcott Green. S Glo 5J 33
Easby. N Yor 3E 60 (nr. Great Ayton)
Easby. N Yor 3A 60 (nr. Richmond)
Easdale. Arg 4E 74
Easebourne. W Sus 3J 27
Easenhall. Warw 4C 42
Eashing. Surr 1K 27
Easington. Buck 2G 35
Easington. Dur 7K 67
Easington. E Yor 4K 57
Easington. Nmbd 6L 73
Easington. Oxon 8C 42 (nr. Banbury)
Easington. Oxon 4G 35 (nr. Watlington)
Easington. Red C 2G 61
Easington Colliery. Dur 7K 67
Easington Lane. Tyne 7J 67
Easingwold. N Yor 7E 60
Easole Street. Kent 8L 37
Eassie. Ang 1J 77
Eassie and Nevay. Ang 1J 77
East Aberthaw. V Glam 7C 32
Eastacombe. Devn 3G 23
Eastacott. Devn 3H 23
East Allington. Devn 5J 21
East Anstey. Devn 3K 23
East Anton. Hants 1D 26
East Appleton. N Yor 4B 60
East Ardsley. W Yor 3M 55
East Ashley. Devn 4H 23
East Ashling. W Sus 5J 27
East Aston. Hants 1E 26
East Ayton. N Yor 5J 61
East Barkwith. Linc 7H 57
East Barnby. N Yor 2H 61
East Barnet. G Lon 4A 36
East Barns. E Lot 2G 73
East Barsham. Norf 4F 52
East Beach. W Sus 6J 27
East Beckham. Norf 3H 53
East Bedfont. G Lon 6L 35
East Bennan. N Ayr 7H 69
East Bergholt. Suff 8G 45
East Bierley. W Yor 3K 55
East Blatchington. E Sus 7C 28
East Bliney. Norf 6F 52
East Bloxworth. Dors 6H 25
East Boldre. Hants 5D 26
East Bolton. Nmbd 8L 73
Eastbourne. Darl 2B 60
Eastbourne. E Sus 8E 28
East Brent. Som 8F 32
East Bridge. Suff 5L 45
East Bridgford. Notts 5C 50
East Briscoe. Dur 2L 59
East Buckland. Devn 2H 23 (nr. Barnstaple)
East Buckland. Devn 5H 21 (nr. Thurlestone)
East Budleigh. Devn 7M 23
Eastburn. W Yor 1J 55
East Burnham. Buck 5K 35
East Burrafirth. Shet 6D 95
East Burton. Dors 7H 25
Eastbury. Herts 4L 35
Eastbury. W Ber 6D 34
East Butsfield. Dur 7G 67
East Butterleigh. Devn 5L 23
East Butterwick. N Lin 5E 56
Eastby. N Yor 8M 59
East Calder. W Lot 3J 71
East Carleton. Norf 1H 45
East Carlton. Nptn 3G 43
East Carlton. W Yor 1L 55
East Chaldon. Dors 7G 25
East Challow. Oxon 5D 34
East Charleton. Devn 5J 21
East Chelborough. Dors 5E 24
East Chiltington. E Sus 6B 28
East Chinnock. Som 4D 24
East Chisenbury. Wilts 8B 34
Eastchurch. Kent 6H 37
East Clandon. Surr 8L 35
East Claydon. Buck 1H 35
East Clevedon. N Som 6G 33
East Clyne. High 1L 87
East Clyth. High 6H 93
East Coker. Som 4E 24
Eastcombe. Glos 3L 33
East Combe. Som 2A 24
East Common. N Yor 2C 56
East Compton. Som 1F 24
East Cornworthy. Devn 4K 21
Eastcote. G Lon 5M 35
Eastcote. Nptn 6E 42
Eastcote. W Mid 4M 41
Eastcott. Corn 4D 22
Eastcott. Wilts 8A 34
East Cottingwith. E Yor 1D 56
East Coulston. Wilts 8M 33
Eastcourt. Wilts 7C 34 (nr. Pewsey)
Eastcourt. Wilts 4M 33 (nr. Tetbury)
East Cowes. IOW 6F 26
East Cowick. E Yor 3C 56
East Cowton. N Yor 3C 60
East Cramlington. Nmbd 4H 67
East Cranmore. Som 1F 24
East Creech. Dors 7J 25
East Croachy. High 1J 81
East Dean. E Sus 8D 28
East Dean. Glos 1J 33
East Dean. Hants 3C 26
East Dean. W Sus 4K 27
East Down. Devn 1H 23
East Drayton. Notts 8D 56
East Dundry. N Som 7H 33
East Ella. Hull 3G 57
East End. Cambs 4M 43
East End. Dors 6J 25
East End. E Yor 8L 61 (nr. Ulrome)
East End. E Yor 3J 57 (nr. Withernsea)
East End. Hants 6D 26 (nr. Lymington)
East End. Hants 7E 34 (nr. Newbury)
East End. Herts 1C 36
East End. Kent 6H 37 (nr. Minster)
East End. Kent 4G 29 (nr. Tenterden)
East End. N Som 6G 33
East End. Oxon 2D 34
East End. Som 8H 33
East End. Suff 8H 45
Easter Ardross. High 4J 87
Easter Balgedie. Per 5G 77
Easter Balmoral. Abers 4C 82
Easter Brae. High 5J 87
Easter Buckieburn. Stir 1F 70
Easter Bush. Midl 3L 71
Easter Compton. S Glo 5H 33
Easter Fearn. High 3J 87
Easter Galcantray. High 7L 87
Eastergate. W Sus 5K 27
Easterhouse. Glas 3E 70
Easter Howgate. Midl 3L 71
Easter Kinkell. High 6H 87
Easter Lednathie. Ang 7D 82
Easter Ogil. Ang 7E 82
Easter Ord. Abers 3J 83
Easter Quarff. Shet 8E 95
Easter Rhynd. Per 4G 77
Easter Skeld. Shet 7D 95
Easter Suddie. High 6J 87
Easterton. Wilts 8A 34
Eastertown. Som 8F 32
Easter Tulloch. Abers 6H 83
East Everleigh. Wilts 8C 34
East Farleigh. Kent 8F 36
East Farndon. Nptn 3F 42
East Ferry. Linc 6E 56
Eastfield. N Lan 3G 71 (nr. Caldercruix)
Eastfield. N Lan 3G 71 (nr. Harthill)
Eastfield. N Yor 5K 61
Eastfield. S Lan 3E 70
Eastfield Hall. Nmbd 1H 67
East Fortune. E Lot 2E 72
East Garforth. W Yor 2A 56
East Garston. W Ber 6D 34
Eastgate. Dur 8E 66
Eastgate. Norf 5H 53
East Ginge. Oxon 5E 34
East Gores. Essx 1G 37
East Goscote. Leics 8C 50
East Grafton. Wilts 7C 34
East Green. Suff 6C 44
East Grimstead. Wilts 3C 26
East Grinstead. W Sus 4B 28
East Guldeford. E Sus 5H 29
East Haddon. Nptn 5E 42
East Hagbourne. Oxon 5F 34
East Halton. N Lin 3H 57
East Ham. G Lon 5C 36
Eastham. Mers 7B 54
Eastham. Worc 5G 41
Eastham Ferry. Mers 7B 54
Easthampstead. Brac 7J 35
Easthampton. Here 5E 40
East Hanney. Oxon 4E 34
East Hanningfield. Essx 3F 36
East Hardwick. W Yor 4A 56
East Harling. Norf 3F 44
East Harlsey. N Yor 4D 60
East Harnham. Wilts 3B 26
East Harptree. Bath 8H 33
East Hartford. Nmbd 4H 67
East Harting. W Sus 4J 27
East Hatch. Wilts 3J 25
East Hatley. Cambs 6L 43
Easthaugh. Norf 6G 53
East Hauxwell. N Yor 4A 60
East Haven. Ang 2L 77
Eastheath. Wok 7J 35
East Heckington. Linc 5H 51
East Hedleyhope. Dur 7G 67
East Helmsdale. High 8F 92
East Hendred. Oxon 5E 34
East Heslerton. N Yor 6J 61
East Hoathly. E Sus 6D 28
East Holme. Dors 7H 25
Easthope. Shrp 2F 40
Easthorpe. Essx 1H 37
Easthorpe. Leics 6E 50
East Horrington. Som 1E 24
East Horsley. Surr 8L 35
East Horton. Nmbd 6K 73
Easthouses. Midl 3M 71
East Howe. Bour 6A 26
East Huntspill. Som 1C 24
East Hyde. C Beds 2M 35
East Ilsley. W Ber 5E 34
Eastington. Devn 5J 23
Eastington. Glos 2B 34 (nr. Northleach)
Eastington. Glos 3K 33 (nr. Stonehouse)
East Keal. Linc 3K 51
East Kennett. Wilts 7B 34
East Keswick. W Yor 1M 55
East Kilbride. S Lan 4E 70
East Kirkby. Linc 3K 51
East Knapton. N Yor 6H 61
East Knighton. Dors 7H 25
East Knowstone. Devn 3K 23
East Knoyle. Wilts 2H 25
East Kyloe. Nmbd 6K 73
East Lambrook. Som 4D 24
East Langdon. Kent 3M 29
East Langton. Leics 2F 42
East Langwell. High 1K 87
East Lavant. W Sus 5J 27
East Lavington. W Sus 4K 27
East Layton. N Yor 3A 60
Eastleach Martin. Glos 3C 34
Eastleach Turville. Glos 3B 34
East Leake. Notts 7B 50
East Learmouth. Nmbd 6H 73
Eastleigh. Devn 3F 22 (nr. Bideford)
East Leigh. Devn 5J 23 (nr. Crediton)
East Leigh. Devn 4H 21 (nr. Modbury)
Eastleigh. Hants 4E 26
East Lexham. Norf 6E 52
East Lilburn. Nmbd 7K 73
Eastling. Kent 8H 37
East Linton. E Lot 2E 72
East Liss. Hants 3H 27
East Lockinge. Oxon 5E 34
East Looe. Corn 4D 20
East Lound. N Lin 6D 56
East Lulworth. Dors 7H 25
East Lutton. N Yor 7J 61
East Lydford. Som 2E 24
East Lyng. Som 3C 24
East Mains. Abers 4G 83
East Malling. Kent 8F 36
East Marden. W Sus 4J 27
East Markham. Notts 8D 56
East Marton. N Yor 8L 59
East Meon. Hants 3G 27
East Mersea. Essx 2J 37
East Mey. High 2J 93
East Midlands Airport. Leics 7A 50
East Molesey. Surr 7M 35
Eastmoor. Norf 1D 44
East Morden. Dors 6J 25
East Morton. W Yor 1K 55
East Ness. N Yor 6F 60
East Newton. E Yor 2J 57
East Newton. N Yor 6F 60
Eastney. Port 6G 27
Eastnor. Here 8H 41
East Norton. Leics 1F 42
East Nynehead. Som 3A 24
East Oakley. Hants 8F 34
Eastoft. N Lin 4E 56
East Ogwell. Devn 8K 23
Easton. Cambs 4K 43
Easton. Cumb 6K 65 (nr. Burgh by Sands)
Easton. Cumb 4M 65 (nr. Longtown)
Easton. Devn 7J 23
Easton. Dors 8F 24
Easton. Hants 2F 26
Easton. Linc 7F 50
Easton. Norf 6H 53
Easton. Som 1E 24
Easton. Suff 6J 45
Easton. Wilts 6L 33
Easton Grey. Wilts 5L 33
Easton-in-Gordano. N Som 6H 33
Easton Maudit. Nptn 6G 43
Easton on the Hill. Nptn 1J 43
Easton Royal. Wilts 7C 34
East Orchard. Dors 4H 25
East Ord. Nmbd 4J 73
East Panson. Devn 6E 22
East Peckham. Kent 3E 28
East Pennard. Som 2E 24
East Perry. Cambs 5K 43
East Pitcorthie. Fife 5L 77
East Portlemouth. Devn 6J 21
East Prawle. Devn 6J 21
East Preston. W Sus 5L 27
East Putford. Devn 4E 22
East Quantoxhead. Som 1A 24
East Rainton. Tyne 7J 67
East Ravendale. NE Lin 6J 57
East Raynham. Norf 5E 52
Eastrea. Cambs 2L 43
East Rhidorroch Lodge. High 2E 86
Eastriggs. Dum 5K 65
East Rigton. W Yor 1M 55
Eastrington. E Yor 2D 56
East Rounton. N Yor 3D 60
East Row. N Yor 2H 61
East Rudham. Norf 5E 52
East Runton. Norf 3H 53
East Ruston. Norf 5K 53
Eastry. Kent 8M 37
East Saltoun. E Lot 3D 72
East Shaws. Dur 2M 59
East Shefford. W Ber 6D 34
Eastshore. Shet 10D 95
East Sleekburn. Nmbd 3H 67
East Somerton. Norf 6L 53
East Stockwith. Linc 6D 56
East Stoke. Dors 7H 25
East Stoke. Notts 5D 50
East Stoke. Som 4D 24
East Stour. Dors 3H 25
East Stourmouth. Kent 7L 37
East Stowford. Devn 3H 23
East Stratton. Hants 1F 26
East Studdal. Kent 3M 29
East Taphouse. Corn 3C 20
East-the-Water. Devn 3F 22
East Thirston. Nmbd 2G 67
East Tilbury. Thur 6E 36
East Tisted. Hants 2H 27
East Torrington. Linc 7H 57
East Tuddenham. Norf 6G 53
East Tytherley. Hants 3C 26
East Tytherton. Wilts 6M 33
East Village. Devn 5K 23
Eastville. Linc 4L 51
East Wall. Shrp 2F 40
East Walton. Norf 6D 52
East Week. Devn 6H 23
Eastwell. Leics 7D 50
East Wellow. Hants 3D 26
East Wemyss. Fife 6J 77
East Whitburn. W Lot 3H 71
Eastwick. Herts 2C 36
Eastwick. Shet 4D 95
East Williamston. Pemb 3E 30
East Winch. Norf 6C 52
East Winterslow. Wilts 2C 26
East Wittering. W Sus 6H 27
East Witton. N Yor 5A 60
Eastwood. Notts 5A 50
Eastwood. S'end 5G 37
East Woodburn. Nmbd 3E 66
Eastwood End. Cambs 2A 44
East Woodhay. Hants 7E 34
East Woodlands. Som 1G 25
East Worldham. Hants 2H 27
East Worlington. Devn 4J 23
East Wretham. Norf 2F 44
East Youlstone. Devn 4D 22
Eathorpe. Warw 5B 42
Eaton. Ches E 3F 48
Eaton. Ches W 3C 48
Eaton. Leics 7D 50
Eaton. Norf 4C 52 (nr. Heacham)
Eaton. Norf 1J 45 (nr. Norwich)
Eaton. Notts 8D 56
Eaton. Oxon 3E 34
Eaton. Shrp 3D 40 (nr. Bishop's Castle)
Eaton. Shrp 2F 40 (nr. Church Stretton)
Eaton Bishop. Here 8E 40
Eaton Bray. C Beds 1K 35
Eaton Constantine. Shrp 1F 40
Eaton Hastings. Oxon 4C 34
Eaton Socon. Cambs 6K 43
Eaton upon Tern. Shrp 7D 48
Eau Brink. Norf 8M 51
Eaves Green. W Mid 3A 42
Ebberley Hill. Devn 4G 23
Ebberston. N Yor 5H 61
Ebbesbourne Wake. Wilts 3J 25
Ebblake. Dors 5B 26
Ebbsfleet. Kent 6E 36
Ebbw Vale. Blae 3D 32
Ebchester. Dur 6G 67
Ebernoe. W Sus 3K 27
Ebford. Devn 7L 23
Ebley. Glos 3L 33
Ebnal. Ches W 5B 48
Ebrington. Glos 7M 41
Ecchinswell. Hants 8F 34
Ecclefechan. Dum 4J 65
Eccles. G Man 6F 54
Eccles. Kent 7F 36
Eccles. Bord 5G 73
Ecclesall. S Yor 7M 55
Ecclesfield. S Yor 6M 55
Eccles Green. Here 7D 40
Eccleshall. Staf 7F 48
Eccleshill. W Yor 2K 55
Ecclesmachan. W Lot 2J 71
Eccles on Sea. Norf 5L 53
Eccles Road. Norf 2G 45
Eccleston. Ches W 3B 48
Eccleston. Lanc 4D 54
Eccleston. Mers 6C 54
Eccup. W Yor 1L 55
Echt. Abers 3H 83
Eckford. Bord 7G 73
Eckington. Derbs 8A 56
Eckington. Worc 7K 41
Ecton. Nptn 5G 43
Edale. Derbs 7K 55
Eday Airport. Orkn 4D 94
Edburton. W Sus 6A 28
Edderside. Cumb 7J 65
Edderton. High 3K 87
Eddington. Kent 7K 37
Eddington. W Ber 7D 34
Eddleston. Bord 5L 71
Eddlewood. S Lan 4F 70
Edenbridge. Kent 3C 28
Edendonich. Arg 3J 75
Edenfield. Lanc 4G 55
Edenhall. Cumb 8A 66
Edenham. Linc 7G 51
Edensor. Derbs 3K 49
Edentaggart. Arg 6L 75
Edenthorpe. S Yor 5C 56
Eden Vale. Dur 8K 67
Edern. Gwyn 6B 46
Edgarley. Som 2E 24
Edgbaston. W Mid 3L 41
Edgcott. Buck 1G 35
Edgcott. Som 2K 23
Edge. Glos 3L 33
Edge. Shrp 1D 40
Edgebolton. Shrp 7C 48
Edge End. Glos 2H 33
Edgefield. Norf 4G 53
Edgefield Street. Norf 4G 53
Edge Green. Ches W 4B 48
Edgehead. Midl 3M 71
Edgeley. Shrp 5C 48
Edgeside. Lanc 3G 55
Edgeworth. Glos 3M 33
Edgiock. Worc 5L 41
Edgmond. Telf 8E 48
Edgmond Marsh. Telf 7E 48
Edgton. Shrp 3D 40
Edgware. G Lon 4M 35
Edgworth. Bkbn 4F 54

Edinbane. High 6H 85
Edinburgh. Edin 2L 71
Edinburgh Airport. Edin 2K 71
Edingale. Staf 8K 49
Edingley. Notts 4C 50
Edingthorpe. Norf 4K 53
Edington. Som 2C 24
Edington. Wilts 8M 33
Edingworth. Som 8F 32
Edistone. Devn 3D 22
Edithmead. Som 1C 24
Edith Weston. Rut 1H 43
Edlaston. Derbs 5J 49
Edlesborough. Buck 2K 35
Edlingham. Nmbd 1G 67
Edlington. Linc 8J 57
Edmondsham. Dors 4A 26
Edmondsley. Dur 7H 67
Edmondthorpe. Leics 8E 50
Edmonstone. Orkn 5D 94
Edmonton. Corn 8A 22
Edmonton. G Lon 4B 36
Edmundbyers. Dur 6F 66
Ednam. Bord 6G 73
Ednaston. Derbs 5K 49
Edney Common. Essx 3E 36
Edrom. Bord 4H 73
Edstaston. Shrp 6C 48
Edstone. Warw 5M 41
Edwalton. Notts 6C 50
Edwardstone. Suff 7F 44
Edwardsville. Mer T 4C 32
Edwinsford. Carm 8J 39
Edwinstowe. Notts 3C 50
Edworth. C Beds 7L 43
Edwyn Ralph. Here 6G 41
Edzell. Ang 7G 83
Efail-fach. Neat 4M 31
Efail Isaf. Rhon 5C 32
Efailnewydd. Gwyn 6C 46
Efail-rhyd. Powy 7L 47
Efailwen. Carm 1F 30
Efenechtyd. Den 4L 47
Effingham. Surr 8M 35
Effingham Common. Surr 8M 35
Effirth. Shet 6D 95
Efflinch. Staf 8J 49
Efford. Devn 5K 23
Efstigarth. Shet 2E 95
Egbury. Hants 8E 34
Egdon. Worc 6K 41
Egerton. G Man 4F 54
Egerton. Kent 3H 29
Egerton Forstal. Kent 3G 29
Eggborough. N Yor 3B 56
Eggbuckland. Plym 4F 20
Eggesford. Devn 4H 23
Eggington. C Beds 1K 35
Egginton. Derbs 7K 49
Egglescliffe. Stoc T 2D 60
Eggleston. Dur 1L 59
Egham. Surr 6L 35
Egham Hythe. Surr 6L 35
Egleton. Rut 1G 43
Eglingham. Nmbd 8L 73
Egloshayle. Corn 8B 22
Egloskerry. Corn 7D 22
Eglwysbach. Cnwy 2H 47
Eglwys Brewis. V Glam 7C 32
Eglwys Fach. Cdgn 2J 39
Eglwyswrw. Pemb 8D 38
Egmanton. Notts 3D 50
Egmere. Norf 4F 52
Egremont. Cumb 2B 58
Egremont. Mers 6B 54
Egton. N Yor 3H 61
Egton Bridge. N Yor 3H 61
Egypt. Buck 5K 35
Egypt. Hants 1E 26
Eight Ash Green. Essx 1H 37
Eight Mile Burn. Midl 4K 71
Eignaig. High 1E 74
Eilanreach. High 2A 80
Eildon. Bord 6E 72
Eileanach Lodge. High 5H 87
Eilean Fhlodaigh. W Isl 6C 84
Eilean Iarmain. High 2M 79
Einacleit. W Isl 6B 90
Eisgein. W Isl 7D 90
Eisingrug. Gwyn 6F 46
Elan Village. Powy 5M 39
Elberton. S Glo 5J 33
Elbridge. W Sus 5K 27
Elburton. Plym 4G 21
Elcho. Per 3G 77
Elcombe. Swin 5B 34
Elcot. W Ber 7D 34
Eldernell. Cambs 2M 43
Eldersfield. Worc 8J 41
Elderslie. Ren 3C 70
Elder Street. Essx 8B 44
Eldon. Dur 1B 60
Eldroth. N Yor 7J 59
Eldwick. W Yor 1K 55
Elfhowe. Cumb 4F 58
Elford. Nmbd 6L 73
Elford. Staf 8J 49
Elford Closes. Cambs 4A 44
Elgin. Mor 3C 88
Elgol. High 2K 79
Elham. Kent 3K 29
Elie. Fife 5K 77
Eling. Hants 4D 26
Eling. W Ber 6F 34
Elishaw. Nmbd 2D 66
Elizafield. Dum 4H 65
Elkesley. Notts 8C 56
Elkington. Nptn 4E 42
Elkins Green. Essx 3E 36
Elkstone. Glos 2M 33
Ellan. High 1L 81
Elland. W Yor 3K 55
Ellary. Arg 2F 68
Ellastone. Staf 5J 49
Ellbridge. Corn 3F 20
Ellel. Lanc 8F 58
Ellemford. Bord 3G 73
Ellenabeich. Arg 4E 74
Ellenborough. Cumb 8H 65
Ellenbrook. Herts 3A 36
Ellenhall. Staf 7F 48
Ellen's Green. Surr 2L 27
Ellerbec. N Yor 4D 60
Ellerburn. N Yor 5H 61
Ellerby. N Yor 2G 61
Ellerdine. Telf 7D 48
Ellerdine Heath. Telf 7D 48
Ellerhayes. Devn 5L 23
Elleric. Arg 1H 75
Ellerker. E Yor 3F 56
Ellerton. E Yor 2D 56
Ellerton. N Yor 4B 60
Ellerton. Shrp 7E 48
Ellesborough. Buck 3J 35
Ellesmere. Shrp 6A 48
Ellesmere Port. Ches W 8C 54
Ellingham. Hants 5B 26
Ellingham. Norf 2K 45
Ellingham. Nmbd 7L 73
Ellingstring. N Yor 5A 60
Ellington. Cambs 4K 43
Ellington. Nmbd 2H 67
Ellington Thorpe. Cambs 4K 43
Elliot. Ang 2M 77
Ellisfield. Hants 1G 27
Ellishadder. High 5K 85
Ellistown. Leics 8A 50
Ellon. Abers 6K 89
Ellonby. Cumb 8M 65
Ellough. Suff 3L 45
Elloughton. E Yor 3F 56
Ellwood. Glos 3H 33
Elm. Cambs 1A 44
Elmbridge. Glos 2L 33
Elmbridge. Worc 5K 41
Elmdon. Essx 8A 44
Elmdon. W Mid 3M 41
Elmdon Heath. W Mid 3M 41
Elmesthorpe. Leics 2C 42
Elmfield. IOW 6F 26
Elm Hill. Dors 3H 25
Elmhurst. Staf 8J 49
Elmley Castle. Worc 7K 41
Elmley Lovett. Worc 5J 41
Elmore. Glos 2K 33
Elmore Back. Glos 2K 33
Elm Park. G Lon 5D 36
Elmscott. Devn 3D 22
Elmsett. Suff 7G 45
Elmstead. Essx 1J 37
Elmstead Heath. Essx 1J 37
Elmstead Market. Essx 1J 37
Elmsted. Kent 3K 29
Elmstone. Kent 7L 37
Elmstone Hardwicke. Glos 1M 33
Elmswell. E Yor 8J 61
Elmswell. Suff 5F 44
Elmton. Derbs 8B 56
Elphin. High 8K 91
Elphinstone. E Lot 2M 71
Elrick. Abers 3J 83
Elrick. Mor 1E 82
Elrig. Dum 7A 64
Elsdon. Nmbd 2E 66
Elsecar. S Yor 6M 55
Elsenham. Essx 1D 36
Elsfield. Oxon 2F 34
Elsham. N Lin 4G 57
Elsing. Norf 6G 53
Elslack. N Yor 1H 55
Elsrickle. S Lan 5J 71
Elstead. Surr 1K 27
Elsted. W Sus 4J 27
Elsted Marsh. W Sus 3J 27
Elsthorpe. Linc 7G 51
Elstob. Dur 1C 60
Elston. Devn 5J 23
Elston. Lanc 2E 54
Elston. Notts 5D 50
Elston. Wilts 1A 26
Elstone. Devn 4H 23
Elstow. Bed 7J 43
Elstree. Herts 4M 35
Elstronwick. E Yor 2J 57
Elswick. Lanc 2C 54
Elswick. Tyne 5H 67
Elsworth. Cambs 5M 43
Elterwater. Cumb 3E 58
Eltham. G Lon 6C 36
Eltisley. Cambs 6L 43
Elton. Cambs 2J 43
Elton. Ches W 8C 54
Elton. Derbs 3K 49
Elton. Glos 2K 33
Elton. G Man 4F 54
Elton. Here 4E 40
Elton. Notts 6D 50
Elton. Stoc T 2D 60
Elton Green. Ches W 8C 54
Eltringham. Nmbd 5F 66
Elvanfoot. S Lan 8H 71
Elvaston. Derbs 6A 50
Elveden. Suff 4E 44
Elvetham Heath. Hants 8H 35
Elvingston. E Lot 2D 72
Elvington. Kent 8L 37
Elvington. York 1D 56
Elwick. Hart 8K 67
Elwick. Nmbd 6L 73
Elworth. Ches E 3E 48
Elworth. Dors 7E 24
Elworthy. Som 2M 23
Ely. Cambs 3B 44
Ely. Card 6D 32
Emberton. Mil 7G 43
Embleton. Cumb 8J 65
Embleton. Dur 1D 60
Embleton. Nmbd 7M 73
Embo. High 2L 87
Emborough. Som 8J 33
Embo Street. High 2L 87
Embsay. N Yor 8M 59
Emery Down. Hants 5C 26
Emley. W Yor 4L 55
Emmbrook. Wok 7H 35
Emmer Green. Read 6H 35
Emmington. Oxon 3H 35
Emneth. Norf 1A 44
Emneth Hungate. Norf 1B 44
Empingham. Rut 1H 43
Empshott. Hants 2H 27
Emsworth. Hants 5H 27
Enborne. W Ber 7E 34
Enborne Row. W Ber 7E 34
Enchmarsh. Shrp 2F 40
Enderby. Leics 2D 42
Endmoor. Cumb 5G 59
Endon. Staf 4G 49
Endon Bank. Staf 4G 49
Enfield. G Lon 4B 36
Enfield Wash. G Lon 4B 36
Enford. Wilts 8B 34
Engine Common. S Glo 5J 33
Englefield. W Ber 6G 35
Englefield Green. Surr 6K 35
Engleseabrook. Ches E 4E 48
English Bicknor. Glos 2H 33
Englishcombe. Bath 7K 33
English Frankton. Shrp 7B 48
Enham Alamein. Hants 1D 26
Enmore. Som 2M 23
Ennerdale Bridge. Cumb 2B 58
Enniscaven. Corn 4A 20
Enoch. Dum 1F 64
Enochdhu. Per 7A 82
Ensay. Arg 1A 74
Ensbury. Bour 6A 26
Ensdon. Shrp 8B 48
Ensis. Devn 3G 23
Enson. Staf 7G 49
Enstone. Oxon 1D 34
Enterkinfoot. Dum 1F 64
Enville. Staf 3J 41
Eolaigearraidh. W Isl 3B 78
Eorabus. Arg 3A 74
Eoropaidh. W Isl 2F 90
Epney. Glos 2K 33
Epperstone. Notts 5C 50
Epping. Essx 3C 36
Epping Green. Essx 3C 36
Epping Green. Herts 3A 36
Epping Upland. Essx 3C 36
Eppleby. N Yor 2A 60
Eppleworth. E Yor 2G 57
Epsom. Surr 7A 36
Epwell. Oxon 7B 42
Epworth. N Lin 5D 56
Epworth Turbary. N Lin 5D 56
Erbistock. Wrex 5A 48
Erbusaig. High 1M 79
Erchless Castle. High 7G 87
Erdington. W Mid 2M 41
Eredine. Arg 5G 75
Eriboll. High 4M 91
Ericstane. Dum 8J 71
Eridge Green. E Sus 4D 28
Erines. Arg 2G 69
Eriswell. Suff 4D 44
Erith. G Lon 6D 36
Erlestoke. Wilts 8M 33
Ermine. Linc 8F 56
Ermington. Devn 4H 21
Ernesettle. Plym 4F 20
Erpingham. Norf 4H 53
Erriottwood. Kent 8H 37
Errogie. High 1H 81
Errol. Per 3H 77
Errol Station. Per 3H 77
Erskine. Ren 2C 70
Erskine Bridge. Ren 2C 70
Ervie. Dum 5K 63
Erwarton. Suff 8J 45
Erwood. Powy 7A 40
Eryholme. N Yor 3C 60
Eryrys. Den 4M 47
Escalls. Corn 7A 19
Escomb. Dur 8G 67
Escrick. N Yor 1C 56
Esgair. Carm 1H 31
(nr. Carmarthen)
Esgair. Carm 2G 31
(nr. St Clears)
Esgairgeiliog. Powy 1K 39
Esh. Dur 7G 67
Esher. Surr 7M 35
Esholt. W Yor 1K 55
Eshott. Nmbd 2H 67
Eshton. N Yor 8L 59
Esh Winning. Dur 7G 67
Eskadale. High 8G 87
Eskbank. Midl 3M 71
Eskdale Green. Cumb 3C 58
Eskdalemuir. Dum 2K 65
Eskham. Linc 6K 57
Esknish. Arg 3B 68
Esk Valley. N Yor 3H 61
Eslington Hall. Nmbd 8K 73
Espley Hall. Nmbd 2G 67
Esprick. Lanc 2C 54
Essendine. Rut 8G 51
Essendon. Herts 3A 36
Essich. High 8J 87
Essington. Staf 1K 41
Eston. Red C 2E 60
Estover. Plym 4G 21
Eswick. Shet 6E 95
Etal. Nmbd 6J 73
Etchilhampton. Wilts 7A 34
Etchingham. E Sus 5F 28
Etchinghill. Kent 4K 29
Etchinghill. Staf 8H 49
Etherley Dene. Dur 1A 60
Ethie Haven. Ang 1M 77
Etling Green. Norf 6G 53
Etloe. Glos 3J 33
Eton. Wind 6K 35
Eton Wick. Wind 6K 35
Etteridge. High 4J 81
Ettersgill. Dur 1K 59
Ettiley Heath. Ches E 3E 48
Ettington. Warw 7A 42
Etton. E Yor 1F 56
Etton. Pet 1K 43
Ettrick. Bord 8L 71
Ettrickbridge. Bord 7M 71
Etwall. Derbs 6K 49
Eudon Burnell. Shrp 3H 41
Eudon George. Shrp 3G 41
Euston. Suff 4E 44
Euxton. Lanc 4D 54
Evanstown. B'end 5B 32
Evanton. High 5J 87
Evedon. Linc 5G 51
Evelix. High 2K 87
Evendine. Here 7H 41
Evenjobb. Powy 5C 40
Evenley. Nptn 8D 42
Evenlode. Glos 1C 34
Even Swindon. Swin 5B 34
Evenwood. Dur 1A 60
Evenwood Gate. Dur 1A 60
Everbay. Orkn 5E 94
Evercreech. Som 2F 24
Everdon. Nptn 6D 42
Everingham. E Yor 1E 56
Everleigh. Wilts 8C 34
Everley. N Yor 5J 61
Eversholt. C Beds 8H 43
Evershot. Dors 5E 24
Eversley. Hants 7H 35
Eversley Centre. Hants 7H 35
Eversley Cross. Hants 7H 35
Everthorpe. E Yor 2F 56
Everton. C Beds 6L 43
Everton. Hants 6C 26
Everton. Mers 6B 54
Everton. Notts 6C 56
Evertown. Dum 4L 65
Evesbatch. Here 7G 41
Evesham. Worc 7L 41
Evington. Leic 1E 42
Ewden Village. S Yor 6L 55
Ewdness. Shrp 2H 41
Ewell. Surr 7A 36
Ewell Minnis. Kent 3L 29
Ewelme. Oxon 4G 35
Ewen. Glos 4A 34
Ewenny. V Glam 6B 32
Ewerby. Linc 5H 51
Ewes. Dum 2L 65
Ewesley. Nmbd 2F 66
Ewhurst. Surr 1L 27
Ewhurst Green. E Sus 5F 28
Ewhurst Green. Surr 2L 27
Ewlo. Flin 3A 48
Ewloe. Flin 3A 48
Ewood Bridge. Lanc 3F 54
Eworthy. Devn 6F 22
Ewshot. Hants 8J 35
Ewyas Harold. Here 1F 32
Exbourne. Devn 5H 23
Exbury. Hants 5E 26
Exceat. E Sus 8D 28
Exebridge. Som 3L 23
Exelby. N Yor 5B 60
Exeter. Devn 6L 23
Exeter International Airport.
Devn 6M 23
Exford. Som 2K 23
Exfords Green. Shrp 1E 40
Exhall. Warw 6M 41
Exlade Street. Oxon 5G 35
Exminster. Devn 7L 23
Exmoor. Som 2K 23
Exmouth. Devn 7M 23
Exnaboe. Shet 10D 95
Exning. Suff 5C 44
Exton. Devn 7L 23
Exton. Hants 3G 27
Exton. Rut 8F 50
Exton. Som 2L 23
Exwick. Devn 6L 23
Eyam. Derbs 8L 55
Eydon. Nptn 6D 42
Eye. Here 5E 40
Eye. Pet 1L 43
Eye. Suff 4H 45
Eye Green. Pet 1L 43
Eyemouth. Bord 3J 73
Eyeworth. C Beds 7L 43
Eyhorne Street. Kent 8G 37
Eyke. Suff 6K 45
Eynesbury. Cambs 6K 43
Eynort. High 1H 79
Eynsford. Kent 7D 36
Eynsham. Oxon 3E 34
Eyre. High 6J 85
(on Isle of Skye)
Eyre. High 8K 85
(on Raasay)
Eythorne. Kent 3L 29
Eyton. Here 5E 40
Eyton. Shrp 3D 40
(nr. Bishop's Castle)
Eyton. Shrp 8A 48
(nr. Shrewsbury)
Eyton. Wrex 5A 48
Eyton on Severn. Shrp 1F 40
Eyton upon the Weald Moors.
Telf 8D 48

F

Faccombe. Hants 8D 34
Faceby. N Yor 3D 60
Faddiley. Ches E 4C 48
Fadmoor. N Yor 5F 60
Fagwyr. Swan 3L 31
Faichem. High 3E 80
Faifley. W Dun 2D 70
Fail. S Ayr 7C 70
Failand. N Som 6H 33
Failford. S Ayr 7C 70
Failsworth. G Man 5H 55
Fairbourne. Gwyn 8F 46
Fairbourne Heath. Kent 8G 37
Fairburn. N Yor 3A 56
Fairfield. Derbs 8J 55
Fairfield. Kent 5H 29
Fairfield. Worc 4K 41
(nr. Bromsgrove)
Fairfield. Worc 7L 41
(nr. Evesham)
Fairford. Glos 3B 34
Fair Green. Norf 6C 52
Fair Hill. Cumb 8A 66
Fairhill. S Lan 4F 70
Fair Isle Airport. Shet 1G 94
Fairlands. Surr 8K 35
Fairlie. N Ayr 4A 70
Fairlight. E Sus 6G 29
Fairlight Cove. E Sus 6G 29
Fairmile. Devn 6M 23
Fairmile. Surr 7M 35
Fairmilehead. Edin 3L 71
Fair Oak. Devn 4M 23
Fair Oak. Hants 4E 26
(nr. Eastleigh)
Fair Oak. Hants 7F 34
(nr. Kingsclere)
Fairoak. Staf 6E 48
Fair Oak Green. Hants 7G 35
Fairseat. Kent 7E 36
Fairstead. Essx 2F 36
Fairstead. Norf 6C 52
Fairwarp. E Sus 5C 28
Fairwater. Card 6D 32
Fairy Cross. Devn 3F 22
Fakenham. Norf 5F 52
Fakenham Magna. Suff 4F 44
Fala. Midl 3D 72
Fala Dam. Midl 3D 72
Falcon. Here 8G 41
Faldingworth. Linc 7G 57
Falfield. S Glo 4J 33
Falkenham. Suff 8J 45
Falkirk. Falk 2G 71
Falkland. Fife 5H 77
Fallin. Stir 6D 76
Fallowfield. G Man 6G 55
Falmer. E Sus 7B 28
Falmouth. Corn 6F 19
Falsgrave. N Yor 5K 61
Falstone. Nmbd 3C 66
Fanagmore. High 5J 91
Fancott. C Beds 1L 35
Fanellan. High 7G 87
Fangdale Beck. N Yor 4E 60
Fangfoss. E Yor 8G 61
Fankerton. Falk 1F 70
Fanmore. Arg 1B 74
Fanner's Green. Essx 2E 36
Fannich Lodge. High 5E 86
Fans. Bord 5F 72
Farcet. Cambs 2L 43
Far Cotton. Nptn 6F 42
Fareham. Hants 5F 26
Farewell. Staf 8H 49
Far Forest. Worc 4H 41
Farforth. Linc 8K 57
Far Green. Glos 3K 33
Far Hoarcross. Staf 7J 49
Faringdon. Oxon 4C 34
Farington. Lanc 3D 54
Farlam. Cumb 6A 66
Farleigh. N Som 7G 33
Farleigh. Surr 7B 36
Farleigh Hungerford. Som 8L 33
Farleigh Wallop. Hants 1G 27
Farleigh Wick. Wilts 7L 33
Farlesthorpe. Linc 8L 57
Farleton. Cumb 5G 59
Farleton. Lanc 7G 59
Farley. High 7G 87
Farley. N Som 6G 33
Farley. Shrp 1D 40
(nr. Shrewsbury)
Farley. Shrp 1G 41
(nr. Telford)
Farley. Staf 5H 49
Farley. Wilts 3C 26
Farley Green. Suff 6D 44
Farley Green. Surr 1L 27
Farley Hill. Wok 7H 35
Farley's End. Glos 2K 33
Farlington. N Yor 7F 60
Farlington. Port 5G 27
Farlow. Shrp 3G 41
Farmborough. Bath 7J 33
Farmcote. Glos 1A 34
Farmcote. Shrp 2H 41
Farmington. Glos 2B 34
Far Moor. G Man 5D 54
Farmoor. Oxon 3E 34
Farmtown. Mor 4F 88
Farnah Green. Derbs 5L 49
Farnborough. G Lon 7C 36
Farnborough. Hants 8J 35
Farnborough. Warw 7C 42
Farnborough. W Ber 5E 34
Farncombe. Surr 1K 27
Farndish. Bed 5H 43
Farndon. Ches W 4B 48
Farndon. Notts 4D 50
Farnell. Ang 8G 83
Farnham. Dors 4J 25
Farnham. Essx 1C 36
Farnham. N Yor 7C 60
Farnham. Suff 5K 45
Farnham. Surr 1J 27
Farnham Common. Buck 5K 35
Farnham Green. Essx 1C 36
Farnham Royal. Buck 5K 35
Farnhill. N Yor 1J 55
Farningham. Kent 7D 36
Farnley. N Yor 1L 55
Farnley Tyas. W Yor 4K 55
Farnsfield. Notts 4C 50
Farnworth. G Man 5F 54
Farnworth. Hal 7D 54
Far Oakridge. Glos 3M 33
Farr. High 3C 92
(nr. Bettyhill)
Farr. High 8J 87
(nr. Inverness)
Farr. High 3L 81
(nr. Kingussie)
Farraline. High 1H 81
Farringdon. Devn 6M 23
Farrington. Dors 4H 25
Farrington Gurney. Bath 8J 33
Far Sawrey. Cumb 4E 58
Farsley. W Yor 2L 55
Farthinghoe. Nptn 8D 42
Farthingstone. Nptn 6E 42
Farthorpe. Linc 8J 57
Fartown. W Yor 4K 55
Farway. Devn 6A 24
Fasag. High 6A 86
Fascadale. High 6K 79
Fasnacloich. Arg 1H 75
Fassfern. High 6C 80
Fatfield. Tyne 6J 67
Faugh. Cumb 6A 66
Fauld. Staf 7J 49
Fauldhouse. W Lot 3H 71
Faulkbourne. Essx 2F 36
Faulkland. Som 8K 33
Fauls. Shrp 6C 48
Faverdale. Darl 2B 60
Faversham. Kent 7J 37
Fawdington. N Yor 6D 60
Fawfieldhead. Staf 3H 49
Fawkham Green. Kent 7D 36
Fawler. Oxon 2D 34
Fawley. Buck 5H 35
Fawley. Hants 5E 26
Fawley. W Ber 5D 34
Fawley Chapel. Here 1H 33
Fawton. Corn 3C 20
Faxfleet. E Yor 3E 56
Faygate. W Sus 4A 28
Fazakerley. Mers 6B 54
Fazeley. Staf 1M 41
Feabuie. High 7K 87
Feagour. High 4H 81
Fearann Dhomhnaill. High 3L 79
Fearby. N Yor 5A 60
Fearn. High 4L 87
Fearnan. Per 1C 76
Fearnbeg. High 6M 85
Fearnhead. Warr 6E 54
Fearnmore. High 5M 85
Featherstone. Staf 1K 41
Featherstone. W Yor 3A 56
Featherstone Castle.
Nmbd 5B 66
Feckenham. Worc 5L 41
Feering. Essx 1G 37
Feetham. N Yor 4L 59
Feizor. N Yor 7J 59
Felbridge. Surr 4B 28
Felbrigg. Norf 4J 53
Felcourt. Surr 3B 28
Felden. Herts 3L 35
Felhampton. Shrp 3E 40
Felindre. Carm 1K 31
(nr. Llandeilo)
Felindre. Carm 8J 39
(nr. Llandovery)
Felindre. Carm 8F 38
(nr. Newcastle Emlyn)
Felindre. Powy 3B 40
Felindre. Swan 3L 31
Felindre Farchog. Pemb 8D 38
Felinfach. Cdgn 6H 39
Felinfach. Powy 8A 40
Felinfoel. Carm 3K 31
Felingwmisaf. Carm 1K 31
Felingwmuchaf. Carm 1K 31
Felin Newydd. Powy 1A 40
(nr. Newtown)
Felin Newydd. Powy 7M 47
(nr. Oswestry)
Felin Wnda. Cdgn 7F 38
Felinwynt. Cdgn 6E 38
Felixkirk. N Yor 5D 60
Felixstowe. Suff 8J 45
Felixstowe Ferry. Suff 8K 45
Felkington. Nmbd 5J 73
Fell End. Cumb 4J 59
Felling. Tyne 5H 67
Fell Side. Cumb 8L 65
Felmersham. Bed 6H 43
Felmingham. Norf 5J 53
Felpham. W Sus 6K 27
Felsham. Suff 6F 44
Felsted. Essx 1E 36
Feltham. G Lon 6M 35
Felthamhill. Surr 6L 35
Felthorpe. Norf 6H 53
Felton. Here 7F 40
Felton. N Som 7H 33
Felton. Nmbd 1G 67
Felton Butler. Shrp 8A 48
Feltwell. Norf 2D 44
Fenay Bridge. W Yor 4K 55
Fence. Lanc 2G 55
Fence Houses. Tyne 6J 67
Fencott. Oxon 2F 34
Fen Ditton. Cambs 5A 44
Fen Drayton. Cambs 5M 43
Fen End. Linc 7J 51
Fen End. W Mid 4A 42
Fenham. Nmbd 5K 73
Fenham. Tyne 5H 67
Fenhouses. Linc 5J 51
Feniscowles. Bkbn 3E 54
Feniton. Devn 6M 23
Fenn Green. Shrp 3H 41
Fenn's Bank. Wrex 6C 48
Fenn Street. Medw 6F 36
Fenny Bentley. Derbs 4J 49
Fenny Bridges. Devn 6A 24
Fenny Compton. Warw 6C 42
Fenny Drayton. Leics 2B 42
Fenny Stratford. Mil 8G 43
Fenrother. Nmbd 2G 67
Fenstanton. Cambs 5M 43
Fen Street. Norf 2G 45
Fenton. Cambs 4M 43
Fenton. Cumb 6A 66
Fenton. Linc 4E 50
(nr. Caythorpe)
Fenton. Linc 8E 56
(nr. Saxilby)
Fenton. Nmbd 6J 73
Fenton. Notts 7D 56
Fenton. Stoke 5F 48
Fentonadle. Corn 8B 22
Fenton Barns. E Lot 1E 72
Fenwick. E Ayr 5C 70
Fenwick. Nmbd 5K 73
(nr. Berwick-upon-Tweed)
Fenwick. Nmbd 4F 66
(nr. Hexham)
Fenwick. S Yor 4B 56
Feochaig. Arg 8F 68
Feock. Corn 6F 19
Feolin Ferry. Arg 3C 68
Feorlan. Arg 8E 68
Ferindonald. High 3L 79
Feriniquarrie. High 6F 84
Fern. Ang 7E 82
Ferndale. Rhon 4B 32
Ferndown. Dors 5A 26
Ferness. High 7M 87
Fernham. Oxon 4C 34
Fernhill. W Sus 3A 28
Fernhill Heath. Worc 6J 41
Fernhurst. W Sus 3J 27
Fernieflatt. Abers 6J 83
Ferniegair. S Lan 4F 70
Fernilea. High 8H 85
Fernilee. Derbs 8J 55
Ferrensby. N Yor 7C 60
Ferriby Sluice. N Lin 3F 56
Ferring. W Sus 5M 27
Ferrybridge. W Yor 3A 56
Ferryden. Ang 8H 83
Ferryhill. Aber 3K 83
Ferry Hill. Cambs 3M 43
Ferryhill. Dur 8H 67
Ferryhill Station. Dur 8H 67
Ferryside. Carm 2H 31
Ferryton. High 5J 87
Fersfield. Norf 3G 45
Fersit. High 6F 80
Feshiebridge. High 3L 81
Fetcham. Surr 8M 35
Fetterangus. Abers 4K 89
Fettercairn. Abers 6G 83
Fewcott. Oxon 1F 34
Fewston. N Yor 8A 60
Ffairfach. Carm 1L 31
Ffair Rhos. Cdgn 5K 39
Ffaldybrenin. Carm 7J 39
Ffarmers. Carm 7J 39
Ffawyddog. Powy 2E 32
Ffodun. Powy 1C 40
Ffont-y-gari. V Glam 7C 32
Fforest. Carm 3K 31
Fforest-fach. Swan 4L 31
Fforest Goch. Neat 3M 31
Ffostrasol. Cdgn 7F 38
Ffos-y-ffin. Cdgn 5G 39
Ffrith. Flin 4M 47
Ffrwdgrech. Powy 1C 32
Ffwl-y-mwn. V Glam 7C 32
Ffynnon-ddrain. Carm 1J 31
Ffynnongroyw. Flin 1L 47
Ffynnon Gynydd. Powy 7B 40
Ffynnonoer. Cdgn 6H 39
Fiag Lodge. High 7M 91
Fidden. Arg 3A 74
Fiddington. Glos 8K 41
Fiddington. Som 1B 24
Fiddleford. Dors 4H 25
Fiddlers Hamlet. Essx 3C 36
Field. Staf 6H 49
Field Assarts. Oxon 2D 34
Field Broughton. Cumb 5E 58
Field Dalling. Norf 4G 53
Fieldhead. Cumb 8M 65
Field Head. Leics 1C 42
Fifehead Magdalen. Dors 3G 25
Fifehead Neville. Dors 4G 25
Fifehead St Quintin. Dors 4G 25
Fife Keith. Mor 4E 88
Fifield. Oxon 2C 34
Fifield. Wilts 8B 34
Fifield. Wind 6K 35
Fifield Bavant. Wilts 3A 26
Figheldean. Wilts 1B 26
Filby. Norf 6L 53
Filey. N Yor 5L 61
Filford. Dors 6D 24
Filgrave. Mil 7G 43
Filkins. Oxon 3C 34
Filleigh. Devn 4J 23
(nr. Crediton)
Filleigh. Devn 3H 23
(nr. South Molton)
Fillingham. Linc 7F 56
Fillongley. Warw 3A 42
Filton. S Glo 6J 33
Fimber. E Yor 7H 61
Finavon. Ang 8E 82
Fincham. Norf 1C 44
Finchampstead. Wok 7H 35
Fincharn. Arg 5G 75
Finchdean. Hants 4H 27
Finchingfield. Essx 8C 44
Finchley. G Lon 4A 36
Findern. Derbs 6L 49
Findhorn. Mor 3A 88
Findhorn Bridge. High 1L 81
Findochty. Mor 3E 88
Findo Gask. Per 3F 76
Findon. Abers 4K 83
Findon. W Sus 5M 27
Findon Mains. High 5J 87
Findon Valley. W Sus 5M 27
Finedon. Nptn 4H 43
Fingal Street. Suff 4J 45
Fingest. Buck 4H 35
Finghall. N Yor 5A 60
Fingland. Cumb 6K 65
Fingland. Dum 8F 70
Finglesham. Kent 8M 37
Fingringhoe. Essx 1J 37
Finiskaig. High 4A 80
Finmere. Oxon 8E 42
Finnart. Per 8H 81
Finningham. Suff 5G 45
Finningley. S Yor 6C 56
Finnyguad. Abers 4G 89
Finsbury. G Lon 5B 36
Finstall. Worc 4K 41
Finsthwaite. Cumb 5E 58
Finstock. Oxon 2D 34
Finstown. Orkn 6B 94
Fintry. Abers 4H 89
Fintry. D'dee 2K 77
Fintry. Stir 1E 70
Finwood. Warw 5M 41
Finzean. Abers 4G 83
Fionnphort. Arg 3A 74
Fionnsabhagh. W Isl 3E 84
Firbeck. S Yor 7B 56
Firby. N Yor 5B 60
(nr. Bedale)
Firby. N Yor 7G 61
(nr. Malton)
Firgrove. G Man 4H 55
Firle. E Sus 7C 28
Firsdown. Wilts 2C 26
First Coast. High 2B 86
Firth. Shet 4E 95
Fir Tree. Dur 8G 67
Fishbourne. IOW 6F 26
Fishbourne. W Sus 5J 27
Fishburn. Dur 8J 67
Fishcross. Clac 6E 76
Fisherford. Abers 6G 89
Fisherrow. E Lot 2M 71
Fisher's Pond. Hants 3E 26
Fisher's Row. Lanc 1C 54
Fisherstreet. W Sus 2K 27
Fisherton. High 6K 87
Fisherton. S Ayr 8A 70
Fisherton de la Mere. Wilts 2J 25
Fishguard. Pemb 8B 38
Fishlake. S Yor 4C 56
Fishley. Norf 6L 53
Fishnish. Arg 1D 74
Fishpond Bottom. Dors 6C 24
Fishponds. Bris 6J 33
Fishpool. Glos 1J 33
Fishpool. G Man 5G 55
Fishpools. Powy 5B 40
Fishtoft. Linc 5K 51
Fishtoft Drove. Linc 5K 51
Fishwick. Bord 4J 73
Fiskavaig. High 8H 85
Fiskerton. Linc 8G 57
Fiskerton. Notts 4D 50
Fitch. Shet 7D 95
Fitling. E Yor 2J 57
Fittleton. Wilts 1B 26
Fittleworth. W Sus 4L 27
Fitton End. Cambs 8L 51
Fitz. Shrp 8B 48
Fitzhead. Som 3A 24
Fitzwilliam. W Yor 4A 56
Fiunary. High 1D 74
Five Ash Down. E Sus 5C 28
Five Ashes. E Sus 5D 28
Five Bells. Som 1M 23
Five Bridges. Here 7G 41
Fivehead. Som 3C 24
Five Lane Ends. Lanc 8G 59
Fivelanes. Corn 7D 22
Five Oak Green. Kent 3E 28
Five Oaks. W Sus 3L 27
Five Roads. Carm 3J 31
Five Ways. Warw 4A 42
Flack's Green. Essx 2F 36
Flackwell Heath. Buck 5J 35
Fladbury. Worc 7K 41
Fladda. Shet 3D 95
Fladdabister. Shet 8E 95
Flagg. Derbs 3J 49
Flamborough. E Yor 6M 61
Flamstead. Herts 2L 35
Flansham. W Sus 5K 27
Flasby. N Yor 8L 59
Flash. Staf 3H 49
Flashader. High 6H 85
Flatt, The. Cumb 4A 66
Flaunden. Herts 3L 35
Flawborough. Notts 5D 50
Flawith. N Yor 7D 60
Flax Bourton. N Som 7H 33
Flaxby. N Yor 8C 60
Flaxholme. Derbs 5L 49
Flaxley. Glos 2J 33
Flaxley Green. Staf 8H 49
Flaxpool. Som 2A 24
Flaxton. N Yor 7F 60
Fleck. Shet 10D 95
Fleckney. Leics 2E 42
Flecknoe. Warw 5D 42
Fledborough. Notts 8E 56
Fleet. Dors 7F 24
Fleet. Hants 8J 35
(nr. Farnborough)
Fleet. Hants 5H 27
(nr. South Hayling)
Fleet. Linc 7K 51
Fleet Hargate. Linc 7K 51
Fleetville. Herts 3M 35
Fleetwood. Lanc 1B 54
Fleggburgh. Norf 6L 53
Fleisirin. W Isl 5F 90
Flemingston. V Glam 6C 32
Flemington. S Lan 3E 70
(nr. Glasgow)
Flemington. S Lan 5F 70
(nr. Strathaven)
Flempton. Suff 5E 44
Fleoideabhagh. W Isl 3E 84
Fletcher's Green. Kent 3D 28
Fletchertown. Cumb 7K 65
Fletching. E Sus 5C 28
Fleuchary. High 2K 87
Flexbury. Corn 5D 22
Flexford. Surr 8K 35
Flimby. Cumb 8H 65
Flimwell. E Sus 4F 28
Flint. Flin 8A 54
Flintham. Notts 5D 50
Flint Mountain. Flin 8A 54
Flinton. E Yor 2J 57
Flintsham. Here 6D 40
Flishinghurst. Kent 4F 28
Flitcham. Norf 5D 52
Flitton. C Beds 8J 43
Flitwick. C Beds 8J 43
Flixborough. N Lin 4E 56
Flixton. G Man 6F 54
Flixton. N Yor 6K 61
Flixton. Suff 3K 45
Flockton. W Yor 4L 55
Flodden. Nmbd 6J 73
Flodigarry. High 4J 85
Flood's Ferry. Cambs 2M 43
Flookburgh. Cumb 6E 58
Flordon. Norf 2H 45
Flore. Nptn 5E 42
Flotterton. Nmbd 1F 66
Flowton. Suff 7G 45
Flushing. Abers 5L 89
Flushing. Corn 6F 19
Fluxton. Devn 6M 23
Flyford Flavell. Worc 6K 41
Fobbing. Thur 5F 36
Fochabers. Mor 4D 88
Fochriw. Cphy 3D 32
Fockerby. N Lin 4E 56
Fodderty. High 6H 87
Foddington. Som 3E 24
Foel. Powy 8J 47
Foffarty. Ang 1K 77
Foggathorpe. E Yor 2D 56
Fogo. Bord 5G 73
Fogorig. Bord 5G 73
Foindle. High 5J 91
Folda. Ang 7B 82
Fole. Staf 6H 49
Foleshill. W Mid 3B 42
Foley Park. Worc 4J 41
Folke. Dors 4F 24
Folkestone. Kent 4L 29
Folkingham. Linc 6G 51
Folkington. E Sus 7D 28
Folksworth. Cambs 2K 43
Folkton. N Yor 6K 61
Folla Rule. Abers 6H 89
Follifoot. N Yor 8C 60
Folly Cross. Devn 5F 22
Folly Gate. Devn 6G 23
Folly, The. Herts 2M 35
Folly, The. W Ber 7E 34
Fonmon. V Glam 7C 32
Fonthill Bishop. Wilts 2J 25
Fonthill Gifford. Wilts 2J 25
Fontmell Magna. Dors 4H 25
Fontwell. W Sus 5K 27
Font-y-gary. V Glam 7C 32
Foodieash. Fife 4J 77
Foolow. Derbs 8K 55
Footdee. Aber 3K 83
Footherley. Staf 1M 41
Foots Cray. G Lon 6C 36
Forbestown. Abers 2D 82
Force Forge. Cumb 4E 58
Force Mills. Cumb 4E 58
Forcett. N Yor 2A 60
Ford. Arg 5F 74
Ford. Buck 3H 35
Ford. Derbs 7A 56
Ford. Devn 3F 22
(nr. Bideford)
Ford. Devn 4H 21
(nr. Holbeton)
Ford. Devn 5J 21
(nr. Salcombe)
Ford. Glos 1A 34
Ford. Nmbd 6J 73
Ford. Plym 4F 20
Ford. Shrp 8B 48
Ford. Som 8H 33
(nr. Wells)
Ford. Som 3M 23
(nr. Wiveliscombe)
Ford. Staf 4H 49
Ford. W Sus 5L 27
Ford. Wilts 6L 33
(nr. Chippenham)
Ford. Wilts 2B 26
(nr. Salisbury)
Forda. Devn 2F 22
Ford Barton. Devn 4L 23
Fordcombe. Kent 3D 28
Fordell. Fife 1K 71
Forden. Powy 1C 40
Ford End. Essx 2E 36
Forder Green. Devn 3J 21
Ford Green. Lanc 1C 54
Fordham. Cambs 4C 44
Fordham. Essx 1H 37
Fordham. Norf 2C 44
Fordham Heath. Essx 1H 37
Ford Heath. Shrp 8B 48
Fordhouses. W Mid 1K 41
Fordie. Per 3C 76
Fordingbridge. Hants 4B 26
Fordington. Linc 8L 57
Fordon. E Yor 6K 61
Fordoun. Abers 6H 83
Ford Street. Essx 1H 37
Ford Street. Som 4A 24
Fordton. Devn 6K 23
Fordwells. Oxon 2D 34
Fordwich. Kent 8K 37
Fordyce. Abers 3F 88
Forebridge. Staf 7G 49
Foremark. Derbs 7L 49
Forest. N Yor 3B 60
Forestburn Gate. Nmbd 2F 66
Foresterseat. Mor 4B 88
Forest Green. Glos 4L 33
Forest Green. Surr 1M 27
Forest Hall. Cumb 3G 59
Forest Head. Cumb 6A 66
Forest Hill. Oxon 3F 34
Forest-in-Teesdale. Dur 1K 59
Forest Lodge. Per 6M 81
Forest Mill. Clac 6E 76
Forest Row. E Sus 4C 28
Forestside. W Sus 4H 27
Forest Town. Notts 3B 50
Forfar. Ang 8E 82
Forgandenny. Per 4F 76
Forge. Powy 2K 39
Forge Side. Torf 3E 32
Forge, The. Here 6D 40
Forgewood. N Lan 4F 70
Forgie. Mor 4D 88
Forgue. Abers 5G 89
Formby. Mers 5A 54
Forncett End. Norf 2H 45
Forncett St Mary. Norf 2H 45
Forncett St Peter. Norf 2H 45
Forneth. Per 1F 76
Fornham All Saints. Suff 5E 44
Fornham St Martin. Suff 5E 44
Forres. Mor 4A 88
Forrestfield. N Lan 3G 71
Forrest Lodge. Dum 3C 64
Forsbrook. Staf 5G 49
Forse. High 6H 93
Forsinard. High 5D 92
Forss. High 3F 92
Forstal, The. Kent 4J 29
Forston. Dors 6F 24
Fort Augustus. High 3F 80
Forteviot. Per 4F 76
Fort George. High 6K 87
Forth. S Lan 4H 71
Forthampton. Glos 8J 41
Forthay. Glos 4K 33
Forth Road Bridge. Fife 2K 71
Fortingall. Per 1C 76
Fort Matilda. Inv 2A 70
Forton. Hants 1E 26
Forton. Lanc 8F 58
Forton. Shrp 8B 48
Forton. Som 5C 24
Forton. Staf 7E 48
Forton Heath. Shrp 8B 48
Fortrie. Abers 5G 89
Fortrose. High 6K 87
Fortuneswell. Dors 8F 24
Fort William. High 6D 80
Forty Green. Buck 4K 35
Forty Hill. G Lon 4B 36
Forward Green. Suff 6G 45
Fosbury. Wilts 8D 34
Foscot. Oxon 1C 34
Fosdyke. Linc 6K 51
Foss. Per 8K 81
Fossebridge. Glos 2A 34
Foster Street. Essx 3C 36
Foston. Derbs 6J 49
Foston. Leics 2E 42
Foston. Linc 5E 50
Foston. N Yor 7F 60
Foston on the Wolds.
E Yor 8L 61
Fotherby. Linc 6K 57
Fothergill. Cumb 8H 65
Fotheringhay. Nptn 2J 43
Foubister. Orkn 7D 94
Foula Airport. Shet 9B 95
Foul Anchor. Cambs 8L 51
Foulbridge. Cumb 7M 65
Foulden. Norf 2D 44
Foulden. Bord 4J 73
Foul Mile. E Sus 6E 28
Foulridge. Lanc 1G 55
Foulsham. Norf 5G 53
Fountainhall. Bord 5D 72
Four Alls, The. Shrp 6D 48
Four Ashes. Staf 1K 41
(nr. Cannock)
Four Ashes. Staf 3J 41
(nr. Kinver)
Four Ashes. Suff 4G 45
Four Crosses. Powy 1A 40
(nr. Llanerfyl)
Four Crosses. Powy 8M 47
(nr. Llanymynech)
Four Crosses. Staf 1K 41
Four Elms. Kent 3C 28
Four Forks. Som 2B 24
Four Gotes. Cambs 8L 51
Four Lane End. S Yor 5L 55
Four Lane Ends. Lanc 8G 59
Four Lanes. Corn 6D 19
Fourlanes End. Ches E 4E 48
Four Marks. Hants 2G 27
Four Mile Bridge. IOA 2B 46
Four Oaks. E Sus 5G 29
Four Oaks. Glos 1J 33
Four Oaks. W Mid 3A 42
Four Roads. Carm 3J 31
Four Roads. IOM 7C 62
Fourstones. Nmbd 5D 66
Four Throws. Kent 5F 28
Fovant. Wilts 3A 26
Foveran. Abers 1K 83
Fowey. Corn 4C 20
Fowlershill. Abers 2K 83
Fowley Common. Warr 6E 54
Fowlis. Ang 2J 77
Fowlis Wester. Per 3E 76
Fowlmere. Cambs 7A 44
Fownhope. Here 8F 40
Foxcombe Hill. Oxon 3E 34
Fox Corner. Surr 8K 35
Foxcote. Glos 2A 34
Foxcote. Som 8K 33
Foxdale. IOM 6C 62
Foxearth. Essx 7E 44
Foxfield. Cumb 5D 58
Foxham. Wilts 6M 33
Fox Hatch. Essx 4D 36
Foxhole. Corn 4A 20
Foxholes. N Yor 6K 61
Foxhunt Green. E Sus 6D 28
Fox Lane. Hants 8J 35
Foxley. Norf 5G 53
Foxley. Nptn 6E 42
Foxley. Wilts 5L 33
Foxlydiate. Worc 5L 41
Fox Street. Essx 1J 37
Foxt. Staf 5H 49
Foxton. Cambs 7A 44
Foxton. Dur 1C 60
Foxton. Leics 3E 42
Foxton. N Yor 4D 60
Foxup. N Yor 6K 59
Foxwist Green. Ches W 3D 48
Foxwood. Shrp 4G 41
Foy. Here 1H 33
Foyers. High 1G 81
Foynesfield. High 6L 87
Fraddam. Corn 6C 19
Fraddon. Corn 4A 20
Fradley. Staf 8J 49
Fradley South. Staf 8J 49
Fradswell. Staf 6G 49
Fraisthorpe. E Yor 7L 61
Framfield. E Sus 5C 28
Framingham Earl. Norf 1J 45
Framingham Pigot. Norf 1J 45
Framlingham. Suff 5J 45
Frampton. Dors 6F 24
Frampton. Linc 6K 51
Frampton Cotterell. S Glo 5J 33
Frampton Mansell. Glos 3M 33
Frampton on Severn. Glos 3K 33
Frampton West End. Linc 5J 51
Framsden. Suff 6H 45
Framwellgate Moor. Dur 7H 67
Franche. Worc 4J 41
Frandley. Ches W 8E 54
Frankby. Mers 7A 54
Frankfort. Norf 5K 53
Frankley. Worc 3K 41
Frank's Bridge. Powy 6B 40
Frankton. Warw 4C 42
Frankwell. Shrp 8B 48
Frant. E Sus 4D 28
Fraserburgh. Abers 3K 89
Frating Green. Essx 1J 37
Fratton. Port 5G 27
Freathy. Corn 4F 20
Freckenham. Suff 4C 44
Freckleton. Lanc 3C 54
Freeby. Leics 7E 50
Freefolk Priors. Hants 1E 26
Freehay. Staf 5H 49
Freeland. Oxon 2E 34
Freester. Shet 6E 95
Freethorpe. Norf 1L 45
Freiston. Linc 5K 51
Freiston Shore. Linc 5K 51
Fremington. Devn 2G 23
Fremington. N Yor 4M 59
Frenchbeer. Devn 7H 23
French Street. Kent 8C 36
Frenich. Stir 5M 75
Frensham. Surr 1J 27
Frenze. Norf 3H 45
Fresgoe. High 3E 92
Freshfield. Mers 5A 54
Freshford. Bath 7K 33
Freshwater. IOW 7D 26
Freshwater Bay. IOW 7D 26
Freshwater East. Pemb 4E 30
Fressingfield. Suff 4J 45
Freston. Suff 8H 45
Freswick. High 3J 93
Fretherne. Glos 3K 33
Frettenham. Norf 6J 53
Freuchie. Fife 5H 77
Freystrop. Pemb 2D 30
Friar's Gate. E Sus 4C 28
Friar Waddon. Dors 7F 24
Friday Bridge. Cambs 1A 44
Friday Street. E Sus 7E 28
Friday Street. Surr 1M 27
Fridaythorpe. E Yor 8H 61
Friden. Derbs 3J 49
Friern Barnet. G Lon 4A 36
Friesthorpe. Linc 7G 57
Frieston. Linc 5F 50
Frieth. Buck 4H 35
Friezeland. Notts 4A 50
Frilford. Oxon 4E 34
Frilsham. W Ber 6F 34
Frimley. Surr 8J 35
Frimley Green. Surr 8J 35
Frindsbury. Medw 7F 36
Fring. Norf 4D 52
Fringford. Oxon 1G 35
Frinsted. Kent 8G 37
Frinton-on-Sea. Essx 2L 37
Friockheim. Ang 1L 77
Friog. Gwyn 8F 46
Frisby. Leics 1F 42
Frisby. Linc 3L 51
Frisby on the Wreake.
Leics 8C 50
Friskney. Linc 4L 51
Friskney Eaudyke. Linc 4L 51
Friston. E Sus 8D 28
Friston. Suff 5L 45
Fritchley. Derbs 4L 49
Fritham. Hants 4C 26
Frith Bank. Linc 5K 51
Frith Common. Worc 5G 41
Frithelstock. Devn 4F 22
Frithelstock Stone. Devn 4F 22
Frithsden. Herts 3L 35
Frithville. Linc 4K 51
Frittenden. Kent 3G 29
Frittiscombe. Devn 5K 21
Fritton. Norf 1L 45
(nr. Great Yarmouth)
Fritton. Norf 2J 45
(nr. Long Stratton)
Fritwell. Oxon 1F 34
Frizinghall. W Yor 2K 55
Frizington. Cumb 2B 58
Frobost. W Isl 1B 78
Frocester. Glos 3K 33
Frochas. Powy 1B 40
Frodesley. Shrp 1F 40
Frodingham. N Lin 4F 56
Frodsham. Ches W 8D 54
Froggat. Derbs 8L 55
Froghall. Staf 5H 49
Frogham. Hants 4B 26
Frogham. Kent 8L 37
Frogmore. Devn 5J 21
Frogmore. Hants 7J 35
Frogmore. Herts 3M 35
Frognall. Linc 8H 51
Frogshall. Norf 4J 53
Frogwell. Corn 3E 20
Frolesworth. Leics 2D 42
Frome. Som 1G 25
Fromefield. Som 1G 25
Frome St Quintin. Dors 5E 24
Fromes Hill. Here 7G 41
Fron. Carm 8K 39
Fron. Gwyn 4E 46
(nr. Caernarfon)
Fron. Gwyn 6C 46
(nr. Pwllheli)
Fron. Powy 5A 40
(nr. Llandrindod Wells)
Fron. Powy 2B 40
(nr. Newtown)
Fron. Powy 1C 40
(nr. Welshpool)
Froncysyllte. Wrex 5M 47

Frongoch. *Gwyn* 6J **47**
Fron Isaf. *Wrex* 5M **47**
Fronoleu. *Gwyn* 6G **47**
Frosterley. *Dur* 8F **66**
Frotoft. *Orkn* 5C **94**
Froxfield. *C Beds* 8H **43**
Froxfield. *Wilts* 7C **34**
Froxfield Green. *Hants* 3H **27**
Fryern Hill. *Hants* 3E **26**
Fryerning. *Essx* 3E **36**
Fryton. *N Yor* 6F **60**
Fugglestone St Peter. *Wilts* 2B **26**
Fulbeck. *Linc* 4F **50**
Fulbourn. *Cambs* 6B **44**
Fulbrook. *Oxon* 2C **34**
Fulflood. *Hants* 2E **26**
Fulford. *Som* 3B **24**
Fulford. *Staf* 6G **49**
Fulford. *York* 1C **56**
Fulham. *G Lon* 6A **36**
Fulking. *W Sus* 6A **28**
Fuller's Moor. *Ches W* 4B **48**
Fuller Street. *Essx* 2F **36**
Fullerton. *Hants* 2D **26**
Fulletby. *Linc* 8J **57**
Full Sutton. *E Yor* 8G **61**
Fullwood. *E Ayr* 4C **70**
Fulmer. *Buck* 5K **35**
Fulmodestone. *Norf* 4F **52**
Fulnetby. *Linc* 8G **57**
Fulney. *Linc* 7J **51**
Fulstow. *Linc* 6K **57**
Fulthorpe. *Stoc T* 1D **60**
Fulwell. *Tyne* 6J **67**
Fulwood. *Lanc* 2D **54**
Fulwood. *Notts* 4A **50**
Fulwood. *Som* 4B **24**
Fulwood. *S Yor* 7L **55**
Fundenhall. *Norf* 2H **45**
Funtington. *W Sus* 5J **27**
Funtley. *Hants* 5F **26**
Funzie. *Shet* 2G **95**
Furley. *Devn* 5B **24**
Furnace. *Arg* 5H **75**
Furnace. *Carm* 3K **31**
Furnace. *Cdgn* 2J **39**
Furner's Green. *E Sus* 5C **28**
Furness Vale. *Derbs* 7J **55**
Furneux Pelham. *Herts* 1C **36**
Furzebrook. *Dors* 7J **25**
Furzehill. *Devn* 1J **23**
Furzehill. *Dors* 5A **26**
Furzeley Corner. *Hants* 4G **27**
Furzey Lodge. *Hants* 5D **26**
Furzley. *Hants* 4C **26**
Fyfield. *Essx* 3D **36**
Fyfield. *Glos* 3C **34**
Fyfield. *Hants* 1C **26**
Fyfield. *Oxon* 4E **34**
Fyfield. *Wilts* 7B **34**
Fylde, The. *Lanc* 2B **54**
Fylingthorpe. *N Yor* 3J **61**
Fyning. *W Sus* 3J **27**
Fyvie. *Abers* 6H **89**

G

Gabhsann bho Dheas. *W Isl* 3E **90**
Gabhsann bho Thuath. *W Isl* 3E **90**
Gabroc Hill. *E Ayr* 4C **70**
Gadbrook. *Surr* 3A **28**
Gaddesby. *Leics* 8C **50**
Gadfa. *IOA* 1D **46**
Gadgirth. *S Ayr* 7C **70**
Gaer. *Powy* 1D **32**
Gaerwen. *IOA* 2D **46**
Gagingwell. *Oxon* 1E **34**
Gaick Lodge. *High* 5K **81**
Gailey. *Staf* 8G **49**
Gainford. *Dur* 2A **60**
Gainsborough. *Linc* 6E **56**
Gainsborough. *Suff* 7H **45**
Gainsford End. *Essx* 8D **44**
Gairletter. *Arg* 1K **69**
Gairloch. *Abers* 3H **83**
Gairloch. *High* 4A **86**
Gairlochy. *High* 5D **80**
Gairney Bank. *Per* 6G **77**
Gairnshiel Lodge. *Abers* 3C **82**
Gaisgill. *Cumb* 3H **59**
Gaitsgill. *Cumb* 7L **65**
Galashiels. *Bord* 6D **72**
Galgate. *Lanc* 8F **58**
Galhampton. *Som* 3F **24**
Gallatown. *Fife* 6H **77**
Galley Common. *Warw* 2B **42**
Galleyend. *Essx* 3F **36**
Galleywood. *Essx* 3F **36**
Gallin. *Per* 1A **76**
Gallowfauld. *Ang* 1K **77**
Gallowhill. *E Dun* 2E **70**
Gallowhill. *Per* 2G **77**
Gallowhill. *Ren* 3C **70**
Gallowhills. *Abers* 4L **89**
Gallows Green. *Staf* 5H **49**
Gallows Green. *Worc* 5K **41**
Gallowstree Common. *Oxon* 5G **35**
Galltair. *High* 1A **80**
Gallt Melyd. *Den* 1K **47**
Galmington. *Som* 3B **24**
Galmisdale. *High* 5J **79**
Galmpton. *Devn* 5H **21**
Galmpton. *Torb* 4K **21**
Galmpton Warborough. *Torb* 4K **21**
Galphay. *N Yor* 6B **60**
Galston. *E Ayr* 6C **70**
Galton. *Dors* 7G **25**
Galtrigill. *High* 6F **84**
Gamblesby. *Cumb* 8B **66**
Gamelsby. *Cumb* 6K **65**
Gamesley. *Derbs* 6J **55**
Gamlingay. *Cambs* 6L **43**
Gamlingay Cinques. *Cambs* 6L **43**
Gamlingay Great Heath. *C Beds* 6L **43**
Gammaton. *Devn* 3F **22**
Gammersgill. *N Yor* 5M **59**
Gamston. *Notts* 6C **50** (nr. Nottingham)
Gamston. *Notts* 8D **56** (nr. Retford)
Ganarew. *Here* 2H **33**
Ganavan. *Arg* 2F **74**
Ganborough. *Glos* 1B **34**
Gang. *Corn* 3E **20**
Ganllwyd. *Gwyn* 7G **47**
Gannochy. *Ang* 6F **82**
Gannochy. *Per* 3G **77**
Gansclet. *High* 5J **93**
Ganstead. *E Yor* 2H **57**
Ganthorpe. *N Yor* 6F **60**
Ganton. *N Yor* 6J **61**
Gants Hill. *G Lon* 5C **36**
Gappah. *Devn* 8K **23**
Garafad. *High* 5J **85**
Garboldisham. *Norf* 3G **45**
Garden City. *Flin* 3A **48**
Gardeners Green. *Wok* 7J **35**
Gardenstown. *Abers* 3J **89**
Garden Village. *S Yor* 8L **55**
Garden Village. *Swan* 4K **31**
Garderhouse. *Shet* 7D **95**
Gardham. *E Yor* 1F **56**
Gardie. *Shet* 5B **95** (on Papa Stour)
Gardie. *Shet* 1G **95** (on Unst)
Gardie Ho. *Shet* 7E **95**
Gare Hill. *Som* 1G **25**
Garelochhead. *Arg* 6K **75**
Garford. *Oxon* 4E **34**
Garforth. *W Yor* 4A **56**
Gargrave. *N Yor* 8L **59**
Gargunnock. *Stir* 6C **76**
Garleffin. *S Ayr* 3K **63**
Garlieston. *Dum* 7B **64**
Garlinge Green. *Kent* 8K **37**
Garlogie. *Abers* 5H **83**
Garmelow. *Staf* 7E **48**
Garmond. *Abers* 4J **89**
Garmondsway. *Dur* 8J **67**
Garmony. *Arg* 1D **74**
Garmouth. *Mor* 3D **88**
Garmston. *Shrp* 1G **41**
Garnant. *Carm* 2L **31**
Garndiffaith. *Torf* 3E **32**
Garndolbenmaen. *Gwyn* 5D **46**
Garnett Bridge. *Cumb* 4G **59**
Garnfadryn. *Gwyn* 6B **46**
Garnkirk. *N Lan* 3E **70**
Garnlydan. *Blae* 2D **32**
Garnsgate. *Linc* 7L **51**
Garnswllt. *Swan* 3L **31**
Garn-yr-erw. *Torf* 2E **32**
Garrabost. *W Isl* 5F **90**
Garrallan. *E Ayr* 8D **70**
Garras. *Corn* 7E **19**
Garreg. *Gwyn* 5F **46**
Garrigill. *Cumb* 7C **66**
Garriston. *N Yor* 4A **60**
Garrogie Lodge. *High* 2H **81**
Garros. *High* 5J **85**
Garrow. *Per* 1D **76**
Garsdale. *Cumb* 5J **59**
Garsdale Head. *Cumb* 4J **59**
Garsdon. *Wilts* 5M **33**
Garshall Green. *Staf* 6G **49**
Garsington. *Oxon* 3F **34**
Garstang. *Lanc* 1C **54**
Garston. *Mers* 7C **54**
Garswood. *Mers* 6D **54**
Gartcosh. *N Lan* 3E **70**
Garth. *B'end* 4A **32**
Garth. *Cdgn* 3J **39**
Garth. *Gwyn* 6E **46**
Garth. *IOM* 6D **62**
Garth. *Powy* 7M **39** (nr. Builth Wells)
Garth. *Powy* 4C **40** (nr. Knighton)
Garth. *Shet* 6C **95** (nr. Sandness)
Garth. *Shet* 6E **95** (nr. Skellister)
Garth. *Wrex* 5M **47**
Garthamlock. *Glas* 3E **70**
Garthbrengy. *Powy* 8A **40**
Gartheli. *Cdgn* 6H **39**
Garthmyl. *Powy* 2B **40**
Garthorpe. *Leics* 7E **50**
Garthorpe. *N Lin* 4E **56**
Garth Owen. *Powy* 2B **40**
Garth Row. *Cumb* 4G **59**
Gartly. *Abers* 6F **88**
Gartmore. *Stir* 6A **76**
Gartness. *N Lan* 3F **70**
Gartness. *Stir* 1D **70**
Gartocharn. *W Dun* 1C **70**
Garton. *E Yor* 2J **57**
Garton-on-the-Wolds. *E Yor* 8J **61**
Gartsherrie. *N Lan* 3F **70**
Gartymore. *High* 8F **92**
Garvald. *E Lot* 2E **72**
Garvamore. *High* 4H **81**
Garvard. *Arg* 6A **74**
Garvault. *High* 6C **92**
Garve. *High* 5F **86**
Garvestone. *Norf* 1G **45**
Garvie. *Arg* 6H **75**
Garvock. *Abers* 6H **83**
Garvock. *Inv* 2A **70**
Garway. *Here* 1G **33**
Garway Common. *Here* 1G **33**
Garway Hill. *Here* 1G **33**
Garwick. *Linc* 5H **51**
Gaskan. *High* 6A **80**
Gasper. *Wilts* 2G **25**
Gastard. *Wilts* 7L **33**
Gasthorpe. *Norf* 3F **44**
Gatcombe. *IOW* 7E **26**
Gateacre. *Mers* 7C **54**
Gatebeck. *Cumb* 5G **59**
Gate Burton. *Linc* 7E **56**
Gateforth. *N Yor* 3B **56**
Gatehead. *E Ayr* 6B **70**
Gate Helmsley. *N Yor* 8F **60**
Gatehouse. *Nmbd* 3C **66**
Gatehouse of Fleet. *Dum* 6D **64**
Gatelawbridge. *Dum* 2G **65**
Gateley. *Norf* 5F **52**
Gatenby. *N Yor* 5C **60**
Gatesgarth. *Cumb* 2C **58**
Gateshead. *Tyne* 5H **67**
Gatesheath. *Ches W* 3B **48**
Gateside. *Ang* 1K **77** (nr. Forfar)
Gateside. *Ang* 1J **77** (nr. Kirriemuir)
Gateside. *Fife* 5G **77**
Gateside. *N Ayr* 4B **70**
Gathurst. *G Man* 5D **54**
Gatley. *G Man* 7G **55**
Gatton. *Surr* 8A **36**
Gattonside. *Bord* 6E **72**
Gatwick (London) Airport. *W Sus* 3A **28**
Gaufron. *Powy* 5M **39**
Gaulby. *Leics* 1E **42**
Gauldry. *Fife* 3J **77**
Gaultree. *Norf* 1A **44**
Gaunt's Common. *Dors* 5A **26**
Gaunt's Earthcott. *S Glo* 5J **33**
Gautby. *Linc* 8H **57**
Gavinton. *Bord* 4G **73**
Gawber. *S Yor* 5M **55**
Gawcott. *Buck* 8E **42**
Gawsworth. *Ches E* 3F **48**
Gawthorpe. *W Yor* 3L **55**
Gawthrop. *Cumb* 5H **59**
Gawthwaite. *Cumb* 5D **58**
Gay Bowers. *Essx* 3F **36**
Gaydon. *Warw* 6B **42**
Gayfield. *Orkn* 2C **94**
Gayhurst. *Mil* 7G **43**
Gayle. *N Yor* 5K **59**
Gayles. *N Yor* 3A **60**
Gay Street. *W Sus* 3L **27**
Gayton. *Mers* 7A **54**
Gayton. *Norf* 6D **52**
Gayton. *Nptn* 6F **42**
Gayton. *Staf* 7G **49**
Gayton le Marsh. *Linc* 7L **57**
Gayton le Wold. *Linc* 7J **57**
Gayton Thorpe. *Norf* 6D **52**
Gaywood. *Norf* 5C **52**
Gazeley. *Suff* 5D **44**
Geanies. *High* 4L **87**
Gearraidh Bhailteas. *W Isl* 1B **78**
Gearraidh Bhaird. *W Isl* 7D **90**
Gearraidh ma Monadh. *W Isl* 2B **78**
Gearraidh na h-Aibhne. *W Isl* 5C **90**
Geary. *High* 5G **85**
Geddes. *High* 6L **87**
Gedding. *Suff* 6F **44**
Geddington. *Nptn* 3G **43**
Gedintailor. *High* 8K **85**
Gedling. *Notts* 5C **50**
Gedney. *Linc* 7L **51**
Gedney Broadgate. *Linc* 7L **51**
Gedney Drove End. *Linc* 7L **51**
Gedney Dyke. *Linc* 7L **51**
Gedney Hill. *Linc* 8K **51**
Gee Cross. *G Man* 6H **55**
Geeston. *Rut* 1H **43**
Geilston. *Arg* 2B **70**
Geirinis. *W Isl* 7B **84**
Geise. *High* 3G **93**
Geisiadar. *W Isl* 5B **90**
Gelder Shiel. *Abers* 5C **82**
Geldeston. *Norf* 2K **45**
Gell. *Cnwy* 3H **47**
Gelli. *Pemb* 2E **30**
Gelli. *Rhon* 4B **32**
Gellifor. *Den* 3L **47**
Gelligaer. *Cphy* 4D **32**
Gellilydan. *Gwyn* 6F **46**
Gellinudd. *Neat* 3M **31**
Gellyburn. *Per* 2F **76**
Gellywen. *Carm* 1G **31**
Gelston. *Dum* 6E **64**
Gelston. *Linc* 5F **50**
Gembling. *E Yor* 8L **61**
Geneva. *Cdgn* 6G **39**
Gentleshaw. *Staf* 8H **49**
Geocrab. *W Isl* 2F **84**
George Green. *Buck* 5K **35**
Georgeham. *Devn* 2F **22**
George Nympton. *Devn* 3J **23**
Georgetown. *Blae* 3D **32**
Georgetown. *Ren* 3C **70**
Georth. *Orkn* 5B **94**
Gerlan. *Gwyn* 3F **46**
Germansweek. *Devn* 6F **22**
Germoe. *Corn* 7C **19**
Gerrans. *Corn* 6F **19**
Gerrard's Bromley. *Staf* 6E **48**
Gerrards Cross. *Buck* 5K **35**
Gerston. *High* 4G **93**
Gestingthorpe. *Essx* 8E **44**
Gethsemane. *Pemb* 7C **38**
Geuffordd. *Powy* 8M **47**
Gibraltar. *Buck* 2H **35**
Gibraltar. *Linc* 4M **51**
Gibraltar. *Suff* 6H **45**
Gibsmere. *Notts* 5D **50**
Giddeahall. *Wilts* 6L **33**
Gidea Park. *G Lon* 5D **36**
Gidleigh. *Devn* 7H **23**
Giffnock. *E Ren* 4D **70**
Gifford. *E Lot* 3E **72**
Giffordtown. *Fife* 4H **77**
Giggetty. *Staf* 2J **41**
Giggleswick. *N Yor* 7K **59**
Gignog. *Pemb* 1C **30**
Gilberdyke. *E Yor* 3E **56**
Gilbert's End. *Worc* 7J **41**
Gilbert's Green. *Warw* 4M **41**
Gilchriston. *E Lot* 3D **72**
Gilcrux. *Cumb* 8J **65**
Gildersome. *W Yor* 3L **55**
Gildingwells. *S Yor* 7B **56**
Gilesgate Moor. *Dur* 7H **67**
Gileston. *V Glam* 7C **32**
Gilfach. *Cphy* 4D **32**
Gilfach Goch. *Rhon* 5B **32**
Gilfachreda. *Cdgn* 6G **39**
Gilgarran. *Cumb* 1B **58**
Gillamoor. *N Yor* 4F **60**
Gillan. *Corn* 7E **19**
Gillar's Green. *Mers* 6C **54**
Gillen. *High* 6G **85**
Gilling East. *N Yor* 6F **60**
Gillingham. *Dors* 3H **25**
Gillingham. *Medw* 7F **36**
Gillingham. *Norf* 2L **45**
Gilling West. *N Yor* 3A **60**
Gillock. *High* 4H **93**
Gillow Heath. *Staf* 4F **48**
Gills. *High* 2J **93**
Gill's Green. *Kent* 4F **28**
Gilmanscleuch. *Bord* 7M **71**
Gilmerton. *Edin* 3L **71**
Gilmerton. *Per* 3D **76**
Gilmonby. *Dur* 2L **59**
Gilmorton. *Leics* 3D **42**
Gilsland. *Nmbd* 5B **66**
Gilsland Spa. *Cumb* 5B **66**
Gilston. *Midl* 4D **72**
Giltbrook. *Notts* 5A **50**
Gilwern. *Mon* 2E **32**
Gimingham. *Norf* 4J **53**
Giosla. *W Isl* 6B **90**
Gipping. *Suff* 5G **45**
Gipsey Bridge. *Linc* 5J **51**
Gipton. *W Yor* 2M **55**
Girdle Toll. *N Ayr* 5B **70**
Girlsta. *Shet* 6E **95**
Girsby. *N Yor* 3C **60**
Girthon. *Dum* 6D **64**
Girton. *Cambs* 5A **44**
Girton. *Notts* 3E **50**
Girvan. *S Ayr* 2L **63**
Gisburn. *Lanc* 1G **55**
Gisleham. *Suff* 3M **45**
Gislingham. *Suff* 4G **45**
Gissing. *Norf* 3H **45**
Gittisham. *Devn* 6A **24**
Gladestry. *Powy* 6C **40**
Gladsmuir. *E Lot* 2D **72**
Glaichbea. *High* 8H **87**
Glais. *Swan* 3M **31**
Glaisdale. *N Yor* 3G **61**
Glame. *High* 7K **85**
Glamis. *Ang* 1J **77**
Glamisdale. *High* 5J **79**
Glanaman. *Carm* 2L **31**
Glan-Conwy. *Cnwy* 4H **47**
Glandford. *Norf* 3G **53**
Glan Duar. *Carm* 7H **39**
Glandwr. *Blae* 3E **32**
Glandwr. *Pemb* 1F **30**
Glan-Dwyfach. *Gwyn* 5D **46**
Glandy Cross. *Carm* 1F **30**
Glandyfi. *Cdgn* 2J **39**
Glangrwyney. *Powy* 2E **32**
Glanmule. *Powy* 2B **40**
Glanrhyd. *Gwyn* 6B **46**
Glanrhyd. *Pemb* 7D **38** (nr. Cardigan)
Glan-rhyd. *Pemb* 8D **38** (nr. Crymych)
Glan-rhyd. *Powy* 3M **31**
Glanton. *Nmbd* 8K **73**
Glanton Pyke. *Nmbd* 8K **73**
Glanvilles Wootton. *Dors* 5F **24**
Glan-y-don. *Flin* 2L **47**
Glan-y-nant. *Powy* 3M **39**
Glan-yr-afon. *Gwyn* 5K **47**
Glan-yr-afon. *IOA* 1F **46**
Glan-yr-afon. *Powy* 1A **40**
Glan-y-wern. *Gwyn* 6F **46**
Glapthorn. *Nptn* 2J **43**
Glapwell. *Derbs* 3A **50**
Glas Aird. *Arg* 6A **74**
Glas-allt Shiel. *Abers* 5C **82**
Glasbury. *Powy* 8B **40**
Glaschoil. *Mor* 6A **88**
Glascoed. *Den* 2J **47**
Glascoed. *Mon* 3F **32**
Glascote. *Staf* 1A **42**
Glascwm. *Powy* 6B **40**
Glasfryn. *Cnwy* 4J **47**
Glasgow. *Glas* 3D **70**
Glasgow Airport. *Ren* 3C **70**
Glasgow Prestwick International Airport. *S Ayr* 7B **70**
Glashvin. *High* 5J **85**
Glasinfryn. *Gwyn* 3E **46**
Glas na Cardaich. *High* 4L **79**
Glasnacardoch. *High* 4L **79**
Glasnakille. *High* 2K **79**
Glaspwll. *Cdgn* 2K **39**
Glassburn. *High* 8F **86**
Glassenbury. *Kent* 4F **28**
Glasserton. *Dum* 8B **64**
Glassford. *S Lan* 5F **70**
Glassgreen. *Mor* 3C **88**
Glasshouse. *Glos* 1K **33**
Glasshouses. *N Yor* 7A **60**
Glasson. *Cumb* 5K **65**
Glasson. *Lanc* 8F **58**
Glassonby. *Cumb* 8A **66**
Glasterlaw. *Ang* 8F **82**
Glaston. *Rut* 1G **43**
Glastonbury. *Som* 2D **24**
Glatton. *Cambs* 3K **43**
Glazebrook. *Warr* 6E **54**
Glazebury. *Warr* 6E **54**
Glazeley. *Shrp* 3H **41**
Gleadless. *S Yor* 7M **55**
Gleadsmoss. *Ches E* 3F **48**
Gleann Dail bho Dheas. *W Isl* 2B **78**
Gleann Tholastaidh. *W Isl* 4F **90**
Gleann Uige. *High* 6L **79**
Gleaston. *Cumb* 6D **58**
Glecknabae. *Arg* 3J **69**
Gledrid. *Shrp* 6M **47**
Gleiniant. *Powy* 2M **39**
Glemsford. *Suff* 7E **44**
Glen. *Dum* 6C **64**
Glenancross. *High* 4L **79**
Glen Audlyn. *IOM* 4E **62**
Glenbarr. *Arg* 6E **68**
Glenbeg. *High* 7K **79**
Glen Bernisdale. *High* 7J **85**
Glenbervie. *Abers* 5H **83**
Glenboig. *N Lan* 3F **70**
Glenborrodale. *High* 7L **79**
Glenbranter. *Arg* 6J **75**
Glenbreck. *Bord* 7J **71**
Glenbrein Lodge. *High* 2G **81**
Glenbrittle. *High* 1J **79**
Glenbuchat Lodge. *Abers* 2D **82**
Glenbuck. *E Ayr* 7F **70**
Glenburn. *Ren* 3C **70**
Glencalvie Lodge. *High* 3G **87**
Glencaple. *Dum* 5G **65**
Glencarron Lodge. *High* 6C **86**
Glencarse. *Per* 3G **77**
Glencassley Castle. *High* 1G **87**
Glencat. *Abers* 4F **82**
Glencoe. *High* 8D **80**
Glen Cottage. *High* 5L **79**
Glencraig. *Fife* 6G **77**
Glendale. *High* 7F **84**
Glendevon. *Per* 5E **76**
Glendoebeg. *High* 3G **81**
Glendoick. *Per* 3H **77**
Glendoune. *S Ayr* 2L **63**
Glenduckie. *Fife* 4H **77**
Gleneagles. *Per* 5E **76**
Glenegedale. *Arg* 4B **68**
Glenegedale Lots. *Arg* 4B **68**
Glenelg. *High* 2A **80**
Glenernie. *Mor* 5A **88**
Glenesslin. *Dum* 3F **64**
Glenfarg. *Per* 4G **77**
Glenfarquhar Lodge. *Abers* 5H **83**
Glenferness Mains. *High* 7M **87**
Glenfeshie Lodge. *High* 4L **81**
Glenfiddich Lodge. *Mor* 6D **88**
Glenfield. *Leics* 1D **42**
Glenfinnan. *High* 5B **80**
Glenfintaig Lodge. *High* 5E **80**
Glenfoot. *Per* 4G **77**
Glenfyne Lodge. *Arg* 4K **75**
Glengap. *Dum* 6D **64**
Glengarnock. *N Ayr* 4B **70**
Glengolly. *High* 3G **93**
Glengorm Castle. *Arg* 8J **79**
Glengrasco. *High* 7J **85**
Glenhead Farm. *Ang* 7C **82**
Glenholm. *Bord* 6K **71**
Glen House. *Bord* 6L **71**
Glenhurich. *High* 7A **80**
Glenkerry. *Bord* 8L **71**
Glenkiln. *Dum* 4F **64**
Glenkindle. *Abers* 2E **82**
Glenkinglass Lodge. *Arg* 2J **75**
Glenkirk. *Bord* 7J **71**
Glenlean. *Arg* 1J **69**
Glenlee. *Dum* 3D **64**
Glenleraig. *High* 6J **91**
Glenlichorn. *Per* 4C **76**
Glenlivet. *Mor* 1B **82**
Glenlochar. *Dum* 5E **64**
Glenlochsie Lodge. *Per* 6A **82**
Glenluce. *Dum* 6L **63**
Glenmarskie. *High* 6F **86**
Glenmassan. *Arg* 1K **69**
Glenmavis. *N Lan* 3F **70**
Glen Maye. *IOM* 6C **62**
Glenmazeran Lodge. *High* 1K **81**
Glenmidge. *Dum* 3F **64**
Glen Mona. *IOM* 5E **62**
Glenmore. *High* 7K **79** (nr. Glenborrodale)
Glenmore. *High* 3M **81** (nr. Kingussie)
Glenmore. *High* 7J **85** (on Isle of Skye)
Glenmoy. *Ang* 7E **82**
Glennoe. *Arg* 2H **75**
Glen of Coachford. *Abers* 5E **88**
Glenogil. *Ang* 7E **82**
Glen Parva. *Leics* 2D **42**
Glenprosen Village. *Ang* 7D **82**
Glenree. *N Ayr* 7H **69**
Glenridding. *Cumb* 2E **58**
Glenrosa. *N Ayr* 6J **69**
Glenrothes. *Fife* 5H **77**
Glensanda. *High* 1F **74**
Glensaugh. *Abers* 6G **83**
Glenshero Lodge. *High* 4H **81**
Glensluain. *Arg* 6H **75**
Glenstockadale. *Dum* 5K **63**
Glenstriven. *Arg* 2J **69**
Glen Tanar House. *Abers* 4E **82**
Glentham. *Linc* 6G **57**
Glenton. *Abers* 1G **83**
Glentress. *Bord* 6L **71**
Glentromie Lodge. *High* 4K **81**
Glentrool Lodge. *Dum* 3B **64**
Glentrool Village. *Dum* 4A **64**
Glentruim House. *High* 4J **81**
Glentworth. *Linc* 7F **56**
Glenuig. *High* 6L **79**
Glen Village. *Falk* 2G **71**
Glen Vine. *IOM* 6D **62**
Glenwhilly. *Dum* 4L **63**
Glenzierfoot. *Dum* 4L **65**
Glespin. *S Lan* 7G **71**
Gletness. *Shet* 6E **95**
Glewstone. *Here* 1H **33**
Glib Cheois. *W Isl* 6D **90**
Glinton. *Pet* 1K **43**
Glooston. *Leics* 2F **42**
Glossop. *Derbs* 6J **55**
Gloster Hill. *Nmbd* 1H **67**
Gloucester. *Glos* 2L **33**
Gloucestershire Airport. *Glos* 1L **33**
Gloup. *Shet* 1F **95**
Glusburn. *N Yor* 1J **55**
Glutt Lodge. *High* 6E **92**
Glutton Bridge. *Staf* 3H **49**
Gluvian. *Corn* 3A **20**
Glympton. *Oxon* 1E **34**
Glyn. *Cnwy* 2H **47**
Glynarthen. *Cdgn* 7F **38**
Glynbrochan. *Powy* 3M **39**
Glyn Ceiriog. *Wrex* 6M **47**
Glyncoch. *Rhon* 4C **32**
Glyncorrwg. *Neat* 4A **32**
Glynde. *E Sus* 7C **28**
Glyndebourne. *E Sus* 6C **28**
Glyndyfrdwy. *Den* 5L **47**
Glyn Ebwy. *Blae* 3D **32**
Glynllan. *B'end* 5B **32**
Glyn-neath. *Neat* 3A **32**
Glynogwr. *B'end* 5B **32**
Glyntaff. *Rhon* 5C **32**
Glyntawe. *Powy* 2A **32**
Glynteg. *Carm* 8F **38**
Gnosall. *Staf* 7F **48**
Gnosall Heath. *Staf* 7F **48**
Goadby. *Leics* 2F **42**
Goadby Marwood. *Leics* 7D **50**
Goatacre. *Wilts* 6A **34**
Goathill. *Dors* 4F **24**
Goathland. *N Yor* 3H **61**
Goathurst. *Som* 2B **24**
Goathurst Common. *Kent* 8C **36**
Goat Lees. *Kent* 3J **29**
Gobernuisgach Lodge. *High* 5M **91**
Gobernuisgeach. *High* 6E **92**
Gobhaig. *W Isl* 1E **84**
Gobowen. *Shrp* 6A **48**
Godalming. *Surr* 1K **27**
Goddard's Corner. *Suff* 5J **45**
Goddard's Green. *Kent* 4G **29** (nr. Benenden)
Goddard's Green. *Kent* 4F **28** (nr. Cranbrook)
Goddards Green. *W Sus* 5A **28**
Godford Cross. *Devn* 5A **24**
Godleybrook. *Staf* 5G **49**
Godmanchester. *Cambs* 4L **43**
Godmanstone. *Dors* 6F **24**
Godmersham. *Kent* 8J **37**
Godolphin Cross. *Corn* 6D **19**
Godre'r-graig. *Neat* 3M **31**
Godshill. *Hants* 4B **26**
Godshill. *IOW* 7F **26**
Godstone. *Staf* 6H **49**
Godstone. *Surr* 8B **36**
Goetre. *Mon* 3F **32**
Goff's Oak. *Herts* 3B **36**
Gogar. *Edin* 2K **71**
Goginan. *Cdgn* 3J **39**
Golan. *Gwyn* 5E **46**
Golant. *Corn* 4C **20**
Golberdon. *Corn* 8E **22**
Golborne. *G Man* 6E **54**
Golcar. *W Yor* 4J **55**
Goldcliff. *Newp* 5F **32**
Golden Cross. *E Sus* 6D **28**
Golden Green. *Kent* 3E **28**
Golden Grove. *Carm* 2K **31**
Golden Grove. *N Yor* 3H **61**
Golden Hill. *Pemb* 1D **30**
Goldenhill. *Stoke* 4F **48**
Golden Pot. *Hants* 1H **27**
Golden Valley. *Glos* 1M **33**
Golders Green. *G Lon* 5A **36**
Goldhanger. *Essx* 3H **37**
Gold Hill. *Norf* 2B **44**
Golding. *Shrp* 1F **40**
Goldington. *Bed* 6J **43**
Goldsborough. *N Yor* 8C **60** (nr. Harrogate)
Goldsborough. *N Yor* 2H **61** (nr. Whitby)
Goldsithney. *Corn* 6C **19**
Goldstone. *Kent* 7L **37**
Goldstone. *Shrp* 7E **48**
Goldthorpe. *S Yor* 5A **56**
Goldworthy. *Devn* 3E **22**
Golfa. *Powy* 7L **47**
Gollanfield. *High* 6L **87**
Gollinglith Foot. *N Yor* 5A **60**
Golsoncott. *Som* 2M **23**
Golspie. *High* 2L **87**
Gomeldon. *Wilts* 2B **26**
Gomersal. *W Yor* 3L **55**
Gometra House. *Arg* 1A **74**
Gomshall. *Surr* 1L **27**
Gonalston. *Notts* 5C **50**
Gonerby Hill Foot. *Linc* 6F **50**
Gonfirth. *Shet* 5D **95**
Gonnabarn. *Corn* 4A **20**
Good Easter. *Essx* 2E **36**
Gooderstone. *Norf* 1D **44**
Goodleigh. *Devn* 2H **23**
Goodmanham. *E Yor* 1E **56**
Goodmayes. *G Lon* 5C **36**
Goodnestone. *Kent* 8L **37** (nr. Aylesham)
Goodnestone. *Kent* 7J **37** (nr. Faversham)
Goodrich. *Here* 2H **33**
Goodrington. *Torb* 4K **21**
Goodshaw. *Lanc* 3G **55**
Goodshaw Fold. *Lanc* 3G **55**
Goodstone. *Devn* 8J **23**
Goodwick. *Pemb* 8B **38**
Goodworth Clatford. *Hants* 1D **26**
Goole. *E Yor* 3D **56**
Goom's Hill. *Worc* 6L **41**
Goonbell. *Corn* 5E **19**
Goonhavern. *Corn* 4E **19**
Goonvrea. *Corn* 5E **19**
Goose Green. *Cumb* 5G **59**
Goose Green. *S Glo* 5K **33**
Gooseham. *Corn* 4D **22**
Goosewell. *Plym* 4G **21**
Goosey. *Oxon* 4D **34**
Goosnargh. *Lanc* 2D **54**
Goostrey. *Ches E* 8F **54**
Gorcott Hill. *Warw* 5L **41**
Gord. *Shet* 9E **95**
Gordon. *Bord* 5F **72**
Gordonbush. *High* 1L **87**
Gordonstown. *Abers* 4F **88** (nr. Cornhill)
Gordonstown. *Abers* 6H **89** (nr. Fyvie)
Gorebridge. *Midl* 3M **71**
Gorefield. *Cambs* 8L **51**
Gores. *Wilts* 8B **34**
Gorgie. *Edin* 2L **71**
Goring. *Oxon* 5G **35**
Goring-by-Sea. *W Sus* 5M **27**
Goring Heath. *Oxon* 6G **35**
Gorleston-on-Sea. *Norf* 1M **45**
Gornalwood. *W Mid* 2K **41**
Gorran Churchtown. *Corn* 5A **20**
Gorran Haven. *Corn* 5B **20**
Gorran High Lanes. *Corn* 5A **20**
Gors. *Cdgn* 4J **39**
Gorsedd. *Flin* 2L **47**
Gorseinon. *Swan* 4K **31**
Gorseness. *Orkn* 6C **94**
Gorseybank. *Derbs* 4K **49**
Gorsgoch. *Cdgn* 6G **39**
Gorslas. *Carm* 2K **31**
Gorsley. *Glos* 1J **33**
Gorsley Common. *Here* 1J **33**
Gorstan. *High* 5F **86**
Gorstella. *Ches W* 3A **48**
Gorsty Common. *Here* 8E **40**
Gorsty Hill. *Staf* 7H **49**
Gortantaoid. *Arg* 2B **68**
Gorteneorn. *High* 7L **79**
Gortenfern. *High* 7L **79**
Gorton. *G Man* 6G **55**
Gosbeck. *Suff* 6H **45**
Gosberton. *Linc* 6J **51**
Gosberton Cheal. *Linc* 7J **51**
Gosberton Clough. *Linc* 7H **51**
Goseley Dale. *Derbs* 7L **49**
Gosfield. *Essx* 1F **36**
Gosford. *Oxon* 2F **34**
Gosforth. *Cumb* 3B **58**
Gosforth. *Tyne* 5H **67**
Gosmore. *Herts* 1M **35**
Gospel End Village. *Staf* 2J **41**
Gosport. *Hants* 5G **27**
Gossabrough. *Shet* 3F **95**
Gossington. *Glos* 3K **33**
Gossops Green. *W Sus* 4A **28**
Goswick. *Nmbd* 5K **73**
Gotham. *Notts* 6B **50**
Gotherington. *Glos* 1M **33**
Gott. *Arg* 8B **78**
Gott. *Shet* 7E **95**
Goudhurst. *Kent* 4F **28**
Goulceby. *Linc* 8J **57**
Gourdon. *Abers* 6J **83**
Gourock. *Inv* 2A **70**
Govan. *Glas* 3D **70**
Govanhill. *Glas* 3D **70**
Goverton. *Notts* 5D **50**
Goveton. *Devn* 5J **21**
Govilon. *Mon* 2E **32**
Gowanhill. *Abers* 3L **89**
Gowdall. *E Yor* 3C **56**
Gowerton. *Swan* 4K **31**
Gowkhall. *Fife* 1J **71**
Gowthorpe. *E Yor* 8G **61**
Goxhill. *E Yor* 1H **57**
Goxhill. *N Lin* 3H **57**
Goxhill Haven. *N Lin* 3H **57**
Goytre. *Neat* 5M **31**
Grabhair. *W Isl* 7D **90**
Graby. *Linc* 7G **51**
Graffham. *W Sus* 4K **27**
Grafham. *Cambs* 5K **43**
Grafham. *Surr* 1L **27**
Grafton. *Here* 8E **40**
Grafton. *N Yor* 7D **60**
Grafton. *Oxon* 3C **34**
Grafton. *Shrp* 8B **48**
Grafton. *Worc* 8K **41** (nr. Evesham)
Grafton. *Worc* 5F **40** (nr. Leominster)
Grafton Flyford. *Worc* 6K **41**
Grafton Regis. *Nptn* 7F **42**
Grafton Underwood. *Nptn* 3H **43**
Grafty Green. *Kent* 3G **29**
Graianrhyd. *Den* 4M **47**
Graig. *Carm* 3J **31**
Graig. *Cnwy* 2H **47**
Graig. *Den* 2K **47**
Graig-fechan. *Den* 4L **47**
Graig Penllyn. *V Glam* 6B **32**
Grain. *Medw* 6G **37**
Grainsby. *Linc* 6J **57**
Grainthorpe. *Linc* 6K **57**
Grainthorpe Fen. *Linc* 6K **57**
Graiselound. *N Lin* 6D **56**
Gramasdail. *W Isl* 6C **84**
Grampound. *Corn* 5A **20**
Grampound Road. *Corn* 4A **20**
Granborough. *Buck* 1H **35**
Granby. *Notts* 6D **50**
Grandborough. *Warw* 5C **42**
Grandpont. *Oxon* 3F **34**
Grandtully. *Per* 8M **81**
Grange. *Cumb* 2D **58**
Grange. *E Ayr* 6C **70**
Grange. *Here* 4E **40**
Grange. *Mers* 7A **54**
Grange. *Per* 3H **77**
Grange Crossroads. *Mor* 4E **88**
Grange Hill. *G Lon* 4C **36**
Grangemill. *Derbs* 4K **49**
Grange Moor. *W Yor* 4L **55**
Grangemouth. *Falk* 1H **71**
Grange of Lindores. *Fife* 4H **77**
Grange-over-Sands. *Cumb* 6F **58**
Grangepans. *Falk* 1J **71**
Grange, The. *N Yor* 4E **60**
Grangetown. *Card* 6D **32**
Grangetown. *Red C* 1E **60**
Grange Villa. *Dur* 6H **67**
Granish. *High* 2L **81**
Gransmoor. *E Yor* 8L **61**
Granston. *Pemb* 8A **38**
Grantchester. *Cambs* 6A **44**
Grantham. *Linc* 6F **50**
Grantley. *N Yor* 7B **60**
Grantlodge. *Abers* 2H **83**
Granton. *Edin* 2L **71**
Grantown-on-Spey. *High* 1A **82**
Grantshouse. *Bord* 3H **73**
Grappenhall. *Warr* 7E **54**
Grasby. *Linc* 5G **57**
Grasmere. *Cumb* 3E **58**
Grasscroft. *G Man* 5H **55**
Grassendale. *Mers* 7B **54**
Grassgarth. *Cumb* 7L **65**
Grassholme. *Dur* 1L **59**
Grassington. *N Yor* 7M **59**
Grassmoor. *Derbs* 3A **50**
Grassthorpe. *Notts* 3D **50**
Grateley. *Hants* 1C **26**
Gratton. *Devn* 4E **22**
Gratton. *Staf* 4G **49**
Gratwich. *Staf* 6H **49**
Graveley. *Cambs* 5L **43**
Graveley. *Herts* 1A **36**
Gravelhill. *Shrp* 8B **48**
Gravel Hole. *G Man* 5H **55**
Gravelly Hill. *W Mid* 2M **41**
Graven. *Shet* 4E **95**
Graveney. *Kent* 7J **37**
Gravesend. *Kent* 6E **36**
Grayingham. *Linc* 6F **56**
Grayrigg. *Cumb* 4G **59**
Grays. *Thur* 6E **36**
Grayshott. *Hants* 2J **27**
Grayson Green. *Cumb* 1A **58**
Grayswood. *Surr* 2K **27**
Graythorp. *Hart* 1E **60**
Grazeley. *Wok* 7G **35**
Grealin. *High* 5K **85**
Greasbrough. *S Yor* 6A **56**
Greasby. *Mers* 7A **54**
Great Abington. *Cambs* 7B **44**
Great Addington. *Nptn* 4H **43**
Great Alne. *Warw* 6M **41**
Great Altcar. *Lanc* 5B **54**
Great Amwell. *Herts* 2B **36**
Great Asby. *Cumb* 2H **59**
Great Ashfield. *Suff* 5F **44**
Great Ayton. *N Yor* 2E **60**
Great Baddow. *Essx* 3F **36**
Great Bardfield. *Essx* 8C **44**
Great Barford. *Bed* 6K **43**
Great Barr. *W Mid* 2L **41**
Great Barrington. *Glos* 2C **34**
Great Barrow. *Ches W* 3B **48**
Great Barton. *Suff* 5E **44**
Great Barugh. *N Yor* 6G **61**
Great Bavington. *Nmbd* 3E **66**
Great Bealings. *Suff* 7J **45**
Great Bedwyn. *Wilts* 7C **34**
Great Bentley. *Essx* 1K **37**
Great Billing. *Nptn* 5G **43**
Great Bircham. *Norf* 4D **52**
Great Blakenham. *Suff* 6H **45**
Great Blencow. *Cumb* 8M **65**
Great Bolas. *Telf* 7D **48**
Great Bookham. *Surr* 8M **35**
Great Bosullow. *Corn* 6B **19**
Great Bourton. *Oxon* 7C **42**
Great Bowden. *Leics* 3F **42**
Great Bradley. *Suff* 6C **44**
Great Braxted. *Essx* 2G **37**
Great Bricett. *Suff* 6G **45**
Great Brickhill. *Buck* 8H **43**
Great Bridgeford. *Staf* 7F **48**
Great Brington. *Nptn* 5E **42**
Great Bromley. *Essx* 1J **37**
Great Broughton. *Cumb* 8H **65**
Great Broughton. *N Yor* 3E **60**
Great Budworth. *Ches W* 8E **54**
Great Burdon. *Darl* 2C **60**
Great Burstead. *Essx* 4E **36**
Great Busby. *N Yor* 3E **60**
Great Canfield. *Essx* 2D **36**
Great Carlton. *Linc* 7L **57**
Great Casterton. *Rut* 1J **43**
Great Chalfield. *Wilts* 7L **33**
Great Chart. *Kent* 3H **29**
Great Chatwell. *Staf* 8E **48**
Great Chesterford. *Essx* 7B **44**
Great Cheverell. *Wilts* 8M **33**
Great Chilton. *Dur* 8H **67**
Great Chishill. *Cambs* 8A **44**
Great Clacton. *Essx* 2K **37**
Great Cliff. *W Yor* 4M **55**
Great Clifton. *Cumb* 1B **58**
Great Coates. *NE Lin* 4J **57**
Great Comberton. *Worc* 7K **41**
Great Corby. *Cumb* 6M **65**
Great Cornard. *Suff* 7E **44**
Great Cowden. *E Yor* 1J **57**
Great Coxwell. *Oxon* 4C **34**
Great Crakehall. *N Yor* 5B **60**
Great Cransley. *Nptn* 4G **43**
Great Cressingham. *Norf* 1E **44**
Great Crosby. *Mers* 6B **54**
Great Cubley. *Derbs* 6J **49**
Great Dalby. *Leics* 8D **50**
Great Doddington. *Nptn* 5G **43**
Great Doward. *Here* 2H **33**
Great Dunham. *Norf* 6E **52**
Great Dunmow. *Essx* 1E **36**
Great Durnford. *Wilts* 2B **26**
Great Easton. *Essx* 1E **36**
Great Easton. *Leics* 2G **43**
Great Eccleston. *Lanc* 1C **54**
Great Edstone. *N Yor* 5G **61**
Great Ellingham. *Norf* 2G **45**
Great Elm. *Som* 1G **25**
Great Eppleton. *Tyne* 7J **67**
Great Eversden. *Cambs* 6M **43**
Great Fencote. *N Yor* 4B **60**
Great Finborough. *Suff* 6G **45**
Greatford. *Linc* 8G **51**
Great Fransham. *Norf* 6E **52**
Great Gaddesden. *Herts* 2L **35**
Great Gate. *Staf* 5H **49**
Great Gidding. *Cambs* 3K **43**
Great Givendale. *E Yor* 8H **61**
Great Glemham. *Suff* 5K **45**
Great Glen. *Leics* 2E **42**
Great Gonerby. *Linc* 6F **50**
Great Gransden. *Cambs* 6L **43**
Great Green. *Norf* 3J **45**
Great Green. *Suff* 6F **44** (nr. Lavenham)
Great Green. *Suff* 4H **45** (nr. Palgrave)
Great Habton. *N Yor* 6G **61**
Great Hale. *Linc* 5H **51**
Great Hallingbury. *Essx* 2D **36**
Greatham. *Hants* 2H **27**
Greatham. *Hart* 1D **60**
Greatham. *W Sus* 4L **27**
Great Hampden. *Buck* 3J **35**
Great Harrowden. *Nptn* 4G **43**
Great Harwood. *Lanc* 2F **54**
Great Haseley. *Oxon* 3G **35**
Great Hatfield. *E Yor* 1H **57**
Great Haywood. *Staf* 7G **49**
Great Heath. *W Mid* 3B **42**
Great Heck. *N Yor* 3B **56**
Great Henny. *Essx* 8E **44**
Great Hinton. *Wilts* 8M **33**
Great Hockham. *Norf* 2F **44**
Great Holland. *Essx* 2L **37**
Great Horkesley. *Essx* 8F **44**
Great Hormead. *Herts* 8A **44**
Great Horton. *W Yor* 2K **55**
Great Horwood. *Buck* 8F **42**
Great Houghton. *Nptn* 6F **42**
Great Houghton. *S Yor* 5A **56**
Great Hucklow. *Derbs* 8K **55**
Great Kelk. *E Yor* 8L **61**
Great Kendale. *E Yor* 7K **61**
Great Kimble. *Buck* 3J **35**
Great Kingshill. *Buck* 4J **35**
Great Langdale. *Cumb* 3D **58**
Great Langton. *N Yor* 4B **60**
Great Leighs. *Essx* 2F **36**
Great Limber. *Linc* 5H **57**
Great Linford. *Mil* 7G **43**
Great Livermere. *Suff* 4E **44**
Great Longstone. *Derbs* 8L **55**
Great Lumley. *Dur* 7H **67**
Great Lyth. *Shrp* 1E **40**
Great Malvern. *Worc* 7H **41**
Great Maplestead. *Essx* 8E **44**
Great Marton. *Bkpl* 2B **54**
Great Massingham. *Norf* 5D **52**
Great Melton. *Norf* 1H **45**
Great Milton. *Oxon* 3G **35**
Great Missenden. *Buck* 3J **35**
Great Mitton. *Lanc* 2F **54**
Great Mongeham. *Kent* 8M **37**
Great Moulton. *Norf* 2H **45**
Great Munden. *Herts* 1B **36**
Great Musgrave. *Cumb* 2J **59**
Great Ness. *Shrp* 8A **48**
Great Notley. *Essx* 1F **36**
Great Oak. *Mon* 3F **32**
Great Oakley. *Essx* 1K **37**
Great Oakley. *Nptn* 3G **43**
Great Offley. *Herts* 1M **35**
Great Ormside. *Cumb* 2J **59**
Great Orton. *Cumb* 6L **65**
Great Ouseburn. *N Yor* 7D **60**
Great Oxendon. *Nptn* 3F **42**
Great Oxney Green. *Essx* 3E **36**
Great Parndon. *Essx* 3C **36**
Great Paxton. *Cambs* 5L **43**
Great Plumpton. *Lanc* 2B **54**
Great Plumstead. *Norf* 6K **53**
Great Ponton. *Linc* 6F **50**
Great Potheridge. *Devn* 4G **23**
Great Preston. *W Yor* 3A **56**
Great Raveley. *Cambs* 3L **43**
Great Rissington. *Glos* 2B **34**
Great Rollright. *Oxon* 8B **42**
Great Ryburgh. *Norf* 5F **52**
Great Ryle. *Nmbd* 8K **73**
Great Ryton. *Shrp* 1E **40**
Great Saling. *Essx* 1E **36**
Great Salkeld. *Cumb* 8A **66**
Great Sampford. *Essx* 8C **44**
Great Sankey. *Warr* 7D **54**
Great Saredon. *Staf* 1K **41**
Great Saxham. *Suff* 5D **44**
Great Shefford. *W Ber* 6D **34**
Great Shelford. *Cambs* 6A **44**
Great Shoddesden. *Hants* 1C **26**
Great Smeaton. *N Yor* 3C **60**
Great Snoring. *Norf* 4F **52**
Great Somerford. *Wilts* 5M **33**
Great Stainton. *Darl* 1C **60**
Great Stambridge. *Essx* 4G **37**
Great Staughton. *Cambs* 5K **43**
Great Steeping. *Linc* 3L **51**
Great Stonar. *Kent* 8M **37**
Greatstone-on-Sea. *Kent* 5J **29**
Great Strickland. *Cumb* 1G **59**
Great Stukeley. *Cambs* 4L **43**
Great Sturton. *Linc* 8J **57**
Great Sutton. *Ches W* 8B **54**
Great Sutton. *Shrp* 3F **40**
Great Swinburne. *Nmbd* 4E **66**
Great Tew. *Oxon* 1D **34**
Great Tey. *Essx* 1G **37**
Great Thirkleby. *N Yor* 6D **60**
Great Thorness. *IOW* 6E **26**
Great Thurlow. *Suff* 6C **44**
Great Torr. *Devn* 5H **21**
Great Torrington. *Devn* 4F **22**
Great Tosson. *Nmbd* 1F **66**
Great Totham North. *Essx* 2G **37**
Great Totham South. *Essx* 2G **37**
Great Tows. *Linc* 6J **57**
Great Urswick. *Cumb* 6D **58**
Great Wakering. *Essx* 5H **37**
Great Waldingfield. *Suff* 7F **44**
Great Walsingham. *Norf* 4F **52**
Great Waltham. *Essx* 2E **36**
Great Warley. *Essx* 4D **36**
Great Washbourne. *Glos* 8K **41**
Great Wenham. *Suff* 8G **45**
Great Whelnetham. *Suff* 6E **44**
Great Whittington. *Nmbd* 4F **66**
Great Wigborough. *Essx* 2H **37**
Great Wilbraham. *Cambs* 6B **44**
Great Wilne. *Derbs* 6A **50**
Great Wishford. *Wilts* 2A **26**
Great Witchingham. *Norf* 5H **53**
Great Witcombe. *Glos* 2M **33**
Great Witley. *Worc* 5H **41**
Great Wolford. *Warw* 8A **42**
Greatworth. *Nptn* 7D **42**
Great Wratting. *Suff* 7C **44**
Great Wymondley. *Herts* 1A **36**
Great Wyrley. *Staf* 1K **41**
Great Wytheford. *Shrp* 8C **48**
Great Yarmouth. *Norf* 1M **45**
Great Yeldham. *Essx* 8D **44**
Grebby. *Linc* 3L **51**
Greeba Castle. *IOM* 5D **62**
Greenbank. *Shet* 1F **95**
Greenbottom. *Corn* 5E **19**
Greenburn. *W Lot* 3H **71**
Greencroft. *Dur* 6G **67**
Greencroft Park. *Dur* 7G **67**
Greendown. *Som* 8H **33**
Greendykes. *Nmbd* 7K **73**
Green End. *Bed* 7J **43** (nr. Bedford)
Green End. *Bed* 5K **43** (nr. St Neots)
Green End. *Herts* 8M **43** (nr. Buntingford)
Green End. *Herts* 1B **36** (nr. Stevenage)
Green End. *N Yor* 3H **61**
Green End. *Warw* 3A **42**
Greenfield. *Arg* 6K **75**
Greenfield. *C Beds* 8J **43**
Greenfield. *Flin* 2L **47**
Greenfield. *G Man* 5H **55**
Greenfield. *Oxon* 4H **35**
Greenfoot. *N Lan* 3F **70**
Greenford. *G Lon* 5M **35**
Greengairs. *N Lan* 2F **70**
Greengate. *Norf* 6G **53**
Greengill. *Cumb* 8J **65**
Greenhalgh. *Lanc* 2C **54**
Greenham. *Dors* 5D **24**
Greenham. *Som* 3M **23**
Greenham. *W Ber* 7E **34**
Green Hammerton. *N Yor* 8D **60**
Greenhaugh. *Nmbd* 3C **66**
Greenhead. *Nmbd* 5B **66**
Green Heath. *Staf* 8G **49**
Greenhill. *Dum* 4J **65**
Greenhill. *Falk* 2G **71**
Greenhill. *Kent* 7K **37**
Greenhill. *S Yor* 7M **55**
Greenhill. *Worc* 4J **41**
Greenhills. *N Ayr* 4B **70**
Greenhithe. *Kent* 6D **36**
Greenholm. *E Ayr* 6D **70**
Greenhow Hill. *N Yor* 7A **60**
Greenigoe. *Orkn* 7C **94**
Greenland. *High* 3H **93**
Greenland Mains. *High* 3H **93**
Greenlands. *Worc* 5L **41**
Green Lane. *Shrp* 7D **48**
Green Lane. *Warw* 5L **41**
Greenlaw. *Bord* 5G **73**
Greenlea. *Dum* 4H **65**
Greenloaning. *Per* 5D **76**
Greenmount. *G Man* 4F **54**
Greenmow. *Shet* 9E **95**
Greenock. *Inv* 2A **70**
Greenock Mains. *E Ayr* 7E **70**
Greenodd. *Cumb* 5E **58**
Green Ore. *Som* 8H **33**
Greenrow. *Cumb* 6J **65**
Greens. *Abers* 5J **89**
Greensgate. *Norf* 6H **53**
Greenside. *Tyne* 5G **67**
Greensidehill. *Nmbd* 8J **73**
Greens Norton. *Nptn* 7E **42**
Greenstead Green. *Essx* 1G **37**
Greensted Green. *Essx* 3D **36**
Green Street. *Herts* 4M **35**
Green Street. *Suff* 4H **45**
Green Street Green. *G Lon* 7C **36**
Green Street Green. *Kent* 6D **36**
Greenstreet Green. *Suff* 7G **45**
Green, The. *Cumb* 5C **58**
Green, The. *Wilts* 2H **25**
Green Tye. *Herts* 2C **36**
Greenwall. *Orkn* 7D **94**
Greenway. *Pemb* 1E **30**
Greenway. *V Glam* 6C **32**
Greenwell. *Cumb* 6A **66**
Greenwich. *G Lon* 6B **36**
Greet. *Glos* 8L **41**
Greete. *Shrp* 4F **40**
Greetham. *Linc* 8K **57**
Greetham. *Rut* 8F **50**
Greetland. *W Yor* 3J **55**
Gregson Lane. *Lanc* 3D **54**
Grein. *W Isl* 3A **78**
Greinetobht. *W Isl* 4C **84**
Greinton. *Som* 2D **24**
Gremista. *Shet* 7E **95**
Grenaby. *IOM* 6C **62**
Grendon. *Nptn* 5G **43**
Grendon. *Warw* 2A **42**
Grendon Common. *Warw* 2A **42**
Grendon Green. *Here* 6F **40**
Grendon Underwood. *Buck* 1G **35**
Grenofen. *Devn* 8F **22**
Grenoside. *S Yor* 6M **55**
Greosabhagh. *W Isl* 2F **84**
Gresford. *Wrex* 4A **48**
Gresham. *Norf* 4H **53**
Greshornish. *High* 6H **85**
Gressenhall. *Norf* 6F **52**
Gressingham. *Lanc* 6G **59**
Greta Bridge. *Dur* 2M **59**
Gretna. *Dum* 5L **65**
Gretna Green. *Dum* 5L **65**
Gretton. *Glos* 8L **41**
Gretton. *Nptn* 2H **43**
Gretton. *Shrp* 2F **40**
Grewelthorpe. *N Yor* 6B **60**
Greygarth. *N Yor* 6A **60**
Grey Green. *N Lin* 5D **56**
Greylake. *Som* 2C **24**
Greysouthen. *Cumb* 1B **58**
Greystoke. *Cumb* 8M **65**
Greystoke Gill. *Cumb* 1F **58**
Greystone. *Ang* 1L **77**
Greystones. *S Yor* 7M **55**
Greywell. *Hants* 8H **35**
Griais. *W Isl* 4E **90**
Grianan. *W Isl* 5E **90**
Gribthorpe. *E Yor* 2D **56**
Gribun. *Arg* 2B **74**
Griff. *Warw* 3B **42**
Griffithstown. *Torf* 4E **32**
Griffydam. *Leics* 8A **50**
Griggs Green. *Hants* 2J **27**
Grimbister. *Orkn* 6B **94**
Grimeford Village. *Lanc* 4E **54**
Grimeston. *Orkn* 6B **94**
Grimethorpe. *S Yor* 5A **56**
Griminis. *W Isl* 6B **84** (on Benbecula)
Griminis. *W Isl* 4B **84** (on North Uist)
Grimister. *Shet* 2E **95**
Grimley. *Worc* 5J **41**
Grimness. *Orkn* 8C **94**
Grimoldby. *Linc* 7K **57**
Grimpo. *Shrp* 7A **48**
Grimsargh. *Lanc* 2D **54**
Grimsbury. *Oxon* 7C **42**
Grimsby. *NE Lin* 4J **57**
Grimscote. *Nptn* 6E **42**
Grimscott. *Corn* 5D **22**
Grimshaw. *Bkbn* 3F **54**
Grimshaw Green. *Lanc* 4C **54**
Grimsthorpe. *Linc* 7G **51**
Grimston. *E Yor* 2J **57**
Grimston. *Leics* 7C **50**
Grimston. *Norf* 5D **52**
Grimston. *York* 8F **60**
Grimstone. *Dors* 6F **24**
Grimstone End. *Suff* 5F **44**
Grinacombe Moor. *Devn* 6F **22**
Grindale. *E Yor* 6L **61**
Grindhill. *Devn* 6F **22**
Grindiscol. *Shet* 8E **95**
Grindle. *Shrp* 1H **41**
Grindleford. *Derbs* 8L **55**
Grindleton. *Lanc* 1F **54**
Grindley. *Staf* 7H **49**
Grindley Brook. *Shrp* 5C **48**
Grindlow. *Derbs* 8K **55**
Grindon. *Nmbd* 5J **73**
Grindon. *Staf* 4H **49**
Gringley on the Hill. *Notts* 6D **56**
Grinsdale. *Cumb* 6L **65**
Grinshill. *Shrp* 7C **48**
Grinton. *N Yor* 4M **59**
Griomsidar. *W Isl* 6E **90**
Grishipoll. *Arg* 8F **78**
Grisling Common. *E Sus* 5C **28**
Gristhorpe. *N Yor* 5K **61**
Griston. *Norf* 2F **44**
Gritley. *Orkn* 7D **94**
Grittenham. *Wilts* 5A **34**
Grittleton. *Wilts* 6L **33**
Grizebeck. *Cumb* 5D **58**
Grizedale. *Cumb* 4E **58**
Grobister. *Orkn* 5E **94**
Grobsness. *Shet* 5D **95**
Groby. *Leics* 1D **42**
Groes. *Cnwy* 3K **47**
Groes. *Neat* 5M **31**
Groes-faen. *Rhon* 5C **32**
Groesffordd. *Gwyn* 6B **46**
Groesffordd. *Powy* 1C **32**
Groeslon. *Gwyn* 4D **46**
Groes-lwyd. *Powy* 8M **47**
Groes-wen. *Cphy* 5D **32**
Grogport. *Arg* 5G **69**
Groigearraidh. *W Isl* 7B **84**
Gromford. *Suff* 6K **45**
Gronant. *Flin* 1K **47**
Groombridge. *E Sus* 4D **28**
Grosmont. *Mon* 1G **33**
Grosmont. *N Yor* 3H **61**
Groton. *Suff* 7F **44**
Grove. *Dors* 8G **25**
Grove. *Kent* 7L **37**
Grove. *Notts* 8D **56**
Grove. *Oxon* 4D **34**
Grovehill. *E Yor* 2G **57**
Grove Park. *G Lon* 6C **36**
Grovesend. *Swan* 3K **31**
Grove, The. *Dum* 4G **65**
Grove, The. *Worc* 7J **41**
Grub Street. *Staf* 7E **48**
Grudie. *High* 5F **86**
Gruids. *High* 1H **87**
Gruinard House. *High* 2B **86**
Gruinart. *Arg* 3A **68**
Grulinbeg. *Arg* 3A **68**
Gruline. *Arg* 1C **74**
Grummore. *High* 6B **92**
Grundisburgh. *Suff* 6J **45**
Gruting. *Shet* 7C **95**
Grutness. *Shet* 10E **95**
Gualachulain. *High* 1J **75**
Gualin House. *High* 4L **91**
Guardbridge. *Fife* 4K **77**
Guarlford. *Worc* 7J **41**
Guay. *Per* 1F **76**
Gubblecote. *Herts* 2K **35**
Guestling Green. *E Sus* 6G **29**
Guestling Thorn. *E Sus* 6G **29**
Guestwick. *Norf* 5G **53**
Guestwick Green. *Norf* 5G **53**
Guide. *Bkbn* 3F **54**
Guide Post. *Nmbd* 3H **67**
Guilden Down. *Shrp* 3D **40**
Guilden Morden. *Cambs* 7L **43**
Guilden Sutton. *Ches W* 3B **48**
Guildford. *Surr* 1K **27**
Guildtown. *Per* 2G **77**
Guilsborough. *Nptn* 4E **42**
Guilsfield. *Powy* 8M **47**
Guineaford. *Devn* 2G **23**
Guisborough. *Red C* 2F **60**
Guiseley. *W Yor* 1K **55**
Guist. *Norf* 5F **52**
Guiting Power. *Glos* 1A **34**
Gulberwick. *Shet* 8E **95**
Gullane. *E Lot* 1D **72**
Gulling Green. *Suff* 6E **44**
Gulval. *Corn* 6B **19**
Gumfreston. *Pemb* 3F **30**
Gumley. *Leics* 2E **42**
Gunby. *E Yor* 2D **56**
Gunby. *Linc* 7F **50**
Gundleton. *Hants* 2G **27**

Gun Green. *Kent* 4F 28
Gun Hill. *E Sus* 6D 28
Gunn. *Devn* 2H 23
Gunnerside. *N Yor* 4L 59
Gunnerton. *Nmbd* 4E 66
Gunness. *N Lin* 4E 56
Gunnislake. *Corn* 8F 22
Gunnista. *Shet* 7E 95
Gunsgreenhill. *Bord* 3J 73
Gunstone. *Staf* 1J 41
Gunthorpe. *Norf* 4G 53
Gunthorpe. *N Lin* 6E 56
Gunthorpe. *Notts* 5C 50
Gunthorpe. *Pet* 1K 43
Gunville. *IOW* 7E 26
Gupworthy. *Som* 2L 23
Gurnard. *IOW* 6E 26
Gurney Slade. *Som* 1F 24
Gurnos. *Powy* 3M 31
Gussage All Saints. *Dors* 4A 26
Gussage St Andrew. *Dors* 4J 25
Gussage St Michael. *Dors* 4J 25
Guston. *Kent* 3M 29
Gutcher. *Shet* 2F 95
Guthram Gowt. *Linc* 7H 51
Guthrie. *Ang* 8F 82
Guyhirn. *Cambs* 1A 44
Guyhirn Gull. *Cambs* 1M 43
Guy's Head. *Linc* 7L 51
Guy's Marsh. *Dors* 3H 25
Guyzance. *Nmbd* 1H 67
Gwaelod-y-garth. *Card* 5D 32
Gwaenynog Bach. *Den* 3K 47
Gwaenysgor. *Flin* 1K 47
Gwalchmai. *IOA* 2C 46
Gwastad. *Pemb* 1E 30
Gwaun-Cae-Gurwen. *Neat* 2M 31
Gwaun-y-bara. *Cphy* 5D 32
Gwbert. *Cdgn* 7D 38
Gweek. *Corn* 7E 19
Gwehelog. *Mon* 3F 32
Gwenddwr. *Powy* 7A 40
Gwennap. *Corn* 5E 19
Gwenter. *Corn* 8E 19
Gwernaffield. *Flin* 3M 47
Gwernesney. *Mon* 3G 33
Gwernogle. *Carm* 8H 39
Gwern-y-go. *Powy* 2C 40
Gwernymynydd. *Flin* 3M 47
Gwersyllt. *Wrex* 4A 48
Gwespyr. *Flin* 1L 47
Gwinear. *Corn* 6C 19
Gwithian. *Corn* 5C 19
Gwredog. *IOA* 1D 46
Gwyddelwern. *Den* 5K 47
Gwyddgrug. *Carm* 8G 39
Gwynfryn. *Wrex* 4M 47
Gwystre. *Powy* 5A 40
Gwytherin. *Cnwy* 3H 47
Gyfelia. *Wrex* 5A 48
Gyffin. *Cnwy* 2G 47

H

Haa of Houlland. *Shet* 1F 95
Habberley. *Shrp* 1D 40
Habblesthorpe. *Notts* 7D 56
Habergham. *Lanc* 2G 55
Habin. *W Sus* 3J 27
Habrough. *NE Lin* 4H 57
Haceby. *Linc* 6G 51
Hacheston. *Suff* 6K 45
Hackenthorpe. *S Yor* 7A 56
Hackford. *Norf* 1G 45
Hackforth. *N Yor* 4B 60
Hackland. *Orkn* 5B 94
Hackleton. *Nptn* 6G 43
Hackman's Gate. *Worc* 4J 41
Hackness. *N Yor* 4J 61
Hackness. *Orkn* 8B 94
Hackney. *G Lon* 5B 36
Hackthorn. *Linc* 7F 56
Hackthorpe. *Cumb* 1G 59
Haclait. *W Isl* 7C 84
Haconby. *Linc* 7H 51
Hadden. *Bord* 6G 73
Haddenham. *Buck* 3H 35
Haddenham. *Cambs* 4A 44
Haddenham End. *Cambs* 4A 44
Haddington. *E Lot* 2E 72
Haddington. *Linc* 3F 50
Haddiscoe. *Norf* 2L 45
Haddo. *Abers* 6J 89
Haddon. *Cambs* 2K 43
Hademore. *Staf* 1M 41
Hadfield. *Derbs* 6J 55
Hadham Cross. *Herts* 2C 36
Hadham Ford. *Herts* 1C 36
Hadleigh. *Essx* 5G 37
Hadleigh. *Suff* 7G 45
Hadleigh Heath. *Suff* 7F 44
Hadley. *Telf* 8D 48
Hadley. *Worc* 5J 41
Hadley End. *Staf* 7J 49
Hadley Wood. *G Lon* 4A 36
Hadlow. *Kent* 3E 28
Hadlow Down. *E Sus* 5D 28
Hadnall. *Shrp* 7C 48
Hadstock. *Essx* 7B 44
Hadston. *Nmbd* 2H 67
Hady. *Derbs* 8M 55
Hadzor. *Worc* 5K 41
Haffenden Quarter. *Kent* 3G 29
Haggate. *Lanc* 2G 55
Haggbeck. *Cumb* 4M 65
Haggersta. *Shet* 7D 95
Haggerston. *Nmbd* 5K 73
Haggrister. *Shet* 4D 95
Hagley. *Here* 7F 40
Hagley. *Worc* 3K 41
Hagnaby. *Linc* 3K 51
Hagworthingham. *Linc* 3K 51
Haigh. *G Man* 5E 54
Haigh Moor. *W Yor* 3L 55
Haighton Green. *Lanc* 2D 54
Haile. *Cumb* 3B 58
Hailes. *Glos* 8L 41
Hailey. *Herts* 2B 36
Hailey. *Oxon* 2D 34
Hailsham. *E Sus* 7D 28
Hail Weston. *Cambs* 5K 43
Hainault. *G Lon* 4C 36
Hainford. *Norf* 6J 53
Hainton. *Linc* 7H 57
Hainworth. *W Yor* 2J 55
Haisthorpe. *E Yor* 7L 61
Hakin. *Pemb* 3C 30
Halam. *Notts* 4C 50
Halbeath. *Fife* 1K 71
Halberton. *Devn* 4M 23
Halcro. *High* 3H 93
Hale. *Cumb* 6G 59
Hale. *G Man* 7F 54
Hale. *Hal* 7C 54
Hale. *Hants* 4B 26
Hale. *Surr* 1J 27
Hale Bank. *Hal* 7C 54
Halebarns. *G Man* 7F 54
Hales. *Norf* 2K 45
Hales. *Staf* 6E 48
Halesgate. *Linc* 7K 51
Hales Green. *Derbs* 5J 49
Halesowen. *W Mid* 3K 41
Hale Street. *Kent* 3E 28
Halesworth. *Suff* 4K 45
Halewood. *Mers* 7C 54
Halford. *Shrp* 3E 40
Halford. *Warw* 7A 42
Halfpenny. *Cumb* 5G 59
Halfpenny Furze. *Carm* 2G 31
Halfpenny Green. *Shrp* 2J 41
Halfway. *Carm* 8J 39
Halfway. *Powy* 8L 39
Halfway. *S Yor* 7A 56
Halfway. *W Ber* 7E 34
Halfway House. *Shrp* 8A 48
Halfway Houses. *Kent* 6H 37
Halgabron. *Corn* 7B 22
Halifax. *W Yor* 3J 55
Halistra. *High* 6G 85
Halket. *E Ayr* 4C 70
Halkirk. *High* 4G 93
Halkyn. *Flin* 8A 54
Hall. *E Ren* 4C 70
Hallam Fields. *Derbs* 5A 50
Halland. *E Sus* 6D 28
Hallands, The. *N Lin* 3G 57
Hallaton. *Leics* 2F 42
Hallatrow. *Bath* 8J 33
Hallbank. *Cumb* 4H 59
Hallbankgate. *Cumb* 6A 66
Hall Dunnerdale. *Cumb* 4D 58
Hallen. *S Glo* 5H 33
Hall End. *Bed* 7J 43
Hallgarth. *Dur* 7J 67
Hall Green. *Ches E* 4F 48
Hall Green. *Norf* 3H 45
Hall Green. *W Mid* 3M 41
Hall Green. *W Yor* 4M 55
Hall Green. *Wrex* 5B 48
Halliburton. *Bord* 5F 72
Hallin. *High* 6G 85
Halling. *Medw* 7F 36
Hallington. *Linc* 7K 57
Hallington. *Nmbd* 4E 66
Halloughton. *Notts* 4C 50
Hallow. *Worc* 6J 41
Hallow Heath. *Worc* 6J 41
Hallowsgate. *Ches W* 3C 48
Hallsands. *Devn* 6K 21
Hall's Green. *Herts* 1A 36
Hallspill. *Devn* 3F 22
Hallthwaites. *Cumb* 5C 58
Hall Waberthwaite. *Cumb* 4C 58
Hallwood Green. *Glos* 8G 41
Hallworthy. *Corn* 7C 22
Hallyne. *Bord* 5K 71
Halmer End. *Staf* 5F 48
Halmond's Frome. *Here* 7G 41
Halmore. *Glos* 3J 33
Halnaker. *W Sus* 5K 27
Halsall. *Lanc* 4B 54
Halse. *Nptn* 7D 42
Halse. *Som* 3A 24
Halsetown. *Corn* 6C 19
Halsham. *E Yor* 3J 57
Halsinger. *Devn* 2G 23
Halstead. *Essx* 8E 44
Halstead. *Kent* 7C 36
Halstead. *Leics* 1F 42
Halstock. *Dors* 5E 24
Halsway. *Som* 2A 24
Haltcliff Bridge. *Cumb* 8L 65
Haltham. *Linc* 3J 51
Haltoft End. *Linc* 5K 51
Halton. *Buck* 3J 35
Halton. *Hal* 7D 54
Halton. *Lanc* 7G 59
Halton. *Nmbd* 5E 66
Halton. *W Yor* 2M 55
Halton. *Wrex* 6A 48
Halton East. *N Yor* 8M 59
Halton Fenside. *Linc* 3L 51
Halton Gill. *N Yor* 6K 59
Halton Holegate. *Linc* 3L 51
Halton Lea Gate. *Nmbd* 6B 66
Halton Moor. *W Yor* 2M 55
Halton Shields. *Nmbd* 5F 66
Halton West. *N Yor* 8K 59
Haltwhistle. *Nmbd* 5C 66
Halvergate. *Norf* 1L 45
Halwell. *Devn* 4J 21
Halwill. *Devn* 6F 22
Halwill Junction. *Devn* 6F 22
Ham. *Devn* 5B 24
Ham. *Glos* 4J 33
Ham. *G Lon* 6M 35
Ham. *High* 2H 93
Ham. *Kent* 8M 37
Ham. *Plym* 4F 20
Ham. *Shet* 9B 95
Ham. *Som* 4B 24 (nr. Ilminster)
Ham. *Som* 3B 24 (nr. Taunton)
Ham. *Som* 3A 24 (nr. Wellington)
Ham. *Wilts* 7D 34
Hambleden. *Buck* 5H 35
Hambledon. *Hants* 4G 27
Hambledon. *Surr* 2K 27
Hamble-le-Rice. *Hants* 5E 26
Hambleton. *Lanc* 1B 54
Hambleton. *N Yor* 2B 56
Hambridge. *Som* 3C 24
Hambrook. *S Glo* 6J 33
Hambrook. *W Sus* 5H 27
Ham Common. *Dors* 3H 25
Hameringham. *Linc* 3K 51
Hamerton. *Cambs* 4K 43
Ham Green. *Here* 7H 41
Ham Green. *Kent* 7G 37
Ham Green. *N Som* 6H 33
Ham Green. *Worc* 5L 41
Ham Hill. *Kent* 7E 36
Hamilton. *Leics* 1E 42
Hamilton. *S Lan* 4F 70
Hamister. *Shet* 5F 95
Hammer. *W Sus* 2J 27
Hammersmith. *G Lon* 6A 36
Hammerwich. *Staf* 1L 41
Hammerwood. *E Sus* 4C 28
Hammill. *Kent* 8L 37
Hammond Street. *Herts* 3B 36
Hammoon. *Dors* 4H 25
Hamnavoe. *Shet* 3C 95 (nr. Braehoulland)
Hamnavoe. *Shet* 8D 95 (nr. Burland)
Hamnavoe. *Shet* 4E 95 (nr. Lunna)
Hamnavoe. *Shet* 3E 95 (on Yell)
Hamp. *Som* 2C 24
Hampden Park. *E Sus* 7E 28
Hampen. *Glos* 1A 34
Hamperden End. *Essx* 8B 44
Hamperley. *Shrp* 3E 40
Hampnett. *Glos* 2A 34
Hampole. *S Yor* 4B 56
Hampreston. *Dors* 6A 26
Hampstead. *G Lon* 5A 36
Hampstead Norreys. *W Ber* 6F 34
Hampsthwaite. *N Yor* 8B 60
Hampton. *Devn* 6B 24
Hampton. *G Lon* 6M 35
Hampton. *Kent* 7K 37
Hampton. *Shrp* 3H 41
Hampton. *Swin* 4B 34
Hampton. *Worc* 7L 41
Hampton Bishop. *Here* 8F 40
Hampton Fields. *Glos* 4L 33
Hampton Hargate. *Pet* 2K 43
Hampton Heath. *Ches W* 5C 48
Hampton in Arden. *W Mid* 3A 42
Hampton Loade. *Shrp* 3H 41
Hampton Lovett. *Worc* 5J 41
Hampton Lucy. *Warw* 6A 42
Hampton Magna. *Warw* 5A 42
Hampton on the Hill. *Warw* 5A 42
Hampton Poyle. *Oxon* 2F 34
Hampton Wick. *G Lon* 7M 35
Hamptworth. *Wilts* 4C 26
Hamrow. *Norf* 5F 52
Hamsey. *E Sus* 6C 28
Hamsey Green. *Surr* 8B 36
Hamstall Ridware. *Staf* 8J 49
Hamstead. *IOW* 6E 26
Hamstead. *W Mid* 2L 41
Hamstead Marshall. *W Ber* 7E 34
Hamsterley. *Dur* 6G 67 (nr. Consett)
Hamsterley. *Dur* 8G 67 (nr. Wolsingham)
Hamsterley Mill. *Dur* 6G 67
Hamstreet. *Kent* 4J 29
Ham Street. *Som* 2E 24
Hamworthy. *Pool* 6J 25
Hanbury. *Staf* 7J 49
Hanbury. *Worc* 5K 41
Hanbury Woodend. *Staf* 7J 49
Hanby. *Linc* 6G 51
Hanchurch. *Staf* 5F 48
Hand and Pen. *Devn* 6M 23
Handbridge. *Ches W* 3B 48
Handcross. *W Sus* 5A 28
Handforth. *Ches E* 7G 55
Handley. *Ches W* 4B 48
Handley. *Derbs* 3L 49
Handsacre. *Staf* 8H 49
Handsworth. *S Yor* 7A 56
Handsworth. *W Mid* 2L 41
Handy Cross. *Buck* 4J 35
Hanford. *Dors* 4H 25
Hanford. *Stoke* 5F 48
Hangersley. *Hants* 5B 26
Hanging Houghton. *Nptn* 4F 42
Hanging Langford. *Wilts* 2A 26
Hangleton. *Brig* 7A 28
Hangleton. *W Sus* 5L 27
Hanham. *S Glo* 6J 33
Hanham Green. *S Glo* 6J 33
Hankelow. *Ches E* 5D 48
Hankerton. *Wilts* 4M 33
Hankham. *E Sus* 7E 28
Hanley. *Stoke* 5F 48
Hanley Castle. *Worc* 7J 41
Hanley Childe. *Worc* 5G 41
Hanley Swan. *Worc* 7J 41
Hanley William. *Worc* 5G 41
Hanlith. *N Yor* 7L 59
Hanmer. *Wrex* 6B 48
Hannaborough. *Devn* 5G 23
Hannaford. *Devn* 3H 23
Hannah. *Linc* 8M 57
Hannington. *Hants* 8F 34
Hannington. *Nptn* 4G 43
Hannington. *Swin* 4B 34
Hannington Wick. *Swin* 4B 34
Hanscombe End. *C Beds* 8K 43
Hanslope. *Mil* 7G 43
Hanthorpe. *Linc* 7G 51
Hanwell. *G Lon* 5M 35
Hanwell. *Oxon* 7C 42
Hanwood. *Shrp* 1E 40
Hanworth. *G Lon* 6M 35
Hanworth. *Norf* 4H 53
Happas. *Ang* 1K 77
Happendon. *S Lan* 6G 71
Happisburgh. *Norf* 4K 53
Happisburgh Common. *Norf* 5K 53
Hapsford. *Ches W* 8C 54
Hapton. *Lanc* 2F 54
Hapton. *Norf* 2H 45
Harberton. *Devn* 4J 21
Harbertonford. *Devn* 4J 21
Harbledown. *Kent* 8K 37
Harborne. *W Mid* 3L 41
Harborough Magna. *Warw* 4C 42
Harbottle. *Nmbd* 1E 66
Harbourneford. *Devn* 3J 21
Harbours Hill. *Worc* 5K 41
Harbridge. *Hants* 4B 26
Harbury. *Warw* 5B 42
Harby. *Leics* 6D 50
Harby. *Notts* 8E 56
Harcombe. *Devn* 6A 24
Harcombe Bottom. *Devn* 6C 24
Harcourt. *Corn* 6F 19
Harden. *W Yor* 2J 55
Hardenhuish. *Wilts* 6M 33
Hardgate. *Abers* 3H 83
Hardgate. *Dum* 5F 64
Hardham. *W Sus* 4L 27
Hardingham. *Norf* 1G 45
Hardingstone. *Nptn* 6F 42
Hardings Wood. *Ches E* 4F 48
Hardington. *Som* 8K 33
Hardington Mandeville. *Som* 4E 24
Hardington Marsh. *Som* 5E 24
Hardington Moor. *Som* 4E 24
Hardley. *Hants* 5E 26
Hardley Street. *Norf* 1K 45
Hardmead. *Mil* 7H 43
Hardraw. *N Yor* 4K 59
Hardstoft. *Derbs* 3A 50
Hardway. *Hants* 5G 27
Hardway. *Som* 2G 25
Hardwick. *Buck* 2J 35
Hardwick. *Cambs* 6M 43
Hardwick. *Norf* 3J 45
Hardwick. *Nptn* 5G 43
Hardwick. *Oxon* 1F 34 (nr. Bicester)
Hardwick. *Oxon* 3D 34 (nr. Witney)
Hardwick. *Shrp* 2D 40
Hardwick. *S Yor* 7A 56
Hardwick. *Stoc T* 1D 60
Hardwick. *W Mid* 2L 41
Hardwicke. *Glos* 1M 33 (nr. Cheltenham)
Hardwicke. *Glos* 2K 33 (nr. Gloucester)
Hardwicke. *Here* 7C 40
Hardwick Village. *Notts* 8C 56
Hardy's Green. *Essx* 1H 37
Hare. *Som* 4B 24
Hareby. *Linc* 3K 51
Hareden. *Lanc* 8H 59
Harefield. *G Lon* 4L 35
Hare Green. *Essx* 1J 37
Hare Hatch. *Wok* 6J 35
Harehill. *Derbs* 6J 49
Harehills. *W Yor* 2M 55
Harehope. *Nmbd* 7K 73
Harelaw. *Dum* 4M 65
Harelaw. *Dur* 6G 67
Hareplain. *Kent* 4G 29
Haresceugh. *Cumb* 7B 66
Harescombe. *Glos* 2L 33
Haresfield. *Glos* 2L 33
Haresfinch. *Mers* 6D 54
Hareshaw. *N Lan* 3G 71
Hare Street. *Essx* 3C 36
Hare Street. *Herts* 1B 36
Harewood. *W Yor* 1M 55
Harewood End. *Here* 1H 33
Harford. *Devn* 4H 21
Hargate. *Norf* 2H 45
Hargatewall. *Derbs* 8K 55
Hargrave. *Ches W* 3B 48
Hargrave. *Nptn* 4J 43
Hargrave. *Suff* 6D 44
Harker. *Cumb* 5L 65
Harkland. *Shet* 3E 95
Harkstead. *Suff* 8H 45
Harlaston. *Staf* 8K 49
Harlaxton. *Linc* 6E 50
Harlech. *Gwyn* 6E 46
Harlequin. *Notts* 6C 50
Harlescott. *Shrp* 8C 48
Harleston. *Devn* 5J 21
Harleston. *Norf* 3J 45
Harleston. *Suff* 5G 45
Harlestone. *Nptn* 5F 42
Harley. *Shrp* 1F 40
Harley. *S Yor* 6M 55
Harling Road. *Norf* 3F 44
Harlington. *C Beds* 8J 43
Harlington. *G Lon* 6L 35
Harlington. *S Yor* 5A 56
Harlosh. *High* 7G 85
Harlow. *Essx* 2C 36
Harlow Hill. *Nmbd* 5F 66
Harlsey Castle. *N Yor* 4D 60
Harlthorpe. *E Yor* 2D 56
Harlton. *Cambs* 6M 43
Harlyn. *Corn* 2F 19
Harman's Cross. *Dors* 7J 25
Harmby. *N Yor* 5A 60
Harmer Green. *Herts* 2A 36
Harmer Hill. *Shrp* 7B 48
Harmondsworth. *G Lon* 6L 35
Harmston. *Linc* 3F 50
Harnage. *Shrp* 1F 40
Harnham. *Nmbd* 3F 66
Harnhill. *Glos* 3A 34
Harold Hill. *G Lon* 4D 36
Haroldston West. *Pemb* 2C 30
Haroldswick. *Shet* 1G 95
Harold Wood. *G Lon* 4D 36
Harome. *N Yor* 5F 60
Harpenden. *Herts* 2M 35
Harpford. *Devn* 6M 23
Harpham. *E Yor* 7K 61
Harpley. *Norf* 5D 52
Harpley. *Worc* 5G 41
Harpole. *Nptn* 5E 42
Harpsdale. *High* 4G 93
Harpsden. *Oxon* 5H 35
Harpswell. *Linc* 7F 56
Harpurhey. *G Man* 5G 55
Harpur Hill. *Derbs* 8J 55
Harraby. *Cumb* 6M 65
Harracott. *Devn* 3G 23
Harrapool. *High* 1L 79
Harrapul. *High* 1L 79
Harrietfield. *Per* 3E 76
Harrietsham. *Kent* 8G 37
Harrington. *Cumb* 1A 58
Harrington. *Linc* 8K 57
Harrington. *Nptn* 3F 42
Harringworth. *Nptn* 2H 43
Harriseahead. *Staf* 4F 48
Harriston. *Cumb* 7J 65
Harrogate. *N Yor* 8C 60
Harrold. *Bed* 6H 43
Harrop Dale. *G Man* 5J 55
Harrow. *G Lon* 5M 35
Harrowbarrow. *Corn* 3E 20
Harrowden. *Bed* 7J 43
Harrowgate Hill. *Darl* 2B 60
Harrow on the Hill. *G Lon* 5M 35
Harrow Weald. *G Lon* 4M 35
Harry Stoke. *S Glo* 6J 33
Harston. *Cambs* 6A 44
Harston. *Leics* 6E 50
Harswell. *E Yor* 1E 56
Hart. *Hart* 8K 67
Hartburn. *Nmbd* 3K 66
Hartburn. *Stoc T* 2D 60
Hartest. *Suff* 6E 44
Hartfield. *E Sus* 4C 28
Hartford. *Cambs* 4L 43
Hartford. *Ches W* 8E 54
Hartford. *Som* 3L 23
Hartfordbridge. *Hants* 8H 35
Hartford End. *Essx* 2E 36
Harthill. *Ches W* 4C 48
Harthill. *N Lan* 3H 71
Harthill. *S Yor* 7A 56
Hartington. *Derbs* 3J 49
Hartland. *Devn* 3D 22
Hartland Quay. *Devn* 3D 22
Hartle. *Worc* 4K 41
Hartlebury. *Worc* 4J 41
Hartlepool. *Hart* 8L 67
Hartley. *Cumb* 3J 59
Hartley. *Kent* 4F 28 (nr. Cranbrook)
Hartley. *Kent* 7E 36 (nr. Dartford)
Hartley. *Nmbd* 4J 67
Hartley Green. *Staf* 6G 49
Hartley Mauditt. *Hants* 2H 27
Hartley Wespall. *Hants* 8G 35
Hartley Wintney. *Hants* 8H 35
Hartlip. *Kent* 7G 37
Hartmount. *High* 4K 87
Hartoft End. *N Yor* 4G 61
Harton. *N Yor* 7G 61
Harton. *Shrp* 3E 40
Harton. *Tyne* 5J 67
Hartpury. *Glos* 1K 33
Hartshead. *W Yor* 3K 55
Hartshill. *Warw* 2B 42
Hartshorne. *Derbs* 7L 49
Hartsop. *Cumb* 2F 58
Hart Station. *Hart* 8K 67
Hartswell. *Som* 3M 23
Hartwell. *Nptn* 6F 42
Hartwood. *Lanc* 4D 54
Hartwood. *N Lan* 4G 71
Harvel. *Kent* 7E 36
Harvington. *Worc* 7L 41 (nr. Evesham)
Harvington. *Worc* 4J 41 (nr. Kidderminster)
Harwell. *Oxon* 5E 34
Harwich. *Essx* 8J 45
Harwood. *Dur* 8D 66
Harwood. *G Man* 4F 54
Harwood Dale. *N Yor* 4J 61
Harworth. *Notts* 6C 56
Hascombe. *Surr* 2K 27
Haselbech. *Nptn* 4F 42
Haselbury Plucknett. *Som* 4D 24
Haseley. *Warw* 5A 42
Haselor. *Warw* 6M 41
Hasfield. *Glos* 1L 33
Hasguard. *Pemb* 3C 30
Haskayne. *Lanc* 5B 54
Hasketon. *Suff* 6J 45
Hasland. *Derbs* 3L 49
Haslemere. *Surr* 2K 27
Haslingden. *Lanc* 3F 54
Haslingden Grane. *Lanc* 3F 54
Haslingfield. *Cambs* 6A 44
Haslington. *Ches E* 4E 48
Hassall. *Ches E* 4E 48
Hassall Green. *Ches E* 4E 48
Hassell Street. *Kent* 3J 29
Hassendean. *Bord* 7E 72
Hassingham. *Norf* 1K 45
Hassness. *Cumb* 2C 58
Hassocks. *W Sus* 6B 28
Hassop. *Derbs* 8L 55
Haste Hill. *Surr* 2K 27
Haster. *High* 4J 93
Hasthorpe. *Linc* 3L 51
Hastigrow. *High* 3H 93
Hastingleigh. *Kent* 3J 29
Hastings. *E Sus* 7G 29
Hastingwood. *Essx* 3C 36
Hastoe. *Herts* 3K 35
Haston. *Shrp* 7C 48
Haswell. *Dur* 7J 67
Haswell Plough. *Dur* 7J 67
Hatch. *C Beds* 7K 43
Hatch Beauchamp. *Som* 3C 24
Hatch End. *G Lon* 4M 35
Hatch Green. *Som* 4C 24
Hatching Green. *Herts* 2M 35
Hatchmere. *Ches W* 8D 54
Hatch Warren. *Hants* 1G 27
Hatcliffe. *NE Lin* 5J 57
Hatfield. *Here* 6F 40
Hatfield. *Herts* 3A 36
Hatfield. *S Yor* 5C 56
Hatfield. *Worc* 6J 41
Hatfield Broad Oak. *Essx* 2D 36
Hatfield Garden Village. *Herts* 3A 36
Hatfield Heath. *Essx* 2D 36
Hatfield Hyde. *Herts* 2A 36
Hatfield Peverel. *Essx* 2F 36
Hatfield Woodhouse. *S Yor* 5C 56
Hatford. *Oxon* 4D 34
Hatherden. *Hants* 8D 34
Hatherleigh. *Devn* 5G 23
Hathern. *Leics* 7B 50
Hatherop. *Glos* 3B 34
Hathersage. *Derbs* 7L 55
Hathersage Booths. *Derbs* 7L 55
Hatherton. *Ches E* 5D 48
Hatherton. *Staf* 8G 49
Hatley St George. *Cambs* 6L 43
Hatt. *Corn* 3E 20
Hattersley. *G Man* 6H 55
Hattingley. *Hants* 2G 27
Hatton. *Abers* 6L 89
Hatton. *Derbs* 6K 49
Hatton. *G Lon* 6L 35
Hatton. *Linc* 8H 57
Hatton. *Shrp* 2E 40
Hatton. *Warr* 7D 54
Hatton. *Warw* 5A 42
Hattoncrook. *Abers* 1J 83
Hatton Heath. *Ches W* 3B 48
Hatton of Fintray. *Abers* 2J 83
Haugh. *E Ayr* 7C 70
Haugh. *Linc* 8L 57
Haugham. *Linc* 7K 57
Haugh Head. *Nmbd* 7K 73
Haughley. *Suff* 5G 45
Haughley Green. *Suff* 5G 45
Haugh of Ballechin. *Per* 8M 81
Haugh of Glass. *Mor* 6E 88
Haugh of Urr. *Dum* 5F 64
Haughton. *Ches E* 4C 48
Haughton. *Notts* 8C 56
Haughton. *Shrp* 2G 41 (nr. Bridgnorth)
Haughton. *Shrp* 7A 48 (nr. Oswestry)
Haughton. *Shrp* 1H 41 (nr. Shifnal)
Haughton. *Shrp* 8C 48 (nr. Shrewsbury)
Haughton. *Staf* 7F 48
Haughton Green. *G Man* 6H 55
Haughton le Skerne. *Darl* 2C 60
Haultwick. *Herts* 1B 36
Haunn. *Arg* 1A 74
Haunn. *W Isl* 2B 78
Haunton. *Staf* 8K 49
Hauxton. *Cambs* 6A 44
Havannah. *Ches E* 3F 48
Havant. *Hants* 5H 27
Haven. *Here* 6E 40
Haven Bank. *Linc* 4J 51
Havenside. *E Yor* 3H 57
Havenstreet. *IOW* 6F 26
Haven, The. *W Sus* 2L 27
Havercroft. *W Yor* 4M 55
Haverfordwest. *Pemb* 2D 30
Haverhill. *Suff* 7C 44
Haverigg. *Cumb* 6C 58
Havering-atte-Bower. *G Lon* 4D 36
Havering's Grove. *Essx* 4E 36
Haversham. *Mil* 7G 43
Haverthwaite. *Cumb* 5E 58
Haverton Hill. *Stoc T* 1D 60
Havyatt. *Som* 2E 24
Hawarden. *Flin* 3A 48
Hawbridge. *Worc* 7K 41
Hawcoat. *Cumb* 6D 58
Hawcross. *Glos* 8H 41
Hawen. *Cdgn* 7F 38
Hawes. *N Yor* 5K 59
Hawes Green. *Norf* 2J 45
Hawick. *Bord* 8E 72
Hawkchurch. *Devn* 5C 24
Hawkedon. *Suff* 6D 44
Hawkenbury. *Kent* 3G 29
Hawkeridge. *Wilts* 8L 33
Hawkerland. *Devn* 7M 23
Hawkesbury. *S Glo* 5K 33
Hawkesbury. *W Mid* 3B 42
Hawkesbury Upton. *S Glo* 5K 33
Hawkes End. *W Mid* 3A 42
Hawk Green. *G Man* 7H 55
Hawkhurst. *Kent* 4F 28
Hawkhurst Common. *E Sus* 6D 28
Hawkinge. *Kent* 3L 29
Hawkley. *Hants* 3H 27
Hawkridge. *Som* 2K 23
Hawksdale. *Cumb* 7L 65
Hawkshaw. *G Man* 4F 54
Hawkshead. *Cumb* 4E 58
Hawkshead Hill. *Cumb* 4E 58
Hawkswick. *N Yor* 6L 59
Hawksworth. *Notts* 5D 50
Hawksworth. *W Yor* 1K 55
Hawkwell. *Essx* 4G 37
Hawley. *Hants* 8J 35
Hawley. *Kent* 6D 36
Hawling. *Glos* 1A 34
Hawnby. *N Yor* 5E 60
Haworth. *W Yor* 2J 55
Hawstead. *Suff* 6E 44
Hawthorn. *Dur* 7K 67
Hawthorn Hill. *Brac* 6J 35
Hawthorn Hill. *Linc* 4J 51
Hawthorpe. *Linc* 7G 51
Hawton. *Notts* 4D 50
Haxby. *York* 8F 60
Haxey. *N Lin* 6D 56
Haybridge. *Shrp* 4G 41
Haybridge. *Som* 1E 24
Haydock. *Mers* 6D 54
Haydon. *Bath* 8J 33
Haydon. *Dors* 4F 24
Haydon. *Som* 3B 24
Haydon Bridge. *Nmbd* 5D 66
Haydon Wick. *Swin* 5B 34
Haye. *Corn* 3E 20
Hayes. *G Lon* 7C 36 (nr. Bromley)
Hayes. *G Lon* 5L 35 (nr. Uxbridge)
Hayfield. *Derbs* 7J 55
Hay Green. *Norf* 8M 51
Hayhill. *E Ayr* 8C 70
Haylands. *IOW* 6F 26
Hayle. *Corn* 6C 19
Hayley Green. *W Mid* 3K 41
Hayling Island. *Hants* 6H 27
Hayne. *Devn* 5K 23
Haynes. *C Beds* 7J 43
Haynes West End. *C Beds* 7J 43
Hay-on-Wye. *Powy* 7C 40
Hayscastle. *Pemb* 1C 30
Hayscastle Cross. *Pemb* 1D 30
Haysden. *Kent* 3D 28
Hayshead. *Ang* 1M 77
Hay Street. *Herts* 1B 36
Hayton. *Aber* 3K 83
Hayton. *Cumb* 7J 65 (nr. Aspatria)
Hayton. *Cumb* 6A 66 (nr. Brampton)
Hayton. *E Yor* 1E 56
Hayton. *Notts* 7D 56
Hayton's Bent. *Shrp* 3F 40
Haytor Vale. *Devn* 8J 23
Haytown. *Devn* 4E 22
Haywards Heath. *W Sus* 5B 28
Haywood. *S Lan* 4H 71
Hazelbank. *S Lan* 5G 71
Hazelbury Bryan. *Dors* 5G 25
Hazeleigh. *Essx* 3G 37
Hazeley. *Hants* 8H 35
Hazel Grove. *G Man* 7H 55
Hazelhead. *S Yor* 5K 55
Hazelslade. *Staf* 8H 49
Hazel Street. *Kent* 4E 28
Hazelton Walls. *Fife* 3J 77
Hazelwood. *Derbs* 5L 49
Hazlemere. *Buck* 4J 35
Hazler. *Shrp* 2E 40
Hazlerigg. *Tyne* 4H 67
Hazles. *Staf* 5H 49
Hazleton. *Glos* 2A 34
Hazon. *Nmbd* 1G 67
Heacham. *Norf* 4C 52
Headbourne Worthy. *Hants* 2E 26
Headcorn. *Kent* 3G 29
Headingley. *W Yor* 2L 55
Headington. *Oxon* 3F 34
Headlam. *Dur* 2A 60
Headless Cross. *Worc* 5L 41
Headley. *Hants* 2J 27 (nr. Haslemere)
Headley. *Hants* 7F 34 (nr. Kingsclere)
Headley. *Surr* 8A 36
Headley Down. *Hants* 2J 27
Headley Heath. *Worc* 4L 41
Headley Park. *Bris* 7H 33
Head of Muir. *Falk* 1G 71
Headon. *Notts* 8D 56
Heads Nook. *Cumb* 6M 65
Heage. *Derbs* 4L 49
Healaugh. *N Yor* 4M 59 (nr. Grinton)
Healaugh. *N Yor* 1B 56 (nr. York)
Heald Green. *G Man* 7G 55
Heale. *Devn* 1H 23
Healey. *G Man* 4G 55
Healey. *Nmbd* 6F 66
Healey. *N Yor* 5A 60
Healeyfield. *Dur* 7F 66
Healey Hall. *Nmbd* 6F 66
Healing. *NE Lin* 4J 57
Heamoor. *Corn* 6B 19
Heanish. *Arg* 8B 78
Heanor. *Derbs* 5A 50
Heanton Punchardon. *Devn* 2G 23
Heapham. *Linc* 7E 56
Heartsease. *Powy* 5B 40
Heasley Mill. *Devn* 2J 23
Heaste. *High* 2L 79
Heath. *Derbs* 3A 50
Heath and Reach. *C Beds* 1K 35
Heath Common. *W Sus* 4M 27
Heathcote. *Derbs* 3J 49
Heath Cross. *Devn* 6J 23
Heathencote. *Nptn* 7F 42
Heath End. *Derbs* 7L 49
Heath End. *Hants* 7F 34
Heath End. *W Mid* 1L 41
Heather. *Leics* 8L 49
Heatherfield. *High* 7J 85
Heatherton. *Derb* 6L 49
Heathfield. *Cambs* 7A 44
Heathfield. *Cumb* 7J 65
Heathfield. *Devn* 8K 23
Heathfield. *E Sus* 5D 28
Heathfield. *Ren* 3B 70
Heathfield. *Som* 2A 24 (nr. Lydeard St Lawrence)
Heathfield. *Som* 3A 24 (nr. Norton Fitzwarren)
Heath Green. *Worc* 4L 41
Heathhall. *Dum* 4G 65
Heath Hayes. *Staf* 8H 49
Heath Hill. *Shrp* 8E 48
Heath House. *Som* 1D 24
Heathrow (London) Airport. *G Lon* 6L 35
Heathstock. *Devn* 5B 24
Heath, The. *Norf* 5J 53 (nr. Buxton)
Heath, The. *Norf* 5F 52 (nr. Fakenham)
Heath, The. *Norf* 5H 53 (nr. Hevingham)
Heath, The. *Staf* 6H 49
Heath, The. *Suff* 8H 45
Heathton. *Shrp* 2J 41
Heathtop. *Derbs* 6J 49
Heath Town. *W Mid* 2K 41
Heatley. *G Man* 7F 54
Heatley. *Staf* 7H 49
Heaton. *Lanc* 7F 58
Heaton. *Staf* 3G 49
Heaton. *Tyne* 5H 67
Heaton. *W Yor* 2K 55
Heaton Moor. *G Man* 6G 55
Heaton's Bridge. *Lanc* 4C 54
Heaverham. *Kent* 8D 36
Heavitree. *Devn* 6L 23
Hebburn. *Tyne* 5J 67
Hebden. *N Yor* 7M 59
Hebden Bridge. *W Yor* 3H 55
Hebden Green. *Ches W* 3D 48
Hebing End. *Herts* 1B 36
Hebron. *Carm* 1F 30
Hebron. *Nmbd* 3G 67
Heck. *Dum* 3H 65
Heckdyke. *Notts* 6D 56
Heckfield. *Hants* 7H 35
Heckfield Green. *Suff* 4H 45
Heckfordbridge. *Essx* 1H 37
Heckington. *Linc* 5H 51
Heckmondwike. *W Yor* 3L 55
Heddington. *Wilts* 7M 33
Heddle. *Orkn* 6B 94
Heddon. *Devn* 3H 23
Heddon-on-the-Wall. *Nmbd* 5G 67
Hedenham. *Norf* 2K 45
Hedge End. *Hants* 4E 26
Hedgerley. *Buck* 5K 35
Hedging. *Som* 3C 24
Hedley on the Hill. *Nmbd* 6F 66
Hednesford. *Staf* 8H 49
Hedon. *E Yor* 3H 57
Hegdon Hill. *Here* 6F 40
Heglibister. *Shet* 6D 95
Heighington. *Darl* 1B 60
Heighington. *Linc* 3G 51
Heightington. *Worc* 4H 41
Heights of Brae. *High* 5H 87
Heights of Fodderty. *High* 5H 87
Heights of Kinlochewe. *High* 5C 86
Heiton. *Bord* 6G 73
Hele. *Devn* 5L 23 (nr. Exeter)
Hele. *Devn* 6E 22 (nr. Holsworthy)
Hele. *Devn* 1G 23 (nr. Ilfracombe)
Hele. *Torb* 3L 21
Helensburgh. *Arg* 1A 70
Helford. *Corn* 7E 19
Helhoughton. *Norf* 5E 52
Helions Bumpstead. *Essx* 7C 44
Helland. *Corn* 8B 22
Helland. *Som* 3C 24
Hellandbridge. *Corn* 8B 22
Hellesdon. *Norf* 6J 53
Hellesveor. *Corn* 5C 19
Hellidon. *Nptn* 6D 42
Hellifield. *N Yor* 8K 59
Hellingly. *E Sus* 6D 28
Hellington. *Norf* 1K 45
Hellister. *Shet* 7D 95
Helmdon. *Nptn* 7D 42
Helmingham. *Suff* 6H 45
Helmington Row. *Dur* 8G 67
Helmsdale. *High* 8F 92
Helmshore. *Lanc* 3F 54
Helmsley. *N Yor* 5F 60
Helperby. *N Yor* 7D 60
Helperthorpe. *N Yor* 6J 61
Helpringham. *Linc* 5H 51
Helpston. *Pet* 1K 43
Helsby. *Ches W* 8C 54
Helsey. *Linc* 8M 57
Helston. *Corn* 7D 19
Helstone. *Corn* 7B 22
Helton. *Cumb* 1G 59
Helwith. *N Yor* 3M 59
Helwith Bridge. *N Yor* 7K 59
Helygain. *Flin* 8A 54
Hemblington. *Norf* 6K 53
Hemel Hempstead. *Herts* 3L 35
Hemerdon. *Devn* 4G 21
Hemingbrough. *N Yor* 2C 56
Hemingby. *Linc* 8J 57
Hemingfield. *S Yor* 5M 55
Hemingford Abbots. *Cambs* 4L 43
Hemingford Grey. *Cambs* 4L 43
Hemingstone. *Suff* 6H 45
Hemington. *Leics* 7A 50
Hemington. *Nptn* 3J 43
Hemington. *Som* 8K 33
Hemley. *Suff* 7J 45
Hemlington. *Midd* 2D 60
Hempholme. *E Yor* 8K 61
Hempnall. *Norf* 2J 45
Hempnall Green. *Norf* 2J 45
Hempriggs. *High* 5J 93
Hemp's Green. *Essx* 1H 37
Hempstead. *Essx* 8C 44
Hempstead. *Medw* 7F 36
Hempstead. *Norf* 4H 53 (nr. Holt)
Hempstead. *Norf* 5L 53 (nr. Stalham)
Hempsted. *Glos* 2L 33
Hempton. *Norf* 5F 52
Hempton. *Oxon* 8C 42
Hemsby. *Norf* 6L 53
Hemswell. *Linc* 6F 56
Hemswell Cliff. *Linc* 7F 56
Hemsworth. *Dors* 5J 25
Hemsworth. *W Yor* 4A 56
Hem, The. *Shrp* 1H 41
Hemyock. *Devn* 4A 24
Henallt. *Carm* 1J 31
Henbury. *Bris* 6H 33
Henbury. *Ches E* 8G 55
Hendomen. *Powy* 2C 40
Hendon. *G Lon* 5A 36
Hendon. *Tyne* 6K 67
Hendra. *Corn* 4A 20
Hendre. *B'end* 5B 32
Hendreforgan. *Rhon* 5B 32
Hendy. *Carm* 3K 31
Heneglwys. *IOA* 2D 46
Henfeddau Fawr. *Pemb* 8E 38
Henfield. *S Glo* 6J 33
Henfield. *W Sus* 6A 28
Henford. *Devn* 6E 22
Hengoed. *Cphy* 4D 32
Hengoed. *Shrp* 6M 47
Hengrave. *Suff* 5E 44
Henham. *Essx* 1D 36
Heniarth. *Powy* 1B 40
Henlade. *Som* 3B 24
Henley. *Dors* 5F 24
Henley. *Shrp* 3E 40 (nr. Church Stretton)
Henley. *Shrp* 4F 40 (nr. Ludlow)
Henley. *Som* 2D 24
Henley. *Suff* 6H 45
Henley. *W Sus* 3J 27
Henley-in-Arden. *Warw* 5M 41
Henley-on-Thames. *Oxon* 5H 35
Henley's Down. *E Sus* 6F 28
Henley Street. *Kent* 7E 36
Henllan. *Cdgn* 7F 38
Henllan. *Den* 3K 47
Henllan. *Mon* 1E 32
Henllan Amgoed. *Carm* 2F 30
Henllys. *Torf* 4E 32
Henlow. *C Beds* 8K 43
Hennock. *Devn* 7K 23
Henny Street. *Essx* 8E 44
Henryd. *Cnwy* 2G 47
Henry's Moat. *Pemb* 1E 30
Hensall. *N Yor* 3B 56
Henshaw. *Nmbd* 5C 66
Hensingham. *Cumb* 2A 58
Henstead. *Suff* 3L 45
Hensting. *Hants* 3E 26
Henstridge. *Som* 4G 25
Henstridge Ash. *Som* 3G 25
Henstridge Bowden. *Som* 3F 24
Henstridge Marsh. *Som* 3G 25
Henton. *Oxon* 3H 35
Henton. *Som* 1D 24
Henwood. *Corn* 8D 22
Heogan. *Shet* 7E 95
Heol Senni. *Powy* 1B 32
Heol-y-Cyw. *B'end* 5B 32
Hepburn. *Nmbd* 7K 73
Hepple. *Nmbd* 1E 66
Hepscott. *Nmbd* 3H 67
Heptonstall. *W Yor* 3H 55
Hepworth. *Suff* 4F 44
Hepworth. *W Yor* 5K 55
Herbrandston. *Pemb* 3C 30
Hereford. *Here* 8F 40
Heribusta. *High* 4J 85
Heriot. *Bord* 4D 72
Hermiston. *Edin* 2K 71
Hermitage. *Dors* 5F 24
Hermitage. *Bord* 2A 66
Hermitage. *W Ber* 6F 34
Hermitage. *W Sus* 5H 27
Hermon. *Carm* 1L 31 (nr. Llandeilo)
Hermon. *Carm* 8F 38 (nr. Newcastle Emlyn)
Hermon. *IOA* 3C 46
Hermon. *Pemb* 8E 38
Herne. *Kent* 7K 37
Herne Bay. *Kent* 7K 37
Herne Common. *Kent* 7K 37
Herne Pound. *Kent* 8E 36
Herner. *Devn* 3G 23
Hernhill. *Kent* 7J 37
Herodsfoot. *Corn* 3D 20
Heronden. *Kent* 8L 37
Herongate. *Essx* 4E 36
Heronsford. *S Ayr* 3L 63
Heronsgate. *Herts* 4L 35
Heron's Ghyll. *E Sus* 5C 28
Herra. *Shet* 2G 95
Herriard. *Hants* 1G 27
Herringfleet. *Suff* 2L 45
Herringswell. *Suff* 5D 44
Herrington. *Tyne* 6J 67
Hersden. *Kent* 7L 37
Hersham. *Corn* 5D 22
Hersham. *Surr* 7M 35
Herstmonceux. *E Sus* 6E 28
Herston. *Dors* 8A 26
Herston. *Orkn* 8C 94
Hertford. *Herts* 2B 36
Hertford Heath. *Herts* 2B 36
Hertingfordbury. *Herts* 2B 36
Hesketh. *Lanc* 3C 54
Hesketh Bank. *Lanc* 3C 54
Hesketh Lane. *Lanc* 1E 54
Hesket Newmarket. *Cumb* 8L 65
Heskin Green. *Lanc* 4D 54
Hesleden. *Dur* 8K 67
Hesleyside. *Nmbd* 3D 66
Heslington. *York* 8F 60
Hessay. *York* 8E 60
Hessenford. *Corn* 4E 20
Hessett. *Suff* 5F 44
Hessilhead. *N Ayr* 4B 70
Hessle. *Hull* 3G 57
Hestaford. *Shet* 6C 95
Hest Bank. *Lanc* 7F 58
Hester's Way. *Glos* 1M 33
Hestinsetter. *Shet* 7C 95
Heston. *G Lon* 6M 35
Hestwall. *Orkn* 6A 94
Heswall. *Mers* 7A 54
Hethe. *Oxon* 1F 34
Hethelpit Cross. *Glos* 1K 33
Hethersett. *Norf* 1H 45
Hethersgill. *Cumb* 5M 65
Hetherside. *Cumb* 5M 65
Hethpool. *Nmbd* 7H 73
Hett. *Dur* 8H 67
Hetton. *N Yor* 8L 59
Hetton-le-Hole. *Tyne* 7J 67
Hetton Steads. *Nmbd* 6K 73
Heugh. *Nmbd* 4F 66
Heugh-head. *Abers* 2D 82
Heveningham. *Suff* 4K 45
Hever. *Kent* 3C 28
Heversham. *Cumb* 5F 58
Hevingham. *Norf* 5H 53
Hewas Water. *Corn* 5A 20
Hewelsfield. *Glos* 3H 33
Hewish. *N Som* 7F 32
Hewish. *Som* 5D 24
Hewood. *Dors* 5C 24
Heworth. *York* 8F 60
Hexham. *Nmbd* 5E 66
Hextable. *Kent* 6D 36
Hexton. *Herts* 8K 43
Hexworthy. *Devn* 8H 23
Heybridge. *Essx* 4E 36 (nr. Brentwood)
Heybridge. *Essx* 3G 37 (nr. Maldon)
Heybridge Basin. *Essx* 3G 37
Heybrook Bay. *Devn* 5F 20
Heydon. *Cambs* 7A 44
Heydon. *Norf* 5H 53
Heydour. *Linc* 6G 51
Heylipol. *Arg* 8A 78
Heyop. *Powy* 4C 40
Heysham. *Lanc* 7F 58
Heyshott. *W Sus* 4J 27
Heytesbury. *Wilts* 1J 25
Heythrop. *Oxon* 1D 34
Heywood. *G Man* 4G 55
Heywood. *Wilts* 8L 33
Hibaldstow. *N Lin* 5F 56
Hickleton. *S Yor* 5A 56
Hickling. *Norf* 5L 53
Hickling. *Notts* 7C 50
Hickling Green. *Norf* 5L 53
Hickling Heath. *Norf* 5L 53
Hickstead. *W Sus* 5A 28
Hidcote Bartrim. *Glos* 7M 41
Hidcote Boyce. *Glos* 7M 41
Higford. *Shrp* 1H 41
High Ackworth. *W Yor* 4A 56
Higham. *Derbs* 4L 49
Higham. *Kent* 6F 36
Higham. *Lanc* 2G 55
Higham. *S Yor* 5M 55
Higham. *Suff* 8G 45 (nr. Ipswich)
Higham. *Suff* 5D 44 (nr. Newmarket)
Higham Dykes. *Nmbd* 4G 67
Higham Ferrers. *Nptn* 5H 43
Higham Gobion. *C Beds* 8K 43
Higham on the Hill. *Leics* 2B 42
Highampton. *Devn* 5F 22
Higham Wood. *Kent* 3D 28
High Angerton. *Nmbd* 3F 66
High Auldgirth. *Dum* 3G 65
High Bankhill. *Cumb* 7A 66
High Banton. *N Lan* 1F 70
High Barnet. *G Lon* 4A 36
High Beech. *Essx* 4C 36
High Bentham. *N Yor* 7H 59
High Bickington. *Devn* 3H 23
High Biggins. *Cumb* 6H 59
High Birkwith. *N Yor* 6K 59
High Blantyre. *S Lan* 4E 70
High Bonnybridge. *Falk* 2G 71
High Borrans. *Cumb* 3F 58
High Bradfield. *S Yor* 6L 55
High Bray. *Devn* 2H 23
Highbridge. *Cumb* 7L 65
Highbridge. *High* 5D 80
Highbridge. *Som* 1C 24
Highbrook. *W Sus* 4B 28
High Brooms. *Kent* 3D 28
High Bullen. *Devn* 3G 23
Highburton. *W Yor* 4K 55
Highbury. *Som* 1F 24
High Buston. *Nmbd* 1H 67
High Callerton. *Nmbd* 4G 67
High Carlingill. *Cumb* 3H 59
High Catton. *E Yor* 8G 61
High Church. *Nmbd* 3G 67
Highclere. *Hants* 7E 34
Highcliffe. *Dors* 6C 26
High Cogges. *Oxon* 3D 34
High Common. *Norf* 1F 44
High Coniscliffe. *Darl* 2B 60
High Crosby. *Cumb* 6M 65
High Cross. *Hants* 3H 27
High Cross. *Herts* 2B 36
High Dougarie. *N Ayr* 6G 69
High Easter. *Essx* 2E 36
High Eggborough. *N Yor* 3B 56
High Ellington. *N Yor* 5A 60
Higher Alham. *Som* 1F 24
Higher Ansty. *Dors* 5G 25
Higher Ashton. *Devn* 7K 23
Higher Ballam. *Lanc* 2B 54
Higher Bartle. *Lanc* 2D 54
Higher Bockhampton. *Dors* 6G 25
Higher Bojewyan. *Corn* 6A 19
High Ercall. *Telf* 8C 48
Higher Cheriton. *Devn* 5A 24
Higher Clovelly. *Devn* 3E 22
Higher Compton. *Plym* 4F 20
Higher Dinting. *Derbs* 6J 55
Higher Dunstone. *Devn* 8J 23
Higher End. *G Man* 5D 54
Higher Gabwell. *Devn* 3L 21
Higher Halstock Leigh. *Dors* 5E 24
Higher Heysham. *Lanc* 7F 58
Higher Hurdsfield. *Ches E* 8H 55
Higher Kingcombe. *Dors* 6E 24
Higher Kinnerton. *Flin* 3A 48
Higher Melcombe. *Dors* 5G 25
Higher Penwortham. *Lanc* 3D 54
Higher Porthpean. *Corn* 4B 20
Higher Poynton. *Ches E* 7H 55
Higher Shotton. *Flin* 3A 48
Higher Shurlach. *Ches W* 8E 54
Higher Slade. *Devn* 1G 23
Higher Tale. *Devn* 5M 23
Highertown. *Corn* 5F 19
Higher Town. *IOS* 2C 19
Higher Town. *Som* 1L 23
Higher Vexford. *Som* 2A 24
Higher Walton. *Lanc* 3D 54
Higher Walton. *Warr* 7D 54
Higher Whatcombe. *Dors* 5H 25
Higher Wheelton. *Lanc* 3E 54
Higher Whiteleigh. *Corn* 6D 22
Higher Whitley. *Ches W* 8E 54
Higher Wincham. *Ches W* 8E 54
Higher Wraxall. *Dors* 5E 24
Higher Wych. *Wrex* 5B 48
Higher Yalberton. *Torb* 4K 21
High Etherley. *Dur* 1A 60
High Ferry. *Linc* 5K 51
Highfield. *E Yor* 2D 56
Highfield. *N Ayr* 4B 70
Highfield. *Tyne* 6G 67
Highfields Caldecote. *Cambs* 6M 43
High Garrett. *Essx* 1F 36
Highgate. *G Lon* 5A 36
Highgate. *N Ayr* 4B 70
Highgate. *Powy* 2B 40
High Grange. *Dur* 8G 67
High Green. *Cumb* 3F 58
High Green. *Norf* 1H 45
High Green. *Shrp* 3H 41
High Green. *S Yor* 6M 55
High Green. *W Yor* 4K 55
High Green. *Worc* 7J 41
Highgreen Manor. *Nmbd* 2D 66
High Halden. *Kent* 4G 29
High Halstow. *Medw* 6F 36
High Ham. *Som* 2D 24
High Harrington. *Cumb* 1B 58
High Haswell. *Dur* 7J 67
High Hatton. *Shrp* 7D 48
High Hawkser. *N Yor* 3J 61
High Hesket. *Cumb* 7M 65
High Hesleden. *Dur* 8K 67
High Hoyland. *S Yor* 4L 55
High Hunsley. *E Yor* 2F 56
High Hurstwood. *E Sus* 5C 28
High Hutton. *N Yor* 7G 61
High Ireby. *Cumb* 8K 65
High Keil. *Arg* 8E 68
High Kelling. *Norf* 3H 53
High Kilburn. *N Yor* 6E 60
High Knipe. *Cumb* 2G 59
High Lands. *Dur* 1A 60
Highlands, The. *Shrp* 3G 41
Highlane. *Ches E* 3F 48
Highlane. *Derbs* 7A 56
High Lane. *G Man* 7H 55
High Lane. *Here* 5G 41
High Laver. *Essx* 3D 36
Highlaws. *Cumb* 7J 65
Highleadon. *Glos* 1K 33
High Legh. *Ches E* 7E 54
Highleigh. *W Sus* 6J 27
High Leven. *Stoc T* 2D 60
Highley. *Shrp* 3H 41
High Littleton. *Bath* 8J 33
High Longthwaite. *Cumb* 7K 65
High Lorton. *Cumb* 1C 58
High Marishes. *N Yor* 6H 61
High Marnham. *Notts* 8E 56
High Melton. *S Yor* 5B 56
High Mickley. *Nmbd* 5F 66
Highmoor. *Cumb* 7K 65
High Moor. *Lanc* 4D 54
Highmoor. *Oxon* 5H 35
Highmoor Cross. *Oxon* 5H 35
Highmoor Hill. *Mon* 5G 33
High Mowthorpe. *N Yor* 7H 61
Highnam. *Glos* 2K 33
High Newport. *Tyne* 6J 67
High Newton. *Cumb* 5F 58
High Newton-by-the-Sea. *Nmbd* 7M 73
High Nibthwaite. *Cumb* 5D 58
High Offley. *Staf* 7E 48
High Ongar. *Essx* 3D 36
High Onn. *Staf* 8F 48
High Orchard. *Glos* 2L 33
High Park. *Mers* 4B 54
High Roding. *Essx* 2E 36
High Row. *Cumb* 8L 65
High Salvington. *W Sus* 5M 27
High Scales. *Cumb* 7J 65
High Shaw. *N Yor* 4K 59
High Shincliffe. *Dur* 7H 67
High Side. *Cumb* 8K 65
High Spen. *Tyne* 5G 67
Highsted. *Kent* 7H 37
High Stoop. *Dur* 7G 67
High Street. *Corn* 4A 20
High Street. *Suff* 6L 45 (nr. Aldeburgh)
High Street. *Suff* 3K 45 (nr. Bungay)
High Street. *Suff* 4L 45 (nr. Yoxford)
Highstreet Green. *Essx* 8D 44
High Street Green. *Suff* 6G 45
Highstreet Green. *Surr* 2K 27
Hightae. *Dum* 4H 65
High Throston. *Hart* 8K 67
Hightown. *Ches E* 3F 48
Hightown. *Mers* 5A 54
High Town. *Staf* 8G 49
Hightown Green. *Suff* 6F 44
High Toynton. *Linc* 3J 51
High Trewhitt. *Nmbd* 1F 66
High Valleyfield. *Fife* 1J 71
Highway. *Here* 7E 40
Highweek. *Devn* 8K 23
High Westwood. *Dur* 6G 67
Highwood. *Staf* 6H 49
Highwood. *Worc* 5G 41
High Worsall. *N Yor* 3C 60
Highworth. *Swin* 4C 34
High Wray. *Cumb* 4E 58
High Wych. *Herts* 2C 36
High Wycombe. *Buck* 4J 35
Hilborough. *Norf* 1E 44
Hilcott. *Wilts* 8B 34
Hildenborough. *Kent* 3D 28
Hildersham. *Cambs* 7B 44
Hilderstone. *Staf* 6G 49
Hilderthorpe. *E Yor* 7L 61
Hilfield. *Dors* 5F 24

Hilgay. Norf 2C 44
Hill. S Glo 4J 33
Hill. Warw 5C 42
Hill. Worc 7K 41
Hillam. N Yor 3B 56
Hillbeck. Cumb 2J 59
Hillberry. IOM 6D 62
Hillborough. Kent 7L 37
Hillbourne. Pool 6A 26
Hillbrae. Abers 5G 89 (nr. Aberchirder)
Hillbrae. Abers 1H 83 (nr. Inverurie)
Hillbrae. Abers 6J 89 (nr. Methlick)
Hill Brow. Hants 3H 27
Hillbutts. Dors 5J 25
Hillclifflane. Derbs 5K 49
Hillcommon. Som 3A 24
Hill Deverill. Wilts 1H 25
Hilldyke. Linc 5K 51
Hill End. Dur 8F 66
Hillend. Fife 1K 71 (nr. Inverkeithing)
Hill End. Fife 6F 76 (nr. Saline)
Hillend. N Lan 3G 71
Hill End. N Yor 8M 59
Hillend. Shrp 2J 41
Hillend. Swan 4J 31
Hillersland. Glos 2H 33
Hillerton. Devn 6J 23
Hillesden. Buck 1G 35
Hillesley. Glos 5K 33
Hillfarrance. Som 3A 24
Hill Furze. Worc 7K 41
Hill Gate. Here 1G 33
Hill Green. Essx 8A 44
Hillgreen. W Ber 6E 34
Hillhead. Abers 6F 88
Hill Head. Hants 5F 26
Hillhead. S Ayr 8C 70
Hillhead. Torb 4L 21
Hillhead of Auchentumb. Abers 4K 89
Hilliard's Cross. Staf 8J 49
Hilliclay. High 3G 93
Hillingdon. G Lon 5L 35
Hillington. Norf 5D 52
Hillington. Ren 3D 70
Hillmorton. Warw 4D 42
Hill of Beath. Fife 6G 77
Hill of Fearn. High 4L 87
Hill of Fiddes. Abers 1K 83
Hill of Keillor. Ang 1H 77
Hill of Overbrae. Abers 3J 89
Hill Ridware. Staf 8H 49
Hillsborough. S Yor 6M 55
Hillside. Abers 4K 83
Hillside. Ang 7H 83
Hillside. Devn 3J 21
Hillside. Mers 4B 54
Hillside. Orkn 5B 94
Hillside. Shet 5E 95
Hillside. Shrp 3G 41
Hill Side. W Yor 4K 55
Hillside. Worc 5H 41
Hillside of Prieston. Ang 2J 77
Hill Somersal. Derbs 6J 49
Hillstown. Derbs 3A 50
Hillstreet. Hants 4D 26
Hillswick. Shet 4C 95
Hill, The. Cumb 5C 58
Hill Top. Dur 1L 59 (nr. Barnard Castle)
Hill Top. Dur 7H 67 (nr. Durham)
Hill Top. Dur 6G 67 (nr. Stanley)
Hill Top. Hants 5E 26
Hill View. Dors 6J 25
Hillwell. Shet 10D 95
Hill Wootton. Warw 5B 42
Hillyland. Per 3F 76
Hilmarton. Wilts 6A 34
Hilperton. Wilts 8L 33
Hilperton Marsh. Wilts 8L 33
Hilsea. Port 5G 27
Hilston. E Yor 2J 57
Hiltingbury. Hants 3E 26
Hilton. Cambs 5L 43
Hilton. Cumb 1J 59
Hilton. Derbs 6K 49
Hilton. Dors 5G 25
Hilton. Dur 1A 60
Hilton. High 3K 87
Hilton. Shrp 2H 41
Hilton. Staf 1L 41
Hilton. Stoc T 2D 60
Hilton of Cadboll. High 4L 87
Himbleton. Worc 6K 41
Himley. Staf 2J 41
Hincaster. Cumb 5G 59
Hinchcliffe Mill. W Yor 5K 55
Hinchwick. Glos 8M 41
Hinckley. Leics 2C 42
Hinderclay. Suff 4G 45
Hinderwell. N Yor 2G 61
Hindford. Shrp 6A 48
Hindhead. Surr 2J 27
Hindley. G Man 5E 54
Hindley. Nmbd 6F 66
Hindley Green. G Man 5E 54
Hindlip. Worc 6J 41
Hindolveston. Norf 5G 53
Hindon. Wilts 2J 25
Hindringham. Norf 4F 52
Hingham. Norf 1G 45
Hinksford. Staf 3J 41
Hinstock. Shrp 7D 48
Hintlesham. Suff 7G 45
Hinton. Hants 6C 26
Hinton. Here 8D 40
Hinton. Nptn 6D 42
Hinton. Shrp 1E 40
Hinton. S Glo 6K 33
Hinton Ampner. Hants 3F 26
Hinton Blewett. Bath 8H 33
Hinton Charterhouse. Bath 8K 33
Hinton-in-the-Hedges. Nptn 8D 42
Hinton Martell. Dors 5A 26
Hinton on the Green. Worc 7L 41
Hinton Parva. Swin 5C 34
Hinton St George. Som 4D 24
Hinton St Mary. Dors 4G 25
Hinton Waldrist. Oxon 4D 34
Hints. Shrp 4G 41
Hints. Staf 1M 41
Hinwick. Bed 5H 43
Hinxhill. Kent 3J 29
Hinxton. Cambs 7A 44
Hinxworth. Herts 7L 43
Hipley. Hants 4G 27
Hipperholme. W Yor 3K 55
Hipsburn. Nmbd 8M 73
Hipswell. N Yor 4A 60
Hiraeth. Carm 1F 30
Hirn. Abers 3H 83
Hirnant. Powy 7K 47
Hirst. N Lan 3G 71
Hirst. Nmbd 3H 67
Hirst Courtney. N Yor 3C 56
Hirwaen. Den 3L 47
Hirwaun. Rhon 3B 32
Hiscott. Devn 3G 23
Histon. Cambs 5A 44
Hitcham. Suff 6F 44
Hitchin. Herts 1M 35
Hittisleigh. Devn 6J 23
Hittisleigh Barton. Devn 6J 23
Hive. E Yor 2E 56
Hixon. Staf 7H 49
Hoaden. Kent 8L 37
Hoar Cross. Staf 7J 49
Hoarwithy. Here 1H 33
Hoath. Kent 7L 37
Hobarris. Shrp 4D 40
Hobbister. Orkn 7B 94
Hobbles Green. Suff 6D 44
Hobbs Cross. Essx 4C 36
Hobkirk. Bord 8E 72
Hobson. Dur 6G 67
Hoby. Leics 8C 50
Hockering. Norf 6G 53
Hockering Heath. Norf 6G 53
Hockerton. Notts 4D 50
Hockley. Essx 4G 37
Hockley. Staf 1A 42
Hockley. W Mid 4A 42
Hockley Heath. W Mid 4M 41
Hockliffe. C Beds 1K 35
Hockwold cum Wilton. Norf 3D 44
Hockworthy. Devn 4M 23
Hoddesdon. Herts 3B 36
Hoddlesden. Bkbn 3F 54
Hoddomcross. Dum 4J 65
Hodgeston. Pemb 4E 30
Hodley. Powy 2B 40
Hodnet. Shrp 7D 48
Hodsoll Street. Kent 7E 36
Hodson. Swin 5B 34
Hodthorpe. Derbs 8B 56
Hoe. Norf 6F 52
Hoe Gate. Hants 4G 27
Hoe, The. Plym 4F 20
Hoff. Cumb 2H 59
Hoffleet Stow. Linc 6J 51
Hogaland. Shet 4D 95
Hogben's Hill. Kent 8J 37
Hoggard's Green. Suff 6E 44
Hoggeston. Buck 1J 35
Hoggrill's End. Warw 2A 42
Hogha Gearraidh. W Isl 4B 84
Hoghton. Lanc 3E 54
Hoghton Bottoms. Lanc 3E 54
Hognaston. Derbs 4K 49
Hogsthorpe. Linc 8M 57
Hogstock. Dors 5J 25
Holbeach. Linc 7K 51
Holbeach Bank. Linc 7K 51
Holbeach Clough. Linc 7K 51
Holbeach Drove. Linc 8K 51
Holbeach Hurn. Linc 7K 51
Holbeach St Johns. Linc 8K 51
Holbeach St Marks. Linc 6K 51
Holbeach St Matthew. Linc 6L 51
Holbeck. Notts 8B 56
Holbeck. W Yor 2L 55
Holbeck Woodhouse. Notts 8B 56
Holberrow Green. Worc 6L 41
Holbeton. Devn 4H 21
Holborn. G Lon 5B 36
Holbrook. Derbs 5L 49
Holbrook. S Yor 7A 56
Holbrook. Suff 8H 45
Holburn. Nmbd 6K 73
Holbury. Hants 5E 26
Holcombe. Devn 8L 23
Holcombe. G Man 4F 54
Holcombe. Som 1F 24
Holcombe Brook. G Man 4F 54
Holcombe Rogus. Devn 4M 23
Holcot. Nptn 5F 42
Holden. Lanc 1F 54
Holdenby. Nptn 5E 42
Holder's Green. Essx 1E 36
Holdgate. Shrp 3F 40
Holdingham. Linc 5G 51
Holditch. Dors 5C 24
Holemoor. Devn 5F 22
Hole Street. W Sus 4M 27
Holford. Som 1A 24
Holker. Cumb 6E 58
Holkham. Norf 3E 52
Hollacombe. Devn 5E 22
Holland. Orkn 2C 94 (on Papa Westray)
Holland. Orkn 5E 94 (on Stronsay)
Holland Fen. Linc 5J 51
Holland Lees. Lanc 5D 54
Holland-on-Sea. Essx 2L 37
Holland Park. W Mid 1L 41
Hollandstoun. Orkn 2F 94
Hollesley. Suff 7K 45
Hollinfare. Warr 6E 54
Hollingbourne. Kent 8G 37
Hollingbury. Brig 7B 28
Hollingdon. Buck 1J 35
Hollingrove. E Sus 5E 28
Hollington. Derbs 5K 49
Hollington. E Sus 6F 28
Hollington. Staf 6H 49
Hollington Grove. Derbs 6K 49
Hollingworth. G Man 6J 55
Hollins. Derbs 8M 55
Hollins. G Man 5G 55 (nr. Bury)
Hollins. G Man 5G 55 (nr. Middleton)
Hollinsclough. Staf 3H 49
Hollinswood. Telf 1G 41
Hollinthorpe. W Yor 2M 55
Hollinwood. G Man 5H 55
Hollinwood. Shrp 6C 48
Hollocombe. Devn 4H 23
Holloway. Derbs 4L 49
Hollow Court. Worc 6K 41
Hollowell. Nptn 4E 42
Hollow Meadows. S Yor 7L 55
Hollows. Dum 4L 65
Hollybush. Cphy 3D 32
Hollybush. E Ayr 8B 70
Hollybush. Worc 8H 41
Holly End. Norf 1A 44
Holly Hill. N Yor 3A 60
Hollyhurst. Ches E 5C 48
Hollym. E Yor 3K 57
Hollywood. Worc 4L 41
Holmacott. Devn 3G 23
Holmbridge. W Yor 5K 55
Holmbury St Mary. Surr 1M 27
Holmbush. Corn 4B 20
Holmcroft. Staf 7G 49
Holme. Cambs 3K 43
Holme. Cumb 6G 59
Holme. N Lin 5F 56
Holme. N Yor 5C 60
Holme. Notts 4E 50
Holme. W Yor 5K 55
Holmebridge. Dors 7H 25
Holme Chapel. Lanc 3G 55
Holme Hale. Norf 1E 44
Holme Lacy. Here 8F 40
Holme Marsh. Here 6D 40
Holmend. Dum 1H 65
Holme next the Sea. Norf 3D 52
Holme-on-Spalding-Moor. E Yor 2E 56
Holme on the Wolds. E Yor 1F 56
Holme Pierrepont. Notts 6C 50
Holmer. Here 7F 40
Holmer Green. Buck 4K 35
Holmes. Lanc 4C 54
Holme St Cuthbert. Cumb 7J 65
Holmes Chapel. Ches E 3E 48
Holmesfield. Derbs 8M 55
Holmeswood. Lanc 4C 54
Holmewood. Derbs 3A 50
Holmfirth. W Yor 5K 55
Holmhead. E Ayr 7D 70
Holmisdale. High 7F 84
Holm of Drumlanrig. Dum 2F 64
Holmpton. E Yor 3K 57
Holmrook. Cumb 4B 58
Holmsgarth. Shet 7E 95
Holmside. Dur 7H 67
Holmwrangle. Cumb 7A 66
Holne. Devn 3J 21
Holsworthy. Devn 5E 22
Holsworthy Beacon. Devn 5E 22
Holt. Dors 5A 26
Holt. Norf 4G 53
Holt. Wilts 7L 33
Holt. Worc 5J 41
Holt. Wrex 4B 48
Holtby. York 8F 60
Holt End. Hants 2G 27
Holt End. Worc 5L 41
Holt Fleet. Worc 5J 41
Holt Green. Lanc 5B 54
Holt Heath. Dors 5A 26
Holt Heath. Worc 5J 41
Holton. Oxon 3G 35
Holton. Som 3F 24
Holton. Suff 4K 45
Holton cum Beckering. Linc 7H 57
Holton Heath. Dors 6J 25
Holton le Clay. Linc 5J 57
Holton le Moor. Linc 6G 57
Holton St Mary. Suff 8G 45
Holt Pound. Hants 1J 27
Holtsmere End. Herts 2L 35
Holtye. E Sus 4C 28
Holwell. Dors 4G 25
Holwell. Herts 8K 43
Holwell. Leics 7D 50
Holwell. Oxon 3C 34
Holwell. Som 1G 25
Holwick. Dur 1L 59
Holworth. Dors 7G 25
Holybourne. Hants 1H 27
Holy City. Devn 5C 24
Holy Cross. Worc 4K 41
Holyfield. Essx 3B 36
Holyhead. IOA 1B 46
Holy Island. Nmbd 5L 73
Holymoorside. Derbs 3L 49
Holyport. Wind 6J 35
Holystone. Nmbd 1E 66
Holytown. N Lan 3F 70
Holywell. Cambs 4M 43
Holywell. Corn 4E 19
Holywell. Dors 5E 24
Holywell. Flin 2L 47
Holywell. Glos 4K 33
Holywell. Nmbd 4J 67
Holywell. Warw 5M 41
Holywell Green. W Yor 4J 55
Holywell Lake. Som 3A 24
Holywell Row. Suff 4D 44
Holywood. Dum 3G 65
Homer. Shrp 1G 41
Homer Green. Mers 5B 54
Homersfield. Suff 3J 45
Hom Green. Here 1H 33
Homington. Wilts 3B 26
Honeyborough. Pemb 3D 30
Honeybourne. Worc 7M 41
Honeychurch. Devn 5H 23
Honeydon. Bed 6K 43
Honey Hill. Kent 7K 37
Honey Street. Wilts 7B 34
Honey Tye. Suff 8F 44
Honeywick. C Beds 1K 35
Honiley. Warw 4A 42
Honing. Norf 5K 53
Honingham. Norf 6H 53
Honington. Linc 5F 50
Honington. Suff 4F 44
Honington. Warw 7A 42
Honiton. Devn 5A 24
Honley. W Yor 4K 55
Honnington. Telf 8E 48
Hoo. Suff 6J 45
Hoobrook. Worc 4J 41
Hood Green. S Yor 5M 55
Hooe. E Sus 7E 28
Hooe. Plym 4G 21
Hooe Common. E Sus 6E 28
Hoohill. Bkpl 2B 54
Hook. Cambs 2A 44
Hook. E Yor 3D 56
Hook. G Lon 7M 35
Hook. Hants 8H 35 (nr. Basingstoke)
Hook. Hants 5F 26 (nr. Fareham)
Hook. Pemb 2D 30
Hook. Wilts 5A 34
Hook-a-Gate. Shrp 1E 40
Hook Bank. Worc 7J 41
Hooke. Dors 5E 24
Hooker Gate. Tyne 6G 67
Hookgate. Staf 6E 48
Hook Green. Kent 4E 28 (nr. Lamberhurst)
Hook Green. Kent 6E 36 (nr. Longfield)
Hook Green. Kent 7E 36 (nr. Meopham)
Hook Norton. Oxon 8B 42
Hook's Cross. Herts 1A 36
Hook Street. Glos 4J 33
Hookway. Devn 6K 23
Hookwood. Surr 3A 28
Hoole. Ches W 3B 48
Hooley. Surr 8A 36
Hooley Bridge. G Man 4G 55
Hooley Brow. G Man 4G 55
Hoo St Werburgh. Medw 6F 36
Hooton. Ches W 8B 54
Hooton Levitt. S Yor 6B 56
Hooton Pagnell. S Yor 5A 56
Hooton Roberts. S Yor 6A 56
Hoove. Shet 7D 95
Hope. Derbs 7K 55
Hope. Flin 4A 48
Hope. High 3M 91
Hope. Powy 1C 40
Hope. Shrp 1D 40
Hope. Staf 4J 49
Hope Bagot. Shrp 4F 40
Hope Bowdler. Shrp 2E 40
Hopedale. Staf 4J 49
Hope Green. Ches E 7H 55
Hopeman. Mor 3B 88
Hope Mansell. Here 2J 33
Hopesay. Shrp 3D 40
Hope's Green. Essx 5F 36
Hopetown. W Yor 3M 55
Hope under Dinmore. Here 6F 40
Hopley's Green. Here 6D 40
Hopperton. N Yor 8D 60
Hop Pole. Linc 8H 51
Hopstone. Shrp 2H 41
Hopton. Derbs 4K 49
Hopton. Powy 2C 40
Hopton. Shrp 7A 48 (nr. Oswestry)
Hopton. Shrp 7C 48 (nr. Wem)
Hopton. Staf 7G 49
Hopton. Suff 4F 44
Hopton Cangeford. Shrp 3F 40
Hopton Castle. Shrp 4D 40
Hoptonheath. Shrp 4D 40
Hopton Heath. Staf 7G 49
Hopton on Sea. Norf 1M 45
Hopton Wafers. Shrp 4G 41
Hopwas. Staf 1M 41
Hopwood. Worc 4L 41
Horam. E Sus 6D 28
Horbling. Linc 6H 51
Horbury. W Yor 4L 55
Horcott. Glos 3B 34
Horden. Dur 7K 67
Horderley. Shrp 3E 40
Hordle. Hants 6C 26
Hordley. Shrp 6A 48
Horeb. Carm 1K 31 (nr. Brechfa)
Horeb. Carm 3J 31 (nr. Llanelli)
Horeb. Cdgn 7F 38
Horfield. Bris 6J 33
Horgabost. W Isl 2E 84
Horham. Suff 4J 45
Horkesley Heath. Essx 1H 37
Horkstow. N Lin 4F 56
Horley. Oxon 7C 42
Horley. Surr 3A 28
Horn Ash. Dors 5C 24
Hornblotton Green. Som 2E 24
Hornby. Lanc 7G 59
Hornby. N Yor 3C 60 (nr. Appleton Wiske)
Hornby. N Yor 4B 60 (nr. Catterick Garrison)
Horncastle. Linc 3J 51
Hornchurch. G Lon 5D 36
Horncliffe. Nmbd 5J 73
Horndean. Hants 4G 27
Horndean. Bord 5H 73
Horndon. Devn 7G 23
Horndon on the Hill. Thur 5E 36
Horne. Surr 3B 28
Horner. Som 1L 23
Horning. Norf 6K 53
Horninghold. Leics 2G 43
Horninglow. Staf 7K 49
Horningsea. Cambs 5A 44
Horningsham. Wilts 1H 25
Horningtoft. Norf 5F 52
Hornsbury. Som 4C 24
Hornsby. Cumb 6A 66
Hornsbygate. Cumb 6A 66
Horns Corner. Kent 5F 28
Horns Cross. Devn 3E 22
Hornsea. E Yor 1J 57
Hornsea Burton. E Yor 1J 57
Hornsey. G Lon 5B 36
Hornton. Oxon 7B 42
Horpit. Swin 5C 34
Horrabridge. Devn 3G 21
Horringer. Suff 5E 44
Horringford. IOW 7F 26
Horrocks Fold. G Man 4F 54
Horrocksford. Lanc 1F 54
Horsbrugh Ford. Bord 6L 71
Horsebridge. Devn 8F 22
Horsebridge. E Sus 6D 28
Horsebridge. Hants 2D 26
Horse Bridge. Staf 4G 49
Horsebrook. Staf 8F 48
Horsecastle. N Som 7G 33
Horsehay. Telf 1G 41
Horseheath. Cambs 7C 44
Horsehouse. N Yor 5M 59
Horsell. Surr 8K 35
Horseman's Green. Wrex 5B 48
Horsenden. Buck 3H 35
Horseway. Cambs 3A 44
Horsey. Norf 5L 53
Horsey. Som 2C 24
Horsford. Norf 6H 53
Horsforth. W Yor 2L 55
Horsham. W Sus 2M 27
Horsham. Worc 6H 41
Horsham St Faith. Norf 6J 53
Horsington. Linc 3H 51
Horsington. Som 3G 25
Horsley. Derbs 5L 49
Horsley. Glos 4L 33
Horsley. Nmbd 5F 66 (nr. Prudhoe)
Horsley. Nmbd 2D 66 (nr. Rochester)
Horsley Cross. Essx 1K 37
Horsleycross Street. Essx 1K 37
Horsleyhill. Bord 8E 72
Horsleyhope. Dur 7F 66
Horsley Woodhouse. Derbs 5L 49
Horsmonden. Kent 3E 28
Horspath. Oxon 3F 34
Horstead. Norf 6J 53
Horsted Keynes. W Sus 5B 28
Horton. Buck 2K 35
Horton. Dors 5A 26
Horton. Lanc 8K 59
Horton. Nptn 6G 43
Horton. Shrp 6B 48
Horton. Som 4C 24
Horton. S Glo 5K 33
Horton. Staf 4G 49
Horton. Swan 5J 31
Horton. Wilts 7A 34
Horton. Wind 6L 35
Horton Cross. Som 4C 24
Horton-cum-Studley. Oxon 2F 34
Horton Grange. Nmbd 4H 67
Horton Green. Ches W 5B 48
Horton Heath. Hants 4E 26
Horton in Ribblesdale. N Yor 6K 59
Horton Kirby. Kent 7D 36
Hortonwood. Telf 8D 48
Horwich. G Man 4E 54
Horwich End. Derbs 7J 55
Horwood. Devn 3G 23
Hoscar. Lanc 4C 54
Hose. Leics 7D 50
Hosh. Per 3D 76
Hosta. W Isl 4B 84
Hoswick. Shet 9E 95
Hotham. E Yor 2E 56
Hothfield. Kent 3H 29
Hoton. Leics 7B 50
Houbie. Shet 2G 95
Hough. Arg 8A 78
Hough. Ches E 4E 48 (nr. Crewe)
Hough. Ches E 8G 55 (nr. Wilmslow)
Hougham. Linc 5E 50
Hough Green. Hal 7C 54
Hough-on-the-Hill. Linc 5F 50
Houghton. Cambs 4L 43
Houghton. Cumb 6M 65
Houghton. Hants 2D 26
Houghton. Nmbd 5G 67
Houghton. Pemb 3D 30
Houghton. W Sus 4L 27
Houghton Bank. Darl 1B 60
Houghton Conquest. C Beds 7J 43
Houghton Green. E Sus 5H 29
Houghton-le-Side. Darl 1B 60
Houghton-le-Spring. Tyne 7J 67
Houghton on the Hill. Leics 1E 42
Houghton Regis. C Beds 1L 35
Houghton St Giles. Norf 4F 52
Houlland. Shet 6D 95 (on Mainland)
Houlland. Shet 4F 95 (on Yell)
Houlsyke. N Yor 3G 61
Hound. Hants 5E 26
Hound Green. Hants 8H 35
Houndslow. Bord 5F 72
Houndsmoor. Som 3A 24
Houndwood. Bord 3H 73
Hounsdown. Hants 4D 26
Hounslow. G Lon 6M 35
Housabister. Shet 6E 95
Housay. Shet 4G 95
Househill. High 6L 87
Housetter. Shet 3D 95
Houss. Shet 8D 95
Houston. Ren 3C 70
Housty. High 6G 93
Houton. Orkn 7B 94
Hove. Brig 7A 28
Hoveringham. Notts 5D 50
Hoveton. Norf 6K 53
Hovingham. N Yor 6F 60
How. Cumb 6A 66
How Caple. Here 8G 41
Howden. E Yor 3D 56
Howden-le-Wear. Dur 8G 67
Howe. High 3J 93
Howe. Norf 1J 45
Howe. N Yor 5C 60
Howe Green. Essx 3F 36 (nr. Chelmsford)
Howegreen. Essx 3G 37 (nr. Maldon)
Howe Green. Warw 3B 42
Howell. Linc 5H 51
How End. C Beds 7J 43
Howe of Teuchar. Abers 5H 89
Howes. Dum 5J 65
Howe Street. Essx 2E 36 (nr. Chelmsford)
Howe Street. Essx 8C 44 (nr. Finchingfield)
Howe, The. Cumb 5F 58
Howe, The. IOM 7B 62
Howey. Powy 6A 40
Howgate. Midl 4L 71
Howgill. Lanc 1G 55
Howgill. N Yor 8M 59
How Green. Kent 3C 28
How Hill. Norf 6K 53
Howick. Nmbd 8M 73
Howle. Telf 7D 48
Howle Hill. Here 1J 33
Howleigh. Som 4B 24
Howlett End. Essx 8B 44
Howley. Som 5B 24
Howley. Warr 7E 54
Hownam. Bord 8G 73
Howsham. N Lin 5G 57
Howsham. N Yor 7G 61
Howtel. Nmbd 6H 73
Howt Green. Kent 7G 37
Howton. Here 1G 33
Howwood. Ren 3B 70
Hoxne. Suff 4H 45
Hoylake. Mers 7A 54
Hoyland. S Yor 5M 55
Hoylandswaine. S Yor 5L 55
Hoyle. W Sus 4K 27
Hubberholme. N Yor 6L 59
Hubberston. Pemb 3C 30
Hubbert's Bridge. Linc 5J 51
Huby. N Yor 1L 55 (nr. Harrogate)
Huby. N Yor 7E 60 (nr. York)
Hucclecote. Glos 2L 33
Hucking. Kent 8G 37
Hucknall. Notts 5B 50
Huddersfield. W Yor 4K 55
Huddington. Worc 6K 41
Huddlesford. Staf 1M 41
Hudswell. N Yor 3A 60
Huggate. E Yor 8H 61
Hugglescote. Leics 8A 50
Hughenden Valley. Buck 4J 35
Hughley. Shrp 2F 40
Hughton. High 7G 87
Hugh Town. IOS 2C 19
Hugus. Corn 5E 19
Huish. Devn 4G 23
Huish. Wilts 7B 34
Huish Champflower. Som 3M 23
Huish Episcopi. Som 3D 24
Huisinis. W Isl 1D 84
Hulcote. Nptn 6F 42
Hulcott. Buck 2J 35
Hulham. Devn 7M 23
Hull. Hull 3G 57
Hulland. Derbs 5K 49
Hulland Moss. Derbs 5K 49
Hulland Ward. Derbs 5K 49
Hullavington. Wilts 5L 33
Hullbridge. Essx 4G 37
Hulme. G Man 6G 55
Hulme. Staf 5G 49
Hulme End. Staf 4J 49
Hulme Walfield. Ches E 3F 48
Hulverstone. IOW 7D 26
Hulver Street. Suff 3L 45
Humber. Devn 8L 23
Humber. Here 6F 40
Humber Bridge. N Lin 3G 57
Humberside International Airport. N Lin 4G 57
Humberston. NE Lin 5K 57
Humberstone. Leic 1E 42
Humbie. E Lot 3D 72
Humbleton. E Yor 2J 57
Humbleton. Nmbd 7J 73
Humby. Linc 6G 51
Hume. Bord 5G 73
Humshaugh. Nmbd 4E 66
Huna. High 2J 93
Huncoat. Lanc 2F 54
Huncote. Leics 2D 42
Hundall. Derbs 8M 55
Hunderthwaite. Dur 1L 59
Hundleby. Linc 3K 51
Hundle Houses. Linc 4J 51
Hundleton. Pemb 3D 30
Hundon. Suff 7D 44
Hundred Acres. Hants 4F 26
Hundred House. Powy 6B 40
Hundred, The. Here 5F 40
Hungarton. Leics 1E 42
Hungerford. Hants 4B 26
Hungerford. Shrp 3F 40
Hungerford. Som 1M 23
Hungerford. W Ber 7D 34
Hungerford Newtown. W Ber 6D 34
Hunger Hill. G Man 5E 54
Hungerton. Linc 6E 50
Hungladder. High 4H 85
Hungryhatton. Shrp 7D 48
Hunmanby. N Yor 6K 61
Hunmanby Sands. N Yor 6L 61
Hunningham. Warw 5B 42
Hunnington. Worc 3K 41
Hunny Hill. IOW 7E 26
Hunsdon. Herts 2C 36
Hunsdonbury. Herts 2C 36
Hunsingore. N Yor 8D 60
Hunslet. W Yor 2M 55
Hunslet Carr. W Yor 3M 55
Hunsonby. Cumb 8A 66
Hunspow. High 2H 93
Hunstanton. Norf 3C 52
Hunstanworth. Dur 7E 66
Hunston. Suff 5F 44
Hunston. W Sus 5J 27
Hunstrete. Bath 7J 33
Hunt End. Worc 5L 41
Hunterfield. Midl 3M 71
Hunters Forstal. Kent 7K 37
Hunter's Quay. Arg 2K 69
Huntham. Som 3C 24
Hunthill Lodge. Ang 6E 82
Huntingdon. Cambs 4L 43
Huntingfield. Suff 4K 45
Huntingford. Wilts 2H 25
Huntington. Ches W 3B 48
Huntington. E Lot 2D 72
Huntington. Here 6C 40
Huntington. Staf 8G 49
Huntington. Telf 1G 41
Huntington. York 8F 60
Huntingtower. Per 3F 76
Huntley. Glos 2K 33
Huntley. Staf 5H 49
Huntly. Abers 5F 88
Huntlywood. Bord 5F 72
Hunton. Hants 2E 26
Hunton. Kent 3F 28
Hunton. N Yor 4A 60
Hunton Bridge. Herts 3L 35
Hunt's Corner. Norf 3G 45
Huntscott. Som 1L 23
Hunt's Cross. Mers 7C 54
Hunts Green. Warw 2M 41
Huntsham. Devn 3M 23
Huntshaw. Devn 3G 23
Huntspill. Som 1C 24
Huntstile. Som 2B 24
Huntstrete. Bath 7J 33
Huntworth. Som 2C 24
Hunwick. Dur 8G 67
Hunworth. Norf 4G 53
Hurcott. Som 4C 24 (nr. Ilminster)
Hurcott. Som 3E 24 (nr. Somerton)
Hurdcott. Wilts 2B 26
Hurdley. Powy 2C 40
Hurdsfield. Ches E 8H 55
Hurlet. Glas 3D 70
Hurley. Warw 2A 42
Hurley. Wind 5J 35
Hurlford. E Ayr 6C 70
Hurliness. Orkn 9A 94
Hurlston Green. Lanc 4B 54
Hurn. Dors 6B 26
Hursey. Dors 5D 24
Hursley. Hants 3E 26
Hurst. G Man 5H 55
Hurst. N Yor 3M 59
Hurst. Som 4D 24
Hurst. Wok 6H 35
Hurstbourne Priors. Hants 1E 26
Hurstbourne Tarrant. Hants 8D 34
Hurst Green. Ches E 5C 48
Hurst Green. E Sus 5F 28
Hurst Green. Essx 2J 37
Hurst Green. Lanc 2E 54
Hurst Green. Surr 8B 36
Hurstley. Here 7D 40
Hurstpierpoint. W Sus 6A 28
Hurstway Common. Here 7C 40
Hurst Wickham. W Sus 6A 28
Hurstwood. Lanc 2G 55
Hurtmore. Surr 1K 27
Hurworth-on-Tees. Darl 2C 60
Hurworth Place. Darl 2B 60
Hury. Dur 2L 59
Husbands Bosworth. Leics 3E 42
Husborne Crawley. C Beds 8H 43
Husthwaite. N Yor 6E 60
Hutcherleigh. Devn 4J 21
Hut Green. N Yor 3B 56
Huthwaite. Notts 4A 50
Huttoft. Linc 8M 57
Hutton. Cumb 1F 58
Hutton. E Yor 8K 61
Hutton. Essx 4E 36
Hutton. Lanc 3C 54
Hutton. N Som 8F 32
Hutton. Bord 4J 73
Hutton Bonville. N Yor 3C 60
Hutton Buscel. N Yor 5J 61
Hutton Conyers. N Yor 6C 60
Hutton Cranswick. E Yor 8K 61
Hutton End. Cumb 8M 65
Hutton Gate. Red C 2E 60
Hutton Henry. Dur 8K 67
Hutton-le-Hole. N Yor 5G 61
Hutton Magna. Dur 2A 60
Hutton Mulgrave. N Yor 3H 61
Hutton Roof. Cumb 6G 59 (nr. Kirkby Lonsdale)
Hutton Roof. Cumb 8L 65 (nr. Penrith)
Hutton Rudby. N Yor 3D 60
Huttons Ambo. N Yor 7G 61
Hutton Sessay. N Yor 6D 60
Hutton Village. Red C 2F 60
Hutton Wandesley. N Yor 8E 60
Huxham. Devn 6L 23
Huxham Green. Som 2E 24
Huxley. Ches W 3C 48
Huxter. Shet 6B 95 (on Mainland)
Huxter. Shet 5F 95 (on Whalsay)
Huyton. Mers 6C 54
Hwlffordd. Pemb 2D 30
Hycemoor. Cumb 5B 58
Hyde. Glos 3L 33 (nr. Stroud)
Hyde. Glos 1A 34 (nr. Winchcombe)
Hyde. G Man 6H 55
Hyde Heath. Buck 3K 35
Hyde Lea. Staf 7G 49
Hyde Park. S Yor 5B 56
Hydestile. Surr 1K 27
Hyndford Bridge. S Lan 5H 71
Hynish. Arg 9A 78
Hyssington. Powy 2D 40
Hythe. Hants 5E 26
Hythe. Kent 4K 29
Hythe End. Wind 6L 35
Hythie. Abers 4L 89
Hyton. Cumb 5B 58

I

Ianstown. Mor 3E 88
Iarsiadar. W Isl 6B 90
Ibberton. Dors 5G 25
Ible. Derbs 4K 49
Ibrox. Glas 3D 70
Ibsley. Hants 5B 26
Ibstock. Leics 8A 50
Ibstone. Buck 4H 35
Ibthorpe. Hants 8D 34
Iburndale. N Yor 3H 61
Ibworth. Hants 8F 34
Icelton. N Som 7F 32
Ichrachan. Arg 2H 75
Ickburgh. Norf 2E 44
Ickenham. G Lon 5L 35
Ickenthwaite. Cumb 5E 58
Ickford. Buck 3G 35
Ickham. Kent 8L 37
Ickleford. Herts 8K 43
Icklesham. E Sus 6G 29
Ickleton. Cambs 7A 44
Icklingham. Suff 4D 44
Ickwell. C Beds 7K 43
Icomb. Glos 1C 34
Idbury. Oxon 1C 34
Iddesleigh. Devn 5G 23
Ide. Devn 6K 23
Ideford. Devn 8K 23
Ide Hill. Kent 8C 36
Iden. E Sus 5H 29
Iden Green. Kent 4G 29 (nr. Benenden)
Iden Green. Kent 4F 28 (nr. Goudhurst)
Idle. W Yor 2K 55
Idless. Corn 5F 19
Idlicote. Warw 7A 42
Idmiston. Wilts 2B 26
Idole. Carm 2J 31
Idridgehay. Derbs 5K 49
Idrigill. High 5H 85
Idstone. Oxon 5C 34
Iffley. Oxon 3F 34
Ifield. W Sus 4A 28
Ifieldwood. W Sus 4A 28
Ifold. W Sus 2L 27
Iford. E Sus 7C 28
Ifton Heath. Shrp 6A 48
Ightfield. Shrp 6C 48
Ightham. Kent 8D 36
Iken. Suff 6L 45
Ilam. Staf 4J 49
Ilchester. Som 3E 24
Ilderton. Nmbd 7K 73
Ilford. G Lon 5C 36
Ilford. Som 4C 24
Ilfracombe. Devn 1G 23
Ilkeston. Derbs 5A 50
Ilketshall St Andrew. Suff 3K 45
Ilketshall St Lawrence. Suff 3K 45
Ilketshall St Margaret. Suff 3K 45
Ilkley. W Yor 1K 55
Illand. Corn 8D 22
Illey. W Mid 3K 41
Illidge Green. Ches E 3E 48
Illington. Norf 3F 44
Illingworth. W Yor 3J 55
Illogan. Corn 5D 19
Illogan Highway. Corn 5D 19
Illston on the Hill. Leics 2F 42
Ilmer. Buck 3H 35
Ilmington. Warw 7A 42
Ilminster. Som 4C 24
Ilsington. Devn 8J 23
Ilsington. Dors 6G 25
Ilston. Swan 4K 31
Ilton. N Yor 6A 60
Ilton. Som 4C 24
Imachar. N Ayr 5G 69
Imber. Wilts 1J 25
Immingham. NE Lin 4H 57
Immingham Dock. NE Lin 4H 57
Impington. Cambs 5A 44
Ince. Ches W 8C 54
Ince Blundell. Mers 5B 54
Ince-in-Makerfield. G Man 5D 54
Inchbae Lodge. High 5G 87
Inchbare. Ang 7G 83
Inchberry. Mor 4D 88
Inchbraoch. Ang 8H 83
Inchbrook. Glos 3L 33
Incheril. High 5C 86
Inchinnan. Ren 3C 70
Inchlaggan. High 3D 80
Inchmichael. Per 3H 77
Inchnadamph. High 7K 91
Inchree. High 7C 80
Inchture. Per 3H 77
Inchyra. Per 3G 77
Indian Queens. Corn 4A 20
Ingatestone. Essx 4E 36
Ingbirchworth. S Yor 5L 55
Ingestre. Staf 7G 49
Ingham. Linc 7F 56
Ingham. Norf 5K 53
Ingham. Suff 4E 44
Ingham Corner. Norf 5K 53
Ingleborough. Norf 8L 51
Ingleby. Derbs 7L 49
Ingleby Arncliffe. N Yor 3D 60
Ingleby Barwick. Stoc T 2D 60
Ingleby Greenhow. N Yor 3E 60
Ingleigh Green. Devn 5H 23
Inglemire. Hull 2G 57
Inglesbatch. Bath 7K 33
Ingleton. Dur 1A 60
Ingleton. N Yor 6H 59
Inglewhite. Lanc 1D 54
Ingoe. Nmbd 4F 66
Ingol. Lanc 2D 54
Ingoldisthorpe. Norf 4C 52
Ingoldmells. Linc 3M 51
Ingoldsby. Linc 6G 51
Ingon. Warw 6A 42
Ingram. Nmbd 8K 73
Ingrave. Essx 4E 36
Ingrow. W Yor 2J 55
Ings. Cumb 4F 58
Ingst. S Glo 5H 33
Ingthorpe. Rut 1H 43
Ingworth. Norf 5H 53
Inkberrow. Worc 6L 41
Inkford. Worc 4L 41
Inkpen. W Ber 7D 34
Inkstack. High 2H 93
Innellan. Arg 3K 69
Inner Hope. Devn 6H 21
Innerleith. Fife 4H 77
Innerleithen. Bord 6M 71
Innerleven. Fife 5J 77
Innermessan. Dum 5K 63
Innerwick. E Lot 2G 73
Innerwick. Per 1A 76
Innsworth. Glos 1L 33
Insch. Abers 1G 83
Insh. High 3L 81
Inshegra. High 4K 91
Inshore. High 2L 91
Inskip. Lanc 2C 54
Instow. Devn 2F 22
Intwood. Norf 1H 45
Inver. Abers 4C 82
Inver. High 3L 87
Inver. Per 1F 76
Inverailort. High 5M 79
Inveralligin. High 6A 86
Inverallochy. Abers 3L 89
Inveramsay. Abers 1H 83
Inveran. High 2H 87
Inveraray. Arg 5H 75
Inverarish. High 8K 85
Inverarity. Ang 1K 77
Inverarnan. Arg 4L 75
Inverarnie. High 8J 87
Inverbeg. Arg 6L 75
Inverbervie. Abers 6J 83
Inverboyndie. Abers 3G 89
Invercassley. High 1G 87
Invercharnan. High 1J 75
Inverchoran. High 6E 86
Invercreran. Arg 1H 75
Inverdruie. High 2M 81
Inverebrie. Abers 6K 89
Invereck. Arg 1K 69
Inveresk. E Lot 2M 71
Inveresragan. Arg 2G 75
Inverey. Abers 5A 82
Inverfarigaig. High 1H 81
Invergarry. High 3F 80
Invergeldie. Per 3C 76
Invergordon. High 5K 87
Invergowrie. Per 2J 77
Inverguseran. High 3M 79
Inverharroch. Mor 6D 88
Inverie. High 3M 79
Inverinan. Arg 4G 75
Inverinate. High 1B 80
Inverkeilor. Ang 1M 77
Inverkeithing. Fife 1K 71
Inverkeithny. Abers 5G 89
Inverkip. Inv 2A 70
Inverkirkaig. High 8H 91
Inverlael. High 3D 86
Inverliever Lodge. Arg 5F 74
Inverliver. Arg 2H 75
Inverloch. High 6D 80
Inverlochlarig. Stir 4M 75
Inverlussa. Arg 1E 68
Inver Mallie. High 5D 80
Invermarkie. Abers 6E 88
Invermoriston. High 2G 81
Invernaver. High 3C 92
Inverneil House. Arg 1G 69
Inverness. High 7J 87
Inverness Airport. High 6K 87
Invernettie. Abers 5M 89
Inverpolly Lodge. High 8H 91
Inverquhomery. Abers 5L 89
Inverroy. High 5E 80
Inversanda. High 8B 80
Invershiel. High 2B 80
Invershin. High 2H 87
Invershore. High 6H 93
Inversnaid. Stir 5L 75
Inverugie. Abers 5M 89
Inveruglas. Arg 5L 75
Inverurie. Abers 1H 83
Invervar. Per 1B 76
Inverythan. Abers 5H 89
Inwardleigh. Devn 6G 23
Inworth. Essx 2G 37
Iochdar. W Isl 7B 84
Iping. W Sus 3J 27
Ipplepen. Devn 3K 21
Ipsden. Oxon 5G 35
Ipstones. Staf 5H 49
Ipswich. Suff 7H 45
Irby. Mers 7A 54
Irby in the Marsh. Linc 3L 51
Irby upon Humber. NE Lin 5H 57
Irchester. Nptn 5H 43
Ireby. Cumb 8K 65
Ireby. Lanc 6H 59
Ireland. Shet 9D 95
Ireleth. Cumb 6D 58
Ireshopeburn. Dur 8D 66
Ireton Wood. Derbs 5K 49
Irlam. G Man 6F 54
Irnham. Linc 7G 51
Iron Acton. S Glo 5J 33
Iron Bridge. Cambs 2A 44
Ironbridge. Telf 1G 41
Iron Cross. Warw 6L 41
Ironville. Derbs 4A 50
Irstead. Norf 5K 53
Irthington. Cumb 5M 65
Irthlingborough. Nptn 4H 43
Irton. N Yor 5K 61
Irvine. N Ayr 6B 70
Irvine Mains. N Ayr 6B 70
Isabella Pit. Nmbd 3J 67
Isauld. High 3E 92
Isbister. Orkn 6B 94
Isbister. Shet 2D 95 (on Mainland)
Isbister. Shet 5F 95 (on Whalsay)
Isfield. E Sus 6C 28
Isham. Nptn 4G 43
Island Carr. N Lin 5F 56
Islay Airport. Arg 4B 68
Isle Abbotts. Som 3C 24
Isle Brewers. Som 3C 24
Isleham. Cambs 4C 44
Isle of Man Airport. IOM 7C 62
Isle of Thanet. Kent 7M 37
Isle of Whithorn. Dum 8B 64
Isleornsay. High 2M 79
Islesburgh. Shet 5D 95
Isles of Scilly (St Mary's) Airport. IOS 2C 19
Islesteps. Dum 4G 65
Isleworth. G Lon 6M 35
Isley Walton. Leics 7A 50
Islibhig. W Isl 6A 90
Islington. G Lon 5B 36
Islington. Telf 7E 48
Islip. Nptn 4H 43
Islip. Oxon 2F 34
Islwyn. Cphy 4E 32
Isombridge. Telf 8D 48
Istead Rise. Kent 7E 36
Itchen. Sotn 4E 26
Itchen Abbas. Hants 2F 26
Itchen Stoke. Hants 2F 26
Itchingfield. W Sus 3M 27
Itchington. S Glo 5J 33
Itlaw. Abers 4G 89
Itteringham. Norf 4H 53
Itteringham Common. Norf 5H 53
Itton. Devn 6H 23
Itton Common. Mon 4G 33
Ivegill. Cumb 7M 65
Ivelet. N Yor 4L 59
Iverchaolain. Arg 2J 69
Iver Heath. Buck 5L 35
Iveston. Dur 6G 67
Ivetsey Bank. Staf 8F 48
Ivinghoe. Buck 2K 35
Ivinghoe Aston. Buck 2K 35
Ivington. Here 6E 40
Ivington Green. Here 6E 40
Ivybridge. Devn 4H 21
Ivychurch. Kent 5J 29
Ivy Hatch. Kent 8D 36
Ivy Todd. Norf 1E 44
Iwade. Kent 7H 37
Iwerne Courtney. Dors 4H 25
Iwerne Minster. Dors 4H 25
Ixworth. Suff 4F 44
Ixworth Thorpe. Suff 4F 44

J

Jackfield. Shrp 1G 41
Jack Hill. N Yor 8B 60
Jacksdale. Notts 4A 50
Jackton. S Lan 4D 70
Jacobstow. Corn 6C 22
Jacobstowe. Devn 5G 23
Jacobswell. Surr 8K 35
Jameston. Pemb 4E 30
Jamestown. Dum 2L 65
Jamestown. Fife 1K 71
Jamestown. High 6G 87
Jamestown. W Dun 1B 70
Janetstown. High 3F 92 (nr. Thurso)
Janetstown. High 4J 93 (nr. Wick)
Jarrow. Tyne 5J 67
Jarvis Brook. E Sus 5D 28
Jasper's Green. Essx 1F 36
Jaywick. Essx 2K 37
Jedburgh. Bord 7F 72
Jeffreyston. Pemb 3E 30
Jemimaville. High 5K 87
Jenkins Park. High 3F 80
Jersey Marine. Neat 4M 31
Jesmond. Tyne 5H 67
Jevington. E Sus 7D 28
Jingle Street. Mon 2G 33
Jockey End. Herts 2L 35
Jodrell Bank. Ches E 8F 54
Johnby. Cumb 8M 65
John o' Gaunts. W Yor 3M 55
John o' Groats. High 2J 93
John's Cross. E Sus 5F 28
Johnshaven. Abers 7H 83
Johnson Street. Norf 6K 53
Johnston. Pemb 2D 30
Johnstone. Ren 3C 70
Johnstonebridge. Dum 2H 65
Johnstown. Carm 2H 31
Johnstown. Wrex 5A 48
Joppa. Edin 2M 71
Joppa. S Ayr 8C 70
Jordan Green. Norf 5G 53
Jordans. Buck 4K 35
Jordanston. Pemb 8B 38
Jump. S Yor 5M 55
Jumpers Common. Dors 6B 26
Juniper. Nmbd 6E 66
Juniper Green. Edin 3K 71
Jurby East. IOM 4D 62
Jurby West. IOM 4D 62
Jury's Gap. E Sus 6H 29

K

Kaber. Cumb 2J 59
Kaimend. S Lan 5H 71
Kaimes. Edin 3L 71
Kaimrig End. Bord 5J 71
Kames. Arg 2H 69
Kames. E Ayr 7E 70
Kea. Corn 5F 19
Keadby. N Lin 4E 56
Keal Cotes. Linc 3K 51
Kearsley. G Man 5F 54
Kearsney. Kent 3L 29
Kearstwick. Cumb 5H 59
Kearton. N Yor 4L 59
Kearvaig. High 2K 91
Keasden. N Yor 7J 59
Keason. Corn 3E 20
Keckwick. Hal 7D 54
Keddington. Linc 7K 57
Keddington Corner. Linc 7K 57
Kedington. Suff 7D 44
Kedleston. Derbs 5L 49
Kedlock Feus. Fife 4J 77
Keekle. Cumb 2B 58
Keelby. Linc 4H 57
Keele. Staf 5F 48
Keeley Green. Bed 7J 43
Keeston. Pemb 2D 30
Keevil. Wilts 8M 33
Kegworth. Leics 7A 50
Kehelland. Corn 5D 19
Keig. Abers 2G 83
Keighley. W Yor 1J 55
Keilarsbrae. Clac 6D 76
Keillmore. Arg 1E 68
Keillor. Per 1H 77
Keillour. Per 3E 76
Keills. Arg 3C 68
Keiloch. Abers 4B 82
Keils. Arg 3D 68
Keinton Mandeville. Som 2E 24
Keir Mill. Dum 2F 64
Keirsleywell Row. Nmbd 6C 66
Keisby. Linc 7G 51
Keisley. Cumb 1J 59
Keiss. High 3J 93
Keith. Mor 4E 88
Keith Inch. Abers 5M 89
Kelbrook. Lanc 1H 55
Kelby. Linc 5G 51
Keld. Cumb 2G 59
Keld. N Yor 3K 59
Keldholme. N Yor 5G 61
Kelfield. N Lin 5E 56
Kelfield. N Yor 2B 56
Kelham. Notts 4D 50
Kellacott. Devn 7F 22
Kellan. Arg 1C 74
Kellas. Ang 2K 77
Kellas. Mor 4B 88
Kellaton. Devn 6K 21
Kelleth. Cumb 3H 59
Kelling. Norf 3G 53
Kellingley. N Yor 3B 56
Kellington. N Yor 3B 56
Kelloe. Dur 8J 67
Kelloholm. Dum 8F 70
Kells. Cumb 2A 58
Kelly. Devn 7E 22
Kelly Bray. Corn 8E 22
Kelmarsh. Nptn 4F 42
Kelmscott. Oxon 4C 34
Kelsale. Suff 5K 45
Kelsall. Ches W 3C 48
Kelshall. Herts 8M 43
Kelsick. Cumb 6J 65
Kelso. Bord 6G 73
Kelstedge. Derbs 3L 49
Kelstern. Linc 6J 57
Kelsterton. Flin 8A 54
Kelston. Bath 7K 33
Keltneyburn. Per 1C 76
Kelton. Dum 4G 65
Kelton Hill. Dum 6E 64
Kelty. Fife 6G 77
Kelvedon. Essx 2G 37
Kelvedon Hatch. Essx 4D 36
Kelvinside. Glas 3D 70
Kelynack. Corn 6A 19
Kemback. Fife 4K 77
Kemberton. Shrp 1H 41
Kemble. Glos 4M 33
Kemerton. Worc 8K 41
Kemeys Commander. Mon 3F 32
Kemnay. Abers 2H 83
Kempe's Corner. Kent 3J 29
Kempley. Glos 1J 33
Kempley Green. Glos 1J 33
Kempsey. Worc 7J 41
Kempsford. Glos 4B 34
Kemps Green. Warw 4M 41
Kempshott. Hants 8G 35
Kempston. Bed 7J 43
Kempston Hardwick. Bed 7J 43
Kempton. Shrp 3D 40
Kemp Town. Brig 7B 28
Kemsing. Kent 8D 36
Kemsley. Kent 7H 37
Kenardington. Kent 4H 29
Kenchester. Here 7E 40
Kencot. Oxon 3C 34
Kendal. Cumb 4G 59
Kendleshire. S Glo 6J 33
Kendray. S Yor 5M 55
Kenfig. B'end 5A 32
Kenfig Hill. B'end 5A 32

Kengharair—Lenacre

- Kengharair. *Arg* —1B 74
- Kenidjack. *Corn* —6A 19
- **Kenilworth.** *Warw* —4A 42
- Kenknock. *Stir* —2M 75
- Kenley. *G Lon* —8B 36
- Kenley. *Shrp* —1F 40
- Kenmore. *High* —6M 85
- Kenmore. *Per* —1C 76
- Kenn. *N Som* —7G 33
- Kennacraig. *Arg* —4H 65
- Kenneggy Downs. Corn —7C 19
- Kennerleigh. *Devn* —4E 22
- Kennet. *Clac* —6E 76
- Kennethmont. *Abers* —3E 81
- Kennett. *Cambs* —5D 44
- Kennford. *Devn* —7L 23
- Kenninghall. *Norf* —3G 45
- Kennington. *Kent* —3J 29
- Kennington. *Oxon* —3C 36
- Kennoway. *Fife* —5J 77
- Kennyhill. *Suff* —4C 44
- Kennythorpe. *N Yor* —7G 85
- Kenovay. *Arg* —4A 78
- **Kensington.** *G Lon* —6A 36
- Kensworth. *C Beds* —7C 48
- Kensworth Common. *C Beds* —2L 35
- Kentallen. *High* —8C 80
- Kentchurch. *Here* —5M 23
- Kentford. *Suff* —5D 44
- Kent International Airport. *Kent* —7M 37
- Kentisbeare. *Devn* —5M 23
- Kentisbury. *Devn* —1H 23
- Kentisbury Ford. *Devn* —1H 23
- Kentmere. *Cumb* —5F 58
- Kenton. *Devn* —7L 23
- Kenton. *G Lon* —5H 35
- Kenton. *Suff* —5H 45
- Kenton Bankfoot. *Tyne* —5F 54
- Kentra. *High* —7L 79
- Kentrigg. *Cumb* —4G 59
- Kents Bank. *Cumb* —6B 58
- Kent's Green. *Glos* —1K 33
- Kent's Oak. *Hants* —3D 26
- Kent Street. *E Sus* —6E 28
- Kent Street. *Kent* —8C 36
- Kent Street. *W Sus* —5A 28
- Kenwick. *Shrp* —6B 48
- Kenwyn. *Corn* —6E 54
- Keoldale. *High* —3L 91
- Keppoch. *High* —1B 80
- Kepwick. *N Yor* —4D 60
- Keresley. *W Mid* —3B 42
- Keresley Newland. *Warw* —3B 42
- Kermoil. *Arg* —6D 62
- Kerne Bridge. *Here* —2F 33
- Kerridge. *Ches E* —2H 41
- Kerris. *Corn* —7B 19
- Kerrow. *High* —3B 40
- Kerrycroy. *Arg* —3K 69
- Kerry's Gate. *Here* —8D 40
- Kersall. *Notts* —3D 50
- Kersbrook. *Devn* —7M 23
- Kerse. *Ren* —7B 54
- Kersey. *Suff* —7G 45
- Kershopefoot. *Cumb* —3M 65
- Kersoe. *Worc* —8K 41
- Kerswell. *Devn* —5M 23
- Kerswell Green. *Worc* —7J 41
- Kesgrave. *Suff* —7J 45
- Kessingland. *Suff* —3M 45
- Kessingland Beach. *Suff* —3M 45
- Kestle. *Corn* —5A 20
- Kestle Mill. *Corn* —4K 33
- Keston. *G Lon* —7C 36
- Keswick. *Cumb* —4K 53
- Keswick. *Norf* —4K 53 (nr. North Walsham)
- Keswick. *Norf* —1J 45 (nr. Norwich)
- **Ketsby.** *Linc* —8K 57
- **Kettering.** *Nptn* —4G 43
- Ketteringham. *Norf* —1H 45
- Kettins. *Per* —2H 77
- Kettlebaston. *Suff* —6F 44
- Kettlebridge. *Fife* —5J 77
- Kettlebrook. *Staf* —1A 42
- Kettleburgh. *Suff* —5J 45
- Kettleholm. *Dum* —4J 65
- Kettleness. *N Yor* —7N 61
- Kettleshulme. *Ches E* —4J 45
- Kettlesing. *N Yor* —8B 60
- Kettlesing Bottom. *N Yor* —8B 60
- Kettlestone. *Norf* —7F 38
- Kettlethorpe. *Linc* —8E 56
- Kettletoft. *Orkn* —1F 90
- Kettlewell. *N Yor* —6L 59
- Ketton. *Rut* —1H 43
- Kew. *G Lon* —6M 35
- Kewaigue. *IOM* —7D 62
- Kewstoke. *N Som* —7B 32
- Kexbrough. *S Yor* —7M 51
- Kexby. *Linc* —1F 52
- Kexby. *York* —8G 61
- Keyford. *Som* —1E 24
- Key Green. *Ches E* —3F 48
- Key Green. *N Yor* —5E 60
- Keyham. *Leics* —1E 42
- Keyhaven. *Hants* —6D 26
- Keyhead. *Abers* —8K 81
- Keyingham. *E Yor* —3L 57
- **Keynsham.** *Bath* —7J 33
- Keysoe. *Bed* —5J 43
- Keysoe Row. *Bed* —5J 43
- Key's Toft. *Linc* —4L 51
- Keyston. *Cambs* —4J 43
- Key Street. *Kent* —7G 37
- Keyworth. *Notts* —6C 50
- Kibblesworth. *Tyne* —6F 54
- Kibworth Beauchamp. *Leics* —2E 42
- Kibworth Harcourt. *Leics* —2E 42
- Kidbrooke. *G Lon* —6A 36
- Kidburngill. *Cumb* —1B 58
- **Kidderminster.** *Worc* —3J 41
- Kiddemore Green. *Staf* —1J 41
- Kiddington. *Oxon* —1E 34
- Kidd's Moor. *Norf* —1H 65
- **Kidlington.** *Oxon* —2C 36
- Kidmore End. *Oxon* —6E 35
- Kidnal. *Ches W* —4C 40
- **Kidsgrove.** *Staf* —4F 48
- Kidstones. *N Yor* —6L 59
- Kidwelly. *Carm* —8L 16
- Kiel Crofts. *Arg* —2G 75
- Kielder. *Nmbd* —3F 66
- Kilbagie. *Fife* —8C 76
- Kilbarchan. *Ren* —3C 70
- Kilberry. *Arg* —3L 78
- Kilbirnie. *N Ayr* —3J 69
- Kilbride. *Arg* —5E 64 (on Muirs of Clac)
- Kilbride. *Arg* —7E 40 (on Arran)
- Kilbucho Place. *Bord* —6J 71
- Kilburn. *Derbs* —5L 49
- Kilburn. *G Lon* —5K 35
- Kilburn. *N Yor* —6E 60
- Kilby. *Leics* —2E 42
- Kilchattan. *Arg* —3L 77 (on Colonsay)
- Kilchattan Bay. *Arg* —4J 69 (on Isle of Bute)
- Kilchenzie. *Arg* —7F 66
- Kilcheran. *Arg* —3A 66
- Kilchoan. *High* —7J 79 (nr. Inverie)
- Kilchoan. *High* —3B 68 (nr. Tobermory)
- Kilchoman. *Arg* —3A 68
- Kilconquhar. *Fife* —5K 75
- Kilcot. *Glos* —8H 79
- Kilcoy. *High* —6H 79
- Kilcreggan. *Arg* —1M 69
- Kildary. *High* —4K 87
- Kildonan. *Dum* —6K 63
- Kildonan. *High* —2K 87 (nr. Helmsdale)
- Kildonan. *High* —1G 69 (on Isle of Skye)
- Kildonan. *N Ayr* —7J 69
- Kildrummy. *Abers* —2E 82
- Kildwick. *N Yor* —5J 79
- Kilfillan. *Dum* —6M 63
- Kilfinan. *Arg* —2H 69
- Kilfinnan. *High* —4E 80
- Kilgetty. *Pemb* —7F 30
- Kilgour. *Fife* —7K 61
- Kilgrammie. *S Ayr* —1M 63
- Kilham. *E Yor* —7K 61
- Kilham. *Nmbd* —6H 73
- Kilkenneth. *Arg* —4A 78
- Kilkenzie. *Arg* —7F 66
- Kilkhampton. *Corn* —5B 22
- Killamarsh. *Derbs* —7A 56
- Killandrist. *Arg* —1F 74
- Killay. *Swan* —5E 68
- Killean. *Arg* —4L 77
- Killearn. *Stir* —1L 68
- Killerby. *Darl* —8E 68
- Killichonan. *Per* —8L 78
- Killichonan. *Per* —6F 74
- Killichronan. *Arg* —3L 77
- Killichronan. *Per* —5D 72
- Killin. *Stir* —2A 76
- Killin Lodge. *High* —4J 79
- Killinghall. *N Yor* —6H 60
- Killinghurst. *Surr* —2K 27
- Killington. *Cumb* —5H 59
- Killingworth. *Tyne* —4H 67
- Killochyett. *Bord* —8J 33
- Killocraw. *Arg* —3J 26
- Killundine. *High* —6F 74
- Killyneeme. *Arg* —6E 74
- Kilmacolm. *Inv* —3B 70
- Kilmahumaig. *Arg* —6E 74
- Kilmahog. *Stir* —8A 80
- Kilmalieu. *High* —4J 85
- Kilmaluag. *High* —3H 83
- Kilmany. *Fife* —2K 79
- Kilmarie. *High* —4J 77
- **Kilmarnock.** *E Ayr* —6C 70
- Kilmartin. *Arg* —4J 77
- Kilmaurs. *E Ayr* —5C 70
- Kilmelford. *Arg* —4E 74
- Kilmeny. *Arg* —3B 68
- Kilmersdon. *Som* —8J 33
- Kilmeston. *Hants* —3C 26
- Kilmichael Glassary. *Arg* —6F 74
- Kilmichael of Inverlussa. *Arg* —1F 68
- Kilmington. *Devn* —6A 24
- Kilmington. *Wilts* —2G 25
- Kilmoluaig. *Arg* —7G 87
- Kilmorack. *High* —8E 86
- Kilmore. *Arg* —3F 74
- Kilmore. *High* —4G 77
- Kilmory. *Arg* —1L 69
- Kilmory. *Arg* —3L 79 (nr. Kilchoan)
- Kilmory. *High* —1L 79 (on Rùm)
- Kilmory. *N Ayr* —7J 69
- Kilmory Lodge. *Arg* —6E 74
- Kilmote. *High* —8E 92
- Kilmuir. *High* —7M 85 (nr. Dunvegan)
- Kilmuir. *High* —4K 87 (nr. Invergordon)
- Kilmuir. *High* —7J 87 (nr. Inverness)
- Kilmuir. *High* —7J 87 (nr. Uig)
- Kilmun. *Arg* —1L 69
- Kiln. *G Lon* —2A 68
- Kilncadzow. *S Lan* —5G 71
- Kilndown. *Kent* —2D 28
- Kiln Green. *Here* —2J 33
- Kiln Green. *Wind* —6J 35
- Kilnhill. *Cumb* —8K 65
- Kilninian. *Arg* —3J 77
- Kilninver. *Arg* —3F 74
- Kiln Pit Hill. *Nmbd* —6F 66
- Kilnsea. *E Yor* —4L 57
- Kilnsey. *N Yor* —7J 59
- Kilnwick. *E Yor* —2H 61
- Kiloran. *Arg* —6A 74
- Kilpatrick. *N Ayr* —7H 69
- Kilpeck. *Here* —8C 40
- Kilpin. *E Yor* —5E 60
- Kilpin Pike. *E Yor* —5D 71
- Kirkton St Michael. *Wilts* —6M 33
- Kilrenny. *Fife* —3H 77
- Kilsby. *Nptn* —4D 42
- Kilspindie. *Per* —5H 77
- Kilsyth. *N Lan* —2F 70
- Kiltarlity. *High* —7H 87
- Kilton. *Som* —1A 24
- Kilton Thorpe. *Red C* —2F 60
- Kilvaxter. *High* —5H 85
- Kilve. *Som* —1A 24
- **Kilwinning.** *N Ayr* —5A 70
- Kimberley. *Norf* —1G 45
- Kimberley. *Notts* —5B 50
- Kimberworth. *S Yor* —3A 50
- Kimble Wick. *Buck* —3B 36
- Kimblesworth. *Dur* —5J 43
- Kimbolton. *Cambs* —5J 43
- Kimbolton. *Here* —5D 40
- Kimcote. *Leics* —3D 42
- Kimmeridge. *Dors* —8H 25
- Kimmerston. *Nmbd* —6H 73
- Kimpton. *Hants* —1M 25
- Kimpton. *Herts* —2K 35
- Kimworthy. *Devn* —4B 22
- Kinbeachie. *High* —7G 87
- Kinbrace. *High* —8L 91
- Kinbuck. *Stir* —7L 75
- Kincaple. *Fife* —6H 77
- Kincardine. *Fife* —1H 71
- Kincardine. *High* —4G 87
- Kincardine Bridge. *Fife* —1H 71
- Kincardine O'Neil. *Abers* —6E 82
- Kinchrackine. *Arg* —4E 74
- Kincorth. *Aber* —5J 83
- Kincraig. *High* —5J 81
- Kincraigie. *Per* —3B 76
- Kindallachan. *Per* —2B 76
- Kineton. *Glos* —1J 34
- Kineton. *Warw* —6L 41
- Kinfauns. *Per* —5F 76
- Kingarth. *Arg* —4J 69
- King Edward. *Abers* —8G 81
- Kingerby. *Linc* —8H 57
- Kingham. *Oxon* —1L 34
- Kingholm Quay. *Dum* —4D 52
- Kinghorn. *Fife* —1L 71
- Kinglassie. *Fife* —8F 76
- Kingledores. *Bord* —7K 71
- Kingodie. *Per* —5H 77
- King O' Muirs. *Clac* —8C 76
- King's Acre. *Here* —7C 40
- Kingsand. *Corn* —4F 20
- Kingsash. *Buck* —3F 35
- Kingsbarns. *Fife* —4L 77
- Kingsbridge. *Devn* —7K 21
- Kingsbridge. *Som* —2K 23
- King's Bromley. *Staf* —6H 35
- Kingsburgh. *High* —1E 76
- Kingsbury. *G Lon* —5K 35
- Kingsbury. *Warw* —2L 41
- Kingsbury Episcopi. *Som* —3D 24
- King's Caple. *Here* —1D 33
- Kingscavil. *W Lot* —2J 71
- King's Cliffe. *Nptn* —2H 43
- Kingscote. *Glos* —4G 33
- Kingscott. *Devn* —4D 22
- King's Coughton. *Warw* —6J 41
- Kingscross. *N Ayr* —7J 69
- Kingsdon. *Som* —3D 24
- Kingsdown. *Kent* —1K 29
- Kingsdown. *Swin* —5J 33
- Kingsdown. *Wilts* —7F 32
- Kingseat. *Fife* —8E 76
- Kingsey. *Buck* —3E 35
- Kingsfold. *Lanc* —5G 53
- Kingsfold. *W Sus* —2J 27
- Kingsford. *E Ayr* —5C 70
- Kingsford. *Worc* —3G 41
- Kingsforth. *N Lin* —4G 59
- Kingsgate. *Kent* —6M 37
- Kingshall Street. *Suff* —5F 44
- Kingsheanton. *Devn* —2E 22
- King's Heath. *W Mid* —3J 41
- Kings Hill. *Kent* —8E 36
- Kingsholme. *Glos* —2L 33
- Kingshouse. *Stir* —3A 76
- Kingshurst. *W Mid* —3K 41
- Kingskerswell. *Devn* —5L 21
- Kingskettle. *Fife* —5J 77
- Kingsland. *Here* —5C 40
- Kingsland. *IOA* —2B 46
- Kings Langley. *Herts* —3H 35
- Kingsley. *Ches W* —2D 48
- Kingsley. *Hants* —2E 26
- Kingsley. *Staf* —5J 49
- Kingsley Green. *W Sus* —2F 26
- Kingsley Holt. *Staf* —5J 49
- **King's Lynn.** *Norf* —7C 52
- King's Meaburn. *Cumb* —3E 58
- Kings Moss. *Mers* —7D 48
- Kingsmuir. *Ang* —3H 77
- Kings Muir. *Bord* —6L 71
- King's Newnham. *Warw* —4C 42
- King's Newton. *Derbs* —7L 49
- Kingsnorth. *Kent* —4G 29
- King's Norton. *Leics* —1E 42
- King's Norton. *W Mid* —4J 41
- King's Nympton. *Devn* —4H 23
- King's Pyon. *Here* —6C 40
- Kings Ripton. *Cambs* —4L 43
- King's Somborne. *Hants* —2A 26
- King's Stag. *Dors* —4F 24
- King's Stanley. *Glos* —3G 33
- King's Sutton. *Nptn* —8B 42
- Kingstanding. *W Mid* —2J 41
- Kingsteignton. *Devn* —7L 21
- Kingsteps. *High* —8J 87
- Kings Thorn. *Here* —8D 40
- Kingsthorpe. *Nptn* —5E 42
- Kingston. *Cambs* —6M 43
- Kingston. *Devn* —5J 21 (nr. Salcombe)
- Kingston. *Devn* —6A 24 (nr. Sturminster Newton)
- Kingston. *Dors* —3F 24
- Kingston. *Dors* —8H 25 (nr. Swanage)
- Kingston. *E Lot* —1C 72
- Kingston. *Hants* —5B 26
- Kingston. *IOW* —7C 26
- Kingston. *Kent* —8J 37
- Kingston. *Mor* —7B 88
- Kingston. *W Sus* —5J 27
- **Kingston Bagpuize.** *Oxon* —4E 34
- Kingston Blount. *Oxon* —4H 35
- Kingston by Sea. *W Sus* —5K 27
- Kingston Deverill. *Wilts* —2H 25
- Kingstone. *Here* —8C 40
- Kingstone. *Som* —4C 24
- Kingstone. *Staf* —7H 49
- Kingston Lisle. *Oxon* —5A 34
- Kingston Maurward. *Dors* —6F 24
- Kingston near Lewes. *E Sus* —7B 28
- Kingston on Soar. *Notts* —7B 50
- Kingston Russell. *Dors* —6E 24
- Kingston St Mary. *Som* —3A 24
- Kingston Seymour. *N Som* —7B 32
- Kingston Stert. *Oxon* —3E 34
- **Kingston upon Hull.** *Hull* —3G 57
- **Kingston upon Thames.** *G Lon* —7J 35
- King's Walden. *Herts* —7M 35
- Kingswear. *Devn* —4K 21
- Kingswells. *Aber* —5H 83
- Kingswinford. *W Mid* —3G 41
- Kingswood. *Buck* —2D 35
- **Kingswood.** *G Lon* —8J 35
- Kingswood. *Glos* —4F 32
- Kingswood. *Here* —5F 40
- Kingswood. *Kent* —8E 36
- Kingswood. *Per* —5D 76
- Kingswood. *Powy* —1L 39
- Kingswood. *S Glo* —6E 32
- Kingswood. *Som* —2M 23
- Kingswood. *Surr* —8K 35
- Kingswood. *Warw* —4K 41
- Kingswood Common. *Staf* —1J 41
- Kings Worthy. *Hants* —2B 26
- Kingthorpe. *Linc* —2J 51
- Kington. *Here* —6A 40
- Kington. *S Glo* —4D 32
- Kington. *Worc* —6K 41
- Kington Langley. *Wilts* —6J 33
- Kington Magna. *Dors* —3F 24
- Kington St Michael. *Wilts* —6H 33
- Kingussie. *High* —5H 81
- Kingweston. *Som* —3K 31
- Kinharrachie. *Abers* —2J 83
- Kinhrive. *High* —5H 87
- Kinkell Bridge. *Per* —6C 76
- Kinknockie. *Abers* —1K 83
- Kinlet. *Shrp* —3F 40
- Kinloch. *Fife* —6F 76
- Kinloch. *High* —5J 85 (nr. Lochaline)
- Kinloch. *High* —6L 91 (nr. Loch More)
- Kinloch. *High* —2L 77 (on Rùm)
- Kinloch. *Per* —3G 77
- Kinlochard. *Stir* —7J 75
- Kinlochbervie. *High* —5J 91
- Kinlocheil. *High* —8K 79
- Kinlochewe. *High* —5B 86
- Kinloch Hourn. *High* —4L 79
- Kinloch Laggan. *High* —6G 81
- Kinlochleven. *High* —1D 74
- Kinloch Lodge. *High* —4J 91
- Kinlochmoidart. *High* —8K 79
- Kinloch Rannoch. *Per* —2K 75
- Kinlochspelve. *Arg* —5L 73
- Kinloss. *Mor* —7K 87
- Kinmel Bay. *Cnwy* —2J 47
- Kinmuck. *Abers* —4H 83
- Kinnadie. *Abers* —1J 83
- Kinnaird. *Per* —4G 77
- Kinneff. *Abers* —1G 77
- Kinnelhead. *Dum* —1H 65
- Kinnell. *Ang* —2K 77
- Kinnerley. *Shrp* —7B 48
- Kinnernie. *Abers* —4G 83
- Kinnersley. *Here* —7B 40
- Kinnersley. *Worc* —7G 41
- Kinnerton. *Powy* —5A 40
- Kinnerton. *Shrp* —2B 40
- Kinnesswood. *Per* —7E 76
- Kinninvie. *Dur* —3J 59
- Kinnordy. *Ang* —2G 77
- Kinoulton. *Notts* —6D 50
- Kinross. *Per* —7E 76
- Kinrossie. *Per* —4F 76
- Kinsbourne Green. *Herts* —2J 35
- Kinsey Heath. *Ches E* —5E 48
- Kinsham. *Here* —5B 40
- Kinsham. *Worc* —8H 41
- Kinsley. *W Yor* —6B 54
- Kinson. *Bour* —6J 25
- Kintbury. *W Ber* —7M 33
- Kintessack. *Mor* —7J 87
- Kintillo. *Per* —6F 76
- Kinton. *Here* —4B 40
- Kinton. *Shrp* —8B 48
- Kintore. *Abers* —4H 83
- Kintour. *Arg* —4D 68
- Kintra. *Arg* —5H 73
- Kintraw. *Arg* —4F 74
- Kinveachy. *High* —5J 81
- Kinver. *Staf* —3G 41
- Kinwarton. *Warw* —6K 41
- Kiplingcotes. *E Yor* —3G 61
- Kippax. *W Yor* —4B 54
- Kippen. *Stir* —8L 75
- Kippford. *Dum* —6C 52
- Kipping's Cross. *Kent* —1C 28
- Kirbister. *Orkn* —8C 88 (nr. Hobbister)
- Kirbister. *Orkn* —6A 88 (nr. Quholm)
- Kirbuster. *Orkn* —5C 88
- Kirby Bedon. *Norf* —1J 45
- Kirby Bellars. *Leics* —8E 50
- Kirby Cane. *Norf* —2K 45

Labost, Lacasaidh, Lacasdal, Laceby, Lacey Green, Lach Dennis, Lache, Lackford, Lacock, Ladbroke, Laddingford, Lade Bank, Ladock, Lady, Ladybank, Ladycross, Lady Hall, Ladykirk, Ladysford, Ladywood, Laga, Lagavulin, Lagg, Laggan, Lagness, Laid, Laide, Laigh Fenwick, Laindon, Lairg, Lairg Muir, Laithes, Laithkirk, Lake, Lakenham, Lakenheath, Lakesend, Lakeside, Laleham, Lamancha, Lamarsh, Lamas, Lambden, Lamberhead Green, Lamberhurst, Lamberhurst Quarter, Lamberton, Lambeth, Lambfell Moar, Lambhill, Lambley, Lambourn, Lambourne End, Lambourn Woodlands, Lambrook, Lambs Green, Lambston, Lamellion, Lamerton, Lamesley, Laminess, Lamington, Lamlash, Lamonby, Lamorick, Lamorna, Lamorran, Lampeter, Lampeter Velfrey, Lamphey, Lamplugh, Lamport, Lamyatt, Lana, Lanark, Lancaster, Lanchester, Lancing, Landbeach, Landcross, Landerberry, Landford, Landhallow, Landimore, Landkey, Landkey Newland, Landore, Landport, Landrake, Land's End, Landscove, Land Shipping, Landshipping, Landulph, Landywood, Lane, Lane Bottom, Lane Bottom, Lane End, Lane End, Lane End, Lane End, Lane Ends, Lane Ends, Lane Ends, Lane Head, Lane Head, Lane Head, Lane Head, Lanehead, Lane Heads, Lanercost, Laneshawbridge, Laney Green, Langais, Langal, Langamull, Langar, Langbank, Langbar, Langburnshiels, Langcliffe, Langdale End, Langdon, Langdon Beck, Langdon Cross, Langdon Hills, Langdown, Langenhoe, Langford, Langford, Langford, Langford, Langford, Langford Budville, Langham, Langham, Langham, Langham, Langham, Langho, Langholm, Langland, Langleeford, Langley, Langley, Langley, Langley, Langley, Langley, Langley, Langley, Langley, Langley, Langley Burrell, Langley Common, Langley Green, Langley Green, Langley Green, Langley Heath, Langley Marsh, Langley Moor, Langley Park, Langley Street, Langney, Langold, Langore, Langport, Langrick, Langridge, Langridgeford, Langrish, Langsett, Langshaw, Langstone, Langthorne, Langthorpe, Langthwaite, Langtoft, Langtoft, Langton, Langton, Langton, Langton, Langton by Wragby, Langton Green, Langton Green, Langton Herring, Langton Long Blandford, Langton Matravers, Langtree, Langwathby, Langwith, Langworth, Lanivet, Lanjeth, Lank, Lanlivery, Lanner, Lanreath, Lansallos, Lanteglos Highway, Lanton, Lanton, Lapford, Laphroaig, Lapley, Lapworth, Larach, Larbert, Larden Green, Larel, Largie, Largiemore, Largoward, Largs, Largue, Largybaan, Largymeanoch, Largymore, Larkfield, Larkhall, Larkhall, Larkhill, Larling, Larport, Lartington, Lary, Lasham, Lashenden, Lassodie, Lastingham, Latchford, Latchingdon, Latchley, Latchmere Green, Lathbury, Latheron, Latheronwheel, Lathom, Lathones, Latimer, Latteridge, Lattiford, Latton, Laudale House, Lauder, Laugharne, Laughterton, Laughton, Laughton, Laughton, Laughton, Laughton Common, Laughton en le Morthen, Launcells, Launceston, Launcherley, Laund, Launton, Laurelvale, Laurencekirk, Laurieston, Laurieston, Lavendon, Lavenham, Laverhay, Laversdale, Laverstock, Laverstoke, Laverton, Laverton, Laverton, Lavister, Lawers, Lawford, Lawhitton, Lawkland, Lawley, Lawnhead, Lawrenny, Lawshall, Lawton, Laxey, Laxfield, Laxfirth, Laxo, Laxton, Laxton, Laxton, Layer Breton, Layer de la Haye, Layer Marney, Laymore, Laysters Pole, Layter's Green, Laytham, Lazenby, Lazonby, Lea, Lea, Lea, Lea, Lea, Leabrooks, Leac a Li, Leachd, Leachkin, Leachpool, Leadenham, Leaden Roding, Leadgate, Leadgate, Leadgate, Leadhills, Leadingcross Green, Lea End, Leafield, Leagrave, Lea Hall, Lea Heath, Leake, Leake Common Side, Leake Fold Hill, Lealholm, Lealt, Lealt, Lea Marston, Leamington Hastings, **Leamington Spa, Royal**, Leamonsley, Leamside, Leargybreck, Lease Rigg, Leasgill, Leasingham, Leasingthorne, Leasowe, **Leatherhead**, Leathley, Leaths, Leaton, Leaton, Lea Town, Leaveland, Leavenheath, Leavening, Leaves Green, Lea Yeat, Leazes, Lebberston, Lechlade on Thames, Leck, Leckford, Leckfurin, Leckgruinart, Leckhampstead, Leckhampstead, Leckhampton, Leckhampton Street, Leckmelm, Leckwith, Leconfield, Ledaig, Ledburn, Ledbury, Ledgemoor, Ledgowan, Ledicot, Ledmore, Lednabirichen, Lednagullin, Ledsham, Ledsham, Ledston, Ledstone, Ledwell, Lee, Lee, Lee, Lee, Lee, Lee, Leebotten, Leebotwood, Lee Brockhurst, Leece, Leechpool, Lee Clump, Leeds, Leeds, **Leeds Bradford International Airport**, Leedstown, Leegomery, **Leek**, Leekbrook, Leek Wootton, Lee Mill, Leeming, Leeming Bar, Lee Moor, Lee Moor, Lee-on-the-Solent, Lees, Lees, Lees, Lee, The, Leeswood, Leetown, Leftwich, Legbourne, Legburthwaite, Legerwood, Legsby, Leicester, **Leicester Forest East**, **Leigh**, Leigh, Leigh, Leigh, Leigh, Leigh, Leigh, Leigh, Leigh, Leigh, The, Leigh Beck, Leigh Common, Leigh Delamere, Leigh Green, Leighland Chapel, Leigh-on-Sea, Leigh Park, Leigh Sinton, Leighterton, Leighton, Leighton, Leighton, Leighton, Leighton Bromswold, **Leighton Buzzard**, Leigh-upon-Mendip, Leigh Woods, Leinthall Earls, Leinthall Starkes, Leintwardine, Leire, Leirinmore, Leishmore, Leitfie, Leith, Leitholm, Lelant, Lelant Downs, Lelley, Lem Hill, Lemington, Lempitlaw, Lemsford, Lenacre

A-Z Great Britain Road Atlas 125

Low Ellington—Millthorpe

- Low Ellington. *N Yor* — 5B 60
- Lower Amble. *Corn* — 8A 22
- Lower Ansty. *Dors* — 5G 25
- Lower Arboll. *High* — 1B 87
- Lower Arncott. *Oxon* — 2G 35
- Lower Auchenreath. *Mor* — 3D 88
- Lower Badcall. *High* — 5J 91
- Lower Ballam. *Lanc* — 2B 54
- Lower Basildon. *W Ber* — 5A 28
- Lower Beeding. *W Sus* — 5A 28
- ...
- Lydgate. *G Man* — 5H 55
- Lydgate. *W Yor* — 3H 55
- Lydham. *Shrp* — 2D 40
- Lydiard Millicent. *Wilts* — 5H 34
- Lydiate. *Mers* — 3M 53
- ...

M

- Mabe Burnthouse. *Corn* — 6E 19
- Mabie. *Dum* — 4D 52
- Mablethorpe. *Linc* — 7M 57
- Macbiehill. *Bord* — 4K 71
- **Macclesfield.** *Ches E* — 8H 55
- Macclesfield Forest. *Ches E* — 8H 55
- Macduff. *Abers* — 7M 81
- ...
- **Maidenhead.** *Wind* — 5D 28
- Maiden Law. *Dur* — 7C 60
- Maiden Newton. *Dors* — 6E 24
- Maidens. *S Ayr* — 1M 59
- ...
- **Mansfield.** *Notts* — 3B 50
- **Mansfield Woodhouse.** *Notts* — 3B 50
- ...
- **Manchester.** *G Man* — 6G 55
- Manchester International Airport. *G Man* — 7G 55
- ...
- **Marlow.** *Buck* — 4E 28
- Marlow. *Here* — 4E 40
- **Margate.** *Kent* — 6M 30
- ...
- **Market Drayton.** *Shrp* — 6E 34
- **Market Harborough.** *Leics* — 3E 28
- **Market Rasen.** *Linc* — 1J 43
- ...
- **Marple.** *G Man* — 1H 49
- **Maryport.** *Cumb* — 8E 52
- **Matlock.** *Derb* — 4L 49
- **Medway Towns.** *Medw* — 7D 30
- **Melksham.** *Wilts* — 7G 35
- **Melton Mowbray.** *Leics* — 8E 36
- **Merthyr Tydfil.** *Mer T* — 3C 32
- **Middlesbrough.** *Midd* — 4B 62
- **Middlewich.** *Ches E* — 3F 34
- **Midhurst.** *W Sus* — 4F 26
- **Midsomer Norton.** *Bath* — 8F 34
- **Mildenhall.** *Suff* — 4D 30
- **Milford Haven.** *Pemb* — 6F 14
- **Millom.** *Cumb* — 6L 53
- **Millport.** *N Ayr* — 3L 57
- Millthorpe. *Derbs* — 2M 49

Newtown. *Nmbd* 1F **66**
(nr. Rothbury)
Newtown. *Nmbd* 7K **73**
(nr. Wooler)
Newtown. *Pool* 6A **26**
Newtown. *Powy* 2B **40**
Newtown. *Rhon* 4C **32**
Newtown. *Shet* 3E **95**
Newtown. *Shrp* 6B **48**
Newtown. *Som* 4B **24**
Newtown. *Staf* 3G **49**
(nr. Biddulph)
Newtown. *Staf* 1K **41**
(nr. Cannock)
Newtown. *Staf* 3H **49**
(nr. Longnor)
New Town. *W Yor* 3A **56**
Newtown. *Wilts* 3J **25**
Newtown-in-St Martin. *Corn* 7E **19**
Newtown Linford. *Leics* 8B **50**
Newtown St Boswells. *Bord* 6E **72**
New Tredegar. *Cphy* 3D **32**
Newtyle. *Ang* 1H **77**
New Village. *E Yor* 2G **57**
New Village. *S Yor* 5B **56**
New Walsoken. *Cambs* 1A **44**
New Waltham. *NE Lin* 5J **57**
New Winton. *E Lot* 2D **72**
New World. *Cambs* 2M **43**
New Yatt. *Oxon* 2D **34**
Newyears Green. *G Lon* 5L **35**
New York. *Linc* 4J **51**
New York. *Tyne* 4J **67**
Nextend. *Here* 6D **40**
Neyland. *Pemb* 3D **30**
Nib Heath. *Shrp* 8B **48**
Nicholashayne. *Devn* 4A **24**
Nicholaston. *Swan* 5K **31**
Nidd. *N Yor* 7C **60**
Niddrie. *Edin* 2L **71**
Niddry. *Edin* 2J **71**
Nigg. *Aber* 3K **83**
Nigg. *High* 4L **87**
Nigg Ferry. *High* 5K **87**
Nightcott. *Som* 3K **23**
Nimmer. *Som* 4C **24**
Nine Ashes. *Essx* 3D **36**
Ninebanks. *Nmbd* 6C **66**
Nine Elms. *Swin* 5B **34**
Ninemile Bar. *Dum* 4F **64**
Nine Mile Burn. *Midl* 4K **71**
Ninfield. *E Sus* 6F **28**
Ningwood. *IOW* 7E **26**
Nisbet. *Bord* 7F **72**
Nisbet Hill. *Bord* 4G **73**
Niton. *IOW* 8F **26**
Nitshill. *E Ren* 4D **70**
Niwbwrch. *IOA* 3D **46**
Noak Hill. *G Lon* 4D **36**
Nobold. *Shrp* 8B **48**
Nobottle. *Nptn* 5E **42**
Nocton. *Linc* 3G **51**
Nogdam End. *Norf* 1K **45**
Noke. *Oxon* 2F **34**
Nolton. *Pemb* 2C **30**
Nolton Haven. *Pemb* 2C **30**
No Man's Heath. *Ches W* 5C **48**
No Man's Heath. *Warw* 1A **42**
Nomansland. *Devn* 4K **23**
Nomansland. *Wilts* 4C **26**
Noneley. *Shrp* 7B **48**
Noness. *Shet* 9E **95**
Nonikiln. *High* 4J **87**
Nonington. *Kent* 8L **37**
Nook. *Cumb* 4M **65**
(nr. Longtown)
Nook. *Cumb* 5G **59**
(nr. Milnthorpe)
Noranside. *Ang* 7E **82**
Norbreck. *Bkpl* 1B **54**
Norbridge. *Here* 7H **41**
Norbury. *Ches E* 5C **48**
Norbury. *Derbs* 5J **49**
Norbury. *Shrp* 2D **40**
Norbury. *Staf* 7E **48**
Norby. *N Yor* 5D **60**
Norby. *Shet* 6B **95**
Norcross. *Lanc* 1B **54**
Nordelph. *Norf* 1B **44**
Norden. *G Man* 4G **55**
Nordley. *Shrp* 2G **41**
Norfolk Broads. *Norf* 1L **45**
Norham. *Nmbd* 5J **73**
Norland Town. *W Yor* 3J **55**
Norley. *Ches W* 8D **54**
Norleywood. *Hants* 6D **26**
Normanby. *N Lin* 4E **56**
Normanby. *N Yor* 5G **61**
Normanby. *Red C* 2E **60**
Normanby-by-Spital. *Linc* 7G **57**
Normanby le Wold. *Linc* 6H **57**
Norman Cross. *Cambs* 2K **43**
Normandy. *Surr* 8K **35**
Norman's Bay. *E Sus* 7E **28**
Norman's Green. *Devn* 5M **23**
Normanton. *Derb* 6L **49**
Normanton. *Leics* 5E **50**
Normanton. *Linc* 5F **50**
Normanton. *Notts* 4D **50**
Normanton. *W Yor* 3M **55**
Normanton le Heath. *Leics* 8L **49**
Normanton on Soar. *Notts* 7B **50**
Normanton-on-the-Wolds. *Notts* 6C **50**
Normanton on Trent. *Notts* 3D **50**
Normoss. *Lanc* 2B **54**
Norrington Common. *Wilts* 7L **33**
Norris Green. *Mers* 6B **54**
Norris Hill. *Leics* 8L **49**
Norristhorpe. *W Yor* 3L **55**
Northacre. *Norf* 2F **44**
Northall. *Buck* 1K **35**
Northallerton. *N Yor* 4C **60**
Northam. *Devn* 3F **22**
Northam. *Sotn* 4E **26**
Northampton. *Nptn* 5F **42**
North Anston. *S Yor* 7B **56**
North Ascot. *Brac* 7K **35**
North Aston. *Oxon* 1E **34**
Northaw. *Herts* 3A **36**
Northay. *Som* 4B **24**
North Baddesley. *Hants* 3D **26**
North Balfern. *Dum* 6B **64**
North Ballachulish. *High* 7C **80**
North Barrow. *Som* 3F **24**
North Barsham. *Norf* 4F **52**
Northbeck. *Linc* 5G **51**
North Benfleet. *Essx* 5F **36**
North Bersted. *W Sus* 5K **27**
North Berwick. *E Lot* 1E **72**
North Bitchburn. *Dur* 8G **67**
North Blyth. *Nmbd* 3J **67**
North Boarhunt. *Hants* 4G **27**
North Bockhampton. *Dors* 6B **26**
Northborough. *Pet* 1K **43**
Northbourne. *Kent* 8M **37**
Northbourne. *Oxon* 5F **34**
North Bovey. *Devn* 7J **23**
North Bowood. *Dors* 6D **24**
North Bradley. *Wilts* 8L **33**
North Brentor. *Devn* 7F **22**
North Brewham. *Som* 2G **25**
Northbrook. *Oxon* 1E **34**
North Brook End. *Cambs* 7L **43**
North Broomhill. *Nmbd* 1H **67**
North Buckland. *Devn* 1F **22**
North Burlingham. *Norf* 6K **53**
North Cadbury. *Som* 3F **24**
North Carlton. *Linc* 8F **56**
North Cave. *E Yor* 2E **56**
North Cerney. *Glos* 3A **34**
North Chailey. *E Sus* 5B **28**
Northchapel. *W Sus* 3K **27**
North Charford. *Hants* 4B **26**
North Charlton. *Nmbd* 7L **73**
North Cheriton. *Som* 3F **24**
North Chideock. *Dors* 6D **24**
Northchurch. *Herts* 3K **35**
North Cliffe. *E Yor* 2E **56**
North Clifton. *Notts* 8E **56**
North Close. *Dur* 8H **67**
North Cockerington. *Linc* 6K **57**
North Coker. *Som* 4E **24**
North Collafirth. *Shet* 3D **95**
North Common. *E Sus* 5B **28**
North Commonty. *Abers* 5J **89**
North Coombe. *Devn* 4K **23**
North Cornelly. *B'end* 5A **32**
North Cotes. *Linc* 5K **57**
Northcott. *Devn* 6E **22**
(nr. Boyton)
Northcott. *Devn* 4M **23**
(nr. Culmstock)
Northcourt. *Oxon* 4F **34**
North Cove. *Suff* 3L **45**
North Cowton. *N Yor* 3B **60**
North Craigo. *Ang* 7G **83**
North Crawley. *Mil* 7H **43**
North Cray. *G Lon* 6C **36**
North Creake. *Norf* 4E **52**
North Curry. *Som* 3C **24**
North Dalton. *E Yor* 8J **61**
North Deighton. *N Yor* 8C **60**
North Dronley. *Ang* 2J **77**
North Duffield. *N Yor* 2C **56**
Northdyke. *Orkn* 5A **94**
Northedge. *Derbs* 3L **49**
North Elkington. *Linc* 6J **57**
North Elmham. *Norf* 5F **52**
North Elmsall. *W Yor* 4A **56**
Northend. *Buck* 4H **35**
North End. *E Yor* 2J **57**
North End. *Essx* 2E **36**
(nr. Great Dunmow)
North End. *Essx* 8D **44**
(nr. Great Yeldham)
North End. *Hants* 7E **34**
North End. *Leics* 8B **50**
North End. *Linc* 5J **51**
North End. *Norf* 2F **44**
North End. *N Som* 7G **33**
North End. *Port* 5G **27**
Northend. *Warw* 6B **42**
North End. *W Sus* 5M **27**
North End. *Wilts* 4A **34**
North Erradale. *High* 3M **85**
North Evington. *Leic* 1E **42**
North Fambridge. *Essx* 4G **37**
North Fearns. *High* 8K **85**
North Featherstone. *W Yor* 3A **56**
North Feorline. *N Ayr* 7H **69**
North Ferriby. *E Yor* 3F **56**
Northfield. *Aber* 3J **83**
Northfield. *Hull* 3G **57**
Northfield. *Som* 2B **24**
Northfield. *W Mid* 4L **41**
Northfleet. *Kent* 6E **36**
North Frodingham. *E Yor* 8L **61**
Northgate. *Linc* 7H **51**
North Gluss. *Shet* 4D **95**
North Gorley. *Hants* 4B **26**
North Green. *Norf* 3J **45**
North Green. *Suff* 5K **45**
(nr. Framlingham)
North Green. *Suff* 4K **45**
(nr. Halesworth)
North Green. *Suff* 5K **45**
(nr. Saxmundham)
North Greetwell. *Linc* 8G **57**
North Grimston. *N Yor* 7H **61**
North Halling. *Medw* 7F **36**
North Hayling. *Hants* 5H **27**
North Hazelrigg. *Nmbd* 6K **73**
North Heasley. *Devn* 2J **23**
North Heath. *W Sus* 3L **27**
North Hill. *Corn* 8D **22**
North Hinksey Village. *Oxon* 3E **34**
North Holmwood. *Surr* 1M **27**
North Huish. *Devn* 4J **21**
North Hykeham. *Linc* 3F **50**
Northiam. *E Sus* 5G **29**
Northill. *C Beds* 7K **43**
Northington. *Hants* 2F **26**
North Kelsey. *Linc* 5G **57**
North Kelsey Moor. *Linc* 5G **57**
North Kessock. *High* 7J **87**
North Killingholme. *N Lin* 4H **57**
North Kilvington. *N Yor* 5D **60**
North Kilworth. *Leics* 3E **42**
North Kyme. *Linc* 4H **51**
North Lancing. *W Sus* 5M **27**
Northlands. *Linc* 4K **51**
Northleach. *Glos* 2B **34**
North Lee. *Buck* 3J **35**
North Lees. *N Yor* 6B **60**
Northleigh. *Devn* 2H **23**
(nr. Barnstaple)
Northleigh. *Devn* 6A **24**
(nr. Honiton)
North Leigh. *Kent* 3K **29**
North Leigh. *Oxon* 2D **34**
North Leverton. *Notts* 7D **56**
Northlew. *Devn* 6G **23**
North Littleton. *Worc* 7L **41**
North Lopham. *Norf* 3G **45**
North Luffenham. *Rut* 1H **43**
North Marden. *W Sus* 4J **27**
North Marston. *Buck* 1H **35**
North Middleton. *Midl* 4M **71**
North Middleton. *Nmbd* 7K **73**
North Molton. *Devn* 3J **23**
North Moor. *N Yor* 5J **61**
Northmoor. *Oxon* 3E **34**
Northmoor Green. *Som* 2C **24**
North Moreton. *Oxon* 5F **34**
Northmuir. *Ang* 8D **82**
North Mundham. *W Sus* 5J **27**
North Murie. *Per* 3H **77**
North Muskham. *Notts* 4D **50**
North Ness. *Orkn* 8B **94**
North Newbald. *E Yor* 2F **56**
North Newington. *Oxon* 8C **42**
North Newnton. *Wilts* 8B **34**
North Newton. *Som* 2B **24**
Northney. *Hants* 5H **27**
North Nibley. *Glos* 4K **33**
North Oakley. *Hants* 8F **34**
North Ockendon. *G Lon* 5D **36**
Northolt. *G Lon* 5M **35**
Northop. *Flin* 3M **47**
Northop Hall. *Flin* 3M **47**
North Ormesby. *Midd* 2E **60**
North Ormsby. *Linc* 6J **57**
Northorpe. *Linc* 8G **51**
(nr. Bourne)
Northorpe. *Linc* 6J **51**
(nr. Donington)
Northorpe. *Linc* 6E **56**
(nr. Gainsborough)
North Otterington. *N Yor* 5C **60**
Northover. *Som* 2D **24**
(nr. Glastonbury)
Northover. *Som* 3E **24**
(nr. Yeovil)
North Owersby. *Linc* 6G **57**
Northowram. *W Yor* 3K **55**
North Perrott. *Som* 5D **24**
North Petherton. *Som* 2B **24**
North Petherwin. *Corn* 7D **22**
North Pickenham. *Norf* 1E **44**
North Piddle. *Worc* 6K **41**
North Poorton. *Dors* 6E **24**
North Port. *Arg* 3H **75**
Northport. *Dors* 7J **25**
North Queensferry. *Fife* 1K **71**
North Radworthy. *Devn* 2J **23**
North Rauceby. *Linc* 5G **51**
Northrepps. *Norf* 4J **53**
North Rigton. *N Yor* 1L **55**
North Rode. *Ches E* 3F **48**
North Roe. *Shet* 3D **95**
North Ronaldsay Airport. *Orkn* 2F **94**
North Row. *Cumb* 8K **65**
North Runcton. *Norf* 6C **52**
North Sannox. *N Ayr* 5J **69**
North Scale. *Cumb* 6C **58**
North Scarle. *Linc* 3E **50**
North Seaton. *Nmbd* 3H **67**
North Seaton Colliery. *Nmbd* 3H **67**
North Sheen. *G Lon* 6M **35**
North Shian. *Arg* 1G **75**
North Shields. *Tyne* 5J **67**
North Shoebury. *S'end* 5H **37**
North Shore. *Bkpl* 2B **54**
North Side. *Cumb* 1B **58**
North Skelton. *Red C* 2F **60**
North Somercotes. *Linc* 6L **57**
North Stainley. *N Yor* 6B **60**
North Stainmore. *Cumb* 2K **59**
North Stifford. *Thur* 5E **36**
North Stoke. *Bath* 7K **33**
North Stoke. *Oxon* 5G **35**
North Stoke. *W Sus* 4L **27**
Northstowe. *Cambs* 5A **44**
North Street. *Hants* 2G **27**
North Street. *Kent* 8J **37**
North Street. *Medw* 6G **37**
North Street. *W Ber* 6G **35**
North Sunderland. *Nmbd* 6M **73**
North Tamerton. *Corn* 6E **22**
North Tawton. *Devn* 5H **23**
North Thoresby. *Linc* 6J **57**
North Town. *Devn* 5G **23**
Northtown. *Orkn* 8C **94**
North Town. *Shet* 10D **95**
North Tuddenham. *Norf* 6G **53**
North Walbottle. *Tyne* 5G **67**
Northwall. *Orkn* 3F **94**
North Walney. *Cumb* 7C **58**
North Walsham. *Norf* 4J **53**
North Waltham. *Hants* 1F **26**
North Warnborough. *Hants* 8H **35**
North Water Bridge. *Ang* 7G **83**
North Watten. *High* 4H **93**
Northway. *Glos* 8K **41**
Northway. *Swan* 5K **31**
North Weald Bassett. *Essx* 3D **36**
North Weston. *N Som* 6G **33**
North Weston. *Oxon* 3G **35**
North Wheatley. *Notts* 7D **56**
North Whilborough. *Devn* 3K **21**
Northwich. *Ches W* 8E **54**
North Wick. *Bath* 7H **33**
Northwick. *Som* 1C **24**
Northwick. *S Glo* 5H **33**
North Widcombe. *Bath* 8H **33**
North Willingham. *Linc* 7H **57**
North Wingfield. *Derbs* 3A **50**
North Witham. *Linc* 7F **50**
Northwold. *Norf* 2D **44**
Northwood. *Derbs* 3K **49**
Northwood. *G Lon* 4L **35**
Northwood. *IOW* 6E **26**
Northwood. *Kent* 7M **37**
Northwood. *Shrp* 6B **48**
Northwood. *Stoke* 5F **48**
Northwood Green. *Glos* 2K **33**
North Wootton. *Dors* 4F **24**
North Wootton. *Norf* 5C **52**
North Wootton. *Som* 1E **24**
North Wraxall. *Wilts* 6L **33**
North Wroughton. *Swin* 5B **34**
North Yardhope. *Nmbd* 1E **66**
North York Moors. *N Yor* 4F **60**
Norton. *Devn* 4K **21**
Norton. *Glos* 1L **33**
Norton. *Hal* 7D **54**
Norton. *Herts* 8L **43**
Norton. *IOW* 7D **26**
Norton. *Mon* 1G **33**
Norton. *Nptn* 5E **42**
Norton. *Notts* 8B **56**
Norton. *Powy* 5D **40**
Norton. *Shrp* 3E **40**
(nr. Ludlow)
Norton. *Shrp* 1H **41**
(nr. Madeley)
Norton. *Shrp* 1F **40**
(nr. Shrewsbury)
Norton. *S Yor* 4B **56**
(nr. Askern)
Norton. *S Yor* 7M **55**
(nr. Sheffield)
Norton. *Stoc T* 1D **60**
Norton. *Suff* 5F **44**
Norton. *Swan* 5L **31**
Norton. *W Sus* 5K **27**
(nr. Arundel)
Norton. *W Sus* 6J **27**
(nr. Selsey)
Norton. *Wilts* 5L **33**
Norton. *Worc* 7L **41**
(nr. Evesham)
Norton. *Worc* 6J **41**
(nr. Worcester)
Norton Bavant. *Wilts* 1J **25**
Norton Bridge. *Staf* 6F **48**
Norton Canes. *Staf* 1L **41**
Norton Canon. *Here* 7D **40**
Norton Corner. *Norf* 5G **53**
Norton Disney. *Linc* 4E **50**
Norton East. *Staf* 1L **41**
Norton Ferris. *Wilts* 2G **25**
Norton Fitzwarren. *Som* 3B **24**
Norton Green. *IOW* 7D **26**
Norton Green. *Stoke* 4G **49**
Norton Hawkfield. *Bath* 7H **33**
Norton Heath. *Essx* 3E **36**
Norton in Hales. *Shrp* 6E **48**
Norton in the Moors. *Stoke* 4F **48**
Norton-Juxta-Twycross. *Leics* 1B **42**
Norton-le-Clay. *N Yor* 6D **60**
Norton Lindsey. *Warw* 5A **42**
Norton Little Green. *Suff* 5F **44**
Norton Malreward. *Bath* 7J **33**
Norton Mandeville. *Essx* 3D **36**
Norton-on-Derwent. *N Yor* 6G **61**
Norton St Philip. *Som* 8K **33**
Norton Subcourse. *Norf* 2L **45**
Norton sub Hamdon. *Som* 4D **24**
Norton Woodseats. *S Yor* 7M **55**
Norwell. *Notts* 3D **50**
Norwell Woodhouse. *Notts* 3D **50**
Norwich. *Norf* 1J **45**
Norwich International Airport. *Norf* 6J **53**
Norwick. *Shet* 1G **95**
Norwood. *Derbs* 7A **56**
Norwood Green. *W Yor* 3K **55**
Norwood Hill. *Surr* 3A **28**
Norwood Park. *Som* 2E **24**
Norwoodside. *Cambs* 2A **44**
Noseley. *Leics* 2F **42**
Noss. *Shet* 10D **95**
Noss Mayo. *Devn* 5G **21**
Nosterfield. *N Yor* 5B **60**
Nostie. *High* 1A **80**
Notgrove. *Glos* 1B **34**
Nottage. *B'end* 6A **32**
Nottingham. *Nott* 5B **50**
Nottington. *Dors* 7F **24**
Notton. *Dors* 6F **24**
Notton. *W Yor* 4M **55**
Notton. *Wilts* 7M **33**
Nounsley. *Essx* 2F **36**
Noutard's Green. *Worc* 5H **41**
Nox. *Shrp* 8B **48**
Noyadd Trefawr. *Cdgn* 7E **38**
Nuffield. *Oxon* 5G **35**
Nunburnholme. *E Yor* 1E **56**
Nuncargate. *Notts* 4A **50**
Nunclose. *Cumb* 7M **65**
Nuneaton. *Warw* 2B **42**
Nuneham Courtenay. *Oxon* 4F **34**
Nun Monkton. *N Yor* 8E **60**
Nunnerie. *S Lan* 8H **71**
Nunney. *Som* 1G **25**
Nunnington. *N Yor* 6F **60**
Nunnykirk. *Nmbd* 2F **66**
Nunsthorpe. *NE Lin* 5J **57**
Nunthorpe. *Red C* 2E **60**
Nunthorpe. *York* 1B **56**
Nunton. *Wilts* 3B **26**
Nunwick. *Nmbd* 4D **66**
Nunwick. *N Yor* 6C **60**
Nupend. *Glos* 3K **33**
Nursling. *Hants* 4D **26**
Nursted. *W Sus* 3H **27**
Nursteed. *Wilts* 7A **34**
Nurston. *V Glam* 7C **32**
Nutbourne. *W Sus* 5H **27**
(nr. Chichester)
Nutbourne. *W Sus* 4L **27**
(nr. Pulborough)
Nutfield. *Surr* 8B **36**
Nuthall. *Notts* 5B **50**
Nuthampstead. *Herts* 8A **44**
Nuthurst. *Warw* 4M **41**
Nuthurst. *W Sus* 3M **27**
Nutley. *E Sus* 5C **28**
Nuttall. *G Man* 4F **54**
Nutwell. *S Yor* 5C **56**
Nybster. *High* 3J **93**
Nyetimber. *W Sus* 6J **27**
Nyewood. *W Sus* 3J **27**
Nymet Rowland. *Devn* 5J **23**
Nymet Tracey. *Devn* 5J **23**
Nympsfield. *Glos* 3L **33**
Nynehead. *Som* 3A **24**
Nyton. *W Sus* 5K **27**

O

Oadby. *Leics* 1E **42**
Oad Street. *Kent* 7G **37**
Oakamoor. *Staf* 5H **49**
Oakbank. *Arg* 2E **74**
Oakbank. *W Lot* 3J **71**
Oakdale. *Cphy* 4D **32**
Oakdale. *Pool* 6A **26**
Oake. *Som* 3A **24**
Oaken. *Staf* 1J **41**
Oakenclough. *Lanc* 1D **54**
Oakengates. *Telf* 8E **48**
Oakenholt. *Flin* 8A **54**
Oakenshaw. *Dur* 8H **67**
Oakenshaw. *W Yor* 3K **55**
Oakerthorpe. *Derbs* 4L **49**
Oakford. *Cdgn* 6G **39**
Oakford. *Devn* 3L **23**
Oakfordbridge. *Devn* 3L **23**
Oakgrove. *Ches E* 3G **49**
Oakham. *Rut* 1G **43**
Oakhanger. *Ches E* 4E **48**
Oakhanger. *Hants* 2H **27**
Oakhill. *Som* 1F **24**
Oakington. *Cambs* 5A **44**
Oaklands. *Powy* 6A **40**
Oakle Street. *Glos* 2K **33**
Oakley. *Bed* 6J **43**
Oakley. *Buck* 2G **35**
Oakley. *Fife* 1J **71**
Oakley. *Hants* 8F **34**
Oakley. *Suff* 4H **45**
Oakley Green. *Wind* 6K **35**
Oakley Park. *Powy* 3M **39**
Oakmere. *Ches W* 3C **48**
Oakridge. *Glos* 3M **33**
Oaks. *Shrp* 1E **40**
Oaksey. *Wilts* 4M **33**
Oaks Green. *Derbs* 6J **49**
Oakshaw Ford. *Cumb* 4A **66**
Oakshott. *Hants* 3H **27**
Oakthorpe. *Leics* 8L **49**
Oak Tree. *Darl* 2C **60**
Oakwood. *Derb* 6L **49**
Oakwood. *W Yor* 2M **55**
Oakwoodhill. *Surr* 2M **27**
Oakworth. *W Yor* 2J **55**
Oape. *High* 1G **87**
Oare. *Kent* 7J **37**
Oare. *Som* 1K **23**
Oare. *W Ber* 6F **34**
Oare. *Wilts* 7B **34**
Oareford. *Som* 1K **23**
Oasby. *Linc* 6G **51**
Oath. *Som* 3C **24**
Oathlaw. *Ang* 8E **82**
Oatlands. *N Yor* 8C **60**
Oban. *Arg* 3F **74**
Oban. *W Isl* 1F **84**
Oborne. *Dors* 4F **24**
Obsdale. *High* 5J **87**
Obthorpe. *Linc* 8G **51**
Occlestone Green. *Ches W* 3D **48**
Occold. *Suff* 4H **45**
Ochiltree. *E Ayr* 7D **70**
Ochtermuthill. *Per* 4D **76**
Ochtertyre. *Per* 3D **76**
Ockbrook. *Derbs* 6A **50**
Ockeridge. *Worc* 5H **41**
Ockham. *Surr* 8L **35**
Ockle. *High* 6K **79**
Ockley. *Surr* 1M **27**
Ocle Pychard. *Here* 7F **40**
Octofad. *Arg* 4A **68**
Octomore. *Arg* 4A **68**
Octon. *E Yor* 7K **61**
Odcombe. *Som* 4E **24**
Odd Down. *Bath* 7K **33**
Oddingley. *Worc* 6K **41**
Oddington. *Oxon* 2F **34**
Oddsta. *Shet* 2F **95**
Odell. *Bed* 6H **43**
Odie. *Orkn* 5E **94**
Odiham. *Hants* 8H **35**
Odsey. *Cambs* 8L **43**
Odstock. *Wilts* 3B **26**
Odstone. *Leics* 1B **42**
Offchurch. *Warw* 5B **42**
Offenham. *Worc* 7L **41**
Offenham Cross. *Worc* 7L **41**
Offerton. *G Man* 7H **55**
Offerton. *Tyne* 6J **67**
Offham. *E Sus* 6C **28**
Offham. *Kent* 8E **36**
Offham. *W Sus* 5L **27**
Offleyhay. *Staf* 7F **48**
Offley Hoo. *Herts* 1M **35**
Offleymarsh. *Staf* 7E **48**
Offord Cluny. *Cambs* 5L **43**
Offord D'Arcy. *Cambs* 5L **43**
Offton. *Suff* 7G **45**
Offwell. *Devn* 6A **24**
Ogbourne Maizey. *Wilts* 6B **34**
Ogbourne St Andrew. *Wilts* 6B **34**
Ogbourne St George. *Wilts* 6C **34**
Ogden. *G Man* 4H **55**
Ogle. *Nmbd* 4G **67**
Ogmore. *V Glam* 6A **32**
Ogmore-by-Sea. *V Glam* 6A **32**
Ogmore Vale. *B'end* 4B **32**
Okeford Fitzpaine. *Dors* 4H **25**
Okehampton. *Devn* 6G **23**
Okehampton Camp. *Devn* 6G **23**
Okraquoy. *Shet* 8E **95**
Okus. *Swin* 5B **34**
Old. *Nptn* 4F **42**
Old Aberdeen. *Aber* 3K **83**
Old Alresford. *Hants* 2F **26**
Oldany. *High* 6J **91**
Old Arley. *Warw* 2A **42**
Old Basford. *Nott* 5B **50**
Old Basing. *Hants* 8G **35**
Oldberrow. *Warw* 5M **41**
Old Bewick. *Nmbd* 7K **73**
Old Bexley. *G Lon* 6C **36**
Old Blair. *Per* 7L **81**
Old Bolingbroke. *Linc* 3K **51**
Oldborough. *Devn* 5J **23**
Old Brampton. *Derbs* 8M **55**
Old Bridge of Tilt. *Per* 7L **81**
Old Bridge of Urr. *Dum* 5E **64**
Old Buckenham. *Norf* 2G **45**
Old Burghclere. *Hants* 8E **34**
Oldbury. *Shrp* 2H **41**
Oldbury. *Warw* 2B **42**
Oldbury. *W Mid* 3K **41**
Oldbury-on-Severn. *S Glo* 4J **33**
Oldbury on the Hill. *Glos* 5L **33**
Old Byland. *N Yor* 5E **60**
Old Cassop. *Dur* 8J **67**
Oldcastle. *Mon* 1F **32**
Oldcastle Heath. *Ches W* 5B **48**
Old Catton. *Norf* 6J **53**
Old Clee. *NE Lin* 5J **57**
Old Cleeve. *Som* 1M **23**
Old Clipstone. *Notts* 3C **50**
Old Colwyn. *Cnwy* 2H **47**
Oldcotes. *Notts* 7B **56**
Old Coulsdon. *G Lon* 8B **36**
Old Dailly. *S Ayr* 2M **63**
Old Dalby. *Leics* 7C **50**
Old Dam. *Derbs* 8K **55**
Old Deer. *Abers* 5K **89**
Old Dilton. *Wilts* 1H **25**
Old Down. *S Glo* 5J **33**
Oldeamere. *Cambs* 2M **43**
Old Edlington. *S Yor* 6B **56**
Old Eldon. *Dur* 1B **60**
Old Ellerby. *E Yor* 2H **57**
Old Fallings. *W Mid* 1K **41**
Oldfallow. *Staf* 8G **49**
Old Felixstowe. *Suff* 8K **45**
Oldfield. *Shrp* 3G **41**
Oldfield. *Worc* 5J **41**
Old Fletton. *Pet* 2K **43**
Oldford. *Som* 8K **33**
Old Forge. *Here* 2H **33**
Old Glossop. *Derbs* 6J **55**
Old Goole. *E Yor* 3D **56**
Old Gore. *Here* 1J **33**
Old Graitney. *Dum* 5L **65**
Old Grimsby. *IOS* 2B **19**
Oldhall. *High* 4H **93**
Old Hall Street. *Norf* 4K **53**
Oldham. *G Man* 5H **55**
Oldhamstocks. *E Lot* 2G **73**
Old Heathfield. *E Sus* 5D **28**
Old Hill. *W Mid* 3K **41**
Old Hunstanton. *Norf* 3C **52**
Old Hurst. *Cambs* 4L **43**
Old Hutton. *Cumb* 5G **59**
Old Kea. *Corn* 5F **19**
Old Kilpatrick. *W Dun* 2C **70**
Old Kinnernie. *Abers* 3H **83**
Old Knebworth. *Herts* 1A **36**
Oldland. *S Glo* 6J **33**
Old Laxey. *IOM* 5E **62**
Old Leake. *Linc* 4L **51**
Old Lenton. *Nott* 6B **50**
Old Llanberis. *Gwyn* 4F **46**
Old Malton. *N Yor* 6G **61**
Oldmeldrum. *Abers* 1J **83**
Old Micklefield. *W Yor* 2A **56**
Old Mill. *Corn* 8E **22**
Oldmixon. *N Som* 8F **32**
Old Monkland. *N Lan* 3F **70**
Old Newton. *Suff* 5G **45**
Old Park. *Telf* 1G **41**
Old Pentland. *Midl* 3L **71**
Old Philpstoun. *W Lot* 2J **71**
Old Quarrington. *Dur* 8J **67**
Old Radnor. *Powy* 6C **40**
Old Rayne. *Abers* 1G **83**
Oldridge. *Devn* 6K **23**
Old Romney. *Kent* 5J **29**
Old Scone. *Per* 3G **77**
Oldshore Beg. *High* 4J **91**
Oldshoremore. *High* 4K **91**
Old Snydale. *W Yor* 3A **56**
Old Sodbury. *S Glo* 5K **33**
Old Somerby. *Linc* 6F **50**
Old Spital. *Dur* 2L **59**
Oldstead. *N Yor* 5E **60**
Old Stratford. *Nptn* 7F **42**
Old Swan. *Mers* 6B **54**
Old Swarland. *Nmbd* 1G **67**
Old Tebay. *Cumb* 3H **59**
Old Town. *Cumb* 7M **65**
Old Town. *E Sus* 8D **28**
Oldtown. *High* 3H **87**
Old Town. *IOS* 2C **19**
Old Town. *Nmbd* 2D **66**
Oldtown of Ord. *Abers* 4G **89**
Old Trafford. *G Man* 6G **55**
Old Tupton. *Derbs* 3L **49**
Oldwall. *Cumb* 5M **65**
Oldwalls. *Swan* 4J **31**
Old Warden. *C Beds* 7K **43**
Oldways End. *Som* 3K **23**
Old Westhall. *Abers* 1G **83**
Old Weston. *Cambs* 4J **43**
Oldwhat. *Abers* 4J **89**
Old Windsor. *Wind* 6K **35**
Old Wives Lees. *Kent* 8J **37**
Old Woking. *Surr* 8L **35**
Oldwood Common. *Worc* 5F **40**
Old Woodstock. *Oxon* 2E **34**
Olgrinmore. *High* 4F **92**
Oliver's Battery. *Hants* 3E **26**
Ollaberry. *Shet* 3D **95**
Ollerton. *Ches E* 8F **54**
Ollerton. *Notts* 3C **50**
Ollerton. *Shrp* 7D **48**
Olmarch. *Cdgn* 6J **39**
Olmstead Green. *Cambs* 7C **44**
Olney. *Mil* 6G **43**
Olrig. *High* 3G **93**
Olton. *W Mid* 3M **41**
Olveston. *S Glo* 5J **33**
Ombersley. *Worc* 5J **41**
Ompton. *Notts* 3C **50**
Omunsgarth. *Shet* 7D **95**
Onchan. *IOM* 6E **62**
Onecote. *Staf* 4H **49**
Onehouse. *Suff* 6G **45**
Onen. *Mon* 2G **33**
Ongar Hill. *Norf* 7M **51**
Ongar Street. *Here* 5D **40**
Onibury. *Shrp* 4E **40**
Onich. *High* 7C **80**
Onllwyn. *Neat* 2A **32**
Onneley. *Shrp* 5E **48**
Onslow Green. *Essx* 2E **36**
Onslow Village. *Surr* 1K **27**
Onthank. *E Ayr* 6C **70**
Openwoodgate. *Derbs* 5L **49**
Opinan. *High* 4M **85**
(nr. Gairloch)
Opinan. *High* 2A **86**
(nr. Laide)
Orasaigh. *W Isl* 7D **90**
Orbost. *High* 7G **85**
Orby. *Linc* 3L **51**
Orchard Hill. *Devn* 3F **22**
Orchard Portman. *Som* 3B **24**
Orcheston. *Wilts* 1A **26**
Orcop. *Here* 1G **33**
Orcop Hill. *Here* 1G **33**
Ord. *High* 2L **79**
Ordale. *Shet* 1G **95**
Ordhead. *Abers* 2G **83**
Ordie. *Abers* 3E **82**
Ordiquish. *Mor* 4D **88**
Ordley. *Nmbd* 6E **66**
Ordsall. *Notts* 8D **56**
Ore. *E Sus* 6G **29**
Oreham Common. *W Sus* 6A **28**
Oreton. *Shrp* 3G **41**
Orford. *Suff* 7L **45**
Orford. *Warr* 6E **54**
Organford. *Dors* 6J **25**
Orgil. *Orkn* 7A **94**
Orgreave. *Staf* 8J **49**
Oridge Street. *Glos* 1K **33**
Orlestone. *Kent* 4H **29**
Orleton. *Here* 5E **40**
Orleton. *Worc* 5G **41**
Orleton Common. *Here* 5E **40**
Orlingbury. *Nptn* 4G **43**
Ormacleit. *W Isl* 8B **84**
Ormathwaite. *Cumb* 1D **58**
Ormesby. *Midd* 2E **60**
Ormesby St Margaret. *Norf* 6L **53**
Ormesby St Michael. *Norf* 6L **53**
Ormiscaig. *High* 2A **86**
Ormiston. *E Lot* 3D **72**
Ormsaigbeg. *High* 7J **79**
Ormsaigmore. *High* 7J **79**
Ormsary. *Arg* 2F **68**
Ormsgill. *Cumb* 6C **58**
Ormskirk. *Lanc* 5C **54**
Orphir. *Orkn* 7B **94**
Orpington. *G Lon* 7C **36**
Orrell. *Lanc* 5D **54**
Orrell. *Mers* 6B **54**
Orrisdale. *IOM* 4D **62**
Orsett. *Thur* 5E **36**
Orslow. *Staf* 8F **48**
Orston. *Notts* 5D **50**
Orthwaite. *Cumb* 8K **65**
Orton. *Cumb* 3H **59**
Orton. *Mor* 4D **88**
Orton. *Nptn* 4G **43**
Orton. *Staf* 2J **41**
Orton Longueville. *Pet* 2K **43**
Orton-on-the-Hill. *Leics* 1B **42**
Orton Waterville. *Pet* 2K **43**
Orton Wistow. *Pet* 2K **43**
Orwell. *Cambs* 6M **43**
Osbaldeston. *Lanc* 2E **54**
Osbaldwick. *York* 8F **60**
Osbaston. *Leics* 1C **42**
Osbaston. *Shrp* 7A **48**
Osbournby. *Linc* 6G **51**
Osclay. *High* 6H **93**
Oscroft. *Ches W* 3C **48**
Ose. *High* 7H **85**
Osgathorpe. *Leics* 8A **50**
Osgodby. *Linc* 6G **57**
Osgodby. *N Yor* 5K **61**
(nr. Scarborough)
Osgodby. *N Yor* 2C **56**
(nr. Selby)
Oskaig. *High* 8K **85**
Oskamull. *Arg* 1B **74**
Osleston. *Derbs* 6K **49**
Osmaston. *Derb* 6L **49**
Osmaston. *Derbs* 5K **49**
Osmington. *Dors* 7G **25**
Osmington Mills. *Dors* 7G **25**
Osmondthorpe. *W Yor* 2M **55**
Osmondwall. *Orkn* 9B **94**
Osmotherley. *N Yor* 4D **60**
Osnaburgh. *Fife* 4K **77**
Ospisdale. *High* 3K **87**
Ospringe. *Kent* 7J **37**
Ossett. *W Yor* 3L **55**
Ossington. *Notts* 3D **50**
Ostend. *Essx* 4H **37**
Ostend. *Norf* 4K **53**
Osterley. *G Lon* 6M **35**
Oswaldkirk. *N Yor* 6F **60**
Oswaldtwistle. *Lanc* 3F **54**
Oswestry. *Shrp* 7M **47**
Otby. *Linc* 6H **57**
Otford. *Kent* 8D **36**
Otham. *Kent* 8F **36**
Otherton. *Staf* 8G **49**
Othery. *Som* 2C **24**
Otley. *Suff* 6J **45**
Otley. *W Yor* 1L **55**
Otterbourne. *Hants* 3E **26**
Otterburn. *Nmbd* 2D **66**
Otterburn. *N Yor* 8K **59**
Otterburn Camp. *Nmbd* 2D **66**
Otterburn Hall. *Nmbd* 2D **66**
Otter Ferry. *Arg* 1H **69**
Otterford. *Som* 4B **24**
Otterham. *Corn* 6C **22**
Otterhampton. *Som* 1B **24**
Otterham Quay. *Kent* 7G **37**
Ottershaw. *Surr* 7L **35**
Otterspool. *Mers* 7B **54**
Otterswick. *Shet* 3F **95**
Otterton. *Devn* 7M **23**
Otterwood. *Hants* 5E **26**
Ottery St Mary. *Devn* 6A **24**
Ottinge. *Kent* 3K **29**
Ottringham. *E Yor* 3J **57**
Oughterby. *Cumb* 6K **65**
Oughtershaw. *N Yor* 5K **59**
Oughterside. *Cumb* 7J **65**
Oughtibridge. *S Yor* 6M **55**
Oughtrington. *Warr* 7E **54**
Oulston. *N Yor* 6E **60**
Oulton. *Cumb* 6K **65**
Oulton. *Norf* 5H **53**
Oulton. *Staf* 7E **48**
(nr. Gnosall Heath)
Oulton. *Staf* 6G **49**
(nr. Stone)
Oulton. *Suff* 2M **45**
Oulton. *W Yor* 3M **55**
Oulton Broad. *Suff* 2M **45**
Oulton Street. *Norf* 5H **53**
Oundle. *Nptn* 3J **43**
Ousby. *Cumb* 8B **66**
Ousdale. *High* 7F **92**
Ousden. *Suff* 6D **44**
Ousefleet. *E Yor* 3E **56**
Ouston. *Dur* 6H **67**
Ouston. *Nmbd* 6C **66**
(nr. Bearsbridge)
Ouston. *Nmbd* 4F **66**
(nr. Stamfordham)
Outer Hope. *Devn* 5H **21**
Outertown. *Orkn* 6A **94**
Outgate. *Cumb* 4E **58**
Outhgill. *Cumb* 3J **59**
Outlands. *Staf* 6E **48**
Outlane. *W Yor* 4J **55**
Out Newton. *E Yor* 3K **57**
Out Rawcliffe. *Lanc* 1C **54**
Outwell. *Norf* 1B **44**
Outwick. *Hants* 4B **26**
Outwood. *Surr* 3B **28**
Outwood. *W Yor* 3M **55**
Outwood. *Worc* 4K **41**
Outwoods. *Leics* 8A **50**
Outwoods. *Staf* 8E **48**
Ouzlewell Green. *W Yor* 3M **55**
Ovenden. *W Yor* 3J **55**
Over. *Cambs* 4M **43**
Over. *Ches W* 3D **48**
Over. *Glos* 2L **33**
Over. *S Glo* 5H **33**
Overbister. *Orkn* 3E **94**
Over Burrows. *Derbs* 6K **49**
Overbury. *Worc* 8K **41**
Overcombe. *Dors* 7F **24**
Over Compton. *Dors* 4E **24**
Over End. *Cambs* 2J **43**
Over Finlarg. *Ang* 1K **77**
Overgreen. *Derbs* 8M **55**
Over Green. *W Mid* 2M **41**
Over Haddon. *Derbs* 3K **49**
Over Hulton. *G Man* 5E **54**
Over Kellet. *Lanc* 6G **59**
Over Kiddington. *Oxon* 1E **34**
Overleigh. *Som* 2D **24**
Overley. *Staf* 8J **49**
Over Monnow. *Mon* 2H **33**
Over Norton. *Oxon* 1D **34**
Over Peover. *Ches E* 8F **54**
Overpool. *Ches W* 8B **54**
Overscaig. *High* 7M **91**
Overseal. *Derbs* 8K **49**
Over Silton. *N Yor* 4D **60**
Oversland. *Kent* 8J **37**
Overstone. *Nptn* 5G **43**
Over Stowey. *Som* 2A **24**
Overstrand. *Norf* 3J **53**
Over Stratton. *Som* 4D **24**
Over Street. *Wilts* 2A **26**
Overthorpe. *Nptn* 7C **42**
Overton. *Aber* 2J **83**
Overton. *Ches W* 8D **54**
Overton. *Hants* 1F **26**
Overton. *High* 6H **93**
Overton. *Lanc* 8F **58**
Overton. *N Yor* 8E **60**
Overton. *Shrp* 3G **41**
(nr. Bridgnorth)
Overton. *Shrp* 4F **40**
(nr. Ludlow)
Overton. *Swan* 5J **31**
Overton. *W Yor* 4L **55**
Overton. *Wrex* 5A **48**
Overtown. *Lanc* 6H **59**
Overtown. *N Lan* 4G **71**
Overtown. *Swin* 6B **34**
Over Wallop. *Hants* 2C **26**
Over Whitacre. *Warw* 2A **42**
Over Worton. *Oxon* 1E **34**
Oving. *Buck* 1H **35**
Oving. *W Sus* 5K **27**
Ovingdean. *Brig* 7B **28**
Ovingham. *Nmbd* 5F **66**
Ovington. *Dur* 2A **60**
Ovington. *Essx* 7D **44**
Ovington. *Hants* 2F **26**
Ovington. *Norf* 1F **44**
Ovington. *Nmbd* 5F **66**
Owen's Bank. *Staf* 7K **49**
Ower. *Hants* 5E **26**
(nr. Holbury)
Ower. *Hants* 4D **26**
(nr. Totton)
Owermoigne. *Dors* 7G **25**
Owlbury. *Shrp* 2D **40**
Owler Bar. *Derbs* 8L **55**
Owlerton. *S Yor* 7M **55**
Owlsmoor. *Brac* 7J **35**
Owlswick. *Buck* 3H **35**
Owmby. *Linc* 5G **57**
Owmby-by-Spital. *Linc* 7G **57**
Ownham. *W Ber* 6E **34**
Owrytn. *Wrex* 5A **48**
Owslebury. *Hants* 3F **26**
Owston. *Leics* 1F **42**
Owston. *S Yor* 4B **56**
Owston Ferry. *N Lin* 5E **56**
Owstwick. *E Yor* 2J **57**
Owthorne. *E Yor* 3K **57**
Owthorpe. *Notts* 6C **50**
Owton Manor. *Hart* 1D **60**
Oxborough. *Norf* 1D **44**
Oxbridge. *Dors* 6D **24**
Oxcombe. *Linc* 8K **57**
Oxen End. *Essx* 1E **36**
Oxenhall. *Glos* 1K **33**
Oxenholme. *Cumb* 4G **59**
Oxenhope. *W Yor* 2J **55**
Oxen Park. *Cumb* 5E **58**
Oxenpill. *Som* 1D **24**
Oxenton. *Glos* 8K **41**
Oxenwood. *Wilts* 8D **34**
Oxford. *Oxon* 3F **34**
Oxgangs. *Edin* 3L **71**
Oxhey. *Herts* 4M **35**
Oxhill. *Warw* 7B **42**
Oxley. *W Mid* 1J **41**
Oxley Green. *Essx* 2H **37**
Oxley's Green. *E Sus* 5E **28**
Oxlode. *Cambs* 3A **44**
Oxnam. *Bord* 8G **73**
Oxshott. *Surr* 7M **35**
Oxspring. *S Yor* 5L **55**
Oxted. *Surr* 8B **36**
Oxton. *Mers* 7A **54**
Oxton. *N Yor* 1B **56**
Oxton. *Notts* 4C **50**
Oxton. *Bord* 4D **72**
Oxwich. *Swan* 5J **31**
Oxwich Green. *Swan* 5J **31**
Oxwick. *Norf* 5F **52**
Oykel Bridge. *High* 1F **86**
Oyne. *Abers* 1G **83**
Oystermouth. *Swan* 5L **31**
Ozleworth. *Glos* 4K **33**

P

Pabail Iarach. *W Isl* 5F **90**
Pabail Uarach. *W Isl* 5F **90**
Pachesham. *Surr* 8M **35**
Packers Hill. *Dors* 4G **25**
Packington. *Leics* 8L **49**
Packmoor. *Stoke* 4F **48**
Packmores. *Warw* 5A **42**
Packwood. *W Mid* 4M **41**
Packwood Gullett. *W Mid* 4M **41**
Padanaram. *Ang* 8E **82**
Padbury. *Buck* 8F **42**
Paddington. *G Lon* 5A **36**
Paddington. *Warr* 7E **54**
Paddlesworth. *Kent* 4K **29**
Paddock. *Kent* 8H **37**
Paddockhole. *Dum* 3K **65**
Paddock Wood. *Kent* 3E **28**
Paddolgreen. *Shrp* 6C **48**
Padeswood. *Flin* 3M **47**
Padiham. *Lanc* 2F **54**
Padside. *N Yor* 8A **60**
Padson. *Devn* 6G **23**
Padstow. *Corn* 8A **22**
Padworth. *W Ber* 7G **35**
Page Bank. *Dur* 8H **67**
Pagham. *W Sus* 6J **27**
Paglesham Churchend. *Essx* 4H **37**
Paglesham Eastend. *Essx* 4H **37**
Paibeil. *W Isl* 5B **84**
(on North Uist)
Paibeil. *W Isl* 2E **84**
(on Taransay)
Paiblesgearraidh. *W Isl* 5B **84**
Paignton. *Torb* 3K **21**
Pailton. *Warw* 3C **42**
Paine's Corner. *E Sus* 5E **28**
Painleyhill. *Staf* 6H **49**
Painscastle. *Powy* 7B **40**
Painshawfield. *Nmbd* 5F **66**
Painsthorpe. *E Yor* 8H **61**
Painswick. *Glos* 3L **33**
Painter's Forstal. *Kent* 8H **37**
Painthorpe. *W Yor* 4M **55**
Pairc Shiaboist. *W Isl* 4C **90**
Paisley. *Ren* 3C **70**
Pakefield. *Suff* 2M **45**
Pakenham. *Suff* 5F **44**
Pale. *Gwyn* 6J **47**
Palehouse Common. *E Sus* 6C **28**
Palestine. *Hants* 1C **26**
Paley Street. *Wind* 6J **35**
Palgowan. *Dum* 3A **64**
Palgrave. *Suff* 4H **45**
Pallington. *Dors* 6G **25**
Palmarsh. *Kent* 4K **29**
Palmer Moor. *Derbs* 6J **49**
Palmers Cross. *W Mid* 1J **41**
Palmerstown. *V Glam* 7D **32**
Palnackie. *Dum* 6F **64**
Palnure. *Dum* 5B **64**
Palterton. *Derbs* 3A **50**
Pamber End. *Hants* 8G **35**
Pamber Green. *Hants* 8G **35**
Pamber Heath. *Hants* 7G **35**
Pamington. *Glos* 8K **41**
Pamphill. *Dors* 5J **25**
Pampisford. *Cambs* 7A **44**
Panborough. *Som* 1D **24**
Panbride. *Ang* 2L **77**
Pancakehill. *Glos* 2A **34**
Pancrasweek. *Devn* 5D **22**
Pandy. *Gwyn* 7H **47**
(nr. Bala)
Pandy. *Gwyn* 1J **39**
(nr. Tywyn)
Pandy. *Mon* 1F **32**
Pandy. *Powy* 1M **39**
Pandy. *Wrex* 6L **47**
Pandy Tudur. *Cnwy* 3H **47**
Panfield. *Essx* 1F **36**
Pangbourne. *W Ber* 6G **35**
Pannal. *N Yor* 8C **60**
Pannal Ash. *N Yor* 8B **60**
Pannanich. *Abers* 4D **82**
Pant. *Shrp* 7M **47**
Pant. *Wrex* 5A **48**
Pantasaph. *Flin* 2L **47**
Pant Glas. *Gwyn* 5D **46**
Pant-glas. *Shrp* 6M **47**
Pantgwyn. *Carm* 1K **31**
Pantgwyn. *Cdgn* 7E **38**
Pant-lasau. *Swan* 4L **31**
Panton. *Linc* 8H **57**
Pant-pastynog. *Den* 3K **47**
Pantperthog. *Gwyn* 1K **39**
Pant-teg. *Carm* 1J **31**
Pant-y-Caws. *Carm* 1F **30**
Pant-y-dwr. *Powy* 4M **39**
Pant-y-ffridd. *Powy* 1B **40**
Pantyffynnon. *Carm* 2L **31**
Pantygasseg. *Torf* 3E **32**
Pant-y-llyn. *Carm* 2L **31**
Pant-yr-awel. *B'end* 5B **32**
Pant y Wacco. *Flin* 2L **47**
Panxworth. *Norf* 6K **53**
Papa Stour Airport. *Shet* 6B **95**
Papa Westray Airport. *Orkn* 2C **94**
Papcastle. *Cumb* 8J **65**
Papigoe. *High* 4J **93**
Papil. *Shet* 8D **95**
Papple. *E Lot* 2E **72**
Papplewick. *Notts* 4B **50**
Papworth Everard. *Cambs* 5L **43**
Papworth St Agnes. *Cambs* 5L **43**
Par. *Corn* 4B **20**
Paramour Street. *Kent* 7L **37**
Parbold. *Lanc* 4C **54**
Parbrook. *Som* 2E **24**
Parbrook. *W Sus* 3L **27**
Parc. *Gwyn* 6H **47**
Parcllyn. *Cdgn* 6E **38**
Parc-Seymour. *Newp* 4G **33**
Pardown. *Hants* 1F **26**
Pardshaw. *Cumb* 1B **58**
Parham. *Suff* 5K **45**
Park. *Abers* 4H **83**
Park. *Arg* 1G **75**
Park. *Dum* 2G **65**
Park Bottom. *Corn* 5D **19**
Parkburn. *Abers* 6H **89**
Park Corner. *E Sus* 4D **28**
Park Corner. *Oxon* 5G **35**
Parkend. *Glos* 3J **33**
Park End. *Nmbd* 4D **66**
Parkeston. *Essx* 8J **45**
Parkfield. *Corn* 3E **20**
Parkgate. *Ches W* 8A **54**
Parkgate. *Cumb* 7K **65**
Parkgate. *Dum* 3H **65**
Park Gate. *Hants* 5F **26**
Parkgate. *Surr* 3A **28**
Park Gate. *Worc* 4K **41**
Parkhall. *W Dun* 2C **70**
Parkham. *Devn* 3E **22**
Parkham Ash. *Devn* 3E **22**
Parkhead. *Cumb* 7L **65**
Parkhead. *Glas* 3E **70**
Park Hill. *Mers* 5C **54**
Parkhouse. *Mon* 3G **33**
Parkhurst. *IOW* 6E **26**
Park Lane. *G Man* 5F **54**
Park Lane. *Staf* 1J **41**
Parkmill. *Swan* 5K **31**
Park Mill. *W Yor* 4L **55**
Parkneuk. *Abers* 6H **83**
Parkside. *N Lan* 4G **71**
Parkstone. *Pool* 6A **26**
Park Street. *Herts* 3M **35**
Park Street. *W Sus* 2M **27**
Park Town. *Oxon* 3F **34**
Park Village. *Nmbd* 5B **66**
Parkway. *Here* 8H **41**
Parley Cross. *Dors* 6A **26**
Parmoor. *Buck* 5H **35**
Parr. *Mers* 6D **54**
Parracombe. *Devn* 1H **23**
Parrog. *Pemb* 8C **38**
Parsonage Green. *Essx* 2F **36**
Parsonby. *Cumb* 8J **65**
Parson Cross. *S Yor* 6M **55**
Parson Drove. *Cambs* 1M **43**
Partick. *Glas* 3D **70**
Partington. *G Man* 6F **54**
Partney. *Linc* 3L **51**
Parton. *Cumb* 1A **58**
(nr. Whitehaven)
Parton. *Cumb* 6K **65**
(nr. Wigton)
Parton. *Dum* 4D **64**
Partridge Green. *W Sus* 4M **27**
Parwich. *Derbs* 4J **49**
Passenham. *Nptn* 8F **42**
Passfield. *Hants* 2J **27**
Passingford Bridge. *Essx* 4D **36**
Paston. *Norf* 4K **53**
Pasturefields. *Staf* 7G **49**
Patchacott. *Devn* 6F **22**
Patcham. *Brig* 7B **28**
Patchetts Green. *Herts* 4M **35**
Patching. *W Sus* 5L **27**
Patchole. *Devn* 1H **23**
Patchway. *S Glo* 5J **33**
Pateley Bridge. *N Yor* 7A **60**
Pathe. *Som* 2C **24**
Pathfinder Village. *Devn* 6K **23**
Pathhead. *Abers* 7H **83**
Pathhead. *E Ayr* 8E **70**
Pathhead. *Fife* 6H **77**
Pathhead. *Midl* 3M **71**
Pathlow. *Warw* 6M **41**
Path of Condie. *Per* 4F **76**
Pathstruie. *Per* 4F **76**
Patmore Heath. *Herts* 1C **36**
Patna. *E Ayr* 8C **70**
Patney. *Wilts* 8A **34**
Patrick. *IOM* 5C **62**
Patrick Brompton. *N Yor* 4B **60**
Patrington. *E Yor* 3K **57**
Patrington Haven. *E Yor* 3K **57**
Patrixbourne. *Kent* 8K **37**
Patterdale. *Cumb* 2E **58**
Pattiesmuir. *Fife* 1J **71**
Pattingham. *Staf* 2J **41**
Pattishall. *Nptn* 6E **42**
Pattiswick. *Essx* 1G **37**
Patton Bridge. *Cumb* 4G **59**
Paul. *Corn* 7B **19**
Paulerspury. *Nptn* 7F **42**
Paull. *E Yor* 3H **57**
Paulton. *Bath* 8J **33**
Pauperhaugh. *Nmbd* 2G **67**
Pave Lane. *Telf* 8E **48**
Pavenham. *Bed* 6H **43**
Pawlett. *Som* 1C **24**
Pawston. *Nmbd* 6H **73**
Paxford. *Glos* 8M **41**
Paxton. *Bord* 4J **73**
Payhembury. *Devn* 5M **23**
Paythorne. *Lanc* 8K **59**
Payton. *Som* 3A **24**
Peacehaven. *E Sus* 7C **28**
Peak Dale. *Derbs* 8J **55**
Peak District. *Derbs* 7K **55**
Peak Forest. *Derbs* 8K **55**
Peak Hill. *Linc* 8J **51**
Peakirk. *Pet* 1K **43**
Pearsie. *Ang* 8D **82**
Peasedown St John. *Bath* 8K **33**
Peaseland Green. *Norf* 6G **53**
Peasemore. *W Ber* 6E **34**
Peasenhall. *Suff* 5K **45**
Pease Pottage. *W Sus* 4A **28**
Peaslake. *Surr* 1L **27**
Peasley Cross. *Mers* 6D **54**
Peasmarsh. *E Sus* 5G **29**
Peasmarsh. *Som* 4C **24**
Peasmarsh. *Surr* 1K **27**
Peaston. *E Lot* 3D **72**
Peastonbank. *E Lot* 3D **72**
Peathill. *Abers* 3K **89**
Peat Inn. *Fife* 5K **77**
Peatling Magna. *Leics* 2D **42**
Peatling Parva. *Leics* 3D **42**
Peaton. *Arg* 1A **70**
Peaton. *Shrp* 3F **40**
Peats Corner. *Suff* 5H **45**
Pebmarsh. *Essx* 8E **44**
Pebworth. *Worc* 7M **41**
Pecket Well. *W Yor* 3H **55**
Peckforton. *Ches E* 4C **48**
Peckham Bush. *Kent* 8E **36**
Peckleton. *Leics* 1C **42**
Pedair-ffordd. *Powy* 7L **47**
Pedham. *Norf* 6K **53**
Pedlinge. *Kent* 4K **29**
Pedmore. *W Mid* 3K **41**
Pedwell. *Som* 2D **24**
Peebles. *Bord* 5L **71**
Peel. *IOM* 5C **62**
Peel. *Bord* 6D **72**
Peel Common. *Hants* 5F **26**
Peening Quarter. *Kent* 5G **29**
Peggs Green. *Leics* 8A **50**
Pegsdon. *C Beds* 8K **43**
Pegswood. *Nmbd* 3H **67**
Peinchorran. *High* 8K **85**
Peinlich. *High* 6J **85**
Pelaw. *Tyne* 5J **67**
Pelcomb Bridge. *Pemb* 2D **30**
Pelcomb Cross. *Pemb* 2D **30**
Peldon. *Essx* 2H **37**
Pelsall. *W Mid* 1L **41**
Pelton. *Dur* 6H **67**
Pelutho. *Cumb* 7J **65**
Pelynt. *Corn* 4D **20**
Pemberton. *Carm* 3K **31**
Pembrey. *Carm* 3J **31**
Pembridge. *Here* 6D **40**
Pembroke. *Pemb* 3D **30**
Pembroke Dock. *Pemb* 3D **30**
Pembroke Ferry. *Pemb* 3D **30**
Pembury. *Kent* 3E **28**
Penallt. *Mon* 2H **33**
Penally. *Pemb* 4F **30**
Penalt. *Here* 1H **33**
Penalum. *Pemb* 4F **30**
Penare. *Corn* 5A **20**
Penarth. *V Glam* 6D **32**
Penbeagle. *Corn* 6C **19**
Penberth. *Corn* 7B **19**
Pen-bont Rhydybeddau. *Cdgn* 3J **39**
Penbryn. *Cdgn* 6E **38**
Pencader. *Carm* 8G **39**
Pen-cae. *Cdgn* 6G **39**
Pencaenewydd. *Gwyn* 5D **46**
Pencaerau. *Neat* 4M **31**
Pencaitland. *E Lot* 3D **72**
Pencarnisiog. *IOA* 2C **46**
Pencarreg. *Carm* 7H **39**
Pencarrow. *Corn* 7C **22**
Pencelli. *Powy* 1C **32**
Pen-clawdd. *Swan* 4K **31**
Pencoed. *B'end* 5B **32**
Pencombe. *Here* 6F **40**
Pencraig. *Here* 1H **33**
Pencraig. *Powy* 7K **47**
Pendeen. *Corn* 6A **19**
Pendeford. *W Mid* 1K **41**
Penderyn. *Rhon* 3B **32**
Pendine. *Carm* 3G **31**
Pendlebury. *G Man* 5F **54**
Pendleton. *G Man* 6G **55**
Pendleton. *Lanc* 2F **54**
Pendock. *Worc* 8H **41**
Pendoggett. *Corn* 8B **22**
Pendomer. *Som* 4E **24**

Q

R

Page contents are an index listing from an A-Z Great Britain Road Atlas, too dense to transcribe meaningfully in full. Representative entries include: Redmarley D'Abitot, Glos 8H 41; Redmarshall, Stoc T 1C 60; Redmile, Leics 6D 50; ... through to Scone.

U

Uppertown—Whitacre Heath

- Uppertown. *Nmbd* — 4D 66
- Upper Tysoe. *Warw* — 7B 42
- Upper Upnor. *Medw* — 6F 36
- Upper Urquhart. *Fife* — 5G 77
- Upper Wardington. *Oxon* — 7C 42
- Upper Weald. *Mil* — 6G 43
- Upper Weedon. *Nptn* — 6E 42
- Upper Wellingham. *E Sus* — 6C 28
- Upper Whiston. *S Yor* — 5H 73
- Upper Wield. *Hants* — 2G 27
- Upper Winchendon. *Buck* — 2H 35
- Upperwood. *Derbs* — 4K 49
- Upper Woodford. *Wilts* — 3H 25
- Upper Wootton. *Hants* — 8F 34
- Upper Wraxall. *Wilts* — 6L 33
- Upper Wyche. *Worc* — 7F 41
- Uppincott. *Devn* — 5K 23
- Uppington. *Shrp* — 1F 40
- Upsall. *N Yor* — 5D 60
- Upsettlington. *Bord* — 5H 73

A-Z Great Britain Road Atlas 131

Whitbeck. Cumb 5C 58
Whitbourne. Here 6H 41
Whitburn. Tyne 5K 67
Whitburn. W Lot 3H 71
Whitburn Colliery. Tyne 5K 67
Whitby. Ches W 8B 54
Whitby. N Yor 2H 61
Whitbyheath. Ches W 8B 54
Whitchester. Bord 4G 73
Whitchurch. Bath 7J 33
Whitchurch. Buck 1J 35
Whitchurch. Card 6D 32
Whitchurch. Devn 8F 22
Whitchurch. Hants 1E 26
Whitchurch. Here 2H 33
Whitchurch. Pemb 1C 30
Whitchurch. Shrp 5C 48
Whitchurch Canonicorum. Dors 6C 24
Whitchurch Hill. Oxon 6G 35
Whitchurch-on-Thames. Oxon 6G 35
Whitcombe. Dors 7G 25
Whitcot. Shrp 2D 40
Whitcott Keysett. Shrp 3C 40
Whiteash Green. Essx 8D 44
Whitebog. High 5K 87
Whitebridge. High 2G 81
Whitebrook. Mon 3H 33
Whitecairns. Abers 2K 83
White Chapel. Lanc 1D 54
Whitechurch. Pemb 8D 38
White Colne. Essx 1G 37
White Coppice. Lanc 4E 54
White Corries. High 8E 80
Whitecraig. E Lot 2M 71
Whitecroft. Glos 3J 33
White Cross. Corn 7D 19 (nr. Mullion)
Whitecross. Corn 8A 22 (nr. Wadebridge)
Whitecross. Falk 2H 71
White End. Worc 8H 41
Whiteface. High 3K 87
Whitefarland. N Ayr 5G 69
Whitefaulds. S Ayr 1M 63
Whitefield. Dors 6J 25
Whitefield. G Man 5G 55
Whitefield. Som 3M 23
Whiteford. Abers 1H 83
Whitegate. Ches W 3D 48
Whitehall. Devn 4A 24
Whitehall. Hants 8H 35
Whitehall. Orkn 5E 94
Whitehall. W Sus 3M 27
Whitehaven. Cumb 2A 58
Whitehaven. Shrp 7M 47
Whitehill. Hants 2H 27
Whitehill. N Ayr 4A 70
Whitehills. Abers 3G 89
Whitehills. Ang 8E 82
White Horse Common. Norf 5K 53
Whitehough. Derbs 7J 55
Whitehouse. Abers 2G 83
Whitehouse. Arg 3G 69
Whiteinch. Glas 3D 70
Whitekirk. E Lot 1E 72
White Kirkley. Dur 8F 66
White Lackington. Dors 6G 25
Whitelackington. Som 4C 24
White Ladies Aston. Worc 6K 41
White Lee. W Yor 3L 55
Whiteley. Hants 4F 26
Whiteley Bank. IOW 7F 26
Whiteley Village. Surr 7L 35
Whitemans Green. W Sus 5B 28
White Mill. Carm 1J 31
Whitemire. Mor 6M 87
Whitemoor. Corn 4A 20
Whitenap. Hants 3D 26
Whiteness. Shet 7E 95
White Notley. Essx 2F 36
Whiteoak Green. Oxon 2D 34
Whiteparish. Wilts 3C 26
White Pit. Linc 8K 57
Whiterashes. Abers 1J 83
White Rocks. Here 1G 33
White Roding. Essx 2D 36
Whiterow. High 5J 93
Whiterow. Mor 4A 88
Whiteshill. Glos 3L 33
Whiteside. Nmbd 5C 66
Whiteside. W Lot 3H 71
Whitesmith. E Sus 6D 28
Whitestaunton. Som 4B 24
Whitestone. Abers 4G 83
Whitestone. Devn 6K 23
White Stone. Here 7F 40
Whitestones. Abers 4J 89
Whitestreet Green. Suff 8F 44
Whitewall Corner. N Yor 6G 61
White Waltham. Wind 6J 35
Whiteway. Glos 2M 33
Whitewell. Lanc 1E 54
Whitewell Bottom. Lanc 3G 55
Whiteworks. Devn 8H 23
Whitewreath. Mor 4C 88
Whitfield. D'dee 2K 77
Whitfield. Kent 3M 29
Whitfield. Nptn 8E 42
Whitfield. Nmbd 6C 66
Whitfield. S Glo 4J 33
Whitford. Devn 6B 24
Whitford. Flin 2L 47
Whitgift. E Yor 3E 56
Whitgreave. Staf 7F 48
Whithorn. Dum 7B 64
Whiting Bay. N Ayr 7J 69
Whitington. Norf 2D 44
Whitkirk. W Yor 2M 55
Whitland. Carm 2G 31
Whitleigh. Plym 4F 20
Whitletts. S Ayr 7B 70
Whitley. N Yor 3B 56
Whitley. Wilts 7L 33
Whitley Bay. Tyne 4J 67
Whitley Chapel. Nmbd 6E 66
Whitley Heath. Staf 7F 48
Whitley Lower. W Yor 4L 55
Whitley Thorpe. N Yor 3B 56
Whitlock's End. W Mid 4M 41
Whitminster. Glos 3K 33
Whitmore. Dors 5A 26
Whitmore. Staf 5F 48
Whitnage. Devn 4M 23
Whitnash. Warw 5B 42
Whitney. Here 7C 40
Whitrigg. Cumb 6K 65 (nr. Kirkbride)
Whitrigg. Cumb 8K 65 (nr. Torpenhow)
Whitsbury. Hants 4B 26
Whitsome. Bord 4H 73
Whitson. Newp 5F 32
Whitstable. Kent 7K 37
Whitstone. Corn 6D 22
Whittingham. Nmbd 8K 73
Whittingslow. Shrp 3E 40
Whittington. Derbs 8A 56
Whittington. Glos 1A 34
Whittington. Lanc 6H 59
Whittington. Shrp 6A 48
Whittington. Staf 3J 41 (nr. Kinver)
Whittington. Staf 1M 41 (nr. Lichfield)
Whittington. Warw 2A 42
Whittington. Worc 6J 41
Whittington Barracks. Staf 1M 41
Whittlebury. Nptn 7E 42
Whittleford. Warw 2B 42
Whittle-le-Woods. Lanc 3D 54
Whittlesey. Cambs 2L 43
Whittlesford. Cambs 7A 44
Whittlestone Head. Bkbn 4F 54
Whitton. N Lin 3F 56
Whitton. Nmbd 1F 66
Whitton. Powy 5C 40
Whitton. Bord 7G 73
Whitton. Shrp 4F 40
Whitton. Stoc T 1C 60
Whittonditch. Wilts 6C 34
Whittonstall. Nmbd 6F 66
Whitway. Hants 8E 34
Whitwell. Derbs 8B 56
Whitwell. Herts 1M 35
Whitwell. IOW 8F 26
Whitwell. N Yor 4B 60
Whitwell. Rut 1H 43
Whitwell-on-the-Hill. N Yor 7G 61
Whitwick. Leics 8A 50
Whitwood. W Yor 3A 56
Whitworth. Lanc 4G 55
Whixall. Shrp 6C 48
Whixley. N Yor 8D 60
Whoberley. W Mid 4A 42
Whorlton. Dur 2A 60
Whorlton. N Yor 3D 60
Whygate. Nmbd 4C 66
Whyle. Here 5F 40
Whyteleafe. Surr 8B 36
Wibdon. Glos 4H 33
Wibtoft. Warw 3C 42
Wichenford. Worc 5H 41
Wichling. Kent 8H 37
Wick. Bour 6B 26
Wick. Devn 5A 24
Wick. High 4J 93
Wick. Shet 8E 95 (on Mainland)
Wick. Shet 1F 95 (on Unst)
Wick. Som 1B 24 (nr. Bridgwater)
Wick. Som 8F 32 (nr. Burnham-on-Sea)
Wick. Som 3D 24 (nr. Somerton)
Wick. S Glo 6K 33
Wick. V Glam 6B 32
Wick. W Sus 5L 27
Wick. Wilts 3B 26
Wick. Worc 7K 41
Wick Airport. High 4J 93
Wicken. Cambs 4B 44
Wicken. Nptn 8F 42
Wicken Bonhunt. Essx 8A 44
Wickenby. Linc 7G 57
Wicken Green Village. Norf 4E 52
Wickersley. S Yor 6A 56
Wicker Street Green. Suff 7F 44
Wickford. Essx 4F 36
Wickham. Hants 4F 26
Wickham. W Ber 6D 34
Wickham Bishops. Essx 2G 37
Wickhambreaux. Kent 8L 37
Wickhambrook. Suff 6D 44
Wickhamford. Worc 7L 41
Wickham Green. Suff 5G 45
Wickham Heath. W Ber 7E 34
Wickham Market. Suff 6K 45
Wickhampton. Norf 1L 45
Wickham St Paul. Essx 8E 44
Wickham Skeith. Suff 5G 45
Wickham Street. Suff 5G 45
Wick Hill. Wok 7H 35
Wicklewood. Norf 1G 45
Wickmere. Norf 4H 53
Wick St Lawrence. N Som 7F 32
Wickwar. S Glo 5K 33
Widdington. Essx 8B 44
Widdrington. Nmbd 2H 67
Widdrington Station. Nmbd 2H 67
Widecombe in the Moor. Devn 8J 23
Widegates. Corn 4D 20
Widemouth Bay. Corn 5D 22
Wide Open. Tyne 4H 67
Widewall. Orkn 8C 94
Widford. Essx 3E 36
Widford. Herts 2C 36
Widham. Wilts 5A 34
Widmer End. Buck 4J 35
Widmerpool. Notts 7C 50
Widnes. Hal 7D 54
Widworthy. Devn 6B 24
Wigan. G Man 5D 54
Wigbeth. Dors 5A 26
Wigborough. Som 4D 24
Wiggaton. Devn 6A 24
Wiggenhall St Germans. Norf 8M 51
Wiggenhall St Mary Magdalen. Norf 8M 51
Wiggenhall St Mary the Virgin. Norf 8M 51
Wiggenhall St Peter. Norf 6C 52
Wiggens Green. Essx 7C 44
Wigginton. Herts 2K 35
Wigginton. Oxon 8B 42
Wigginton. Staf 1A 42
Wigginton. York 8E 60
Wigglesworth. N Yor 8K 59
Wiggonby. Cumb 6K 65
Wiggonholt. W Sus 4L 27
Wighill. N Yor 1A 56
Wighton. Norf 3F 52
Wightwick. Staf 2J 41
Wigley. Hants 4D 26
Wigmore. Here 5E 40
Wigmore. Medw 7G 37
Wigsley. Notts 8E 56
Wigsthorpe. Nptn 3J 43
Wigston. Leics 2E 42
Wigtoft. Linc 6J 51
Wigton. Cumb 7K 65
Wigtown. Dum 6B 64
Wigtwizzle. S Yor 6L 55
Wike. W Yor 1M 55
Wilbarston. Nptn 3G 43
Wilberfoss. E Yor 8G 61
Wilburton. Cambs 4A 44
Wilby. Norf 3G 45
Wilby. Nptn 5G 43
Wilby. Suff 4J 45
Wilcot. Wilts 7B 34
Wilcott. Shrp 8A 48
Wilcove. Corn 4F 20
Wildboarclough. Ches E 3G 49
Wilden. Bed 6J 43
Wilden. Worc 4J 41
Wildern. Hants 4E 26
Wilderspool. Warr 7E 54
Wilde Street. Suff 4D 44
Wildhern. Hants 8D 34
Wildmanbridge. S Lan 4G 71
Wildmoor. Worc 4K 41
Wildsworth. Linc 6E 56
Wildwood. Staf 7G 49
Wilford. Nott 6B 50
Wilkesley. Ches E 5D 48
Wilkhaven. High 3M 87
Wilkieston. W Lot 3K 71
Wilksby. Linc 3J 51
Willand. Devn 4M 23
Willaston. Ches E 4D 48
Willaston. Ches W 8B 54
Willaston. IOM 6D 62
Willen. Mil 7G 43
Willenhall. W Mid 4B 42 (nr. Coventry)
Willenhall. W Mid 2K 41 (nr. Wolverhampton)
Willerby. E Yor 2G 57
Willerby. N Yor 6K 61
Willersey. Glos 8M 41
Willersley. Here 7D 40
Willesborough. Kent 3J 29
Willesborough Lees. Kent 3J 29
Willesden. G Lon 5A 36
Willesley. Wilts 5L 33
Willett. Som 2A 24
Willey. Shrp 2G 41
Willey. Warw 3C 42
Willey Green. Surr 8K 35
Williamscot. Oxon 7C 42
Williamsetter. Shet 9D 95
Willian. Herts 8L 43
Willingale. Essx 3D 36
Willingdon. E Sus 7D 28
Willingham. Cambs 4A 44
Willingham by Stow. Linc 7E 56
Willingham Green. Cambs 6C 44
Willington. Bed 7K 43
Willington. Derbs 7K 49
Willington. Dur 8G 67
Willington. Tyne 5J 67
Willington. Warw 8A 42
Willington Corner. Ches W 3C 48
Willisham Tye. Suff 6G 45
Willitoft. E Yor 2D 56
Williton. Som 1M 23
Willoughbridge. Staf 5E 48
Willoughby. Linc 8L 57
Willoughby. Warw 5D 42
Willoughby-on-the-Wolds. Notts 7C 50
Willoughby Waterleys. Leics 2D 42
Willoughton. Linc 6F 56
Willow Green. Worc 6H 41
Willows Green. Essx 2F 36
Willsbridge. S Glo 6J 33
Willslock. Staf 6H 49
Wilmcote. Warw 6M 41
Wilmington. Bath 7J 33
Wilmington. Devn 6B 24
Wilmington. E Sus 7D 28
Wilmington. Kent 6D 36
Wilmslow. Ches E 7G 55
Wilnecote. Staf 1A 42
Wilney Green. Norf 3G 45
Wilpshire. Lanc 2E 54
Wilsden. W Yor 2J 55
Wilsford. Linc 5G 51
Wilsford. Wilts 2B 26 (nr. Amesbury)
Wilsford. Wilts 8B 34 (nr. Devizes)
Wilsill. N Yor 7A 60
Wilsley Green. Kent 4F 28
Wilson. Here 1H 33
Wilson. Leics 7A 50
Wilsontown. S Lan 4H 71
Wilstead. Bed 7J 43
Wilsthorpe. E Yor 7L 61
Wilsthorpe. Linc 8G 51
Wilstone. Herts 2K 35
Wilton. Cumb 2B 58
Wilton. N Yor 5H 61
Wilton. Red C 2E 60
Wilton. Bord 8E 72
Wilton. Wilts 7C 34 (nr. Marlborough)
Wilton. Wilts 2A 26 (nr. Salisbury)
Wimbish. Essx 8B 44
Wimbish Green. Essx 8C 44
Wimblebury. Staf 8H 49
Wimbledon. G Lon 6A 36
Wimblington. Cambs 2A 44
Wimboldsley. Ches W 3D 48
Wimborne Minster. Dors 5A 26
Wimborne St Giles. Dors 4A 26
Wimbotsham. Norf 1C 44
Wimpole. Cambs 7M 43
Wimpstone. Warw 7A 42
Wincanton. Som 3G 25
Winceby. Linc 3K 51
Wincham. Ches W 8E 54
Winchburgh. W Lot 2J 71
Winchcombe. Glos 1A 34
Winchelsea. E Sus 6H 29
Winchelsea Beach. E Sus 6H 29
Winchester. Hants 3E 26
Winchet Hill. Kent 3F 28
Winchfield. Hants 8H 35
Winchmore Hill. Buck 4K 35
Winchmore Hill. G Lon 4B 36
Wincle. Ches E 3G 49
Windermere. Cumb 4F 58
Winderton. Warw 7B 42
Windhill. High 7H 87
Windle Hill. Ches W 8B 54
Windlesham. Surr 7K 35
Windley. Derbs 5L 49
Windmill. Derbs 8K 55
Windmill Hill. E Sus 6E 28
Windmill Hill. Som 4C 24
Windrush. Glos 2B 34
Windsor. Wind 6K 35
Windsor Green. Suff 6E 44
Windyedge. Abers 4K 83
Windygates. Fife 5J 77
Windyharbour. Ches E 8G 55
Windyknowe. W Lot 3H 71
Wineham. W Sus 5A 28
Winestead. E Yor 3K 57
Winfarthing. Norf 3H 45
Winford. IOW 7F 26
Winford. N Som 7H 33
Winforton. Here 7C 40
Winfrith Newburgh. Dors 7H 25
Wing. Buck 1J 35
Wing. Rut 1G 43
Wingate. Dur 8J 67
Wingates. G Man 5E 54
Wingates. Nmbd 2G 67
Wingerworth. Derbs 3L 49
Wingfield. C Beds 1L 35
Wingfield. Suff 4J 45
Wingfield. Wilts 8L 33
Wingfield Park. Derbs 4L 49
Wingham. Kent 8L 37
Wingmore. Kent 3K 29
Wingrave. Buck 2J 35
Winkburn. Notts 4D 50
Winkfield. Brac 6K 35
Winkfield Row. Brac 6J 35
Winkhill. Staf 4H 49
Winklebury. Hants 8G 35
Winkleigh. Devn 5H 23
Winksley. N Yor 8L 60
Winkton. Dors 6B 26
Winlaton. Tyne 5G 67
Winlaton Mill. Tyne 5G 67
Winless. High 4J 93
Winmarleigh. Lanc 1C 54
Winnal Common. Here 8E 40
Winnard's Perch. Corn 3A 20
Winnersh. Wok 6H 35
Winnington. Ches W 2E 48
Winnington. Staf 6E 48
Winnothdale. Staf 5H 49
Winscales. Cumb 1B 58
Winscombe. N Som 8G 33
Winsford. Ches W 3D 48
Winsford. Som 2L 23
Winsham. Devn 2G 23
Winsham. Som 5C 24
Winshill. Staf 7K 49
Winsh-wen. Swan 4L 31
Winskill. Cumb 8A 66
Winslade. Hants 1G 27
Winsley. Wilts 7K 33
Winslow. Buck 1H 35
Winson. Glos 3A 34
Winson Green. W Mid 3L 41
Winsor. Hants 4D 26
Winster. Cumb 4F 58
Winster. Derbs 3K 49
Winston. Dur 2A 60
Winston. Suff 5H 45
Winstone. Glos 3M 33
Winswell. Devn 4F 22
Winterborne Clenston. Dors 5H 25
Winterborne Herrington. Dors 7F 24
Winterborne Houghton. Dors 5H 25
Winterborne Kingston. Dors 6H 25
Winterborne Monkton. Dors 7F 24
Winterborne St Martin. Dors 7F 24
Winterborne Stickland. Dors 5H 25
Winterborne Whitechurch. Dors 5H 25
Winterborne Zelston. Dors 6J 25
Winterbourne. S Glo 5J 33
Winterbourne. W Ber 6E 34
Winterbourne Abbas. Dors 6F 24
Winterbourne Bassett. Wilts 6B 34
Winterbourne Dauntsey. Wilts 2B 26
Winterbourne Earls. Wilts 2B 26
Winterbourne Gunner. Wilts 2B 26
Winterbourne Monkton. Wilts 6A 34
Winterbourne Steepleton. Dors 7F 24
Winterbourne Stoke. Wilts 1A 26
Winterbrook. Oxon 5G 35
Winterburn. N Yor 8L 59
Winter Gardens. Essx 5F 36
Winterhay Green. Som 4C 24
Winteringham. N Lin 3F 56
Winterley. Ches E 4E 48
Wintersett. W Yor 4M 55
Winterton. N Lin 4F 56
Winterton-on-Sea. Norf 6L 53
Winthorpe. Linc 3M 51
Winthorpe. Notts 4E 50
Winton. Bour 6A 26
Winton. Cumb 2J 59
Winton. E Sus 7D 28
Wintringham. N Yor 6H 61
Winwick. Cambs 3K 43
Winwick. Nptn 4E 42
Winwick. Warr 6E 54
Wirksworth. Derbs 4K 49
Wirswall. Ches E 5C 48
Wisbech. Cambs 8L 51
Wisbech St Mary. Cambs 1A 44
Wisborough Green. W Sus 3L 27
Wiseton. Notts 7D 56
Wishaw. N Lan 4G 71
Wishaw. Warw 2M 41
Wisley. Surr 8L 35
Wispington. Linc 8J 57
Wissenden. Kent 3H 29
Wissett. Suff 4K 45
Wistanstow. Shrp 3E 40
Wistanswick. Shrp 7D 48
Wistaston. Ches E 4D 48
Wiston. Pemb 2E 30
Wiston. S Lan 6H 71
Wiston. W Sus 4M 27
Wistow. Cambs 3L 43
Wistow. N Yor 2B 56
Wiswell. Lanc 2F 54
Witcham. Cambs 3A 44
Witchampton. Dors 5J 25
Witchford. Cambs 4B 44
Witham. Essx 2G 37
Witham Friary. Som 1G 25
Witham on the Hill. Linc 8G 51
Witham St Hughs. Linc 3E 50
Withcall. Linc 7J 57
Witherenden Hill. E Sus 5E 28
Withergate. Norf 5J 53
Witheridge. Devn 4K 23
Witheridge Hill. Oxon 5G 35
Witherley. Leics 2B 42
Withermarsh Green. Suff 8G 45
Withern. Linc 7L 57
Withernsea. E Yor 3K 57
Withernwick. E Yor 1H 57
Withersdale Street. Suff 3J 45
Withersfield. Suff 7C 44
Witherslack. Cumb 5F 58
Withiel. Corn 3A 20
Withiel Florey. Som 2L 23
Withington. Glos 2A 34
Withington. G Man 6G 55
Withington. Here 7F 40
Withington. Shrp 8C 48
Withington. Staf 6H 49
Withington Green. Ches E 8G 55
Withington Marsh. Here 7F 40
Withleigh. Devn 4L 23
Withnell. Lanc 3E 54
Withnell Fold. Lanc 3E 54
Withybrook. Warw 3C 42
Withycombe. Som 1M 23
Withycombe Raleigh. Devn 7M 23
Withyham. E Sus 4C 28
Withypool. Som 2K 23
Witley. Surr 1K 27
Witnesham. Suff 6H 45
Witney. Oxon 2D 34
Wittering. Pet 1J 43
Wittersham. Kent 5H 29
Witton. Norf 1K 45
Witton. Worc 5K 41
Witton Bridge. Norf 4K 53
Witton Gilbert. Dur 7H 67
Witton-le-Wear. Dur 8G 67
Witton Park. Dur 8G 67
Wiveliscombe. Som 3M 23
Wivelrod. Hants 2G 27
Wivelsfield. E Sus 5B 28
Wivelsfield Green. E Sus 6B 28
Wivenhoe. Essx 1J 37
Wiveton. Norf 3G 53
Wix. Essx 1K 37
Wixford. Warw 6L 41
Wixhill. Shrp 7C 48
Wixoe. Suff 7D 44
Woburn. C Beds 8H 43
Woburn Sands. Mil 8H 43
Woking. Surr 8L 35
Wokingham. Wok 7J 35
Wolborough. Devn 8K 23
Woldingham. Surr 8B 36
Wold Newton. E Yor 6K 61
Wold Newton. NE Lin 6J 57
Wolferlow. Here 5G 41
Wolferton. Norf 5C 52
Wolfhill. Per 2G 77
Wolf's Castle. Pemb 1D 30
Wolfsdale. Pemb 1D 30
Wolgarston. Staf 8G 49
Wollaston. Nptn 5H 43
Wollaston. Shrp 8A 48
Wollaston. W Mid 3J 41
Wollaton. Nott 5B 50
Wollerton. Shrp 6D 48
Wollescote. W Mid 3K 41
Wolseley Bridge. Staf 7H 49
Wolsingham. Dur 8F 66
Wolstanton. Staf 5F 48
Wolston. Warw 4C 42
Wolsty. Cumb 6J 65
Wolterton. Norf 4H 53
Wolvercote. Oxon 3E 34
Wolverhampton. W Mid 2K 41
Wolverley. Shrp 6B 48
Wolverley. Worc 4J 41
Wolverton. Hants 8F 34
Wolverton. Mil 7G 43
Wolverton. Warw 5A 42
Wolverton. Wilts 2G 25
Wolverton Common. Hants 8F 34
Wolvesnewton. Mon 4G 33
Wolvey. Warw 3C 42
Wolvey Heath. Warw 3C 42
Wolviston. Stoc T 1D 60
Womaston. Powy 5C 40
Wombleton. N Yor 5F 60
Wombourne. Staf 2J 41
Wombwell. S Yor 5M 55
Womenswold. Kent 8L 37
Womersley. N Yor 4B 56
Wonersh. Surr 1L 27
Wonson. Devn 7H 23
Wonston. Dors 5G 25
Wonston. Hants 2E 26
Wooburn. Buck 5K 35
Wooburn Green. Buck 5K 35
Wood. Pemb 1C 30
Woodacott. Devn 5E 22
Woodale. N Yor 6M 59
Woodall. S Yor 7A 56
Woodbank. Ches W 8B 54
Woodbastwick. Norf 6K 53
Woodbeck. Notts 8D 56
Woodborough. Notts 5C 50
Woodborough. Wilts 8B 34
Woodbridge. Devn 6A 24
Woodbridge. Dors 4G 25
Woodbridge. Suff 7J 45
Wood Burcote. Nptn 7E 42
Woodbury. Devn 7M 23
Woodbury Salterton. Devn 7M 23
Woodchester. Glos 3L 33
Woodchurch. Kent 4H 29
Woodchurch. Mers 7A 54
Woodcock Heath. Staf 7H 49
Woodcombe. Som 1L 23
Woodcote. Oxon 5G 35
Woodcote Green. Worc 4K 41
Woodcott. Hants 8E 34
Woodcroft. Glos 4H 33
Woodcutts. Dors 4J 25
Wood Dalling. Norf 5G 53
Woodditton. Cambs 6C 44
Woodeaton. Oxon 2F 34
Wood Eaton. Staf 8F 48
Wood End. Bed 5J 43
Wood End. Herts 1B 36
Woodend. Cumb 4C 58
Woodend. Nptn 7E 42
Woodend. Staf 7J 49
Wood End. Warw 3A 42 (nr. Bedworth)
Wood End. Warw 2A 42 (nr. Dordon)
Wood End. Warw 4M 41 (nr. Tanworth-in-Arden)
Woodend. W Sus 5J 27
Wood Enderby. Linc 3J 51
Woodend Green. Essx 1D 36
Woodfalls. Wilts 3B 26
Woodfield. Oxon 1F 34
Woodfields. Lanc 2E 54
Woodford. Corn 4D 22
Woodford. Devn 4J 21
Woodford. Glos 4J 33
Woodford. G Lon 4B 36
Woodford. G Man 7G 55
Woodford. Nptn 4H 43
Woodford. Plym 4G 21
Woodford Green. G Lon 4C 36
Woodford Halse. Nptn 6D 42
Woodgate. Norf 6G 53
Woodgate. W Mid 3K 41
Woodgate. W Sus 5K 27
Woodgate. Worc 5K 41
Wood Green. G Lon 4A 36
Woodgreen. Hants 4B 26
Woodgreen. Oxon 2D 34
Wood Hall. E Yor 2H 57
Woodhall. Inv 2B 70
Woodhall. Linc 3J 51
Woodhall. N Yor 4L 59
Woodhall Spa. Linc 3H 51
Woodham. Surr 7L 35
Woodham Ferrers. Essx 4F 36
Woodham Mortimer. Essx 3G 37
Woodham Walter. Essx 3G 37
Woodhaven. Fife 3K 77
Wood Hayes. W Mid 1K 41
Woodhead. Abers 3K 89 (nr. Fraserburgh)
Woodhead. Abers 6H 89 (nr. Fyvie)
Woodhill. N Som 6G 33
Woodhill. Shrp 3H 41
Woodhill. Som 3C 24
Woodhorn. Nmbd 3J 67
Woodhouse. Leics 8B 50
Woodhouse. S Yor 7A 56
Woodhouse. W Yor 2L 55 (nr. Leeds)
Woodhouse. W Yor 3M 55 (nr. Normanton)
Woodhouse Eaves. Leics 8B 50
Woodhouses. Ches W 8D 54
Woodhouses. G Man 5H 55 (nr. Failsworth)
Woodhouses. G Man 6F 54 (nr. Sale)
Woodhouses. Staf 8J 49
Woodhuish. Devn 4L 21
Woodhurst. Cambs 4M 43
Woodingdean. Brig 7B 28
Woodland. Devn 3J 21
Woodland. Dur 1M 59
Woodland Head. Devn 6J 23
Woodlands. Abers 4H 83
Woodlands. Dors 5A 26
Woodlands. Hants 4D 26
Woodlands. Kent 7D 36
Woodlands. N Yor 8C 60
Woodlands. S Yor 5B 56
Woodlands Park. Wind 6J 35
Woodlands St Mary. W Ber 6D 34
Woodlane. Shrp 7D 48
Woodlane. Staf 7J 49
Woodleigh. Devn 5J 21
Woodlesford. W Yor 3M 55
Woodley. G Man 6H 55
Woodley. Wok 6H 35
Woodmancote. Glos 1M 33 (nr. Cheltenham)
Woodmancote. Glos 3A 34 (nr. Cirencester)
Woodmancote. W Sus 5H 27 (nr. Chichester)
Woodmancote. W Sus 6A 28 (nr. Henfield)
Woodmancote. Worc 7K 41
Woodmancott. Hants 1F 26
Woodmansey. E Yor 2G 57
Woodmansgreen. W Sus 3J 27
Woodmansterne. Surr 8A 36
Woodmanton. Devn 7M 23
Woodmill. Staf 7J 49
Woodminton. Wilts 3A 26
Woodnesborough. Kent 8M 37
Woodnewton. Nptn 2J 43
Woodnook. Linc 6F 50
Wood Norton. Norf 5G 53
Woodplumpton. Lanc 2D 54
Woodrising. Norf 1F 44
Woodrow. Cumb 7K 65
Woodrow. Dors 4G 25 (nr. Fifehead Neville)
Woodrow. Dors 5G 25 (nr. Hazelbury Bryan)
Wood Row. W Yor 3M 55
Woods Eaves. Here 7C 40
Woodseaves. Shrp 6D 48
Woodseaves. Staf 7E 48
Woodsend. Wilts 6C 34
Woodsetts. S Yor 7B 56
Woodsford. Dors 6G 25
Wood's Green. E Sus 4E 28
Woodshaw. Wilts 5A 34
Woodside. Aber 3K 83
Woodside. Brac 6K 35
Woodside. Derbs 5L 49
Woodside. Dum 4H 65
Woodside. Dur 1A 60
Woodside. Fife 5K 77
Woodside. Herts 3A 36
Woodside. Per 2H 77
Wood Stanway. Glos 8L 41
Woodstock. Oxon 2E 34
Woodstock Slop. Pemb 1E 30
Woodston. Pet 2K 43
Wood Street. Norf 5K 53
Wood Street Village. Surr 8K 35
Woodthorpe. Derbs 8A 56
Woodthorpe. Leics 8B 50
Woodthorpe. Linc 7L 57
Woodthorpe. York 1B 56
Woodton. Norf 2J 45
Woodtown. Devn 3F 22 (nr. Bideford)
Woodtown. Devn 3F 22 (nr. Littleham)
Woodvale. Mers 4B 54
Woodville. Derbs 8L 49
Woodwalton. Cambs 3L 43
Woodwick. Orkn 5B 94
Woodyates. Dors 4A 26
Woody Bay. Devn 1H 23
Woofferton. Shrp 5F 40
Wookey. Som 1E 24
Wookey Hole. Som 1E 24
Wool. Dors 7H 25
Woolacombe. Devn 1F 22
Woolage Green. Kent 3L 29
Woolage Village. Kent 8L 37
Woolaston. Glos 4H 33
Woolavington. Som 1C 24
Woolbeding. W Sus 3J 27
Woolcotts. Som 2L 23
Wooldale. W Yor 5K 55
Wooler. Nmbd 7J 73
Woolfardisworthy. Devn 3E 22 (nr. Bideford)
Woolfardisworthy. Devn 5K 23 (nr. Crediton)
Woolfords. S Lan 4J 71
Woolgarston. Dors 7J 25
Woolhampton. W Ber 7F 34
Woolhope. Here 8G 41
Woolland. Dors 5G 25
Woollard. Bath 7J 33
Woolley. Bath 7K 33
Woolley. Cambs 4K 43
Woolley. Corn 4D 22
Woolley. Derbs 3L 49
Woolley. W Yor 4M 55
Woolley Green. Wilts 7L 33
Woolmere Green. Worc 5K 41
Woolmer Green. Herts 2A 36
Woolminstone. Som 5D 24
Woolpit. Suff 5F 44
Woolridge. Glos 1L 33
Woolscott. Warw 5C 42
Woolsery. Devn 3E 22
Woolsington. Tyne 5G 67
Woolstaston. Shrp 2E 40
Woolsthorpe By Belvoir. Linc 6E 50
Woolsthorpe-by-Colsterworth. Linc 7F 50
Woolston. Devn 5J 21
Woolston. Shrp 3E 40 (nr. Church Stretton)
Woolston. Shrp 7A 48 (nr. Oswestry)
Woolston. Som 3F 24
Woolston. Sotn 4E 26
Woolston. Warr 6E 54
Woolstone. Glos 8K 41
Woolstone. Oxon 5C 34
Woolston Green. Devn 3J 21
Woolton. Mers 7C 54
Woolton Hill. Hants 7E 34
Woolverstone. Suff 8H 45
Woolverton. Som 8K 33
Woolwell. Devn 3G 21
Woolwich. G Lon 6C 36
Woonton. Here 6D 40 (nr. Kington)
Woonton. Here 5F 40 (nr. Leominster)
Wooperton. Nmbd 7K 73
Woore. Shrp 5E 48
Wooth. Dors 6D 24
Wooton. Shrp 3H 41
Wootton. Bed 7J 43
Wootton. Hants 6C 26
Wootton. IOW 6F 26
Wootton. Kent 3L 29
Wootton. Nptn 6F 42
Wootton. N Lin 4G 57
Wootton. Oxon 3E 34 (nr. Abingdon)
Wootton. Oxon 2E 34 (nr. Woodstock)
Wootton. Shrp 4E 40 (nr. Ludlow)
Wootton. Shrp 7A 48 (nr. Oswestry)
Wootton. Staf 7F 48 (nr. Eccleshall)
Wootton. Staf 5J 49 (nr. Ellastone)
Wootton Bridge. IOW 6F 26
Wootton Common. IOW 6F 26
Wootton Courtenay. Som 1L 23
Wootton Fitzpaine. Dors 6C 24
Wootton Rivers. Wilts 7B 34
Wootton St Lawrence. Hants 8F 34
Wootton Wawen. Warw 5M 41
Worcester. Worc 6J 41
Worcester Park. G Lon 7A 36
Wordsley. W Mid 3J 41
Worfield. Shrp 2H 41
Work. Orkn 6C 94
Workhouse Green. Suff 8F 44
Workington. Cumb 1A 58
Worksop. Notts 8B 56
Worlaby. N Lin 4G 57
Worlds End. Hants 4G 27
Worldsend. Shrp 2E 40
World's End. W Ber 6E 34
Worlds End. W Mid 3M 41
World's End. W Sus 6B 28
Worle. N Som 7F 32
Worleston. Ches E 4D 48
Worley. Glos 4L 33
Worlingham. Suff 2L 45
Worlington. Suff 4C 44
Worlingworth. Suff 5J 45
Wormbridge. Here 8E 40
Wormegay. Norf 6C 52
Wormelow Tump. Here 8E 40
Wormhill. Derbs 8K 55
Wormingford. Essx 8F 44
Worminghall. Buck 3G 35
Wormington. Glos 8L 41
Worminster. Som 1E 24
Wormit. Fife 3J 77
Wormleighton. Warw 6C 42
Wormley. Herts 3B 36
Wormley. Surr 2K 27
Wormshill. Kent 8G 37
Wormsley. Here 7E 40
Worplesdon. Surr 8K 35
Worrall. S Yor 6M 55
Worsbrough. S Yor 5M 55
Worsley. G Man 5F 54
Worstead. Norf 5K 53
Worsthorne. Lanc 2G 55
Worston. Lanc 1F 54
Worth. Kent 8M 37
Worth. W Sus 4B 28
Wortham. Suff 4G 45
Worthen. Shrp 1D 40
Worthenbury. Wrex 5B 48
Worthing. Norf 6F 52
Worthing. W Sus 5M 27
Worthington. Leics 7A 50
Worth Matravers. Dors 8J 25
Worting. Hants 8G 35
Wortley. Glos 4K 33
Wortley. S Yor 6M 55
Wortley. W Yor 2L 55
Worton. N Yor 4L 59
Worton. Wilts 8M 33
Wortwell. Norf 3J 45
Wotherton. Shrp 1C 40
Wothorpe. Nptn 1J 43
Wotter. Devn 3G 21
Wotton. Glos 2L 33
Wotton. Surr 1M 27
Wotton-under-Edge. Glos 4K 33
Wotton Underwood. Buck 2G 35
Wouldham. Kent 7F 36
Wrabness. Essx 8H 45
Wrafton. Devn 2F 22
Wragby. Linc 8H 57
Wragby. W Yor 4A 56
Wramplingham. Norf 1H 45
Wrangbrook. W Yor 4A 56
Wrangle. Linc 4L 51
Wrangle Lowgate. Linc 4L 51
Wrangway. Som 4A 24
Wrantage. Som 3C 24
Wrawby. N Lin 5G 57
Wraxall. N Som 6G 33
Wraxall. Som 2F 24
Wray. Lanc 7H 59
Wraysbury. Wind 6L 35
Wrayton. Lanc 6H 59
Wrea Green. Lanc 2B 54
Wreay. Cumb 7M 65 (nr. Carlisle)
Wreay. Cumb 1F 58 (nr. Penrith)
Wrecclesham. Surr 1J 27
Wrecsam. Wrex 4A 48
Wrekenton. Tyne 6H 67
Welton. N Yor 5G 61
Wrenbury. Ches E 5C 48
Wreningham. Norf 2H 45
Wrentham. Suff 3L 45
Wrenthorpe. W Yor 3M 55
Wrentnall. Shrp 1E 40
Wressle. E Yor 2D 56
Wressle. N Lin 5F 56
Wrestlingworth. C Beds 7L 43
Wretton. Norf 2C 44
Wrexham. Wrex 4A 48
Wrexham Industrial Estate. Wrex 5A 48
Wreyland. Devn 7J 23
Wrickton. Shrp 3G 41
Wrightlington Bar. Lanc 4D 54
Wright's Green. Essx 2D 36
Wrinehill. Staf 5E 48
Wrington. N Som 7G 33
Writtle. Essx 3E 36
Wrockwardine. Telf 8D 48
Wroot. N Lin 5D 56
Wrotham. Kent 8E 36
Wrotham Heath. Kent 8E 36
Wroughton. Swin 5B 34
Wroxall. IOW 7F 26
Wroxall. Warw 4A 42
Wroxeter. Shrp 1F 40
Wroxham. Norf 6K 53
Wroxton. Oxon 7C 42
Wyaston. Derbs 5J 49
Wyatt's Green. Essx 4D 36
Wybers Wood. NE Lin 5J 57
Wyberton. Linc 5K 51
Wyboston. Bed 6K 43
Wybunbury. Ches E 5D 48
Wychbold. Worc 5K 41
Wych Cross. E Sus 4C 28
Wychnor. Staf 8J 49
Wychnor Bridges. Staf 8J 49
Wyck. Hants 2H 27
Wyck Hill. Glos 1B 34
Wyck Rissington. Glos 1B 34
Wycliffe. Dur 2A 60
Wycombe Marsh. Buck 4J 35
Wyddial. Herts 8M 43
Wye. Kent 3J 29
Wyesham. Mon 2H 33
Wyfold Grange. Oxon 5G 35
Wyfordby. Leics 8D 50
Wyke. Devn 6K 23
Wyke. Dors 3G 25
Wyke. Shrp 1G 41
Wyke. Surr 8K 35
Wyke. W Yor 3K 55
Wyke Champflower. Som 2F 24
Wykeham. Linc 7J 51
Wykeham. N Yor 6H 61 (nr. Malton)
Wykeham. N Yor 5J 61 (nr. Scarborough)
Wyken. Shrp 2H 41
Wyken. W Mid 3B 42
Wyke Regis. Dors 8F 24
Wyke, The. Shrp 1H 41
Wykey. Shrp 7A 48
Wykin. Leics 2C 42
Wylam. Nmbd 5G 67
Wylde Green. W Mid 2M 41
Wylye. Wilts 2A 26
Wymering. Port 5G 27
Wymeswold. Leics 7C 50
Wymington. Bed 5H 43
Wymondham. Leics 8E 50
Wymondham. Norf 1H 45
Wyndham. B'end 4B 32
Wynford Eagle. Dors 6E 24
Wyng. Orkn 8B 94
Wynyard Village. Stoc T 1D 60
Wyre Piddle. Worc 7K 41
Wysall. Notts 7C 50
Wyson. Here 5F 40
Wythall. Worc 4L 41
Wytham. Oxon 3E 34
Wythenshawe. G Man 7G 55
Wythop Mill. Cumb 1C 58
Wyton. Cambs 4L 43
Wyton. E Yor 2H 57
Wyverstone. Suff 5G 45
Wyverstone Street. Suff 5G 45
Wyville. Linc 7F 50
Wyvis Lodge. High 4G 87

Y

Yaddlethorpe. N Lin 5E 56
Yafford. IOW 7E 26
Yafforth. N Yor 4C 60
Yalding. Kent 8E 36
Yanley. N Som 7H 33
Yanwath. Cumb 1G 59
Yanworth. Glos 2A 34
Yapham. E Yor 8G 61
Yapton. W Sus 5K 27
Yarburgh. Linc 6K 57
Yarcombe. Devn 5B 24
Yarde. Som 2M 23
Yardley. W Mid 3M 41
Yardley Gobion. Nptn 7F 42
Yardley Hastings. Nptn 6G 43
Yardley Wood. W Mid 3M 41
Yardro. Powy 6C 40
Yarhampton. Worc 5H 41
Yarkhill. Here 7G 41
Yarlet. Staf 7G 49
Yarley. Som 1E 24
Yarlington. Som 3F 24
Yarm. Stoc T 2D 60
Yarmouth. IOW 7D 26
Yarnbrook. Wilts 8L 33
Yarnfield. Staf 6F 48
Yarnscombe. Devn 3G 23
Yarnton. Oxon 2E 34
Yarpole. Here 5E 40
Yarrow. Nmbd 3C 66
Yarrow. Bord 7M 71
Yarrow. Som 1C 2[illegible]
Yarrow Feus. Bord 7M 7[illegible]
Yarrow Ford. Bord 6D 72
Yarsop. Here 7E 4[illegible]
Yarwell. Nptn 2J [illegible]
Yate. S Glo 5K 3[illegible]
Yateley. Hants 7J 3[illegible]
Yatesbury. Wilts 6A 3[illegible]
Yattendon. W Ber 6F 3[illegible]
Yatton. Here 5E 4[illegible] (nr. Leominster)
Yatton. Here 8G 41 (nr. Ross-on-Wye)
Yatton. N Som 7G 33
Yatton Keynell. Wilts 6L 33
Yaverland. IOW 7G 27
Yawl. Devn 6C 24
Yaxham. Norf 6G 5[illegible]
Yaxley. Cambs 2K 4[illegible]
Yaxley. Suff 4H 4[illegible]
Yazor. Here 7E 40
Y Bala. Gwyn 6J 4[illegible]
Y Bont-Faen. V Glam 6B 3[illegible]
Y Clun. Neat 3A 3[illegible]
Y Dref. Gwyn 6D 46
Y Drenewydd. Powy 2B 40
Yeading. G Lon 5M 35
Yeadon. W Yor 1L 55
Yealand Conyers. Lanc 6G 59
Yealand Redmayne. Lanc 6G 59
Yealand Storrs. Lanc 6F 58
Yealmpton. Devn 4G 21
Yearby. Red C 1F 60
Yearngill. Cumb 7J 65
Yearsett. Here 6H 41
Yearsley. N Yor 6E 60
Yeaton. Shrp 8B 48
Yeaveley. Derbs 5J 49
Yeavering. Nmbd 6J 73
Yedingham. N Yor 6H 61
Yeldersley Hollies. Derbs 5K 49
Yelford. Oxon 3D 34
Yelland. Devn 2F 22
Yelling. Cambs 5L 43
Yelsted. Kent 7G 37
Yelvertoft. Nptn 4D 42
Yelverton. Devn 3G 21
Yelverton. Norf 1J 45
Yenston. Som 3G 25
Yeoford. Devn 6J 23
Yeolmbridge. Corn 7E 22
Yeo Mill. Devn 3K 23
Yeovil. Som 4E 24
Yeovil Marsh. Som 4E 24
Yeovilton. Som 3E 24
Yerbeston. Pemb 3E 30
Yesnaby. Orkn 6A 94
Yetlington. Nmbd 1F 66
Yetminster. Dors 4E 24
Yett. N Lan 4F 70
Yett. S Ayr 7C 70
Yettington. Devn 7M 23
Yetts o' Muckhart. Clac 5F 76
Y Fali. IOA 2B 46
Y Felinheli. Gwyn 3E 46
Y Fenni. Mon 2F 32
Y Ferwig. Cdgn 7D 38
Y Fflint. Flin 8A 54
Y Ffor. Gwyn 6C 46
Y Gelli Gandryll. Powy 7C 40
Yielden. Bed 5J 43
Yieldshields. S Lan 4G 71
Yiewsley. G Lon 5L 35
Yinstay. Orkn 6D 94
Ynysboeth. Rhon 4C 32
Ynysddu. Cphy 4D 32
Ynysforgan. Swan 4L 31
Ynyshir. Rhon 4C 32
Ynyslas. Cdgn 2J 39
Ynysmaerdy. Rhon 5C 32
Ynysmeudwy. Neat 3M 31
Ynystawe. Swan 3L 31
Ynyswen. Powy 2A 32
Ynys-wen. Rhon 4B 32
Ynys y Barri. V Glam 7D 32
Ynysybwl. Rhon 4C 32
Ynysymaerdy. Neat 4M 31
Yockenthwaite. N Yor 6L 59
Yockleton. Shrp 8B 48
Yokefleet. E Yor 3E 56
Yoker. Glas 3D 70
Yonder Bognie. Abers 5F 88
Yonderton. Abers 6K 89
York. York 8F 60
Yorkletts. Kent 7J 37
Yorkley. Glos 3J 33
Yorkshire Dales. N Yor 6K 59
Yorton. Shrp 7C 48
Yorton Heath. Shrp 7C 48
Youlgreave. Derbs 3K 49
Youlthorpe. E Yor 8G 61
Youlton. N Yor 7D 60
Young's End. Essx 2F 36
Young Wood. Linc 8H 57
Yoxall. Staf 8J 49
Yoxford. Suff 5K 45
Yr Hôb. Flin 4A 48
Y Rhws. V Glam 7C 32
Yr Wyddgrug. Flin 3M 47
Ysbyty Cynfyn. Cdgn 4K 39
Ysbyty Ifan. Cnwy 5H 47
Ysbyty Ystwyth. Cdgn 4K 39
Ysceifiog. Flin 2L 47
Yspitty. Carm 4K 31
Ystalyfera. Neat 3M 31
Ystrad. Rhon 4B 32
Ystrad Aeron. Cdgn 6H 39
Ystradfellte. Powy 2B 32
Ystradffin. Carm 7K 39
Ystradgynlais. Powy 2M 31
Ystradmeurig. Cdgn 5K 39
Ystrad Mynach. Cphy 4D 32
Ystradowen. Carm 2M 31
Ystradowen. V Glam 6C 32
Ystumtuen. Cdgn 4K 39
Ythanbank. Abers 6K 89
Ythanwells. Abers 6G 89
Y Trallwng. Powy 1C 40
Y Tymbl. Carm 2K 31
Y Waun. Wrex 6M 47

Z

Zeal Monachorum. Devn 5J 23
Zeals. Wilts 2G 25
Zelah. Corn 4F 19
Zennor. Corn 6B 19
Zouch. Notts 7B 50

Printed and bound in the United Kingdom by Polestar Wheatons Ltd., Exeter.